T0183418

Lecture Notes in Computer Science 12862

Founding Editors

Gerhard Goos
Karlsruhe Institute of Technology, Karlsruhe, Germany
Juris Hartmanis
Cornell University, Ithaca, NY, USA

Editorial Board Members

Elisa Bertino
Purdue University, West Lafayette, IN, USA
Wen Gao
Peking University, Beijing, China
Bernhard Steffen
TU Dortmund University, Dortmund, Germany
Gerhard Woeginger
RWTH Aachen, Aachen, Germany
Moti Yung
Columbia University, New York, NY, USA

More information about this subseries at http://www.springer.com/series/7407

Ignacio Rojas · Gonzalo Joya ·
Andreu Català (Eds.)

Advances in Computational Intelligence

16th International Work-Conference
on Artificial Neural Networks, IWANN 2021
Virtual Event, June 16–18, 2021
Proceedings, Part II

 Springer

Editors
Ignacio Rojas (iD)
University of Granada
Granada, Spain

Gonzalo Joya
University of Málaga
Málaga, Spain

Andreu Català
Technical University of Catalonia
Barcelona, Spain

ISSN 0302-9743   ISSN 1611-3349   (electronic)
Lecture Notes in Computer Science
ISBN 978-3-030-85098-2   ISBN 978-3-030-85099-9   (eBook)
https://doi.org/10.1007/978-3-030-85099-9

LNCS Sublibrary: SL1 – Theoretical Computer Science and General Issues

© Springer Nature Switzerland AG 2021, corrected publication 2021
This work is subject to copyright. All rights are reserved by the Publisher, whether the whole or part of the material is concerned, specifically the rights of translation, reprinting, reuse of illustrations, recitation, broadcasting, reproduction on microfilms or in any other physical way, and transmission or information storage and retrieval, electronic adaptation, computer software, or by similar or dissimilar methodology now known or hereafter developed.
The use of general descriptive names, registered names, trademarks, service marks, etc. in this publication does not imply, even in the absence of a specific statement, that such names are exempt from the relevant protective laws and regulations and therefore free for general use.
The publisher, the authors and the editors are safe to assume that the advice and information in this book are believed to be true and accurate at the date of publication. Neither the publisher nor the authors or the editors give a warranty, expressed or implied, with respect to the material contained herein or for any errors or omissions that may have been made. The publisher remains neutral with regard to jurisdictional claims in published maps and institutional affiliations.

This Springer imprint is published by the registered company Springer Nature Switzerland AG
The registered company address is: Gewerbestrasse 11, 6330 Cham, Switzerland

Preface

We are proud to present the set of final accepted papers for the 16th edition of the IWANN conference - the International Work-Conference on Artificial Neural Networks - held online during June 16–18, 2021. Unfortunately, the 2021 edition of the conference had to be carried out remotely due to the consequences of the COVID-19 pandemic, but interactive digital platforms were used to preserve the participatory climate of previous editions.

IWANN is a biennial conference that seeks to provide a discussion forum for scientists, engineers, educators, and students about the latest ideas and realizations in the foundations, theory, models, and applications of hybrid systems inspired by nature (neural networks, fuzzy logic, and evolutionary systems) as well as in emerging areas related to these topics. As in previous editions of IWANN, this year's conference aimed to create a friendly environment that could lead to the establishment of scientific collaborations and exchanges among attendees. The proceedings include all the communications presented at the conference. Extended versions of selected papers will also be published in special issues of relevant journals (such as *PeerJ Computer Science* and *Neural Proccesing Letters*).

Since the first edition in Granada (LNCS 540, 1991), the conference has evolved and matured. The list of topics in the successive Call for Papers has also evolved, resulting in the following list for the present edition:

1. **Mathematical and theoretical methods in computational intelligence**: mathematics for neural networks; RBF structures; self-organizing networks and methods; support vector machines and kernel methods; fuzzy logic; and evolutionary and genetic algorithms.
2. **Neurocomputational formulations**: single-neuron modeling; perceptual modeling; system-level neural modeling; spiking neurons; and models of biological learning.
3. **Learning and adaptation**: adaptive systems; imitation learning; reconfigurable systems; and supervised, non-supervised, reinforcement, and statistical algorithms.
4. **Emulation of cognitive functions**: decision-making; multi-agent systems; sensor mesh; natural language; pattern recognition; perceptual and motor functions (visual, auditory, tactile, virtual reality, etc.); robotics; and planning motor control.
5. **Bio-inspired systems and neuro-engineering**: embedded intelligent systems; evolvable computing; evolving hardware; microelectronics for neural, fuzzy, and bioinspired systems; neural prostheses; retinomorphic systems; brain-computer interfaces (BCI) nanosystems; and nanocognitive systems.
6. **Advanced topics in computational intelligence**: intelligent networks; knowledge-intensive problem-solving techniques; multi-sensor data fusion using computational intelligence; search and meta-heuristics; soft computing; neuro-fuzzy systems; neuro-evolutionary systems; neuro-swarm; and hybridization with novel computing paradigms.

7. **Applications**: expert systems; image and signal processing; ambient intelligence; biomimetic applications; system identification, process control, and manufacturing; computational biology and bioinformatics; parallel and distributed computing; human computer interaction, internet modeling, communication and networking; intelligent systems in education; human-robot interaction; multi-agent systems; time series analysis and prediction; and data mining and knowledge discovery.

At the end of the submission process, and after a careful peer review and evaluation process (each submission was reviewed by at least 2, and on average 2.8, Program Committee members or additional reviewers), 85 papers were accepted for oral presentation, according to the reviewers' recommendations.

During IWANN 2021, several special sessions were held. Special sessions are a very useful tool for complementing the regular program with new and emerging topics of particular interest for the participating community. Special sessions that emphasize multi-disciplinary and transversal aspects, as well as cutting-edge topics are especially encouraged and welcome, and in this edition of IWANN 2019 comprised the following:

- SS01: Agent-based Models for Policy Design Towards a More Sustainable World.
  Organized by Amparo Alonso-Betanzos, Bertha Guijarro-Berdiñas, Noelia Sánchez-Maroño, and Alejandro Rodríguez-Arias
- SS02: Convolutional Neural Networks: Beyond Traditional Solutions.
  Organized by Irina Perfilieva, Jan Platos, and Jan Hula
- SS03: Quality Control Charts Based on Imprecise Information.
  Organized by Gholamreza Hesamian
- SS04: Neural Networks for Time Series Forecasting.
  Organized by Grzegorz Dudek
- SS05: Randomization in Deep Learning.
  Organized by Claudio Gallicchio, Massimo Panella, and Ponnuthurai Nagaratnam Suganthan
- SS06: Intelligent Computing Solutions for SARS-CoV-2 COVID-19 (INClutions COVID-19).
  Organized by Carmen Paz Suárez Araujo and Juan Luis Navarro Mesa
- SS07: Multi-valued Cognitive Intelligence.
  Organized by Prem Kumar Singh
- SS08: Meta-learning and Other Automatic Learning Approaches in Intelligent Systems.
  Organized by Rashedur M Rahman, Ahsanur Rahman, Tanzilur Rahman, Shafin Rahman, Luis Garcia, and Ali Cheraghian
- SS09: New Advances in Artificial Intelligence for Green Computing.
  Organized by Antonello Rosato and Massimo Panella
- SS10: Attentive Models and Visual Attention in Computer Vision and AI.
  Organized by Lorenzo Baraldi and Marcella Cornia
- SS11: Biosignals Processing.
  Organized by Antonio Fernandez-Caballero, Roberto Sánchez-Reolid, and Beatriz García-Martínez

– SS12: Information Fusion in Deep Learning for Biomedicine.
Organized by Miguel Atencia, Francisco Veredas, and Ruxandra Stoean

In this edition of IWANN, we were honored to have the presence of the following invited speakers:

1. Pierre Baldi, University of California, Irvine, USA
2. Jeanna Matthews, Division of Mathematics and Computer Science, Clarkson University, USA
3. Davide Anguita, University of Genova, Italy

It is important to note that, for the sake of consistency and readability of the book, the presented papers are not organized as they were presented in the IWANN 2021 sessions but classified under 13 chapters. The organization of the papers is in two volumes arranged basically following the topics list included in the Call for Papers. The first volume (LNCS 12861), entitled Advances on Computational Intelligence, IWANN 2021, Part I, is divided into seven main parts and includes contributions on

1. Information Fusion in Deep Learning for Biomedicine
2. Intelligent Computing Solutions for SARS-CoV-2 COVID-19 (INClutions COVID-19)
3. Advanced Topics in Computational Intelligence
4. Biosignals Processing
5. Deep Learning
6. Meta-learning and Other Automatic Learning Approaches in Intelligent Systems
7. Artificial Intelligence and Biomedicine

The second volume (LNCS 12862), entitled Advances on Computational Intelligence, IWANN 2021, Part II, is divided into six main parts and includes contributions on

1. Convolutional Neural Networks: Beyond Traditional Solutions
2. Bio-inspired Systems and Neuro-Engineering
3. Agent-based Models for Policy Design Towards a More Sustainable World
4. Randomization in Deep Learning
5. Neural Networks for Time Series Forecasting
6. Applications in Artificial Intelligence

The 16th edition of the IWANN conference was organized by the University of Granada, the University of Malaga, and the Polytechnic University of Catalonia, Spain.

We would also like to express our gratitude to the members of the different committees for their support, collaboration, and good work. We specially thank our Steering Committee (David Anguita, Andreu Catalá, Marie Cotrell, Gonzalo Joya, Kurosh Madani, Madalina Olteanu, Ignacio Rojas, and Ulrich Rückert), the Technical Assistant Committee (Miguel Atencia, Francisco García-Lagos, Luis Javier Herrera, and Fernando Rojas), the Program Committee, the reviewers, invited speakers, and special session organizers. Finally, we want to thank Springer and especially Ronan Nugent, Alfred Hofmann, and Anna Kramer for their continuous support and cooperation.

June 2021   Ignacio Rojas
                                                                             Gonzalo Joya
                                                                             Andreu Catala

The original version of the book was revised: the affiliations of Gonzalo Joya and Andreu Català as well as the last name of Andreu Català were not correct. This is now corrected. The correction to the book is available at https://doi.org/10.1007/978-3-030-85099-9_36

Organization

Program Committee

Kouzou Abdellah	Djelfa University, Algeria
Vanessa Aguiar-Pulido	Cornell University, USA
Arnulfo Alanis Garza	Instituto Tecnologico de Tijuana, Mexico
Amparo Alonso-Betanzos	University of A Coruña, Spain
Jhon Edgar Amaya	University of Tachira, Venezuela
Gabriela Andrejkova	Pavol Jozef Safarik University, Slovakia
Anastassia Angelopoulou	University of Westminster, UK
Davide Anguita	University of Genoa, Italy
Javier Antich Tobaruela	University of the Balearic Islands, Spain
Miguel Atencia	University of Málaga, Spain
Jorge Azorín-López	University of Alicante, Spain
Davide Bacciu	University of Pisa, Italy
Antonio Bahamonde	University of Oviedo at Gijon, Spain
Halima Bahi	University of Annaba, Algeria
Juan Pedro Bandera Rubio	University of Malaga, Spain
Oresti Banos	University of Granada, Spain
Emilia Barakova	Einhoven University of Technology, The Netherlands
Lorenzo Baraldi	University of Modena and Reggio Emilia, Italy
Andrzej Bartoszewicz	Technical University of Lodz, Poland
Bruno Baruque	University of Burgos, Spain
Lluís Belanche	Universitat Politècnica de Catalunya, Spain
Sergio Bermejo	Universitat Politècnica de Catalunya, Spain
Francisco Bonin-Font	University of the Balearic Islands, Spain
Julio Brito	University of La Laguna, Spain
Joan Cabestany	Universitat Politècnica de Catalunya, Spain
Eldon Glen Caldwell	University of Costa Rica
Tomasa Calvo	University of Alcala, Spain
Azahara Camacho	WATA Factory, Spain
Hoang-Long Cao	Vrije Universiteit Brussel, Belgium
Carlos Carrascosa	Universidad Politecnica de Valencia, Spain
Francisco Carrillo Pérez	University of Granada, Spain
Luis Castedo	University of A Coruña, Spain
Pedro Castillo	University of Granada, Spain
Daniel Castillo-Secilla	University of Granada, Spain
Andreu Catala	Universitat Politècnica de Catalunya, Spain
Ana Rosa Cavalli	Institut Mines-Telecom/Telecom SudParis, France
Miguel Cazorla	University of Alicante, Spain
Pablo C. Cañizares	Universidad Complutense de Madrid, Spain

Ali Cheraghian	Australian National University, Australia
Zouhair Chiba	Hassan II University of Casablanca, Morocco
Maximo Cobos	University of Valencia, Spain
Valentina Colla	Scuola Superiore S. Anna, Italy
Feijoo Colomine	Universidad Nacional Experimental del Táchira, Venezuela
Pablo Cordero	University of Málaga, Spain
Marcella Cornia	University of Modena and Reggio Emilia, Italy
Francesco Corona	Aalto University, Finland
Marie Cottrell	Université Paris 1 Panthéon-Sorbonne, France
Raúl Cruz-Barbosa	Universidad Tecnológica de la Mixteca, Mexico
Miguel Damas	University of Granada, Spain
Daniela Danciu	University of Craiova, Romania
Luiza de Macedo Mourelle	State University of Rio de Janeiro, Brazil
Angel Pascual Del Pobil	Universidad Jaime I, Spain
Enrique Dominguez	University of Malaga, Spain
Grzegorz Dudek	Czestochowa University of Technology, Poland
Richard Duro	University of A Coruna, Spain
Gregorio Díaz	University of Castilla-La Mancha, Spain
Marcos Faundez-Zanuy	Escola Superior Politècnica, Tecnocampus, Spain
Francisco Fernandez De Vega	University of Extremadura, Spain
Enrique Fernandez-Blanco	University of A Coruña, Spain
Carlos Fernandez-Lozano	University of A Coruña, Spain
Antonio Fernández-Caballero	University of Castilla-La Mancha, Spain
Jose Manuel Ferrandez	Politecnic University of Cartagena, Spain
Leonardo Franco	University of Málaga, Spain
Claudio Gallicchio	University of Pisa, Italy
Luis Garcia	University of Brasília, Brazil
Esther Garcia Garaluz	Eneso Tecnología de Adaptación SL, Spain
Beatriz Garcia Martinez	University of Castilla-La Mancha, Spain
Emilio Garcia-Fidalgo	University of the Balearic Islands, Spain
Francisco Garcia-Lagos	University of Malaga, Spain
Jose Garcia-Rodriguez	University of Alicante, Spain
Patricio García Báez	University of La Laguna, Spain
Rodolfo García-Bermúdez	Universidad Técnica de Manabí, Ecuador
Patrick Garda	Sorbonne Université, France
Peter Gloesekoetter	Münster University of Applied Sciences, Germany
Juan Gomez Romero	University of Granada, Spain
Pedro González Calero	Politecnic University of Madrid, Spain
Juan Gorriz	University of Granada, Spain
Karl Goser	Technical University Dortmund, Germany
M. Grana Romay	UPV/EHU, Spain
Jose Guerrero	Universitat de les Illes Balears, Spain
Bertha Guijarro-Berdiñas	University of A Coruña, Spain

Alberto Guillen	University of Granada, Spain
Pedro Antonio Gutierrez	University of Cordoba, Spain
Luis Herrera	University of Granada, Spain
Cesar Hervas	University of Cordoba, Spain
Wei-Chiang Hong	Jiangsu Normal University, China
M. Dolores Jimenez-Lopez	Rovira i Virgili University, Spain
Gonzalo Joya	University of Málaga, Spain
Vicente Julian	Universitat Politècnica de València, Spain
Nuno Lau	University of Aveiro, Portugal
Otoniel Lopez Granado	Miguel Hernandez University, Spain
Rafael Marcos Luque Baena	University of Málaga, Spain
Fernando López Pelayo	University of Castilla-La Mancha, Spain
Ezequiel López-Rubio	University of Málaga, Spain
Kurosh Madani	LISSI/Université PARIS-EST Creteil, France
Mario Martin	Universitat Politècnica de Catalunya, Spain
Bonifacio Martin Del Brio	University of Zaragoza, Spain
Jesús Medina	University of Cádiz, Spain
Jj Merelo	University of Granada, Spain
Jose M. Molina	Universidad Carlos III de Madrid, Spain
Miguel A. Molina-Cabello	University of Málaga, Spain
Angel Mora Bonilla	University of Málaga, Spain
Juan Carlos Morales Vega	University of Granada, Spain
Gines Moreno	University of Castilla-La Mancha, Spain
Juan Moreno Garcia	University of Castilla-La Mancha, Spain
Juan L. Navarro-Mesa	University of Las Palmas de Gran Canaria, Spain
Nadia Nedjah	State University of Rio de Janciro, Brazil
Alberto Núñez	Universidad Complutense de Madrid, Spain
Julio Ortega	University of Granada, Spain
Alberto Ortiz	Universitat de les Illes Balears, Spain
Osvaldo Pacheco	University of Aveiro, Portugal
Esteban José Palomo	University of Malaga, Spain
Massimo Panella	University of Rome "La Sapienza", Italy
Irina Perfilieva	University of Ostrava, Czech Republic
Hector Pomares	University of Granada, Spain
Alberto Prieto	University of Granada, Spain
Alexandra Psarrou	University of Westminster, UK
Pablo Rabanal	Universidad Complutense de Madrid, Spain
Md. Ahsanur Rahman	North South University, Bangladesh
Shafin Rahman	North South University, Bangladesh
Tanzilur Rahman	North South University, Bangladesh
Sivarama Krishnan Rajaraman	National Library of Medicine, USA
Mohammad Rashedur Rahman	North South University, Bangladesh
Ismael Rodriguez	Universidad Complutense de Madrid, Spain
Alejandro Rodríguez Arias	Universidade da Coruña

Fernando Rojas	University of Granada, Spain
Ignacio Rojas	University of Granada, Spain
Ricardo Ron-Angevin	University of Málaga, Spain
Antonello Rosato	"Sapienza" University of Rome, Italy
Fabrice Rossi	SAMM - Université Paris 1, France
Peter M. Roth	Graz University of Technology, Austria
Fernando Rubio	Universidad Complutense de Madrid, Spain
Ulrich Rueckert	Bielefeld University, Germany
Addisson Salazar	Universitat Politècnica de València, Spain
Roberto Sanchez Reolid	Universidad de Castilla-La Mancha, Spain
Noelia Sanchez-Maroño	University of A Coruña, Spain
Jorge Santos	ISEP
Jose Santos	University of A Coruña, Spain
Jose A. Seoane	Vall d'Hebron Institute of Oncology, Spain
Prem Singh	GITAM University-Visakhapatnam, India
Jordi Solé-Casals	University of Vic - Central University of Catalonia, Spain
Ruxandra Stoean	University of Craiova, Rumania
Carmen Paz Suárez-Araujo	University of Las Palmas de Gran Canaria, Spain
Claude Touzet	Aix-Marseille University, France
Daniel Urda	University of Burgos, Spain
Oscar Valero	University of Islas Baleares, Spain
Francisco Velasco-Alvarez	University of Málaga, Spain
Marley Vellasco	Pontifical Catholic University of Rio de Janeiro (PUC-Rio), Brazil
Alfredo Vellido	Universitat Politècnica de Catalunya, Spain
Francisco J. Veredas	University of Málaga, Spain
Michel Verleysen	Universite catholique de Louvain, Belgium
Ivan Volosyak	Rhine-Waal University of Applied Sciences, Germany
Mauricio Zamora	Universidad de Costa Rica

Contents – Part II

Randomization in Deep Learning

Neural Networks for Time Series Forecasting

Applications in Artificial Intelligence

Contents – Part I

Advanced Topics in Computational Intelligence

Biosignals Processing

Deep Learning

Meta-Learning and Other Automatic Learning Approaches in Intelligent Systems

Artificial Intelligence and Biomedicine

Convolutional Neural Networks: Beyond Traditional Solutions

Error-Correcting Output Codes in the Framework of Deep Ordinal Classification

Javier Barbero-Gómez[✉], Pedro Antonio Gutiérrez,
and César Hervás-Martínez

University of Córdoba, 14014 Córdoba, Spain
{jbarbero,pagutierrez,chervas}@uco.es

Abstract. Automatic classification tasks have been revolutionized by Convolutional Neural Networks (CNNs), but the focus has been on binary and nominal classification tasks. Only recently, ordinal classification (where class labels present a natural ordering) has been tackled through the framework of CNNs, such as adapting the classic Proportional Odds Model to deep architectures. Also, ordinal classification datasets commonly present a high imbalance in the number of samples of each class, making it an even harder problem. In this work, we present a new CNN architecture based on the Ordinal Binary Decomposition (OBD) technique using Error-Correcting Output Codes (ECOC) and show how it can improve performance over previously proposed methods.

1 Introduction

Classification tasks in Machine Learning (ML) are traditionally addressed in one of two ways: binary or nominal classification, depending on the number of classes.

In the last decade, a third approach referred to as "ordinal classification" (sometimes referred as "ordinal regression") has gained popularity. This concept, halfway between nominal classification and regression, allows the exploitation of extra information when a natural ordering of the classes is present [1,3]. Certain applications of this concept have been proven to outperform purely nominal methods in the context of unstructured data [5,11].

However, for structured information such as 2D images, domain-specific feature extraction is still necessary. In this regard, Convolutional Neural Networks (CNNs) provide an automatic method for extracting learned features from structured data in classification tasks. Adapting CNNs to work with ordinal information is a recent line of research that still needs extensive work. Some methodologies have very recently been explored, like adapting Cumulative Link Models (CLMs) [13], but there is still much work to do in this context [7].

In this work we propose a novel general methodology for ordinal classification tasks of 2D images including the adaptation of a CNN architecture and a prediction scheme based on Error-Correcting Output Codes (ECOC). This can

© Springer Nature Switzerland AG 2021
I. Rojas et al. (Eds.): IWANN 2021, LNCS 12862, pp. 3–13, 2021.
https://doi.org/10.1007/978-3-030-85099-9_1

be applied to a large variety of ordinal classification tasks. Our hypothesis is that this exploitation of ordinal information in the context of image classification can improve performance, not only on ordinal metrics but also in nominal ones.

This work is structured as follows: in Sect. 2, three different architectures, two based on previous works and one novel architecture, are described. In Sect. 3, the experiments for the comparison of these three approaches are presented, including the used dataset. Finally, in Sect. 4, the experiment results are shown, and Sect. 5 concludes with a discussion of these results.

2   Adapting CNNs for Ordinal Classification

In the following section, the baseline ordinal classification framework is presented, and it is explained how we have adapted a traditional CNN architecture to work with ordinal label information.

2.1   Ordinal Classification Framework

Like in a nominal classification framework, an ordinal classification task is characterised as the prediction process of assigning a label y to an input vector $\mathbf{x}$, where $\mathbf{x} \in \mathcal{X} \subseteq \mathbb{R}^K$ and $y \in \mathcal{Y} = \{C_1, C_2, \ldots, C_Q\}$, i.e., $\mathbf{x}$ is a K-dimensional vector and y is a class label in a finite set. The goal is to obtain some classification rule $r : \mathcal{X} \to \mathcal{Y}$ that predicts the categories of new patterns given a dataset $D = \{(\mathbf{x}_i, y_i) \mid \mathbf{x}_i \in \mathcal{X}, y_i \in \mathcal{Y}, i \in \{1, \ldots, N\}\}$.

Where the ordinal framework differs from the nominal framework is in the presence of a natural ordering of the class labels: $C_1 \prec C_2 \prec \cdots \prec C_Q$, where $\prec$ is an order relation. This is similar to regression, where $y \in \mathbb{R}$, and real values can be ordered by the $<$ operator, but, in this case, the labels are discrete and include qualitative information instead of quantitative [7].

2.2   Base Nominal Architecture

We have considered a well-known and competitive CNN architecture such as VGG11 [12] in order to have a good performance baseline. Some readers will already be familiar with its design:

- First, several blocks of convolution operations ending with a max-pooling are applied to the input image.
- Then, two hidden fully-connected layers, each with 4096 units are added.
- Finally, an output layer with as many units as classes and the softmax activation is used, whose value represent the probability of each class label $(P(y = C_q \mid \mathbf{x}))$.

The ReLU activation function is used in all layers except the final output layer, where the softmax activation function is applied.

Table 1 describes this architecture similarly to the original paper [12] under the column "Nominal". This architecture is use as a baseline for traditional nominal classification. In the following sections, several modifications are presented in order to adapt it to work with ordinal label information.

Decision Rule. During evaluation of the model, the maximum probability class of $\mathbf{x}_i$ is selected as the predicted class label $\hat{y}_i$:

$$\hat{y}_i = \underset{\mathcal{C}_1 \preceq \mathcal{C}_q \preceq \mathcal{C}_Q}{\text{argmax}} P(y_i = \mathcal{C}_q \,|\, \mathbf{x}_i). \tag{1}$$

Loss Function. For the baseline nominal methodology, cross-entropy is used as the loss function during training:

$$\ell(\mathbf{x}_i) = -\sum_{q=1}^{Q} \mathbb{1}\{y_i = \mathcal{C}_q\} \log(P(y_i = \mathcal{C}_q \,|\, \mathbf{x}_i)), \tag{2}$$

where $\mathbb{1}\{y_i = \mathcal{C}_q\}$ is the indicator function that is equal to 1 when $y_i = \mathcal{C}_q$ and 0 otherwise, and $P(y_i = \mathcal{C}_q \,|\, \mathbf{x}_i)$ is the probability predicted by the network for class q.

2.3   The Cumulative Link Model Approach

For the CLM framework, only a small modification to the model is needed: the output is reduced to only a single unit in the last layer, and the `logit` cumulative link function is used as the activation function, as proposed by the Proportional Odds Model (POM) [10]:

$$P(y \preceq \mathcal{C}_q \,|\, \mathbf{x}) = \sigma(b_q - f(\mathbf{x})) , \ 1 \le q < Q, \tag{3}$$

where $f(\mathbf{x})$ is the output of the model, σ is the sigmoid function and b_q is one of the $Q - 1$ thresholds learned as additional parameters to the model.

The model architecture is shown in Table 1 under column "CLM".

Decision Rule. During evaluation, elementary probability rules are used to combine the cumulative probabilities from Eq. (3) into individual probabilities [6]:

$$P(y_i = \mathcal{C}_q \,|\, \mathbf{x}_i) = \begin{cases} P(y_i \preceq \mathcal{C}_1 \,|\, \mathbf{x}_i), & \text{if } q = 1, \\ P(y_i \preceq \mathcal{C}_q \,|\, \mathbf{x}_i) - P(y_i \preceq \mathcal{C}_{q-1} \,|\, \mathbf{x}_i), & \text{if } 1 < q < Q, \\ 1 - P(y_i \preceq \mathcal{C}_{Q-1} \,|\, \mathbf{x}_i), & \text{if } q = Q, \end{cases} \tag{4}$$

and the maximum probability class is then selected as the predicted label $\hat{y}_i$:

$$\hat{y}_i = \underset{\mathcal{C}_1 \preceq \mathcal{C}_q \preceq \mathcal{C}_Q}{\text{argmax}} P(y_i = \mathcal{C}_q \,|\, \mathbf{x}_i). \tag{5}$$

Loss Function. Cross-entropy loss is used as the loss function in the same manner as in the nominal model.

2.4   Our Approach: Ordinal Binary Decomposition

For our ordinal approach, we decompose the original Q-class ordinal problem into $Q-1$ binary decision problems, what is known as Ordinal Binary Decomposition (OBD). Each q problem consists on deciding if label $y \succ C_q$ conditioned to sample $\mathbf{x}$ $(1 \leq q < Q)$ (this is referred to as the "Ordered partitions" scheme in [7]).

To adapt the outputs of the model to this, the fully-connected block is substituted by $Q-1$ fully-connected blocks, each one with $\lfloor 4096/(Q-1) \rfloor$ units layers (in order to maintain a similar number of parameters) and a single output unit with sigmoid activation. Each of the $Q-1$ outputs of the model o_q is trying to predict the probability $P(y \succ C_q \mid \mathbf{x})$. The result of this modification is obtaining $Q-1$ different models, which share their convolutional feature extraction parameters and are trained simultaneously.

The whole architecture is illustrated in Table 1 under the column "OBD".

Decision Rule. In the case of the OBD model, because the outputs are not individual probabilities but cumulative ones ($o_k = P(y \succ C_k \mid \mathbf{x})$), the decision rule requires combining several outputs. Moreover, these probabilities may be inconsistent: nothing forces them to fulfil $P(y \succ C_i) \geq P(y \succ C_{i+1})$ and $\sum_{i=1}^{Q} P(y = C_i) = 1$. For this reason, Eq. 4 cannot be applied as for the CLM.

In order to circumvent this problem, a stable approach based on the ECOC framework is used: the ideal output vector $\mathbf{v}(C_i)$ for each class C_i is considered, $\mathbf{v}(C_i) = (c_1, \ldots, c_{Q-1})$ where $c_j = 1\{C_j \prec C_i\}$, i.e. a vector with ones in all positions corresponding with classes which are lower or equal than C_i in the ordinal scale. This makes the ideal zero-one output for a sample $\mathbf{x}_i$ with label $y_i = C_k$ the vector:

$$\mathbf{v}(C_k) = (c_1, \ldots, c_{k-1}, c_k, \ldots, c_{Q-1}) = (1, \ldots, 1, 0, \ldots, 0), \tag{6}$$

i.e., for a 4 class ordinal problem with labels C_1, C_2, C_3, and C_4 the ideal outputs would be $\mathbf{v}(C_1) = (0,0,0)$, $\mathbf{v}(C_2) = (1,0,0)$, $\mathbf{v}(C_3) = (1,1,0)$, and $\mathbf{v}(C_4) = (1,1,1)$.

The decision rule is based on determining the ideal vector which minimizes the distance to the obtained output vector $\mathbf{o}$:

$$\hat{y}_i = \operatorname*{argmin}_{C_1 \preceq C_q \preceq C_Q} \|\mathbf{o} - \mathbf{v}(C_q)\|_2. \tag{7}$$

The L_2 norm is selected as the distance metric to align it with the loss function of the optimization process.

Loss Function. For the OBD methodology, categorical cross-entropy has been substituted by the Squared Error loss because it copes better with the distance function used for the ECOC decision:

$$\ell(\mathbf{x}_i) = \sum_{k=1}^{Q-1} (1\{y_i \succ C_k\} - P(y_i \succ C_k \mid \mathbf{x}_i))^2. \tag{8}$$

Table 1. The three proposed models. Convolutional layers are denoted by "conv⟨kernel size⟩-⟨no. features⟩" and fully-connected layers as "FC-⟨output size⟩".

	Nominal	CLM	OBD		
	Input	Input	Input		
Feature extraction	conv3-64	conv3-64	conv3-64		
	maxpool	maxpool	maxpool		
	conv3-128	conv3-128	conv3-128		
	maxpool	maxpool	maxpool		
	conv3-256	conv3-256	conv3-256		
	conv3-256	conv3-256	conv3-256		
	maxpool	maxpool	maxpool		
	conv3-512	conv3-512	conv3-512		
	conv3-512	conv3-512	conv3-512		
	maxpool	maxpool	maxpool		
	conv3-512	conv3-512	conv3-512		
	conv3-512	conv3-512	conv3-512		
	maxpool	maxpool	maxpool		
Classification	FC-4096	FC-4096	FC-$\lfloor 4096/(Q-1)\rfloor$	[...]	FC-$\lfloor 4096/(Q-1)\rfloor$
	FC-4096	FC-4096	FC-$\lfloor 4096/(Q-1)\rfloor$		FC-$\lfloor 4096/(Q-1)\rfloor$
	FC-Q	FC-1	FC-1		FC-1
	softmax	link function	sigmoid		sigmoid

$$Q - 1 \text{ times}$$

3 Experiment Design

3.1 Dataset

The diabetic retinopathy dataset from Kaggle[1] is used for testing the model performance. It consists on a total of 88 702 retina images labelled by a clinician on a 0 to 4 scale evaluating the presence of diabetic retinopathy. It contains 65 343 images labelled as class 0, 6205 images labelled as class 1, 13 153 images

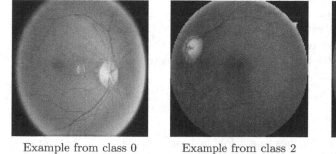

Example from class 0   Example from class 2   Example from class 4

Fig. 1. Sample images from the diabetic retinopathy dataset.

[1] https://www.kaggle.com/c/diabetic-retinopathy-detection.

labelled as class 2, 2087 images labelled as class 3, and 1914 images labelled as class 4. Three sample images can be seen in Fig. 1.

We consider this database to be a good benchmark for performance because of the clear and direct ordering of the class labels, as well as the high imbalance ratio between the classes, a very common pattern of medical datasets.

3.2   Training Scheme

Before training, all images are normalized to a resolution of 128×128 pixels.

Three different models are tested: the unmodified VGG nominal approach described in Sect. 2.2, the CLM model described in Sect. 2.3 and the proposed OBD model described in Sect. 2.4.

In all cases, weights are initialized randomly using the He initialization scheme described in [8]. They are then adjusted using the Adam method [9] with a learning rate $\eta = 10^{-4}$. Dropout and L_2 regularization is applied in the fully-connected layers like in the original VGG proposal [12]. The nominal model has approximately 128.79×10^6 trainable parameters, the CLM has 128.77×10^6 trainable parameters, and the OBD model has 116.18×10^6 trainable parameters.

In order to help overcome the class imbalance, class weighting is applied to the loss function based on n_q (number of training samples for class C_q):

$$w_q = \frac{e^{-Cn_q}}{\sum_{i=1}^{Q} e^{-Cn_i}}, \tag{9}$$

where C is a constant defined as $C = 3 \times 10^{-5}$. Thus, we define a new loss function with the form of:

$$\ell_w(\mathbf{x}_i) = w_k \ell(\mathbf{x}_i) \tag{10}$$

where the class label of sample $\mathbf{x}_i$ is $y_i = C_k$. In this way, the least represented classes contribute more and vice versa.

Before training, 10% of training samples are reserved for validation. Model weights are updated in batches of 72 training samples and loss performance is monitored on both training and validation. If validation performance does not increase for 5 full epochs, training is halted, and the best performing parameters over the validation set are restored.

Values for η, C and the batch size have been selected heuristically because of resource constraints.

3.3   Cross-Validation

The experiment is repeated 5 times in a 5-fold fashion, where the original dataset is split into 5 disjoint subsets, and, at each step, one of the subsets is used for test and the rest are used for training. This leaves 70 962 training samples (of which 7096 are reserved for validation) and 17 740 test samples per fold.

In Sect. 4, mean results and standard deviation are reported for each methodology.

3.4   Performance Metrics

Given that the dataset presents a very high class imbalance, the traditional Correct Classification Rate (CCR) will not be a representative measure of model performance: a dummy classifier that always assign the majority class label (class 0) would obtain a CCR of 73%.

In order to monitor per-class performance, the classification can be partitioned into Q binary problems (using a One-vs-Rest approach), and traditional binary performance metrics such as Accuracy, Precision, Sensitivity or F-1 score can be computed for each class. Additionally, the Receiver Operating Characteristic (ROC) curve for each class can be obtained. Moreover, global metrics such as the Average Area Under the ROC curve ($AvAUC$), minimum sensitivity (MS) and geometric mean of the sensitivities (GMS) [5] will be also included.

Also, for ordinal classification problems, rank agreement metrics including the Root of Mean Squared Error ($RMSE$) (comparing actual and predicted labels, represented as consecutive integers in the ordinal scale), Spearman's rank correlation coefficient (r_s) [4] or the Quadratic Weighted Cohen's Kappa (κ) [2] have been selected as well for evaluation.

4   Results

The per-fold average experimental results are shown in Table 2. The CLM is able to improve ordinal metrics by a little, at the cost of worsening metrics related to the imbalance problem ($AvAUC$, MS, and GMS). Meanwhile, the OBD model improves the ordinal metrics further while also improving class balancing metrics. This is done at the cost of worsening CCR, but only because of the high class imbalance.

In order to have a more granular view of the performance, the binary results per-class are provided in Fig. 2, and the corresponding ROC curves are included in Fig. 3. Furthermore, the weighted confusion matrices for each model are shown in Fig. 4.

From Fig. 2 it can be noted that, although Table 2 shows that the CLM improves on the ordinal metrics, it fails on every class balancing metric compared to the nominal model, as it ignores both classes 1 and 3. The OBD model, on the other hand, is able to improve both class balancing and ordinal metrics This is achieved at the cost of losing some performance on the extreme classes, but note how sensitivity and precision never fall to zero when using the OBD model on any class, that is, no class is ignored systematically. This is easily seen on the confusion matrices for each model (Fig. 4).

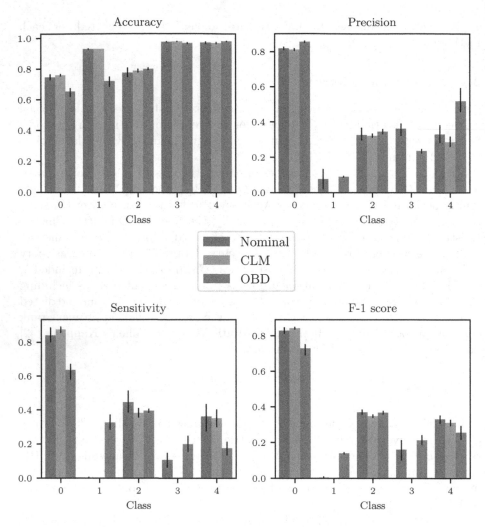

Fig. 2. Per-class (One-vs-Rest) binary results. The black line on each bar represents ± the standard deviation. (Color figure online)

The OBD model maintains a good balance between Precision and Recall for all classes in the One-vs-Rest scheme, as can be seen in Fig. 3: it is able to maintain or improve AUC for all classes, unlike the CLM. Note also that it is able to achieve this with 9.8% less parameters than the other two models.

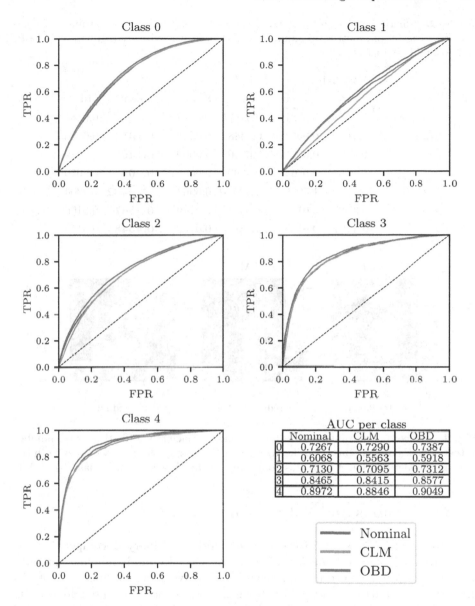

Fig. 3. Per-class (One-vs-Rest) ROC curves, along with their area under the curve (AUC).

Table 2. Experimental results for all three methodologies. Metrics to maximize are marked with (↑) and metrics to minimize with (↓). Best results are highlighted in **bold** and second best in *italics*.

	Nominal		CLM		OBD	
	Mean	Std. dev.	Mean	Std. dev.	Mean	Std. dev.
CCR (↑)	*0.6965*	0.0281	**0.7097**	0.0098	0.5583	0.0384
$AvAUC$ (↑)	*0.7620*	0.0073	0.7448	0.0049	**0.7655**	0.0046
MS (↑)	*0.0023*	0.0027	0.0000	0.0000	**0.1466**	0.0229
GMS (↑)	*0.0771*	0.0704	0.0000	0.0000	**0.3056**	0.0050
$RMSE$ (↓)	28.1576	1.4299	*27.1670*	0.6964	**25.9482**	0.4304
r_s (↑)	0.3738	0.0198	*0.3785*	0.0109	**0.3867**	0.0106
κ (↑)	0.4284	0.0175	*0.4462*	0.0126	**0.4548**	0.0155

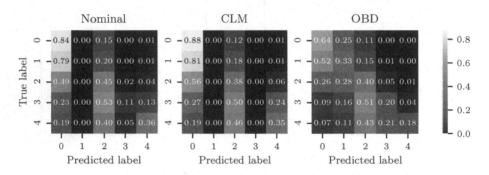

Fig. 4. Weighted confusion matrices for each model. Each row is divided by the number of test samples of that class in order to account for class imbalance. Note how both the Nominal model and CLM fail catastrophically on the classification of classes 1 and 3.

5   Conclusions and Future Work

A new ordinal CNN architecture based on Ordinary Binary Decomposition has been proposed, showing that it is able to outperform a purely nominal approach as well as a previous ordinal approach in a highly imbalanced scenario as the diabetic retinopathy dataset from Kaggle. This dataset was used for testing the model performance. Specifically, the proposed OBD methodology is able to improve both class balancing and ordinal metrics as Root of Mean Squared Error, Spearman's rank correlation coefficient and Quadratic Weighted Cohen's Kappa. This architecture is easy to adapt to other medical diagnosis tasks and also other popular ordinal 2D image classification tasks, like age prediction.

While VGG is a widely tested and overall well performing model, different and more novel architectures could also be adapted in the same manner. This adds a new fairly generic tool for classification tasks where ordinal information can be exploited.

In a future work, more complex data structures like 3D images can be studied, and better class balancing approaches than loss weighting, such as data augmentation, can be applied.

Acknowledgments. This work has been partially subsidised by the Spanish Ministry of Economy and Competitiveness (MINECO) [project reference TIN2017-85887-C2-1-P], the "Consejería de Economía, Conocimiento, Empresas y Universidad" of the "Junta de Andalucía" [project reference UCO-1261651] and FEDER funds of the European Union. Javier Barbero-Gómez research has been subsidised by the FPI Predoctoral Program of the Spanish Ministry of Science, Innovation and Universities (MCIU) [grant reference PRE2018-085659].

References

1. Agresti, A.: Analysis of Ordinal Categorical Data. Wiley Series in Probability and Statistics, Wiley, Hoboken (2010)
2. Ben-David, A.: Comparison of classification accuracy using Cohen's weighted Kappa. Expert Syst. Appl. **34**(2), 825–832 (2008)
3. Cardoso, J.S., Pinto da Costa, J.F.: Learning to classify ordinal data the data replication method. J. Mach. Learn. Res. **8**, 1393–1429 (2007)
4. Cardoso, J.S., Sousa, R.: Measuring the performance of ordinal classification. Int. J. Pattern Recogn. Artif. Intell. **25**(08), 1173–1195 (2011)
5. Dorado-Moreno, M., Pérez-Ortiz, M., Gutiérrez, P.A., Ciria, R., Briceño, J., Hervás-Martínez, C.: Dynamically weighted evolutionary ordinal neural network for solving an imbalanced liver transplantation problem. Artif. Intell. Med.. **77**, 1–11 (2017)
6. Frank, E., Hall, M.: A simple approach to ordinal classification. In: De Raedt, L., Flach, P. (eds.) ECML 2001. LNCS (LNAI), vol. 2167, pp. 145–156. Springer, Heidelberg (2001). https://doi.org/10.1007/3-540-44795-4_13
7. Gutiérrez, P.A., Pérez-Ortiz, M., Sánchez-Monedero, J., Fernández-Navarro, F., Hervás-Martínez, C.: Ordinal regression methods: survey and experimental study. IEEE Trans. Knowl. Data Eng. **28**(1), 127–146 (2016)
8. He, K., Zhang, X., Ren, S., Sun, J.: Delving Deep into Rectifiers: Surpassing Human-Level Performance on ImageNet Classification. arXiv:1502.01852 [cs], February 2015
9. Kingma, D.P., Ba, J.: Adam: A Method for Stochastic Optimization. arXiv:1412.6980 [cs], January 2017
10. McCullagh, P.: Regression models for ordinal data. J. Roy. Stat. Soc. Ser. B (Methodol.) **42**(2), 109–127 (1980)
11. Sánchez-Monedero, J., Pérez-Ortiz, M., Sáez, A., Gutiérrez, P.A., Hervás-Martínez, C.: Partial order label decomposition approaches for melanoma diagnosis. Appl. Soft Comput. **64**, 341–355 (2018)
12. Simonyan, K., Zisserman, A.: Very Deep Convolutional Networks for Large-Scale Image Recognition. arXiv:1409.1556 [cs], April 2015
13. Vargas, V.M., Gutiérrez, P.A., Hervás-Martínez, C.: Cumulative link models for deep ordinal classification. Neurocomputing **401**, 48–58 (2020)

Features as Keypoints and How Fuzzy Transforms Retrieve Them

Irina Perfilieva$^{(\boxtimes)}$ (iD) and David Adamczyk

Institute for Research and Applications of Fuzzy Modeling, Centre of Excellence IT4Innovations, University of Ostrava, 30. dubna 22, Ostrava, Czech Republic
{irina.perfilieva,david.adamczyk}@osu.cz

Abstract. We are focused on a new fast and robust algorithm of image/signal feature extraction in the form of representative keypoints. We analyze various multi-scale representations of a one-dimensional signal in spaces with a closeness relation determined by a symmetric and positive semi-definite kernel. We show that kernels arising from generating functions of fuzzy partitions can be used in a scale space representation of a one-dimensional signal. We show that the reconstruction from the proposed multi-scale representations is of better quality than the reconstruction from MLP with almost double the number of neurons in 4 hidden layers. Finally, we propose a new algorithm of keypoints localization and description and test it on financial time series with high volatility.

Keywords: Multi-scale representation · Keypoint · Fuzzy partition · Fuzzy transform

1 Introduction

We are focused on a new fast and robust algorithm of image/signal feature extraction in the form of representative keypoints. This problem closely relates to the data processing by neural networks, extraction of stable features that are invariant under various geometric transformations.

Our motivation is supported by the recently published overview of the explainability of artificial intelligence [1], the authors of which pointed out that "The sophistication of AI-powered systems has lately increased to such an extent that almost no human intervention is required for their design and deployment. When decisions derived from such systems ultimately affect humans' lives (as in e.g. medicine, law or defense), there is an emerging need for understanding how such decisions are furnished by AI methods." They propose to link explainability to understanding how the data is processed by the model, which means how the results obtained contribute to solving the imposed problem. This forces us to focus on feature extraction because it is the first step in every machine learning algorithm.

© Springer Nature Switzerland AG 2021
I. Rojas et al. (Eds.): IWANN 2021, LNCS 12862, pp. 14–27, 2021.
https://doi.org/10.1007/978-3-030-85099-9_2

Depending on feature extractors, we distinguish between local, semi-local, and non-local features. The character of their extraction (by means of convolution) depends on a receptive field of the corresponding kernel. The latter is connected with semantics of the extracted value and by this, contributes to the explainability. Therefore, to increase the level of explainability, we shall consciously select convolution kernels.

In image processing tasks, features are associated with keypoints and their descriptors. In early works, both were identified with local areas of the image that correspond to its content (not related to the background). Thus, the processing was computationally consuming and depending on many space-environment conditions: illumination, position, resolution, etc. In the seminal work [12], it was shown that invariant local features (Harris corners and their rotation invariant descriptors) can contribute to solving general problems of image recognition. In detail, an invariant image description in a neighborhood of a point can be described by the set of its convolutions with Gaussian derivatives. Because the Harris corner detector is sensitive to changes in image scale, it was expanded in [8] to the descriptor known in the literature as SIFT to achieve scale and rotation invariance and to provide reliable matching over a wide range of affine distortions. The publication of SIFT has inspired many modifications: SURF, PCA-SIFT, GLOH, Gauss-SIFT, etc., (see [7] and references therein), aimed at improving its efficiency in various senses: reliability, computation time, etc. However, the main stages and their semantics have been preserved.

Our contribution to this topic is as follows: we use the basic methodology of SIFT and its modifications, but use non-traditional kernels derived from the theory of F-transforms [9]. This allows you to simplify the scaling and selection of key points, as well as reduce their number and enhance robustness. We also propose a new keypoint descriptor and test it on matching financial time series with high volatility.

The main theoretical result that we arrive at here is that the Gaussian kernel as the predominant in the scale-space theory can be replaced with the same success by a special symmetric positive semi-definite kernel with a local support. In particular, we show that generating function of a triangular-based uniform fuzzy partition of $\mathbb{R}$ can be used for determining such kernel. This fact allows us to base upon the theory of F-transforms and its ability to extract features (keypoints) with a clear understanding of their semantic meaning [10].

2 Briefly About the Theory of Scale-Space Representations

We start with a brief overview of the mentioned theory because it explains the proposed methods. Perhaps, the quad-tree methodology [4] is the first type of multi-scale representation of image data. It focuses on recursively dividing an image into smaller areas controlled by the intensity range. A low-pass pyramid representation was proposed in [3], where the added benefit to multi-scaling was that the image size decreased exponentially compared to scale level.

Koenderink [5] emphasized that scaling up and down the internal scope of observations and handling image structures at all scales (in accordance with the task) contribute to a successful image analysis. The challenge is to understand the image at all relevant scales at the same time, but not as an unrelated set of derived images at different levels of blur.

The basic idea (in Lindeberg [6]) how to obtain a multi-scale representation of an object is to embed it into a one-parameter family of gradually smoothed ones where fine-scale details are sequentially suppressed. Under fairly general conditions, the author showed that the Gaussian kernel and its derivatives are the only possible smoothing kernels. These conditions are mainly linearity and shift invariance, combined with various ways of formalizing the notion that structures on a coarse scale should correspond to simplifications of corresponding structures on a fine scale.

A scale-space representation differs from a multi-scale representation in that it uses the same spatial sampling at all scales and one continuous scale parameter as the generator. By the construction in Witkin [13], a scale-space representation is a one-parameter family of derived signals constructed using convolution with a one-parameter family of Gaussian kernels of increasing width.

Formally, a scale-space family of a continuous signal is constructed as follows. For a signal $f : \mathbb{R}^N \to \mathbb{R}$, the scale-space representation $L : \mathbb{R}^N \times \mathbb{R}_+ \to \mathbb{R}$ is defined by:

$$L(\cdot, 0) = f(\cdot),$$
$$L(\cdot, t) = g(\cdot, t) \star f, \tag{1}$$

where $t \in \mathbb{R}_+$ is the scale parameter and $g : \mathbb{R}^N \times \mathbb{R}_+ \to \mathbb{R}$ is the Gaussian kernel as follows:

$$g(x, t) = \frac{1}{(2\pi t)^{N/2}} \exp - \sum_{i=1}^{N} \frac{x_i^2}{2t}.$$

The scale parameter t relates to the standard deviation of the kernel g, and is a natural measure of spatial scale at the level t.

As an important remark, we note that the scale-space family L can be defined as the solution to the diffusion (heat) equation

$$\partial_t L = \frac{1}{2} \nabla^T \nabla L, \tag{2}$$

with initial condition $L(\cdot, 0) = f$. The Laplace operator, $\nabla^T \nabla$ or Δ, the divergence of the gradient, is taken in the spatial variables.

The solution to (2) in one-dimension and in the case where the spatial domain is R is known as the convolution ($\star$) of f (initial condition) and the fundamental solution:

$$L(\cdot, t) = g(\cdot, t) \star f, \tag{3}$$

$$g(x, t) = \frac{1}{(\sqrt{2\pi t})} \exp -\frac{x^2}{2t}. \tag{4}$$

The following two questions arise: is this approach the only reasonable way to perform low-level processing, and are Gaussian kernels and their derivatives the only smoothing kernels that can be used? Many authors cite Lind94, Wit83, Koen84 answer these questions positively, which leads to the default choice of Gaussian kernels in most image processing tasks. In this article, we want to expand on the set of useful kernels suitable for performing scale-space representations. In particular, we propose to use kernels arising from generating functions of fuzzy partitioning.

3   Space with a Fuzzy Partition

In this section, we introduce space that plays an important role in our research. A space with a fuzzy partition is considered as a space with a proximity (closeness) relation, which is a weak version of a metric space. Our goal is to show that the diffusion (heat conduction) equation in (2) can be extended to spaces with closeness, where the concepts of derivatives are adapted to nonlocal cases.

Let us first recall the basic definitions. As we indicated at the beginning, our goal is to extend the Laplace operators to those that take into account the specifics of spaces with fuzzy partitions. For this reason, in the following sections, we recall the basic concepts on this topic.

3.1   Fuzzy Partition

Definition 1: Fuzzy sets $A_1, \ldots, A_n : [a, b] \to \mathbb{R}$, establish a *fuzzy partition* of the real interval $[a, b]$ with nodes $a = x_1 < \ldots < x_n = b$, if for all $k = 1, \ldots, n$, the following conditions are valid (we assume $x_0 = a$, $x_{n+1} = b$):

1. $A_k(x_k) = 1$, $A_k(x) > 0$ if $x \in (x_{k-1}, x_{k+1})$;
2. $A_k(x) = 0$ if $x \notin (x_{k-1}, x_{k+1})$;
3. $A_k(x)$ is continuous,
4. $A_k(x)$, for $k = 2, \ldots, n$, strictly increases on $[x_{k-1}, x_k]$ and $A_k(x)$ strictly decreases on $[x_k, x_{k+1}]$ for $k = 1, \ldots, n-1$,

The membership functions $A_1, \ldots, A_n$ are called *basic functions* [9].

Definition 2: The fuzzy partition $A_1, \ldots, A_n$, where $n \geq 2$, is *h-uniform* if nodes $x_1 < \cdots < x_n$ are *h*-equidistant, i.e. for all $k = 1, \ldots, n-1$, $x_{k+1} = x_k + h$, where $h = (b - a)/(n - 1)$, and the following additional properties are fulfilled [9]:

1. for all $k = 2, \ldots, n-1$ and for all $x \in [0, h]$, $A_k(x_k - x) = A_k(x_k + x)$,

2. for all $k = 2, \ldots, n-1$, and for all $x \in [x_k, x_{k+1}]$, $A_k(x) = A_{k-1}(x-h)$, and $A_{k+1}(x) = A_k(x-h)$.

Proposition 1: If the fuzzy partition $A_1, \ldots, A_n$ of $[a, b]$ is h-uniform, then there exists an even function $A_0 : [-1, 1] \to [0, 1]$, such that for all $k = 1, \ldots, n$:

$$A_k(x) = A_0 \left(\frac{x - x_k}{h} \right), \quad x \in [x_{k-1}, x_{k+1}].$$

A_0 is called a *generating function* of uniform fuzzy partition [9].

Remark 1. Generating function $A_h(x) = A_0(x/h)$ of an h-uniform fuzzy partition produces the corresponding to it kernel $A_h(x-y)$ and the normalized kernel $\frac{1}{h}A_h(x-y)$, so that for all $x \in \mathbb{R}$,

$$\frac{1}{h} \int_{-\infty}^{\infty} A_h(x - y) dy = 1.$$

Remark 2. A fuzzy partition of an interval can be easily generalized to any (finite) direct product of intervals and by this, to an arbitrary n-dimensional region. As an example, we take two intervals $[a, b]$ and $[c, d]$ and consider $[a, b] \times [c, d]$ as a rectangular area in the 2D space. If fuzzy sets $A_1, \ldots, A_n : [a, b] \to \mathbb{R}$, and $B_1, \ldots, B_m : [c, d] \to \mathbb{R}$, establish fuzzy partitions of the corresponding intervals $[a, b]$ and $[c, d]$, then their products $A_i B_j$, $i = 1, \ldots, n; j = 1, \ldots, m$, establish a fuzzy partition of $[a, b] \times [c, d]$.

3.2   Discrete Universe and Its Fuzzy Partition

From the point of view of image/signal processing, we assume that the domain of the corresponding functions is finite, i.e. finitely sampled in $\mathbb{R}$, and the functions are identified with high-dimensional vectors of their values at the selected samples in the discretized domain. Moreover, we assume that the domain and the range of all considered functions are equipped with the corresponding relations of closeness.

The best formal model of all these assumptions is a weighted graph $G = (V, E, w)$ where $V = \{v_1, \ldots, v_\ell\}$ is a finite set of vertices, and E ($E \subset V \times V$) is a set of weighted edges so that $w : E \to \mathbb{R}_+$. The edge $e = (v_i, v_j)$ connects two vertices v_i and v_j, and then the weight of e is $w(v_i, v_j)$ or just w_{ij}. Weights are set using the function $w : V \times V \to \mathbb{R}_+$, which is symmetric ($w_{ij} = w_{ji}, \forall 1 \le i, j \le \ell$), non-negative ($w_{ij} \ge 0$) and $w_{ij} = 0$ if $(v_i, v_j) \notin E$. The notation $v_i \sim v_j$ denotes two adjacent vertices v_i and v_j with an existing edge connecting them.

Let $H(V)$ denote the Hilbert space of real-valued functions on the set of vertices V of the graph, where if $f, h \in H(V)$ and $f, h : V \to \mathbb{R}$, then the inner product $\langle f, h \rangle_{H(V)} = \sum_{v \in V} f(v)h(v)$. Similarly, $H(E)$ denotes the space of real-valued functions defined on the set E of edges of a graph G. This space has the inner product $\langle F, H \rangle_{H(E)} = \sum_{(u,v) \in E} F(u, v)H(u, v) = \sum_{u \in V} \sum_{v \sim u} F(u, v)H(u, v)$, where $F, H : E \to \mathbb{R}$ are two functions on $H(E)$.

We assume that the set of vertices V is identified with the set of indices $V = \{1, \ldots, \ell\}$ and that $[1, \ell]$ is h-uniform fuzzy partitioned with normalized basic functions $A_1^h, \ldots A_\ell^h$, so that $A_k^h(x) = A_h(x - k)/h$, $k = 1, \ldots, \ell$, $A_h(x) = A_0(x/h)$ and A_0 is the generating function.

Definition 3: A weighted graph $G = (V, E, w)$ is fuzzy weighted, if $V = \{1, \ldots, \ell\}$, $A_1^h, \ldots A_\ell^h$ is an h-uniform fuzzy partition, generated by A_0, and $w_{ij} = A_i^h(j)$, $i, j = 1, \ldots, \ell$. The fuzzy weighted graph $G = (V, E, w)$, corresponding to the h-uniform fuzzy partition, will be denoted $G_h = (V, E, A_h)$.

4   Discrete Laplace Operator

In this section, we recall the definition of (non-local) Laplace operator as a differential operator given by the divergence of the gradient of a function (see [2]).

Let $G = (V, E, w)$ be a weighted graph, and let $f : V \to \mathbb{R}$ be a function in $H(V)$. The difference operator $d : H(V) \to H(E)$ of f, is defined on $(u, v) \in E$ by

$$(df)(u, v) = \sqrt{w(u, v)}\,(f(v) - f(u)). \tag{5}$$

The directional derivative of f, at vertex $v \in V$, along the edge $e - (u, v)$, is defined as:

$$\partial_v f(u) = (df)(u, v). \tag{6}$$

The adjoint to the difference operator $d^* : H(E) \to H(V)$, is a linear operator defined by:

$$\langle df, H\rangle_{H(E)} = \langle f, d^* H\rangle_{H(V)}, \tag{7}$$

for any function $H \in H(E)$ and function $f \in H(V)$.

Proposition 2: The adjoint operator d^* can be expressed at a vertex $u \in V$ by the following formula:

$$(d^* H)(u) = \sum_{v \sim u} \sqrt{w(u, v)}\,(H(v, u) - H(u, v)). \tag{8}$$

The divergence operator, defined by $-d^*$, measures the network outflow of a function in $H(E)$, at each vertex of the graph.

The weighted gradient operator of $f \in H(V)$, at vertex $u \in V$, $\forall (u, v_i) \in E$, is a column vector:

$$\nabla_w f(u) = (\partial_v f(u) : v \sim u)^T = (\partial_{v_1} f(u), \ldots, \partial_{v_k} f(u))^T.$$

The weighted Laplace operator $\Delta_w : H(V) \to H(V)$, is defined by:

$$\Delta_w f = -\frac{1}{2} d^*(df). \tag{9}$$

Proposition 3 [2]**:** The weighted Laplace operator Δ_w at $f \in H(V)$ acts as follows:

$$(\Delta_w f)(u) = -\sum_{v \sim u} w(u,v)(f(v) - f(u)).$$

This Laplace operator is linear and corresponds to the graph Laplacian.

Proposition 4 [11]**:** Let $G_h = (V, E, A_h)$ be a fuzzy weighted graph, corresponding to the h-uniform fuzzy partition of $V = \{1, \ldots \ell\}$. Then, the weighted Laplace operator Δ_h at $f \in H(V)$ acts as follows:

$$(\Delta_h f)(i) = -\sum_{i \sim j} A_i^h(j)(f(j) - f(i)) = f(i) - F^h[f]_i,$$

where $F^h[f]_i$, $i = 1, \ldots, \ell$, is the i-th discrete F-transform component of f, cf. [9].

5   Multi-scale Representation in a Space with a Fuzzy Partition

Taking into account the introduced notation, we propose the following scheme for the multi-scale representation L_{FP} of the signal $f : V \to \mathbb{R}$, where $V = \{1, \ldots, \ell\}$ and subscript "FP" stands for an h-uniform fuzzy partition determined by parameter $h \in \mathbb{N}$, $h \geq 1$:

$$L_{FP}(\cdot, 0) = f(\cdot),$$
$$L_{FP}(\cdot, t) = F^{2^t h}[f], \tag{10}$$

where $t \in \mathbb{N}$ is the scale parameter and $F^{2^t h}[f]$ is the whole vector of F-transform components of f. The scale parameter t relates to the length of the support of the corresponding basic function. As in the case of (1), it is a natural measure of spatial scale at level t. To show the relationship to the diffusion equation, we formulate the following general result.

Proposition 5: Assume that two time continuously differentiated real function $f : [a, b] \to \mathbb{R}$, and $[a, b]$ is h- and $2h$-uniform fuzzy partitioned by $\Lambda_1^h, \ldots, \Lambda_n^h$ and $A_1^{2h}, \ldots, A_n^{2h}$, where basic functions A_i^h (A_i^{2h}), $i = 1, \ldots, n$, are generated by $A_0(x) = 1 - |x|$ with the node at $x_i = a + \frac{b-a}{n-1}(i-1)$. Then,

$$F^{2h}[f]_i - F^h[f]_i \approx \frac{h^2}{4} f''(x_i). \tag{11}$$

The semantic meaning of this proposition in relation to the proposed scheme (10) of multi-scale representation L_{FP} of f is as follows:

The FT-based Laplacian of f (11) can be approximated by the (weighted) differences of two adjacent convolutions determined by the triangular-shaped generating function of a fuzzy partition.

6 Experiments with Time Series

6.1 Reconstruction from FT-based Laplacians

To demonstrate the effectiveness of the proposed representation, we first show that an initial time series can be (with a sufficient precision) reconstructed from a sequence of FT-based Laplacians. Below, we illustrate this claim on a financial time series with high volatility. With each value of $t = 1, 2, \ldots$ we obtain the corresponding FT-based Laplacian as the difference between two adjacent convolutions (vectors with F-transform components), so that we obtain the sequence

$$\{L_{FP}(\cdot, t+1) - L_{FP}(\cdot, t) \mid t = 1, 2, \ldots\}$$

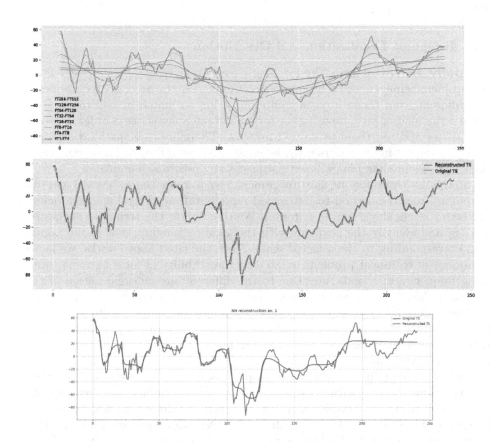

Fig. 1. *Top.* The sequence of reconstruction steps, where with each value $t = 1, 2, \ldots$ we improve the quality of the reconstruction by adding the corresponding Laplacian to the previous one. *Middle.* The original time series (blue) against its reconstruction (red) from a sequence of FT-based Laplacians with the distance 89.6. *Bottom.* The original time series (blue) against its MLP reconstruction (in red) with the distance 159.3. (Color figure online)

The stop criterion is closeness to zero of the current difference. We then compute the reconstruction by summing all the elements in the sequence. Figure 1 shows the step-by-step reconstruction and the final reconstructed time series. The latter is plotted on the bottom image along with the original time series to give confidence in a perfect fit. The estimated Euclidean distance is 89.6.

In the same Fig. 1, we show one MLP reconstructions of the same time series with the following configurations: 4 hidden layers with 4086 neurons in each layer (common setting) and learning rate 0.001. It is obvious that the proposed multi-scale representation and subsequent reconstruction are computationally cheaper and give results with better reconstruction quality. To confirm, we give estimates of the Euclidean distances between the original time series and its reconstructions: (from a sequence of FT-based Laplacians) against 159.3 (using MLP).

6.2   Keypoint Localization and Description

Keypoint Localization. The localization accuracy of key points depends on the problem being solved. When analyzing time series, the accuracy requirements are different from those used in computer vision to match or register images. Time series focuses on comparing the target and reference series in order to detect similarities and use them to make a forecast. Therefore, the spatial coordinate is not so important in contrast to the comparative analysis of local trends and their changes in time intervals with adjacent key points as boundaries.

Taking into account the above arguments, we propose to localize and identify keypoints from the second-to-last scaled representation of the Laplacian before the latter meets the stopping criterion. We then follow the technique suggested in [7, 8] and identify the keypoint with the local extremum point of the Laplacian corresponding to the selected scale. As in the cited above works, we faced a number of technical problems related to the stability of local extrema, sampling frequency in a scale, etc. Due to the different spatial organization of the analyzed objects (time series versus images), we found simpler solutions to the problems raised. For example, in order to exclude extrema close to each other (and therefore they are very unstable), we leave only one representative, the value of which gives the best semantic correlation with the characteristic of this particular extremum.

Below, we give illustrations to some processed by us time series. They were selected from the cite with historical data in Yahoo Finance. We analyzed the 2016 daily adjusting closing prices using international stock indices, namely Prague (PX), Paris (FCHI), Frankfurt (GDAXI) and Moscow (MOEX). Due to the daily nature of the time series, they all have high volatility, which is additional support for the proposed method. In Fig. 2, we show the time series with stock indices PX (Prague) and its last three scaled representations of the Laplacian, where the latter satisfies the stopping criterion. Selected (filtered out) keypoints are marked with red (blue) dots.

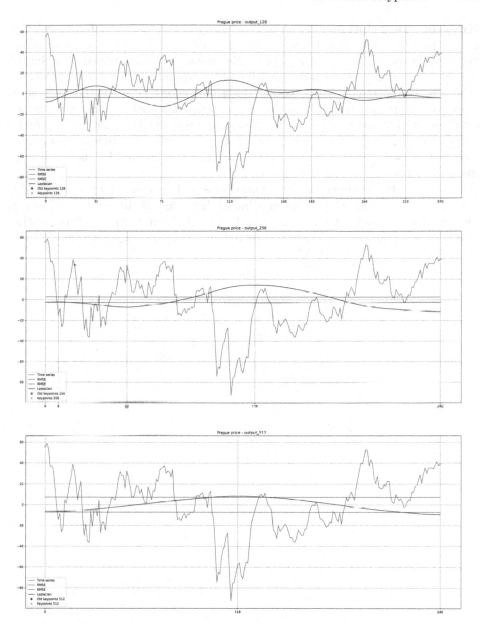

Fig. 2. The time series with stock indices PX (Prague) and its last three scaled representations of the Laplacian, where the latter *bottom image* satisfies the stopping criterion. Selected (filtered out) keypoints are marked with red (blue) dots. (Color figure online)

Keypoint Description. Due to the specificity of time series with high volatility, we propose a keypoint descriptor as a vector that includes only the Laplacian values at keypoints from two adjacent scales and in an area bounded by an interval with boundaries set by adjacent left/right keypoints from the same scale. In addition, we normalize the keypoint descriptor coordinates by the Laplacian value of the principal keypoint. As our experiments with matching keypoint descriptors of different time series show, the proposed keypoint descriptor is robust to noise and invariant with respect to spatial shifts and time series ranges. The last remark is that the quality of matching is estimated by the Euclidean distance between keypoint descriptors.

To illustrate the assertion about robustness and invariance, we show (Fig. 3) with the results of matches between principal keypoints of time series with stock indices PX (Prague), FCHI (Paris), and GDAXI (Frankfurt). In all cases, the stock indices PX were considered as tested and compared against the reference stock indices FCHI and GDAXI.

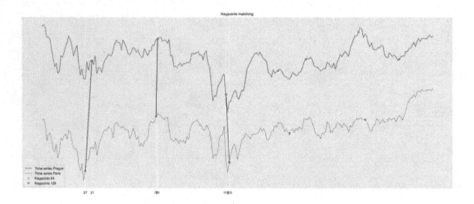

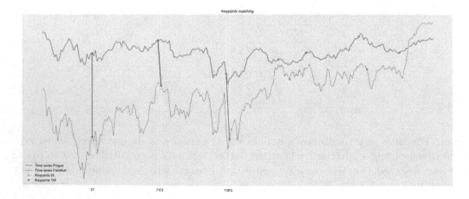

Fig. 3. The results of matches between principal keypoints of time series with stock indices PX (Prague), FCHI (Paris), and GDAXI (Frankfurt). The stock indices PX are considered as tested and compared against the reference stock indices FCHI *top image* and GDAXI *bottom image*.

7   Experiments with Images

In this section, we test our theory and methodology on images. We aim to show that the similar approach to that for the keypoints time series detection is applicable for images. In the latter case, we use the 2D space and a fuzzy partition of a rectangular area described in Remark 2, Sect. 3.1. We use triangular-shaped generating functions for each space dimension.

We show that for a given image, key points can be selected as extreme values of differences of scale-space convolutions of the image with triangular-shaped kernels. The two nearby scales are separated by the constant multiplicative factor $k = 2$. Each of the two stacks of scale-space convolutions consists of three images that are repeatedly convolved with kernels obtained from triangular-shaped generating functions. Adjacent images are subtracted to produce the Laplacian images. Finally, detection of local maxima and minima of the Laplacian images is based on the same procedure as in SIFT [8]. The initial image of the second scale-space stack is the result of down-sampling of the original one by factor 2.

The procedure is robust and simpler than in the e.g., method of SIFT [8]. We focus on keypoints as centers of fuzzy partition units, and therefore, their exact location as points where the Laplacian takes its extreme values is not that important.

As the last step, we compute two descriptors of each keypoint: the magnitude of the most influential gradient and the scale value.

Below, we illustrate the obtained results on the RGB-image "Seagull"[1] of dimension 852×480 (Fig. 4).

Fig. 4. The 852×480 image "Seagull": original (left); and with 115 keypoints from the two scale-spaces (right).

We got the following numbers of keypoints: 45 in the first scale-space, 70 in the second scale-space, and 115 in both. It is important to emphasize that some of the keypoints can be merged, so that their total number can be reduced. However, this step requires further analysis and it is computationally expensive. Therefore, we created three different fuzzy partitions: one for each set of

---

[1] https://ak2.picdn.net/shutterstock/videos/4928582/thumb/1.jpg.

keypoints and calculated three different direct and inverse F-transforms using the corresponding sets of keypoints as nodes of the partition units. The quality estimates are given in Table 1.

Table 1. MSE and SSIM quality indicators

Keypoints number	MSE	SSIM
45	1.665	0.998
70	1.312	0.998
115	1.853	0.998

8   Conclusion

We are focused on a new fast and robust algorithm of image/signal feature extraction in the form of representative keypoints. We have contributed to this topic by showing that the use of non-traditional kernels derived from the theory of F-transforms [9] leads to simplified algorithms and comparable efficiency in the selection of keypoints. Moreover, we reduced their number and enhanced robustness. This has been shown at the theoretical and experimental levels. We also proposed a new keypoint descriptor and tested it on matching financial time series with high volatility.

Acknowledgment. The work was supported from ERDF/ESF by the project "Centre for the development of Artificial Inteligence Methods for the Automotive Industry of the region" No. $CZ.02.1.01/0.0/0.0/17_049/0008414$. Additional support of the grant project SGS18/PrF-MF/2021 (Ostrava University) is kindly announced.

References

1. Arrieta, A.B., et al.: Explainable artificial intelligence (XAI): concepts, taxonomies, opportunities and challenges toward responsible AI. Inf. Fusion **58**, 82–115 (2020)
2. Elmoataz, A., Lezoray, O., Bougleux, S.: Discrete regularization on weighted graphs: a framework for image and manifold processing. IEEE Trans. Image Process. **17**, 1047–1060 (2008)
3. Burt, P.J.: Fast filter transform for image processing. Comput. Graph. Image Process. **16**, 20–51 (1981)
4. Klinger, A.: Pattern and search statistics. In: Proceedings of Symposium Held at the Center for Tomorrow, the Ohio State University, 14–16 June, pp. 303–337 (1971)
5. Koenderink, J.J.: The structure of images. Biol. Cybern. **50**, 363–370 (1984)
6. Lindeberg, T.: Scale-space theory: a basic tool for analyzing structures at different scales. J. Appl. Stat. **21**, 225–270 (1994)

7. Lindeberg, T.: Image matching using generalized scale-space interest points. J. Math. Imaging Vision **52**(1), 3–36 (2015)
8. Lowe, D.G.: Distinctive image features from scale-invariant keypoints. Int. J. Comput. Vision **60**(2), 91–110 (2004)
9. Perfilieva, I.: Fuzzy transforms: theory and applications. Fuzzy Sets Syst. **157**(8), 993–1023 (2006)
10. Molek, V., Perfilieva, I.: Deep learning and higher degree F-transforms: interpretable kernels before and after learning. Int. J. Comput. Intell. Syst. **13**(1), 1404–1414 (2020)
11. Perfilieva, I., Vlasanek, P.: Total variation with nonlocal FT-Laplacian for patch-based inpainting. Soft Comput. **23**, 1833–1841 (2019)
12. Schmid, C., Mohr, R.: Local grayvalue invariants for image retrieval. IEEE Trans. Pattern Anal. Mach. Intell. **19**(5), 530–535 (1997)
13. Witkin, A.P.: Scale-space filtering. In: Proceedings of 8th International Joint Conference on Artificial Intelligence, IJCAI 1983, vol. 2, pp. 1019–1022 (1983)

Instagram Hashtag Prediction Using Deep Neural Networks

Anna Beketova[1] and Ilya Makarov[1,2]([✉])

[1] HSE University, Moscow, Russia
ambeketova@edu.hse.ru, iamakarov@hse.ru
[2] Artificial Intelligence Research Institute, Moscow, Russia

Abstract. Instagram is one of the most popular photos sharing services. For more convenient content search people use hashtags (#nature, #love, etc.) in posts with photos. The author's aim is to make hashtag prediction possible and convenient for users.

The paper provides a reader with a detailed theoretical overview of Multi-Label Image Classification, Knowledge Distillation, and an overview of ResNet architecture. Next, the author proposes improvements on ResNet architecture allowing the model to boost quality and converge faster. Finally, the model type Self-Improving-Modified-Resnet (SIMR) is presented. Their main feature is the additional bottleneck block used as the tool incorporating benefits from a combination of self-training and knowledge distillation.

Keywords: Deep learning · Multi-label image classification · Knowledge distillation · Multimedia

1 Introduction

Every minute 11.6 TB of content is uploaded onto the Internet. Most of the publicly available photos are uploaded into Image and Video sharing Social Network Instagram. While ordinary users share their photos with friends, companies, and bloggers concerned about gaining more popularity. Instagram allows users to search for specific content by using #hashtags - user-generated tags that a user may or may not add to their post. The more popular hashtag is the more people tend to monitor it and, therefore, setting appropriate and popular hashtags for photos leads to an increase in user's fame faster.

This paper examines methods of multi-label image classification for the automatic generation of human-like Instagram Hashtags based on a photo. In addition, the author's own architecture is proposed and compared with other methods. Our goal is hashtag prediction in a multi-label image classification task. ResNet model and its modifications are used for predicting models. The author introduces the Self-Improving-Modified-Resnet (SIMR) architecture and examines its performance.

© Springer Nature Switzerland AG 2021
I. Rojas et al. (Eds.): IWANN 2021, LNCS 12862, pp. 28–42, 2021.
https://doi.org/10.1007/978-3-030-85099-9_3

As hashtags on Instagram are user-generated they may differ from person to person and do not have to relate to the photo content directly - some may contain personal opinion (#beautiful) or personal experience (#memory). Building a good human-like hashtag prediction system will lead to better human understanding. Firstly, such a system can make bloggers' life easier - it automatically generates better tags based on photo content and current trends. Secondly, with a more advanced understanding of people's feelings and life experience companies can personalize their products and advertising, gain customers' loyalty, and earn more money. The second part is not covered in the paper as each company can decide to what extent to use customers' data.

2   Methodology and Related Work

This chapter covers the main theoretical aspects of experiments. Every section presents its topic and refers to original related scientific papers. In the end, the author proposes a new architecture SIMR that incorporates benefits from the novel self distillation method, model improvements, and author's experiments.

2.1   Multi-Label Classification

Multi-Label Image Classification (MLIC) is a fundamental task in Computer Vision. It aims to tell whether an image has certain objects, features, etc. denoted by labels. Typical tasks of MLIC include human attribute recognition [1, 9, 15, 31, 34], scene understanding [49], retail checkout recognition [12, 55], facial attribute recognition [18]. Multi-label classification is more challenging than multi-class classification due to the combinatorial nature of the predictions.

MLIC problem has been widely explored, covering both label-separate and label-correlated methods. The first approach implies the conversion of MLIC to multiple binary image classification problems using binary relevance strategy [2, 53]. Label-correlated methodologies such as matrix completion [4], probabilistic label enhancement model (PLEM) [33] are proposed to model the semantic correlations between labels for MLIC. PLEM requires the construction of a maximum spanning tree (MST) of labels to take their co-occurrence into account and then use MST to solve MLIC problem.

Often researchers compare single-class image classification models using ImageNet [8] dataset. It contains images for 1000 classes. With the introduction of ImageNet Challenge many powerful Convolutional Neural Networks (CNN) appeared such as AlexNet [29], VGG [50], ResNet [20], DenseNet [24]. With them MLIC improved significantly. For large class numbers specific methods were suggested [47, 48] with applications to selecting based frames in video for recognition problem [26]. In combination with Recurrent Neural Networks (RNN) researchers propose CNN-RNN [54]. Applications to automated video editing and multimedia retrieval may also rely on image embeddings taken from classification neural networks latent representation [37, 52]. Additionally, we showed that ResNet family of deep CNNs and RNNs is widely used in other computer vision tasks, such as depth estimation [28, 39, 40, 43, 44].

Some researchers model label dependencies with graphs [32,41,57] or even graph-text features [42]. The approach is to model the co-occurrence dependencies with pairwise co-occurrence probabilities and use Markov random fields [17] to construct the final joint label probability.

Notations. The author denotes by L the number of labels and N the number of images. The training data $\mathcal{D} = \left\{ \left(\mathcal{I}^{(1)}, \mathbf{y}^{(1)} \right), \ldots, \left(\mathcal{I}^{(N)}, \mathbf{y}^{(N)} \right) \right\}$, where $\mathcal{I}^{(i)}$ is the ith image and $\mathbf{y}^{(i)} = \left[y_1^{(i)}, \ldots, y_L^{(i)} \right] \in \mathcal{Y} \subseteq \{0,1\}^L$ the label vector. For a given image i and label l, $y_l^{(i)} = 1$ (respectively 0) means that the label l is present in the image i (respectively - not present).

Loss. Various loss functions have been used for MLIC, such as Rank Loss [7] and Cross Entropy Loss [15,30,31,34,36]. When using the Cross Entropy Loss, MLIC task is defined as multiple binary classification problems. Author parsed Instagram photos and tags dataset from Instagram.com official web page. As the dataset is not balanced, the author adopts the Weighted Sigmoid Cross Entropy (WSCE) Loss in [30]:

$$\text{loss} = -\frac{1}{N} \sum_{i=1}^{N} \sum_{l=1}^{L} \omega_i^{(l)} \left(y_i^{(l)} \log \frac{1}{1 + e^{-x_i^{(l)}}} + \left(1 - y_i^{(l)} \right) \log \frac{e^{-x_i^{(l)}}}{1 + e^{-x_i^{(l)}}} \right) \quad (1)$$

$$\omega_i^{(l)} = \begin{cases} e^{1-p^{(l)}} & \text{if } y_i^{(l)} = 1 \\ e^{p^{(l)}} & \text{if } y_i^{(l)} = 0 \end{cases} \quad (2)$$

where $x_i^{(l)} \in \mathbb{R}$ is the output of the model - the predicted presence of label l in the image i and $y_i^{(l)} \in \{0,1\}$ - ground truth presence. Then presence score is calculated via sigmoid activation $1 / \left(1 + e^{-x_i^{(l)}} \right) \in [0,1]$. The weighting coefficient $\omega_i^{(l)}$ is used to balance training samples which is calculated with $p^{(l)}$ - the proportion of positive samples with label l in the training set.

WSCE loss function is modified from Cross Entropy Loss and has been used in several prior works on MLIC [16,31,36].

Metrics. Researchers in [5,11,59] compared different Deep Learning architectures on MS-COCO dataset (in more detail in the following chapter). The dataset has 2.9 tags per image that is similar to the author's dataset having 3.1 tags per image. As in these researches, the author evaluates models quality based on Recall@3 (the share of relevant items in top3 out of all relevant items) and Precision@3 (the share of relevant items in top3 out of 3 - the number of selected items).

2.2   Knowledge Distillation

Knowledge Distillation (KD) [22] was first introduced for model compression tasks [3]. In experiments the more layer a model has the more powerful it is keeping architectures equal. Initially the aim of KD was to build a powerful and complex neural network with many layers or an ensemble of them and distill (transfer) the collected knowledge to a smaller neural network, so-called a student-teacher paradigm.

FitNet architecture [45] introduced intermediate-level hints from the teacher hidden layers to guide the training process of the student network. Such methodology helps a student to learn better through the prediction of a teacher hidden hint layer regularizing the model. The student model may suffer from over-regularization if the guided by the teacher layer is set deeper. Therefore, to provide a student model with more flexibility researchers choose to use the teacher's middle layer as a hint layer and the student's middle layer as the guided layer.

Authors of [22] suggest using class probabilities produced by teacher network as "soft targets" for training student network. Soft targets are those probabilities q_i computed from the model logits z_i using Softmax layer $q_i = \frac{\exp(z_i/T)}{\sum_j \exp(z_j/T)}$, where T is a temperature. The higher T is set, the softer probability distribution over classes are calculated. Authors use a weighted loss from two components. The first component is the cross entropy of teacher and student soft labels with high temperature. The second component is cross entropy of student predictions with correct labels (temperature is set to 1). As the magnitudes of the gradients produced by the soft targets scaled by $1/T^2$ it is important to multiply them by T^2 when using both hard and soft targets.

Kullback-Leibler divergence is used in loss functions to compare how the distribution of x differs from the distribution of y via $\mathrm{loss}(x, y) = y \cdot (\log y - \log x) = y \cdot \left(\log \frac{y}{x} \right)$.

Self Distillation Training. Knowledge Distillation operates in a student-teacher paradigm, while self distillation (SD) considers both student and teacher models as one model. It was shown by [58] that with SD training is significantly faster (no need to train deeper and more complicated teacher model) and SD trained student model even reached higher accuracy scores.

The methodology of SD resembles the one with the student-teacher paradigm but in this case a student model tries to boost its own performance.

2.3   ResNet Architecture and Its Modification

Before ResNet architectures [20], it was impossible to build significantly deep neural network due to the problem of vanishing gradients. The depth (number of stacked layers) plays a crucial role in model performance [50,51].

The vanishing gradients problem is eliminated using shortcut connections. Shortcuts are applied to several consecutive stacked layers and form so-called building block $\mathbf{y} = \mathcal{F}(\mathbf{x}, \{W_i\}) + \mathbf{x}$, where $\mathbf{y}$ and $\mathbf{x}$ are output and input vectors of the layers, $\mathcal{F}(\mathbf{x}, \{W_i\})$ represents residual mapping to be learned, can represent multiple convolutional layers.

ResNet18 network has an input stem, four subsequent stages - residual blocks - and a final output layer. The input stem starts with 7×7 convolution layer (stride=2, output channel=64), followed by a 3×3 max pooling layer (stride=2). The input stem reduces the input from 224×224 to 112×112 and increases its channel size to 64. Each res block has 2 branches: bottleneck and shortcut connection. Bottleneck is presented as three 1×1, 3×3, 1×1 convolution, where the 1×1 layers are used for reducing and then increasing (restoring) dimensions. There are batch normalization and activation layers after every conv layer. Output sizes after each res block are 56×56, 28×28, 14×14 and 7×7 with depth increasing from 64 to 512 channels. The final output layer is responsible for flattening with average pooling (leaves vectors of 512 for every sample in batch), then a fully connected layer is applied to transform a vector of 512 to the required number of final classes. So in case of ImageNet Challenge the number of classes is 1000, and in the author's research, there are 212 labels.

The model benefits from Batch Normalization (BN) layers [25] as they add stability to the learning process. BN layers are located after convolution layers before activation in accordance with [25].

Proposed Model Improvements. The first improvement initially appeared in a Torch implementation of ResNet [14] and then adopted by multiple works [13,23,56]. The improvement is the switch of the stride size of the first two convolutions in a downsampling block of ResNet. The output shape remains unchanged. Secondly, paper [21] recommends adding a 2×2 average pooling layer (stride=2) before the convolution layer in the shortcut connection and set stride=1 in the convolution layer. It was found that initially, this shortcut connection ignored $3/4$ of image information as kernel size was 1×1 while stride equaled 2. Thirdly, the author replaces all activations to Leaky ReLU $LeakyReLU(x) = \max(0, x) + negativeslope * \min(0, x)$, as it leads to faster convergence in experiments [38]. Author selects $negativeslope = 0.2$ according to experiment dynamics.

2.4   Proposed Architecture SIMR

Paper [46] proposes the usage of "hints" for better training of a student model with a teacher model. Researchers describe "hint" as the output of the teacher model hidden layers. Such output reflects feature maps in the teacher model and allows the student model to learn faster more complex patterns.

Inspired by the novel self distillation method [58], training with "hints" [46], useful model tweaks [21] and own experiment improvements author proposes Self-Improving-Modified-Resnet (SIMR) architecture. The model is built upon the improved and modified ResNet version mentioned above i.e. contains Average pooling in shortcut connections, changes in the downsampling block, and Leaky ReLU as activation. The author proposes two modifications of SIMR models: SIMR1 with the bottleneck after 1 res block and SIMR2 with the bottleneck after 2 res block. These two modifications are used for comparison as it is not clear theoretically which model should perform better. SIMR2 architecture is illustrated in Fig. 1.

As for SIMR2: the shapes of output after second and fourth residual blocks are different ($128 \times 28 \times 28$ and $512 \times 7 \times 7$). So to add L2 loss from hints Bottleneck

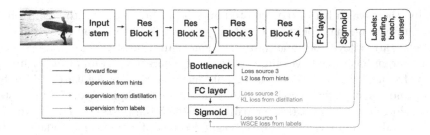

Fig. 1. SIMR2 model scheme - bottleneck after 2 residual block

layer consists of 3 blocks of convolution, batch normalization, and leaky ReLU layers. First is 1×1 convolution (stride=1), second 4×4 convolution (stride=4), third 1×1 convolution (stride=1). The number of channels remains 128 for 1 and 2 convolutions and increases to 512 channels after 3 convolutions. By doing so the bottleneck outputs $512 \times 7 \times 7$ as well as the final layer in the network. After average pooling is applied there is a 512 vector of feature maps to compare from the bottleneck layer and final layer. In our model, we use

In the research author uses three kinds of losses:

– Weighted Sigmoid Cross Entropy Loss. For network final output q^f and true labels y as WSCE (q^f, y). For network bottleneck output q^b as WSCE (q^b, y). By doing so the knowledge hidden in the dataset is introduced directly from labels to both classifiers WSCE$_{\text{total}}$ = WSCE$_f$ (q^f, y) + WSCE$_b$ (q^b, y).
– KL (Kullback-Leibler) divergence loss under the teacher's guidance. It helps to improve distribution received from the bottleneck layer according to the distribution of the final model layer KL_{bf} $(q^b, q^f) = q^f \cdot (\log q^f - \log q^b) = q^f \cdot \left(\log \frac{q^f}{q^b} \right)$.
L2 loss from hints. It takes into account the sum of squared differences between features map of the final classifier F_f and the feature maps from the bottleneck F_b motivating bottleneck feature maps to fit with ones of the final classifier $L2_F = \| F_b - F_f \|_2^2$.

The final architecture is trained to improve combined loss

$$\text{loss} = (1 - \alpha) \cdot \text{WSCE}_{\text{total}} + \alpha \cdot KL_{bf} \left(q^b, q^f \right) + \lambda \cdot \text{L2}_{\text{F}} \tag{3}$$

where α, λ are the hyperparameters used for weighting.

3 Dataset

3.1 Collection Method

The dataset was parsed from the official Instagram.com web page using Python3 programming language. The total number of images downloaded is 543 065.

Initially, there was a list of tags created and the author expected to download an equal number of images per tag. Due to tags co-occurrences, some tags (#nature, #travel, #art, #love) became more frequent than others.

Instagram hashtags have some patterns of generation. Comparing with popularity frequently there is let us call it "main tag" like #nature (515.5 bln posts) and its modified versions like #naturephotography (106.7 bln posts), #naturelover (26.6 bln posts), #naturelovers (65.5 bln posts). Other found patterns include: "main tag" + ofinstagram (#dogssofinstagram, #cakesofinstagram), "main tag" + instagram or instagram + "main tag" (#selfieinstagram, #instagramcats), #insta + "main tag" (#instafashion, #instafood). To standardise targets the author derived "main tag" out of these patterns.

The next steps were filtering tags that are hard to predict at all, for example, #nikon, #canon - types of camera a photo was taken on. After that author selected tags with higher frequency. Finally, there are 354 635 photos and 212 tags.

3.2 Dataset Description

The final dataset consists of 354.6k photos and 212 tags. Some tags tend to appear together. Tag frequencies are imbalanced ranging from 2361 to 19442 images per class.

Tags might be divided into the following categories (some tags appear in several categories):

Scene details: #forest, #sea, #beach, #interior, #trail, #snow, etc.

Objects: #airplane, #animal, #bike, #boat, #book, #bird, #train, etc.

Person's occupation: #chef, #driver, #gamer, #programmer, #soldier, etc.

People's attitude to photo content: #beautiful, #cute, #yummy (used to describe tasty food), #love, #healthylifestyle, etc.

Actions: #basketball, #fitness, #wedding, #concert, #conference, #party, #cooking, #swim, #sailing, etc.

Specific details to stress attention: #hair, #blouse, #dress, #smile, etc.

Abstract things: #digital, #education, #success, #hobby, #outdoors, #hiphop, #technology, #engineering, #science, #cosmos, #style, etc.

Collective information about photo: #nofilter, #illustration, #memory, #art, #nature, #design, #selfie, #healthy, #christmas, #blackandwhite, etc.

3.3 Comparison with Other Multi-Label Datasets

Common multi-label classification datasets:

- MS-COCO [35] contains 123 287 images with 80 object labels. This dataset was collected for object recognition tasks and now it is widely used in multi-label classification [5, 10, 16, 59];
- NUS-WIDE [6] consists of 269 648 images and 5 018 unique tags. The source is the image and video hosting service Flickr. Tags are divided into categories: event/activity, scene/location, people, program, objects, graphics. Tag frequencies are highly imbalanced; unique tags;

- WIDER Attribute [34] - the dataset with 14k images belonging to 30 scene categories (picnic, soccer, hockey, parade, etc.) and 58k human bounding boxes each annotated with 14 binary attributes (male, long hair, no sunglasses, hat, jeans, etc.). It is used for attribute recognition tasks;

For 1-class classification, the dataset benchmark is ImageNet dataset [8] (1000 classes, 1.28 million images, 50k validation images). Models trained on ImageNet and then finetuned on specific datasets show better quality as a trained model benefits from gained feature maps allowing it search for specific details on images (color differences, edges, and more high level as geometric shapes, patterns).

The author's Dataset has on average 3.1 tags per image approximately the same as MS-COCO (2.9 tags per image), NUS WIDE and WIDER Attribute have more than 15. The author's dataset and MS-COCO have the class imbalance problem as well as the range of the number of tags per image varies a lot. Still, the author's dataset contains 3 times more images and 2.5 times more tags than MS COCO. The author's dataset is also more challenging as MC-COCO has labels of physical objects actually containing on an image.

Collected dataset difficulties are attributed to tags human-generated nature. People do not have to mark with tags everything on their photos, they tend to show their opinions, expectations, experience, or just follow the popular trend to gain fame. Below author presents the main findings:

Noisy labels can dramatically decrease model generalization power. Researchers in [10] trained models on MS COCO in two ways: 1) with only 20% of clean partial labels (removing other 80% from the dataset) and 2) with 80% of clean labels and 20% of wrong randomly added labels. Models trained with 1) method showed better performance.

Nevertheless, exploration of people's attitudes is a significant and beneficial study. According to more advanced knowledge derived from such datasets, companies can suggest people personalized promotions and boost loyalty.

4 Experiments

4.1 Experimental Setup

The input size of an image for models is 224×224 with 3 red, green, and blue channels. In the author's experiments optimizer Adam [27] showed faster convergence, therefore, it was chosen for training. Learning rate starts from 0.002 and halves every 10 epochs. Batch size varied from 64 to 256 according to GPU CUDA available memory.

For the non-linear activation function author chose LeakyReLU [38] (negative slope is set to 0.2) as it leads to faster convergence in experiments. The model consists of 4 consecutive basic blocks, each the following block operates with twice as large tensors in depth starting from 64. Layer weights are initialized with Kaiming normal initialization [19].

The split on train and test is done stratifying by tags. By doing so the author kept label distribution in both sets almost equal with the shares of tags in the test ranging from 18% to 21.5%.

Data Augmentation. Taking a picture of a car and flipping it horizontally a person still see a car. If all cars in the dataset are always turned left, a model is likely to overfit and only learn to correctly distinguish turned left cars. In order to decrease overfitting and increase robustness in predictions researchers use augmentation techniques. The author uses the following augmentations: image rotation by up to 15° in both directions, every time applied the angle is chosen randomly; change the brightness, contrast, and saturation of an image; random resized crop with a random aspect ratio of 3/4 to 4/3 and to downscale an image up to 0.8 of initial scale; random horizontal flip with a probability of 0.5; resize to the network input size 224×224; normalization of an image tensor with mean and standard deviation.

4.2   Models Quality Comparison

In Table 1 the best metrics on train set are in *italic* and the best metrics on test set are in **bold**. ResNet* refers to ResNet model with suggested improvements; P@3, R@3, F1@3 refer to precision, recall, and their geometric mean F1 score metrics keeping only the top 3 model predictions.

Table 1. Models quality comparison. Higher values refer to better quality

Model	Phase	P@3	R@3	F1@3
SIMR2	Train	0.7867	*0.7378*	*0.7538*
	Test	**0.6855**	**0.6428**	**0.6566**
SIMR1	Train	0.7753	0.7230	0.7397
	Test	0.6763	0.6265	0.6426
ResNet*	Train	*0.8059*	0.7188	0.7465
	Test	0.6645	0.6034	0.6227
ResNet	Train	0.7905	0.7064	0.7331
	Test	0.6587	0.6008	0.6196

ResNet improved shows a bit better results in comparison with plain ResNet. Switched stride in the first 2 convolutions in every 4 residual blocks leaves the model with mode data to analyze. Also, added average pooling to shortcut connections helps the model to take into account more details. It is seen that initial ResNet architectures overfit more than proposed SIMR as the difference of train and test statistics is wider. Also, SIMR models reach better quality on the test set. SIMR2 performed slightly better than the modification with bottleneck added to the first residual block SIMR1. This happens due to over regularization of SIMR1 model in loss associated with feature maps that is partially proved in Table 2. $WSCE_f$ is Weighted Sigmoid Cross Entropy loss of true labels with final layer of the network, $WSCE_b$ - WSCE loss of true labels with bottleneck layer.

Table 2. Test loss values for SIMR1 and SIMR2 (smaller values are better)

Model	Epoch	$WSCE_f$	$WSCE_b$	KL_{bf}	$L2_F$
SIMR1	1	0.6206	0.6294	0.2544	0.0131
	5	0.5776	0.5929	0.2435	0.0039
	10	0.5565	0.5781	0.2422	0.0042
	15	0.5491	0.5722	0.2396	0.0067
	20	**0.5477**	0.5693	0.2387	0.0083
	25	**0.5477**	0.5657	0.2383	0.0107
SIMR2	1	0.6265	0.6321	0.2529	0.0094
	5	0.5742	0.5856	0.2425	0.0028
	10	0.5604	0.5754	0.2412	0.0038
	15	0.5489	0.5634	0.2360	0.0052
	20	**0.5466**	0.5496	0.2353	0.0066
	25	**0.5456**	0.5530	0.2340	0.0088

All metrics are balanced according to their significance. WSCE values are multiplied by 10 for more convenience, KL multiplied by 0.05, L2 loss from features are multiplied by 0.00001. WSCE with final layer continues to decrease from 20 to 25 epoch for SIMR2 and stays almost the same in SIMR1 experiments.

Bottleneck added to the second res block provides the SIMR model with more flexibility. Loss from hints - L2 loss from feature maps firstly decreases and then begins to rise a bit. This might be mitigated by choosing the lower weight of this component in the total loss as the model is slightly over regularized by this term. Kullback-Leibler divergence decreases gradually in both architectures showing that the output of the final layer improves the whole architecture with self-knowledge distillation technique. It means that the bottleneck mimics the distribution of the final guiding layer which is deeper and more accurate in predictions. WSCE scores are also decreasing which illustrates that the model predicts more accurate results. The author took models after 25 epochs that are not overfitted according to $WSCE_f$.

4.3 Error Analysis

Most of the errors model makes are associated with initial dataset quality. As people's opinions could be biased (different people may prefer a different set of tags for the same picture stressing on various aspects), it also has false co-occurrences. People who travel to other countries and surprised and amused by architecture there tend to post #travel and #architecture tags together. Instagram hashtags are biased so are models (see Fig. 2).

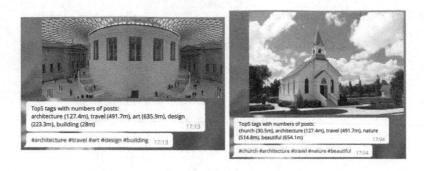

Fig. 2. Common Instagram false co-occurrences: #architecture and #travel

Moreover, some people tend to emphasize the fact that they are doing things they love or just insert tag #love to almost all pictures. It is also much harder to find a person with a sad face on an image accompanied by hashtag #sad in comparison with a happy person and #happy hashtag. People do not like to show their failures and frustrating moments, they would rather show how great they and their lives are. As Instagram hashtags are not exhaustive. Performance drops because a lot of ground-truth positive labels are initialized as negative labels. For example, an easily fixable problem: some people add #animal or #pet to photos of #dog. Much harder is when people add opinion tags (like #beautiful, #cute, #happy, #new, #love, etc.) or draw attention to specific details.

5   Conclusion

In the current paper author successfully completed all the project tasks stated in the introduction part. Covering a substantial number of related works, the author proposed improvements for ResNet models and own Self-Improving-Modified-Resnet (SIMR) architecture. The training process is done with the novel method of self-knowledge distillation presented in 2019. Then the author compares models performance on the collected dataset from Instagram.com contains 355k images with 212 various unique tags. Due to SIMR architecture's ability to use self-knowledge distillation and improving middle layers feature maps with final layer feature maps, SIMR2 model with bottleneck applied to second residual block reached Precision of 0.69, Recall of 0.64 and F1 score of 0.66 - better than other models in comparison.

These are great results on a challenging dataset incorporating human-induced bias and noise in tags. People upload photos of their achievements not failures, photos of their happy moments not while they are in depression. Telegram Chat Bot works better with photos that potentially could be uploaded into Instagram. In other way it leads to unfair comparison.

When discussing directions for future work, it seems to be beneficial for understanding people's opinions and attitudes to various aspects of their life, large companies could take advantage of this research in order to suggest more personalized products to their customers and increase brand loyalty. Also, from a technical aspect, experiments with loss functions and increasing dataset size may benefit resulting quality.

References

1. Bourdev, L., Maji, S., Malik, J.: Describing people: a poselet-based approach to attribute classification. In: In 2011 International Conference on Computer Vision, pp. 1543–1550. IEEE (2011)
2. Boutell, M.R., Luo, J., Shen, X., Brown, C.M.: Learning multi-label scene classification. Pattern Recognit. **37**(9), 1757–1771 (2004)
3. Buciluǎ, C., Caruana, R., Niculescu-Mizil, A.: Model compression. In: Proceedings of the 12th ACM SIGKDD International Conference on Knowledge Discovery and Data Mining, pp. 535–541 (2006)
4. Cabral, R., De la Torre, F., Costeira, J.P., Bernardino, A.: Matrix completion for weakly-supervised multi-label image classification. IEEE Trans. Pattern Anal. Mach. Intell. **37**(1), 121–135 (2014)
5. Chen, Z.M., Wei, X.S., Wang, P., Guo, Y.: Multi-label image recognition with graph convolutional networks. In: Proceedings of the IEEE Conference on Computer Vision and Pattern Recognition, pp. 5177–5186 (2019)
6. Chua, T.S., Tang, J., Hong, R., Li, H., Luo, Z., Zheng, Y.: Nus-wide: a real-world web image database from National University of Singapore. In: Proceedings of the ACM International Conference on Image and Video Retrieval, pp. 1–9 (2009)
7. Dembczynski, K., Kotlowski, W., Hüllermeier, E.: Consistent multilabel ranking through univariate losses. arXiv preprint arXiv:1206.6401 (2012)
8. Deng, J., Dong, W., Socher, R., Li, L.J., Li, K., Fei-Fei, L.: ImageNet: a large-scale hierarchical image database. In: CVPR09 (2009)
9. Deng, Y., Luo, P., Loy, C.C., Tang, X.: Pedestrian attribute recognition at far distance. In: Proceedings of the 22nd ACM International Conference on Multimedia, pp. 789–792 (2014)
10. Durand, T., Mehrasa, N., Mori, G.: Learning a deep convnet for multi-label classification with partial labels. In: Proceedings of the IEEE Conference on Computer Vision and Pattern Recognition, pp. 647–657 (2019)
11. Ge, W., Yang, S., Yu, Y.: Multi-evidence filtering and fusion for multi-label classification, object detection and semantic segmentation based on weakly supervised learning. In: Proceedings of the IEEE Conference on Computer Vision and Pattern Recognition, pp. 1277–1286 (2018)
12. George, M., Floerkemeier, C.: Recognizing products: a per-exemplar multi-label image classification approach. In: Fleet, D., Pajdla, T., Schiele, B., Tuytelaars, T. (eds.) ECCV 2014. LNCS, vol. 8690, pp. 440–455. Springer, Cham (2014). https://doi.org/10.1007/978-3-319-10605-2_29
13. Goyal, P., et al.: Accurate, large minibatch sgd: Training imagenet in 1 hour. arXiv preprint arXiv:1706.02677 (2017)
14. Gross, S., Wilber, M.: Training and investigating residual nets. Facebook AI Research **6** (2016)
15. Guo, H., Fan, X., Wang, S.: Human attribute recognition by refining attention heat map. Pattern Recogn. Lett. **94**, 38–45 (2017)
16. Guo, H., Zheng, K., Fan, X., Yu, H., Wang, S.: Visual attention consistency under image transforms for multi-label image classification. In: Proceedings of the IEEE Conference on Computer Vision and Pattern Recognition, pp. 729–739 (2019)

17. Guo, Y., Gu, S.: Multi-label classification using conditional dependency networks. In: Twenty-Second International Joint Conference on Artificial Intelligence (2011)
18. Hand, E.M., Castillo, C., Chellappa, R.: Doing the best we can with what we have: multi-label balancing with selective learning for attribute prediction. In: Thirty-Second AAAI Conference on Artificial Intelligence (2018)
19. He, K., Zhang, X., Ren, S., Sun, J.: Delving deep into rectifiers: surpassing human-level performance on imagenet classification. In: Proceedings of the IEEE International Conference on Computer Vision, pp. 1026–1034 (2015)
20. He, K., Zhang, X., Ren, S., Sun, J.: Deep residual learning for image recognition. In: Proceedings of the IEEE Conference on Computer Vision and Pattern Recognition, pp. 770–778 (2016)
21. He, T., Zhang, Z., Zhang, H., Zhang, Z., Xie, J., Li, M.: Bag of tricks for image classification with convolutional neural networks. In: Proceedings of the IEEE Conference on Computer Vision and Pattern Recognition, pp. 558–567 (2019)
22. Hinton, G., Vinyals, O., Dean, J.: Distilling the knowledge in a neural network. arXiv preprint arXiv:1503.02531 (2015)
23. Hu, J., Shen, L., Sun, G.: Squeeze-and-excitation networks. In: Proceedings of the IEEE Conference on Computer Vision and Pattern Recognition, pp. 7132–7141 (2018)
24. Huang, G., Liu, Z., Van Der Maaten, L., Weinberger, K.Q.: Densely connected convolutional networks. In: Proceedings of the IEEE Conference on Computer Vision and Pattern Recognition, pp. 4700–4708 (2017)
25. Ioffe, S., Szegedy, C.: Batch normalization: accelerating deep network training by reducing internal covariate shift. arXiv preprint arXiv:1502.03167 (2015)
26. Kharchevnikova, A., Savchenko, A.V.: Efficient video face recognition based on frame selection and quality assessment. PeerJ Comput. Sci. **7**, e391 (2021)
27. Kingma, D.P., Ba, J.: Adam: a method for stochastic optimization. arXiv preprint arXiv:1412.6980 (2014)
28. Korinevskaya, A., Makarov, I.: Fast depth map super-resolution using deep neural network. In: 2018 IEEE International Symposium on Mixed and Augmented Reality Adjunct (ISMAR-Adjunct), pp. 117–122. IEEE (2018)
29. Krizhevsky, A., Sutskever, I., Hinton, G.E.: Imagenet classification with deep convolutional neural networks. In: Advances in Neural Information Processing Systems, pp. 1097–1105 (2012)
30. Li, D., Chen, X., Huang, K.: In: Multi-attribute learning for pedestrian attribute recognition in surveillance scenarios. In: 2015 3rd IAPR Asian Conference on Pattern Recognition (ACPR), pp. 111–115. IEEE (2015)
31. Li, D., Zhang, Z., Chen, X., Ling, H., Huang, K.: A richly annotated dataset for pedestrian attribute recognition. arXiv preprint arXiv:1603.07054 (2016)
32. Li, Q., Qiao, M., Bian, W., Tao, D.: Conditional graphical lasso for multi-label image classification. In: Proceedings of the IEEE Conference on Computer Vision and Pattern Recognition, pp. 2977–2986 (2016)
33. Li, X., Zhao, F., Guo, Y.: Multi-label image classification with a probabilistic label enhancement model. UAI **1**, 3 (2014)
34. Li, Y., Huang, C., Loy, C.C., Tang, X.: Human attribute recognition by deep hierarchical contexts. In: Leibe, B., Matas, J., Sebe, N., Welling, M. (eds.) ECCV 2016. LNCS, vol. 9910, pp. 684–700. Springer, Cham (2016). https://doi.org/10.1007/978-3-319-46466-4_41
35. Lin, T.-Y., et al.: Microsoft COCO: common objects in context. In: Fleet, D., Pajdla, T., Schiele, B., Tuytelaars, T. (eds.) ECCV 2014. LNCS, vol. 8693, pp. 740–755. Springer, Cham (2014). https://doi.org/10.1007/978-3-319-10602-1_48

36. Liu, X., et al.: Hydraplus-net: attentive deep features for pedestrian analysis. In: Proceedings of the IEEE International Conference on Computer Vision, pp. 350–359 (2017)
37. Lomotin, K., Makarov, I.: Automated image and video quality assessment for computational video editing. In: AIST, pp. 243–256 (2020)
38. Maas, A.L., Hannun, A.Y., Ng, A.Y.: Rectifier nonlinearities improve neural network acoustic models. Proc. icml. **30**, 3 (2013)
39. Makarov, I., Aliev, V., Gerasimova, O.: In: Semi-dense depth interpolation using deep convolutional neural networks. In: Proceedings of the 25th ACM International Conference on Multimedia, MM 2017, pp. 1407–1415. Association for Computing Machinery, New York (2017). https://doi.org/10.1145/3123266.3123360
40. Makarov, I., Aliev, V., Gerasimova, O., Polyakov, P.: Depth map interpolation using perceptual loss. In: 2017 IEEE International Symposium on Mixed and Augmented Reality (ISMAR-Adjunct), pp. 93–94. IEEE (2017)
41. Makarov, I., Kiselev, D., Nikitinsky, N., Subelj, L.: Survey on graph embeddings and their applications to machine learning problems on graphs. PeerJ Comput. Sci. **7**, 1–62 (2021)
42. Makarov, I., Makarov, M., Kiselev, D.: Fusion of text and graph information for machine learning problems on networks. PeerJ Comput. Sci. **7**, 1–26 (2021)
43. Makarov, I., et al.: On reproducing semi-dense depth map reconstruction using deep convolutional neural networks with perceptual loss. In: Proceedings of the 27th ACM International Conference on Multimedia, pp. 1080–1084 (2019)
44. Maslov, D., Makarov, I.: Online supervised attention-based recurrent depth estimation from monocular video. PeerJ Comput. Sci. **6**, e317 (2020)
45. Romero, A., Ballas, N., Kahou, S.E., Chassang, A., Gatta, C., Bengio, Y.: Fitnets: hints for thin deep nets. arXiv preprint arXiv:1412.6550 (2014)
46. Romero, A., Ballas, N., Kahou, S.E., Chassang, A., Gatta, C., Bengio, Y.: Fitnets: hints for thin deep nets. arXiv preprint arXiv:1412.6550 (2015)
47. Savchenko, A.: Sequential analysis with specified confidence level and adaptive convolutional neural networks in image recognition. In: 2020 International Joint Conference on Neural Networks (IJCNN), pp. 1–8. IEEE (2020)
48. Savchenko, A.V.: Fast inference in convolutional neural networks based on sequential three-way decisions. Inf. Sci. **560**, 370–385 (2021)
49. Shao, J., Kang, K., Change Loy, C., Wang, X.: Deeply learned attributes for crowded scene understanding. In: Proceedings of the IEEE Conference on Computer Vision and Pattern Recognition, pp. 4657–4666 (2015)
50. Simonyan, K., Zisserman, A.: Very deep convolutional networks for large-scale image recognition. arXiv preprint arXiv:1409.1556 (2014)
51. Szegedy, C., et al.: Going deeper with convolutions. In: Proceedings of the IEEE Conference on Computer Vision and Pattern Recognition, pp. 1–9 (2015)
52. Tseytlin, B., Makarov, I.: Content based video retrieval system for distorted video queries. In: Proceedings of MacsPro 2020 (2020)
53. Tsoumakas, G., Katakis, I.: Multi-label classification: an overview. Int. J. Data Warehouse. Min. (IJDWM) **3**(3), 1–13 (2007)
54. Wang, J., Yang, Y., Mao, J., Huang, Z., Huang, C., Xu, W.: CNN-RNN: a unified framework for multi-label image classification. In: Proceedings of the IEEE Conference on Computer Vision and Pattern Recognition, pp. 2285–2294 (2016)
55. Wei, X.S., Cui, Q., Yang, L., Wang, P., Liu, L.: RPC: a large-scale retail product checkout dataset. arXiv preprint arXiv:1901.07249 (2019)

56. Xie, S., Girshick, R., Dollár, P., Tu, Z., He, K.: Aggregated residual transformations for deep neural networks. In: Proceedings of the IEEE Conference on Computer Vision and Pattern Recognition, pp. 1492–1500 (2017)
57. Xue, X., Zhang, W., Zhang, J., Wu, B., Fan, J., Lu, Y.: Correlative multi-label multi-instance image annotation. In: 2011 International Conference on Computer Vision, pp. 651–658. IEEE (2011)
58. Zhang, L., Song, J., Gao, A., Chen, J., Bao, C., Ma, K.: Be your own teacher: improve the performance of convolutional neural networks via self distillation. In: Proceedings of the IEEE International Conference on Computer Vision, pp. 3713–3722 (2019)
59. Zhu, F., Li, H., Ouyang, W., Yu, N., Wang, X.: Learning spatial regularization with image-level supervisions for multi-label image classification. In: Proceedings of the IEEE Conference on Computer Vision and Pattern Recognition, pp. 5513–5522 (2017)

Bio-inspired Systems
and Neuro-Engineering

Temporal EigenPAC for Dyslexia Diagnosis

Nicolás J. Gallego-Molina[1]([⊠]), Marco Formoso[1], Andrés Ortiz[1,3],
Francisco J. Martínez-Murcia[2,3], and Juan L. Luque[4]

[1] Department of Communications Engineering, University of Malaga, Malaga, Spain
njgm@ic.uma.es
[2] Department of Signal Theory, Telematic and Communications,
University of Granada, Granada, Spain
[3] Andalusian Data Science and Computational Intelligence Institute (DasCI),
Granada, Spain
[4] Department of Developmental Psychology, University of Malaga, Malaga, Spain

Abstract. Electroencephalography (EEG) signals allow to explore the functional activity of the brain cortex in a non-invasive way. However, the analysis of these signals is not straightforward due to the presence of different artifacts and the very low signal-to-noise ratio. Cross-Frequency Coupling (CFC) methods provide a way to extract information from EEG, related to the synchronization among frequency bands. CFC methods are usually applied in a local way, computing the interaction between phase and amplitude at the same electrode. In this work we show a method to compute Phase-Amplitude Coupling (PAC) features among electrodes to study the functional connectivity. Moreover, this has been applied jointly with Principal Component Analysis (PCA) to explore patterns related to Dyslexia in 7-years-old children. The developed methodology reveals the temporal evolution of PAC-based connectivity. Directions of greatest variance computed by PCA are called eigenPACs here, since they resemble the classical *eigenfaces* representation. The projection of PAC data onto the eigenPACs provide a set of features that has demonstrates their discriminative capability, specifically in the Beta-Gamma bands.

Keywords: Dyslexia diagnosis · Phase-amplitude coupling · EigenPAC · Classification

1 Introduction

Developmental Dyslexia (DD) is one of the learning disability disorders with higher prevalence, affecting between 5% and 13% of the population [2]. It has an important social impact causing effects in children like low self-esteem and depression and may be a cause for school failure. The diagnostic of DD is an important issue for procure the intervention programs that help to adapt the learning process for dyslexic children. In this way, an early diagnosis is essential, which has historically been a complex task due to the use of behavioural

© Springer Nature Switzerland AG 2021
I. Rojas et al. (Eds.): IWANN 2021, LNCS 12862, pp. 45–56, 2021.
https://doi.org/10.1007/978-3-030-85099-9_4

tests. These tests depend on the motivation of each children and also have the inconvenient of include writing and reading tasks which postpone the start of diagnosis (i.e. it is not possible to diagnose pre-readers).

This aspect is changing with the use of biomedical signals, which provide objective and quantifiable measures to study the neural basis of the healthy brain and its pathologies. A relevant method to obtain information of brain activity is the electroencephalography (EEG), which allows to acquire brain signals in a non-invasive way. This technique can be used to quantify the functional activity of the brain while developing a specific task. In particular, EEG signals have been used to explore the neurological origin of DD [3–5], towards the advance in the knowledge of dyslexia and its objective diagnosis. Regarding the classification approach, different works have used EEG signals and Support Vector Machine (SVM) [21–25] achieving moderate to high classification performance showing the potential of this machine learning method.

One way to build functional models is through connectivity. This helps to understand the brain processes developed while the subject is developing a specific task. In other words, it consists in measuring how the different brain areas cooperates in any manner while processing information. On the other hand, neural oscillations are produced mainly in five frequency bands: Delta (0.5–4) Hz, Theta (4–8) Hz, Alpha (8–12) Hz, Beta (12–30) Hz and Gamma (>30 Hz). The exploration of the relationship among these bands has demonstrated to provide useful information to characterize the brain activity. This way, Cross-Frequency Coupling is a technique to explore interactions (also called couplings) between frequency bands and has undergone a special attention in recent years.

In the present work, EEG signals are used to explore the functional connectivity. Specifically, the Phase-Amplitude Coupling, a type of CFC, is calculated to analyze and identify temporal patterns in dyslexic and non-dyslexic subjects. Then, Principal Component Analysis is used to identify and extract patterns in order to perform a classification using SVM for a differential diagnosis.

The paper is organized as follows, Sect. 2 presents details of the database and describes the auditory stimulus and the methods used. Then, Sect. 3 presents and discusses the classification results, and finally, Sect. 4 draws the main conclusions and the future work.

2   Materials and Methods

2.1   Dataset and Stimulus

The EEG data used in this work was provided by the Leeduca Study Group at the University of Málaga [6]. EEG signals were recorded using the Brainvision acticHamp Plus with 32 active electrodes (actiCAP, Brain Products GmbH, Germany) at a sampling rate 500 Hz during 15 min sessions, while presenting an auditory stimulus to the subject. A session consisted of a sequence of white noise stimuli modulated in amplitudes at rates 2, 8, 20 Hz presented sequentially for 5 min each.

The present experiment was carried out with the understanding and written consent of each child's legal guardian and in the presence thereof. Forty-eight participants took part in the present study, including 32 skilled readers (17 males) and 16 dyslexic readers (7 males) matched in age. The mean age of the control group was 94.1 ± 3.3 months, and 95.6 ± 2.9 months for the dyslexic group. All participants were right-handed Spanish native speakers with no hearing impairments and normal or corrected–to–normal vision. Dyslexic children in this study have all received a formal diagnosis of dyslexia in the school. None of the skilled readers reported reading or spelling difficulties or have received a previous formal diagnosis of dyslexia. The locations of 32 electrodes used in the experiments is in the 10–20 standardized system.

2.2   Signal Prepocessing

The EEG signals recorded were processed to remove artifacts related to eye blinking and impedance variation due to movements. Blind source separation was employed with Independent Component Analysis (ICA) to remove artifacts corresponding to eye blinking signals in the EEG signals. Then, EEG signal of each channel was normalized independently to zero mean and unit variance and referenced to the signal of electrode Cz. Baseline correction was also applied. Finally, the EEG signals were segmented into 15.02 s long windows in order to analyze PAC temporal patterns correctly [7]. This is the minimum appropriate window length for which a sufficiently high number of slow oscillation cycles are analyzed, shorter windows lead to overestimates of coupling and lower significance. This adequate window length is one of the main requisites for robust PAC estimation and appropriate statistical validation of the result by surrogate tests without using long data windows that assumes stationarity of the signals within the window.

2.3   Phase-Amplitude Coupling (PAC)

Cross-frequency Coupling has been proposed to coordinate neural dynamics across spatial and temporal scales [8], it serve as a mechanism to transfer information from large scale brain networks and has a potential relevance for understanding healthy and pathological brain function. In particular, Phase-Amplitude Coupling has received significant attention [7,10] and may play an important functional role in local computation and long-range communication in large-scale brain networks [9].

PAC describes the coupling between the phase of a slower oscillation and the amplitude of a faster oscillation. Concretely, in this work we explore the modulation of the amplitude of the Gamma (30–100) Hz frequency band by the phase of the Delta (0.5–4) Hz, Theta (4–8) Hz, Alpha (8–12) Hz and Beta (12–25) Hz bands. There are different PAC descriptors for measuring PAC [1]. In this work, we use the Modulation Index (MI) [11,12], although there is no convention yet of how to calculate Phase-Amplitude Coupling and much heterogeneity of phase-amplitude calculation methods used in the literature [13].

For calculating MI [11], first all phases are binned into eighteen 20 degrees intervals. The average amplitude of the amplitude-providing frequency in each phase bin of the phase-providing frequency is computed and normalized by the following formula:

$$P(j) = \frac{\bar{a}(j)}{\sum_{k=1}^{N} \bar{a}(k)} \tag{1}$$

where $\bar{a}$ is the average amplitude of one bin, k is the running index for the bins, and $N = 18$ is the total amount of bins; P is a vector of N values.

Then, Shannon entropy $H(P)$ is computed by means of

$$H(P) = -\sum_{j=1}^{N} P(j) log P(j) \tag{2}$$

where P is the vector of normalized averaged amplitudes per phase bin. This represents the inherent amount of information of a variable. If the Shannon entropy is maximal, all the phase bins present the same amplitude (uniform distribution). Thus, the existence of Phase-Amplitude Coupling is characterized by a deviation of the amplitude distribution from the uniform distribution in a phase-amplitude plot. To measure this, the Kullback–Leibler (KL) divergence of a discrete distribution P from a distribution Q is used and it is defined as

$$KL(P,Q) = \sum_{j=1}^{N} P(j) log \frac{P(j)}{Q(j)} \tag{3}$$

and the KL distance is relate to the Shannon entropy by the following formula

$$KL(P,U) = log N - H(P) \tag{4}$$

where U is the uniform distribution and P is the amplitude distribution. Finally, the raw MI is calculated by the following formula:

$$MI = \frac{KL(P,U)}{log N} \tag{5}$$

In this work, PAC is measured by MI in each data segment, enabling the exploration of the temporal evolution of the response to specific auditory stimuli. This is achieved with the use of Tensorpac [14], an open-source Python toolbox dedicated to PAC analysis of neurophysiological data. Tensorpac provides a set of efficient methods and functions to implements the most common PAC estimation methods, such as the Modulation Index used in the present work.

2.4 Dimensionality Reduction and Classification

Principal Component Analysis is a widely used method to perform dimensionality reduction. It is a well known multivariate analysis technique used in many studies [15,16]. It is employed to significantly reduce the original high-dimensional feature space to a lower-dimensional subspace spanned by a number

(n) of Principal Components (PC). Preserving as much of the variation of the data set in the original space as possible.

A well known application of PCA the so-called eigenimage decomposition, which results from the application of PCA to images. This is used in different works such as [17,18] and adapted from the eigenface approach of Turk and Pentland [19]. In this work this approach is used allowing to detect underlying patterns that differentiate individuals within a population, even if the differences are subtle.

Here, PCA is applied in the time axis to compute the maximum variance directions of the PAC along the EEG segments. Thus, we obtain the PCs or eigenvectors of the covariance matrix of the a dataset composed by N vectors, corresponding to the MI values of each 31 electrodes for the ten segments of every subject. These eigenvectors describe a set of features that characterize the variation between the PAC measured in each temporal segment. As usual, they are sorted in decreasing explained variance order. We can display these eigenvectors in topoplots, representing the principal components at each electrode position. In order to keep the traditional notation, we called these PC as *eigenPACs*. Then, we selected the eigenPACs that have the largest eigenvalues which therefore account for the most variance within the set of PAC matrix, composing a M-dimensional subspace.

For the sake of clarity, let the measured PAC vector set be $\Gamma_1, \Gamma_2, ..., \Gamma_N$ of length equal to the number of electrodes. The average PAC of the dataset is defined as $\Psi = \frac{1}{N} \sum_{n=1}^{N} \Gamma_n$. Each measured PAC differs from the average by the vector $\Phi_i = \Gamma_i - \Psi$ with $i = 1, 2, ..., N$. On this set, a PCA transformation is applied obtaining M orthogonal vectors u_i which best describes the distribution of the data. This vectors satisfy that

$$\lambda_i = \frac{1}{N} \sum_{n-1}^{N} (u_i^T \Phi_n)^2 \tag{6}$$

is maximum, subject to

$$u_i^T u_j = \delta_{ij} \tag{7}$$

where δ_{ij} is the Kronecker delta, and u_i and λ_i are the eigenvectors and eigenvalues, respectively, of the covariance matrix:

$$C = \frac{1}{N} \sum_{n=1}^{N} \Phi_n \Phi_n^T = AA^T \tag{8}$$

where the matrix $A = \Phi_1, ..., \Phi_N$. These eigenvectors are what we refer as eigenPAC. Usually, the first few eigenPACs explain almost the whole variance, so only a number $M' < M$ is necessary to appropriately describe the dataset [18]. Thus, the computacional complexity of the diagonalization process to obtain the eigenPAC basis is significantly reduced.

In essence, the eigenPACs define a new space in which each component explains the maximum variance in the data represented by its eigenvalue and its correlation is minimized. The projection of the PAC vectors onto the eigenPAC space, will determine the coordinates of each PAC vector in this subspace. It is expected that this projection produce a pattern more suitable for class separation than the projection onto the average PAC space, due to the eigenPAC decorrelation [17].

For the classification we use this projections of the data on the new basis to train a Support Vector Machine. This machine learning method is one of the most used method for dyslexia detection [26] and it is specially suited for cases where the number of dimensions is greater than the number of samples and for overlapping and non-separable data sets [20]. Furthermore, SVM have regularization parameters to prevent over-fitting such as kernel, degree, C and gamma. Hence, the PAC vectors measured for the ten segments EEG signals are projected on the eigenPAC basis obtaining N vectors each of them with its corresponding class label defined as control and dyslexic. Then, using the training data the SVM separates this set of binary labelled data with a hyperplane that is maximally distant from the two classes [18].

3   Experimental Results

In this section, we show the experimental results obtained in with the PAC analysis, eigenPAC representation and classification. As mentioned before, the EEG data was segmented into ten temporal windows of 15.02 s for the analysis of the temporal evolution of the response to the stimulus. This analysis was performed with the measure of PAC over each segment.

PAC Results. To analyze PAC connectivity we used the tensorpac tool [14]. Thus, we defined the frequency bands in which the PAC is measured (phase band and amplitude band) and we expected an identifiable temporal behaviour. This set of frequency band pairs are: Delta-Gamma, Theta-Gamma, Alpha-Gamma and Beta-Gamma. We measured the PAC for each subject and each temporal segment obtaining results for all the frequency bands. This results are represented with a set of ten topoplots showing the temporal evolution of the average PAC of dyslexic subjects and control subjects in each frequency pair. Figure 1 shows the differences between the average MI value for the dyslexic group and the control group. In this Figure we represented each combination of frequency bands for which the PAC has been measured. These topoplots denote differences between the response of dyslexic and control subjects.

EigenPAC Results. PCA has been applied in two different ways. In the first case, PAC features from all the subjects have been used to obtain the PCs, as in the case of *eigenfaces* problem. This aims to obtain a representation of the overall database in terms of the maximum variance directions. To carry out this experiment, a matrix is created containing the MI value computed from temporal segments of all subjects. Specifically, this matrix contains N*(number of

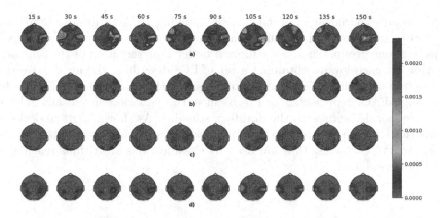

Fig. 1. Difference average MI topoplot 2 Hz. a) Delta-Gamma b) Theta-Gamma c) Alpha-Gamma d) Beta-Gamma

segments) rows corresponding to the number of subjects multiplied by the number of segments and M columns corresponding to MI of each of the 31 electrodes. Then, PCA is applied and we obtain a set of PCs of which the first five represent the most part of the variance. In Fig. 2 we can see the representation of the eigenPAC for the first 5 PC indicating the area where there is a major temporal variation in the measured MI for the Beta-Gamma PAC. This eigenPAC are different for each stimulus and the first topoplot describes the maximal data variation.

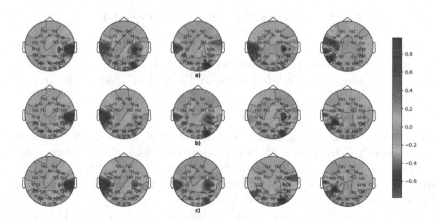

Fig. 2. First 5 eigenPAC for Beta-Gamma. a) 2 Hz b) 8 Hz c) 20 Hz

A second experiment is performed by applying PCA to dyslexic and control groups separately. This results similar as the previous case, but only with subjects of one group. Thus, we achieve a better representation of the temporal variation for each group, obtaining a set of PCs describing the maximal variation for the dyslexic subjects and another set of PCs for the control subjects. These eigenPAC, represented in Fig. 3, show the variation specifically related to the temporal response to the auditory stimulus. As shown, we found global similarities for each group. Furthermore, this helps to identify the characteristic patterns of each class that are used by classifications algorithms reaching a better performance.

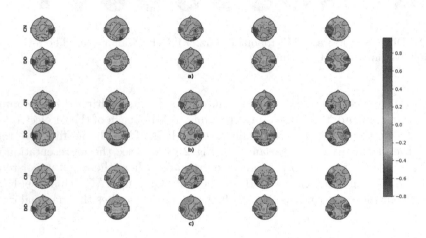

Fig. 3. First 5 eigenPAC. a) 2 Hz b) 8 Hz c) 20 Hz

In Fig. 3, for each case there are represented in the upper row the topoplots containing the information related to control eigenPAC and in the row below the dyslexic eigenPAC.

Classification. Once the application cases of PCA are defined, we used the resulting eigenPAC to train a SVM classifier. Therefore, there are two ways of perform a classification depending on how we compute the PCs that form the eigenPAC. These are used to project the data into the lower-dimensional space to obtain the feature space of the SVM classifier.

In the first case, the PCs are obtained from the application of PCA over all the subjects, dyslexic and control. Then, this PCs correspond to the eigenPAC that we use to project the data for the SVM. In this part, a k-fold stratified cross validation scheme is employed to separate the data into train sets and test set, specifically, 5-fold cross-validation is used.

In the second case, the application of PCA separately over the two classes provide a set of PCs for each class. Then each subject data is projected onto the control and DD components, and these projections are concatenated to compose the feature vector. The process of cross validation is the same as in the above case just with a different set of PCs.

The metrics used in the classification are the accuracy, sensitivity, specificity and Area Under ROC Curve (AUC). The evaluation metrics are described in Table 1. The results show the performance of the two classification scenarios for the best case, which corresponds to the Beta-Gamma PAC as represented in Fig. 4. In Table 1 we can see that there is a improvement related with the application of PCA separately for the two classes. This denotes that the second case helps to identify the characteristic patterns of each class. Thus, providing a feature vector with differential information related to the temporal response to the auditory stimulus.

Table 1. Classification comparative using the Beta-Gamma PAC

Metrics	PCA with all the subjects			PCA with each class separately		
	2 Hz	8 Hz	20 Hz	2 Hz	8 Hz	20 Hz
Accuracy	0.572	0.611	0.561	0.654	0.653	0.594
Sensitivity	0.501	0.551	0.515	0.651	0.635	0.551
Specificity	0.743	0.757	0.675	0.661	0.696	0.7
AUC	0.65	0.705	0.622	**0.699**	**0.721**	**0.65**

Therefore, the application of PCA separately generates higher metrics achieving a better classification performance with a greater AUC and accuracy 2 Hz, 8 Hz 20 Hz. In this case, after model selection, the selected hyperparameters for the SVM classifier are RBF kernel and 3.59, 3.59 and 10 values for C 2 Hz, 8Hz 20 Hz, respectively. We present the results for this case in Fig. 4 where the max AUC is represented for each band combination and each stimulus. Showing that in the Beta-Gamma there are temporal pattern that are distinctive of each class. In the case of Beta-Gamma we perform a PC number sweep obtaining the explained variance and the max AUC for the classification with each number of components in Fig. 5.

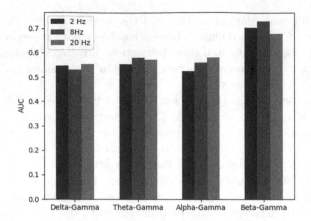

Fig. 4. Max AUC for each band combination and stimulus

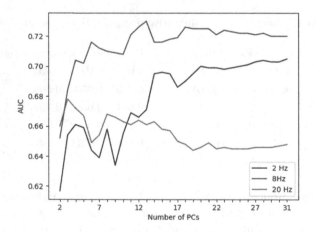

Fig. 5. Max AUC for each number of PCs

4 Conclusions and Future Work

In this work we present a classification method for EEG signals. It is based on the study of functional connectivity PAC and the use of eigenPAC resulting of applying PCA. To this end, the PAC data is projected onto this new basis to train a SVM classifier. This classifier is selected over other machine learning methods due to its advantages and its potential to classify overlapping and non-separable data sets. The concept of eigenPAC helps to extract the underlying pattern that differentiates the temporal response between control and dyslexic subjects. Also, it can be represented in topographic plots to visualize the areas with a greater variation principally corresponding to the temporal evolution.

The classification results suggest differential patterns in the Beta-Gamma bands that allows to discriminate between control and dyslexic subjects, obtaining the highest AUC for 8 Hz stimulus. This is achieved using the second approach explained above, where the feature vector is composed with the maximum variance direction obtained for each class separately. These results point the bands in which the response to the stimulus has differences across the temporal segments and encourage continuing the approach shown in this work. As future work, it is interesting to study the effect of using other windows length and to improve the necessary PAC analysis with the use of decomposition methods such as MEMD to accurately extracts the oscillatory components of the EEG signals.

Acknowledments. This work was supported by project PGC2018-098813-B-C32 (Spanish "Ministerio de Ciencia, Innovacin y Universidades"), and by European Regional Development Funds (ERDF). We gratefully acknowledge the support of NVIDIA Corporation with the donation of one of the GPUs used for this research. Work by F.J.M.M. was supported by the MICINN "Juan de la Cierva - Incorporación" Fellowship. We also thank the *Leeduca* research group and Junta de Andalucí for the data supplied and the support.

References

1. Tabassum, T.M., Munia, K., Aviyente, S.: Time-frequency based phase-amplitude coupling measure for neuronal oscillations. Sci. Rep. **9**, 1–15 (2019)
2. Peterson, R.L., Pennington, B.F.: Developmental dyslexia. Lancet **379**(9830), 1997–2007 (2012). https://doi.org/10.1016/S0140-6736(12)60198-6
3. Power, A.J., Colling, L.J., Mead, N., Barnes, L., Goswami, U.: Neural encoding of the speech envelope by children with developmental dyslexia. Brain Lang. **160**, 1–10 (2016). https://doi.org/10.1016/j.bandl.2016.06.006
4. Ortiz, A., Martínez-Murcia, F.J., Formoso, M.A., Luque, J.L., Sánchez, A.: Dyslexia detection from EEG signals using SSA component correlation and convolutional neural networks. In: de la Cal, E.A., Villar Flecha, J.R., Quintián, H., Corchado, E. (eds.) HAIS 2020. LNCS (LNAI), vol. 12344, pp. 655–664. Springer, Cham (2020). https://doi.org/10.1007/978-3-030-61705-9_54
5. Ortiz, A., López, P.J., Luque, J.L., Martínez-Murcia, F.J., Aquino-Britez, D.A., Ortega, J.: An anomaly detection approach for dyslexia diagnosis using EEG signals. In: Ferrández Vicente, J.M., Álvarez-Sánchez, J.R., de la Paz López, F., Toledo Moreo, J., Adeli, H. (eds.) IWINAC 2019. LNCS, vol. 11486, pp. 369–378. Springer, Cham (2019). https://doi.org/10.1007/978-3-030-19591-5_38
6. Ortiz, A., Martinez-Murcia, F.J., Luque, J.L., Giménez, A., Morales-Ortega, R., Ortega, J.: Dyslexia diagnosis by EEG temporal and spectral descriptors: an anomaly detection approach. Int. J. Neural Syst. **30**(7), 2050029 (2020). https://doi.org/10.1142/S012906572050029X
7. Dvorak, D., Fenton, A.A.: Toward a proper estimation of phase-amplitude coupling in neural oscillations. J. Neurosci Methods **30**(225), 42–56 (2014)
8. Aru, J., Aru, J., Priesemann, V., Wibral, M., Lana, L., Pipa, G., Singer, W., Vicente, R.: Untangling cross-frequency coupling in neuroscience. Curr. Opin. Neurobiol. **31**, 51–61 (2015). https://doi.org/10.1016/j.conb.2014.08.002
9. Canolty, R.T., Knight, R.T.: The functional role of cross-frequency coupling. Trends Cogn. Sci. **14**(11), pp. 506–515 (2010). ISSN 1364–6613. https://doi.org/10.1016/j.tics.2010.09.001

10. van der Meij, R., Kahana, M., Maris, E.: Phase-amplitude coupling in human electrocorticography is spatially distributed and phase diverse. J. Neurosci. **32**(1), 111–23 (2012). https://doi.org/10.1523/JNEUROSCI.4816-11.2012
11. Tort, A.B.L., Komorowski, R., Eichenbaum, H., Kopell, N.: Measuring phase-amplitude coupling between neuronal oscillations of different frequencies. J. Neurophysiol. **104**, 1195–1210 (2010). https://doi.org/10.1152/jn.00106.2010
12. Tort, A.B.L., Kramer, M.A., Thorn, C., Gibson, D.J., Kubota, Y., Graybiel, A.M., et al.: Dynamic cross-frequency couplings of local field potential oscillations in rat striatum and hippocampus during performance of a T-maze task. Proc. Natl. Acad. Sci. U.S.A. **105**, 20517–20522 (2008). https://doi.org/10.1073/pnas.0810524105
13. Hülsemann, M.J., Naumann, E., Rasch, B.: Quantification of phase-amplitude coupling in neuronal oscillations: comparison of phase-locking value, mean vector length, modulation index, and generalized-linear-modeling-cross-frequency-coupling. Front Neurosci. **7**(13), 573 (2019). https://doi.org/10.3389/fnins.2019.00573
14. Combrisson, E., Nest, T., Brovelli, A., Ince, R.A.A., Soto, J.L.P., Guillot, A., et al.: Tensorpac: an open-source Python toolbox for tensor-based phase-amplitude coupling measurement in electrophysiological brain signals. PLoS Comput. Biol. **16**(10), e1008302 (2020). https://doi.org/10.1371/journal.pcbi.1008302
15. Subasi, A., Gursoy, M.I.: EEG signal classification using PCA, ICA, LDA and support vector machines. Expert Syst. Appl. **37**(12), pp. 8659–8666 (2010)
16. Markiewicz, P.J., Matthews, J.C., Declerck, J., Herholz, K.: Robustness of multivariate image analysis assessed by resampling techniques and applied to FDG-PET scans of patients with Alzheimer's disease. NeuroImage **46**(2), 472–485 (2009)
17. Illán, I.A., et al.: 18F-FDG PET imaging analysis for computer aided Alzheimer's diagnosis. Inf. Sci. **181**(4), pp. 903–916 (2011). ISSN 0020–0255. https://doi.org/10.1016/j.ins.2010.10.027
18. Álvarez, I., et al.: Alzheimer's diagnosis using Eigenbrains and support vector machines. In: Cabestany, J., Sandoval, F., Prieto, A., Corchado, J.M. (eds.) IWANN 2009. LNCS, vol. 5517, pp. 973–980. Springer, Heidelberg (2009). https://doi.org/10.1007/978-3-642-02478-8_122
19. Turk, M., Pentland, A.: Eigenfaces for recognition. J. Cogn. Neurosci. **3**(1), pp. 71–86 (1991). https://doi.org/10.1162/jocn.1991.3.1.71
20. Perera, H., Shiratuddin, M.F., Wong, K.W.: Review of EEG-based pattern classification frameworks for dyslexia. Brain Inf. **5**(2), 1–14 (2018)
21. Cui, Z., Xia, Z., Su, M., Shu, H., Gong, G.: Disrupted white matter connectivity underlying developmental dyslexia: a machine learning approach. Hum. Brain Mapp. **37**(4), 1443–58 (2016)
22. Frid, A., Manevitz, L.M.: Features and machine learning for correlating and classifying between brain areas and Dyslexia. arXiv e-prints (2018)
23. Perera, H., et al.: EEG signal analysis of writing and typing between adults with dyslexia and normal controls. Int. J. Interact. Multimedia Artif. Intell. **5**(1), 62 (2018)
24. Rezvani, Z., et al.: Machine learning classification of dyslexic children based on EEG local network features. BioRxiv, p. 569996 (2019)
25. Frid, A., Breznitz, Z.: An SVM based algorithm for analysis and discrimination of dyslexic readers from regular readers using ERPs. In: 2012 IEEE 27th Convention of Electrical and Electronics Engineers in Israel, 14 Nov 2012, pp. 1–4 (2012)
26. Usman, O.L., Muniyandi, R.C., Omar, K., Mohamad, M.: advance machine learning methods for dyslexia biomarker detection: a review of implementation details and challenges. IEEE Access **9**, pp. 36879–36897 (2021)

Autonomous Driving of a Rover-Like Robot Using Neuromorphic Computing

Enrique Piñero-Fuentes[1,2(✉)] 🆔, Salvador Canas-Moreno[1,2] 🆔,
Antonio Rios-Navarro[1,2] 🆔, Tobi Delbruck[3] 🆔,
and Alejandro Linares-Barranco[1,2] 🆔

[1] Robotics and Technology of Computers Lab, ETSII-EPS, Universidad de Sevilla,
Seville, Spain
epinerof@us.es
[2] Smart Computer Systems Research and Engineering Lab (SCORE),
Research Institute of Computer Engineering (I3US), Universidad de Sevilla,
Seville, Spain
[3] Institute of Neuroinformatics, University of Zurich and ETH Zurich,
Zurich, Switzerland

Abstract. Autonomous driving solutions are based on artificial vision
and machine learning for understanding the environment and facilitate
decision making tasks. Similar techniques are used for indoor robot navigation. Deep learning architectures, which are usually computationally
expensive, are impacting our daily lives. This technology is evolving with
a notable improvement of cost-efficiency in terms of energy consumption,
enabling AI-edge computing. However, these architectures are usually
trained on powerful GPUs, what represents the limit for edge computing.
Nevertheless, after this training, efficient edge computing devices can
process these architectures locally. Neuromorphic engineering shows off
on solving the energy bottleneck problem through bio-inspired sensors,
processors and spike-based computation techniques. This work presents
a mobile robotic platform commanded through the Robotic Operating
System (ROS), which obeys the classification output of an AI-edge CNN
accelerator for FPGA connected to a neuromorphic dynamic vision sensor. The classification system is able to process up to 200 fps for 64×64
histograms collected with 2k events per frame and executing a 5 layer
CNN with 18MOPs for indoor robot navigation. A traffic sign dataset
has been used for training achieving a measured accuracy of 97.62% and
99.96% in the validation and test datasets respectively.

Keywords: Autonomous navigation · Neuromorphic · DVS · CNN ·
ROS

This research was partially supported by the Spanish grant (with support from the
European Regional Development Fund) MINDROB (PID2019-105556GB-C33/AEI/
10.13039/501100011033) and the CHIST-ERA H2020 grant SMALL (PCI2019-111841-
2/AEI/10.13039/501100011033).

© Springer Nature Switzerland AG 2021
I. Rojas et al. (Eds.): IWANN 2021, LNCS 12862, pp. 57–68, 2021.
https://doi.org/10.1007/978-3-030-85099-9_5

1   Introduction

Pattern recognition represents a fundamental cognitive process and it forms the basis for learning processes in the central nervous system. These processes are part of our lives through AI facial recognition, language comprehension, object classification, danger identification, etc. For the human (or mammalian) visual system, pattern recognition begins in the retina. Since the brain is capable of carrying out all computations with only 20 W [9], it is still a challenge for electronic and computer engineers to perform similar V1 visual-only tasks with only a few watts.

Early in the 1990s, researchers from Caltech designed the first silicon retina [10,11,13], inspired by some cells present in the human visual system (i.e. the retina). That represented the start of the field of neuromorphic engineering (**NE**), which aims to understand the biological nervous system by mimicking it and applying their modeled behavior to solve engineering problems. Other sensors developed since then are the dynamic vision sensors (**DVS**) [6], DAVIS [3], ATIS [15], auditory sensors such as AEREAR [4], NAS [5], DAS [19], among others.

Like the brain, NE addresses computing hardware energy bottlenecks through processors and computation techniques inspired by biological systems. For example, control of neuromorphic robots with spikes, such as ED-BioRob [8] that implements spike-based PID controllers for the joints of a light robotic arm by expanding output spikes to drive the motors; or through classic digital controllers based on pulse-width modulation (**PWM**), as the NeoN [14] controller for robot navigation, or Loihi PID implementations for UAV [18] or one motor [17].

This NE field is evolving by leaps and bounds, but they are still one step behind from the development of complex deep-learning architectures, such as powerful CNNs deployed in the cloud or powerful GPU-based computers for safe autonomous vehicle navigation. To close the gap between Von Neumann oriented deep-learning architectures and Neuromorphic deep-learning architectures, engineers use neuromorphic sensors to produce effective datasets to be used on training deep-learning architectures that could be executed with relatively low computational demand for robot navigation. For example, in [12], a DVS retina was used for recording a data set for car driving for 1000km with steering angle, what was later used for training conventional CNN architectures. Nevertheless, to enable the edge computing, and therefore, the Edge-AI specialised hardware, artifacts for CNN inference with effective latency and low power are needed. This is the case of novel CNN hardware accelerators, such as NullHop [2].

In this work we present the use of an improved version of Nullhop, called *Elements*, for safe indoor robotic navigation through traffic signs. A neuromorphic dataset has been collected and labelled accordingly for this purpose with a DAVIS [3] retina to exploit the sparsity of the data with Elements accelerator. A CNN has been trained to be executed in an FPGA version of the Elements, deployed in a multiprocessor programmable SoC from Xilinx. Visual classification output is used to autonomously command, through the Robotic Operating System (**ROS**), a mobile robot. The whole setup is mounted in the robot, representing an Edge-AI computing platform.

The rest of the paper is structured as follows: Sect. 2 provides more information on the system itself and its components, Sect. 3 gives details about the data set and its collection, Sect. 4 presents the CNN training results, in Sect. 5 an example application scenario is proposed and in Sect. 6 conclusions are given.

2   System Description

The proposed system has several parts. In this section, we will provide a full description of them and their relevance to the work, as well as a detailed explanation of how these parts interact with each other. There are two different, well-defined parts: hardware and software. Each of these parts has also various elements in them. We proceed to detail them one by one.

2.1   Hardware

Vehicle: the platform used in the present work is a SummitXL mobile robot from Robotnik[1]. It is a versatile rover-like robot with several features. It can move up to 3 m/s, has a maximum autonomy of 5 h and 4 brushless servomotors, one for each wheel. It also allows for connectivity through various interfaces, such as USB or Ethernet and its batteries can be used to power external devices, as a 12 V power outlet is also included in the back of its case. The Ethernet interface comes from an integrated router inside the case of the robot, next to its embedded computer. This router creates a Wi-Fi local network that allows users to interact with the robot, both wiredly and wirelessly. The robot uses the Robotic Operating System (ROS for short) to move, which allows for an autonomous navigation.

MPSoC: the hardware that performs all the processing is a Multiprocessor System On Chip (MPSoC). These kind of devices allow to develop an FPGA implementation but also have multi-purpose CPU cores (ARM in this case) that can run standard operating systems. The FPGA part of the device is called Programmable Logic (PL) and the "standard" part is called Processing System (PS) In this case, a Xilinx Zynq UltraScale + MPSoC XCZU15EG Trenz SOM module with 4 GB DDR4 RAM is used. It is mounted on a Trenz' carrier board, model TEBF0808-04A[2]. Inside this device, a CNN is executed to make the image classification. It is powered through the robot's 12V power outlet and it is also connected to its embedded computer through an Ethernet connection. The MPSoC PS communicates with the vehicle built-in ROS, to make it move according to the detected image autonomously. Figure 1b shows a block diagram of the system and the data flow.

It is important to note that communication between the MPSoC PL and PS is implemented through a special driver that allows for low-latency data

---

[1] https://robotnik.eu/es/productos/robots-moviles/summit-xl/ (accessed on 1/Mar/2021).

[2] https://shop.trenz-electronic.de/en/Products/Programmable-Logic/Xilinx-UltraScale/ (accessed on 10/05/2021).

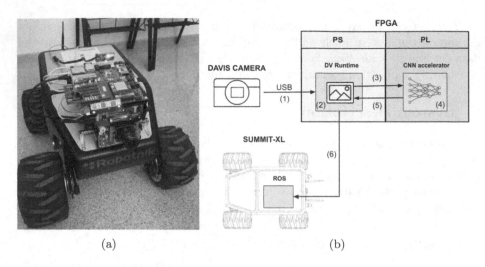

Fig. 1. (a) Summit XL mobile robot, MPSoC and camera. (b) Setup data flow

transfers. It is almost 30% faster on real-time tasks than the native Linux driver [16] and because of that the CNN Accelerator is capable of running the same image through all the inference layers of the network in 5 ms, a very short time for a single image given the depth of the model.

Neuromorphic Camera: one of the prominent features of this work is that it uses a neuromorphic vision sensor in order to retrieve visual data. These kind of sensors differ from conventional cameras radically in the way they work. DVS sensors, also referred to as retinas, have a pixel matrix of a given resolution, like 128 × 128, in which each pixel holds the amount of light it perceives and produces a signal, also commonly known as spike or event, when it registers a log-change in that value bigger than a certain threshold. The generated spike carries very few information, only the address of the affected pixel and the polarity of the event, which is set depending on whether the value change was positive or negative. Conventional cameras capture light at a specific frequency and then display all the images in a sequence, and they do this so quickly it appears to the human eye that the scene is moving, but it is really a sequence of static images. The use of the neuromorphic sensors offers a few advantages to this: less energy consumption, reduced latency and quicker computation, as you don't have to compute full images in order to produce results.

The camera used in this work is a DAVIS346 camera with a resolution of 346 × 260 pixels. It is connected to the MPSoC's PS through a USB connection. It ultimately feeds the accelerator with the events that stimulate it. The CNN used in this work does not actually process the data as events but rather does it conventionally, i.e. it takes a frame as its input, a frame that represents a histogram of the latest received events. This contravenes one of the camera's essential features, but it still benefits from the data recollection aspect, as frames are generated way quicker and contain less way information, essentially improving the CNN's noise robustness. Collected events are integrated by packing 2k events per histogram, and each histogram is normalized using a 3-sigma filter, as shown in Eqs. 1 through 4:

$$S = \sum_{a=0}^{N} \sum_{b=0}^{N} F_{in}(a,b) \qquad c = \sum_{a=0}^{N} \sum_{b=0}^{N} f(F_{in}(a,b)) \qquad (1)$$

$$f(X) = \begin{cases} 0, \text{if } X = 0 \\ 1, \text{otherwise} \end{cases} \qquad mean = S/c \qquad (2)$$

$$\sigma = \sqrt{\frac{\sum_{a=0}^{N} \sum_{b=0}^{N} [F_{in}(a,b) - mean]^2}{c}} \qquad (3)$$

$$F_{norm}(i,j) = \frac{F_{in}(i,j) + 3\sigma}{6\sigma}, \forall i,j \in [0,N] \qquad (4)$$

Where S is the accumulation of all values of non-zero pixels, c is the number of non-zero pixels, $mean$ is the averaged pixel value from those greater than zero and σ is the square-root of the variance, which is used to normalise the pixels of the histogram to be processed by the CNN.

2.2   Software

Dynamic Vision Platform[3], or DV for short, is the software that allows the use of Dynamic Vision Sensors (DVS/DAVIS). It consists of a modular environment and each module is a compiled C/C++ shared library, so almost any program you can code in C/C++ can be executed in this framework. There are actually two core parts of the program that allow for its execution, the runtime and the graphical interface, named *dv-runtime* and *dv-gui* respectively. The runtime is the part of the software that actually performs computations while the graphical interface allows users to enable, disable and interconnect modules dynamically. This division is inherent to the execution environment, as computations are done in the MPSoC edge-computing device and the runtime's behaviour is managed from a graphical interface in other device, typically a laptop connected to the same network as the MPSoC running the runtime, which in this case would be the Summit's local network. Figure 2 shows *dv-gui*'s graphical interface.

Therefore, this piece of software serves as the main execution platform in this work, as everything computing-related is done by the modules loaded in it. Specifically, input from the neuromorphic camera (image-related events) is taken and then passed through a series of modules that process it. The core module in this task is the one that sends the data to the CNN accelerator embedded in the PL and retrieves the accelerator's output, which is an integer representing the class of the image fed to the CNN. This output is then used to make decisions that affect the behaviour of the vehicle, which is then able to navigate autonomously in indoor environments.

---

[3] https://inivation.gitlab.io/dv/dv-docs/ (accessed on 10/May/2021).

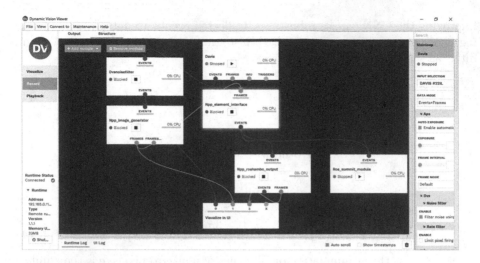

Fig. 2. DV interface with modules

Robotic Operating System: every serious digital system must have a software that controls it in a deterministic way, so that it does not get out of control because of unexpected conditions or reactions. This software is commonly the operating system, and given how dangerous a robot can be if controlled incorrectly, they also need to have one. The Robotic Operating System, or just ROS for short, is an open source framework for writing robot software that tries to make general-purpose robot programming easier for everyone. It provides a complete set of libraries and specifications that allow users to define their robot's models and also control them, keeping robustness as a core part of the design objectives.

The SummitXL uses it as its default controller, and in this work the robot is controlled by issuing commands to that controller. There is a listening process running on the vehicle's embedded computer that receives and executes orders from the MPSoC, which also implements a light-weight ROS node that issues said commands.

Vivado software was used to synthesize the design contained in the FPGA, that is, the CNN. Vivado is a software suite developed by Xilinx Inc to synthesize, implement and generate the bitstream that will be loaded into the FPGA. For this project, Vivado version 2018.2 was used.

PetaLinux is a Yocto based tool used to customize, build and deploy Embedded Linux solutions on Xilinx processing systems targeting Xilinx SoC designs. In this work it has been used to generate a light-weight Linux kernel that runs on the PS ARM cores and that provides a basic Operating System that runs just with what it needs and nothing else, so that unneeded software does not interfere with the rest of the workflow. This approach is greatly beneficial because it allows for a better use of a limited set of resources; this is very important, as edge-computing devices are usually required to be as cost-efficient as possible.

Summarizing, the steps performed are: (1) the retina sends spikes via USB to the DV Runtime which is located in the PS, (2) the DV Runtime integrates these events into a histogram and normalizes them, creating the frame, (3) the DV Runtime sends the frames to the CNN accelerator deployed on the FPGA where the computation is done, (4) the CNN classifies the image, (5) the classification output is sent back to the DV Runtime, and (6) the DV Runtime Summit module implements a light ROS node that communicates with the built-in ROS inside the robot via Ethernet, commanding it to move based on the classified image.

3 Datasets

This paper introduces the IDETSv1 dataset which has been recorded using the DAVIS346 neuromorphic sensor. The dataset includes a reduced number of traffic signals and samples of the interior of a building representing the absence of traffic signs. The dataset has four different traffic signs, turn left, turn right, stop, no entry, a person crossing in front of the robot and images of the corridor which represent background, when no traffic signs nor obstacles are in the scene. The traffic signs have been placed inside a building and have been recorded using the neuromorphic sensor which is deployed in the mobile robot. These recordings were taken approximating the robot to each sign from different trajectories and distances. There is a total of six classes in the dataset, where the training set has a total of 123584 samples, while the testing set has a total of 31286 samples and the validation set has a total of 1554 samples. Figure 3a shows a picture taken during the dataset collection.

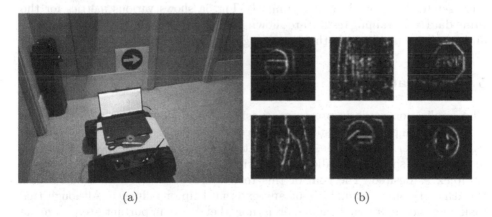

(a)   (b)

Fig. 3. (a) System as seen during dataset collection. (b) Dataset class samples. Top row from left to right: not entry, corridor and stop. Bottom row from left to right, person crossing, turn left and turn right

The recordings of each class that compose the dataset have been captured and labeled using jAER software [1]. This software interfaces with neuromorphic sensors and can also process and save the information provided by them. As mentioned above, this type of sensor provides a constant flow of information, known as events. For each class we have made different event recordings and then we have generated 64 × 64 pixel 2D histograms of a constant number of events. Each histogram has been normalized by using a 3-sigma filter, using 200 grey levels, thus generating the frames. The data augmentation mechanism consists of sampling the original recording creating the histogram using four different numbers of accumulated events: 4k, 2k, 1.5k and 1k. The final training dataset consists of 137061 images and is available online[4]. Figure 3b shows a sample of each class.

4   CNN Training Results

The CNN architecture used in this paper has five quantized convolutional stages as in Aimar et al. [2]. Each stage consists of a convolutional layer using the ReLU activation function followed by 2 × 2 max pooling. Kernels are square with dimension (5 × 5), (3 × 3), (3 × 3), (3 × 3) and (1 × 1) respectively and have the same bit precision as activation, 16 bits. This quantized precision is imposed by the CNN accelerator where the network is computed. The network has 114k weights parameters, making a total of 18 MOp to classify one image.

100 training epochs were performed in TensorFlow 1.14, requiring about 0.5 h on an Nvidia GTX1080 GPU (around 16 s per epoch). Robust accuracy was achieved by collecting sufficient data and systematic architecture exploration. Accuracy of 99.967% was achieved for the test set.

Figure 5b shows the confusion matrix that results from passing the validation data set to the trained model. Similarly, Fig. 5a shows various metrics for the same data set. Training results are shown in Figs. 4a–4d. Loss, accuracy, precision and recall are displayed both for training and test data set.

5   Application

The application scenario presented consists of an indoors circuit in which the features of the proposed system can be tested. Traffic signs may be placed at the end of a corner, for example, indicating the robot to turn in a specific direction or to stop. Using these indications, various itineraries can be constructed, as complex as desired. The goal of this test would be to have the robot follow the itinerary on its own, without any external help or influence. Although this task may not seem challenging, it is nonetheless an important step to make autonomous robots without general knowledge of the environment.

---

[4] https://lara.eii.us.es/cloud/sharing/S1gilrYDM (accessed on 10/May/2021).

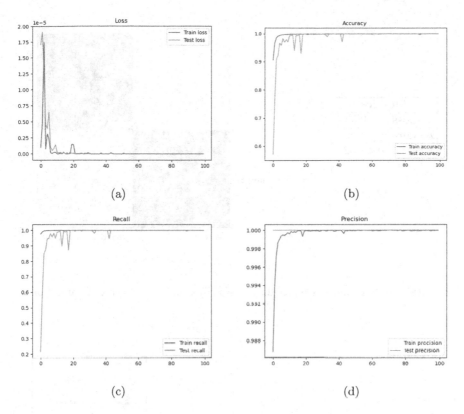

Fig. 4. (a) Loss, (b) accuracy, (c) recall and (d) precision per epoch on train/test dataset

An example circuit could have the robot perform an 8-like trajectory around some obstacles. For this purpose, several signs would be needed, one for each turn and one for stopping at the end of the circuit. Figure 6 shows an itinerary like the one described above. One important aspect that needs to be taken into account when testing systems that use a DVS like this work does is that, as these retinas react to change in every pixel's lighting, they are very sensitive to artificial lights, that flicker at a 50–60 Hz frequency. These effects can be palliated thanks to the normalization implemented in this work, or by adding a post-processing layer to the sensor output, like in [7].

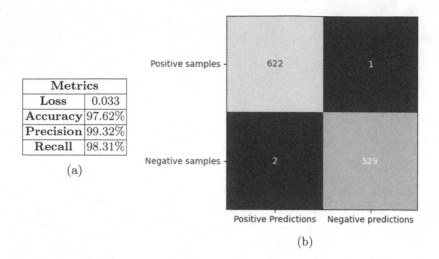

Metrics	
Loss	0.033
Accuracy	97.62%
Precision	99.32%
Recall	98.31%

(a)

(b)

Fig. 5. (a) Different metrics of validation set (b) Confusion matrix of validation set

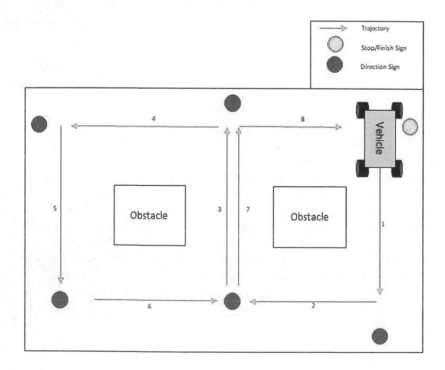

Fig. 6. Proposed test circuit

6   Conclusions

In this work, we present a proof of concept that autonomous navigation can be done both with neuromorphic sensors and Edge-AI computing devices. Key aspects of this process are the integration of events into histograms, the normalization of said histograms to create frames that are used to collect a data set and the training of a neural network with this data set. The CNN accelerator implemented is what finally allows for a viable real-time Edge-AI computing dedicated solution, and everything is possible thanks to the sparsity that exists inherently both in event-driven systems and in the deeper layers of the CNN due to ReLu activations.

There has been an extensive integration work for the present article, as a lot of heterogeneous systems have been used and made to communicate between each other . We believe that this kind of work will encourage fellow researchers to develop their own systems, circuits and strategies, that can later be shared to improve overall knowledge on the field. Following this philosophy, possible test circuits are endless and there is even the chance that one or more of these tests or datasets will become part of a standard "get started" task in the future for autonomous driving.

Results from the CNN are more than satisfactory for the task, having a performance of more than 95% for every metric taking, both during the training and validation process. However, this CNN is still conventional, i.e. it does not process events directly but rather a histogram created from a set of events, which is a downside we would like to address in the future by developing an algorithm that works the other way round (not with frames but with events), hoping that it would achieve even better performance latency and consumption-wise.

References

1. jAER open source project: real time sensory-motor processing for event based sensors and systems. available online at: http://www.jaerproject.org
2. Aimar, A., et al.: NullHop: a flexible convolutional neural network accelerator based on sparse representations of feature maps. IEEE Trans. Neural Netw. Learn. Syst. **30**(3), 644–656 (2019). https://doi.org/10.1109/TNNLS.2018.2852335
3. Brandli, C., Berner, R., Yang, M., Liu, S., Delbruck, T.: A 240 × 180 130 db 3 us latency global shutter spatiotemporal vision sensor. IEEE J. Solid-State Circuits **49**(10), 2333–2341 (2014). https://doi.org/10.1109/JSSC.2014.2342715
4. Chan, V., Liu, S., van Schaik, A.: AER EAR: a matched silicon cochlea pair with address event representation interface. IEEE Trans. Circuits Syst. I Regul. Pap. **54**(1), 48–59 (2007). https://doi.org/10.1109/TCSI.2006.887979
5. Jiménez-Fernández, A., et al.: A binaural neuromorphic auditory sensor for FPGA: a spike signal processing approach. IEEE Trans. Neural Netw. Learn. Syst. **28**(4), 804–818 (2017). https://doi.org/10.1109/TNNLS.2016.2583223
6. Lichtsteiner, P., Posch, C., Delbruck, T.: A 128 × 128 120 dB 15 us latency asynchronous temporal contrast vision sensor. IEEE J. Solid-State Circuits **43**(2), 566–576 (2008). https://doi.org/10.1109/JSSC.2007.914337

7. Linares-Barranco, A., et al.: Low latency event-based filtering and feature extraction for dynamic vision sensors in real-time FPGA applications. IEEE Access **7**, 134926–134942 (2019). https://doi.org/10.1109/ACCESS.2019.2941282

8. Linares-Barranco, A., Perez-Peña, F., Jimenez-Fernandez, A., Chicca, E.: ED-BioRob: a neuromorphic robotic arm with FPGA-based infrastructure for bio-inspired spiking motor controllers. Front. Neurorobotics **14**, 96 (2020). https://doi.org/10.3389/fnbot.2020.590163

9. Maass, W., et al.: Brain Computation: A Computer Science Perspective, pp. 184–199. Springer International Publishing (2019). https://doi.org/10.1007/978-3-319-91908-9-11

10. Mahowald, M.: VLSI analogs of neuronal visual processing: a synthesis of form and function (1992)

11. Mahowald, M.A.: Silicon retina with adaptive photoreceptors. In: Visual Information Processing: From Neurons to Chips, vol. 1473, pp. 52–58. International Society for Optics and Photonics, SPIE (1991). https://doi.org/10.1117/12.45540

12. Maqueda, A.I., et al.: Event-based vision meets deep learning on steering prediction for self-driving cars. In: 2018 IEEE/CVF Conference on Computer Vision and Pattern Recognition (2018). https://doi.org/10.1109/cvpr.2018.00568

13. Mead, C.A., Mahowald, M.: A silicon model of early visual processing. Neural Netw. **1**(1), 91–97 (1988). https://doi.org/10.1016/0893-6080(88)90024-X

14. Mitchell, J.P., et al.: NeoN: neuromorphic control for autonomous robotic navigation. In: 2017 IEEE International Symposium on Robotics and Intelligent Sensors (IRIS), pp. 136–142 (2017). https://doi.org/10.1109/IRIS.2017.8250111

15. Posch, C., Matolin, D., Wohlgenannt, R.: A QVGA 143 dB dynamic range frame-free PWM image sensor with lossless pixel-level video compression and time-domain CDS. IEEE J. Solid-State Circuits **46**(1), 259–275 (2011). https://doi.org/10.1109/JSSC.2010.2085952

16. Rios-Navarro, A., et al.: Efficient memory organization for DNN hardware accelerator implementation on PSoC. Electronics **10**(1), 94 (2021). https://doi.org/10.3390/electronics10010094

17. Stagsted, R.K., et al.: Event-based PID controller fully realized in neuromorphic hardware: a one DoF study. In: 2020 IEEE/RSJ International Conference on Intelligent Robots and Systems (IROS), pp. 10939–10944 (2020). https://doi.org/10.1109/IROS45743.2020.9340861

18. Stagsted, R., et al.: Towards neuromorphic control: a spiking neural network based PID controller for UAV. In: Robotics: Science and Systems 2020. RSS (2020). https://doi.org/10.15607/rss.2020.xvi.074

19. Yang, M., Chien, C., Delbruck, T., Liu, S.: A 0.5 v 55 uw 64 × 2 channel binaural silicon cochlea for event-driven stereo-audio sensing. IEEE J. Solid-State Circuits **51**(11), 2554–2569 (2016). https://doi.org/10.1109/JSSC.2016.2604285

Effects of Training on BCI Accuracy in SSMVEP-based BCI

Piotr Stawicki, Aya Rezeika, and Ivan Volosyak

Rhine-Waal University of Applied Sciences, 47533 Kleve, Germany
ivan.volosyak@hochschule-rhein-waal.de

Abstract. This paper investigates the effects of the training process on the classification accuracy for a steady-state motion visual evoked potentials (SSMVEP)-based brain-computer interface (BCI) paradigm.

An SSMVEP-based BCI works similar to SSVEP with the main difference that the stimulus is smoothly changing its appearance, with a continuous motion, leading to less user fatigue. Typical SSMVEP classification utilises correlation algorithms to compare the incoming Electroencephalography (EEG) data with a sine-cosine template.

To increase the classification performance of BCI algorithms, collecting user training data has been a common practice recently, usually for template-matching detection algorithms. The incoming EEG data are compared with an individually created template from the user's own pre-recorded EEG response to the stimulus. In this offline study, previously recorded data (3 s of training EEG data), which were collected during an online experiment with 86 participants, were used.

Task-related component analysis (TRCA), a state of the art classification method, was modified with the spatial filter W generated by the canonical-correlation analysis (CCA). The TRCA and the sine+cosine templates were compared. The cross paradigm utilisation of the training data was also investigated, e.g. the TRCA model built from SSVEP training data was used to classify the SSMVEP data and vice versa.

Results show a significant difference in favour of the usage of the training data over the sine-cosine template for the SSMVEP paradigm classification. A cross-paradigm validation shows promising results (accuracy >70%) for a time window of 1.5 s, similar to the sine+cosine templates. The trained TRCA models achieved an accuracy of 94% and 97% for the SSMVEP and SSVEP paradigms, respectively, in the mentioned time window. Overall, we conclude that training can significantly improve the SSMVEP target classification.

Keywords: Brain-computer interface (BCI) · Training · Steady-state motion visual evoked potentials (SSMVEP) · Steady-state visual evoked potentials (SSVEP) · Task-related component analysis (TRCA) · Canonical correlation analysis (CCA)

© Springer Nature Switzerland AG 2021
I. Rojas et al. (Eds.): IWANN 2021, LNCS 12862, pp. 69–80, 2021.
https://doi.org/10.1007/978-3-030-85099-9_6

1 Introduction

Brain-computer interface (BCI) designs based on the visual evoked potentials (VEP) have been a popular choice over the past decades [6,8]. These systems have proven to achieve high information transfer rates in various implementations [2,7]. The most common types of VEPs used for BCIs are steady-state VEPs (SSVEPs), code-modulated VEPs (cVEPs), and, recently, steady-state motion VEPs (SSMVEPs). In our recent BCI literacy study, the c-VEP paradigm achieved the most reliable control out of the three compared types of VEP-based BCIs [10]. For these VEP-based BCI modalities, users faced flickering target objects (for example, boxes with letters), which were blinking with different code patterns. When the user gazed at one of these stimuli, VEPs were evoked, which may be recorded via electroencephalography (EEG), where the desired target was identified through a template matching approach based on of the EEG data.

There are different known approaches to achieve the template required for a successful VEP-based BCIs classification process. Zerafa et al. [13] categorises them into three main types: Training-free methods, which allows immediate usage of the BCI application; subject-independent training methods that utilise data sets recorded from many subjects to optimize system parameters to be used for all users; and subject-specific training methods, which require a user-specific recording session prior to the system usage.

Each of the previously mentioned VEP modalities has its advantages and disadvantages. For example, the SSVEP approach has the advantage that it can be used with zero training, using e.g. sinusoidal reference signals as templates [9]. However, many users report that it can cause discomfort and fatigue [1] when compared to the SSMVEP, where the stimulus is in continuous motion, which is more comfortable to the eyes and can also be used without the need for training data [5,9](EEG signals are compared against generic sinusoidal templates [9,10]).

The general assumption is that long training sessions ensure good signal-to-noise ratios. Subject-specific classification approaches with long training sessions have achieved the fastest and most reliable performances (e.g. [7]). However, with respect to user-friendliness, these training sessions may be tedious as subjects are required to focus their gaze for a relatively long time on a flickering or moving stimulus, usually, multiple times in a row. This approach is very time consuming and causes visual fatigue [10]. When the BCI system is developed for everyday use, alternative approaches are desirable, like training-free methods or subject-independent methods. Recent popular approaches are to transfer the subject-specific learning across stimulus frequencies [12], by transferring the learning knowledge within subject and between subjects [11], or with transferring training data from one session to another [3].

The herein paper utilises previously recorded EEG data, from one of the biggest known BCI studies, with three most commonly-used BCI-speller paradigms (SSVEP, SSMVEP, and cVEP), which included 86 subjects [10]. During this study (further referred to as the original study), training data was also recorded for each of the paradigms (see [10] for more details). However, training data were only utilised to classify SSVEP and cVEP (training is essential for cVEP) and not for SSMVEP-based speller classification. The SSMVEP paradigm was classified with a sine-cosine based template. In this study, we ran an offline analysis to investigate the efficacy of training sessions compared with fix-template (cosine- and sine reference template) classification methods, for different classification time-windows on the SSVEP and SSMVEP training data collected during the original study. We also investigated the transfer learning approach by utilising the task-related component analysis (TRCA) training and classification with cross paradigm training models, e.g. classifying the SSMVEP training EEG data with SSVEP TRCA model, and vice versa.

2   Materials and Methods

2.1   Original Study

Participants. Data of all 86 participants of the original experiment [10] were utilised in this offline analysis. Subjects were recruited from Rhine-Waal University of Applied Sciences (58 male, 27 female, 1 diverse), with a mean (SD) age of 25.24 years (4.16). The experiment was approved by the ethical committee of the medical faculty of the University Duisburg-Essen, Germany; written informed consent was given before the experiment was conducted. Participants had little to no prior BCI experience and normal or corrected-to-normal vision. All participants received a financial reward for their participation.

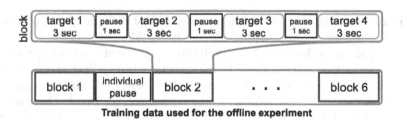

Fig. 1. Diagram representing the training/calibration data recording of the original study. This data were utilised in the offline analysis study presented in this paper. Each subject carried out six blocks of training, where they had to focus their gaze on each of the four targets for three seconds, with one second pause in between.

Stimulus Presentation. The stimuli were presented on a 24.5 in. monitor (Acer predator XB252Q) with a refresh rate 240 Hz and the resolution 1920 × 1080 pixels. The design of the stimulus consisted of four white round targets with the size of 230 × 230 pixels, presented over a black background. The current target, on which the participants needed to fix their gaze was marked with a green frame. The stimulation frequencies of the targets were 8, 10, 12, 15 Hz, for targets 1, 2, 3, and 4, respectively. Further details regarding the stimulus design can be found in [10].

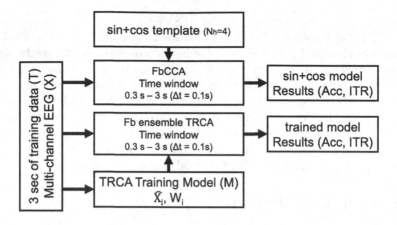

Fig. 2. Diagram, how the offline analyses was performed.

For the stimulus presentation, on the computer screen, the G-Sync® technology was disabled, instead, the fixed refresh-rate (240 Hz) was used.

The number of pre-rendered frames (in the graphics card memory) was set to 1 (minimal available value) to reduce the stimulus drawing delay from graphics card memory to the actual drawing on the screen during the screen refresh. Additionally, thanks to the high refresh rate of the utilised monitor (240 Hz), a single frame was drawn within 4.17 ms.

Training Phase. During the training phase, each of the four stimuli was fixated six times (grouped in six training blocks, $n_b = 6$). The stimuli pattern was repeated for three cycles $3 \times 1 = 3$ s. Initially, subjects pressed the space bar to start the stimulation, and a green frame around a box indicated on which one the user had to fixate their gaze. In each block, every stimulus was attended once, resulting in $6 \times 4 = 24$ total trials in one dataset, see Fig. 1. These datasets were created for both paradigms (SSVEP and SSMVEP), resulting in a total count of $2 \times 86 = 172$ datasets.

2.2 This Study

Hardware and Software. The hardware used for the offline analysis is the same as for the online data analysis [10], Dell Precision 3630, equipped with Intel processor (Intel Core i7-8700K, @3.70 GHz) and 16 GB of RAM, running Windows 10 Education. The software utilized for the offline analysis was MATLAB® 2019a.

CCA-Based Spatial Filter Design and Template Generation

In BCI research, CCA is frequently used to find a linear transformation that maximizes the correlation between the recorded signal and the averaged template signals. Typically, only the first canonical correlation and corresponding weights are used for classification and construction of filters [7].

Here, we applied the improved method (details in [4]), which utilised the CCA to create class-specific spatial filters (see Fig. 2).

Since the CCA is a widely used method for VEP-based BCI system designs [13], we applied it to design the spatial filters by conducting it on the data collected during the training sessions (as proposed in [7] and [4]). Given two multi-dimensional variables $\mathbf{X} \in \mathbb{R}^{m_1 \times n}$ and $\mathbf{Y} \in \mathbb{R}^{m_2 \times n}$, CCA identifies weights $\mathbf{a} \in \mathbb{R}^{m_1}$ and $\mathbf{b} \in \mathbb{R}^{m_2}$ that maximize the correlation, ρ, between the so called canonical variates $\mathbf{x} = \mathbf{X}^T \mathbf{a}$ and $\mathbf{y} = \mathbf{Y}^T \mathbf{b}$ by solving

$$\rho(x, y) = \max_{\mathbf{a}, \mathbf{b}} \frac{\mathbf{a}^T \mathbf{X} \mathbf{Y}^T \mathbf{b}}{\sqrt{\mathbf{a}^T \mathbf{X} \mathbf{X}^T \mathbf{a} \, \mathbf{b}^T \mathbf{Y} \mathbf{Y}^T \mathbf{b}}}. \tag{1}$$

The correlation value ρ that solves (1) is the canonical correlation. For VEP-based BCI, most researchers use only the first canonical correlation weights ($\mathbf{a}$, $\mathbf{b}$) for classification or for the spatial filter design.

Each training trial was stored in an $m \times n$ matrix, where m denotes the number of electrode channels (here, $m = 16$) and n denotes the number of sample points (here, three 1.0 s stimulus cycles, $n = 1.0 \cdot F_S \cdot 3 = 1800$).

For a target T_i in the first filter bank, the trials of all 6 training blocks, corresponding to a specific class, were averaged by calculating the arithmetic mean. This mean was then concatenated yielding the template $\hat{X}$. All trials Ti were also concatenated horizontally yielding the matrix $\hat{T}$. The weight vector W is the Wx obtained with the CCA formula (1) from $\hat{X}$ and $\hat{T}$.

Classification. For the training model target classification the ensemble TRCA-based method introduced in [7] was utilised, and for the sin+cos template classification the filter bank-based CCA method introduced in [2] was used. For the filter bank design, the lower and upper cut-off frequencies for the m-th sub-band were selected as $m \times 5$ and 60 Hz filtered with an 8th order Butterworth filter. In order to cancel the phase response, forward and reverse filtering were applied.

The stored training EEG data were divided into time windows with the lengths from 0.3 s till 3.0 s, increasing every 0.1 s (see Fig. 2).

The output command (C) was calculated based on the weighted linear combinations of the CCA correlation coefficient (ρ in Eq. 1) and the filter bank sub-bands (K) amplitude (a_k),

$$C = \arg \max_{k=1,\dots,K} \lambda_k \,, \text{ where } \lambda_K = \sum_{k=1}^{K} a_k \rho_k \tag{2}$$

for every time window.

Transfer Learning. For every subject the model (M) was used to classify the training data (T) across all other subjects to validate the transfer learning theory, especially for SSMVEP-based BCI (m) and was compared to SSVEP-based BCI (f). In other words, the SSMVEP model of subject 1 ($M_{m,S1}$) was used to classify the training datasets of subjects 2 to 86 $T_{m, Si}$, where i = 2,...,86 of same paradigm (m), or opposite paradigm (f) $T_{f, Si}$, all with an leave-one-out cross-validation. From the combination of $M_{f,m}$ and $T_{f,m}$ four combinations were built: $M_m T_m$, $M_m T_f$, $M_f T_m$ vs $M_f T_f$. This transfer learning approach was analysed for a time window (tw) of lengths 0.5, 1.0, 1.5, 2.0, 2.5, and 3.0 s, with additional detailed analysis for 1.5 s.

3 Results

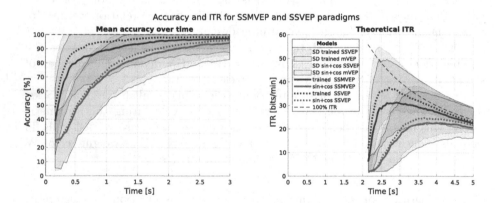

Fig. 3. Mean accuracy and ITR theoretically achievable based on the collected training data averaged across all 86 subjects. The models were build with the training data (trained, utilising TRCA) and with sin+cos templates (Nh = 4, Fb = 5). These results are based on a dynamic time window increasing from 0.3s (minimal time window utilised in the original study [10]) up to 3.0s with a step of 0.1s. The theoretical ITR results include a gaze shift period of 2s added at the beginning of the plot data to simulate the parameters of the original study [10]. Blue colour marks the training model as a template, red marks sin+cos templates, solid lines represent the SSMVEP results, the dotted lines are the SSVEP results, and the dashed black line shows the theoretical ideal results for 100% accuracy. The shaded areas mark the corresponding standard deviation (SD). (Color figure online)

Figure 3 shows the results of the offline analysis results for both TRCA-models (trained) and sin+cos templates in both scenarios (SSVEP and SSMVEP). What can be clearly seen in Fig. 3 is the stabilising of the results after approx. 1.5 s, that is why we focus on this time window performance in further analysis.

Paired t-test showed significant differences in the accuracy and the ITR between the TRCA trained model and the sin+cos model (see Fig. 3), for both paradigms. p-values for the SSMVEP are 1.08E-08 and 1.77E-10 for accuracy and ITR, respectively, and the p-values for the SSVEP are 4.68E-07 and 2.15E-08 for accuracy and ITR, respectively.

3.1   Transfer Learning: Cross-Paradigm Modality Intrasubject Validation

Table 1 summarises the investigation of the average accuracy performance validating the transfer learning theory across paradigms for 6 popular time window lengths (0.5 s, 1.0 s, 1.5 s, 2.0 s, 2.5 s, and 3.0 s). Figure 4 shows the statistical significance of a paired t-test between the different models M and training data T for SSVEP (f) and SSMVEP (m).

Table 1. Average accuracy (SD) transfer learning across paradigms for different time window lenghts (0.5 s, 1.0 s, 1.5 s, 2.0 s, 2.5 s, and 3.0 s).

			TRCA model (M)	
			(f) SSVEP	(m) SSMVEP
Training EEG data (T)	0.5 s	(f) SSVEP	87.45 (12.42)	54.99 (17.94)
		(m) SSMVEP	55.18 (18.40)	79.75 (15.81)
	1.0 s	(f) SSVEP	95.16 (7.42)	68.27 (18.76)
		(m) SSMVEP	69.23 (20.21)	90.26 (12.78)
	1.5 s	(f) SSVEP	96.95 (6.11)	73.30 (17.82)
		(m) SSMVEP	71.61 (20.33)	93.90 (9.14)
	2.0 s	(f) SSVEP	97.97 (4.86)	76.74 (16.67)
		(m) SSMVEP	75.92 (20.13)	95.54 (7.93)
	2.5 s	(f) SSVEP	98.26 (4.63)	79.22 (15.49)
		(m) SSMVEP	78.54 (18.46)	96.56 (6.24)
	3.0 s	(f) SSVEP	98.50 (4.09)	81.20 (15.36)
		(m) SSMVEP	80.23 (18.29)	97.34 (5.42)

A paired t-test was conducted on the same-subject's (diagonals) accuracy for the cross-paradigm classification vs. same-paradigm classification. The results in Fig. 4 showed that using the same paradigm for classification and for building the model achieved a better classification performance.

Figure 5 shows the accuracy when the same paradigm was used for building the model and for classification, across subjects. In other words, for example, the model built from subject 25 data was used to classify all the 86 subjects, and the same was repeated for all the 86 subjects. The accuracy results were plotted in Fig. 5 as an 86 × 86 matrix. The yellow diagonal shows the accuracy when the model and the classified data were from the same subject.

The same analysis was repeated across-paradigms; i.e. if the model was built from the SSVEP training data, it was used for classifying the SSMVEP training data, and vice versa for all 86 subjects (see Fig. 6).

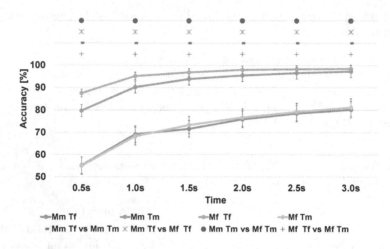

Fig. 4. Statistical results of the cross paradigm transfer learning approach utilising a paired t-test between the different TRCA-based models M and training EEG data T for SSVEP (f) and SSMVEP (m). From the combination of $M_{f,m}$ and $T_{f,m}$ six pairs can be built, out of which five were interested to investigate: $M_m T_f$ vs $M_m T_m$ (-), $M_m T_f$ vs $M_f T_f$ (*), $M_m T_m$ vs $M_f T_m$ (•), $M_f T_f$ vs $M_f T_m$ (+), and $M_m T_f$ vs $M_f T_m$. The last pair showed no statistically significant results. The error bars represent the standard error.

3.2   Transfer Learning: Cross-Paradigm Modality Intersubject Validation for 1.5 s Time Window

Figure 7 shows by how far other subjects SSMVEP models were good for the SSMVEP training data classification for each individual subject, for the 1.5 second window. This corresponds to the data in Fig. 5 (right side) MmTm. Further, the efficiency of transfer learning for same paradigm and cross-paradigm approach was evaluated. The box plot in Fig. 7 and 8 compares each subject's performance when its own model was used against all other 85 models, for SSMVEP, and SSVEP paradigm, respectively. The x marks signifies the mean accuracy, top and bottom whiskers indicates the maximum and minimum values, respectively.

4   Discussion

This paper focuses on the offline analysis of the training data only, since it was unifying for all participants and the tested paradigms.

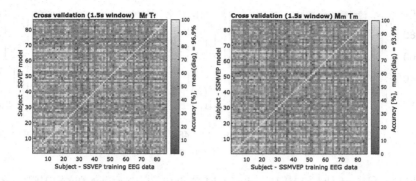

Fig. 5. Cross validation of the training EEG data for 1.5 s time window. This figure shows the accuracy of M_mT_m and M_fT_f tested across all participants, where e.g. the SSVEP (f) model (M) was used to classify the SSVEP (f) training EEG data (T).

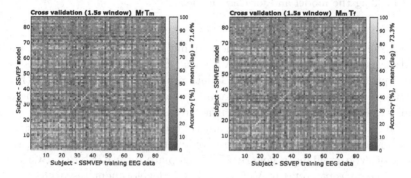

Fig. 6. Cross validation of the training EEG data across paradigms for 1.5 s time window. This figure shows the accuracy of M_fT_m and M_mT_f tested across all participants, where e.g. the SSVEP (f) model (M) was used to classify the SSMVEP (m) training EEG data (T).

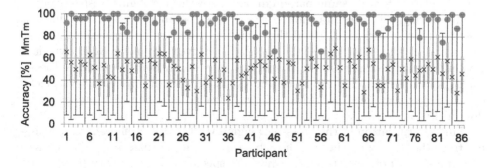

Fig. 7. Box plot of the SSMVEP training EEG data (T_m) against the SSMVEP TRCA training models (M_m) for the 1.5 s window. The x marks signifies the mean accuracy, top and bottom whiskers indicates the maximum and minimum values, respectively. The big dots on the top indicates the accuracy achieved for using the same subject's data for building the model and for classification. (Color figure online)

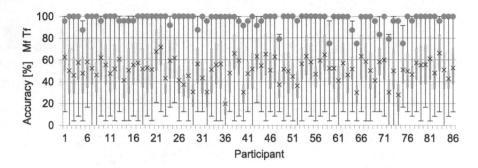

Fig. 8. Box plot of the SSVEP training EEG data (T_f) against the SSVEP TRCA training models (M_f) for the 1.5 s window. The x marks signifies the mean accuracy, top and bottom whiskers indicates the maximum and minimum values, respectively. The big dots on the top indicates the accuracy achieved for using the same subject's data for building the model and for classification.

The results in Fig. 3 show that the training was far better than the sin+cos template classification for the SSMVEP and SSVEP paradigms. This proves the concept, that the users own EEG data are a far better template than the sine-cosine templates. On the other hand, it was observed that the sine-cosine templates can still achieve reliable accuracy results above 70% for a time window of at least 1.5 s. This shows the importance of the training for reliable target classification. Minimising the training time, online re-training while typing, reusing old data, or even creating a generic EEG template for VEP-based BCI classifications is the current trend in VEP-based BCI development research.

In order to explore the possible learning transfer of one subject across other subjects, we compared the training models with the raw EEG training data of all other participants for the SSVEP and SSMVEP paradigms, for an optimal classification time window. Figure 5 and 6 show such a comparison for the time window of 1.5 s for the same paradigm, and between paradigms, respectively.

Interestingly, the results showed that a cross-paradigm usage of training is possible ($M_m T_f$ and $M_f T_m$) and the achieved results are quite similar, in both directions. For most subjects, the accuracy achieved for using their own data was higher than using cross-subject models. However, in some cases (27 subjects, $M_m T_m$) of the SSMVEP cross-subject validation, the accuracy achieved using other subject's models (top whiskers) was higher than their own model (green dot) in Fig. 7.

Further validation of the cross-paradigm ($M_m T_f$, $M_f T_m$) showed that, starting from the 1.5 s time window, the achieved accuracy surpass 70%. This parameters may be a possible starting scenario to speed up the necessary preparation (see Fig. 4), which can be usefull for some subjects in e.g. clinical conditions.

Further investigation should focus on an unified/universal training data set that can be used for initial classification of SSVEP or SSMVEP based BCI paradigms.

5   Conclusion

The presented paper investigated the effectiveness of the training session for SSMVEP-based BCIs with offline analysis from previously recorded subjects' EEG data. The results demonstrated that a training session is not required for most users as an accuracy of 70% can be reached with sin+cos templates with 1.5 s time window (see Fig. 3); when the training is performed, it increases the possible result significantly. Furthermore, a subjective training from one frequency-based VEP paradigm (SSVEP) can be successfully utilised to classify the SSMVEP paradigm to an accepted level of accuracy (70% for 1.5 s time window, Fig. 4).

In comparison with other approaches, such as unsupervised retraining, a major disadvantage of the VEP BCI paradigm (i.e. the repeated tedious training sessions), may be almost entirely circumvented (a one-time initial training session, i.e., when using the system for the first time, is still required).

This offline study is a step towards the reduction of the preparation time to a bare minimum. The findings of the study are relevant for potential use-cases in clinical scenarios, where a patient may want to use the system on a weekly basis.

References

1. Benda, M., et al.: Different feedback methods for an SSVEP-based BCI. In: 2018 40th Annual International Conference of the IEEE Engineering in Medicine and Biology Society (EMBC), pp. 1939–1943. IEEE (2018)
2. Chen, X., Wang, Y., Gao, S., Jung, T.P., Gao, X.: Filter bank canonical correlation analysis for implementing a high-speed SSVEP-based brain-computer interface. J. Neural Eng **12**(046008), 046008 (2015)
3. Gembler, F., Stawicki, P., Rezeika, A., Benda, M., Volosyak, I.: Exploring session-to-session transfer for brain-computer interfaces based on code-modulated visual evoked potentials. In: 2020 IEEE International Conference on Systems, Man, and Cybernetics (SMC), pp. 1505–1510 (2020)
4. Gembler, F., Stawicki, P., Saboor, A., Volosyak, I.: Dynamic time window mechanism for time synchronous VEP-based BCIs—Performance evaluation with a dictionary-supported BCI speller employing SSVEP and c-VEP. PLOS ONE **14**(6), e0218177 (2019)
5. Han, C., Xu, G., Xie, J., Chen, C., Zhang, S.: Highly interactive brain-computer interface based on flicker-free steady-state motion visual evoked potential. Sci. Rep. **8**(1), 1–13 (2018)
6. Li, M., He, D., Li, C., Qi, S.: Brain–computer interface speller based on steady-state visual evoked potential: a review focusing on the stimulus paradigm and performance. Brain Sciences **11**(4), 450 (2021)
7. Nakanishi, M., Wang, Y., Chen, X., Wang, Y.T., Gao, X., Jung, T.P.: Enhancing detection of SSVEPs for a high-speed brain speller using task-related component analysis. IEEE Trans. Biomed. Eng. **65**(1), 104–112 (2018). https://doi.org/10.1109/TBME.2017.2694818
8. Rezeika, A., Benda, M., Stawicki, P., Gembler, F., Saboor, A., Volosyak, I.: Brain–computer interface spellers: a review. Brain Sci. 8(4), 57 (2018)

9. Stawicki, P., Rezeika, A., Saboor, A., Volosyak, I.: Investigating ICKER-free steady- state motion stimuli for VEP–based BCIS. In: 2019 E-Health and Bioengineering Conference (EHB), pp. 1–4. IEEE (2019)
10. Volosyak, I., Rezeika, A., Benda, M., Gembler, F., Stawicki, P.: Towards solving of the illiteracy phenomenon for VEP-based brain-computer interfaces. Biomed. Phys. Eng. Express **6**(3), 035034 (2020)
11. Wang, H., et al.: Cross-subject assistance: inter-and intra-subject maximal correlation for enhancing the performance of SSVEP-based BCIS. IEEE Trans. Neural Syst. Rehabil. Eng. **29**, 517–526 (2021)
12. Wong, C.M. et al.: Transferring subject-specific knowledge across stimulus frequencies in SSVEP-based BCIS. IEEE Trans. Autom. Sci. Eng. 18, 552–563 (2021)
13. Zerafa, R., Camilleri, T., Falzon, O., Camilleri, K.P.: To train or not to train? A survey on training of feature extraction methods for SSVEP-based BCIs. J. Neural Eng. **15**(5), 051001 (2018)

Effect of Electrical Synapses in the Cycle-by-Cycle Period and Burst Duration of Central Pattern Generators

Blanca Berbel[1]($\boxtimes$), Alicia Garrido-peña[1]($\boxtimes$), Irene Elices[2]($\boxtimes$),
Roberto Latorre[1]($\boxtimes$), and Pablo Varona[1]($\boxtimes$)

[1] Grupo de Neurocomputación Biológica, Dpto. de Ingeniería Informática, Escuela Politécnica Superior, Universidad Autónoma de Madrid, 28049 Madrid, Spain
blanca.berbel@inv.uam.es,
{alicia.garrido,roberto.latorre,pablo.varona}@uam.es
[2] Sorbonne Université, INSERM, CNRS, Institut de la Vision, 17 rue Moreau, 75012 Paris, France
irene.elices@inserm.fr

Abstract. Central Pattern Generators (CPGs) are neural circuits that generate robust coordinated neural activity to control motor rhythms. Many CPGs are convenient neural circuits for locomotion control in autonomous robots. In this context, invertebrate CPGs are key networks to understand rhythm generation and coordination, as their cells and connections can be identified and mapped, like in the crustacean pyloric CPG. Experiments during the last decades have shown that mutual inhibition by chemical synapses together with electrical coupling underlie the timing of neuron activations that shape each rhythm cycle of this CPG. Due to the presence of inhibitory and electrical synapses, regular and irregular triphasic spiking-bursting activity can be found in the pyloric CPG, always preserving the same neuron activation sequence. In this study, we use a model of this well-known CPG to assess the role of electrical synapses in shaping the cycle-by-cycle period and individual cell burst duration. We show that electrical coupling strength asymmetrically affects the burst duration of each individual neuron, as well as the overall cycle-by-cycle duration. Our results support the view that electrical coupling largely contributes to shape the intervals that define functional sequences in CPGs, which can be applied in bioinspired autonomous robotic motor control.

Keywords: CPG · Rhythm coordination · Autonomous rhythm generation · Sequential neural activity

1 Introduction

The most common mechanism for signaling among neurons are chemical synapses, which can be excitatory or inhibitory and they display distinct temporal dynamics as a function of the neurotransmitters and neuroreceptors involved

© Springer Nature Switzerland AG 2021
I. Rojas et al. (Eds.): IWANN 2021, LNCS 12862, pp. 81–92, 2021.
https://doi.org/10.1007/978-3-030-85099-9_7

in this kind of communication [1]. Electrical synapses, on the other hand, are faster and simpler. They consist of specialized gap junctions that allow the direct flow of ionic currents between neurons [2,3]. Both chemical and electrical synapses are often combined in neural circuit topologies to produce robust sequential activations of their constituent neurons [4–6].

A central question in the study of neuronal oscillations is what is the mechanism that underlies the generation of such robust and highly coordinated sequential activity and how this activity is regulated, balancing flexibility and robustness. In particular, the role of electrical coupling is of special interest, as it has been less studied from this perspective. Electrical coupling is responsible for a wide variety of coordination phenomena in neural networks [2], especially those related with rhythmic activity. In simple circuits like central pattern generators (CPGs), electrical coupling is responsible for rhytmogenesis, synchronization, and motor pattern formation [7,8]. The role of electrical coupling in the coordination and synchronization of multiple cells is intuitively clear since the current that flows between cells through gap junctions is proportional to the difference of their membranes voltage, and thus tends to equalize their electrical activity. This function has been shown experimentally and theoretically in networks of varying complexity [2,8–12]. It is important to emphasize that moderate coupling leads to moderate synchronization and spiking activity among electrically coupled cells is usually not fully synchronized [13]. Theoretical studies have shown the effect of gap junctions on the oscillation frequency of electrically coupled neurons [14,15]. In large networks of electrically coupled cells, gap junctions lead to coordinated spatio-temporal patterns [15,16].

CPGs are neural networks that generate and coordinate robust sequences of neuronal activations that build-up a rhythm in motor systems. They are specialized for the production of stereotyped sequential rhythmic motor patterns like those needed for locomotion. These circuits have evolved to autonomously produce rhythmic, but at the same time flexible, spatio-temporal motor patterns [17,18].

CPGs are key neural circuit for understanding the generation of rhythm and coordination [19,20], since their cells and connections have been widely identified and mapped, as is the case of the crustacean pyloric CPG that we used in this study [17]. CPG neurons typically have rich dynamics and individual neurons can show a highly irregular spiking-bursting activity when isolated from other CPG members [7,17]. In the intact circuit, neurons generate different robust patterns that keep the same sequence but are nevertheless flexible to manage their constituent time intervals [4]. Such sequential neural activity controls a wide variety of motor movements in activities like chewing, walking or swimming and has been used to propose autonomous locomotion mechanisms in bioinspired robots [21–23].

The CPGs' topology is non-open in most cases, this means that all neurons in the CPG receive input from the other cells in the circuit, which is useful for their transient closed-loop computation [24]. Another essential component of network circuits is reciprocal chemical inhibition between pairs of neurons. This inhibition, together with electrical coupling and other non-reciprocal interactions, are responsible for the order of the activation of the neurons in the circuit, leading to a characteristic shape in each cycle. A recent study has revealed the presence of dynamical invariants in the form of robust linear relationships between two of the intervals that build the pyloric CPG sequence, which are kept even under strong perturbations in the CPG [4]. Although the maintenance of phase and the linear relationship between rhythmic intervals and the period have been previously studied, the role of gap-junctions in shaping the variability of the sequence intervals and the duration of the intervals building the sequence has not been assessed yet. In this work, we use a biophysical model to characterize the cycle-by-cycle period and burst duration as a function of the coupling conductance of its electrical synapses. For this task, we will vary the electrical conductance between three of the CPG neurons to measure the period and burst duration, including also their associated variability.

2   Methods

2.1   Neuron Models

The dynamics of the single neuron models used in this study are based on the Komendantov-Kononenko model [25], a conductance-based Hodgkin-Huxley type model [26] with eight dynamical variables. The model equations and the associated parameters used in this study are described in Appendix A and B.

2.2   CPG Network Model

The crustacean pyloric CPG is built from 14 neurons of different cell types: one anterior buster (AB), two pyloric dilator (PDs) neurons, one lateral pyloric (LP), one inferior cardiac (IC), one ventricular dilator (VD) and eight pyloric (PYs) neurons [17]. In this study we will consider a simplified version built with five neurons: one AB, two PDs, one LP and one PY (that represents eight PYs neurons electrically coupled). Following previously reported modeling approaches [27,28], we did not include the action of IC and VD since these neurons do not innervate the pyloric muscles. The CPG topology scheme considered here is shown in Fig. 1A.

2.3   Synapses

The total synaptic current received by a cell (I_{Syn}) is different for each neuron. This current is built from the summation of all electrical and chemical inputs. Below we describe the models of electrical and chemical currents used in this study.

Electrical Synapses. When an electrical synapse occurs, the membranes of the presynaptic and postsynaptic neuron are joined by a gap junction. The cytoplasm of both neurons is united and there is a direct flow of ions between the two neurons. To model this union, we will use Ohm's law. In this way, the

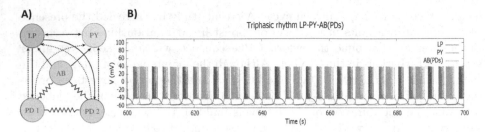

Fig. 1. A) Circuit used to model the crustacean pyloric CPG in this study. The resistors represent electrical synapses. The dotted lines represent slow inhibitory chemical synapses and solid lines represent fast inhibitory chemical connections. Note the presence of two subcircuits: the AB-PD1-PD2 with electrical coupling and the AB/PDs-LP-PY with chemical connectivity. PDs neurons are presynaptic for all slow chemical synapses between the two subcircuits, while LP is connected to both PDs with fast chemical synapses. Also, AB is connected to LP and PY with fast chemical synapses and the same occurs between LP and PY. B) Triphasic rhythm in the CPG circuit, note that the order of the sequence is robust but the activity is not completely regular.

synaptic current from the electrical coupling which goes from the presynaptic to the postsynaptic neuron can be described as:

$$I^{ec}_{post} = g_{prepost}(V_{post} - V_{pre}) \tag{1}$$

where $g_{prepost}$ is the maximal synaptic conductance constant, and $V_{pre,post}$ is the membrane potential of the presynaptic and postsynaptic neuron respectively. The current is proportional to the difference between the membrane potential of both neurons. The other neuron receives the same current with opposite sign as we considered bidirectional symmetric electrical synapses.

In the pacemaker group (AB-PD1-PD2), the electrical connectivity is symmetric and the membrane potential of these neurons are synchronized. In our figures we will only show the activity of neuron AB.

For the isolated dynamics of the AB neuron, the model was set to regular bursting (see parameters in Appendix B). For LP, PY and PD1, the parameters were set for the chaotic mode. Finally, the PD2 neuron was set in the chaotic bursting mode. This in agreement with *in vitro* experiments [17].

Chemical Synapses. The pacemaker group is connected with LP and PY by fast and slow graded chemical synapses [17]. To simulate fast currents we used the following equation [27,29]:

$$I^{f}_{post} = \frac{g^{f}_{prepost}(V_{post} - E_{Syn})}{1.0 + \exp\left(s^{f}(V^{f} - V_{pre})\right)} \tag{2}$$

where $g^{f}_{prepost}$ is the maximum synaptic conductance of the postsynaptic neuron, V_{post} is the membrane potential of the postsynaptic neuron, E_{syn} is the synaptic

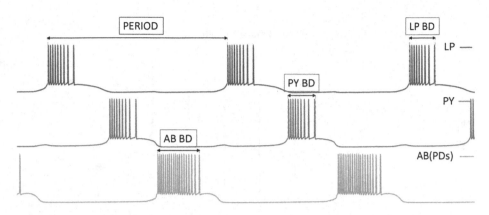

Fig. 2. Definition of the burst duration and the cycle-by-cycle period of the triphasic rhythm of the pyloric CPG, as reproduced by the model described in this study. The definition applies for each cycle. BD stands for burst duration.

reversal potential, V^f determines the threshold of graded synapse and V_{pre} is the membrane potential of the presynaptic neuron.

The slow synaptic current is described with a similar approach [27,29]:

$$I_{post}^s = g_{prepost}^s m_{post}^s (V_{post} - E_{Syn}) \tag{3}$$

where m is described as

$$\frac{dm_{post}^s}{dt} = \frac{k_1(1.0 - m_{post}^s)}{1.0 + \exp\left(s^s(V^s - V_{pre})\right)} - k_2 m_{post}^s \tag{4}$$

Here $g_{prepost}^s$ is the maximal synaptic conductance of the postsynaptic neuron, k_1 and k_2 are time constants that control the speed and duration of the synaptic current and V^s determines the threshold of the graded slow synapse.

3   Results

With the circuit described above, we performed an analysis of the cycle-by-cycle period and burst duration, including their variability, as a function of the coupling strength of several of the electrical connections. To study the temporal variability of each sequence, we detected the spikes using a threshold protocol and the sign of the first derivative of the signals. We distinguished between the first and last spikes within each burst to measure the period and the burst duration as intervals that build up the CPG rhythm sequence.

We executed the code implementing the model for 1000 s of the model time unit containing a total of approximately 100 bursts. We discarded the first 20 s to avoid transient effects from the initial state in the simulation. Simulations of the crustacean pyloric CPG were implemented in C. We solved the eight differential

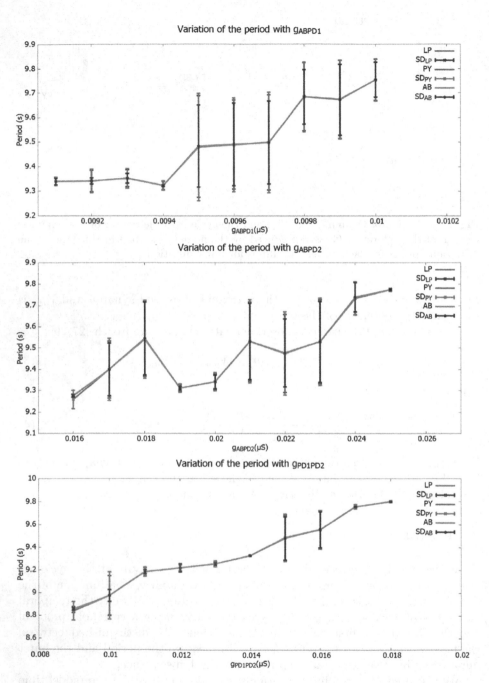

Fig. 3. Evolution of the period for each CPG neuron when changing the electrical synaptic conductance and its associated variability indicated by the standard deviation (SD).

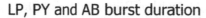

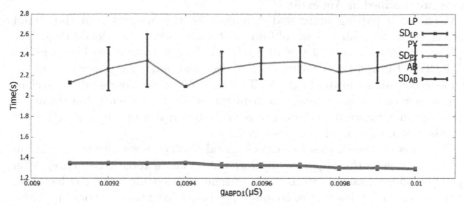

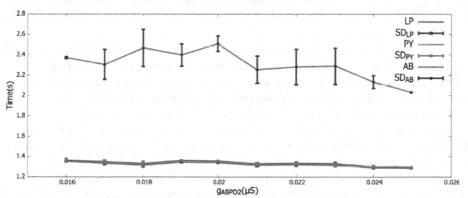

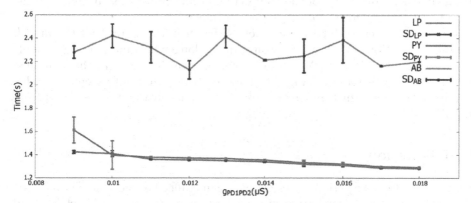

Fig. 4. Evolution of the burst duration for each CPG neuron when changing the electrical synaptic conductance and its associated variability indicated by the standard deviation (SD).

equations of the KK model with a Runge-Kutta method (6th order). Parameter values are specified in Appendix B.

With the departing individual dynamics for the neurons, and the circuit topology described above, we obtain a characteristic triphasic rhythm. The triphasic rhythm consists of the alternation of largely regularized bursts of AB (PD1-PD2), LP and PY activity, in this sequential order. An illustration of the triphasic rhythm is shown in Fig. 1B. The main objective of our study is to characterize how the sequence intervals displayed in Fig. 2 vary with changes in the electrical conductance between neurons in the pacemaker group. The statistical analysis was implemented in Python 3.6.

The criterion chosen to select the electrical conductance range to vary in our study was to keep the triphasic rhythm and its characteristic sequence. After exploring different ranges, we used 10 different values of electrical conductances in each case, leaving the rest of conductance values fixed with the ones provided in [27]. Thus, we varied g_{ABPD1} between $0,0091 - 0,01$ µS (increase of $0,0001$ µS), g_{ABPD2} between $0,016 - 0,025$ µS (increase of $0,001$ µS) and g_{PD1PD2} between $0,009 - 0,018$ µS (increase also of $0,001$ µS). The results of the analysis is described below.

The cycle-by-cycle period is defined as the time interval from the start of one burst to the start of the next burst in the same neuron. As in the living CPG [17], the rhythm in the model is not completely periodic, allowing for restricted variability within the otherwise robust sequential activity. The average of the period calculated from all bursts in the recording time series is identical for the three neurons, thus ensuring the maintenance of the triphasic rhythm. We display the evolution of the period as a function of the explored conductance in Fig. 3, including a characterization of the period variability. In general, we can observe that the period increases with increasing conductance in all three cases of the studied electrical connections. This increased period could be explained in terms of the reduced cell excitability arising from the increase of the coupling strength. There are values of the conductance that reduce the variability of the period, particularly for the g_{PD1PD2} conductance.

On the other hand, for the parameters chosen in the analysis of the model, the burst duration of the AB neuron is much longer and much more variable than that for the LP and PY neurons, as we can see in Fig. 4. In the simplified circuit used in this study, changes in burst duration variability seem to be due mainly to the AB, which in this circuit does not receive direct inhibition from the LP and PY.

4   Discussion

In our study, we have varied the electrical conductance between the neurons AB-PD1-PD2 (i.e., the pacemaker group) to assess how the period of each cell and the associated burst duration change, while robustly sustaining the sequence of the neuron activations, LP-PY-AB(PDs) in all simulations. We quantified the variability of all intervals (period and burst duration as defined in Fig. 2) by identifying the beginning and the end of the bursts in each cycle, and measuring the associated time intervals in a set of long simulations. We have studied how these intervals change with the induction of variability through the change in electrical conductance between neurons of the CPG pacemaker group. Three cases have been studied: variability induced by the change in g_{ABPD1}, in g_{ABPD2} and in g_{PD1PD2}.

The results described above show that conductances of electric gap junctions, and not only inhibitory synapses, can regulate the variability of the intervals that build up the cycle-by-cycle period while robustly keeping the CPG activation sequence. In the assessed circuit, the period of each neuron increases with the value of the electrical coupling conductance. The change is larger when we increase g_{PD1PD2}, where, starting from a lower value, the period values are greater than those reached by increasing the other two electrical conductances within the pacemaker group (g_{ABPD1} and g_{ABPD2}). Note that the connections from/to each member of the pacemaker group of electrically coupled cells are not the same. The current that each pacemaker neuron receives from other cells can be invested in two complementary ways: (i) a change in excitability of the neuron to fire bursts of action potentials and (ii) the distribution of currents to other neurons through the electrical synapses. Current flowing out in a neuron because of an electric synapse means a reduction of its excitability, and thus an increase in its period. On the other hand, the LP and PY burst duration has low variability, while AB burst duration can undergo larger changes and the variability is larger especially with changes in g_{PD1PD2} conductance.

Our study shows that electrical coupling in CPGs can largely affect interval duration and, thus, it is a parameter to be considered in robot CPGs which typically do not display such types of connection. This is because it is frequently assumed that gap junctions play only a synchronization role in such circuits.

This work could be extended by assessing other intervals building the CPG sequence beyond neuron period and burst duration, e.g. intervals defined as the time between the first spike of a neuron's burst and the following first spike of another neuron, or as the time delay between the last spike of one neuron's burst and the following first spike of another neuron. Several of such intervals are known to participate in dynamical invariants in the form of robust relationships with the period and create coordination rules for autonomous CPG function [4]. Dynamical invariants have been proposed to balance flexibility and robustness of CPG sequences and their associated rhythm, and are highly appealing for autonomous robotics. The model results discussed in this paper could be tested in hybrid circuits by modulating the strength of existing electrical connections or by adding new ones through advanced dynamic clamp protocols in a living CPG [30–32].

Acknowledgments. This research was supported by AEI/FEDER PGC2018-095895-B-I00.

A   Equations of Komendantov-Kononenko (KK) Model

The equation that describes the membrane potential in this model is:

$$- C_m dV(t)/dt = I_{Na(TTX)} + I_{K(TEA)} + I_K + I_{Na} + I_{Na}(V) + I_B + I_{Ca} + I_{Ca-Ca} + I_{Syn} \quad (5)$$

where C_m is the capacitance of the membrane and V the membrane potential in mV. I_{Syn} represents the total synaptic current, electrical or chemical, which is different for each neuron in the CPG.

The model is defined with four components describing distinct ionic currents:

1. A slow wave generating mechanism, given by sodium, potassium and chemosensitive currents:

$$I_{Na}(V) = g^*_{Na}(V)(1/1 + \exp(-0.2(V(t) + 45))))(V(t) - V_{Na})); \quad (6)$$

$$I_{Na} = g^*_{Na}(V(t) - V_{Na}); \quad (7)$$

$$I_K = g^*_K(V(t) - V_K); \quad (8)$$

$$I_B = g^*_B m_B(t) h_B(t)(V(t) - V_B); \quad (9)$$

$$dm_B(t)/dt = (1/(1 + \exp(0.4(V(t) + 34))) - m_B(t))/0.05; \quad (10)$$

$$dh_B(t)/dt = (1/(1 + \exp(-0.55(V(t) + 43))) - h_B(t))/1.5; \quad (11)$$

where $m_B(t)$ and $h_B(t)$ are conductance variables that describe the activation and deactivation of the ionic conductance. The parameters $g^*_{Na}(V)$, g^*_{Na}, g^*_K, g^*_B are the maximal conductances of these ionic channels and V_{Na}, V_K and V_B are the corresponding reversal potentials. We will use the same notation for the channels described bellow.

2. A spike-generating mechanism, which is described by TTX-sensitive sodium and TEA-sensitive potassium Hodgkin-Huxley type currents:

$$I_{Na(TTX)} = g^*_{Na(TTX)} m^3(t) h(t)(V(t) - V_{Na}); \quad (12)$$

$$I_{K(TEA)} = g^*_{K(TEA)} n^4(t)(V(t) - V_K) \quad (13)$$

$$dm(t)/dt = (1/(1 + \exp(-0.4(V(t) + 31))) - m(t))/0.0005; \quad (14)$$

$$dh(t)/dt = (1/(1 + \exp(0.25(V(t) + 45))) - h(t))/0.01; \quad (15)$$

$$dn(t)/dt = (1/(1 + \exp(-0.18(V(t) + 25))) - n(t))/0.015; \quad (16)$$

3. A calcium transient voltage-dependent current, described by:

$$I_{Ca} = g^*_{Ca} m^2_{Ca}(V(t) - V_{Ca}); \quad (17)$$

$$dm_{Ca}(t)/dt = (1/(1 + \exp(-0.2(V(t))) - m_{Ca}(t))/0.01; \quad (18)$$

4. A calcium stationary $[Ca^{2+}]_{in}$ inhibited current given by:

$$I_{Ca-Ca} = g^* Ca - Ca \frac{1}{1 + \exp(-0.06(V(t) + 45))} \frac{1}{1 + \exp(K_\beta([Ca](t) - \beta))} (V(t) - V_{Ca}); \quad (19)$$

$$d[Ca](t)/dt = \rho - I_{Ca}/2F\nu - K_s[Ca](t); \quad (20)$$

where $\nu = 4\pi R^3/3$ is the volume of the cell; $[Ca]$ is $[Ca^{2+}]_{in}$ (mM), F is Faraday number $(96,485$ $Cmol^{-1})$, K_s is the rate constant of intracellular Ca-uptake by intracellular stores and ρ is the endogenous Ca buffer capacity.

B   Parameters Used in the KK Model

$V_{Na} = 40\,mV$; $V_K = -70\,mV$; $V_B = -58\,mV$; $V_{Ca} = 150\,mV$; $C_m = 0.02\,\mu F$; $R = 0.1\,mm$; $k_s = 50\,1/s$; $\rho = 0.002$; $k_\beta = 15000\,mV$; $\beta = 0.00004\,mM$;
CHAOTIC MODE: $g_K^* = 0.25\,\mu S$; $g_{Na}^* = 0.0231\,\mu S$; $g_{Na}^*(V) = 0.11\,\mu S$; $g_B^* = 0.1372\,\mu S$; $g_{Na(TTX)}^* = 400\,\mu S$; $g_{K(TEA)}^* = 10\,\mu S$; $g_{Ca}^* = 1.5\,\mu S$; $g_{Ca-Ca}^* = 0.02\,\mu S$;
CHAOTIC BURSTING MODE: $g_K^* = 0.25\,\mu S$; $g_{Na}^* = 0.02\,\mu S$; $g_{Na}^*(V) = 0.13\,\mu S$; $g_B^* = 0.18\,\mu S$; $g_{Na(TTX)}^* = 400\,\mu S$; $g_{K(TEA)}^* = 10\,\mu S$; $g_{Ca}^* = 1\,\mu S$; $g_{Ca-Ca}^* = 0.01\,\mu S$;
REGULAR MODE: $g_K^* = 0.25\,\mu S$; $g_{Na}^* = 0.02\,\mu S$; $g_{Na}^*(V) = 0.13\,\mu S$; $g_B^* = 0.165\,\mu S$; $g_{Na(TTX)}^* = 400\,\mu S$; $g_{K(TEA)}^* = 10\,\mu S$; $g_{Ca}^* = 1\,\mu S$; $g_{Ca-Ca}^* = 0.01\,\mu S$;
INITIAL CONDITIONS: $V = -55\,mV$; $[Ca^{2+}]_{in} = 0$;

References

1. Kandel, E.R., Schwartz, J.H., Jessell, T.M.: Principles of Neural Science, 5th edn. McGraw-Hill Education, New York (2012)
2. Connors, B.W., Long, M.A.: Electrical synapses in the mammalian brain. Annu. Rev. Neurosci. **27**, 393–418 (2004)
3. Sánchez, A., Castro, C., Flores, D.L., Gutiérrez, E., Baldi, P.: Gap junction channels of innexins and connexins: relations and computational perspectives. Int. J. Mol. Sci. **20**, 2476 (2019)
4. Elices, I., Levi, R., Arroyo, D., Rodriguez, F.B., Varona, P.: Robust dynamical invariants in sequential neural activity. Sci. Rep. **9**, 9048 (2019)
5. Buzsáki, G., Tingley, D.: Space and time: the hippocampus as a sequence generator. Trends Cogn. Sci. **22**(10), 853–869 (2018)
6. Paton, J.J., Buonomano, D.V.: The neural basis of timing: distributed mechanisms for diverse functions. Neuron **98**(4), 687–705 (2018)
7. Varona, P., Torres, J.J., Abarbanel, H., Rabinovich, M., Elson, R.: Dynamics of two electrically coupled chaotic neurons: experimental observations and model analysis. Biol. Cybern. **84**(2), 91–101 (2001)
8. Nadim, F., Li, X., Gray, M., Golowasch, J.: The role of electrical coupling in rhythm generation in small networks. In: Jing, J. (ed.) Network Functions and Plasticity, pp. 51–78. Academic Press (2017)
9. Varona, P., Torres, J., Huerta, R., Abarbanel, H., Rabinovich, M.: Regularization mechanisms of spiking-bursting neurons. Neural Netw. **14**(6–7), 865–875 (2001)
10. Venaille, A., Varona, P., Rabinovich, M.I.: Synchronization and coordination of sequences in two neural ensembles. Phys. Rev. E Stat. Nonlin. Soft Matter Phys. **71**(6 Pt 1), 61909 (2005)
11. Chorev, E., Yarom, Y., Lampl, I.: Rhythmic episodes of subthreshold membrane potential oscillations in the rat inferior olive nuclei in vivo. J. Neurosci. **27**(19), 5043–5052 (2007)
12. Jing, J., Cropper, E., Weiss, K.: Network functions of electrical coupling present in multiple and specific sites in behavior-generating circuits. In: Jing, J. (ed.) Network Functions and Plasticity, pp. 79–107. Academic Press (2017)
13. Varona, P., Aguirre, C., Torres, J., Rabinovich, M., Abarbanel, H., Rabinovich, M.: Spatio-temporal patterns of network activity in the inferior olive. Neurocomputing **44–46**, 685–690 (2002)
14. Kepler, T.B., Marder, E., Abbott, L.F.: The effect of electrical coupling on the frequency of model neuronal oscillators. Science **248**, 83–85 (1990)

15. Latorre, R., Aguirre, C., Rabinovich, M., Varona, P.: Transient dynamics and rhythm coordination of inferior olive spatio-temporal patterns. Front. Neural Circ. **7**, 138 (2013)
16. Leznik, E., Llinás, R.: Role of gap junctions in synchronized neuronal oscillations in the inferior olive. J. Neurophysiol. **94**(4), 2447–2456 (2005)
17. Selverston, A.J., et al.: Reliable circuits from irregular neurons: a dynamical approach to understanding central pattern generators. J. Physiol. Paris **94**(5–6), 357–374 (2000)
18. Katz, P.S., Quinlan, P.D.: The importance of identified neurons in gastropod molluscs to neuroscience. Curr. Opin. Neurobiol. **56**, 1–7 (2019)
19. Marder, E., Bucher, D.: Understanding circuit dynamics using the stomatogastric nervous system of lobsters and crabs. Annu. Rev. Physiol. **69**(1), 291–316 (2007)
20. Katz, P., et al.: Vertebrate versus invertebrate neural circuits. Curr. Biol. **23**(12), R504–R506 (2013)
21. Ijspeert, A.J.: Central pattern generators for locomotion control in animals and robots: a review. Neural Netw. **21**(4), 642–653 (2008)
22. Herrero-Carrón, F., Rodríguez, F.B., Varona, P.: Bio-inspired design strategies for central pattern generator control in modular robotics. Bioinspiration Biomimetics **6**(1), 016006 (2011)
23. Suzuki, S., Kano, T., Ijspeert, A.J., Ishiguro, A.: Sprawling quadruped robot driven by decentralized control with cross-coupled sensory feedback between legs and trunk. Front. Neurorobotics **14**, 116 (2021)
24. Huerta, R., Varona, P., Rabinovich, M., Abarbanel, H.: Topology selection by chaotic neurons of a pyloric central pattern generator. Biol. Cybern. **84**(1), L1–L8 (2001)
25. Komendantov, A.O., Kononenko, N.I.: Deterministic chaos in mathematical model of pacemaker activity in bursting neurons of snail. Helix Pomatia. J. Theor. Biol. **183**, 219–230 (1996)
26. Hodgkin, A.L., Huxley, A.F.: A quantitative description of membrane current and its application to conduction and excitation in nerve (1952)
27. Latorre, R., Rodríguez, F.B., Varona, P.: Characterization of triphasic rhythms in central pattern generators (I): interspike interval analysis. In: Dorronsoro, J.R. (ed.) ICANN 2002. LNCS, vol. 2415, pp. 160–166. Springer, Heidelberg (2002). https://doi.org/10.1007/3-540-46084-5_27
28. Latorre, R., Rodríguez, F.B., Varona, P.: Effect of individual spiking activity on rhythm generation of central pattern generators. Neurocomputing **58–60**, 535–540 (2004)
29. Rodríguez, F.B., Latorre, R., Varona, P.: Characterization of triphasic rhythms in central pattern generators (II): burst information analysis. In: Dorronsoro, J.R. (ed.) ICANN 2002. LNCS, vol. 2415, pp. 167–173. Springer, Heidelberg (2002). https://doi.org/10.1007/3-540-46084-5_28
30. Chamorro, P., Muñiz, C., Levi, R., Arroyo, D., Rodríguez, F.B., Varona, P.: Generalization of the dynamic clamp concept in neurophysiology and behavior. PLoS ONE **7**(7), e40887 (2012)
31. Amaducci, R., Reyes-Sanchez, M., Elices, I., Rodriguez, F.B., Varona, P.: RTHybrid: a standardized and open-source real-time software model library for experimental neuroscience. Front. Neuroinformatics **13**, 11 (2019)
32. Reyes-Sanchez, M., Amaducci, R., Elices, I., Rodriguez, F.B., Varona, P.: Automatic adaptation of model neurons and connections to build hybrid circuits with living networks. Neuroinformaticcs **18**, 377–393 (2020)

Operation of Neuronal Membrane Simulator Circuit for Tests with Memristor Based on Graphene and Graphene Oxide

Marina Sparvoli[1]([✉]), Jonas S. Marma[1], Gabriel F. Nunes[1], and Fábio O. Jorge[2]

[1] Universidade Federal do ABC, Santo André, São Paulo, Brazil
[2] Universidade de São Paulo, São Paulo, Brazil

Abstract. Artificial neural networks have been developed by researchers based on the understanding of different brain skills, such as learning and remembering. Memristors can simulate from memory process to neural membrane functioning. Since the first neural networks were proposed, research has been divided into two areas: one aimed at simulating biological phenomena and the other directed at applications. In this work, we intend to carry out a study on the reproduction of neuronal membrane behavior through a resistor-capacitor (RC) circuit associated with a memristor. RC circuit has the property of simulating neural membrane at the moment of the action potential, through charge and discharge curve of a capacitor. Memristor will be the component responsible for the non-linear behavior of circuit due to its resistive switching (RS) property, where it switches from a high resistance state (HRS) to low resistance state (LRS), or vice versa, depending on the voltage; this phenomenon can be reproduced many times. Two types of experiments were performed: the first one, temporal, where the output voltage was obtained as a function of time and time constant could be calculated for each section of the graph. In the second measure, it was possible to obtain the output voltage behavior as a function of input voltage; non-linearity could be observed through hysteresis formation and changes could be perceived by the formation of a step in some cases, which indicates a change in the continuity of behavior in relation to voltage. Important observations were made regarding the operation of the RC circuit; both resistance and capacitor influenced output voltage curve behavior. Together with memristor, it was possible to verify that the behavior of neurotransmitters in action potential could be simulated.

Keywords: Graphene · Memristor · Neuronal membrane · Resistive switching

1 Introduction

A neuron is an animal cell covered by a thin membrane (60 to 70 Å thick) that separates it from an intercellular medium, called neuronal membrane. The neuronal membrane is formed by lipids and proteins. Lipids are arranged in a double layer in which proteins are immersed. Some proteins cross the membrane from side to side, forming channels or pores [1].

© Springer Nature Switzerland AG 2021
I. Rojas et al. (Eds.): IWANN 2021, LNCS 12862, pp. 93–102, 2021.
https://doi.org/10.1007/978-3-030-85099-9_8

A neuronal membrane is generally compared to a capacitor due to its property of storing and separating a charge. In an electrical circuit, the capacitor is a component that has two regions made of conductive material separated by an insulator between them. When one of the regions accumulates charge, an electric field is created, which causes the charges to flow to another conductive region. This phenomenon lasts for a brief period, producing an ephemeral electrical current, where electrical current depends inversely on time [2, 3].

RC circuit associated with memristor is nonlinear. In addition to dependence on time, there is a dependence on tension. Memristor was initially postulated by Chua in 1971 as the fourth fundamental element of circuits and validated experimentally by an HP laboratory in 2008. Memristor based on graphene oxide and graphene has resistive switching (RS) phenomenon; it is a change from a high resistance state (HRS) to low resistance state (LRS) and vice versa. This phenomenon is reversible and can be reproduced countless times. Typically, the change in resistance is non-volatile [4–6].

For applications in computing inspired by neural networks and neuromorphic engineering, memristors have advantages over CMOS (Complementary Metal Oxide Semiconductor) technology, which requires active components and more space to achieve behavior comparable to neural functions [7, 8]. Another advantage that must be taken into account is the fact that all apparatus and technology for the development of CMOS can be used in resistive memories manufacture; the transfer of deposition and manufacturing methods prevents costs from becoming higher [7].

This paper intends to show a new methodology to obtain the electrical parameters of a memristor. Used circuit emulates the behavior of action potential in a neuronal membrane. In the first step, circuit parameters were tested, without the memristor. A study was made with an auxiliary resistance and a capacitor with fixed values (second mesh), varying the resistance placed in the memristor position. In the second step, characteristics of memristor were obtained. Initially, a study was carried out to verify which capacitor would produce an observable change in its resistance. Then, measurement was made with 1000 μF capacitor to characterize the charge and discharge curve due to the fact that there was a change in resistance during discharge.

2 Experimental

A device with three layers was manufactured (Fig. 1): lower contact (54 nm thickness) was obtained through deposition of graphene by dip coating; the insulating layer of graphene oxide was also deposited by dip coating (36 nm thickness); the upper contact was made with the evaporation of aluminum (Al) (300 nm thickness).

Electrical characterization was done through neuronal membrane simulation. An RC circuit was built and the measurements were made using a 16-bit ADC with an input impedance of 10 MΩ, to which the three-layer memristor was associated. Two graphs were obtained: voltage as a function of time for charge and discharge ramp and current as a function of voltage for charge and discharge.

In Fig. 2, the arrangement shows a memristor associated with an auxiliary resistor and a capacitor, imitating a biological neuronal membrane. The memristor device was placed in structure A so that the contacts were fixed with a probe and with the intention

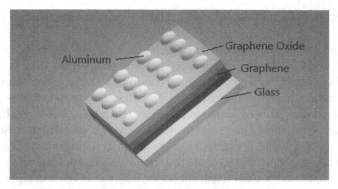

Fig. 1. Memristor structure.

that there would be no noise during the measurements. Circuit B played the role of simulating the neuronal membrane. Data were read by module C which contains an Arduino and 16-bit ADC. Analog to digital conversion is done in module D and data are shown in software written in LabVIEW that shows the graphs being built in real-time.

Fig. 2. Circuit arrangement to measure memristor behavior related to time and input voltage.

Circuit B (Fig. 2 and Fig. 3), considering only the first mesh composed of resistors R3 and R4 and capacitor C2, has its values fixed and serves to generate the ascending ramp with the aid of a PWM to charge the capacitor in the second mesh; PWM serves to generate pulses whose time at a high logic level increases by 1/255 s each cycle, so the time at a high or low logic level changes along the ascending ramp. Resistor R2 and capacitor C1 belong to the second mesh, as well as resistor R1, which may have a memristor in its place; Fig. 3 shows a resistor R1 with the same value as the memristor used in this work. The second mesh contains an RC circuit that generates the charge and discharge curve in order to simulate neuronal membrane; these components do not have a fixed value.

R2 is an auxiliary resistor where data reading is made and this resistor must have a value lower than R1 in order to have an adequate data outlet: if the value is higher, data are not valid because the voltage on auxiliary resistor R2 will be greater than on resistor or memristor in R1. Capacitor C1 must be chosen to take into account that its value alters time constant and may interfere with circuit ability to read memristor non-linearity.

This circuit is based on Zhang and his team work [7], which aims to simulate the behavior of an integrate-and-fire neuron with the aid of a memristor based on the threshold switching phenomenon. But there are differences: the fact that the values of components of the second mesh are not fixed, allows the behavior of the action potential curve to be controlled and it is possible to simulate the behavior of specific action potentials as in the case of neurotransmitters [9].

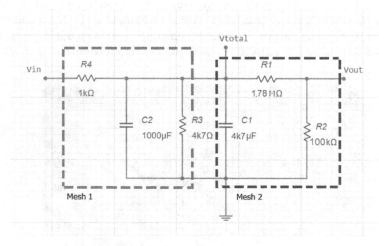

Fig. 3. Schematic circuit with two meshes for simulation of the neuronal membrane.

Through the Fig. 3 circuit and based on Dabrowski work [3], where $\tau = RC$, it is possible to extract the time constant equation for discharge curve from the resistance and capacitance. The equation is based on mesh 2 due to mesh 1 removal from the circuit by opening the switch:

$$\tau_{discharge} = (R_1 + R_2).C_1 \qquad (1)$$

This study has two steps: one that refers to a study of circuit parameters where ohmic resistors are used (10 kΩ, 100 kΩ and 1 MΩ), without memristor, varying linearly. The resulting charge and discharge curves are exponential.

In the second step, an auxiliary resistance of 100 kΩ was set and the memristor was used. Since this device has no linear behavior, curves will behave differently. From the measurement with different capacitors (1000 μF, 4700 μF and 10000 μF), it was possible to choose the curve in which memristor presents a strongly non-linear behavior.

Thus, a curve simulating an action potential, whose capacitor used was 1000 μF, and which showed a different behavior, even with a discontinuity in the discharge curve, was chosen to analyze the time constant. Then, memristor resistance calculation (based on Eq. 1) in each region was performed. This variable memristor resistance can be used as a parameter for characterizing the device when it is a component of a system simulating a neuronal membrane.

3 Results

Through the RC circuit associated with the memristor, it is possible to obtain two measurements: first one, temporal, a graph of output voltage (V_{out}) as a function of time can be obtained and time constant can be calculated for each section of the graph. In the second measure, it is possible to obtain the behavior of output voltage as a function of input voltage (V_{in}); non-linearity can be observed through the formation of hysteresis and the changes can be perceived by the formation of a step in some cases, which indicates a change in the continuity of the behavior in relation to tension.

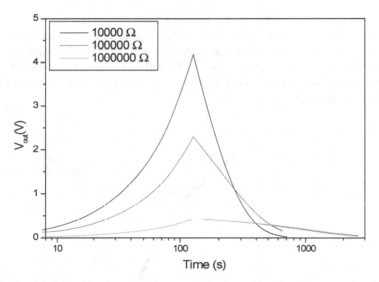

Fig. 4. Study of the behavior of output voltage as a function of time for different resistance values.

The first test of this research refers to circuit behavior for different resistances in place of the memristor. These devices can have different values depending on the type of material and structure with which they were manufactured. In Fig. 4, output voltage in relation to time curves for capacitor charge and discharge of resistors with values 10 kΩ, 100 kΩ and 1 MΩ are shown. A value of 1000 μF was set for capacitor and 100 kΩ for an auxiliary resistor in mesh 2.

It is possible to notice that the time constant τ in the discharge increases with higher resistances (Fig. 5). There is a linear dependence on the resistance value.

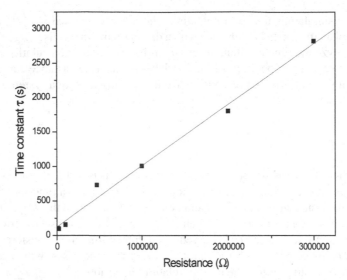

Fig. 5. Linear behavior of time constant in relation to the resistance value.

In the second test, a memristor based on an insulating graphene oxide structure with graphene and aluminum electrodes was used. The auxiliary resistor value was set at 100 kΩ, but three capacitor values were used: 1000 μF, 4700 μF and 10000 μF. The resistance between memristor contacts was measured (through a multimeter) at 1.78 MΩ before being connected to the circuit.

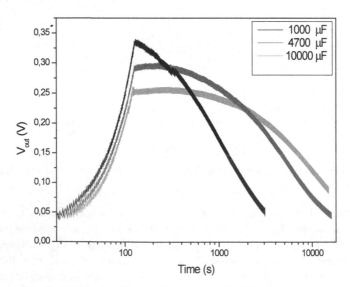

Fig. 6. RC circuit with memristor: test with different capacitors.

In Fig. 6, it is possible to observe a comparison of temporal curves of capacitor charge and discharge. Memristor time constants $\tau_{discharge}$ for 4700 µF and 10000 µF capacitors were 5434.26 s and 10029.69 s, respectively.

The discharge curve for 1000 µF capacitor is not continuous: it has two time constants τ (Fig. 7). It is possible to extract a time constant value for the charge curve and two values for the discharge curve. The time constant of the charge curve is not important because the time interval of the loading ramp for all measurements is the same, regardless of the values of the components that compose the circuit. But it is possible to notice that memristor changes the behavior of exponential curve for polynomial. In a future study, it may be interesting to increase the step time between each measurement, which leads to a longer charging time, to verify if the capacitor used in mesh 2 could store more charge. In this study, the step time used was 500 ms.

For the discharge curve, change of this time constant from region II to III indicates that there was a transition in memristor resistance since capacitor and auxiliary resistance values are fixed. Memristor causes discontinuity in discharge curve, splitting it into two regions that are two exponential curves and where the time constant in region III,

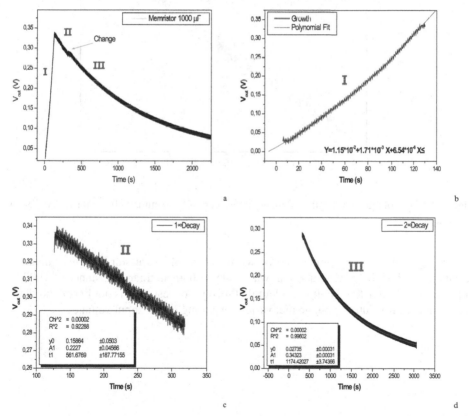

Fig. 7. The temporal curve of the RC circuit is associated with the memristor with a 1000 µF capacitor: a) charge and discharge response, b) region I, c) region II and d) region III.

1174.42 s, is more than twice the value of the time constant in region II, 561.67 s. These values, when substituted in (1), show resistance for memristor of 461.67 KΩ in region II and 1.07 MΩ in region III.

It was also possible to obtain output voltage as a function of input voltage curves for memristor behavior with different capacitors, as seen in Fig. 8. It is noted that the hysteresis slope is the same, but peak output voltage decreases as capacitor values increase.

Even with a high time to complete the measurements, the prototype worked as expected. In future research, the use of capacitors with smaller values is intended. The goal is to miniaturize the devices and fabricate the circuit together with the memristor on a smaller scale using microelectronic processes.

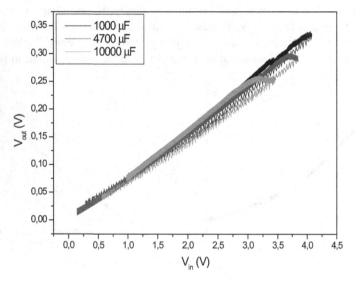

Fig. 8. Output voltage as a function of input voltage curves for memristor behavior with different capacitors.

In Fig. 9 there is a comparison between curves of memristor and an equivalent resistance of 1.78 MΩ. Measurement was made with an auxiliary resistance of 100 kΩ and a capacitor of 1000 μF. It is evident that memristor response is not linear and there is a hysteresis for output voltage that varies depending on the input voltage.

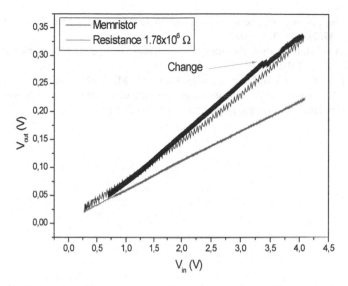

Fig. 9. Comparison between curves of memristor and an equivalent resistance.

4 Conclusion

This work aimed to simulate the fire behavior of neuronal membrane through an RC circuit associated with a memristor manufactured based on graphene and graphene oxide. Memristor affects the curve behavior of the RC circuit so that it becomes non-linear; unlike a common resistance that has a linear behavior, memristor generates a hysteresis in output voltage in relation to the input voltage.

Important observations were made regarding the operation of the RC circuit. Both resistance and capacitor influenced output voltage curve behavior. Together with memristor, it was possible to verify that the behavior of neurotransmitters in action potential could be simulated.

References

1. Xu, T., et al.: Viability and electrophysiology of neural cell structures generated by the inkjet printing method. Biomaterials **27**(19), 3580–3588 (2006)
2. Bédard, C., Destexhe, A.: A modified cable formalism for modeling neuronal membranes at high frequencies. Biophys. J. **94**(4), 1133–1143 (2008)
3. Dabrowski, K.M., Castaño, D.J., Tartar, J.L.: Basic neuron model electrical equivalent circuit: an undergraduate laboratory exercise. J. Undergraduate Neurosci. Educ. **12**(1), A49–A52 (2013)
4. Yoo, D., Cuong, T.V., Hahn, S.H.: Effect of copper oxide on the resistive switching responses of graphene oxide film. Curr. Appl. Phys. **14**(9), 1301–1303 (2014)
5. Xu, J., Xie, D., Feng, T., et al.: Scaling-down characteristics of nanoscale diamond-like carbon based resistive switching memories. Carbon **75**, 255–261 (2014)
6. Tanaka, H., Kinoshita, K., Yoshihara, M., Kishida, S.: Correlation between filament distribution and resistive switching properties in resistive random access memory consisting of binary transition-metal oxides. AIP Adv. **2**(2), 022141-1–022141-6 (2012)

7. Zhang, X., et al.: An artificial neuron based on a threshold switching memristor. IEEE Electron Device Lett. **39**(2), 308–311 (2017)
8. Sung, H.J., et al.: Nanoscale memristor device as synapse in neuromorphic systems. Nano Lett. **10**(4), 1297–1301 (2010)
9. Suzuki, I., Fukuda, M., Shirakawa, K., Jiko, H., Gotoh, M.: Carbon nanotube multi-electrode array chips for non-invasive real-time measurement of dopamine, action potentials, and postsynaptic potentials. Biosens. Bioelectron. **49**, 270–275 (2013)

Agent-Based Models for Policy Design
Towards a More Sustainable World

Informing Agent-Based Models of Social Innovation Uptake

Patrycja Antosz[1]([envelope]) [iD], Wander Jager[2], Gary Polhill[3] [iD], and Douglas Salt[3] [iD]

[1] NORCE Norwegian Research Centre AS, Tromsø, Norway
paan@norceresearch.no
[2] University of Groningen, Groningen, The Netherlands
w.jager@rug.nl
[3] The James Hutton Institute, Aberdeen, UK
{gary.polhill,douglas.salt}@hutton.ac.uk

Abstract. This paper discusses how data and theory were used to inform ten agent-based models in an EU Horizon 2020 project SMARTEES. The project investigates cases of social innovations implemented in different European cities, which promote low-carbon energy sources, ranging from communities insulating houses to cycling for urban transportation. The aim is to support local governments of cities in transitioning to energy efficiency and sustainability through simulating plausible effects of implementing similar social innovations in new contexts. We describe the concept for using theory together with quantitative and qualitative data to inform model assumption, calibration and validation, and the consequences of that concept for the research design in the ten case studies conducted in the project. We outline the role of (1) primary data collection of individual in-depth interviews, questionnaires and stakeholder workshops, and (2) secondary desk research including socio-demographic data and media analysis in developing agent-based models. We emphasize challenges encountered in how to use data from different sources to calibrate and validate agent-based models. The article is a compendium of lessons learned from the project, which can be useful for future collaborations in multi-case study, multi-research teams, and mixed-methods projects where one of the methods used is agent-based modelling.

Keywords: Social innovation · HUMAT · Agent-based modelling · Mixed methods

1 Introduction

There is a general agreement that agent-based models (ABMs) constitute a valuable element of mixed-method research designs, as they are capable of integrating information (including data and theory) from different sources in coherent propositions of causal mechanisms responsible for eliciting emergent phenomena in

The work reported here is part of the SMARTEES project, which has received funding from the European Union's Horizon 2020 research and innovation programme under grant agreement No. 763912.

© Springer Nature Switzerland AG 2021

I. Rojas et al. (Eds.): IWANN 2021, LNCS 12862, pp. 105–117, 2021.
https://doi.org/10.1007/978-3-030-85099-9_9

complex systems. However, real-life examples of more complex research designs (i.e. combining more than two methods) are still relatively scarce. This paper is an effort in the direction of filling the gap. It discusses how data and theory were used to inform ten agent-based models in an EU Horizon 2020 project SMARTEES. The aim is to present what information was integrated into the agent-based models, and what role various pieces of information played in the entire process of model development.

Mixed-method approaches are usually praised for providing a wider picture, more confidence in findings, an improved study component, a wider variety of views, a way of researching an issue that was otherwise impossible, or an understanding of why and where a study component failed [21]. In the current study that combines ABM with other approaches, three primary data collection techniques were aided by desk research and social scientific theory. The main body of the paper (Sect. 3) describes in detail how data and theory was used in (1) devising model assumptions, (2) calibrating and (3) validating the models. Subsequently, in the discussion section, we reflect on the process of model elicitation, emphasizing the role of external stakeholders. To give the readers a better overview of the context in which the agent-based models were developed, the next section briefly describes the SMARTEES project

2   The SMARTEES Project

SMARTEES is an interdisciplinary H2020 research project framed within the carbon reduction objectives of the EU (https://local-social-innovation.eu/). The aim is to support local governments of cities in transitioning to energy efficiency and sustainability through simulating plausible effects of implementing social innovations. The entire process recognizes the importance of residents forming local communities, and the pivotal role of their support for successful implementation of social innovations. Five different types of energy-related social innovations, represented by ten European cities that successfully implemented them in the past Table 1, are analysed and modelled in the project: (1) urban mobility, (2) island renewable energy, (3) district regeneration, (4) mobility in superblocks, and (5) fighting energy poverty through energy efficiency. Using a mix of methods, the project identifies mechanisms bringing about a fruitful implementation of social innovations, and uses this knowledge to aid new cities in copying the successes. Therefore, in each investigated case cluster, on top of two historical cases, additional cities interested in implementing similar energy transitions participate in the study. Knowledge on how to design and carry out effective strategies for engaging citizens and stakeholders of different types to foster social innovations feeds into a policy sandbox tool. The tool's goal is to stimulate stake-holders' imaginations about how change takes place in complex systems. The sand-box tool helps to anticipate social dynamics resulting from simulated policy scenarios. It's important to highlight that social dynamics in complex systems are by nature uncertain. Therefore, offering a tool to reflect on how policy can become more adaptive to the initial context and changes of that context over time introduces added value for stakeholders.

Table 1. Social innovations (SIs) and ABM focus in each case cluster (CC).

CC1: Urban mobility (Groningen, NL and Zurich, CH)	SI: city planning follows a coordinated approach to reduce car traffic
	ABM depicts a referendum on closing a road for car traffic
CC2: Island renewable energy (Samsø, DK and El Hierro, ES)	SI: mobilizing residents towards achieving energy independence through renewable energy sources and efficiency measures
	ABM depicts resident acceptability of renewable energy projects
CC3: District regeneration (Stockholm, SE and Malmö, SE)	SI: public and private organizations ally with citizens triggering district regeneration processes
	ABM depicts resident acceptability of various dwelling energy renovation strategies
CC4: Superblocks (Vitoria Gasteiz, ES and Barcelona, ES)	SI: reorganizing urban districts to minimize motorized modes of transportation and maximize public space
	ABM depicts citizen acceptability of the implementation of superblocks
CC5: Fuel poverty (Aberdeen, UK and Timişoara, RO)	SI: coordination of public authorities, supply companies and civil organizations to fight fuel poverty
	ABM depicts the uptake of district heating among residents

3   Informing ABM Development

Work in each case study began with desk research aimed at collecting relevant knowledge about each investigated case study, and a theoretical review focused on processes crucial to the success of social innovations (Fig. 1). Subsequent model building started with identifying the process of interest (as outlined in Table 1), and translating that process into a concept of a programmable causal mechanism. The causal mechanism became the core of the ABM and allowed for specifying the search for all of the model elements, which had to be present for the model to run. Following targeted desk research and theory review, primary data collection in the forms of individual in-depth interviews, surveys and stakeholder workshops was carried out (Table 2).

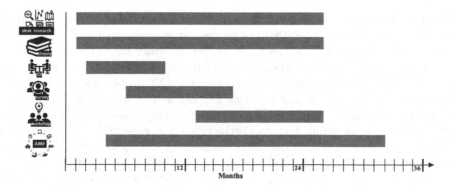

Fig. 1. Execution of empirical work in SMARTEES over time.

Table 2. Primary data collection by case study. Key to survey mode column: CAWI – Computer Assisted Web Interviews, PAPI – Pen and Paper Interviews, CAPI – Computer Assisted Personal Interviews, CATI – Computer Assisted Telephone Interviews.

		IDI N	Survey mode	Survey N	Workshops N
CC1: Urban mobility	Zurich (CH)	8	CAWI	1001	3
	Groningen (NL)	6	CAWI	703	
CC2: Island renewable energy	Samsø (DK)	9	-	-	3
	El Hierro (ES)	8	PAPI	373	3
CC3: District regeneration	Malmö (SE)	5	-	-	3
	Stockholm (SE)	5	-	-	3
CC4: Superblocks	Vitoria Gasteiz (ES)	11	CAPI/CATI	865	3
	Barcelona (ES)	13	CAPI	643	3
CC5: Fuel poverty	Aberdeen (UK)	14	CAWI/PAPI	840	3
	Timişoara (RO)	6	CAWI	439	3

3.1   Model Assumptions

SMARTEES cases differ with respect to their location in Europe, the type of implemented social innovation, and their behavioural context. Hence, the challenge was to create an integrated, general and flexible methodological framework that allowed for representing unique, relevant aspects of the different cases, while assuring a degree of standardization across investigated ABMs. As a result, each model comprises of five standardised components/building blocks:

- Attitude formation among individuals;
- Social innovation and its diffusion in local communities;
- Critical stakeholders;
- Policy scenarios;
- Context.

  Standardisation of building blocks took various forms. For example, the uptake of social innovation was generally implemented as an emergent phenomenon that result-ed from interactions between agents. On the other hand, the attitude formation in individual agents was standardized to a high level of detail by developing the HUMAT socio-cognitive architecture. HUMAT proposes a mechanism of attitude formation through introspection and cognitively motivated information exchange in social networks. The architecture is flexible regarding the object of the attitude. It can be anything from an abstract idea (e.g. renewable energy projects in El Hierro (ES)) to a specific one-off behaviour (e.g. voting in a referendum on a car-free city park in Groningen (NL)). The proposed mechanism of attitude formation brings together assumptions present in social theories and previous empirical studies. Rules for how agents evaluate an idea or a behaviour (i.e. the subject of the attitude) were informed by needs theories [14,16,17], cognitive inconsistency theories [10,13], and studies on the role of direct experiences in memory formation

[8,9]. Moreover, in the information exchange between agents in a social network, persuasiveness of an agent is influenced by the results of alter-ego comparisons [2,3], and alter's source credibility [18,24].

3.2 Model Calibration

In traditional mathematical modelling, calibration is the process of adjusting unknown parameters of the function(s) in the model so as to achieve best numerical fit to data set aside for this purpose. Model calibration in ABMs is the use of empirical data to inform the appropriate values of model components [5]. These data may be qualitative or quantitative. The scope of this paper does not allow detailed discussion of how each of the models was calibrated; the ensuing description highlights illustrative activities from specific case studies. In general, SMARTEES ABMs were calibrated to the investigated cases with respect to (1) timeline of relevant events, (2) geo-socio-demographic characteristics of the resident population, (3) motives/needs of the residents, which were activated by the social innovation, (4) social networks of residents and (5) implemented policy interventions.

Timeline of Relevant Events – Samsø Example. Assuring a sufficient level of correspondence between the historical timeline of the case study and ABM process scheduling was prioritized to facilitate the feeling of familiarity and understanding among stakeholders who use the ABMs. Even though a fair number of relevant documents allowing for a recreation of the history of each case was identified during the extensive desk research phase (e.g. scientific publications, local newspaper articles, other archival materials available online), assistance provided by local stakeholders cooperating with the researchers was invaluable. For example, the help of the Samsø Energy Academy, who supported the community bottom-up efforts to establish the district heating networks (social innovation in Samsø), enabled the researchers to access rare documents (including copies of minutes from 14 meetings of the Onsbjerg district heating working group, which met regularly between October 2000 and October 2001 to plan detailed actions and lobby for the social innovation among other Onsbjerg residents) and arrange four supplementary in-depth interviews with key informants. Privileged information allowed for a detailed recreation of the case timeline and allowed for sufficient level of correspondence between the case and its depiction (Fig. 2).

Geo-Socio-Demographic Characteristics of the Resident Population – Groningen Example. For the purpose of ABM calibration, the population of Groningen from 1994 was recreated on the basis of available statistical data from the 1999 Statistical yearbook and Gemeente Groningen's report from the referendum. Information about geo-socio-demographic characteristics of individual residents and household data from 17 tables was combined into one complex contingency table. Harmonizing data from various tables proved challenging because of different categorizations assumed in different chapters of

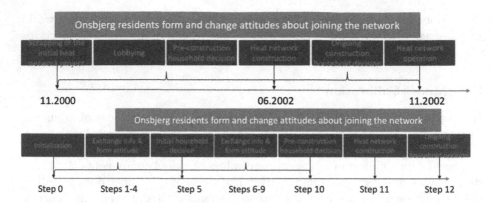

Fig. 2. History of the Onsbjerg district heating case study (top) and the process overview of the Samsø case study ABM (bottom).

the statistical yearbook (e.g. some tables reported five levels of completed education, while other tables used a 3-level categorisation). Meaningful, standardised categories were thereby devised with respect to age, education and geolocation of households. The choice of particular characteristics relevant in each case was related to motives driving attitudes towards social innovation. Consequently, the Groningen ABM population represents the actual 1994 Groningen population with respect to:

- size (scale of 1:10);
- gender (2 categories: M, F);
- age (3 categories: 18–24, 25–64, 65+);
- education level (3 categories: short, medium, long);
- main economic activity (4 categories: student, employee, not working, retired);
- Groningen city districts (13 categories),

and all the known dependencies among these characteristics. As a result, every agent in the ABM belongs to one of 936 homogenous groups i.e., intersections of the five socio-demographic characteristics. All groups comprise a fraction of the modelled population that matches the actual fraction of Groningen residents in 1994 with the same set of geo-socio-demographic characteristics. As a result, there is no stochasticity in the model with this respect introduced at the stage of model initialization.

Motives/Needs of Residents – Vitoria-Gasteiz Example. The exchange of information between residents about why a new behaviour may be preferred was identified as the core process guiding the formation of attitude towards social innovation. For this reason, ABMs were calibrated with respect to the motives/needs that influence attitudes and a survey was carried out in relevant

SMARTEES cases. The core of the questionnaire containing the most important indicators was standardized, and suitable questions were added to that base when case-specific indicators were needed. In Vitoria Gasteiz (ES), the social innovation of creating superblocks is seen as a viable solution to reclaiming public space and decreasing car traffic within city districts. The solution was successful in the past, and policy makers consider upscaling the idea further. Therefore, motives that drive the acceptance of superblocks are relevant for calibrating the ABM. The survey enabled investigating how satisfaction with existing superblocks, combined with importance of needs, motives and values, influences the support of various groups of residents for creating new superblocks in the city. Results of the analyses are fed into the ABM in the form of initial values for motive importances among geo-socio-demographically heterogeneous groups of residents. The solution of using quantitative data to inform agent motives worked well in ongoing SMARTEES cases (e.g. Vitoria Gasteiz or Aberdeen). However, in historical cases where the modelled social innovation took place a quarter of a century ago (e.g. Zurich, Groningen), a present-day survey offered limited calibration usability, and other sources were used to recreate the past conditions. The attitudes changed so significantly, that using present-day distributions simply did not allow for the emergence of the past voting patterns. Nonetheless, even in those cases the survey results were useful to compare the assumptions about the past with the current situation and track long-term changes in attitudes. Thus, the survey recognized the interests of various researchers who, additionally to agent-based modellers, participate in the complex H2020 project.

Social Networks of Residents – Samsø Example. When representing a particular community in an ABM all actors who play a role in the social dynamics should be accounted for. Nodes in the SMARTEES ABMs represent both the critical stakeholders (individual and collective key actors important for co-creation and diffusion of the social innovation) and individual residents. Critical stakeholders and their agendas in investigated cases were identified at the stage of desk research and individual in-depth interviews. The important actors were divided into four groups: promoters of the social innovation, supporters, opponents and media. Subsequent policy scenario workshops helped in outlining critical stakeholders' actual strategies and specifying counterfactual scenarios for model simulations (i.e. alternative strategies that could have but did not take place). Since many strategies were related to information sharing (e.g. organizing a meeting with interested residents in the neighbourhood, sending a letter to all inhabitants), data collected through the SMARTEES surveys allowed for estimating how persuasive information from critical stakeholders is for heterogeneous groups of residents.

Individual residents in the ABMs are grouped into homogeneous clusters with respect to geo-socio-demographic characteristics that define typical motives important for formation of attitude towards the investigated social innovation. The same geo-socio-demographic characteristics are also used to inform the topology of social net-works between agents. In the Samsø ABM, residents are embedded in three distinct social networks that are defined on the basis of homophily. Friends are similar with respect to age and education level, co-workers resemble one another in terms of education level and disposable income, and neighbours live close by. Detailed decisions about network structure were inspired both by theories of homophily [19] and by the implementation of the social circles [11].

Implemented Policy Interventions – Aberdeen Example. Stakeholder workshops play an important role of providing all SMARTEES cases with a catalogue of counterfactual scenarios used in ABM simulations. Co-definition of these scenarios with historical and prospective promoters of the social innovations takes place over a series of structured meetings during which stakeholders define meaningful actions and observe their effects on the system. Modellers in the Aberdeen case decided to go an extra mile to involve historically important stakeholders in the co-development of the entire ABM, not only the counterfactual scenarios for model simulations. The Aberdeen City Council was interested in exploring scenarios leading to greater adoption of its district heating network, with specific attention to opportunities emerging from its implementation of an energy from waste plant. As with all infrastructure projects, the Council has established procedures for analysing feasibility, costs and benefits, budget allocation and approval. The approach was not to seek to supplant those processes with some 'fancy new science', but instead to ask how the opportunity presented by SMARTEES allowed the agent-based social simulation work to augment what they were already planning to do. As might be expected, the chief value is in using simulations to explore scenarios focusing on the social dynamics of heating decisions made by households; these not typically being considered in the engineering practicalities of laying insulated hot-water pipes connecting housing to the heat network. From an academic perspective, there are interesting social-environmental dynamics with respect to the infrastructure costs of laying pipe and the level of adoption of district heating by households in a street that can make adding a section of pipeline viable or not; this also acting to determine which other streets can then be given the option to join. The ABM was developed iteratively over a series of meetings involving modellers, (other) social scientists and representatives of the City Council, following agile software development principles insofar as they entail planning to include or remove features in response to reactions to the current prototype, and welcoming changes throughout the process. To belabour the point somewhat, the current prototype has utility to the stakeholders (academic and non-academic) in its ability to spark discussion and elicit ideas that might otherwise not have been articulated – albeit that this can be challenging to verify scientifically given the absence of a parallel universe in which the prototype was not part of the discussion.

3.3   Model Validation

Empirical validation of simulation results through intensive analysis and comparison with data on empirical reality [5], is the final step of SMARTEES model development that was augmented with information from external sources. In validation, data not used in the calibration process, usually of quantitative nature, serve as a benchmark against which the performance of a model is evaluated [28]. Different types of inputs were used in various models. For example, in the Groningen model that recreates the diffusion of accepting the idea of a car-free park, available voting data from the 1994 referendum served as reference. Summary of reports from 96 voting locations included, among others, the number of residents eligible to vote, number of persons voting yes/no, turnout and city district. The main challenge in harmonizing the available voting data with information from statistical yearbooks and the survey carried out in 2019 was posed by an administrative change of district boundaries that took place over the years in Groningen. Therefore, harmonization began with identifying the addresses and geolocations of 96 voting stations. Newly acquired information was used to re-assign the voting stations to a district classification that matched the one present in the statistical yearbook. Stand-ardized geo representation enabled us to validate the model not only against the city-level turnout and support for a car-free park, but also against the voting patterns ob-served in all city districts. Validation of the Samsø case model took a processual approach, as the computational tool was tasked with replicating the uptake of the district heating in three consecutive points in time: initial, pre-construction and ongoing constructions household decision, as they were recorded in the minutes from the Onsbjerg working group meetings, a 2002 issue of a local newspaper Samsø weekend and in the Energy Academy's internal sources (Onsbjerg district heating factsheet). Hence, the process of model validation recognizes the shift of emphasis from making single-point predictions to predicting meaningful patterns in data.

4   Discussion

Social simulation models are generally used to understand and explain social process-es, in particular the dynamics of micro-macro interactions that lead to the emergence of particular phenomena. Increasingly, policy makers are becoming aware of the relevance of self-organisational bottom-up processes in the diffusion of low-carbon community behaviours. Whereas policy makers are keen on developing policy tools that support such processes, they are also aware of the sensitivities and unpredictability of the associated social dynamics. Seasoned policy makers usually have the experience to derive an educated gut-feeling about the possible dynamics after digesting a lot of information on a specific case. The SMARTEES project provides an example of how complex studies can make this anticipation of possible dynamics more explicit by bringing together a variety of data into an integrated simulation framework. Experimentation with the dynamics of a simulated case and exploring the sensitivities for different events support discussions among stakeholders on possible impacts of policies, help to anticipate opportunities and threats, and encourage preparation of adaptive policies.

Assuring such usability in SMARTEES would be very difficult without the engagement of non-scientific partners that represent policy stakeholders. Awareness of their crucial role has been growing in the agent-based community with a long history of participatory agent-based model-building (see [25]), and companion modelling [7] in particular having a strong 'identity'. Agent-based social simulation is a highly interdisciplinary endeavour at the interface(s) of the social and computing sciences (e.g., [12,26], not to mention geographical (e.g. [4]) and ecological (e.g. [27]). Development of an agent-based model is an exercise in software engineering as much as it is an exercise in understanding, exploring or predicting dynamics of social systems. In software engineering, methods have shifted away from so-called 'waterfall' methods in which requirements analysis, feasibility, design, implementation, testing and roll-out formed a chained sequence of discrete activities. Instead, iterative approaches, such as 'Rapid Applications Development' and more recently 'Agile', have become more popular. Iterative methods start from prototype applications (which might literally comprise a graphical user interface design with no implemented functionality), and, through a series of discussions with end-users, (co-)evolve the applications such that (financial constraints permitting) they provide maximum value with minimum waste of developers' time. The social sciences also have established traditions of participatory research (e.g. [6,20]).

Maintaining stakeholder engagement together with a high value of the modelling process are necessary but insufficient to ensure ABM usability. The process should also elicit trust in a model's performance – the value and validity of the final version of the model and the findings. The first challenge is related to how we assess model validity. Quantitative metrics applied when comparing model out-puts with empirical reality, such as the AIC [1], often include penalty terms for models having large numbers of parameters, embodying modellers' heuristic preferences for parsimony. However, Polhill and Salt [23] observe that such quantitative metrics cannot the sole basis of trust in a model, drawing both on Oreskes et al.'s [22] critique of validation in open systems as affirming the consequent, and the fact that a more complicated model would less reliably fit the course of history (from which data were obtained) through being able to simulate the multiplicity of outcomes that could have occurred. They introduce the 'ontology' of a model as a further basis on which its representation of the empirical world could be assessed, and note that (1) ABMs have more expressive ontological capabilities than other kinds of models, and (2) there is a paucity of ready-to-use methods for assessing the degree to which one ontology matches another – something that might form the basis of measuring ontological validity. The second challenge related to ensuring model validity is related to the empirical benchmark itself, and stems from the fact that empirical reality as we know it has only one manifestation, yet the past could have been different. Quantitative assessment of model performance is associated with a rather simplistic view on causation, in which the particular course that history took is the only possible one. It is somehow often easier for us to think about potential futures than about potential pasts. What follows, is that any model that fails to replicate that history should not be trusted. Acknowledging that the empirical reality is only one instance from an unknown distribution of potential realities places validation as we know it in a wider perspective. Whereas an ABM of a particular case should be capable of replicating its empirical reality, the empirical reality alone might not provide the benchmark to validate the model against. Though quantitative assessment cannot be ignored (the particular path history took should still be possible in the model), these issues place greater emphasis on the ontological aspects of model validation: assessment by experts, collaborators and stakeholders of the processes, entities and variables that are simulated. This creates challenges around communicating model structure to non-ABM-experts such that they understand it sufficiently to make a judgement.

Provided open-minded and experienced individuals are involved in trans-disciplinary collaborations, the combined traditions of iterative software development and participatory social research create propitious circumstances for working with non-academic stakeholders to build agent-based models of policy scenarios that are useful, and of scientific interest. Models that are useful to stakeholders do not necessarily intersect with models that are of scientific interest. Ethical engagement with non-academic stakeholders means that usefulness must take priority, which can interfere with academic involvement in transdisciplinary research. That said, Lang et al. [15, p. 27] define transdisciplinary research as "creating knowledge that is ... transferable to both *scientific* and *societal practice*" [emphasis ours]. For now at least, empirical agent-based social simulation is still in the stage where methodological development through case studies of working with stakeholders will generate knowledge of general interest to the scientific community. SMARTEES's cases shows that agent-based models are capable of constituting an integrative platform for theory, qualitative and quantitative data. As integration tools, they impose standardization and harmonization of data of different sources, types and measurement levels. Moreover, they aid in implementing data triangulation and help identify inconsistencies of information from various origins. It is precisely such integration between methods in a single study that offers a unique contribution of mixed-method approaches.

References

1. Akaike, H.: A new look at the statistical model identification. IEEE Trans. Autom. Control **19**(6), 716–723 (1974)
2. Austin, E.W., Meili, H.K.: Effects of interpretations of televised alcohol portrayals on children's alcohol beliefs. J. Broadcast. Electron. Media **38**(4), 417–435 (1994)
3. Bandura, A.: Social cognitive theory of mass communication. Media Psychol. **3**, 265–299 (2001)
4. Bithell, M., Brasington, J., Richards, K.: Discrete-element, individual-based and agent-based models: Tools for interdisciplinary enquiry in geography? Geoforum **39**(2), 625–642 (2008)
5. Boero, R., Squazzoni, F.: Does empirical embeddedness matter? Methodological issues on agent-based models for analytical social science. J. Artif. Soc. Soc. Simul. **8**(4), 6 (2005). http://jasss.soc.surrey.ac.uk/8/4/6.html
6. Cornwall, A., Jewkes, R.: What is participatory research? Soc. Sci. Med. **41**(12), 1667–1676 (1995)

7. Barreteau, O., Bousquet, F., Étienne, M., Souchère, V., d'Aquino, P.: Companion modelling: a method of adaptive and participatory research. In: Étienne, M. (ed.) Companion Modelling, pp. 13–40. Springer, Dordrecht (2014). https://doi.org/10.1007/978-94-017-8557-0_2
8. Fazio, R.H., Powell, M.C., Herr, P.M.: Toward a process model of the attitude-behavior relation: accessing one's attitude upon a mere observation of the attitude object. J. Pers. Soc. Psychol. **44**(4), 723–735 (1983)
9. Fazio, R.H., Zanna, M.P.: Direct experience and attitude-behavior consistency. Adv. Exp. Soc. Psychol. **14**, 161–202 (1981)
10. Festinger, L.: A Theory of Cognitive Dissonance. Stanford University Press, California (1957)
11. Hamill, L., Gilbert, N.: Social circles: a simple structure for agent-based social network models. J. Artif. Soc. Soc. Simul. **12**(2), 3 (2009). http://jasss.soc.surrey.ac.uk/12/2/3.html
12. Hansen, P., Liu, H., Morrison, G.: Agent-based modelling and socio-technical energy transitions: a systematic literature review. Energy Res. Soc. Sci. **49**, 41–52 (2019)
13. Harmon-Jones, E., Harmon-Jones, C.: Testing the action-based model of cognitive dissonance: the effect of action orientation on postdecisional attitudes. Pers. Soc. Psychol. Bull. **28**(6), 711–723 (2002)
14. Kenrick, D., Griskevicius, V., Neuberg, S., Schaller, M.: Renovating the pyramid of needs: contemporary extensions built upon ancient foundations. Perspect. Psychol. Sci. **5**(3), 292–314 (2010)
15. Lang, D., et al.: Transdisciplinary research in sustainability science: practice, principles, and challenges. Sustain. Sci. **7**(S1), 25–43 (2012). https://doi.org/10.1007/s11625-011-0149-x
16. Maslow, A.: Motivation and Personality. Harper and Row, New York (1954)
17. Max-Neef, M.: Development and human needs. In: Ekins, P., Max-Neef, M. (eds.) Real-Life Economics: Understanding Wealth Creation, pp. 197–213. Routledge, London (1992)
18. McGinnies, E., Ward, C.D.: Better liked than right: trustworthiness and expertise as factors in credibility. Pers. Soc. Psychol. Bull. **6**(3), 467–472 (1980)
19. McPherson, M., Smith-Lovin, L., Cook, J.M.: Birds of a feather: homophily in social networks. Ann. Rev. Sociol. **27**, 415–444 (2001)
20. McTaggart, R.: Principles for participatory action research. Adult Educ. Q. **41**(3), 168–187 (1991)
21. O'Cathain, A., Thomas, K.: Combining qualitative and quantitative methods. In: Pope, C., Mays, N. (eds.) Qualitative Research in Health Care, pp. 102–111. Blackwell Publishing, Toronto (2006)
22. Oreskes, N., Shrader-Frechette, K., Belitz, K.: Verification, validation and confirmation of numerical models in the earth sciences. Science **263**(5147), 641–646 (1994)
23. Polhill, G., Salt, D.: The importance of ontological structure: why validation by 'fit-to-data' is insufficient. In: Edmonds, B., Meyer, R. (eds.) Simulating Social Complexity. UCS, pp. 141–172. Springer, Cham (2017). https://doi.org/10.1007/978-3-319-66948-9_8
24. Pornpitakpan, C.: The persuasiveness of source credibility: a critical review of five decades' evidence. J. Appl. Soc. Psychol. **34**(2), 243–281 (2004)
25. Ramanath, A.M., Gilbert, N.: The design of participatory agent-based social simulations. J. Artif. Soc. Soc. Simul. **7**(4), 1 (2004). http://jasss.soc.surrey.ac.uk/7/4/1.html

26. Reilly, A.C., Dillon, R.L., Guikema, S.D.: Agent-based models as an integrating boundary object for interdisciplinary research. Risk Analysis (in press). https://doi.org/10.1111/risa.13134
27. Schulze, J., Müller, B., Groeneveld, J., Grimm, V.: Agent-based modelling of social-ecological systems: achievements, challenges, and a way forward. J. Artif. Soc. Soc. Simul. **20**(2), 8 (2017). http://jasss.soc.surrey.ac.uk/20/2/8.html
28. van Vliet, J., Bregt, A.K., Brown, D.G., van Delden, H., Heckbert, S., Verburg, P.H.: A review of current calibration and validation practices in land change modeling. Environ. Model. Softw. **82**, 174–182 (2016)

Sensitivity Analysis of an Empirical Agent-Based Model of District Heating Network Adoption

Gary Polhill[1]([⊠]) ⓘ, Doug Salt[1] ⓘ, Tony Craig[2] ⓘ, Ruth Wilson[2] ⓘ,
and Kathryn Colley[2] ⓘ

[1] Information and Computational Sciences Department, The James Hutton Institute,
Craigiebuckler, Aberdeen AB15 8QH, UK
{gary.polhill,doug.salt}@hutton.ac.uk
[2] Social, Economic and Geographical Sciences Department, The James Hutton
Institute, Craigiebuckler, Aberdeen AB15 8QH, UK
{tony.craig,ruth.wilson,kathryn.colley}@hutton.ac.uk
https://www.hutton.ac.uk/

Abstract. We present results from a sensitivity analysis study of an
agent-based model of district heating network adoption in an area of
Aberdeen, Scotland.

Keywords: Agent-based model · District heating · Sensitivity analysis

1 Introduction

Fuel poverty has been defined in Scotland as a condition in which a household
would have to spend 10% or more of its income on heating in order to maintain thermal comfort, with *extreme* fuel poverty applying when that figure is
20% or more. More recently, particularly in preparation for the Scottish Government's Fuel Poverty (Targets, Definition and Strategy) (Scotland) Act, passed
in 2019, the definition has been refined to take into account remaining income
after housing and childcare costs, which must be 90% of UK Minimum Income
Standard.

In Scotland, approximately a quarter (24.6%) of households are in fuel
poverty; about half of them (12.4%) are in extreme fuel poverty [1]. The 2019
Fuel Poverty Act sets a target of reducing these numbers to 5% and 1% by 2040,
both in Scotland as a whole, and in each council in Scotland. Though its use
as a base for the UK's North Sea oil industry means Aberdeen is a relatively
wealthy city, the latest figure available (for 2019) is as high as 23% of households, with 11% in extreme fuel poverty [3]. Partly with a view to addressing
fuel poverty, in 2003 Aberdeen City Council created Aberdeen Heat and Power

The work reported here is part of the SMARTEES project, which has received funding
from the European Union's Horizon 2020 research and innovation programme under
grant agreement No 763912.

© Springer Nature Switzerland AG 2021
I. Rojas et al. (Eds.): IWANN 2021, LNCS 12862, pp. 118–127, 2021.
https://doi.org/10.1007/978-3-030-85099-9_10

as an independent not-for-profit organization to build and run a district heating network. Nearly twenty years later, with several district heating systems successfully installed, especially in social housing tower blocks around the city (where the cost per household of installation is lowest), the Council are keen to expand the network.

To help with exploring scenarios that allow the expansion of the district heating network, as part of an EU Horizon 2020 project, we have built the model ACHSIUM (Aberdeen Central Heating Social Innovation Uptake Model). ACHSIUM simulates households being offered and deciding whether or not to adopt connection to the district heating network. In this paper, we are concerned with analysing the sensitivity the model has when simulating an area in the south-east of the city called 'Torry'.

2   The ACHSIUM Model

The ACHSIUM model is an agent-based model implemented in NetLogo [6], which simulates the adoption of a district heating network by households in Aberdeen, Scotland. A screenshot of the model's interface is shown in Fig. 1. In early experiments with the model, such as those reported here, we are concentrating on a district in Aberdeen named Torry. ACHSIUM simulates household agents living their daily lives over a ten-year period with a daily time step. Agents are also used to explicitly represent information sources such as mainstream media, the government, energy companies (including Aberdeen Heat and Power), and an organization set up by Aberdeen City Council to provide impartial energy advice called 'SCARF' (Save Costs And Reduce Fuel). Besides paying bills, attending school and going to work, household agents in the model are given the option to decide whether or not to join the district heating network when a neighbouring street has the network installed. However, since it is inefficient to install the network for just one house in a street, the network is installed in a street only if a sufficient number of households in the street want it. This partial interaction of scale means there is an element of social complexity to the emergent heat network in the model.

In what follows, we briefly describe the ACHSIUM model using parts of the ODD protocol [2] – an emerging standard for documenting social simulation models.

2.1   Ontology

The classes of entity in the model, and their attributes (in which nof- is short for 'number of'), are:

- buildings: building-street-name (from GIS data), postcode (from GIS data), nof-households, energy-rating (A-G), council-tax-band (A-H), building-fuel-poverty (0 – no fuel poverty, 1 – fuel poverty or 2 – severe fuel poverty). Of these only building-fuel-poverty is affected by model dynamics. Buildings also have data about the infrastructure they have for heating: electric, gas and heat network.

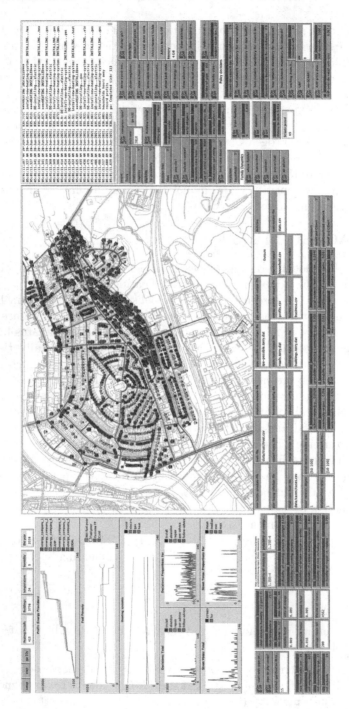

Fig. 1. Rotated screengrab of the interface of ACHSIUM, showing the Torry area of Aberdeen. This is provided to give an idea of the appearance of the model. Note that the colouring of the houses shows the status of the agents living in each building and does not reflect any data from real people living there.

- `heat-pipes`
- `persons`: age (0–81), sex (M or F), `degree` (number of network connections), `trust`, `income` (GBP), `ongoing-costs` (GBP), `hours-away-from-household`, and psychodemographic profile (see below).
- `households`: `trust`, `degree`, `dynamic`, `income` (GBP), `owns-property?` (Boolean), `owns-outright?` (Boolean), `ongoing-costs` (GBP), `balance` (GBP), `heating-status`, `heating-system`, `heating-system-age`, `boiler-size` (kWh), `air-conditioner-size`, `last-energy-provider`, `max-units-of-energy-per-day`, `min-units-of-energy-per-day`, `units-of-energy-used`, `hours-away-from-household`, `last-bill`, `fuel-poverty`, `history-of-fuel-poverty`. Households also store information on whether their rent includes energy build, payments they have made, whether yearly maintenance is required for their heating system, and whether that maintenance has taken place.
- `main-stream-media`: `organization-type` (national or local).
- `businesses`: `min-electrical-units-of-energy-per-day`, `units-of-energy-per-day-for-heating`, `units-of-energy-used`, `rateable-value` (GBP), `heating-system`, `last-bill`, `balance` (GBP). Businesses also store data on payments they make.
- `banks`: Details about purpose, principal, payment, frequency and `nof-payments` for loans they create.
- `landlords`: `rent` (GBP) for each property, frequency of rent payment for each property.
- `energy-providers`: `profitability` (GBP), `profits`, `retail-unit-cost` (GBP), `wholesale-unit-cost` (GBP), frequency (of billing: daily, weekly, monthly, quarterly or yearly), and details of tariffs including `energy-type`, `standing-charge`, `disconnection-cost`, `installation-cost` and `yearly-maintenance` for each tariff.
- `grant-bodies`: `energy-type`, `amount` (GBP), `maximum-income` (GBP – income of applicant above which not eligible), and the x, y and radius of a circle defining where the grant applies.
- `advisory-bodies`: `action` (information about what clients could do), `energy-type`, `recommended-institution`, `finance`, `calendar`, and the x, y and radius of locations in which awareness and advice offered by the advisory body applies.
- `institutions`: `organization-type`, `catchment-radius`, `calendar`, `fixed-holidays`, `floating-holidays`, `probability-of-attendance`, `working-from-home`.
- pixels, `patches` or discrete regular cells of land: `pipe-present?` (Boolean), `pipe-possible?` (Boolean), `street-name`, `voted?` (Boolean)

2.2 Process Overview and Scheduling

The schedule in ACHSIUM operates on a daily time step. Various 'events' can occur daily depending on input to the model and probabilistic parameters. There are then a series of activities that take place per day, per week, per month, per quarter, and per year. Activities at time resolutions of coarser grain than daily effectively take place on the appropriate day. Hence, weekly activities take place every seventh day, and monthly activities take place on the last day of each month, etc.

The following is a list of the daily 'events':

- New pipe is laid
- New homes are built
- Households move out
- New households move in to buildings with vacancies
- City-wide energy infrastructure failures are fixed
- Regional energy infrastructure failures are fixed
- New city-wide energy infrastructure failures can occur
- New regional energy infrastructure failures can occur
- New whole building energy infrastructure failures can occur
- New household energy infrastructure failures can occur
- Advisory bodies can run awareness-raising events

The following lists the daily, weekly, monthly, quarterly and yearly 'activities':

- Daily
  - Businesses consume electricity, and (other) energy for heating
  - Businesses pay energy providers for energy consumed if the tariff is daily
  - Household heating systems age
  - Households consume energy
  - Households pay energy providers for energy consumed if the tariff is daily
  - Households maintain their gas or electric heating system if it is time to do so
  - Households or individuals attend work, school and/or community events
  - Energy providers record profits
- Weekly
  - Businesses pay energy providers for energy consumed if the tariff is weekly
  - Households pay energy providers for energy consumed if the tariff is weekly
  - Households pay banks for loans if the frequency of repayment is weekly
  - Households pay rent to landlords if the frequency is weekly
  - Street voting can take place
- Monthly
  - Businesses pay energy providers for energy consumed if the tariff is monthly
  - Households pay energy providers for energy consumed if the tariff is monthly
  - Households pay banks for loans if the frequency of repayment is monthly
  - Households pay council tax
  - Households pay rent to landlords if the frequency is monthly
  - Households determine their disposable income

- Energy providers update their tariff according to the scenario
- Pipe may be laid
- Quarterly
  - Households pay energy providers for energy consumed if the tariff is quarterly
- Yearly
  - Grant bodies update the grants they offer
  - Energy providers update their tariffs according to the scenario
  - Landlords update their rents according to the scenario
  - Banks update their interest rates according to the scenario
  - Advisory bodies update their status according to the scenario
  - Households update their heating and demographic status
  - Weather data is updated
  - Holiday data is updated

2.3 Input Data

The following is a summary of data that can be input to the model to affect its dynamics while it is running:

- Heat pipe laying scenario data – GIS data from Aberdeen City Council
- New build housing data – GIS data from the local plan
- Tariffs for energy providers
- Grants available
- Rents required by landlords
- Interest rates on loans
- Advisory body data
- Weather data
- Holiday data

2.4 Submodels

This section briefly describes the decision-making, which is based on Moore's [4] interpretation of Rogers' [5] theory of innovation adoption. The population is divided into five 'psychodemographic' profiles: *innovators*, who are drawn to new technology simply because it is new; *early adopters*, who need the new technology to be useful; the *early majority*, who can be a challenging community to sell to (Moore's [4] book is mostly about how to reach them); the *late majority*, who need the new technology to be easy to use; and the *laggards* who adopt because there is no other option.

In the model, we treat the district heating as though it is new technology. A parameter `innovators` is the percentage proportion of the population who will be attracted because it is new. Another parameter `early-adopters` is the percentage breakpoint between the early adopters and the (early) majority. (So the percentage of early adopters is `early-adopters` − `innovators`.) Since we don't simulate ease of use in the model, the parameter `majority` determines the breakpoint between the early and late majority together, and the laggards. Rogers' [5] diffusion of innovation would put these parameters at around 3%, 16% and 84% respectively, though we have used larger values for `early-adopters`.

Tenure is also important in the model, as social housing that is owned by the Council can automatically have district heating installed as part of the Council's housing policy. (In practice, there can be negotiation, especially to manage social tenants with complex needs.) For private tenants and home owners (whether with a mortgage or owned outright), the innovation diffusion principles are applied. Those who are innovators will adopt if they have not experienced the heat network before. The early adopters will adopt the heat network if they can afford it, and people they know who have adopted it tell them it keeps them warm. The majority will adopt the heat network if most of the people they know have adopted it (a simplification of Moore). Laggards will adopt if there is no other choice.

Constraints on pipe installation means that households can only adopt the heat network if it is present in their street. This only happens if the street votes (by simple majority) to join the heat network when a neighbouring street already has it. Agents that voted to join (using the decision algorithm as described above) then connect to the heat network once it is installed.

3   Experiment

In this experiment, we were interested in a sensitivity analysis of the ACHSIUM model, to see how various of its parameters affected key outcome variables. Parameters in agent-based models do not necessarily have the same meanings as parameters in traditional mathematical models. *Traditional* parameters act in the same way as the factors on a polynomial, changing the shape of a fitting function. They have no real-world meaning as such, and can only be measured by calibrating them to minimize fitting error of the function as a whole to a set of observed data. By contrast, what might be called *Ontological* parameters, while they can be calibrated using error minimization methods, do have some level of real-world meaning, and could theoretically be measured. There are two subtypes of ontological parameter according to whether a governing organization could make adjustments to them: *Controllable* and *Non-controllable*. The parameters explored are as listed in Table 1, using 'T' for traditional parameter types, 'OC' for ontological controllable, and 'ON' for ontological non-controllable.

The outcome variable we are interested in is the number of households who have joined the district heating by the 1095th time step of the model run (the end of year 3). We reject runs from the analysis when this number is less than 1500, and use this as a basis for examining histograms of the parameters. We test the significance of a parameter's functional influence on the outcome using a Kruskal-Wallis test in which the population of accepted runs is grouped by number of adopters of the heat network a, five at a time (i.e. group $= 1 + \lfloor \frac{a}{5} \rfloor$).

Table 1. Parameters explored for sensitivity using ACHSIUM. Types of parameter are 'T' for traditional, 'OC' for ontological controllable, and 'ON' for ontological non-controllable. The p-value column shows 0 where the statistical test returned a value less than 10^{-15}.

Parameter	Type	Range sampled	p-value
all-adults?	ON	{true, false}	0.166
b	T	[1.0, 2.0]	0.05875
combined-factor	T	[0.001, 0.02]	0.8573
early-adopters	ON	[30, 60]	0
humidity-factor	T	[0.001, 0.02]	0.9909
ideal-absolute-humidity	ON	[5.0, 10.0]	0.03167
ideal-temperature	ON	[15.0, 25.0]	0.9869
innovators	ON	[1, 15]	0
majority	ON	[76, 100]	0
probability-of-moving-in	ON	[0.00012, 0.00013]	0.4039
probability-of-moving-out	ON	[0.00012, 0.00013]	0.6957
probability-of-owning-property	OC	[0.2, 0.6]	0.0003207
probability-of-owning-property-outright	ON	[0.0, 1.0]	0.9852
probability-of-private-rental-vs-public	OC	[0.0, 1.0]	0
temperature-factor	T	[0.001, 0.03]	0.6808
units-of-energy-per-degree	T	[0.001, 0.02]	0.8631

4   Results

Monte Carlo samples of 2353 runs of ACHSIUM, sampling uniformly from the parameters in Table 1. Of these runs, 1208 had at least 1500 households who joined the heat network by time step 1095, which provides a reasonable sample size from which to examine the effect on parameters. The results of the Kruskal-Wallis tests are shown in Table 1, and reveal that the psychodemographic parameters innovators, early-adopters, and majority are all significant. Two parameters affecting tenure of properties – the probability of owning a property rather than renting it, and the probability of the rental being public rather than private, are also significant. These parameters are assumed to potentially be in the control of governments through planning and housing policies. Finally, the ideal-absolute-humidity parameter is also significant, but only just so at the 0.05 level.

As Fig. 2 shows, when we plot the histograms of the distribution of the proportion of accepted runs, the significant result for ideal-absolute-humidity becomes more questionable, and a larger sample size would be needed to check whether this result persists. The other significant results, however, are verified.

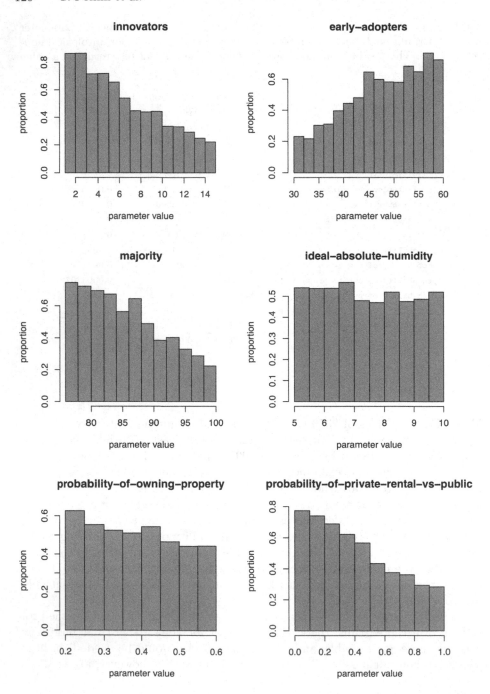

Fig. 2. Histograms those selected parameters from Table 1 with significant results.

5   Discussion

Ideally our analysis would be based on a larger sample of runs, but it is clear that there are a number of parameters that have a significant effect on the number of households who are simulated as having joined the heat network by time step 1095. All the significant results verified by the plots in Fig. 2 were for *ontological* parameters, including two over which governments may potentially have control through planning and housing policy. The psychodemographic parameters would theoretically be measurable using questionnaire surveys, though, as noted earlier, they already have standard values.

The reasons for these parameters' significance are down to the algorithms in the model that use them. Given that they join automatically, it is a surprise to see that higher values for the `innovators` parameter leads to lower levels of adoption – further investigation with the model is needed to confirm this result is not an artefact. Similarly, the direction of the `majority` parameter is unexpected, as the percentage of laggards is 100 − `majority`, and laggards will only adopt if there is no other option. The `early-adopters` parameter behaves as expected, as do the parameters determining tenure. The smaller the proportion of the population who owns their property, the greater the number of people renting, and hence the bigger the effect the probability of private rental. Since public rentals automatically join the heat network because the Council owns the properties, the smaller the proportion of private rentals, the greater the adoption. This sensitivity to tenure, which is borne out by anecdotal experience empirically, means that for the model to simulate policy scenarios, the spatial distribution of tenure will be relevant.

References

1. Clarkson, A., Amin, R., Wood, C.: Scottish House Condition Survey: 2019 key findings. Technical report, The Scottish Government, The Scottish Government, St Andrew's House, Edinburgh EH1 3DG, UK, December 2020. https://www.gov.scot/publications/scottish-house-condition-survey-2019-key-findings/
2. Grimm, V., et al.: The ODD protocol for describing agent-based and other simulation models: a second update to improve clarity, replication, and structural realism. J. Artif. Soc. Soc. Simul. **23**(2), 7 (2020). https://doi.org/10.18564/jasss.4259
3. Housing and Social Justice Directorate: Latest estimates of fuel poverty and extreme fuel poverty under the proposed new definition - following Stage 2 of the Fuel Poverty (Targets, Definition and Strategy) (Scotland) Bill. Technical report, The Scottish Government, The Scottish Government, St Andrew's House, Edinburgh EH1 3DG, UK, May 2019. https://www.gov.scot/publications/latest-estimates-fuel-poverty-extreme-fuel-poverty-under-proposed-new-definition-following-stage-2-fuel-poverty-targets-definition-strategy-scotland-bill/
4. Moore, G.A.: Crossing the Chasm: Marketing and Selling Disruptive Products to Mainstream Customers, 3rd edn. Harper Collins, New York (2014)
5. Rogers, E.M.: Diffusion of Innovations, 5th edn. Free Press, New York (2003)
6. Wilensky, U.: Netlogo (1999). http://ccl.northwestern.edu/netlogo/

Generating a Synthetic Population of Agents Through Decision Trees and Socio Demographic Data

Amparo Alonso-Betanzos[iD], Bertha Guijarro-Berdiñas[(✉)][iD],
Alejandro Rodríguez-Arias[iD], and Noelia Sánchez-Maroño[iD]

Center on Information and Communication Technologies (CITIC) - Universidade da
Coruña, 15071 A Coruña, Spain
{amparo.alonso.betanzos,berta.guijarro,alejandro.rodriguez.arias,
noelia.sanchez}@udc.es
https://citic.udc.es/

Abstract. Agent based models (ABM) are computational models employed for simulating the actions and interactions of autonomous agents with the objective of assessing their effects on the system as a whole. They have been extensively applied in social sciences because ABM simulations, under different running conditions, can help to test the implications of a policy intervention or to observe the population dynamics in different scenarios. We have developed an ABM to model how citizens behave with respect to superblocks, i.e., a type of social innovation where the urban space is reorganized to maximize public space and foster social and economic interactions while minimizing private motorized transports. In this model, the main entity is the citizen agent, so we must acquire personal attribute information to calibrate, validate, and apply the model to test different policy scenarios. Two main data sources were used to derive this information: census data and a survey. However, both were insufficient to generate a realistic population for the model. In this work we present how decision trees were used to generate a synthetic population using both types of data sources.

Keywords: Agent-based models · Synthetic populations · Sample based method · Decision trees · Social innovations · Policy scenarios

1 Introduction

Very often, we need to analyze systems in order to better understand how they work, to be able to make predictions about them or to explain previously observed patterns of behavior. Managing real systems directly for this purpose is sometimes too complex, expensive, time consuming, or even directly unfeasible.

Work in this paper has been supported by the European Commission's Horizon 2020 project SMARTEES (grant agreement no. 763912).

© Springer Nature Switzerland AG 2021
I. Rojas et al. (Eds.): IWANN 2021, LNCS 12862, pp. 128–140, 2021.
https://doi.org/10.1007/978-3-030-85099-9_11

As a solution we can use models, understood as *purposeful* and *simpler* representations of the real system under study. Those models can be approached in a number of ways, and among them agent-based modelling has become a well-established methodology. Unlike other techniques that represent a system through variables describing its state as a whole, agent-based models (ABM) represent systems by simulating the actions of their individual components (agents), which act as autonomous entities, the interaction between them and the interaction with their environment, thus allowing to face complex systems and processes. In the specific field of social sciences, ABMs have become a main tool [7] to study phenomena as it is a natural way of representing societies. Agents might be an individual or collective entities such as organizations, depending on the granularity needed. Of special importance in this field is that ABMs can also allow observing and evaluating problems related to the concept of *emergency*: dynamics of the system as a whole that arise from how its autonomous agents react to interactions with other agents and to changes in their environment. For these reasons they are becoming very popular tools in the social sciences, as they provide a powerful tool for exploring collective social consequences of individuals' characteristics and behavior [4] and have been applied to many different problems like those related to sustainability or education [1,8,12].

ABMs range from abstract worlds to high-dimensional worlds where agents have many attributes, the environment contains a great deal of information and may even have its own dynamics [4]. These last ABMs can be used as a virtual "laboratory" to test the implications of a political intervention or predict future population dynamics thanks to the execution of ABM simulations under different running conditions. Therefore, in social sciences, an interesting application is to provide policy makers and stakeholders with relevant scientific information that can be used to support their planning and decision-making processes by running possible future or alternative policy scenarios. The work presented in this paper was developed under the SMARTEES project[1], which aims to support the energy transition in Europe and improve policy design by developing alternative and robust policy pathways that foster citizen inclusion and take local peculiarities into account. Different implemented social innovation (SI) cases are under study in SMARTEES. Using ABM to model how citizens behave with respect to those SI, the goal is to analyze the effects of certain policy measures, thus supporting better policy design and decision-making in other SI that would take place in local contexts, similar but different from those originally modeled.

In this paper we focus on superblocks. These are a type of social innovation that reorganise urban spaces to maximize public space and foster social and economic interactions at the street level while keeping motorized modes of transportation outside of the neighbourhoods, the minimizing the use of it. Specifically, the superblock project in the city of Vitoria-Gasteiz, in northern Spain, is the case to be modeled. The research question to be answered by running the model is how is the acceptability of this project by its population and its

---

[1] SMARTEES: Social Innovation Modelling Approaches to Realizing Transition to Energy Efficiency and Sustainability (https://local-social-innovation.eu/).

dynamics throughout the years that the project implementation lasted (2006–2012). Being able to simulate this timeline in an ABM will allow experimenting with hypothetical scenarios to study what changes in political decisions, communication campaigns or behaviors would increase or decrease the acceptability of the project. Under these conditions, it becomes clear that a "high-dimensional" realism model is necessary for which it is crucial to correctly represent the population of Vitoria-Gasteiz. Each individual has an opinion about the superblocks project that is influenced, among other factors, by conditions such as where he/she lives, his/her level of studies, age, whether he/she has children or not, etc. When the number of such conditions is high, it is not possible to consider all the profiles that result from all their possible combinations. In this paper we present an approach to this problem based on the use of decision trees trained with data from questionnaires that were filled out by citizens for this study. The combination of the results of this tree with sociodemographic statistics available for Vitoria-Gasteiz has allowed us to create in our model a population of agents that realistically represent the population of Vitoria-Gasteiz.

2   State of the Art

The generation of synthetic yet realistic representations of populations is an important aspect for agent-based modeling. The methods to achieve such synthesized population have their origin in micro-simulation techniques. They follow two steps: first, a population is fit to a set of relevant attributes and constraints, and afterwards, they generate individual units on the fitted population. These methods can be classified as sample-free or sample-based methods [5].

Sample-free methods are used when no sample is available but only the distributions of attributes (of individuals, households or other aggregations) [3].

In sample-based methods, there are two major approaches: synthetic reconstruction (SR) and combinatorial optimisation (CO). The SR approach was first presented by Wilson and Pownall [16]. This approach typically involves a sequential process of random sampling from a set of conditional probabilities, which is generally derived using a sample of the target population from which the joint distributions of the attributes of interest are obtained. CO methods create a synthetic population per zone. The process [15] first randomly selects a group of individuals (or households) from a disaggregated data set (for example, a survey of a sample of the population in a large region) to match the size of the population of the small area. The observed sample is then statistically compared to a predefined set of demographic characteristics from this small area [10].

Between the SR techniques, Iterative Proportional Fitting (IPF) is a procedure used in a variety of applications. From a practical point of view, it enables the calculation of the maximum likelihood estimate of the presence of given individuals in specific zones [13]. An improved over the IPF algorithms, called Iterative Proportional Updating (IPU), was presented in [17] allowing the creation of artificial populations with a distribution at the household level close to the estimated one, and improving the alignment of the distribution at the individual level with the census data. Another variation is the hierarchical IPF (HIPF), a useful algorithm when it is necessary in the model to simulate certain relationships between agents, such as people grouped in households. This algorithm weights the initial population against certain restrictions of interest, and then chooses the households that belong to that population. Its biggest advantage is that it allows for person-level control to be taken into account while generating synthetic households through an entropy optimization tuning step that constantly changes between the household and the person's domain [14].

One critical assumption in the aforementioned population synthesizers is the availability of disaggregated data from which household records are drawn to form the resulting population in the target area. This assumption is not always accurate either because such a survey does not exist or, more often, it is inaccessible. Even when such survey data is available, the sample size needs to be large and spatially distributed enough to be fully representative of the demographic distributions of each target area. This condition is critical to the convergence of the iterative processes previously commented (IPF, IPU, HIPF) [11].

The CO approaches are far less common [3], and a deep and interesting comparative study between SR and CO techniques can be found in [9].

In this paper we present a sample-based method although, in our case we wish to focus only on maintaining a distribution at the individual level as similar as possible to the census information and the characteristics provided by the surveys, completely ignoring the household level. However, as the number of relevant variables to fit the population is high, we have designed a strategy based on the use of decision trees as will be explained below.

3 The Agent-Based Model. General Ideas and Basic Architecture

An important goal in the SMARTEES project is to guide city authorities in their transition to energy efficiency and sustainability through simulating plausible effects of implementing different social innovations actions that promote low-carbon energy sources. The main idea is to recognize the importance of the acceptability of the innovation by the locals and how to better motivate their support for the successful implementation of the SI. Therefore, an ABM architecture was designed in order to study the diffusion of social innovations in a local community and thus allow systematic comparisons of the effects of different policy scenarios on the diffusion of the innovations contemplated in the project.

Citizen agents are the main entity in the model and are characterized by socio-demographic variables and also different categories of personal needs such as wellness or comfort. As citizens live in a society, these needs also include social needs, referring to feeling close to and accepted by other people, or groups, relevant to the citizen. The objective in the model of any citizen agent is to see her needs satisfied to the maximum while feeling socially accepted with regard to the *behavioural alternative* she chooses, that could be, for example, to accept or reject the SI. With this objective, for every behavioral alternative, citizen agents calculate their overall satisfaction in it as a weighted sum that takes into account how an alternative satisfies each of the categories of their needs as well as the importance that each citizen gives to each need. As a result, the overall satisfaction as well as the satisfaction per groups of needs are derived for each citizen. Sometimes a behavioural alternative is perfect, and all groups of needs are satisfied but, very often, alternatives have both pros and cons causing the agent a cognitive dissonance. To identify this situation, along with satisfaction, citizens calculate the global dissonance caused by each alternative as a balance between consonant and dissonant cognitions. Finally, citizen agents will choose the alternative that maximizes their overall satisfaction over the groups of needs; if this is similar, they will choose the one that generates the lowest level of dissonance; if still similar, they will choose the one that best meets their needs following a hedonistic behavior and, finally, they will choose at random [2].

Citizen agents belong to different social networks (family, coworkers...) in which they communicate in order to convince or allow themselves to be convinced about an alternative behavior. Interaction occurs mainly through two processes: signaling and inquiring. Signaling implies informing other agents on one's opinion about the SI project, while inquiring implies asking other agents for their opinion.

Critical nodes are another type of entities in our model, representing persons and/or organizations (key-stakeholders) important in co-creation and diffusion of the SI, such as city councils. Critical nodes can influence citizen agents in the behavioural alternative to select and, for this, they can apply different strategies. In this model, a strategy is always a communicative act about the SI (one-time or repeated over a certain period).

The model begins by initializing the state parameters of the citizen agents and computing their satisfaction levels. Then the critical nodes begin to apply their strategies. When the citizen experiences its effects first-hand, she updates her levels of satisfaction of needs and dissonances for every alternative. When the dissonance's strength in the chosen behaviour exceeds a given tolerance level, the citizen *signals* her satisfaction or disappointment to other citizens in her network or *inquires* to get more information on the subject. In addition, even if a citizen does not experience dissonance, she maintains random conversations with other agents that can possibly cause a change of opinion. During the evolution of the model, it can be observed how the different communicative acts, and especially the strategies of the critical nodes, will make the citizen's choice fluctuate.

4   Modeling the Acceptance of Superblocks in Vitoria-Gasteiz

As mentioned, in this work we are going to focus on how the population was created for the model that represents the response of the population to the reorganization of urban districts into superblocks, taking the historical case of Vitoria-Gasteiz (Spain) to reproduce and calibrate the ABM, which could then be used by other cities interested in implementing similar ideas.

The purpose of the Vitoria-Gasteiz model is to simulate the temporal evolution of citizens' opinions about the superblocks project and how it changes as policy actions take place in order to answer the question: what percentage of citizens will be against, and what percentage in favour of the superblock project based on different policy scenarios? According to this purpose, two behavioural alternatives were considered: accept or reject the superblocks innovation.

The model follows the general architecture presented in the previous section, therefore, in this section we will describe how the main components, that is a) sociodemographic variables and groups of citizen agent needs, b) Critical Nodes, and c) social networks, have been specified.

Different quantitative and qualitative procedures were used to collect relevant information for the case. Among them, a survey was designed to collect data from citizens about their needs, trust and other socio-demographic aspects. This survey was conducted in Vitoria-Gasteiz in November 2020. After the joint analysis of the survey data together with the sociologists of the team, six different groups of needs were identified for each citizen agent:

1. Wellness needs, which, among others, refer to health and security,
2. Environmental quality needs, referring to air and noise pollution,
3. Comfort which, among others, refer to house price and parking,
4. City prestige,
5. Participation needs, referring to the possibility of participating in city decisions, and
6. Social needs, referring to belongingness, social safety, social status, etc.

Table 1. Sociodemographic variables included in the survey and their correspondence with the variables of the citizen's state.

Variables	States
Age	Integer in [18 100]
Gender	Male/female
Education level	Primary/secondary/tertiary
Economic activity	Employed/unemployed/inactive/student
Location	Neighbourhood section code
Non-independent children	Yes/no
Time in the neighbourhood (years)	<3/3–10/10–30/> 30

Moreover, the survey was also used to obtain socio-demographic variables of the citizens (see Table 1). Among these variables is the code of the neighborhood section in which they live (location), that allows us to locate them on the map shown in the system's user interface (see Fig. 1) in addition to being able to determine if they live in a neighbourhood affected by a superblock.

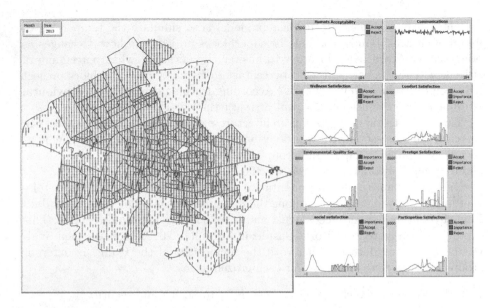

Fig. 1. Representation of the Vitoria-Gasteiz map and the levels of satisfaction of the groups of needs in the model interface. In the graphs of the right hand side, the y axis represents the number of agents, while in the x axis the meaning is the following: in the two top graphs it represents the number of tics (15 days each tic), and in the rest of the graphs it means the agent satisfaction (between −1 and 1)

In addition to citizens, four critical nodes known for their relevance have been included after an exhaustive documentary analysis: the city council, merchants associations, other associations (neighbors, cyclists, pedestrians, etc.) and local media. These critical nodes use communicative acts to convince the citizen agents to accept (or reject) the superblock innovation project. To represent these acts, there are weighted one-way links from critical nodes to citizens. The weight of the link indicates the trust that the citizen has in the critical node and determines the level of impact that the communication will have on the citizen's opinion. The number of links created in the model for each critical node was determined using secondary information sources, such as the number of Twitter followers.

Finally, two different social networks were considered for citizen agents: neighbors and friends. Similar to critical nodes, links on these social networks are weighted with a number that represents trust between agents. These links are bidirectional and the weights are not supposed to be reciprocal.

The number of links that will be created for each citizen's social networks as well as their level of trust both in other citizens and in critical nodes were obtained from the survey data.

5   Generating the Population

The presented model operates at the level of citizens, so one needs personal attribute information for the entire population in Vitoria-Gasteiz to calibrate, validate, and apply the model to test different policy scenarios. In fact, the following data are necessary to represent a citizen agent in this model:

- Socio-demographic variables
- Satisfaction and importance for each group of needs
- Trust in each critical node
- Trust in other agents
- Number of links to form social networks

However, such information is not available at the disaggregate level for the entire city of Vitoria-Gasteiz. We have two main data sources to generate our population: on the one hand census data (from the city council or the National Institute of Statistics of Spain) and, on the other hand, relevant information of some citizens acquired by the survey that have been conducted in the project. The different sample-based techniques presented in Sect. 2 could allow us to generate the socio-demographic variables of a large synthetic population combining both sources of data. However, up to our knowledge, there is no information available referred to trust between citizens/organizations or satisfaction of needs apart from the data gathered in the survey. As presented in Sects. 3 and 4, these data are extremely important for the model to behave properly. Besides, there are seven socio-demographic variables (see Table 1) and, considering the combination of all their possible states to replicate population is unfeasible. For these reasons, we have to design a procedure to generate the population using mainly the data from the valid responses obtained from the survey.

There are 865 available questionnaires to define the population of agents for a city which, according to the National Institute of Statistics of Spain, in 2018 had a population of 249.176 inhabitants. Thus, we needed to replicate agents to better represent the real population. These agents cannot be replicated at random but we must adjust the population to the socio-demographic characteristics of the city. Therefore, we establish an automatic procedure in which a decision tree was constructed from the data survey, using as the variable to be predicted the intention of the agent in voting (accept/reject) for the superblocks innovation (one of the questions in the survey). The reason for using decision trees over other machine learning techniques was the importance of the explicability of the results in our model. Our aim was to derive a tree in which each leaf node represents a *citizen profile*. Once we had those profiles its prevalence in the model is determined by the socio-demographical data, and each new agent to be added to the system will be assigned a questionnaire randomly chosen among those belonging to the same profile. The following subsections explain these steps in detail.

5.1   Generation of the Decision Tree

The decision tree was generated using the standard CART algorithm. Questions of the survey related to socio-demographic variables (see Table 1) were considered as inputs and the citizen's voting intention regarding superblocks was the desired output. It is important to note that agents in the model only have two behaviours (accept or reject the SI), whereas the survey included other options such as *undecided*. Unfortunately, there were a significant number of undecided responses, so this class must be included in the decision tree, leading to a final classification problem with three classes. The following preprocessing steps were carried out before training the decision tree:

- Samples with missing data from the survey were removed (33 samples).
- Most input variables are discrete such as Table 1 indicates. The variable *age* is used as a continuous variable in the model to allow the generation of friendships relations following a homophilia principle (friends usually have similar age). However, for training the decision tree, it was discretized in the intervals considered in the census data, that is: <=24, 25–44, 45–64 >=65.
- The survey is clearly unbalanced, with those who accept the SI being the majority class (67% of samples) and those who reject it the minority (11%), while the undecided constitute 22% of the samples. Therefore, the SMOTE oversampling algorithm [6] was applied to expand the less populated classes.

Different configurations were trained by changing parameters such as the maximum number of splits or the minimum number of samples ($minLeafSize$) in each leaf node, but always trying to guarantee a representative profile in each leaf. A final tree using $minLeafSize = 40$ (5% of the samples) and impurity as the prune criterion was selected as the one with the best performance (up to 72% of accuracy). This decision tree is shown in Fig. 2. Each leaf node in this tree constitutes a *citizen profile*, which leads to 17 different profiles. Note that these profiles are used to establish the initial values of the population, but it is the execution of the model the one determining the decision of each citizen agent (accept/reject the SI).

5.2   Completing Missing Survey Data in Agent Generation

Most missing data values were found in the output variable (blank responses in the voting question) and, as a consequence, they were discarded for the construction of the decision tree. However, for the generation of agents in the model it is possible to extrapolate them using the sociodemographic data and the decision tree and then assigning the corresponding output to their *citizen profile*.

Samples with missing values in the inputs were also completed using the citizen profile. The missing variable (or variables) was filled in using the median for the corresponding citizen profile instead of using the median of all the data. Note that this procedure is only suitable for completing those variables that are not used to determine the profile (for example, needs). If there was a missing value implying a variable of a relevant tree node to derive the profile, the sample

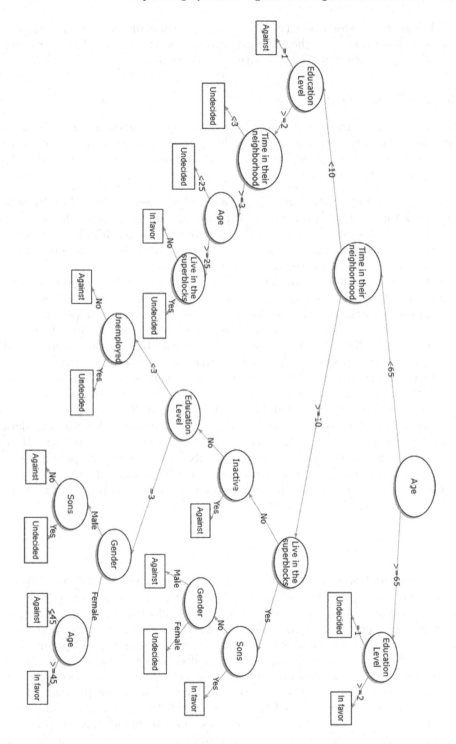

Fig. 2. Decision tree for the Vitoria-Gastciz citizen profiles

would have to be discarded (however, this situation did not occur). Finally, thanks to this procedure, the 865 questionnaires were completed for being the base of the generation of real population in the model.

5.3 Profile Replication

Once the tree with the population profiles has been obtained, we use it to generate new agents, maintaining the sociodemographic distribution of Vitoria. To generate this synthetic population from the responses to the survey and the citizen profiles, the following steps were applied:

1. *Generate synthetic population based on available census data.* The Vitoria-Gasteiz City Council provided us with the distributions by gender and age for each census region of the city. Therefore, as many citizen agents were created as there are citizens in Vitoria-Gasteiz, maintaining the proportions of age and gender indicated for each census section.
2. *Assign values to the remaining socio-demographic variables.* Except for age, gender and zip code, our citizen agents, located on the map according to the census data, lack the other sociodemographic data of interest (see Table 1). To complete this data we use the data provided by the surveys. First, we calculate the distributions of these relevant variables in the survey based on age range and gender. Then, they were assigned a value following the calculated distributions. For example, for a woman between 25 and 44 years old, the probability of having a low educational level is 0.14, for a medium level the probability is 0.29 and for a high level is 0.57.
3. *Replicate agents based on citizen profiles.* Once all the socio-demographic data are generated, the last step consists on selecting the corresponding citizen profile using the decision tree and randomly pick a citizen of that profile to replicate the data. So, the data on satisfaction, importance, trust, and size of the social networks of a random agent belonging to the corresponding profile is transferred to the new agent.

6 Conclusions

Agent-based models in social sciences are used to simulate the evolution of populations with an explicit representation of each individual. A frequent problem is how to properly initialize a large number of these individuals with the appropriate attributes, since very often, for reasons of privacy, costs, etc., only aggregated data and very little individual data are available from a sample of the population. In this work we present an approach based on decision trees trained on a sample obtained through questionnaires. The resulting tree allowed us to determine the relevant variables to categorize the entire population in various profiles. Subsequently, these profiles were used to generate synthetic agents, also taking into account the census data. This procedure was used to model the acceptability of the population about the superblock project in the city of Vitoria-Gasteiz.

As validation criteria, several workshops were carried out with stakeholders and promoters of the superblock in Vitoria-Gasteiz, so as to fit the model obtained to adequately simulate the acceptability of the SI. Finally, it was demonstrated that with the population generated following the method described above, we were able to successfully reproduce the evolution of citizens's opinion throughout the time line that the project lasted (2006–2012).

References

1. Alonso-Betanzos, A., et al. (eds.): Agent-Based Modeling of Sustainable Behaviors. UCS, Springer, Cham (2017). https://doi.org/10.1007/978-3-319-46331-5
2. Antosz, P., et al.: Smartees simulation implementations (2020). https://local-social-innovation.eu/resources/deliverables/, Deliverable 7.3, SMARTEES project
3. Barthelemy, J., Toint, P.L.: Synthetic population generation without a sample. Transp. Sci. **47**(2), 266–279 (2013)
4. Bruch, E., Atwell, J.: Agent-based models in empirical social research. Sociol. Methods Res. **44**(2), 186–221 (2015)
5. Burger, A., Oz, T., Crooks, A., Kennedy, W.G.: Generation of realistic mega-city populations and social networks for agent-based modeling. In: Proceedings of the 2017 International Conference of The Computational Social Science Society of the Americas, pp. 1–7 (2017)
6. Chawla, N.V., Bowyer, K.W., Hall, L.O., Kegelmeyer, W.P.: SMOTE: synthetic minority over-sampling technique. J. Artif. Intell. Res. **16**, 321–357 (2002)
7. Gilbert, N., Terna, P.: How to build and use agent-based models in social science. Mind Soc. **1**, 57–72 (2020)
8. Gu, X., Blackmore, K.: A systematic review of agent-based modelling and simulation applications in the higher education domain. Higher Educ. Res. Dev. **34**(5), 883–898 (2015)
9. Huang, Z., Williamson, P.: A comparison of synthetic reconstruction and combinatorial optimisation approaches to the creation of small-area microdata. Department of Geography, University of Liverpool (2001)
10. Huynh, N., Namazi-Rad, M.R., Perez, P., Berryman, M., Chen, Q., Barthelemy, J.: Generating a synthetic population in support of agent-based modeling of transportation in sydney. In : Adapting to Change: The Multiple Roles of Modelling. 20th International Congress on Modelling and Simulation (MODSIM2013), Adelaide, Australia, December, pp. 1–6 (2013)
11. Huynh, N.N., Barthelemy, J., Perez, P.: A heuristic combinatorial optimisation approach to synthesising a population for agent-based modelling purposes. J. Artif. Soc. Soc. Simul. **19**(4), 11 (2016)
12. Jager, W., Scholz, G., Mellema, R., Kurahashi, S.: The energy transition game: experiences and ways forward. In: Kurahashi, S., Takahashi, H. (eds.) Innovative Approaches in Agent-Based Modelling and Business Intelligence. ASS, vol. 12, pp. 237–252. Springer, Singapore (2018). https://doi.org/10.1007/978-981-13-1849-8_17
13. Lovelace, R., Birkin, M., Ballas, D., Leeuwen, E.S.: Evaluating the performance of iterative proportional fitting for spatial microsimulation: new tests for an established technique. J. Artif. Soc. Social Simul. **18**, 21 (2015). https://doi.org/10.18564/jasss.2768

14. Müller, K., Axhausen, K.W.: Hierarchical IPF: generating a synthetic population for switzerland. Arbeitsberichte Verkehrs-und Raumplanung **718** (2011)
15. Williamson, P., Birkin, M., Rees, P.H.: The estimation of population microdata by using data from small area statistics and samples of anonymised records. Environ. Plan. A **30**(5), 785–816 (1998)
16. Wilson, A.G., Pownall, C.E.: A new representation of the urban system for modelling and for the study of micro-level interdependence. In: Area, pp. 246–254 (1976)
17. Ye, X., Konduri, K., Pendyala, R.M., Sana, B., Waddell, P.: A methodology to match distributions of both household and person attributes in the generation of synthetic populations. In: 88th Annual Meeting of the Transportation Research Board, Washington, DC (2009)

Randomization in Deep Learning

Improved Acoustic Modeling for Automatic Piano Music Transcription Using Echo State Networks

Peter Steiner[1]([✉]) [ID], Azarakhsh Jalalvand[2,3] [ID], and Peter Birkholz[1] [ID]

[1] Institute for Acoustics and Speech Communication, Technische Universität
Dresden, Dresden, Germany
{peter.steiner,peter.birkholz}@tu-dresden.de
[2] IDLab, Ghent University–imec, Ghent, Belgium
azarakhsh.jalalvand@ugent.be
[3] Mechanical and Aerospace Engineering Department, Princeton University,
Princeton, USA

Abstract. Automatic music transcription (AMT) is one of the challenging problems in Music Information Retrieval with the goal of generating a score-like representation of a polyphonic audio signal. Typically, the starting point of AMT is an acoustic model that computes note likelihoods from feature vectors. In this work, we evaluate the capabilities of Echo State Networks (ESNs) in acoustic modeling of piano music. Our experiments show that the ESN-based models outperform state-of-the-art Convolutional Neural Networks (CNNs) by an absolute improvement of 0.5 F_1-score without using an extra language model. We also discuss that a two-layer ESN, which mimics a hybrid acoustic and language model, achieves better results than the best reference approach that combines Invertible Neural Networks (INNs) with a biGRU language model by an absolute improvement of 0.91 F_1-score.

Keywords: Automatic piano transcription · Acoustic modeling · Echo state network

1 Introduction

Automatic Music Transcription (AMT) is one of the most challenging problems in Music Information Retrieval. The goal of AMT is to generate a score-like representation of a polyphonic audio signal. Due to many concurrently played notes from various instruments, complex overlapping of harmonics occurs in the acoustic signal. In many cases, the polyphony, e.g. the number of simultaneously active notes, is unknown and can vary over time. In recent years, AMT was successfully treated as a multi-label classification problem, in which every possible note is treated as one class. Recurrent Neural Networks (RNNs) define the state-of-the-art for acoustic modeling in piano transcription. In [2], one of the first approaches for acoustic modeling with recurrent neural networks was

© Springer Nature Switzerland AG 2021
I. Rojas et al. (Eds.): IWANN 2021, LNCS 12862, pp. 143–154, 2021.
https://doi.org/10.1007/978-3-030-85099-9_12

presented. The authors used multi-resolution features as input for an LSTM network that performed onset and pitch detection on the frame-level. Later, in [10], a large-scale study to determine features and different neural network architectures was conducted to find general guidelines towards simple acoustic modeling for piano transcription. The outcome was that feature design is important, and the best features are spectrum-like representations with log-spaced frequency bins and log-scaled magnitudes. Furthermore, it turned out that the Convolutional Neural Network (CNN) performed significantly better than a Deep Neural Network (DNN) and the All Convolutional Neural Network (AllConv).

Sigtia et al. [13] also used a CNN as acoustic model, but with an additional music language model that is supposed to learn the relationship between successive notes, similar as in speech recognition. The language model is the combination of a Recurrent Neural Network (RNN) and a Neural Autoregressive Distribution Estimator (NADE). This combination of an acoustic and language model led to smoother outputs compared to the purely acoustic model and thus improved the transcription results. Kelz et al. [11] recently showed that Invertible Neural Networks (INNs) together with RNNs as language models are performing slightly better than the CNN. So far, this is the best performing combination of an acoustic and language model that uses simple spectral features as input and output note probabilities for each frame.

In different studies [3, 21], it was shown that incorporating onset information can boost piano transcription. Therefore, several systems combine onset information as language model with acoustic models. In [5], a complex multitask-approach was introduced. It consisted of models for onset detection, frame-wise pitch tracking, and for combining the information from onset detection and pitch tracking. All models were trained jointly. The ADSR model [9] incorporated attack, decay, sustain and release for each piano note. Currently, models that utilize onset and offset information in combination with larger models and a large-scale dataset [6] define the state-of-the-art in piano transcription.

In this paper, we investigate the potential of Echo State Networks (ESNs) [7] as *simple but effective* neural acoustic models for automatic transcription of piano music. In our prior work, it was shown that the performance of ESNs is similar to CNNs for automatic music transcription on the MusicNet dataset [17, 19] and for note onset detection [14, 16]. However, as only a few types of models were evaluated on the MusicNet dataset and all of them were conceptionally complex and computationally intensive, it is difficult to objectively compare ESN with the contenders. On the other hand, the MAPS piano dataset [4], has been considered as a benchmark for many acoustic and hybrid models. This allows for a fair comparison with Deep Neural Networks (DNNs) and Convolutional Neural Networks (CNNs), which are frequently used nowadays.

We compare our ESN-based acoustic model to a CNN-based acoustic model as a reference system and to several hybrid models that have an RNN in the second layer and show that a purely ESN-based approach outperforms a wide range of models.

The remainder of the paper is structured as follows: In Sect. 2, we introduce acoustic modeling using Echo State Networks. We explain our extracted features and the ESN model. Section 3 gives an overview about the utilized MAPS dataset and the metrics utilized to evaluate our model. After presenting our main results in Sect. 4, we end with conclusions and outlook in Sect. 5.

2   Acoustic Modeling Using Echo State Networks

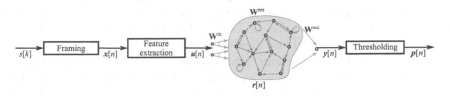

Fig. 1. Outline of the proposed ESN-based acoustic model from [17]: The audio signal $s[k]$ is divided into overlapping frames $\mathbf{x}[n]$ (hop size 10 ms). A filter-bank with logarithmic-spaced center frequencies and logarithmic magnitudes is used to extract spectral features $\mathbf{u}[n]$ for each frame n. The sequence of feature vectors is fed through the ESN-based acoustic model that computes the likelihoods $\mathbf{y}[n]$ for the presence of each note in the frame n. To obtain the binary piano-roll representation $\mathbf{p}[n]$, a global threshold is applied on the likelihoods.

Echo State Networks (ESNs) [7] are a variant of Recurrent Neural Networks (RNNs). In contrast to widely used RNN architectures, which usually consist of sequential layers that need to be trained jointly using iterative algorithms, the input and recurrent connections of ESNs are fixed by random values, and only the output weights are trained in one shot using linear regression. This one-shot training has two advantages compared to iterative algorithms:

- Fast training: All available data is presented *in one time* during training, which is time-efficient.
- Adaptability: The model can be *adapted to new data* in a later stage without presenting old data again.

In [17], we have summarized several properties that make ESNs interesting for multipitch tracking. Relying on our previous work, we adapted the system from [17] and evaluated its capability on acoustic modeling for piano transcription. The main outline of the proposed ESN-based acoustic model for piano transcription is depicted in Fig. 1.

2.1   Framing

The acoustic model works with feature vectors extracted from a discrete input signal $s[k]$, where k is the sample index. It is sampled with a sampling frequency $f_s = 44.1$ kHz. For the subsequent feature extraction, it is divided into overlapping frames $\mathbf{x}[n]$ of length 46.4 ms with a hop size of 10 ms, and with n being the discrete frame index.

2.2   Feature Extraction

For each frame, the short-term Fourier transform was computed. A triangular filter-bank with semitone-spaced center frequencies from 30 Hz to 17 000 Hz was applied on the short-term spectra to reduce the feature dimension. In order to avoid large negative values and to compress large magnitudes in the feature vector, the $\log_{10}$ was applied to the magnitude m plus 1, i.e. $\log_{10}(m+1)$.

To enrich the input feature vector with more temporal information, the first derivative of the computed magnitude spectrum was considered. Therefore, a first-order difference filter kernel with length of 3 frames was used to compute the temporal differences based on one frame before and after. The magnitude spectrum and its derivative were concatenated, so that each feature vector consisted of a spectrum and the first derivative.

We did not apply any additional standardization or normalization steps, and directly supplied these features as input $\mathbf{u}[n]$ to the ESN. This is a result from our previous work about note onset detection [14], where we found that any kind of standardization over-emphasized less important features with a very low variance. This is visualized in Fig. 2.

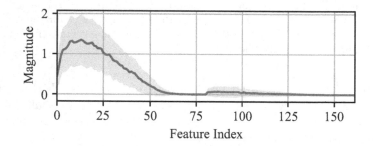

Fig. 2. Mean and variance for each feature. In higher frequencies, any kind of standardization would over-emphasize less important features with a very low variance.

2.3   Basic Echo State Network

The basic ESN outline that was used in this paper is depicted in in the center of Fig. 1 and is based on our general description of an ESN for multipitch tracking in [17], which was adapted in this paper. We briefly summarize the initialization of the ESN here. Basically, it consists of three weight matrices: The input weights $\mathbf{W}^{\mathrm{in}}$ pass the input features to the reservoir, an unordered group of N^{res} nonlinear neurons. Since the reservoir weights $\mathbf{W}^{\mathrm{res}}$ basically connect the reservoir neurons to each other in a recurrent fashion, past information can "echo" for some time inside the reservoir. The output weights $\mathbf{W}^{\mathrm{out}}$ connect the neurons inside the reservoir to the output nodes.

Both, $\mathbf{W}^{\mathrm{in}}$ and $\mathbf{W}^{\mathrm{res}}$, were initialized from random distributions. The reservoir weights $\mathbf{W}^{\mathrm{res}}$ fulfill the *Echo State Property* (ESP), which says that, for a finite input sequence, the reservoir states need to decay in a finite time [7]. This was done by normalizing $\mathbf{W}^{res}$ to its maximum absolute eigenvalue.

In summary, the key difference between ESNs and typical RNN architectures is that $\mathbf{W}^{in}$ and $\mathbf{W}^{res}$ are initialized randomly and kept fixed during the training. Only the output weights $\mathbf{W}^{out}$ are trained using linear regression, whereas all weights need to be jointly optimized in typical RNN architectures.

To briefly recapitulate the main equations of an ESN, let $\mathbf{r}[n]$ represent the reservoir state. The two Eqs. (1) and (2) are then used to describe ESNs.

$$\mathbf{r}[n] = (1 - \lambda)\mathbf{r}[n-1] + \lambda f_{res}(\mathbf{W}^{in}\mathbf{u}[n] + \mathbf{W}^{res}\mathbf{r}[n-1] + \mathbf{w}^{bi}) \tag{1}$$

$$\mathbf{y}[n] = \mathbf{W}^{out}\mathbf{r}[n] \tag{2}$$

Equation (1) is a leaky integration of the reservoir states $\mathbf{r}[n]$ with $\lambda \in (0,1]$ being the leakage, and $f_{res}(\cdot)$ is the non-linear reservoir activation, in this paper the tanh-function. Every neuron in the reservoir receives a bias input using the bias weight vector $\mathbf{w}^{bi}$, which is initialized and fixed from a uniform distribution between ± 1. Equation (2) describes the N^{out}-dimensional output $\mathbf{y}[n]$ as a linear combination of a given reservoir state $\mathbf{r}[n]$.

During the training phase, all reservoir states $\mathbf{r}[n]$ were expanded by a constant of 1 as the intercept term for linear regression, and then collected in the reservoir state collection matrix $\mathbf{R}$. The desired binary outputs $\mathbf{d}[n]$, which are 0 for non-active and 1 for active pitches, are collected into the desired output collection matrix $\mathbf{D}$. Afterwards, $\mathbf{W}^{out}$ is obtained using ridge regression $\mathbf{W}^{out} = (\mathbf{R}\mathbf{R}^T + \epsilon\mathbf{I})^{-1}(\mathbf{D}\mathbf{R}^T)$, where the regularization parameter $\epsilon = 0.01$ penalizes large values in $\mathbf{W}^{out}$, and $\mathbf{I}$ is the identity matrix. The size of the output weight matrix $N^{out} \times (N^{res} + 1)$ determines the total number of free parameters to be trained in ESNs. The output $\mathbf{y}[n]$ indicated whether each note is active or not.

An ESN has several control parameters, which need to be tuned task-dependently: α_u, ρ, and α_{bi} control the absolute importance of the input feature vector, old reservoir state and the constant bias inputs, respectively. They are global scaling factors of the weight matrices $\mathbf{W}^{in}$, $\mathbf{W}^{res}$ and $\mathbf{w}^{bi}$. The leakage λ is a control parameter for the leaky integration and matches the input and output dynamics. The workflow to optimize the hyper-parameters is described detailed in [14, 16, 17].

2.4   Bidirectional Reservoirs

In the case of bidirectional reservoirs, the ESN is able to incorporate future information to compute the outputs. Therefore, the feature vectors are first fed through the ESN and the reservoir states are collected as described before. Next, the input is reversed in time and again fed through exactly the same model. This results in new reservoir states that are reversed in time. Afterwards, the reservoir states of both directions are concatenated to compute the output.

Bidirectional ESNs are usually more powerful than unidirectional models because (1) they have twice the number of free parameters in W^{out} and (2) they use future information to compute the output.

2.5 Stacked Reservoirs

In the case of stacked reservoirs, several ESN models are chained sequentially in layers as in [20]. Typically, subsequent ESNs receive the output of the previous layer as input. The target outputs of all layers are usually the same, and the layers are trained sequentially. By stacking reservoirs, the temporal modeling capacity of a single layer model is extended. This can be done for unidirectional as well as for bidirectional reservoirs.

In [8,17,20], it was shown that this improved the results for phoneme and image recognition, and for multipitch tracking, because subsequent layers are able to smooth the output of previous layers. In this paper, we also used a second layer to smooth the outputs of the first layer.

2.6 Thresholding

In [17], we have discussed that the output of an ESN after linear regression would ideally be zero in case of an absent and one in case of a present note. In practice, this is not always valid and the output is neither bounded between zero and one, nor truly binary. We used a simple thresholding method to convert the raw output values of the ESN into a binary piano roll representation. All output values above the threshold were set to one, the remaining to zero. The threshold was empirically set to 0.36 and tuned to maximize the F_1-Measure on the validation set.

3 Experimental Setup

The model was implemented in Python 3 using the `madmom` [2] framework for feature extraction and PyRCN[1] [15] for developing the ESN models. The code together with pre-trained models is available online in our GitHub repository.

3.1 MAPS Dataset

We use the MAPS dataset [4] to compare our proposed acoustic model with reference models. It contains audio files and annotations of isolated notes, chords, and piano pieces. All audio files are sampled with 44.1 kHz and are stored as stereo WAV files. We considered only the complete piano pieces. The MAPS dataset contains audio files rendered by software synthesizers and recordings from a Yamaha Disklavier player piano. In [13], the dataset was split into subsets for a 4-fold cross validation in different configurations. The most real-world case

---

[1] https://github.com/TUD-STKS/PyRCN.

that was used for later studies is called "Configuration 2" and uses just the synthetic audio files for training/optimization. The Disklavier recordings were held back as an unseen test set. In [5], the authors modified "Configuration 2" and removed music pieces from the training set that are present in both, training and test sets. For the sake of fair comparison and as they have re-trained several reference models based on this reduced training set, we opted for the same MAPS configuration as [5,11].

3.2 Evaluation Metrics

The evaluation was based on standard frame-level metrics proposed in [1], namely Precision P, Recall R and F_1. We used the library mir_eval [12] to compute P and R. The F_1-Measure in Eq. (3) is the harmonic mean of both, P and R. For details on the metrics, we refer to [1].

$$F_1 = 2\frac{P \cdot R}{P + R} \tag{3}$$

4 Results on the MAPS Dataset

4.1 Hyperparameter Optimization

We sequentially optimized the hyper-parameters minimizing the mean squared error as in [17] in the steps (a) ρ and α_u, (b) λ, and (c) α_bi, respectively using 5-fold cross validation. Figure 3 shows the cross validation scores (negative mean squared error) for each step. We can see that the ESN model benefits from recurrent connections, because $\rho = 0.1$ and $\lambda = 0.1$. The bias has only a small impact on the final performance. We also checked the regularization parameter ϵ that, however, did not influence the results.

4.2 General Observations

Figure 4 compares the performance of uni- and bidirectional ESNs next to a reference CNN model. It can be observed that the F_1-Measure strongly depends on the reservoir size N_res. Incorporating future information by using bidirectional architectures strongly improves the results over unidirectional architectures. In fact, the proposed bidirectional model with 12000 neurons outperforms the reference CNN [10] (marked by the dashed line), the best performing acoustic model with comparable features. Of course, we need to note that the CNN utilizes a limited amount of future information (two frames) compared to the ESN.

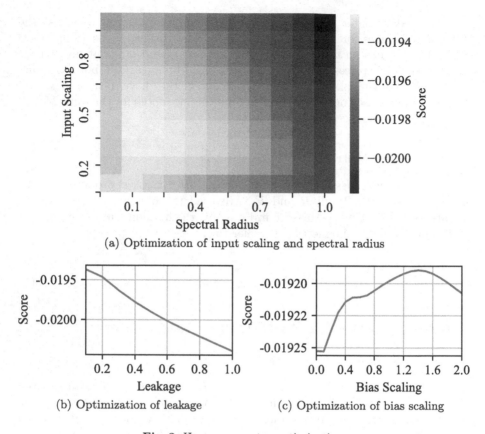

(a) Optimization of input scaling and spectral radius

(b) Optimization of leakage

(c) Optimization of bias scaling

Fig. 3. Hyperparameter optimization

Training and inference of this ESN model with ca. 12M free parameters on a modern laptop CPU is still feasible, which is an important aspect for real-world applications. Further enlarging the reservoir still slightly improves the performance of the model, but at the cost of many more free parameters.

Figure 5 shows the transcription result for the first 30 s of the piano piece "MAPS_MUS-bk_xmas5_ENSTDkCl" computed with the bidirectional ESN model with 24 000 neurons (ESN 24 000bi). It can be seen that many false positive notes (green) were recognized in higher pitch areas. In many cases, a pitch was recognized along with a higher harmonic of itself, leading to an octave error. The missing notes often occurred for low pitches. However, most of the notes were recognized properly.

4.3   Comparison to the State of the Art

In Table 1, we summarize the performance of the proposed ESN-based acoustic models along with some reference models. It is worth to mention that all models but the CNN + LSTM [5] and ADSRNet [9] are supplied only with the extracted

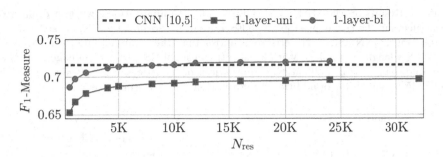

Fig. 4. Pitch detection results on the MAPS test dataset in the modified configuration 2 [5]: A strong dependency of the F_1-Measure from the reservoir size N_{res} and a uni- or bidirectional architectures can be observed.

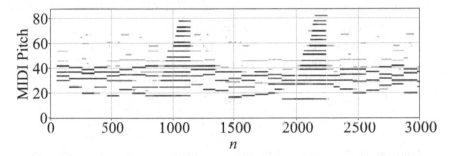

Fig. 5. Transcription result for the first 30 s of the piano piece "MAPS_MUS-bk_xmas5_ENSTDkCl" computed with the model "ESN 24 000b". The blue color (true positive) indicates that most of the notes are transcribed correctly. The green color (false positive) shows that the acoustic model recognized many additional notes, especially in the higher frequency ranges. The red color (false negative) indicates that, especially for lower pitches, several notes were not recognized. (Color figure online)

acoustic features and their derivatives. The latter onces also take advantage of much more information about, e.g., on-/offset or sustain pedal information in addition to the conventional acoustic features.

This comparison suggests that the bidirectional ESN as acoustic model outperforms the CNN-based model [10]. Furthermore, we suppose that the ESN is better than the INN for acoustic modeling, as it even suppresses the INNs with small language models (e.g. GRU (S) and LSTM (S)) as well. Only in case of a large bi-directional language model (biGRU), the models from [11,13] perform slightly better. In order to compare simple combinations of acoustic and language models more fairly, we have also trained a second layer that should denoise and smoothen the frame-based output of the acoustic model. We can see that this strongly improves the results. The middle rows of Table 1 show that our two-layer system perform better than the typical combinations of acoustic and language model.

Table 1. Results on the MAPS test dataset under Configuration 2 without duplicated music pieces in the training set [5]. The ESN has outperformed the CNN-based acoustic model. Both, CNN and ESN performed better than the combination of the INN with small RNN language models. With an additional small ESN-based language model, we were able to outperform all classic combinations of acoustic and language models. The models [5,9] with a lot of additional information still perform better.

Method	P	R	F_1	Only spectral features
CNN only [5,10]	**81.18**	65.07	71.60	x
ESN 32 000u	71.63	67.89	69.71	x
ESN 24 000b	72.89	**71.33**	**72.10**	x
INN + GRU (S) [11]	79.74	63.73	70.84	x
INN + LSTM (S) [11]	80.12	63.91	71.10	x
INN + biGRU (L) [11]	**81.72**	64.81	72.29	
CNN + RNN-NADE [5,13]	71.99	**73.32**	72.22	x
ESN 24 000b, 5000b	81.06	66.73	**73.20**	x
CNN + LSTM [5]	88.53	**70.89**	**78.30**	–
ADSRNet [9]	**90.73**	67.85	77.16	–

The models [5,9] are quite different in terms of utilizing additional information about on- and offset etc., and can thus be not entirely compared to the proposed ESN model. Table 1 shows that the additional information is very useful for piano transcription and significantly improves the recognition results. In the future, we will extend the current approach towards incorporating additional information in a similar way. We have not listed the results of [22] because in those experiments there is some overlap between the training and testing data.

5   Conclusions and Outlook

Our proposed ESN-based acoustic model for piano transcription, which relies on simple spectral features, outperformed a wide variety of deep learning models, such as CNN, INN, and hybrid models which benefit from combination of acoustic and language models. All approaches have in common that they purely rely on spectral feature vectors, from which note likelihoods are computed. Encouraged by promising results for onset detection using ESNs [14], one way to move forward would be to incorporate additional information about on-/offsets [5,6,9] in the current system and also to use the MAESTRO dataset. In [18], data augmentation was also shown to improve multipitch tracking.

Furthermore, we will investigate the length of effective future information in bidirectional ESNs. If only a limited window of future frames is required, ESNs could be incorporated into real-time systems for piano transcription.

Acknowledgement. The parameter optimizations were performed on a Bull Cluster at the Center for Information Services and High Performance Computing (ZIH) at TU Dresden. This research was also partially funded by Ghent University (BOF19/PDO/134).

References

1. Bay, M., Ehmann, A.F., Downie, J.S.: Evaluation of multiple-F0 estimation and tracking systems. In: Proceedings of the 10th International Society for Music Information Retrieval Conference, ISMIR 2009, 26–30 October 2009, Kobe, Japan, pp. 315–320 (2009). http://ismir2009.ismir.net/proceedings/PS2-21.pdf
2. Böck, S., Schedl, M.: Polyphonic piano note transcription with recurrent neural networks. In: ICASSP 2012–2012 IEEE International Conference on Acoustics, Speech and Signal Processing (ICASSP), pp. 121–124, March 2012
3. Cheng, T., Mauch, M., Benetos, E., Dixon, S.: An attack/decay model for piano transcription. In: Mandel, M.I., Devaney, J., Turnbull, D., Tzanetakis, G. (eds.) Proceedings of the 17th International Society for Music Information Retrieval Conference, ISMIR 2016, 7–11 August 2016, New York City, USA, pp. 584–590 (2016). https://archives.ismir.net/ismir2016/paper/000085.pdf
4. Emiya, V., Badeau, R., David, B.: Multipitch estimation of piano sounds using a new probabilistic spectral smoothness principle. IEEE Trans. Audio Speech Lang. Process. **18**(6), 1643–1654 (2010)
5. Hawthorne, C., et al.: Onsets and frames: dual-objective piano transcription. In: Gómez, E., Hu, X., Humphrey, E., Benetos, E. (eds.) Proceedings of the 19th International Society for Music Information Retrieval Conference, ISMIR 2018, 23–27 September 2018, Paris, France, pp. 50–57 (2018). http://ismir2018.ircam.fr/doc/pdfs/19_Paper.pdf
6. Hawthorne, C., et al.: Enabling factorized piano music modeling and generation with the MAESTRO dataset. In: International Conference on Learning Representations (2019). https://openreview.net/forum?id=r1lYRjC9F7
7. Jaeger, H.: The echo state approach to analysing and training recurrent neural networks. Technical report GMD Report 148, German National Research Center for Information Technology (2001). http://www.faculty.iu-bremen.de/hjaeger/pubs/EchoStatesTechRep.pdf
8. Jalalvand, A., Demuynck, K., Neve, W.D., Martens, J.P.: On the application of reservoir computing networks for noisy image recognition. Neurocomputing **277**, 237–248 (2018). hierarchical Extreme Learning Machines
9. Kelz, R., Böck, S., Widmer, G.: Deep polyphonic ADSR Piano note transcription. In: ICASSP 2019–2019 IEEE International Conference on Acoustics, Speech and Signal Processing (ICASSP), pp. 246–250, May 2019
10. Kelz, R., Dorfer, M., Korzeniowski, F., Böck, S., Arzt, A., Widmer, G.: On the potential of simple framewise approaches to piano transcription. In: Mandel, M.I., Devaney, J., Turnbull, D., Tzanetakis, G. (eds.) Proceedings of the 17th International Society for Music Information Retrieval Conference, ISMIR 2016, 7–11 August 2016, New York City, United States, pp. 475–481 (2016). https://wp.nyu.edu/ismir2016/wp-content/uploads/sites/2294/2016/07/179_Paper.pdf
11. Kelz, R., Widmer, G.: Towards interpretable polyphonic transcription with invertible neural networks. In: Flexer, A., Peeters, G., Urbano, J., Volk, A. (eds.) Proceedings of the 20th International Society for Music Information Retrieval Conference, ISMIR 2019, 4–8 November 2019, Delft, The Netherlands, pp. 376–383 (2019). http://archives.ismir.net/ismir2019/paper/000044.pdf

12. Raffel, C., et al.: mir_eval:a transparent implementation of common MIR metrics. In: Wang, H., Yang, Y., Lee, J.H. (eds.) Proceedings of the 15th International Society for Music Information Retrieval Conference, ISMIR 2014, Taipei, Taiwan, 27–31 October 2014, pp. 367–372 (2014). https://archives.ismir.net/ismir2014/paper/000320.pdf

13. Sigtia, S., Benetos, E., Dixon, S.: An end-to-end neural network for polyphonic piano music transcription. IEEE/ACM Trans. Audio Speech Lang. Process. **24**(5), 927–939 (2016)

14. Steiner, P., Jalalvand, A., Stone, S., Birkholz, P.: feature engineering and stacked echo state networks for musical onset detection. In: 2020 25th International Conference on Pattern Recognition (ICPR), pp. 9537–9544, January 2021

15. Steiner, P., Jalalvand, A., Stone, S., Birkholz, P.: PyRCN: Exploration and Application of ESNs (2021)

16. Steiner, P., Stone, S., Birkholz, P.: Note Onset Detection using Echo State Networks. In: Böck, R., Siegert, I., Wendemuth, A. (eds.) Studientexte zur Sprachkommunikation: Elektronische Sprachsignalverarbeitung 2020, pp. 157–164. TUDpress, Dresden (2020)

17. Steiner, P., Stone, S., Birkholz, P., Jalalvand, A.: Multipitch tracking in music signals using Echo state networks. In: 2020 28th European Signal Processing Conference (EUSIPCO), pp. 126–130 (2020). https://www.eurasip.org/Proceedings/Eusipco/Eusipco2020/pdfs/0000126.pdf

18. Thickstun, J., Harchaoui, Z., Foster, D.P., Kakade, S.M.: Invariances and data augmentation for supervised music transcription. In: ICASSP 2018–2018 IEEE International Conference on Acoustics, Speech and Signal Processing (ICASSP), pp. 2241–2245, April 2018

19. Thickstun, J., Harchaoui, Z., Kakade, S.M.: Learning features of music from scratch. In: 5th International Conference on Learning Representations, ICLR 2017, 24–26 April 2017, Toulon, France, Conference Track Proceedings (2017). https://openreview.net/forum?id=rkFBJv9gg

20. Triefenbach, F., Jalalvand, A., Schrauwen, B., Martens, J.P.: Phoneme recognition with large hierarchical reservoirs. In: Advances in Neural Information Processing Systems 23, pp. 2307–2315. Curran Associates, Inc. (2010). http://papers.nips.cc/paper/4056-phoneme-recognition-with-large-hierarchical-reservoirs.pdf

21. Wang, Q., Zhou, R., Yan, Y.: A two-stage approach to note-level transcription of a specific piano. Appl. Sci. **7**(9), 901 (2017)

22. Wu, Y., Chen, B., Su, L.: Polyphonic music transcription with semantic segmentation. In: ICASSP 2019–2019 IEEE International Conference on Acoustics, Speech and Signal Processing (ICASSP), pp. 166–170, May 2019

On Effects of Compression with Hyperdimensional Computing in Distributed Randomized Neural Networks

Antonello Rosato[1], Massimo Panella[1(✉)], Evgeny Osipov[2], and Denis Kleyko[3,4]

[1] University of Rome "La Sapienza", Rome, Italy
{antonello.rosato,massimo.panella}@uniroma1.it
[2] Luleå University of Technology, Luleå, Sweden
evgeny.osipov@ltu.se
[3] Research Institutes of Sweden, Kista, Sweden
denis.kleyko@ri.se
[4] University of California, Berkeley, USA

Abstract. A change of the prevalent supervised learning techniques is foreseeable in the near future: from the complex, computational expensive algorithms to more flexible and elementary training ones. The strong revitalization of randomized algorithms can be framed in this prospect steering. We recently proposed a model for distributed classification based on randomized neural networks and hyperdimensional computing, which takes into account cost of information exchange between agents using compression. The use of compression is important as it addresses the issues related to the communication bottleneck, however, the original approach is rigid in the way the compression is used. Therefore, in this work, we propose a more flexible approach to compression and compare it to conventional compression algorithms, dimensionality reduction, and quantization techniques.

Keywords: Distributed randomized neural networks · Compression · Vector symbolic architectures · Hyperdimensional computing

1 Introduction

In this work, we are exploring the use of compression in a framework for distributed classification. The main motivation of this work is the optimization of the distributed machine learning algorithm when computational and communication costs are to be preserved as is the case in, e.g., resource-constrained scenarios (e.g., edge machine learning [43], smart sensing and privacy-preserving algorithms [8]). Broadly, the objective for compression can be formulated as

The work of D.K. was supported by the European Union's Horizon 2020 Programme under the Marie Skłodowska-Curie Individual Fellowship Grant (839179) and in part by the DARPA's AIE (HyDDENN) program and by AFOSR FA9550-19-1-0241.

© Springer Nature Switzerland AG 2021
I. Rojas et al. (Eds.): IWANN 2021, LNCS 12862, pp. 155–167, 2021.
https://doi.org/10.1007/978-3-030-85099-9_13

finding the best trade-off between classification performance and the communication overhead, which is crucial in the distributed scenario, instead of adopting direct methods for data compression on specific frameworks, as typical for multimedia applications [34]. In this scenario, and generally in distributed solutions, the communication bottleneck is often overlooked, since the tendency is to focus on efficient algorithmic choices and implementations improving classification performance. We, however, aim at developing a flexible solution, which allows controlling the trade-off between classification performance and reduction of the communication overheads. In [36] we presented a novel concept for distributed learning based on a class of randomized neural networks known as Random Vector Functional Link (RVFL) networks [14,16,37] using framework of hyperdimensional computing also known as vector symbolic architectures (HDC/VSA) [10,11,20,32,33].

The main contribution of this article is the in-depth empirical evaluation of the effect of compressing information shared between agents participating in the distributed learning. We present the trade-offs between the accuracy of the neural model and various compression approaches as means of reducing the risk for the communication bottleneck. These results further extend the functionality of our distributed RVFL learning solution with a generalized approach for controlling the compression ratio under different communication bottleneck conditions.

The experiments reported in this paper were done with two approaches to forming network's classifier: regularized least squares (RLS) and centroids. Though, other alternatives are available [1,5,22,38]. The activations of the hidden layer of the network were formed according to a recently proposed version of RVFL network [25], which simplifies the conventional architecture [16] using some of the HDC/VSA principles [24,27].

When studying the effect of compressing the classifier, we focused on analysing our inherently lossy compression approach in a range of compression ratios, along with the conventional, entropic lossless compression. It was also important to contrast the proposed approach with some other conventional lossy approaches. However, we have not identified such an approach, which would compress generic numeric matrices (i.e., classifiers) without assuming a particular data modality (e.g., images) since for such data lossy compression is well performed based on perceptual (e.g., visual) models. However, a lossy compression of the matrix containing the classifier can be done with the conventional methods for dimensionality reduction. In particular, we implemented a lossy approach, which relies on the eigenvectors and eigenvalues obtained from the Singular Value Decomposition (SVD) of the classifier. The approach uses the fact that some of the eigenvalues with the smallest values and the corresponding eigenvectors can be ignored when reconstructing the classifier.

2   Compression Algorithms

As already stated, the main purpose of the compression in the considered distributed scenario is in reducing the communication overhead, thus, improving the feasibility and applicability of the distributed classification. We are particularly interested in the lossy compression, which might results in decreased classification performance compared to the uncompressed solution, since it should allow controlling the trade-off between the compression ratio and classification performance losses.

To better understand the experiments reported hereafter, in which we assess and analyse the performance of the proposed approach, it is important to clarify the parts of the model involved in the compression. The network consists of connected agents (we assume full connectivity in our experiments); each agent has its own training dataset. We form agents' datasets by equally splitting samples of the whole dataset between agents without replacement. So each agent has the access to a subset of samples of the whole dataset with all the features. Each agent trains its own local model with its portion of the dataset and shares information about its own classifier (denoted as $\mathbf{W}^{out}$) with all other agents (due to the full connectivity), thus, the training data are not actually shared but kept private. Additionally, in this work, before sharing values of its local classifier with others, each agent compresses it. At the receiving end, each agent decompresses the data it received and incorporates them in the aggregated model to be able to create a more powerful classifier.

Below, we describe three compression approaches used herein highlighting their differences. Classification performance obtained with these approaches is reported and discussed in Sect. 3.2.

2.1   Compression Based on Conventional Algorithms

We describe hereafter the two compression approaches used to compare with the proposed approach. As already stated, they are general and, although, implemented specifically for the purpose of the presented distributed classification, they only make use of well-known conventional algorithms.

Lossless Compression. The most common and effective way to perform compression on a matrix is using one of the many conventional lossless compression algorithms readily available and widely assessed. We opted for the ones in the zlib software library for data compression, which use the public domain ZLIB Deflator algorithm. The algorithm uses the Deflate file format, employing a combination of LZSS and Huffman coding (see [4] for more details). In this work, the lossless compression is given as a baseline of how strong is the gain of the proposed approach in terms of information compression. Since it is impractical from the application point of view, given that the operations needed to perform it at the local nodes are computationally expensive with respect to the actual classification model. Moreover, when using the lossless compression, the classification performance of the model is the same as in the uncompressed case but the compression ratio is fixed to the one obtained by the compression algorithm.

Lossy Compression. Lossy quantization of a data matrix is well performed in the case of audio and video applications, using specific techniques. Such techniques are not of interest herein since they are based on auditory and visual perceptual models that are not applicable in our scenario. Nevertheless, one way to decrease the size of the classifier is by quantizing matrix values to some fixed number of quantization levels. We will discuss this approach in Sect. 4.3.

In the absence of quantization, dimensionality reduction methods can serve for the purpose of compression. In particular, we use the eigenvectors and eigenvalues obtained from the SVD and the compression is based on the fact that eigenvalues with smaller, negligible norm can be discarded.

In practice, we carry out the SVD-based compression by first transforming the classifier $\mathbf{W}^{out}$ with the SVD. Given that the values of $\mathbf{W}^{out}$ are real, this results in the well-known factorization: $\mathbf{U\Sigma V}$. Given the properties of the SVD, if the eigenvalues and both the left and right eigenvectors are transmitted as is, another agent is able to losslessly reconstruct the original matrix. Of course, this is completely impractical for compression and sharing, since the dimension of the transmitted information in the form of the three matrices $\mathbf{U}$, $\mathbf{\Sigma}$ and $\mathbf{V}$ is much larger than the original classifier $\mathbf{W}^{out}$.

For the compression purpose, to ensure the reduction of the size of the matrices to be transmitted, each agent selects and transmits only a portion of the SVD matrices, corresponding to a number t of the largest eigenvalues, resulting in what is often called a "truncated SVD" ($\mathbf{U}_t$, $\mathbf{\Sigma}_t$ and $\mathbf{V}_t$), as it is used for proper dimensionality reduction [41]. This way, the receiving agent is able to reconstruct a version of the original classifier: $\hat{\mathbf{W}}^{out} = \mathbf{U}_t\mathbf{\Sigma}_t\mathbf{V}_t$, which is not an exact replica, since some information is lost due to the truncation. To be able to effectively control the lossy compression ratio of the classifier, we reshape $\mathbf{W}^{out}$ into a square matrix (with zero padding if necessary) and then select t eigenvalues based on the desired compression ratio.

2.2   Compression Based on HDC/VSA Principles

In our previous work [36], we proposed how to use the principles of HDC/VSA to compress the classifier $\mathbf{W}^{out}$. Here we recapitulate it. The key idea is that before being shared with the other agents a locally computed version of $\mathbf{W}^{out(p)}$ can be compressed into a single D-dimensional vector (hypervector, denoted as $\mathbf{w}$) For the proposed approach we use Holographic Reduced Representations model [32].

The compression procedure uses the idea of key-value pair representations in HDC/VSA[1]. In the compression context, a key hypervector is generated randomly where a value hypervector contains some of the values from $\mathbf{W}^{out(p)}$. The hypervector of a key-value pair is formed via the binding operation. In the Holographic Reduced Representations model, the binding operation is realized via

---

[1] This is possible since HDC/VSA provide primitives for representing structured data in hypervectors such as sequences [9,12,20,40], sets [20], [29], state automata [44], [31], hierarchies, or predicate relations [32], [33]. Please consult [23] for a general overview.

the circular convolution (denoted as ⊛), which is formulated through the outer product of the hypervectors being bound. The value of the jth component of $\mathbf{z}$ is calculated as:

$$\mathbf{z}_j = \sum_{k=0}^{D-1} \mathbf{y}_k \mathbf{x}_{j-k} \mod D$$

In [36], it was proposed to form L key-value pairs where L denotes the number of classes in the task. The disadvantage of this proposal is that the compression ratio is fixed to L to so the procedure is inflexible. Here we show that the procedure can be simply modified so that the compression ratio can take any positive integer value. To do so, for the chosen compression ratio (denoted as R), we first calculate the number of dimensions D in $\mathbf{w}$ as: $D = \lceil HL/R \rceil$, where H denotes the size of the hidden layer. Then $\mathbf{W}^{\text{out}}$ should be reshaped (denoted as $\mathbf{S}$) such that is has D rows and R columns. Note that some zero padding might be necessary when HL is not a multiple of R. Next, R random hypervectors (denoted as $\mathbf{K}_i$) are generated. They act as keys. Each column in $\mathbf{S}$ is then bound with the corresponding key: $\mathbf{K}_i \circledast \mathbf{S}_i$. Finally, these key-value hypervectors are used to form the compressed version of the classifier:

$$\mathbf{w} = \sum_{i=1}^{R} \mathbf{K}_i \circledast \mathbf{S}_i;$$

$\mathbf{w}$ can be shared with other agents in an attempt to improve the classification.

When the agent p receives $\mathbf{w}$ from its neighbour q it needs to decompress $\mathbf{W}^{\text{out}(q)}$ from $\mathbf{w}$. The decompression is done for each $\mathbf{S}_i^{(q)}$ using the inverses of the corresponding key hypervectors of q (see [32] for the details) as:

$$\hat{\mathbf{S}}_i^{(q)} \approx \mathbf{w} \circledast \mathbf{K}_i^{-1}.$$

Finally, $\hat{\mathbf{S}}^{(q)}$ has to be reshaped to get $\hat{\mathbf{W}}^{\text{out}(q)}$. Note that the reconstructed classifier $\hat{\mathbf{W}}^{\text{out}(q)}$ will not be the exact replica of the original one. This is explained by the fact that the superposition operation is lossy in a sense that hypervectors of other key-value pairs add their crosstalk noise to the resultant hypervector [9,30]. It was, however, shown in [36] that when many reconstructed classifiers are combined, the noise will average out without affecting much the classification performance. At the same time, it is expected that the compression ratio R will regulate how lossy is the compression and, therefore, it will affect the classification performance. The effect of R on the classification performance is shown experimentally in Sect. 3.2.

3   Experiments

3.1   Data and Setup

The experiments reported in this paper were performed on a collection of 18 real-world classifications datasets from the UCI Machine Learning Repository [6]. The

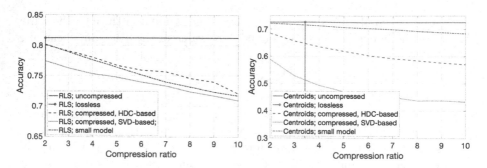

Fig. 1. The average accuracy on the datasets against different compression ratios in the proposed procedure. The number of agents was set to 10.

datasets are a subset of a larger collection used in the seminal work [7]. The only addition, which was introduced to the preprocessing, was the normalization of input features to $[0, 1]$ range as this is necessary to form the thermometer codes used in the model. In the distributed scenario, it is important that each agent gets some training samples. Since we limited ourselves to splitting training data between agents without the replacement, only datasets with more than $1,000$ samples in the training part were considered. Another requirement was the size of the hidden layer, H. In order to be able to make a comparison between compressed classifiers and smaller models of the corresponding size, only the datasets where the optimal H was more than $1,300$ were picked. Only 18 datasets in the collection satisfied both requirements[2].

The optimal hyperparameters of the models (H, λ, and κ) for each dataset were obtained with the grid search using the same steps as in [7] using the centralized scenario with the RLS classifier. H varied in the range $[50,1500]$ with step 50; λ varied in the range $2^{[-10,5]}$ with step 1; and κ varied between $\{1, 3, 7, 15\}$. The chosen values were used for both classifiers and in all the experiments reported below. To avoid the influence of a particular random initialization on the performance, all results reported below were averaged for 10 random initializations of $\mathbf{W}^{in}$, which is the input projection matrix.

3.2   Results

For the lossless compression, the results were analysed only in terms of a single compression ratio. This is straightforward because, being lossless, no information is missing at the decompression receiving end of the network, and each agent can retrieve the exact copy of the classifier sent by its neighbours. Thus, in Fig. 1 for

---

[2] The names of the datasets were: Abalone, Cardiotocography (10 classes) Chess (King-Rook vs. King-Pawn), Letter, Oocytes merluccius nucleus 4D, Oocytes merluccius states 2F, Pendigits, Plant margin, Plant shape, Plant texture, Ringnorm,Semeion, Spambase, Statlog landsat, Steel plates, Waveform, Waveform noise, Yeast.

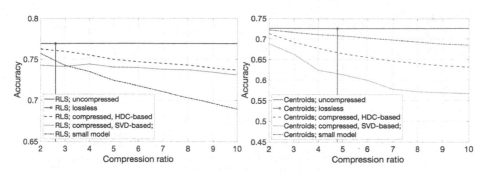

Fig. 2. The average accuracy on the datasets against different compression ratios in the proposed procedure. The number of agents was set to 100.

$N = 10$ agents and Fig. 2 for $N = 100$ agents, the achieved compression ratio for the lossless algorithm is depicted by bars. Naturally, the accuracies were equal to the corresponding uncompressed versions of the classifiers. We stress the fact that this case has only the effect of making the lossy results be examined in terms of compression ratio, giving us the comparison with a compression procedure optimized for much larger models and agents with superior computational power.

The advantage of the lossless compression is that it preserves all of the accuracy but there is no way to control its compression ratio. The proposed compression procedure (Sect. 2.2) and the SVD-based one (Sect. 2.1) are lossy but they allow varying the compression ratio.

In order to investigate the effect of the compression ratio on the accuracy, we performed the experiments in the distributed scenario with both procedures for both classifiers. Figure 1 presents the results of the experiments for the case when the number of agents was set $N = 10$ while Fig. 2 reports the results for $N = 100$. As the baseline, the figures depict the accuracies of the distributed scenario when no compression was evolved (solid lines). For both classifiers, this baseline acted as an upper bound as losses introduced to the classifiers during the decompression incurred decreased classification performance. Obviously, the accuracy of both classifiers was getting worse with the increased compression ratio but given the same ratio, the RLS classifier always outperformed the centroids one.

Note that an approach alternative to the compression would be to train a smaller model and share it with other agents without involving any compression. Therefore, for each compression ratio we trained a model with smaller hidden layer (denoted as "small model" in the figure) such that the size of smaller model's classifier would equal to the compressed classifier of the full-size model. In the case of the centroids classifier for both N, small models (dash-dotted line) performed much closer to the baseline than the compressed centroids. The explanation is likely rooted in the fact that to have a fair comparison in the experiments we used the size of the hidden layer optimized for the RLS classifier. Since the centroids classifier is much simpler it is likely that it would need smaller

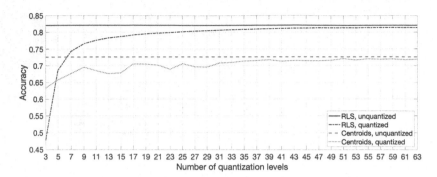

Fig. 3. The average accuracy against different number of quantization levels for $\mathbf{W}^{\mathrm{out}}$.

size of the hidden layer to get most of its classification performance and so its small models were pretty close to the baseline. In contrast, for the RLS classifier and the proposed approach when $N = 10$, for small compression ratios (2 or 3) the compressed classifier and small model performed on a par. However, when the compression ratio was increasing, the compressed classifier was performing better than the corresponding small model. In the case of $N = 100$, the proposed approach was noticeably better than the small models. That is expected because in the proposed approach noise introduced to the decompressed classifiers gets averaged out and the more classifiers get aggregated the better it is for mitigating the noise.

With respect to the SVD-based compression, for both values of N, the trend of results in terms of accuracy/compression ratio trade-off was as expected. In particular, the mean values follow the same trend as for the proposed approach, with the difference that the achieved accuracy was always lower. This can be likely caused by the fact that even least significant eigenvectors bear important information about the classifier so when truncated, the decompressed classifier misses important information. Results indicated that SVD-based compression, while remaining a solid dimensionality reduction method, was inferior in terms of accuracy/compression ratio trade-off compared to the proposed approach.

4 Discussion

4.1 Results

The main point is that, when choosing the compression approach, it is important to consider the burden of the cost of performing the compression procedure for each local agent, given that the studied solution should be deployed on resource-constrained devices. To this end, we note that the proposed compression approach based on HDC/VSA is the most efficient one, being tailored for such devices, while, to a greater extent, the SVD and the lossless ones can be considered as having a lower efficiency but the exact comparison in terms of computational costs is outside the scope of this paper.

4.2   Relation to Other Areas

The proposed approach hinges on principles and premises, which are studied in the federated learning framework [19, 42]. Namely, the availability of raw data only at local agents (i.e., "siloed data") and the impossibility of sharing such raw data are a standard premise in the federated learning. In fact, depending on the definition used, there are certain aspects which might differ; in particular, in our work, there is an absence of a "master" agent orchestrating the training, which is often present in the federated learning. This fundamental distinction makes our work challenging in several aspects (computation, combination) that are specific to the fully distributed scenarios. Thus, while this work could be considered as a particular case of the federated learning, our work has a significance and purpose by itself and should be studied as a distinct field, given also the different practical application. Similarly, there are previous studies in HDC/VSA domain [17, 28], which investigated the distributed scenario but all of them assumed some elements of centralization.

It also worth noting that while the experiments reported here were done with shallow randomized neural networks, the proposed approach is applicable to deep randomized neural networks [2], which recently gained quite a lot of attraction. This is so since the same principle can be used – only information about the trainable part of the model (i.e., classifier) should be exchanged by the agents, while the randomly chosen part of the network can be the same for every agent. In principle, the proposed compression approach could be used even for fully trained neural networks; there is, however, a risk that decompression losses at earlier layers might results in additional errors at the later layers. Nevertheless, it is worth clarifying this in the experiments.

The proposed compression approach is conceptually related to the recent idea of using the binding and superposition operations of HDC/VSA to represent parameters of many deep neural networks in a single hypervector [3, 13, 45]. The difference with the proposed approach is that the classifier is decompressed back to its original shape, which was not the case in [3]. The attempts to apply HDC/VSA in the communication domain [18, 21, 26, 39] are also of relevance but there the goal would usually be to extract the data back from the hypervector without any losses, which is not the case in this work.

4.3   Quantization of the Classifier

In the previous experiments, the weights in $\mathbf{W}^{\text{out}}$ being compressed were real-valued since the proposed compression approach is real-valued as well. It is, however, known that neural networks can perform well even when the weights are limited to a few quantization levels [15, 35]. Therefore, we did an experiment to demonstrate what to potentially expect for the quantization of $\mathbf{W}^{\text{out}}$. For the sake of simplicity, the experiment was done using the centralized scenario so $N = 1$. The goal of this experiment was to explore whether it is worth considering quantizing the classifier before the compression.

Figure 3 presents the average accuracy of the RLS (dash-dotted line) and centroids (dotted line) classifiers (uncompressed) on all 18 datasets against the number quantization levels being used. The corresponding accuracies (solid and dashed lines) from the unquantized real-valued $\mathbf{W}^{out}$ were used as the baselines. When $\mathbf{W}^{out}$ of the RLS classifier was quantized to very few levels (3 or 5) the accuracy was affected significantly. It is, however, clear that for the increased number of levels the accuracy of both classifier started to reach their unquantized baselines. The results, thus, suggest that allocating one byte per weight should preserve most of the classification performance. Note that in the proposed approach, $\mathbf{w}$ with the compressed version of $\mathbf{W}^{out}$ can also be represented with fewer than 32 bits per weight. It is expected that decreasing the precision of $\mathbf{w}$ will just add some additional noise during the reconstruction. Obtaining the quantitative results to characterize the effect of this noise will be a part of the future extension of this work.

5   Conclusions

We presented a study exploring the effect of compression on classification performance in a distributed classification scenario. The main goal was to explore the proposed compression approach, which is based on HDC/VSA principles. By examining the numerical results obtained on a collection of 18 datasets for three compression approaches, it is concluded that the proposed approach has a favourable trade-off in terms of accuracy and communication costs. Also, the finding that small models perform well or on a par with respect to other schemes is worth exploring, and can be considered as enriching the presently relevant discussion regarding the convenience of training large, deep models. Further, future studies should investigate the sensitivity of the overall performance of the proposed approach with respect to residual coding schemes of matrix coefficients, similarly to what is performed in linear predictive coding and adaptive coding of spectral coefficients, as well as considering some parsimonious model representation strategies as, for instance, Minimum Description Length (MDL) and Bayesian Information Criterion (BIC).

References

1. Alonso, P., Shridhar, K., Kleyko, D., Osipov, E., Liwicki, M.: HyperEmbed: HyperEmbed: Trade-offs Between Resources and Performance in NLP Tasks with Hyperdimensional Computing enabled Embedding of n-gram Statisticss. In: International Joint Conference on Neural Networks (IJCNN), pp. 1–9 (2021)
2. Ben-Nun, T., Hoefler, T.: Demystifying parallel and distributed deep learning: an in-depth concurrency analysis. ACM Comput. Surv. **52**(4), 1–43 (2019)
3. Cheung, B., Terekhov, A., Chen, Y., Agrawal, P., Olshausen, B.A.: Superposition of Many Models into One. In: Advances in Neural Information Processing Systems (NeurIPS), pp. 10868–10877 (2019). https://papers.nips.cc/paper/2019/file/4c7a167bb329bd92580a99ce422d6fa6-Paper.pdf

4. Deutsch, P., Gailly, J.L.: RFC1950: ZLIB Compressed Data Format Specification Version, vol. 3, p. 3 (1996)
5. Diao, C., Kleyko, D., Rabaey, J.M., Olshausen, B.A.: Generalized Learning Vector Quantization for Classification in Randomized Neural Networks and Hyperdimensional Computing. In: International Joint Conference on Neural Networks (IJCNN), pp. 1–9 (2021)
6. Dua, D., Graff, C.: UCI Machine Learning Repository (2017). http://archive.ics.uci.edu/ml
7. Fernández-Delgado, M., Cernadas, E., Barro, S., Amorim, D.: Do we need hundreds of classifiers to solve real world classification problems? J. Mach. Learn. Res. **15**(90), 3133–3181 (2014)
8. Fierimonte, R., Scardapane, S., Uncini, A., Panella, M.: Fully decentralized semi-supervised learning via privacy-preserving matrix completion. IEEE Trans. Neural Netw. Learn. Syst. **28**(11), 2699–2711 (2017)
9. Frady, E.P., Kleyko, D., Sommer, F.T.: A theory of sequence indexing and working memory in recurrent neural networks. Neural Comput. **30**, 1449–1513 (2018)
10. Frady, E.P., Kleyko, D., Sommer, F.T.: Variable binding for sparse distributed representations: theory and applications. arXiv:2009.06734, pp. 1–16 (2020)
11. Gayler, R.W.: Multiplicative binding, representation operators and analogy. In: Advances in Analogy Research: Integration of Theory and Data from the Cognitive, Computational, and Neural Sciences, pp. 1–4 (1998)
12. Hannagan, T., Dupoux, E., Christophe, A.: Holographic string encoding. Cogn. Sci. **35**(1), 79–118 (2011)
13. Hersche, M., Rupp, P., Benini, L., Rahimi, A.: Compressing subject-specific brain-computer interface models into one model by superposition in hyperdimensional space. In: 2020 Design, Automation and Test in Europe Conference and Exhibition (DATE), pp. 246–251. IEEE (2020)
14. Huang, G., Zhu, Q., Siew, C.: Extreme learning machine: theory and applications. Neurocomputing **70**(1–3), 489–501 (2006)
15. Hubara, I., Courbariaux, M., Soudry, D., El-Yaniv, R., Bengio, Y.: Quantized neural networks: training neural networks with low precision weights and activations. J. Mach. Learn. Res. **18**, 1–30 (2018)
16. Igelnik, B., Pao, Y.: Stochastic choice of basis functions in adaptive function approximation and the functional-link net. IEEE Trans. Neural Netw. **6**, 1320–1329 (1995)
17. Imani, M., et al.: A framework for collaborative learning in secure high-dimensional space. In: 2019 IEEE 12th International Conference on Cloud Computing (CLOUD), pp. 435-446. IEEE (2019)
18. Jakimovski, P., Schmidtke, H.R., Sigg, S., Chaves, L.W.F., Beigl, M.: Collective communication for dense sensing environments. J. Ambient Intell. Smart Environ. **4**(2), 123–134 (2012)
19. Kairouz, P., McMahan, H.B., Avent, B., Bellet, A., Bennis, M., et al.: Advances and Open Problems in Federated Learning. arXiv:1912.04977, pp. 1–121 (2019)
20. Kanerva, P.: Hyperdimensional computing: an introduction to computing in distributed representation with high-dimensional random vectors. Cogn. Comput. **1**(2), 139–159 (2009)
21. Kim, H.: HDM: Hyper-dimensional modulation for robust low-power communications. In: 2018 IEEE International Conference on Communications (ICC), pp. 1–6. IEEE (2018)

22. Kim, Y., Imani, M., Rosing, T.S.: Efficient human activity recognition using hyper-dimensional computing. In: Proceedings of the 8th International Conference on the Internet of Things, pp. 1–6 (2018)
23. Kleyko, D., et al.: Vector Symbolic Architectures as a Computing Framework for Nanoscale Hardware. arXiv:2106.05268, pp. 1–28 (2021)
24. Kleyko, D., Frady, E.P., Kheffache, M., Osipov, E.: Integer echo state networks: efficient reservoir computing for digital hardware. IEEE Trans. Neural Netw. Learn. Syst. **PP(99)**, 1–14 (2020)
25. Kleyko, D., Kheffache, M., Frady, E.P., Wiklund, U., Osipov, E.: Density encoding enables resource-efficient randomly connected neural networks. IEEE Trans. Neural Netw. Learn. Syst. **32**(8), 3777–3783 (2021)
26. Kleyko, D., Lyamin, N., Osipov, E., Riliskis, L.: Dependable MAC layer architecture based on holographic data representation using hyper-dimensional binary spatter codes. In: Multiple Access Communications (MACOM). Lecture Notes in Computer Science, vol. 7642, pp. 134–145 (2012)
27. Kleyko, D., Osipov, E., De Silva, D., Wiklund, U., Alahakoon, D.: Integer self-organizing maps for digital hardware. In: 2019 International Joint Conference on Neural Networks (IJCNN), pp. 1–8. IEEE (2019)
28. Kleyko, D., Osipov, E., Papakonstantinou, N., Vyatkin, V.: Hyperdimensional computing in industrial systems: the use-case of distributed fault isolation in a power plant. IEEE Access **6**, 30766–30777 (2018)
29. Kleyko, D., Rahimi, A., Gayler, R.W., Osipov, E.: Autoscaling bloom filter: controlling trade-off between true and false positives. Neural Comput. Appl. **32**, 3675–3684 (2020)
30. Kleyko, D., Rosato, A., Frady, E.P., Panella, M., Sommer, F.T.: Perceptron Theory for Predicting the Accuracy of Neural Networks. arXiv:2012.07881, pp. 1–12 (2020)
31. Osipov, E., Kleyko, D., Legalov, A.: Associative synthesis of finite state automata model of a controlled object with hyperdimensional computing. In: IECON 2017-43rd Annual Conference of the IEEE Industrial Electronics Society, pp. 3276-3281. IEEE (2017)
32. Plate, T.A.: Holographic Reduced Representations: Distributed Representation for Cognitive Structures. Center for the Study of Language and Information (CSLI), Stanford (2003)
33. Rachkovskij, D.A.: Representation and processing of structures with binary sparse distributed codes. IEEE Trans. Knowl. Data Eng. **3**(2), 261–276 (2001)
34. Rizzi, A., Buccino, N.M., Panella, M., Uncini, A.: Genre classification of compressed audio data. In: 2008 IEEE 10th Workshop on Multimedia Signal Processing, pp. 654–659. IEEE (2008)
35. Rosato, A., Altilio, R., Panella, M.: Finite precision implementation of random vector functional-link networks. In: 2017 22nd International Conference on Digital Signal Processing (DSP), pp. 1–5. IEEE (2017)
36. Rosato, A., Panella, M., Kleyko, D.: Hyperdimensional Computing for Efficient Distributed Classification with Randomized Neural Networks. In: International Joint Conference on Neural Networks(IJCNN), pp. 1–10 (2021)
37. Scardapane, S., Wang, D.: Randomness in neural networks: an overview. Data Min. Knowl. Disc. **7**(2), 1–18 (2017)
38. Shridhar, K., Jain, H., Agarwal, A., Kleyko, D.: End to end binarized neural networks for text classification. In: Workshop on Simple and Efficient Natural Language Processing (SustaiNLP), pp. 29–34 (2020)

39. Simpkin, C., Taylor, I., Bent, G.A., de Mel, G., Rallapalli, S., Ma, L., Srivatsa, M.: Constructing distributed time-critical applications using cognitive enabled services. Futur. Gener. Comput. Syst. **100**, 70–85 (2019)
40. Thomas, A., Dasgupta, S., Rosing, T.: Theoretical Foundations of Hyperdimensional Computing. arXiv:2010.07426, pp. 1–32 (2020)
41. Xu, P.: Truncated SVD methods for discrete linear Ill-posed problems. Geophys. J. Int. **135**(2), 505–514 (1998)
42. Yang, Q., Liu, Y., Chen, T., Tong, Y.: Federated machine learning: concept and applications. ACM Trans. Intell. Syst. Technol. **10**(2), 1–19 (2019)
43. Yazici, M.T., Basurra, S., Gaber, M.M.: Edge machine learning: enabling smart internet of things applications. Big Data Cogn. Comput. **2**(3), 1–17 (2018)
44. Yerxa, T., Anderson, A., Weiss, E.: The hyperdimensional stack machine. In: Cognitive Computing, pp. 1–2 (2018)
45. Zeman, M., Osipov, E., Bosnic, Z.: Compressed Superposition of Neural Networks for Deep Learning in Edge Computing. In: International Joint Conference on Neural Networks (IJCNN), pp. 1–8 (2021)

Benchmarking Reservoir and Recurrent Neural Networks for Human State and Activity Recognition

Davide Bacciu[ID], Daniele Di Sarli[(✉)][ID], Claudio Gallicchio[ID],
Alessio Micheli[ID], and Niccolò Puccinelli

University of Pisa, Pisa, Italy
bacciu@di.unipi.it, daniele.disarli@phd.unipi.it,
{claudio.gallicchio,alessio.micheli}@unipi.it,
n.puccinelli1@studenti.unipi.it

Abstract. Monitoring of human states from streams of sensor data is an appealing applicative area for Recurrent Neural Network (RNN) models. In such a scenario, Echo State Network (ESN) models from the Reservoir Computing paradigm can represent good candidates due to the efficient training algorithms, which, compared to fully trainable RNNs, definitely ease embedding on edge devices.

In this paper, we provide an experimental analysis aimed at assessing the performance of ESNs on tasks of human state and activity recognition, in both shallow and deep setups. Our analysis is conducted in comparison with vanilla RNNs, Long Short-Term Memory, Gated Recurrent Units, and their deep variations. Our empirical results on several datasets clearly indicate that, despite their simplicity, ESNs are able to achieve a level of accuracy that is competitive with those models that require full adaptation of the parameters. From a broader perspective, our analysis also points out that recurrent networks can be a first choice for the class of tasks under consideration, in particular in their deep and gated variants.

Keywords: Recurrent neural networks · Echo state networks · Human psychological state recognition · Human activity recognition

1 Introduction

The class of recurrent neural networks provides a comprehensive framework for learning in the context of sequential data. Besides canonical applications in the area of speech and text processing, recurrent neural networks are often considered the primary choice for learning tasks over time series data such as sensor streams. In particular, the inductive biases of recurrent networks [9] (such as

This work is supported by the EC H2020 programme under project TEACHING (grant n. 871385).

© Springer Nature Switzerland AG 2021
I. Rojas et al. (Eds.): IWANN 2021, LNCS 12862, pp. 168–179, 2021.
https://doi.org/10.1007/978-3-030-85099-9_14

their fading memory property) can be particularly suited for a variety of tasks. For example, an intuitively good fit of their bias is for tasks related to human state and activity recognition from physiological sensors.

Being able to accurately identify and predict the cognitive, physical or psychological state of a human is of fundamental relevance across multiple application scenarios, such as ambient assisted living, healthcare and wellness applications [2]. When humans are subjected to the decisions and operations of an autonomous application, a precise and timely characterization of their psychophysical state becomes a necessary step to ensure their safety and comfort. Notable applications, in this sense, are autonomous transportation and cooperative human-robot assembly lines. Within such a context, the human state is not only a watchdog for controlling the execution of the autonomous routines, but it can also become a proxy to a non-supervised form of teaching signal that can drive the adaptation of the autonomous system, following the responses that its actions elicit on the humans. The work presented in this paper has been developed within the context of the H2020 project TEACHING[1] [3], which is an ongoing research endeavor targeting specifically the provisioning of innovative methods and systems to enable the development of the next-generation of adaptive autonomous applications. TEACHING puts forward a human-centric perspective based on a synergistic collaboration between the human and the autonomous application, mediated by human psycho-physical reactions, that becomes a driver for adaptation and personalization of the application. The work described in this paper is prodromal to the identification of the candidate learning model to realize a system capable of inferring human state from wearable and environmental sensing devices.

The prediction of the physical or psychological state of a human from sensors requires strong tolerance to noise [1], flexibility to the different personal characteristics of each subject, and, in most practical context, computational efficiency due to the embedding of the models on board of low-power devices. It has been previously shown that Echo State Networks (ESNs) [14,15], from the paradigm of Reservoir Computing [30], are efficient recurrent models [11] which can achieve high predictive performance in human activity recognition applications [4,21]. Recently, it has even been shown that ESN models are capable of an optimal form of federated learning [5], which is often instrumental in human-centric tasks. However, to the best of our knowledge, in the literature there exists no study comprehensively analyzing the performance of ESNs with that achievable by fully trainable alternatives on this kind of tasks or on those regarding the classification of the psychological state.

With this study we set the goal of benchmarking recurrent neural network models for tasks of human state and activity recognition. We do so in a uniform context, and through rigorous experimental settings, considering several datasets from the literature. For our comparison, in addition to the aforementioned ESNs, we will employ the most popular fully trainable recurrent neural architectures, namely the vanilla Recurrent Neural Network (RNN), the Long

---

[1] www.teaching-h2020.eu.

Short-Term Memory (LSTM) [13] and the Gated Recurrent Unit (GRU) [7]. Moreover, given the architectural and training differences of these models, we also discuss the effects of layering.

The rest of this paper is organized as follows. In Sect. 2 we introduce the neural network models under consideration, which will be used for the experimental comparison described in Sect. 3, where we also discuss the results of the study. Finally, in Sect. 4 we draw the conclusions.

2 Background

In this section we provide a brief overview of the recurrent neural network models under consideration. In doing so, we will consider general learning tasks based on sequence classification. In particular, we introduce Vanilla RNNs in Sect. 2.1, ESNs in Sect. 2.2, LSTMs in Sect. 2.3, and GRUs in Sect. 2.4. Note that, for simplicity of exposition, we omit the bias term from all equations.

2.1 Vanilla Recurrent Neural Networks

Vanilla Recurrent Neural Networks (RNNs) are one of the simplest and most widely known recurrent models [18]. The discrete-time evolution of the internal state $\mathbf{h}(t) \in \mathbb{R}^{N_R}$ is described by the recurrent equation

$$\mathbf{h}(t) = \tanh(\mathbf{W}\mathbf{x}(t) + \mathbf{U}\mathbf{h}(t-1)), \tag{1}$$

where $\mathbf{x}(t)$ is the driving input signal, and $\mathbf{W}$ and $\mathbf{U}$ are parameter matrices of the model. The output for a sequence of length T can then be computed as

$$\mathbf{y} = \mathbf{V}\mathbf{h}(T), \tag{2}$$

where $\mathbf{V}$ is another parameter matrix. In the specific setting of time-series classification, which is the context of this work, the output $\mathbf{y} \in \mathbb{R}^{N_Y}$ can be interpreted as a vector of scores, one for each class. All the parameters ($\mathbf{V}$, $\mathbf{W}$, and $\mathbf{U}$) are jointly learned by gradient descent.

A multi-layer – or deep – RNN [12] can be constructed by stacking the recurrent layers. The first layer will take as input the time-series $\mathbf{x}(t)$ as in Eq. 1, while the successive layers will take as input the state of the preceding layer. The output is then computed as in Eq. 2, but using as state the one produced by the last layer.

For what concerns the (architectural) hyper-parameters of a RNN, the most important one is arguably the number N_R of recurrent units. In the case of a multi-layer RNN, another crucial hyper-parameter to optimize is the number L of layers.

2.2   Echo State Networks

Echo State Networks (ESNs) [14,15] are recurrent networks from the paradigm of Reservoir Computing [19,30]. A common way to instantiate the approach consists of using leaky-integrator neurons [16], which leads to the following state update equation:

$$\mathbf{h}(t) = (1 - \alpha)\mathbf{h}(t - 1) + \alpha \tanh(\mathbf{W}\mathbf{x}(t) + \mathbf{U}\mathbf{h}(t - 1)), \tag{3}$$

where $\mathbf{W}$ and $\mathbf{U}$ are (typically sparse and high-dimensional) matrices that encode the recurrent and input connections in the model, respectively, while $\alpha \in (0, 1]$ is a scalar leaking rate. The peculiar characteristic of ESNs is that the values in $\mathbf{W}$ and $\mathbf{U}$ are not learned. In fact, they are initialized from a random distribution according to mathematical properties of stability of the underlying dynamical system [14] and then they are left fixed. The only parameters that are trained are those in the (typically linear) output layer, or *readout*, whose output in case of a sequence of length T can be computed as in Eq. 2.

The key advantage of ESNs is their training efficiency [15], which has been extensively confirmed by experimental comparisons [11]. Since only the linear readout is trained, it is possible to compute the weights in $\mathbf{V}$ without incurring in the problems associated with gradient descent training and backpropagation through time for the recurrent layers [6]. Moreover, since the linear readout is the only part of the model to be trained, it is also possible to employ closed form methods such as ridge regression for the computation of the optimal weights.

Deep versions of the ESN model can be constructed by stacking the recurrent layers while preserving the efficient training method [10]. In this case, it is common practice to concatenate the outputs of all layers into a vector in $\mathbb{R}^{LN_R}$ and use this as input to the readout. This is the setting that we use in this work.

Initialization. Initialization is a crucial phase for ESN training, as it is strictly related to the stable dynamics of the state. It is common to initialize both $\mathbf{W}$ and $\mathbf{U}$ in Eq. 3 with random values drawn from a uniform distribution on $[-1, 1]$, and then re-scaling $\mathbf{W}$ by an input scaling value $\omega_{in} \in \mathbb{R}^+$, and $\mathbf{U}$ to have a desired spectral radius[2] $\rho \in \mathbb{R}^+$. The values of ω_{in} and ρ, together with the leaking rate $\alpha \in (0, 1]$, constitute the major hyper-parameters for the design of reservoir layers in ESNs.

2.3   Long Short-Term Memory

Long Short-Term Memory (LSTM) [13] has been introduced to overcome the classical gradient-propagation limitations of Vanilla RNNs. It introduces the concept of *gates* that regulate the flow of information across states. The evolution of the internal state $\mathbf{h}(t) \in \mathbb{R}^{N_R}$ is described by the equations

---

[2] I.e., its maximum eigenvalue in absolute value.

$$f(t) = \sigma(\mathbf{W}_f \mathbf{x}(t) + \mathbf{U}_f \mathbf{h}(t-1))$$
$$i(t) = \sigma(\mathbf{W}_i \mathbf{x}(t) + \mathbf{U}_i \mathbf{h}(t-1))$$
$$o(t) = \sigma(\mathbf{W}_o \mathbf{x}(t) + \mathbf{U}_o \mathbf{h}(t-1))$$
$$\tilde{\mathbf{c}}(t) = \tanh(\mathbf{W}_c \mathbf{x}(t) + \mathbf{U}_c \mathbf{h}(t-1)) \tag{4}$$
$$\mathbf{c}(t) = \mathbf{f}(t) \odot \mathbf{c}(t-1) + \mathbf{i}(t) \odot \tilde{\mathbf{c}}(t)$$
$$\mathbf{h}(t) = \mathbf{o}(t) \odot \sigma(\mathbf{c}(t)),$$

in which $\mathbf{f}(t)$, $\mathbf{i}(t)$, and $\mathbf{o}(t)$ respectively indicate the activations of the forget, input, and output gate. The matrices $\mathbf{W}_f, \mathbf{W}_i, \mathbf{W}_o, \mathbf{W}_c$ and $\mathbf{U}_f, \mathbf{U}_i, \mathbf{U}_o, \mathbf{U}_c$ contain the model parameters. An output is computed from $\mathbf{h}(t)$ just like for the RNN as in Eq. 2, and all the parameters are trained by gradient descent.

A multi-layer – or deep – LSTM can be constructed in the same way as for a RNN. Likewise, the most important hyper-parameters are again the number N_R of recurrent units and, for a multi-layer LSTM, the number L of layers.

2.4 Gated Recurrent Unit

Gated Recurrent Unit (GRU) [7] is a gated recurrent network that has been introduced in the context of statistical machine translation. Compared to LSTM, it employs a fewer number of gates and a fewer number of parameters. The evolution of the internal state $\mathbf{h}(t) \in \mathbb{R}^{N_R}$ is described by the equations

$$\mathbf{z}(t) = \sigma(\mathbf{W}_z \mathbf{x}(t) + \mathbf{U}_r \mathbf{h}(t-1))$$
$$\mathbf{r}(t) = \sigma(\mathbf{W}_z \mathbf{x}(t) + \mathbf{U}_r \mathbf{h}(t-1))$$
$$\hat{\mathbf{h}}(t) = \tanh(\mathbf{W}\mathbf{x}(t) + \mathbf{U}(\mathbf{r}(t) \cdot \mathbf{h}(t-1))) \tag{5}$$
$$\mathbf{h}(t) = (1 - \mathbf{z}(t)) \cdot \mathbf{h}(t-1) + \mathbf{z}(t) \cdot \hat{\mathbf{h}}(t),$$

in which $\mathbf{z}(t)$ and $\mathbf{r}(t)$ respectively indicate the activations of the update gate and reset gate. The matrices $\mathbf{W}_z, \mathbf{W}_r, \mathbf{W}$ and $\mathbf{U}_z, \mathbf{U}_r, \mathbf{U}$ contain the parameters of the model. An output is computed from $\mathbf{h}(t)$ just like for the RNN as in Eq. 2, and all the parameters are trained by gradient descent.

The multi-layer (i.e., deep) architectural setup and the hyper-parameters considerations are as in the case of LSTM (Sect. 2.3).

3 Experimental Comparison

In the following we compare the performance of 4 recurrent models (RNN, ESN, LSTM, and GRU) over several datasets for human state and activity recognition. In Sect. 3.1 we describe the general experimental setup, then in Sect. 3.2 we provide details about the datasets and their preprocessing. In Sect. 3.3 we then present and discuss the results.

Table 1. Summary of the amount of data that we have selected from each dataset to support our study. The sequence lengths are to be intended after resampling.

Dataset		Sequences	Seq. length	Features	Classes
WESAD	[26]	952	100 (3 s)	14	4
HHAR	[28]	960	100 (2 s)	12	6
PAMAP2	[22]	930	350 (10 s)	31	4
OPPORTUNITY	[23]	480	75 (3 s)	130	4
ASCERTAIN	[29]	3360	160 (5 s)	17	4

3.1 General Setup

For the experimental comparison of the models we have divided the data from each dataset into subsequences of fixed length, each associated to a given label (the target class), and we have trained the networks to classify them. In Sect. 3.2 we describe the details about the datasets and their preprocessing. For the convenience of the reader we have also reported a summary in Table 1.

For what concerns the experimental methodology, for each dataset we have split the data in different folds to perform hold-out validation. In particular, about 80% of the data of each dataset has been used for training, 10% for validation, and the remaining 10% for testing. For a fair comparison we have constrained the number of total trainable parameters to be the same for all models, and for each combination of model and dataset we have selected the numbers of recurrent units that allowed to meet the constraint. To choose the reference number of trainable parameters to use in all experiments we have taken the number of trainable parameters exhibited by the best performing ESN on the validation set, with a number of recurrent layers fixed to 1.

For uniformity of experimental conditions, all models including the ESN have been trained by the Adam algorithm [17] and regularized by a combination of L1 and L2 penalties. The loss function that has been employed is the cross-entropy.

The hyperparameters that have been explored are the number of layers ($L \in [1, 6]$), the learning rate of the optimizer ($\eta \in [1e^{-3}, 1e^{-2}]$), the decay rates of Adam ($\beta_1 \in [0.8, 0.99]$ and $\beta_2 \in [0.98, 0.999]$), and the regularization strength (kernel regularization, bias regularization, and activity regularization, all in $[1e^{-6}, 1e^{-4}]$). For the ESN-only hyperparameters, we have optimized the input scaling ($\omega_{in} \in [0.5, 2.0]$, also used as intra-layer scaling), leaking rate ($\alpha \in [0.3, 1.0]$) and spectral radius of the recurrent matrix $\mathbf{U}$ ($\rho \in [0.5, 1.5]$). The best configuration of the hyperparameters has been selected through 100 iterations of random search.

3.2 Datasets

We briefly describe here the datasets used and their preprocessing. For those datasets that are publicly available, we also publish our preprocessed data.[3]

---

[3] https://github.com/danieleds/Benchmarking_RNN_for_HSM.

WESAD. The WESAD (*WEarable Stress and Affect Detection*) dataset [26] contains physiological measurements recorded from 15 subjects performing activities designed to induce different mental states, such as stress or amusement. The participants to the study have been exposed to different situation in order to induce a state of stress, amusement, or meditation. Recordings from a neutral mental state have also been collected as a baseline. We consider the aforementioned 4 states (baseline, stress, amusement, and meditation) as classes for a task of classification of the sensor data.

Preprocessing. The time series are resampled 32 Hz and standardized. After splitting we obtain a training set of 771 sequences, a validation set of 86 sequences, and a test set of 95 sequences.

HHAR. The HHAR (*Heterogeneity Human Activity Recognition*) dataset [28] contains inertial measurements recorded from 9 subjects performing physical activities. The sensors used (gyroscopes and accelerometers) were part of smartphones or smartwatches which were carried or worn by the subjects. To each subject it was requested to perform 6 different physical activities (in no particular order): standing, sitting, walking, waking up the stairs, walking down the stairs, and biking. The sensor data is labeled with the associated activity: we consider these activities as classes for a task of classification of the sensor data.

Preprocessing. The time series are resampled 70 Hz, and we consider 16,000 samples for each activity. After splitting we obtain a training set of 768 sequences, a validation set of 96 sequences, and a test set of 96 sequences.

PAMAP2. The PAMAP2 (*Physical Activity Monitoring*) dataset [22] contains physiological and inertial measurements recorded from a heart rate monitor and 3 inertial measurement units. To each of the 9 subjects it was requested to perform 18 activities (of which 6 were optional) such as running, watching TV, car driving, and so on. For our purposes we only select the top 4 activities in terms of how many participants did actually perform it. These are lying, sitting, standing, and walking, which have been used for a classification task.

Preprocessing. The features related to the second accelerometer are removed (it is defective). The orientation features are also removed. The time series are upsampled 100 Hz. After splitting we obtain a training set of 753 sequences, a validation set of 84 sequences, and a test set of 93 sequences.

OPPORTUNITY. The OPPORTUNITY Activity Recognition dataset [23] includes measurements from body-worn sensors (7 inertial measurement units, 12 3D acceleration sensors, 4 3D localization information) and other sensors associated to objects in a controlled environment. For the purposes of our study, we only consider the body-worn sensors, in particular the 3D acceleration, 3D rate of turn, 3D magnetic field, and orientation of the sensors. The 4 participants were required to perform several activities in different contexts (e.g., making coffee, eating a sandwich, cleaning the room), and the data was labeled according to four basic motor activities (standing, walking, lying, and sitting). We employ these basic motor activities in a classification task.

Preprocessing. Sequences containing null data are excluded. The features are already at a uniform sampling rate 30 Hz. After splitting we obtain a training set of 389 sequences, a validation set of 43 sequences, and a test set of 48 sequences.

ASCERTAIN. The ASCERTAIN dataset [29] has been built to support tasks of emotion and personality recognition from commercially available sensors. Signals include electrocardiogram, electroencephalogram, galvanic skin response, and facial activity, which were recorded while the subjects were watching affective movie clips (36 clips per subject). After each clip, the 58 subjects were required to give a rating of their state of arousal (indicating a value between 0 and 6) and valence (-3 to 3). We consider these values as axes of the circumplex model [24] and we classify the quadrant. This yields the following four classes: high arousal - high valence, high arousal - low valence, low arousal - high valence, and low arousal - low valence.

Preprocessing. Sequences containing invalid data are excluded. The features are resampled 32 Hz. After splitting we obtain a training set of 2722 sequences, a validation set of 302 sequences, and a test set of 336 sequences.

3.3   Results and Discussion

In Table 2 we report the accuracy obtained by the four models under consideration. We highlight how the values of accuracy obtained by the different models are mostly above 90% on all datasets. In fact, the average accuracy across all models and datasets is 94.67%, with a standard deviation of 4.34%. This indicates that, in general, recurrent neural network models are indeed particularly fit for predicting the mental or physical state of human subjects from sensors.

Due to the complex preprocessing of the datasets, which involves many choices that are difficult to replicate without the source code available, it is not always easy to compare the results that we have obtained with those found in the literature for non-recurrent models. That said, we have observed that the recurrent models that we have tested almost consistently surpass non-recurrent models in the literature on the same datasets. This is especially true for the datasets of emotional state (WESAD and ASCERTAIN) and OPPORTUNITY, where the improvement can be as high as 15% [20,25,26,29]. In particular, for WESAD, the studies in [20,26] reach an accuracy of 80% while limiting to the classification of 3 classes, which is significantly lower than the multi-layer recurrent models which we have shown to be able to achieve an accuracy above 94% for the classification of all 4 classes (with a peak at 98% for GRU). On PAMAP2

Table 2. Average accuracy and standard deviation on the test set. The averages and standard deviations are computed by retraining the models 5 times, each with a different random initialization of the weights.

	WESAD		HHAR		PAMAP2		OPPORTUN.		ASCERTAIN	
	Avg	Std	Avg	Std	Avg	Std	Avg	Std	Avg	Std
RNN	94.62	2.84	78.54	2.04	96.00	3.39	96.84	2.58	94.77	0.78
ESN	94.96	2.60	89.79	3.81	97.50	2.74	94.74	5.77	96.54	0.77
LSTM	95.48	1.17	92.71	2.72	96.50	1.22	93.08	2.88	94.63	0.00
GRU	98.13	1.16	98.54	0.83	98.50	2.00	96.84	2.58	94.63	0.00

[22], we can observe accuracies that are in line with our results (97–98% for our RNNs and 94–99% for the non-recurrent models reported in the study). For HHAR, the accuracy obtained by the ESN (90%) and the LSTM (93%) is similar to the one obtained by k-NN (91%) [28] and a feedforward DNN (93%) [27], but the GRU (98.5%) shows superior performance by more than 5% points. We also point out that for DNN the number of trainable parameters is 4 times larger than those employed by our RNNs (24,000 vs 6000).

Still from Table 2, it can be particularly interesting to focus on the performance of ESN. For this relatively simple model, in which the recurrent and input connections are not trained, we can observe how the accuracy is often comparable to that of the fully trained recurrent models. On average, in the results reported in Table 2 the accuracy of ESN is only 2.65% points below that of the best performing model, and in the case of ASCERTAIN the ESN actually surpasses all other models.

As a further observation, we can also see that gated models perform generally better than non-gated models. In fact, across all datasets, the gated networks (LSTM and GRU) achieve an average accuracy of 95.90%, while the non-gated networks (ESN and RNN) achieve a lower 93.43%. This difference shows that gating mechanisms are indeed useful in the context of sensor data for human state and activity recognition, even if the long-term dependencies in this kind of data are arguably less complicated than those found in other contexts such as natural language processing [7]. Since the use of gates appears to provide a critical advantage in terms of predictive performance, our results motivate further research on how to construct gated ESNs [8].

In Table 3 we have reported the number of layers, recurrent units, and trainable parameters for each combination of model and dataset. From the table we can observe how in almost all cases the reported models have more than one layer. Since the configurations that have been reported are the best performing ones, this means that to achieve maximum performance – under the constraint of a fixed number of trainable parameters – the architecture needs to exploit layering. In order to quantify the advantage of layering we also report in Table 4 the same results of Table 2, but only selecting the best performing non-layered models instead of the overall best performing models. In this case the average

Table 3. Number of layers (L), recurrent units per layer (N_R), and trainable parameters (P) for the best performing hyperparametrization of each model, across all tasks under consideration. The number of recurrent units has been scaled to obtain almost the same number of trainable parameters across models for each given task.

Model	WESAD			HHAR			PAMAP2			OPPORTUN.			ASCERTAIN		
	L	N_R	P	L	N_R	P	L	N_R	P	L	N_R	P	L	N_R	P
RNN	3	26	3930	4	28	6110	3	21	3007	3	18	4090	2	30	3394
ESN	3	750	4004	2	668	6018	3	550	2932	3	750	4004	4	625	3124
LSTM	2	16	4164	3	16	6182	2	11	2952	1	6	4260	5	8	3044
GRU	2	18	3964	3	18	5946	2	14	3294	3	8	4252	2	16	3380

Table 4. Average accuracy and standard deviation on the test set, restricting the number of recurrent layers to 1. The averages and standard deviations are computed by retraining the models 5 times, each with a different random initialization.

	WESAD		HHAR		PAMAP2		OPPORTUN.		ASCERTAIN	
	Avg	Std	Avg	Std	Avg	Std	Avg	Std	Avg	Std
RNN	83.09	8.00	74.78	5.04	95.27	1.45	87.59	1.69	91.83	0.14
ESN	92.44	0.75	88.96	2.24	95.64	0.89	87.50	3.73	91.76	0.00
LSTM	94.23	3.49	91.50	4.37	96.36	1.99	93.08	2.88	91.76	0.00
GRU	97.73	1.01	97.08	1.21	96.36	0.00	92.31	2.43	91.76	0.00

accuracy of all models across all tasks is 91.55%, while allowing layering as in Table 2 yields an average of 94.67% (again, while keeping the total number of trainable parameters fixed). It is clear then how layered architectures allow to better model the different time-scales that are present in the sensor data.

4 Conclusions

In this paper, we have benchmarked recurrent neural network models on tasks on human state and activity recognition from streams of sensor-gathered data. In particular, our analysis comprised 4 different recurrent neural network models and 5 datasets of human state and activity recognition. In most cases, the recurrent models are able to obtain a level of accuracy well above 90%: this allows to state that this kind of models is particularly suited to the task and can be used as a reasonable starting point to build effective predictive systems.

We have shown how a simple and efficient recurrent model such as the ESN is still highly effective for this kind of tasks. This is a significant result in light of practical applications of human state and activity recognition, which often require the implementation of predictive models on small low-power devices and thus can benefit from the efficient training process of ESNs.

We can thus conclude that ESNs are valid alternatives to the most popular (fully trainable) recurrent models and allow effective predictive performances. This is accompanied by advantages in terms of training efficiency and optimal federation: both these aspects are unique to ESNs, have previously been demonstrated in the literature, and are often key to human-centric tasks. Additional advantages in practical applications include privacy preservation (there is no need to transmit the data to a central server, since training can happen locally) and light bandwidth requirements for model transmission over the network (since most of the weights are fixed).

Furthermore, our results suggest that employing deep *and* gated architectures is particularly relevant for these tasks. While the techniques for layering recurrent models are well established for RNNs, LSTMs, GRUs and ESNs [10], applying an ESN-like training methodology to a gated architecture is more tricky and subject of ongoing research efforts [8].

In conclusion, we have shown the effectiveness of recurrent neural networks for tasks of human state and activity recognition, and of ESNs in particular, which thanks to their characteristics can serve as the first choice in human-centric tasks.

References

1. Bacciu, D., Bertoncini, G., Morelli, D.: Randomized neural networks for preference learning with physiological data. Neural Computing Applications (2021)
2. Bacciu, D., Colombo, M., Morelli, D., Plans, D.: Randomized neural networks for preference learning with physiological data. Neurocomputing **298**, 9–20 (2018)
3. Bacciu, D., et al.: Teaching - trustworthy autonomous cyber-physical applications through human-centred intelligence. In: Submitted (2021)
4. Bacciu, D., Barsocchi, P., Chessa, S., Gallicchio, C., Micheli, A.: An experimental characterization of reservoir computing in ambient assisted living applications. Neural Comput. Appl. **24**(6), 1451–1464 (2013). https://doi.org/10.1007/s00521-013-1364-4
5. Bacciu, D., Di Sarli, D., Faraji, P., Gallicchio, C., Micheli, A.: Federated reservoir computing neural networks. In: IJCNN. IEEE (2021)
6. Bengio, Y., Simard, P.Y., Frasconi, P.: Learning long-term dependencies with gradient descent is difficult. IEEE Trans. Neural Netw. **5**(2), 157–166 (1994)
7. Cho, K., et al.: Learning phrase representations using RNN encoder-decoder for statistical machine translation. In: EMNLP, pp. 1724–1734. ACL (2014)
8. Di Sarli, D., Gallicchio, C., Micheli, A.: Gated echo state networks: a preliminary study. In: INISTA, pp. 1–5. IEEE (2020)
9. Gallicchio, C., Micheli, A.: Architectural and Markovian factors of echo state networks. Neural Netw. **24**(5), 440–456 (2011)
10. Gallicchio, C., Micheli, A., Pedrelli, L.: Design of deep echo state networks. Neural Netw. **108**, 33–47 (2018)
11. Gallicchio, C., Micheli, A., Pedrelli, L.: Comparison between DeepESNs and gated RNNS on multivariate time-series prediction. In: ESANN (2019)
12. Hermans, M., Schrauwen, B.: Training and analysing deep recurrent neural networks. Adv. Neural Inf. Process. Syst. **26**, 190–198 (2013)

13. Hochreiter, S., Schmidhuber, J.: Long short-term memory. Neural Comput. **9**(8), 1735–1780 (1997)
14. Jaeger, H.: The "echo state" approach to analysing and training recurrent neural networks - with an erratum note. German National Research Center for Information Technology GMD Technical Report, Bonn (2001)
15. Jaeger, H., Haas, H.: Harnessing nonlinearity: predicting chaotic systems and saving energy in wireless communication. Science **304**(5667), 78–80 (2004)
16. Jaeger, H., Lukoševičius, M., Popovici, D., Siewert, U.: Optimization and applications of echo state networks with leaky-integrator neurons. Neural Netw. **20**(3), 335–352 (2007)
17. Kingma, D.P., Ba, J.: Adam: a method for stochastic optimization. In: ICLR (Poster) (2015)
18. Kolen, J.F., Kremer, S.C.: A field guide to dynamical recurrent networks. John Wiley & Sons (2001)
19. Lukoševičius, M., Jaeger, H.: Reservoir computing approaches to recurrent neural network training. Comput. Sci. Rev. **3**(3), 127–149 (2009)
20. Nkurikiyeyezu, K., Yokokubo, A., Lopez, G.: The effect of person-specific biometrics in improving generic stress predictive models. arXiv:1910.01770 (2019)
21. Palumbo, F., Gallicchio, C., Pucci, R., Micheli, A.: Human activity recognition using multisensor data fusion based on reservoir computing. J. Ambient Intell. Smart Environ. **8**(2), 87–107 (2016)
22. Reiss, A., Stricker, D.: Introducing a new benchmarked dataset for activity monitoring. In: ISWC, pp. 108–109. IEEE Computer Society (2012)
23. Roggen, D., et al.: Collecting complex activity datasets in highly rich networked sensor environments. In: INSS, pp. 233–240 (2010)
24. Russell, J.A.: A circumplex model of affect. J. Pers. Soc. Psychol. **39**(6), 1161 (1980)
25. Sagha, H., et al.: Benchmarking classification techniques using the opportunity human activity dataset. In: SMC, pp. 36–40. IEEE (2011)
26. Schmidt, P., Reiss, A., Dürichen, R., Marberger, C., Laerhoven, K.V.: Introducing wesad, a multimodal dataset for wearable stress and affect detection. In: ICMI, pp. 400–408. ACM (2018)
27. Sozinov, K., Vlassov, V., Girdzijauskas, S.: Human activity recognition using federated learning. In: ISPA/IUCC/BDCloud/SocialCom/SustainCom, pp. 1103–1111. IEEE (2018)
28. Stisen, A., et al.: Smart devices are different: assessing and mitigatingmobile sensing heterogeneities for activity recognition. In: Proceedings of the 13th ACM Conference on Embedded Networked Sensor Systems, pp. 127–140. SenSys 2015, Association for Computing Machinery, New York (2015)
29. Subramanian, R., Wache, J., Abadi, M.K., Vieriu, R.L., Winkler, S., Sebe, N.: ASCERTAIN: emotion and personality recognition using commercial sensors. IEEE Trans. Affect. Comput. **9**(2), 147–160 (2018)
30. Verstraeten, D., Schrauwen, B., d'Haene, M., Stroobandt, D.: An experimental unification of reservoir computing methods. Neural Netw. **20**(3), 391–403 (2007)

Neural Networks for Time Series Forecasting

Learning to Trade from Zero-Knowledge Using Particle Swarm Optimization

Stefan van Deventer and Andries Engelbrecht[✉][iD]

University of Stellenbosch, Cape Town, South Africa
engel@sun.ac.za

Abstract. Competitive co-evolutionary particle swarm optimization (CEPSO) algorithms have been developed to train neural networks (NNs) to predict trend reversals. These approaches considered the optimization problem, i.e. training of the NNs to maximize net profit and to minimize risk, as a static optimization problem. Based on the dynamic nature of the financial stock market, this paper proposes that the training should rather be treated as a dynamic optimization problem. A new dynamic CEPSO is proposed and used to train a NN on technical market indicators to predict trade actions. In addition, this paper incorporates approaches to combat saturation of the activation functions – an aspect neglected in previous research. The dynamic CEPSO is evaluated and compared with the static CEPSO approach, a buy-and-hold strategy, and a rule based strategy. Results show that the new CEPSO performs significantly better on a selection of South African stocks.

Keywords: Particle swarm optimization · Competitive co-evolution · Neural networks · Financial trading · Dynamic optimization problem

1 Introduction

The task of buying and selling securities is notoriously difficult and non-trivial. This is due to the fluctuations in the stock price that can be caused by a number of factors such as supply and demand of the stock, news, market sentiment, trends, liquidity, demographic of traders and incidental transactions [9] to name a few. Producing a model that combines all these factors has proven to be beyond the capabilities of the human mind. This problem needs to be simplified in order to model the behaviour of the market. Technical analysis provides such a solution by mainly interpreting historic and current security prices to derive approximations of market trends. The assumption is that all price fluctuation factors can be described by the price of the security. This provides the tools known as technical market indicators (TMI) which can be used to describe different market attributes. The TMIs used in this paper are Bollinger bands, moving average convergence and divergence, and the Aroon and relative strength index.

Supervised NN approaches do exist to predict trading actions. The focus of this paper is on competitive co-evolutionary approaches to train NNs to predict

© Springer Nature Switzerland AG 2021
I. Rojas et al. (Eds.): IWANN 2021, LNCS 12862, pp. 183–195, 2021.
https://doi.org/10.1007/978-3-030-85099-9_15

trend reversals without using any target information. Specifically, this paper improves on a CEPSO approach developed in [14]. This CEPSO was developed under the assumption that training of NNs on time series of TMIs is a static optimization problem. While the results presented in [14] showed that the CEPSO outperformed classical trading strategies, this paper instead hypothesizes that the optimization problem is dynamic, and that better prediction performance can be obtained if a particle swarm optimization (PSO) algorithm developed specifically to solve dynamic optimization problems, is used in the competitive co-evolutionary algorithm to adjust NN weights and biases. In addition, cognizance is taken of the activation function saturation problem [17], and mechanisms are implemented to prevent premature saturation. The resulting competitive co-evolutionary QPSO (CEQPSO) is evaluated on South African stocks and found to perform significantly better than the original static CEPSO, a buy-and-hold strategy, and a rule-based strategy.

The rest of the paper is organized as follows: Sect. 2 provides the necessary background. The CEQPSO is presented in Sect. 3. The empirical process is described in Sect. 4, and the results are discussed in Sect. 5.

2 Background

This section provides background on the key topics that are studied in this paper.

2.1 Technical Market Indicators

A technical market indicator (TMI) is said to be a time series derived from the price data of a security by applying a mathematical formula to it. This exposes behaviour and properties about the security that may prove difficult to observe by the price alone. This provides insight to the strength and direction of the future price of the security. To achieve optimal performance, multiple TMIs, depicting different properties of the security, are used together and as a result the insight to the future price movements become more consistent. The interested reader is referred to Colby's encyclopedia for a complete list of TMIs [5].

2.2 Competitive Co-evolution

Co-evolution is the complementary evolution of closely associated species [8]. Complementary evolution is achieved through some relative fitness function that depicts the relationship between the species. Competitive co-evolution relies on a bootstrapping process to produce optimal competing species. This means that no expert knowledge about the problem space is supplied. Two populations evolve simultaneously by competing against each other to produce the best solution, resulting in a relationship where one population's success is observed as the other population's failure. At each generation, the populations compete to produce individuals that outperform the other. This is done through some relative fitness function. The relative fitness function is a performance measure that evaluates the performance of an individual relative to other individuals. Competitve co-evolutionary approaches have been developed to train NNs as evaluation functions for game trees [4,6,12] and as trend reversal predictors [14].

2.3   Particle Swarm Optimization

Particle swarm optimization (PSO) [11] is an optimization technique inspired by a simple bird flock model. A swarm consists of particles moving around in n-dimensional space. As these particles move about, they attempt to move the swarm to an optimal position in the problem search space.

Every particle i has a position, $\mathbf{x}_i$, and a velocity, $\mathbf{v}_i$. The position of a particle is a candidate solution, while the velocity can be seen as a step size and search direction with which the solution will change over the next iteration. The position of a particle is initially uniformly distributed within the problem space and the update rule is given as

$$\mathbf{x}_i(t+1) = \mathbf{x}_i(t) + \mathbf{v}_i(t+1) \tag{1}$$

where t is the current iteration and i is the current particle. Assuming the inertia PSO [18], the velocity of a particle is updated as

$$v_{ij}(t+1) = \omega v_{ij}(t) + c_1 r_{1j}(t)[y_{ij}(t) - x_{ij}(t)] + c_2 r_{2j}(t)[\hat{y}_{ij}(t) - x_{ij}(t)] \tag{2}$$

where y_{ij} and $\hat{y}_{ij}$ are respectively the personal best and neighborhood best positions for particle i in dimension j; ω, c_1, and c_2 represent the control parameters, and r_{1j} and r_{2j} are sampled from a uniform distribution in $[0, 1]$.

2.4   Dynamic Environments

The objective function of a dynamic optimization problem (DOP) changes over time which causes the optima to change positions and their quality. This may even cause existing optima to disappear and new optima to appear. In order to solve a DOP, the optimization algorithm should be able to track the movements of optima throughout the changing search landscape. Two aspects of PSO prevent it to be applied to DOPs in general:

- Loss of diversity: Particles move towards a single point in the search space, with swarm diversity and velocities moving towards zero. When an optimum moves, or a new optimum appears, the swarm does not have sufficient diversity in order to track these changes.
- Outdated memory: As the search landscape changes, current personal best and neighbourhood best posistions may no longer be best positions, with the consequence that particles are attracted to non-optimal positions.

PSO has to be adapted to address these problems in order to solve DOPs.

2.5   Quantum Particle Swarm Optimization

QPSO [2] is an adaptation of the PSO to solve DOPs. QPSO uses quantum and neutral particles. Quantum particle update their positions by sampling a new position from some distribution, centered around the global best position, rather than making use of the update rule in Eq. (1). This injects diversity into the swarm, preventiing all particles from convergiing to a single point. Quantum particles enable detection of changes in optima positions. Neutral particles perform the standard PSO updates to facilitate exploitation of a found optimum. Early application of the QPSO sampled quantum particles from a uniform distribution. This distribution was shown to perform sub-par by Harrison et al. [10]. Rather, a non-uniform distribution was shown to perform exceedingly well for all dynamic environments. The outdated memory problem is addressed by re-evaluating best positions whenever an environment change is detected.

2.6   Activation Function Saturation

A NN makes use of an activation function to produce an output from all the weighted inputs. The activation function must be chosen correctly to optimize the performance of the NN. An issue known as activation function saturation can arise when the function is bounded [17]. This issue can cause a node to primarily return a value near the asymptotic ends of the activation function, which impairs the ability of the network to encode information and could lead to ineffective training. This has been shown to be particularly problematic when considering a PSO as training algorithm for a FFNN [19]. Attempts have been made to address or control saturation. Some of the methods used include scaling the inputs, velocity clamping, weight decay, and tuning the initialization range of particles. An in depth assessment of such methods across a variety of activation functions are made by Dennis *et al.* [7].

3   Competitive Co-evolutionary Quantum Particle Swarm Optimization

Papacostantis and Engelbrecht [14] developed a static CEPSO that forms the basis of this paper. Trend reversals were predicted using a standard feed forward NN trained by a coevolutionary approach using a local best (lbest) PSO. This paper continues the research by making use of a QPSO variant, which is more suitable for the dynamic nature of the stock market. This section presents the implementation of the CEQPSO.

3.1   Neural Network

As with CEPSO [14], the CEQPSO is used to train a NN with one hidden layer. The NN has six input nodes, four hidden nodes and three output nodes. The six input nodes correspond to six TMIs, namely the Aroon up, Aroon down,

Bollinger bands, moving average convergence, moving average divergence, and relative strength index. The three output nodes correspond to the three trading actions considered, namely the buy, sell and hold actions. The sigmoid function is used as the activation function for both the hidden and output layers. Each particle in the swarm represents a NN and is therefore considered a NN trader. The weights and biases of the NN are represented by the position of the particle.

3.2   Relative Fitness Function

Particles require a fitness (objective) function to evaluate the quality of the NN represented by the particle. Since no target information is available, a loss function such as sum-squared error cannot be used. Instead, a relative fitness function is used to approximate a particle's fitness relative to that of other particles. The fitness of a particle is evaluated based on net profit and risk. An ideal trading agent is one that maximises profit while minimising risk. Profit and loss (net profit) is calculated as

$$P\&L = CG - CL - TC \tag{3}$$

where CG, CL and TC denote capital gains, capital loss and transaction cost respectively. Risk is approximated by the Sharpe ratio [1], defined as

$$SR = \frac{r_S - r_F}{\sigma_S} \tag{4}$$

where r_S represents the securities' annualised return, r_F is an annualised benchmark risk free rate, and σ_S denotes the annualised standard deviation on returns of the security. The relative fitness function is therefore given as

$$f = \left[\frac{P\&L - min_{P\&L}}{max_{P\&L} - min_{P\&L}}\right] + \left[\frac{SR - min_{SR}}{max_{SR} - min_{SR}}\right] \tag{5}$$

where $min_{P\&L}$ and $max_{P\&L}$ represent the minimum and maximum profit and loss of the trading agents in the neighborhood. Likewise, min_{SR} and max_{SR} represent the minimum and maximum Sharpe ratios of the trading agents.

Equation (5) is a relative fitness function since the performance of a trading agent is only measured relative to the other agents in its neighbourhood. The function returns a value in $[0, 2]$ with a score of 2 being the highest and a score of 0 being the lowest. Note also that since this is a relative score, it cannot be compared with the score of a particle in another neighborhood since the range of values considered in the different neighborhoods may vary.

3.3   Quantum Particle Swarm Optimization

The quantum PSO (QPSO) is a variation of the lbest PSO. Each neighborhood contains three particles selected from their index and not using spatial distance. The QPSO introduces two additional control parameters: The first is the center of the cloud, which is selected as the global best position. The second control parameter is the cloud radius, r_{cloud}. The radius of the quantum cloud determines how far a quantum particle can search for changing optima. A too small radius will cause the particles to be ineffective in tracking changing optima and a too large radius will cause the particles to not assist in the exploitation of found optima. The radius of the quantum cloud therefore depends on the current swarm. A dynamic radius is proposed by Pamparà and Engelbrecht [13] to adapt the radius of the quantum cloud. This process requires no prior knowledge of the problem space and removes the necessity of tuning the parameter.

3.4   Activation Function Saturation

Component-wise velocity clamping and weight decay is used to address saturation [7]. Component-wise velocity clamping effectively limits the size of the NN weights by imposing a limit on the velocity of a particle and is implemented as

$$v_{i,j}(t) = \begin{cases} v_{i,j}(t) & |v_{i,j}(t)| < V_{max,j} \\ V_{max,j} & V_{max,j} < v_{i,j}(t) \\ -V_{max,j} & v_{i,j}(t) < V_{max,j} \end{cases} \tag{6}$$

where $\mathbf{V}_{max}$ is the maximum velocity. This imposes a restriction on the amount by which NN weights and biases are adjusted.

Weight decay penalises the overall magnitude of weights in the NN. The objective function is changed to [16]

$$F(\mathbf{x}) = f(\mathbf{x}) + \lambda E_p \tag{7}$$

where $f(\mathbf{x})$ denotes the relative fitness function, λ is the strength of regularisation and E_p is the penalty term, calculated as

$$E_p = \frac{1}{2} \sum_{l=1}^{W} w_l^2 \tag{8}$$

W denotes the total number of weights and biases; w_l is the lth weight. This approach was examined for PSO based FFNN training in [16] and was found to significantly reduce saturation.

3.5   The CEQPSO Model Step-by-Step

Algorithm 1. CEQPSO

1: Calculate the TMI time series and divide it into an *in_sample* and an *out_sample* set, representing the training and test sets;
2: Create a swarm of n_s particles. Select 50% particles to be neutral and randomly initialise their position in the range $[-r, r]$ for random variable r. The rest of the particles are quantum particles, with positions sampled from a non-uniform distribution;

3: Set the velocity of each particle to zero;

4: Initialise the personal best of each particle to the current position;

5: **for** n epochs **do**

6:    Create a swarm of NNs using the particle position vectors;

7:    Use the *in_sample* to produce NN trend reversal time series;

8:    Simulate the trading action (buy, hold or sell) using the trend reversal time series for each solution in the swarm;

9:    Calculate the relative fitness for each solution;

10:    Add the global best particle to the hall of fame;

11:    Update the fitness of each particle to the calculated relative fitness;

12:    Update the personal best position of each particle;

13:    Update the neighborhood best position of each particle;

14:    Update the velocity of each particle;

15:    Update the position of each neutral particle;

16:    Sample a new position for each quantum particle;

17: **end for**

18: Use the *out_sample* data set to derive trend reversal time series for each solution in the hall of fame;

19: Simulate the trading actions using the trend reversal time series for each solution in the hall of fame;

20: Calculate the relative fitness of each solution in the hall of fame and return the solution with the highest fitness as the best solution;

4   Empirical Process

This section provides details on the empirical procedure followed to evaluate the CEQPSO model. Section 4.1 lists the data sets, and control parameters values are provided in Sect. 4.2. The performance measures and the statistical tests are discussed in Sect. 4.3.

4.1   Data Sets

This paper considers the stocks of eight companies situated in South Africa. These companies are: Anglo American plc (AGL), Gold Fields Ltd (GFI), Impala Platinum Ltd (IMP), Nedbank Group Ltd (NED), Remgro Ltd (REM), Standard Bank Group (SBK), Steinhoff International Hldgs (SNH), and Sasol Ltd (SOL). The historic prices for each company is retrieved form www.finance.yahoo.com. The time period used is 01-01-2000 to 30-06-2008. The price data is split into two continuous groups referred to as the *in_sample* (training data) and *out_sample* (testing data) which represents 80% and 20% of the datasets respectively.

4.2   Control Parameters

Standard PSO and the QPSO posses the same control parameters, set as $\omega = 0.729844$ and $c_1 = c_2 = 1.496180$ to satisfy theoretically derived stability conditions [15]. The swarm consists of 150 particles, of which 50% are quantum particles and 50% are neutral particles. The penalty term for the weight decay is a new control parameter that the optimization algorithm is sensitive to. A too small value causes the penalty introduced to be negligible and will have no effect on the algorithm, and a too large penalty drastically alters the search space which could lead to false optima. Bosman *et al.* [3] empirically found that the optimal value for the weight decay penalty term, λ is in $[0.001, 0.1]$. A value of 0.005 is used in this paper.

4.3   Performance Measures and Statistical Tests

The two benchmark strategies were used, i.e. the 'buy and hold' (B&H) strategy and a 'rule-based' strategy. The B&H strategy is the most commonly used benchmark for trading applications. This strategy requires the trader to buy stock and hold it indefinitely. One advantage that this has is that it keeps transaction costs low as there are only ever two transactions, the initial buying of the stock and the eventual selling thereof. The rule-based strategy is made up of the Bollinger-bands and relative strength index TMIs. The combination of these two TMIs is considered a popular strategy in stock trading.

Annualised return ratios are reported as the performance measure. Saturation is evaluated by observing the distribution of the NNs hidden layer output. Saturation causes the network to produce values close to the boundary of the activation function. If this is the case, it is easily visible by observing the distribution of these values.

The Mann-Whitney U test is used at a significance level of 95% to test if one model performs significantly better for a stock than the other models. The CEQPSO is evaluated against the CEPSO, the B&H and the rule-based strategies. The algorithms were run for 350 epochs and each performance measure was taken as the average over 30 independent runs.

5   Research Results

This section examines the results obtained. Section 5.1 examines the standard CEPSO model when applied to South African stocks. Section 5.2 examines the CEQPSO model before and after addressing hidden layer saturation.

5.1   CEPSO

The first objective of this paper is to show that the CEPSO model can be successfully applied to South African stocks. To do this, the CEPSO model is applied to the eight companies and compared to the buy-and-hold strategy with an initial investable amount of R1,000,000. The annualised return ratios are given in Table 1. It is clear that the CEPSO model performs well on South African stocks and outperforms the buy-and-hold benchmark strategy.

Table 1. Annualised return ratios for the CEPSO

Company	In-sample		Out-sample	
	CEPSO	B&H	CEPSO	B&H
AGL	33.491%	18.562%	25.355%	26.711%
GFI	42.374%	24.973%	4.2%	−1.515%
IMP	37.283%	23.624%	72.198%	56.515%
NED	15.883%	−4.739%	23.262%	5.52%
REM	36.817%	24.275%	40.402%	23.336%
SBK	32.445%	19.901%	24.914%	4.716%
SNH	40.526%	20.263%	17.029%	−2.938%
SOL	41.878%	27.171%	39.092%	27.163%
Average	35.088%	19.254%	30.807%	17.439%

Table 2. Mann-Whitney U test for the out-sample

Company	Median		Symbol
	CEPSO	CEQPSO	
AGL	26.771%	24.431%	−
GFI	3.318%	9.966%	+
IMP	73.659%	73.782%	−
NED	27.395%	17.222%	−
REM	40.341%	40.191%	+
SBK	26.353%	26.965%	+
SNH	17.502%	12.951%	−
SOL	39.351%	42.288%	+

5.2 CEQPSO

The saturated CEQPSO model is compared with the CEPSO, B&H and rule-based models in Figs. 1 and 2. These figures illustrate the annualised return ratios for the different models for each company. The averages are indicated on the far right. It is noted that the CEQPSO model outperforms the B&H and Rule-based models for the in-sample and out-sample data.

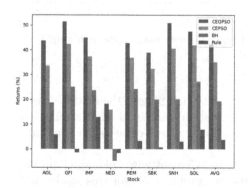

Fig. 1. Annualised return ratios of each stock for all models (In-sample)

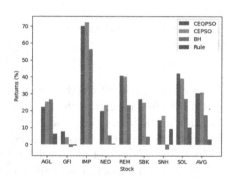

Fig. 2. Annualised return ratios of each stock for all models (Out-sample)

The results of the Mann-Whitney U test applied to the saturated CEQPSO and the CEPSO models are displayed in Table 2. The symbols '+', '−' and '=' indicate that the CEQPSO model is better, worse or the same as the CEPSO model. The Mann-Whitney U test indicates that the CEQPSO model is better than the CEPSO model for four companies and worse for four.

This CEQPSO model suffers from hidden layer saturation as is depicted in
Fig. 5 for the Nedbank stock. This is the common trend throughout the different
companies. This histogram depicts the normalised output values for the hidden
layers of the NN. Note the relatively high number of outputs close to zero and
one. This indicates that the NN is saturated and that the activation function
will be more likely to return values that are close to zero or one.

The effects of weight decay on the velocity of a particle is depicted in Figs. 3
and 4. This illustrates the growth of the velocity magnitude of a single particle.
Without the use of weight decay it is noted that the velocity magnitude grows
indefinitely. Once weight decay is added the velocity magnitude grows until
the penalty is realised and the velocity magnitudes shrinks. It is clear that the
penalty added with weight decay succeeds in lowering the velocity of a particle
once it becomes too large. This allows the particle positions to be updated with
smaller step sizes.

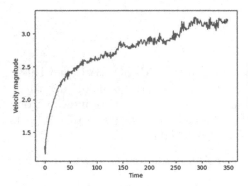

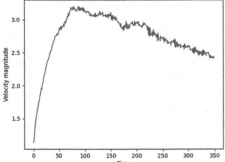

Fig. 3. Velocity magnitude without weight decay

Fig. 4. Velocity magnitude with weight decay

The result of adding weight decay and velocity clamping to the model is visu-
alised in Fig. 6. This figure shows that these methods are successful in reducing
saturation in the hidden layer of the NN, because no values close to the boundary
of the activation function are returned.

The CEQPSO model with weight decay and element wise velocity clamping
provides a better model. The results of the out-sample data for this model and
the benchmark models are given in Fig. 7. The results of the Mann-Whitney
U test are displayed in Table 3. The symbols '+', '−' and '=' indicate that
the CEQPSO model is better, worse or the same as the CEPSO model. The
CEQPSO model is better than the CEPSO model for six companies and worse
for two. The unsaturated CEQPSO model therefore performs better than the
previous saturated model and now outperforms the CEPSO model on average.

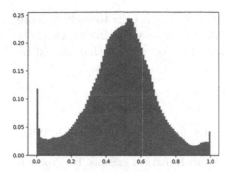

Fig. 5. Histogram of the normalised hidden layer outputs for Nedbank

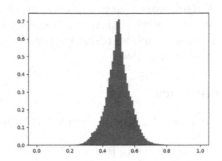

Fig. 6. Histogram of the normalised hidden layer outputs for Nedbank (no saturation)

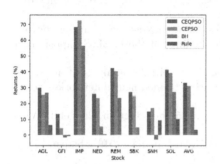

Fig. 7. Annualised return ratios of each stock for all models (Out-sample, no saturation)

Table 3. Mann-Whitney U test for the out-sample

	Median		
Company	CEPSO	CEQPSO	Symbol
AGL	26.771%	30.413%	+
GFI	3.318%	12.635%	+
IMP	73.659%	72.085%	−
NED	27.395%	28.326%	+
REM	40.341%	42.334%	+
SBK	26.353%	27.342%	+
SNH	17.502%	14.327%	−
SOL	39.351%	42.463%	+

6   Conclusion

This paper set out to achieve two objectives. The first objective was to show that the competitive co-evolutionary particle swarm optimization (CEPSO) model introduced by Papacostantis and Engelbrecht [14] is applicable to South African stocks. The second objective was to propose a dynamic variant of the PSO algorithm to better track optima in the dynamic environment of the stock market. The CEPSO model was applied to eight publicly traded South African companies and outperformed the popular buy-and-hold strategy showing that it is effective in discovering trading agents. A quantum PSO hybrid model, CEQPSO, was developed and applied to the eight aforementioned companies and made use of four technical market indicators to produce the necessary market data. The discovered strategies indicated high profit at low risk and outperformed the original CEPSO model.

Future work will expand the inputs to the neural networks to include more technical market indicators. The approach will also be adapted from a classifier to regression model to rather predict the percentage of a stock that should be bought or sold.

References

1. Bacon, C.R.: Practical Portfolio Performance Measurement and Attribution. Wiley (2004)
2. Blackwell, T.M., Bentley, P.J.: Dynamic search with charged swarms. In: Proceedings of the Genetic and Evolutionary Computation Conference, pp. 19–26 (2002)
3. Bosman, A.S., Engelbrecht, A.P., Helbig, M.: Fitness landscape analysis of weight-elimination neural networks. Neural Process. Lett. **48**, 353–373 (2018)
4. Chellapilla, K., Fogel, D.B.: Evolving neural networks to play checkers without expert knowledge. IEEE Trans. Neural Networks **10**(6), 1382–1391 (1999)
5. Colby, R.W.: The Encyclopedia of Technical Market Endicators, 2nd edn. McGraw-Hill Professional (2004)
6. Conradie, J., Engelbrecht, A.P.: Training bao game-playing agents using coevolutionary particle swarm optimization. In: Proceedings of the IEEE Symposium on Computational Intelligence in Games (2006)
7. Dennis, C., Engelbrecht, A.P., Ombuki-Berman, B.M.: An analysis of activation function saturation in particle swarm optimization trained neural networks. Neural Process. Lett. **52**, 1123–1153 (2020)
8. Engelbrecht, A.P.: Computational Intelligence: An Introduction, 2nd end. Wiley (2007)
9. Harper, D.R.: Forces that move stock prices. Investopedia (2019). https://www.investopedia.com/articles/basics/04/100804.asp
10. Harrison, K., Ombuki-Berman, B.M., Engelbrecht, A.P.: The effect of probability distributions on the performance of quantum particle swarm optimization for solving dynamic optimization problems. In: Proceedings of the IEEE Swarm Intelligence Symposium, pp. 242–250 (2015)
11. Kennedy, J., Eberhart, R.: Particle swarm optimization. In: Proceedings of the IEEE International Conference on Neural Networks, pp. 1942–1948 (1995)
12. Messerschmidt, L., Engelbrecht, A.P.: Learning to play games using a PSO-based competitive learning approach. IEEE Trans. Evol. Comput **8**(3), 280–288 (2004)
13. Pamparà, G., Engelbrecht, A.P.: Self-adaptive quantum particle swarm optimization for dynamic environments. In: Dorigo, M., Birattari, M., Blum, C., Christensen, A.L., Reina, A., Trianni, V. (eds.) ANTS 2018. LNCS, vol. 11172, pp. 163–175. Springer, Cham (2018). https://doi.org/10.1007/978-3-030-00533-7_13
14. Papacostantics, E., Engelbrecht, A.: Coevolutionary particle swarm optimization for evolving trend reversal indicators. In: Proceedings of the IEEE Symposium on Computational Intelligence for Financial Engineering & Economics (2011)
15. Poli, R.: Mean and variance of the sampling distribution of particle swarm optimizers during stagnation. IEEE Trans. Evol. Comput **13**, 712–721 (2009)
16. Rakitianskaia, A., Engelbrecht, A.P.: Weight regularisation in particle swarm optimisation neural network training. In: Proceedings of the IEEE Symposium on Swarm Intelligence (2014)
17. Rakitianskaia, A., Engelbrecht, A.P.: Saturation in PSO neural network training: Good or evil? In: Proceedings of the IEEE Congress on Evolutionary Computation, pp. 125–132 (2015)

18. Shi, Y., Eberhart, R.: Parameter selection in particle swarm optimization. In: Proceedings of the Seventh Annual Conference on Evolutionary Programming, pp. 591–600 (1998)
19. van Wyk, A., Engelbrecht, A.P.: Overfitting by PSO trained feedforward neural networks. In: Proceedings of the IEEE Congress on Evolutionary Computation (2010)

Randomized Neural Networks for Forecasting Time Series with Multiple Seasonality

Grzegorz Dudek[✉][ID]

Electrical Engineering Faculty, Czestochowa University of Technology,
Czestochowa, Poland
grzegorz.dudek@pcz.pl

Abstract. This work contributes to the development of neural forecasting models with novel randomization-based learning methods. These methods improve the fitting abilities of the neural model, in comparison to the standard method, by generating network parameters in accordance with the data and target function features. A pattern-based representation of time series makes the proposed approach useful for forecasting time series with multiple seasonality. In the simulation study, we evaluate the performance of the proposed models and find that they can compete in terms of forecasting accuracy with fully-trained networks. Extremely fast and easy training, simple architecture, ease of implementation, high accuracy as well as dealing with nonstationarity and multiple seasonality in time series make the proposed model very attractive for a wide range of complex time series forecasting problems.

Keywords: Multiple seasonality · Pattern representation of time series · Randomized neural networks · Short-term load forecasting · Time series forecasting

1 Introduction

Time series (TS) expressing different phenomena and processes may include multiple seasonal cycles of different lengths. They can be observed in demand variations for various goods, weather conditions, customer numbers, stock market indicators or results of experimental research. Multiple seasonality in TS as well as nonstationarity, nonlinear trend and random fluctuations place high demands on forecasting models. The model should be flexible enough to capture these features without imposing too much computational burden. Over the years, many sophisticated forecasting models for TS with multiple seasonality have been proposed including statistical and machine learning (ML) ones.

One of the most commonly employed classical approaches, the autoregressive moving average model (ARMA), can be extended to multiple seasonal cycles by

Supported by Grant 2017/27/B/ST6/01804 from the National Science Centre, Poland.

© Springer Nature Switzerland AG 2021

I. Rojas et al. (Eds.): IWANN 2021, LNCS 12862, pp. 196–207, 2021.
https://doi.org/10.1007/978-3-030-85099-9_16

including additional seasonal factors [1]. Another popular statistical model, Holt–Winters exponential smoothing (ETS), was developed for forecasting TS data that exhibits both a trend and a seasonal variation. ETS was extended to incorporate a second and a third seasonal component in [2]. Both these models, ARMA and seasonal Holt–Winters model, have a significant weakness. They require the same cyclical behavior for each period. In [3], to cope with changing seasonal patterns, innovations state space models for ETS were proposed. The limitation of the model is that it can only be used for double seasonality where one seasonal length is a multiple of the other. A further extension of ETS was proposed in [4]. To deal with multiple seasonal periods, high-frequency, non-integer seasonality, and dual-calendar effects, it combines an ETS state space model with Fourier terms, a Box-Cox transformation and ARMA error correction.

As an alternative to statistical models, ML models have the ability to learn relationships between predictors and forecasted variables from historical data. One of the most popular in the well-stocked arsenal of ML methods are neural networks (NNs). A huge number of forecasting models based on different NN architectures have been proposed [5]. They deal with multiple seasonality differently, depending on the specific architectural features and the creativity of the authors. For example, the model that won the renowned M4 Makridakis competition combines ETS and recurrent NN (RNN) [6]. In this approach, ETS produces two seasonal components for TS deseasonalization and adaptive normalization during on-the-fly preprocessing, while RNN, i.e. long short term memory (LSTM), predicts the preprocessed TS.

Another example of using LSTM for forecasting TS with multiple seasonal patterns was proposed recently in [7]. To deal with multiple seasonal cycles, the model initially deseasonalizes TS using different strategies including Fourier transformation. RNNs, such as LSTM, gated recurrent units, and DeepAR [8], dominate today as NN architectures for TS forecasting thanks to their powerful ability to process sequential data and capture long-term dependencies. But other deep architectures are also useful for forecasting multiple seasonal TS. For example, N-Beats [9] was designed specifically for TS with multiple seasonality. It is distinguished by a specific architecture including backward and forward residual links and a very deep stack of fully-connected layers.

The above presented approaches to forecasting TS with multiple seasonal periods rely on incorporating into the model mechanisms which allow it to deal with seasonal components. This complicates the model and makes it difficult to train and optimize. An alternative approach is to simplify the forecasting problem by TS decomposition or preprocessing. In [10], TS with three seasonal cycles was represented by patterns expressing unified shapes of the basic cycle. This preprocessing simplified the relationship between TS elements, making decomposition unnecessary and removing the need to build a complex model. Instead, simple shallow NNs can be used [10] or nonparametric regression models [11]. Experimental research has confirmed that these models can compete in terms of accuracy with state-of-the-art deep learning models, like the winning M4 submission [12].

In this study, we use a pattern representation of TS to simplify the forecasting problem with multiple seasonality and propose randomization-based shallow NNs to solve it. Randomized learning was proposed as an alternative to gradient-based learning as the latter is known to be time-consuming, sensitive to the initial parameter values and unable to cope with the local minima of the loss function. In randomized learning, the parameters of the hidden nodes are selected randomly and stay fixed. Only the output weights are learned. This makes the optimization problem convex and allows us to solve it without tedious gradient descent backpropagation, but using a standard linear least-squares method instead [13]. This leads to a very fast training. The main problem in randomized learning is how to select the random parameters to ensure the high performance of the NN [14, 15]. In this study, to generate the random parameters we use three methods recently proposed in [16, 17]. These methods distribute the activation functions (sigmoids) of hidden nodes randomly in the input space and adjust their weights (or a weight interval) to the target function (TF) complexity using different approaches.

The main goal of this study is to show that randomization-based NNs can compete in terms of forecasting accuracy with fully-trained NNs. The contribution of this study can be summarized as follows:

1. A new forecasting model for TS with multiple seasonality based on randomized NNs is proposed. To deal with multiple seasonality and nonstationarity, the model applies pattern representation of TS in order to simplify the relationship between input and output data.
2. Three randomization-based methods are used to generate the NN hidden node parameters. They introduce steep fragments of sigmoids in the input space, which improves modeling of highly nonlinear TFs. A randomized approach leads to extremely fast and easy training, simple NN architecture and ease of implementation.
3. Numerical experiments on several real-world datasets demonstrate the efficiency of the proposed randomization-based models when compared to fully-trained NNs.

The remainder of this work is structured as follows. Section 2 presents the proposed forecasting model based on randomized NNs, and a TS representation using patterns of seasonal cycles and three methods of generating NN parameters are described. The performance of the proposed approach is evaluated in Sect. 3. Finally, Sect. 4 concludes the work.

2   Forecasting Model

The proposed forecasting model is shown in Fig. 1. It is composed of encoder and decoder modules and a randomized feedforward NN (FNN). The model architecture, its specific features, and components are described below.

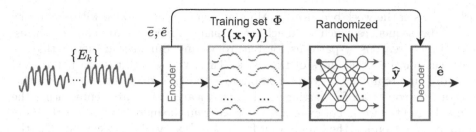

Fig. 1. Block diagram of the proposed forecasting model.

2.1 Encoder

The task of the encoder is to convert an original TS into unified input and output patterns of its seasonal cycles. To create input patterns, the TS expressing multiple seasonality, $\{E_k\}_{k=1}^{K}$, is divided into seasonal sequences of the shortest length. Let these sequences be expressed by vectors $\mathbf{e}_i = [E_{i,1}, E_{i,2}, \ldots, E_{i,n}]^T$, where n is the seasonal sequence length and $i = 1, 2, \ldots, K/n$ is the sequence number. These sequences are encoded in input patterns $\mathbf{x}_i - [x_{i,1}, x_{i,2}, \ldots, x_{i,n}]^T$ as follows:

$$\mathbf{x}_i = \frac{\mathbf{e}_i - \overline{e}_i}{\widetilde{e}_i} \tag{1}$$

where $\overline{e}_i$ is a mean value of sequence $\mathbf{e}_i$, and $\widetilde{e}_i = \sqrt{\sum_{t=1}^{n}(E_{i,t} - \overline{e}_i)^2}$ is a measure of sequence $\mathbf{e}_i$ dispersion.

Note that the x-patterns are normalized versions of centered vectors $\mathbf{e}_i$. All x-patterns, representing successive seasonal sequences, have zero mean, the same variance and the same unity length. However, they differ in shape. Thus, the original seasonal sequences, which have a different mean value and dispersion, are unified. This is shown in Fig. 2 on the example of the hourly electricity demand TS expressing three seasonalities: daily, weekly, and yearly. Note that the x-patterns representing the daily cycles are all normalized and differ only in shape.

The output patterns $\mathbf{y}_i = [y_{i,1}, y_{i,2}, \ldots, y_{i,n}]^T$ represent the forecasted sequences $\mathbf{e}_{i+\tau} = [E_{i+\tau,1}, E_{i+\tau,2}, \ldots, E_{i+\tau,n}]^T$, where $\tau \geq 1$ is a forecast horizon. The y-patterns are determined as follows:

$$\mathbf{y}_i = \frac{\mathbf{e}_{i+\tau} - \overline{e}_i}{\widetilde{e}_i} \tag{2}$$

where $\overline{e}_i$ and $\widetilde{e}_i$ are the same as in (1).

Note that in (2), for the i-th output pattern, we use the same coding variables $\overline{e}_i$ and $\widetilde{e}_i$ as for the i-th input pattern. This is because the coding variables for the forecasted sequence, $\overline{e}_{i+\tau}$ and $\widetilde{e}_{i+\tau}$, are unknown for the future period. Using the coding variables determined from the previous period has consequences which are demonstrated in Fig. 2. Note that y-patterns in this figure reveal the weekly seasonality. The y-patterns of Mondays are much higher than the patterns of other days of the week because the Monday sequences are coded with the means of Sunday sequences which are much lower than the means of Monday sequences. For similar reasons, y-patterns for Saturdays and Sundays are lower than y-patterns for the other days of the week. Thus, the y-patterns are not unified globally but are unified in groups composed of the same days of the week. For this reason, we construct forecasting models that learn from data representing the same days of the week. For example, when we train the model to forecast the daily sequence for Monday, the training set for it, $\Phi = \{(\mathbf{x}_i, \mathbf{y}_i)\}_{i=1}^{N}$, is composed of the y-patterns representing all Mondays from history and corresponding x-patterns representing the previous days (depending on the forecast horizon; Sundays for $\tau = 1$).

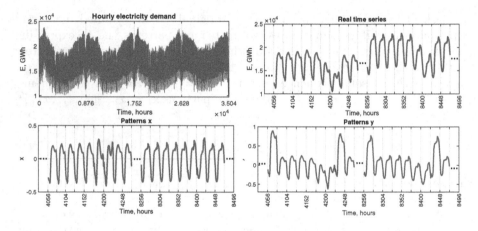

Fig. 2. Real hourly electricity demand TS and its x- and y-patterns.

2.2 Decoder

The decoder converts a forecasted output pattern into a TS seasonal cycle. The output pattern predicted by randomized FNN is decoded using the coding variables of the input query pattern, $\mathbf{x}$, using transformed Eq. (2):

$$\widehat{\mathbf{e}} = \widehat{\mathbf{y}}\widetilde{e} + \overline{e} \tag{3}$$

where $\widehat{\mathbf{e}}$ is the forecasted seasonal sequence, $\widehat{\mathbf{y}}$ is the forecasted output pattern, $\widetilde{e}$ and $\overline{e}$ are the coding variables determined from the TS sequence encoded in query pattern $\mathbf{x}$.

2.3 Randomized FNN

The randomized FNN is composed of n inputs, one hidden layer with m nonlinear nodes, and n outputs. Logistic sigmoid activation functions are employed for hidden nodes. The training set is $\Phi = \{(\mathbf{x}_i, \mathbf{y}_i)\}_{i=1}^{N}$, $\mathbf{x}_i, \mathbf{y}_i \in \mathbb{R}^n$. The randomized learning algorithm consists of three steps [18].

1. Randomly generate hidden node parameters, i.e. weights $\mathbf{a}_j = [a_{j,1}, a_{j,2}, \ldots, a_{j,n}]^T$ and biases $b_j, j = 1, 2, \ldots, m$, according to any continuous sampling distribution.
2. Calculate the hidden layer output matrix:

$$\mathbf{H} = \begin{bmatrix} \mathbf{h}(\mathbf{x}_1) \\ \vdots \\ \mathbf{h}(\mathbf{x}_N) \end{bmatrix} \tag{4}$$

where $\mathbf{h}(\mathbf{x}) = [h_1(\mathbf{x}), h_2(\mathbf{x}), \ldots, h_m(\mathbf{x})]$ is a nonlinear feature mapping from n-dimensional input space to m-dimensional feature space, and $h_j(\mathbf{x})$ is an activation function of the j-th node (a sigmoid in our case).
3. Calculate the output weights:

$$\beta = \mathbf{H}^+ \mathbf{Y} \tag{5}$$

where $\beta \in \mathbb{R}^{m \times n}$ is a matrix of output weights, $\mathbf{Y} \in \mathbb{R}^{N \times n}$ is a matrix of target output patterns, and $\mathbf{H}^+ \in \mathbb{R}^{m \times N}$ is the Moore-Penrose generalized inverse of matrix $\mathbf{H}$.

Typically, the hidden node weights and biases are i.i.d random variables both generated from the same symmetrical interval $a_{j,i}, b_j \sim U(-u, u)$. It was pointed out in [18] and [16] that as the weights and biases have different functions they should be selected separately. The weights decide about the sigmoid slopes and should reflect the TF complexity, while the biases decide about the sigmoid shift and should ensure the placement of the most nonlinear sigmoid fragments, i.e. the fragments around the sigmoid inflection points, into the input hypercube. These fragments, unlike saturation fragments, are most useful for modeling TF fluctuations.

Recently, to improve the performance of randomized FNNs, several new methods of generating the hidden node parameters have been proposed. Among them is the random a method (RaM) which was proposed in [16]. In the first step, this method randomly selects weights from the interval whose bounds u are adjusted to the TF complexity, $a_{j,i} \sim U(-u, u)$. Then, to ensure the introduction of the sigmoid inflection points into the input hypercube, the biases are calculated from:

$$b_j = -\mathbf{a}_j^T \mathbf{x}_j^* \tag{6}$$

where $\mathbf{x}_j^*$ is one of the training x-patterns selected for the j-th hidden node at random.

The second method proposed in [16], called the random α method (RαM), instead of generating weights, generates the slope angles of sigmoids. This changes the distribution of weights, which typically is a uniform one. This new distribution ensures that the slope angles of sigmoids are uniformly distributed, and so improves results by preventing overfitting, especially for highly nonlinear TFs. This method, in the first step, selects randomly the slope angles of the sigmoids, $\alpha_{j,i} \sim U(\alpha_{min}, \alpha_{max})$. Then, the the weights are calculated from:

$$a_{j,i} = 4 \tan \alpha_{j,i} \qquad (7)$$

Finally, the biases are determined from (6). To simplify the optimization process, the lower bound for the angles, α_{min}, can be set as $0°$. In such a case only one parameter decides about the model flexibility, i.e. $\alpha_{max} \in (0°, 90°)$. This is what we used in our simulation study.

To improve further FNN randomized learning, a data-driven method (DDM) was proposed in [17]. This method introduces the sigmoids into randomly selected regions of the input space and adjusts the sigmoid slopes to the TF slopes in these regions. As a result, the sigmoids mimic the TF locally, and their linear combination approximates smoothly the entire TF. In the first step, DDM selects the input space regions by selecting randomly the set of training points, $\{\mathbf{x}_j^*\}_{j=1}^m$. Then, the hyperplanes are fitted to the TF locally in the neighbourhoods of all points $\mathbf{x}_j^*$. The neighborhood of point $\mathbf{x}_j^*$, $\Psi(\mathbf{x}_j^*)$, contains this point and its k nearest neighbors in Φ. The weights are determined based on the hyperplane coefficients from:

$$a_{j,i} = 4a'_{j,i} \qquad (8)$$

where $a'_{j,i}$ are the coefficients of the hyperplane fitted to neighbourhood $\Psi(\mathbf{x}_j^*)$.

The hidden node biases are calculated from (6).

Note that the biases in the above-described approaches are determined based on the weights selected first and the data points. Unlike in the standard approach, they are not chosen randomly from the same interval as the weights. Randomized FNN has two hyperparameters to adjust: number of hidden nodes m, and the smoothing parameter, i.e. u, α_{max} or k, depending on the method of generating parameters chosen. These hyperparameters decide about the fitting performance of the model and its bias-variance tradeoff. Their optimal values should be selected by cross-validation for a given forecasting problem.

3   Simulation Study

In this section, we apply the proposed randomization-based neural models to forecasting hourly TS with three seasonalities: yearly, weekly and daily. These TS express electricity demand for four European countries: Poland (PL), Great Britain (GB), France (FR) and Germany (DE). We use real-world data collected from www.entsoe.eu. The data period covers the 4 years from 2012 to 2015. Atypical days such as public holidays were excluded from these data (between 10 and 20 days a year). The forecast horizon τ is one day, i.e. 24 h. We forecast the daily load profile for each day of 2015. For each forecasted day, a new training set is created and a new randomized model is optimized and trained. The results presented below are averaged over 100 independent training sessions.

The hyperparameters of randomized FNNs were selected using grid search and 5-fold cross-validation. The number of hidden nodes was selected from the set $\{5, 10, ..., 50\}$. The bounds for weights in RαM were selected from $\{0.02, 0.04, ..., 0.2, 0.4, ..., 1\}$. The α_{max} in RαM was selected from $\{2°, 4°, ..., 40°, 45°, ..., 90°\}$. The number of nearest neighbors in DDM was selected from $\{25, 27, ..., 69\}$.

For comparison, we applied a multilayer perceptron (MLP) for the same forecasting problems. MLP was composed of a single hidden layer with m sigmoid nodes whose number was selected using 5-fold cross-validation from the set $\{2, 4, ..., 24\}$. MLP was trained using Levenberg-Marquardt backpropagation with early stopping to avoid overtraining (20% of training samples were used as validation samples).

Forecasting quality metrics for the test data are presented in Table 1. They include: mean absolute percentage error (MAPE), median of APE, root mean square error (RMSE), mean percentage error (MPE), and standard deviation of percentage error (PE) as a measure of the forecast dispersion.

Table 1. Forecasting results.

		RαM	RαM	DDM	MLP
PL data	MAPE	1.32	1.32	1.35	1.37
	Median(APE)	0.93	0.94	0.94	0.96
	RMSE	358.86	364.13	380.77	374.86
	MPE	0.40	0.39	0.39	0.26
	Std(PE)	1.94	1.98	2.09	2.07
GB data	MAPE	2.61	2.62	2.80	2.93
	Median(APE)	1.88	1.90	1.99	2.17
	RMSE	1187.60	1184.58	1382.97	1314.78
	MPE	0.61	−0.61	−0.58	0.60
	Std(PE)	3.57	3.56	4.16	3.99
FR data	MAPE	1.67	1.69	1.81	1.87
	Median(APE)	1.15	1.16	1.25	1.31
	RMSE	1422.60	1433.90	1530.15	1565.70
	MPE	−0.42	−0.39	−0.45	−0.39
	Std(PE)	2.60	2.61	2.78	2.85
DE data	MAPE	1.38	1.39	1.43	1.58
	Median(APE)	0.96	0.98	0.99	1.09
	RMSE	1281.14	1242.36	1333.79	1452.54
	MPE	0.14	0.14	0.10	0.04
	Std(PE)	2.22	2.13	2.34	2.50

More detailed results, i.e. distributions of APE, are shown in Fig. 3. Based on APE, we performed a Wilcoxon signed-rank test with $\alpha = 0.05$ to indicate the most accurate models. Figure 4 depicts pairwise comparisons of the models. The arrow lying at the intersection of the two models indicates which of them gave the significantly lower error. A lack of an arrow means that both models gave statistically indistinguishable errors.

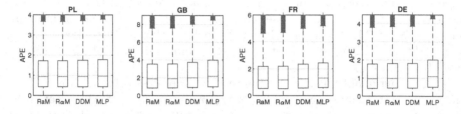

Fig. 3. Boxplots of APE.

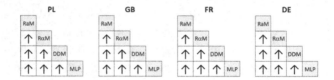

Fig. 4. Results of the Wilcoxon signed-rank test for APE.

As can be seen from Table 1 and Fig. 4, the randomization-based FNNs gave significantly lower errors than fully-trained MLP for each dataset. According to the Wilcoxon test, RaM outperformed the other approaches.

MPE shown in Table 1 allows us to asses the bias of the forecasts produced by different models. A positive value of MPE indicates underprediction, while a negative value indicates overprediction. As can be seen from Table 1, for PL and DE data the bias was positive, whilst for GB and FR data it was negative. The forecasts produced by MLP for PL and DE were less biased than the forecast produced by randomized FNNs.

Figure 5 presents examples of forecasts of the daily load profiles produced by the examined models. Note that the proposed models generate multi-output response, maintaining the relationships between the output variables (y-pattern components). In the case of single-output models, these relationships are ignored because the variables are predicted independently. This may cause a lack of smoothness in the forecasted curve (zigzag effect; see for example [19]).

Figure 6 shows the optimal numbers of hidden nodes selected in the cross-validation procedure. Obviously, the number of hidden nodes is dependent on TF complexity. The forecasting problem for PL required the greatest number of

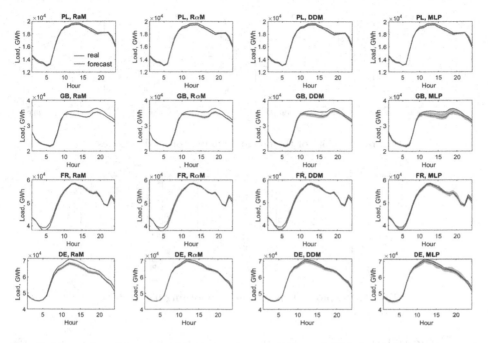

Fig. 5. Examples of forecasts (shaded regions are 5th and 95th percentiles, measured over 100 trials).

nodes for randomized FNNs, around 30, regardless of the learning method. MLP for PL needed many fewer nodes, 12 on average. Other forecasting problems were solved by randomized FNNs with fewer hidden nodes, from 20 to 30 on average. For these problems, the difference in the number of nodes between MLP and randomized FNNs was not as large as for PL data. The relatively small number of hidden nodes in randomized FNNs (note that randomized learning usually requires hundreds or even thousands of nodes) results from TS representation by unified patterns and the decomposition of the forecasting problem (a separate model for each forecasting task, i.e. every day in 2015, trained on the selected patterns).

The optimal values of smoothing parameters for the randomized learning methods are depicted in Fig. 7. As can be seen from this figure, the optimal value of the bound for weights in RaM varies from 0.2 for FR to 0.7 for GB on average, which correspond to sigmoid slope angles from around 3° to 10° (see [16]). The optimal value of the bound for slope angle in RαM varies from 12° for FR to 32° for DE on average. Note also the high value of k in DDM (from 49 for PL to 65 for FR on average) in relation to the number of training points, which ranged from 150 to 200. Thus, for our forecasting problems we can expect flat TFs without fluctuations. Such TFs can be modeled using RaM. Its competitors, RαM and DDM, reveal their strengths in modeling highly nonlinear TFs with fluctuations (see [16,17]).

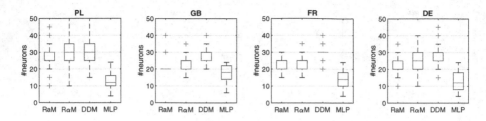

Fig. 6. Boxplots of the optimal number of hidden nodes.

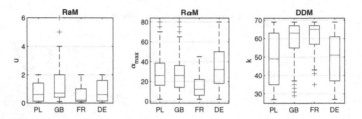

Fig. 7. Boxplots of the optimal smoothing parameters.

4   Conclusion

Forecasting TS with multiple seasonality is a challenging problem, which we propose to solve with randomized FNNs. Unlike fully-trained FNNs, randomized FNNs learn extremely fast and are easy to implement. The simulation study showed that their forecasting accuracy is comparable to the accuracy of fully-trained NNs. To deal with nonstationary TS with multiple seasonal periods, the proposed approach employs a pattern representation of the TS. This representation simplifies the relationship between input and output data and makes the problem easier to solve using simple regression models.

The effectiveness of the randomized FNNs in modeling nonlinear target functions was achieved due to the application of new methods of generating hidden node parameters. These methods, using different approaches, introduce the steepest fragments of sigmoids, which are most useful for modeling TF fluctuations, into the input hypercube and adjust their slopes to TF complexity. This makes the model more flexible, more data-dependent, and more dependent on the complexity of the solved forecasting problem.

In a future study, we plan to introduce an attention mechanism into our randomization-based forecasting models to select training data and develop an ensemble approach for these models.

References

1. Box, G.E.P., Jenkins, G.M., Reinsel, G.C.: Time Series Analysis: Forecasting and Control, 3rd edn. Prentice Hall, New Jersey (1994)

2. Taylor, J.W.: Triple seasonal methods for short-term load forecasting. Eur. J. Oper. Res. **204**, 139–152 (2010)
3. Gould, P.G., Koehler, A.B., Ord, J.K., Snyder, R.D., Hyndman, R.J., Vahid-Araghi, F.: Forecasting time-series with multiple seasonal patterns. Eur. J. Oper. Res. **191**, 207–222 (2008)
4. De Livera, A.M., Hyndman, R.J., Snyder, R.D.: Forecasting time series with complex seasonal patterns using exponential smoothing. J. Am. Stat. Assoc. **106**(496), 1513–1527 (2011)
5. Benidis, K., et al.: Neural forecasting: Introduction and literature overview. arXiv:2004.10240 (2020)
6. Smyl, S.: A hybrid method of exponential smoothing and recurrent neural networks for time series forecasting. Int. J. Forecast. **36**(1), 75–85 (2020)
7. Bandara, K., Bergmeir, C., Hewamalage, H.: LSTM-MSNet: leveraging forecasts on sets of related time series with multiple seasonal patterns. IEEE Trans. Neural Netw. Learn. Syst. **32**(4), 1586–1599 (2021)
8. Salinas, D., Flunkert, V., Gasthaus, J., Januschowski, J.: DeepAR: probabilistic forecasting with autoregressive recurrent networks. Int. J. Forecast. **36**(3), 1181–1191 (2020)
9. Oreshkin, B.N., Carpov, D., Chapados, N., Bengio, Y.: N-BEATS: neural basis expansion analysis for interpretable time series forecasting. In: 8th International Conference on Learning Representations, ICLR (2020)
10. Dudek, G.: Neural networks for pattern-based short-term load forecasting: a comparative study. Neurocomputing **205**, 64–74 (2016)
11. Dudek, G.: Pattern similarity-based methods for short-term load forecasting - Part 1: Principles. Appl. Soft Comput. **37**, 277–287 (2015)
12. Dudek, G., Pełka, P., Smyl, S.: A hybrid residual dilated LSTM and exponential smoothing model for mid-term electric load forecasting. IEEE Trans. Neural Netw. Learn. Syst. (2020) https://doi.org/10.1109/TNNLS.2020.3046629
13. Principe, J., Chen, B.: Universal approximation with convex optimization: gimmick or reality? IEEE Comput. Intell. Mag. **10**(2), 68–77 (2015)
14. Cao, W., Wang, X., Ming, Z., Gao, J.: A review on neural networks with random weights. Neurocomputing **275**, 278–287 (2018)
15. Zhang, L., Suganthan, P.: A survey of randomized algorithms for training neural networks. Inf. Sci. **364–365**, 146–155 (2016)
16. Dudek, G.: Generating random parameters in feedforward neural networks with random hidden nodes: drawbacks of the standard method and how to improve it. In: Yang, H., Pasupa, K., Leung, A.C.-S., Kwok, J.T., Chan, J.H., King, I. (eds.) ICONIP 2020. CCIS, vol. 1333, pp. 598–606. Springer, Cham (2020). https://doi.org/10.1007/978-3-030-63823-8_68
17. Dudek, G.: Data-driven randomized learning of feedforward neural networks. In: 2020 International Joint Conference on Neural Networks (IJCNN), Glasgow, United Kingdom, pp. 1–8 (2020)
18. Dudek, G.: Generating random weights and biases in feedforward neural networks with random hidden nodes. Inf. Sci. **481**, 33–56 (2019)
19. Dudek, G.: Multivariate regression tree for pattern-based forecasting time series with multiple seasonal cycles. In: Borzemski, L., Swatek, J., Wilimowska, Z. (eds.) ISAT 2017. AISC, vol. 655, pp. 85–94. Springer, Cham (2018). https://doi.org/10.1007/978-3-319-67220-5_8

Prediction of Air Pollution Using LSTM

Stanislaw Osowski[1,2]([✉])

[1] Faculty of Electrical Engineering, Warsaw University of Technology,
Koszykowa 75, Warsaw, Poland
stanislaw.osowski@ee.pw.edu.pl
[2] Electronic Faculty, Military University of Technology, Koszykowa 75, Warsaw, Poland

Abstract. The paper describes the application of long short-term memory (LSTM) for air pollution forecasting. LSTM is a special design of deep structure recurrent neural networks, which is very well suited for the prediction of the sequences of data. This work investigates its properties in the task of the short-time one-hour ahead and the one day ahead prediction of air pollutants such as PM10, SO2, NO2, and ozone in Warsaw, Poland. The results of numerical investigations have shown very good accuracy in online prediction, exceeding the corresponding values obtained at the application of feedforward neural structures.

Keywords: LSTM · Time series prediction · Air pollution

1 Introduction

Air pollution refers to the presence of pollutants, such as solid and liquid particles and certain gases that are suspended in the air. They come from car exhaust, factories, the burning of fossil fuels, agriculture activities volcanoes, or wildfires. To the common air pollutants belong particulate matters (typical PM10 and PM2.5), nitrogen dioxide NO2, sulfur dioxide (SO2), or ozone.

Exposure to high levels of air pollution can cause health problems, such as the risk of respiratory infections, heart disease, or even lung cancer. It can also harm pets and wildlife. The acid rain caused by air pollution raises the acidity in rivers and streams and in this way destroys plants and trees.

Accurate forecasting helps people to make some prevention which might lead to decreasing the effects on health and the costs associated. Therefore, many mathematical models of prediction have been developed in the past. These models are mathematical simulations of how airborne pollutants disperse in the air.

The most general approaches are based on the models of linear autoregression and artificial neural networks (nonlinear models) [1–4]. Especially neural networks have shown very good results and high advantage over linear autoregressive approaches. Typical neural solutions include such predictive tools as multilayer perceptron, radial basis function network, support vector machine, and ensembles built on their basis. Their accuracy depends on the type of neural solution as well as the region, in which the measurements have been done.

© Springer Nature Switzerland AG 2021
I. Rojas et al. (Eds.): IWANN 2021, LNCS 12862, pp. 208–219, 2021.
https://doi.org/10.1007/978-3-030-85099-9_17

Nowadays, because of the flexibility of the network framework, many complex deep learning networks have been developed for air quality prediction. In the era of deep learning, the most effective time series prediction seems to be the application of the so-called long short-term memory (LSTM) deep network [5–8]. Many papers applying different forms of it have been presented. Its application is very simple since it memorizes naturally the sequences of process and uses this information in predicting the next step.

The paper will show the forecasting system based on the application of LSTM networks combined in an ensemble. The architecture of the predicting system is very simple. The past values of pollution levels are delivered to the input of the LSTM network and based on this information the prediction of the pollution for the next period is generated. Many runs of the algorithm produce the predicted results. All of them are aggregated in the final predictive model for the next hour or the next day.

The numerical simulations have been concerned with four types of pollutants: PM10, SO2, NO2, and ozone. The system is trained for predicting at the same time all four pollutants levels. The numerical results will be presented for the one-hour ahead and one day ahead prediction problem of air pollution in Warsaw applying the real measurement results gathered in 4 years. The results have shown significant improvement in comparison to the application of a feedforward neural network solution.

2 Prediction System Based on LSTM

2.1 Problem Statement

The general procedure used in forecasting the time series can be presented as the sequence of the following operations.

- Separate the time series $x(t)$ used for learning ($x_l(t)$ and testing ($x_t(t)$) parts.
- Perform the normalization of the data using the standardization with the mean and standard deviation estimated for the known learning part.
- Train the LSTM network using the normalized learning data.
- Test the trained LSTM using the testing data set.
- De-normalize the forecasted values applying the known values of the mean and standard deviation (the same as estimated for the learning data) and calculate the assumed quality measures estimated for the testing results.

The applied standardization procedure is defined on the learning data set as follows

$$x(n) := \frac{x(n) - m_l}{s_l} \tag{1}$$

The mean value $m_l = mean(x_l)$ and standard deviation $s_l = std(x_l)$ are estimated only for learning data x_l and then used directly for testing data x_t, which did not take part in the learning stage. This form of normalization is preferred due to the very high difference between the single maximum and minimum values observed in the time series. The de-normalization procedure of the predicted normalized data $x_t(n)$ is the inverse of the normalization process, i.e.

$$x_t(n) = x_t(n) \cdot s_l + m_l \tag{2}$$

The LSTM predictor is learned on the learning samples and the parameters of the network are fixed. Then, the learned LSTM structure is tested using the testing data.

2.2   LSTM Time Series Predictor

The recurrent LSTM network was developed by Hochreiter & Schmidhuber in 1997 [9, 10]. We can recognize the input signal layer, one hidden layer of mutual feedback between neurons (so-called LSTM cells), and the feedforward output layer fed by the output signals of the LSTM memory cells in the hidden layer. The general form of a single LSTM cell is presented in Fig. 1.

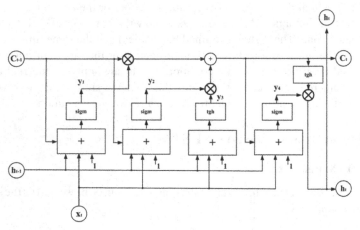

Fig. 1. The structure of the single memory LSTM cell. It contains 4 typical feedforward subnetworks of sigmoidal activations and 3 multiplicative gates denoted in the figure by symbol ×.

The two succeeding time points; the actual t and the previous t-1 representing the previous point of time are taken into account in cell operation. The performance of the cell can be described by the mathematical function that takes three inputs and generates two output signals,

$$(h_t, c_t) = L(h_{t-1}, c_{t-1}, \mathbf{x}_t) \qquad (3)$$

- $\mathbf{x}_t$ – the input signal (vector) in the actual time point t; it represents the actual value of the time series in time t.
- c_{t-1} – the memory signal called cell state, representing the internal cell state from the previous time point t-1.
- h_{t-1} – the output signal of the cell corresponding to the previous time point t-1.

In each time point t the cell generates two output signals:

- c_t – the internal state of the memory cell corresponding to the actual time point t

- h_t – the output signal of the cell in the actual time point t. This signal of the neuron in the hidden layer is delivered to all neurons in the output layer (the feedforward direction of signal transmission).

Both output signals (c_t and h_t) leave the cell at time point t and are fed back to that same cell at a time $t + 1$. Additionally, the elements forming the actual time sequence x_{t+1} are also fed into the cell and start processing the signals in the next time point $t + 1$.

The LSTM cell applies three multiplication gates, denoted in the figure by the symbol $\times$. The upper gate seen on the left side of the figure represents the controlled memory. It defines the percentage of the memory from the previous state which is transferred to the state of a cell in the actual time (the ratio from 0 to 1 of the signal y_1 is transferred further).

The second gate shown in the middle of the figure controls the amount of information c_{t-1}, which will form the state of a cell in the actual (next) time point t. The output signal h_t of the cell is created using the multiplicative gate shown in the right of the figure. It is the product of the created memory signal c_t (after hyperbolic tangential activation) and the output signal of the sigmoidal neuron supplied by the actual vector x_t, signal h_{t-1}, and bias. The signal of this gate defines how much information from the past is transmitted to the cell in the next time point.

Assume the notation of LSTM signals in the form of double indexes: the first one represents the notation of signals y_i (here $i = 1, 2, 3$, and 4) and the second represents the symbol of the input (supply) signal (here c, h, and x). For example, w_{1h} means the weight matrix of the first gate processing the output signals h_{t-1} of the previous time point. The unipolar sigmoidal function is denoted symbolically by $sigm$ and bipolar hyperbolic tangent function by tgh. In such case, the signals y_1, y_2, y_3, and y_4 are described by the following equations [9, 10]

$$y_1 = sigm(w_{1c}c_{t-1} + w_{1h}h_{t-1} + \mathbf{w}_{1x}\mathbf{x}_t + w_{10}) \tag{4}$$

$$y_2 = sigm(w_{2c}c_{t-1} + w_{2h}h_{t-1} + \mathbf{w}_{2x}\mathbf{x}_t + w_{20}) \tag{5}$$

$$y_3 = tgh(w_{3c}h_{t-1} + \mathbf{w}_{3x}\mathbf{x}_t + w_{30}) \tag{6}$$

$$y_4 = sigm(w_{4c}c_t + w_{4h}h_{t-1} + \mathbf{w}_{4x}\mathbf{x}_t + w_{40}) \tag{7}$$

Based on these signal values the actual memory state c_t and output signal h_t of the cell are calculated

$$c_t = y_2y_3 + c_{t-1}y_1 \tag{8}$$

$$h_t = y_4 \cdot tgh(c_t) \tag{9}$$

The additional problem is the calculation of gradient in a recurrent architecture. However, the great help in this problem is so-called backpropagation in time, representing the deep structure of backward direction in time. This interpretation is presented in Fig. 2. The gradient computation needed in the learning stage is now easily implemented in the typical form of backpropagation through time realized within the assumed time window T, as shown in Fig. 2 for one input signal $\mathbf{x}$ represented in different time points: t, $t + 1$, $t + 2 \ldots T$.

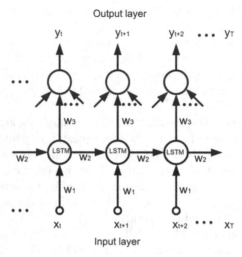

Fig. 2. The scheme of the forward propagation through time representing feedback in the recurrent network. It shows connections of only one hidden neuron (LSTM cell) in a feedforward form at the application of time sequence x_t of input signals. In backpropagation, through time the direction of the flow of signals is simply reversed and the former output signals are replaced by the actual errors at the particular points of time.

The hidden states of LSTM cells are passed through time, and the recurrent network can accept an input sequence of any length $t \rightarrow T$ and generate an output sequence of any length. The layer of n LSTM cells corresponds to the concatenation of n cells, each with a different set of internal weight parameters. This can be written in a vector form

$$(\mathbf{h}_t, \mathbf{c}_t) = \mathbf{L}(\mathbf{h}_{t-1}, \mathbf{c}_{t-1}, \mathbf{x}_t) \tag{10}$$

The LSTM units are trained in a supervised mode using the set of training sequences. The signals from the previous time are put into the network and are associated with the required signals in the next time point. The inputs are fed into the network, pass through the hidden layer to an output and the error between the expected output and actual output is quantified as a loss function. The error is backpropagated through the network and allows calculating the gradient, used in the learning procedure.

After the model has been trained the next out-of-sample multi-step time series can be produced by the network. At given time series $[x_{t1}, x_{t2} \ldots x_T]$ we want to forecast the next k time points into the future to get $[x_{T+1}, x_{T+2} \ldots x_{T+k}]$. The value k may be just one step producing the next step time series element.

3   Numerical Experiments

3.1   Database

The numerical experiments have been performed using the database of four air pollutants (PM10, SO2, NO2, and ozone) collected in Warsaw (Ursynów place) within four years [4]. They might be available on request. The total number of samples used in experiments we 36831. The measured samples represent the hourly values. The dataset may be available publicly upon request. The data are characterized by a very large variety (high standard deviation compared to their mean values). The important (in MAPE calculation) is also the minimum values since they deteriorate the MAPE in a significant way. Especially susceptible to this is ozone, for which the minimum achieved a very small value. This is well seen by analyzing the corresponding values collected in Table 1.

Table 1. The chosen statistical parameters of the data corresponding to four pollutants

	PM10	SO2	NO2	Ozone
Mean $\left[\mu g/m^3\right]$	33.56	9.89	24.82	48.43
Std/mean [%]	78.20	88.82	71.92	64.20
Max $\left[\mu g/m^3\right]$	414.91	57.84	203.86	189.12
Min $\left[\mu g/m^3\right]$	0.70	0.71	0.42	0.09

The scale of difficulty in forecasting these pollutants in one-hour ahead prognosis mode is well illustrated on the distribution of samples, presented in the coordinate system representing two neighboring hours. This is shown in Fig. 3. The wider is the diagonal band, the higher dispersion of data and the more different are the neighboring pollution levels. It is evident, that the most difficult is the task of predicting SO2 changes.

3.2   Applied Network and Quality Measures

Based on the past measured values representing time series the next hour or next day pollution was predicted. The applied structure of the LSTM network developed after series of introductory experiments with validation data was 4-300-4 (4 preceding input values of 4 pollutants: PM10, SO2, No2 and ozone, 300 LSTM cells in the hidden layer, and the predicted values of all pollutants on the output of the network corresponding to the succeeding hour). 80% of data have been used in learning and the remaining 20% are left for testing. Different arrangements of learning and testing data have been investigated. Only the results of testing are presented in the paper.

The applied learning algorithm was the typical gradient descent method. It was implemented in Matlab with the ADAM algorithm, initial learning rate 0.005, learning rate schedule piecewise, learning rate drop period 125, and learning rated drop factor

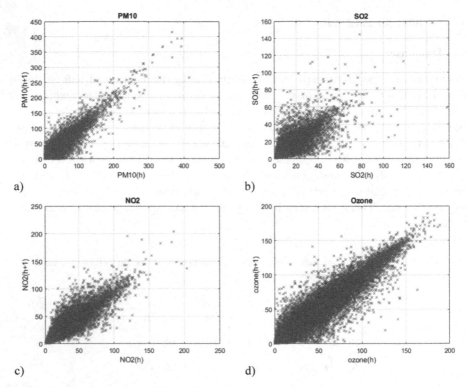

Fig. 3. The distribution of pollution of the next hour versus their values in the previous hour: a) PM10, b) SO2, c) NO2 and d) ozone.

0.2. The network was trained on the learning data, and 10% of this data was used in the validation of learning progress. The parameters of the trained network were fixed and the circuit was tested using the testing data. In the testing phase, the known data vector representing the previous day is delivered as the input to the network, and based on this information the prediction for the actual day is made.

The different quality measures of the system performance have been applied [11]: the mean absolute percentage error (MAPE), mean absolute error (MAE), root mean squared error (RMSE), mean percentage statistical error (MPSE), and correlation coefficient (R). They are defined as follows: $MAPE = \frac{1}{n}(\sum_{i=1}^{n} \frac{|d_i - y_i|}{d_i}) \cdot 100\%$, $MAE = \frac{1}{n}(\sum_{i=1}^{n} |d_i - y_i|)$,

$RMSE = \sqrt{\frac{1}{n} \sum_{i=1}^{n} |d_i - y_i|^2}$, $MPSE \cong \frac{\|\mathbf{d} - \mathbf{y}\|}{\|\mathbf{d}\|} \cdot 100\%$, and $R = R_{yd}/std(y)std(d)$. The

variables $\mathbf{d}$ and $\mathbf{y}$ represent vectors of the destination (the true values of output) and the actual values generated by the predictor, respectively. The symbol R_{yd} represents the covariance of $\mathbf{y}$ and $\mathbf{d}$ and std the appropriate standard deviation. The MPSE is similar to MAPE, however, avoids the trap of close to zero destination values, since it operates on the norms of vectors, instead of ratios computed for the individual samples.

3.3 Numerical Results

The results of simulations will be presented for two cases: the individual modes of predictors and combining the results of them in the so-called ensemble, integrated in an average way to create the final verdict of prediction. This is not a typical way of ensemble creation, since it is based on many runs of the algorithm with different starting parameters, instead of using different types of members. The ensemble was created by 5 members. Each member is represented by the results of the run of the LSTM predictor at the same set of testing data (the runs start at different arrangement of the learning data, therefore, their results differ). All experiments have been conducted using Matlab2020a [12].

Table 2. The statistical results of PM10 in hourly prediction

PM10	MAPE [%]	MAE $\left[\frac{\mu g}{m^3}\right]$	RMSE $\left[\frac{\mu g}{m^3}\right]$	MPSE [%]	R
Mean of individuals	13.86	4.27	7.40	11.91	0.9649
Ensemble	13.80	4.11	7.36	11.74	0.9653

Table 2 presents the quality measures of hourly prediction of PM10 obtained in an individual mode of predictors (the average of their quality measures) and combining the predicted values of all members to one final verdict by averaging their results. It is seen that assembling the individual predicted results into one final verdict leads to some improvement of the quality of the system.

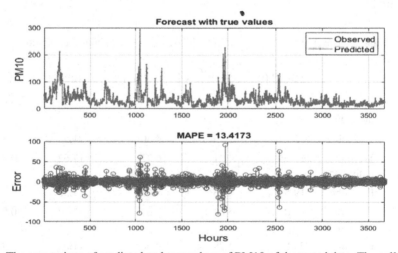

Fig. 4. The comparison of predicted and true values of PM10 of the tested data. The pollution is presented in $\left[\mu g/m^3\right]$.

It is interesting to compare the results of the prediction with the real measured values of the tested data in a graphical way. This is done in Fig. 4 in the form of predicted versus really observed time series in the upper figure, and the error (the difference between the observed and predicted hourly values) in the bottom figure. They represent the result of one chosen run. Such a large period of presentation does not allow us to see the details of the time series. Therefore, Fig. 5 depicts the detailed results for a small chosen period.

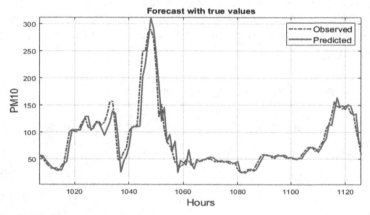

Fig. 5. The detailed curves of predicted versus really observed values of PM10 in a small period.

The experiments performed for the other pollutants have shown similar results. Tables 3, 4, and 6 depict the corresponding statistical quality values for SO2, NO2, and ozone, respectively (the mean of individual predictors and the forecasted results of the ensemble).

Table 3. The statistical results of SO2, NO2, and ozone in hourly prediction

Pollutant		MAPE [%]	MAE $\left[\frac{\mu g}{m^3}\right]$	RMSE $\left[\frac{\mu g}{m^3}\right]$	MPSE [%]	R
SO2	Mean of individuals	23.48	2.22	4.40	22.20	0.8488
	Ensemble	22.82	2.15	4.30	21.52	0.8556
NO2	Mean of individuals	19.95	4.21	6.72	17.62	0.9157
	Ensemble	19.53	4.13	6.63	17.30	0.9180
Ozone	Mean of individuals	26.00	5.81	8.62	11.24	0.9592
	Ensemble	25.93	5.79	8.60	11.31	0.9593

The level of quality measures for these pollutants is slightly worse compared to PM10. This is due mainly to a higher level of instantaneous changes of their values.

Very interesting is the large difference between MAPE and MPSE values for ozone (MAPE = 25.93% and MPSE = 11.31%). This is the result of very high number of the very small (close to zero) observed values of the samples in the database.

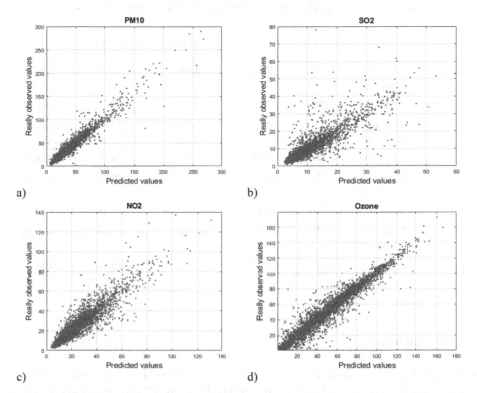

Fig. 6. The distribution of samples representing the predicted values (horizontal axis) and the observed values (vertical axis) for testing data of a) PM10, b) SO2, c) NO2 and d) ozone.

Figure 6 presents the distribution of testing samples in the coordinate system formed by the predicted values of samples (horizontal) and true observed (vertical). Comparing it with the learning data distribution in Fig. 3 we can see a significant difference (the diagonal band is now much narrower for each pollutant).

Additional experiments have been performed for predicting the daily average values of the pollutants. This is a much easier task since the average values are characterized by smaller variations compared to the hourly changes. It should be noted, that the daily averaged values are very useful in practice.

Table 4 presents the MAPE, MAE, MPSE, and RMSE errors, as well as the correlation coefficient R in this particular case. The prediction of the next element of the time series was based on the input value representing the preceding value of the particular pollutant. Despite the very simple prediction architecture (1–300–1) the results are of very good quality, especially compared to the one-hour ahead prediction for the whole day pattern, presented in Table 3. For example, the MAPE of PM10 was reduced this time from

13.80% to only 4.28%. Similar reductions are also observed for other pollutants, for example MAPE in the case of ozone was reduced from 25.93% to 15.23%.

Table 4. The statistical results of pollutant predictions in daily mean mode

Pollutant		MAPE [%]	MAE $\left[\frac{\mu g}{m^3}\right]$	RMSE $\left[\frac{\mu g}{m^3}\right]$	MPSE [%]	R
PM10	Mean of individuals	4.85	0.27	0.33	5.39	0.8823
	Ensemble	4.28	0.24	0.29	5.12	0.8828
SO2	Mean of individuals	15.05	0.49	0.57	19.04	0.7785
	Ensemble	14.79	0.41	0.55	18.07	0.7832
NO2	Mean of individuals	17.27	0.75	0.93	20.18	0.7512
	Ensemble	17.10	0.73	0.91	19.19	0.7527
Ozone	Mean of individuals	15.47	0.79	1.05	15.91	0.8153
	Ensemble	15.23	0.72	1.03	15.76	0.8160

4   Conclusions

The paper has presented the application of the LSTM network to the online prediction of air pollutant levels. The LSTM network has shown very good performance in this task. The recurrent nature included in such operation is very well suited to the prediction problems, in which the previous state has a great influence on the next value. Such property is absent in the feed-forward structure of neural networks, where there is no feedback (multilayer perceptron, radial basis function network, or support vector machine). Despite the very simple architecture of LSTM, the results of prediction ae good and better than those obtained in a very sophisticated structure based on the feed-forward architectures presented in [4]. Moreover, the computation time is relatively low. For example, the time of one run in predicting the daily mean of a single pollutant at 1228 learning samples was about 20 s in a laptop with GPU.

Due to the flexibility of neural frameworks, many complex learning networks have been developed for air quality prediction in the past. As far as we know, there is no unified dataset in the current air quality prediction research. Therefore, the fair comparison of the results is difficult because they depend on the localization of the measurement site and the characteristics of the pollution mechanisms. Particular regions of the world have different pollution generation mechanisms, which may lead to various difficulties in prediction process.

Table 5. The comparative results of MAPE in daily mean prediction

PM10	PM10	SO2	NO2	Ozone
Results of [4]	17.83%	18.35%	18.27%	17.31%
Present best results	4.28%	14.79%	17.10%	15.23%

Therefore, the comparison to other methods will be presented here only for the same data, that has been used previously in [4]. Table 5 presents such a comparison concentrated on MAPE for all considered pollutants.

All results obtained at the application of LSTM are much better. Especially high improvement is visible in the case of PM10. Similar levels of improvements have been observed for other quality measures of all pollutants.

In future studies, more emphasis will be placed on considering the longer prediction period as well as the influence of other meteorological parameters such as the wind, temperature, humidity, etc.

References

1. Taşpınar, F.: Improving artificial neural network model predictions of daily average PM10 concentrations by applying principle component analysis and implementing the seasonal model. J. Air Waste Manag. Assoc. **65**, 800–809 (2015)
2. Agirre-Basurko, E., Ibarra-Berastegi, G., Madriaga, I.: Regression and multilayer perceptron-based models for forecast hourly O3 and NO2 levels in the Bilbao area. Environ. Model. Softw. **21**(4), 430–446 (2006)
3. Grivas, G., Chaloulakou, A.: Artificial neural network models for predictions of PM10 hourly concentrations in greater area of Athens. Atmos. Environ. **40**(7), 1216–1229 (2006)
4. Siwek, K., Osowski, S.: Data mining methods for prediction of air pollution. Int. J. Appl. Math. Comput. Sci. **26**(2), 467–478 (2016)
5. Chang, Y.S., Chiao, H.T., Abimannan, S., Huang, Y.P., Tsai, Y.T., Ming, L.K.: An LSTM-based aggregated model for air pollution forecasting. Atmos. Pollut. Res. **11**(8), 1451–1463 (2020)
6. Li, X., et al.: Long short-term memory neural network for air pollutant concentration predictions: Method development and evaluation. Environ. Pollut. **231**(1), 997–1004 (2017)
7. Xayasouk, T., Lee, H.M., Lee, G.: Air pollution prediction using long short-term memory (LSTM) and deep autoencoder (DAE) models. Sustainability **12**, 2570 (2020). https://doi.org/10.3390/su12062570
8. Guo, C., Liu, G., Chen, C.H.: Air pollution concentration forecast method based on the deep ensemble neural network. Wirel. Commun. Mob. Comput. **8854649**, 1–13 (2020). https://doi.org/10.1155/2020/8854649
9. Hochreiter, S., Schmidhuber, J.: Long short-term memory. Neural Comput. **9**(8), 1735–1780 (1997). https://doi.org/10.1162/neco.1997.9.8.1735
10. Greff, K., Srivastava, R.K., Koutník, J., Steunebrink, B.R., Schmidhuber, J.: LSTM: a search space odyssey. IEEE Trans. Neural Netw. Learn. Syst. **28**(10), 2222–2232 (2017). https://doi.org/10.1109/TNNLS.2016.2582924
11. Tan, P.N., Steinbach, M., Kumar, V.: Introduction to Data Mining. Pearson Education Inc., Boston (2014)
12. Matlab user manual. MathWorks, Natick (2020)

Applications in Artificial Intelligence

Detection of Alzheimer's Disease Versus Mild Cognitive Impairment Using a New Modular Hybrid Neural Network

Alberto Sosa-Marrero[1], Ylermi Cabrera-León[1], Pablo Fernández-López[1],
Patricio García-Báez[2], Juan Luis Navarro-Mesa[3], Carmen Paz Suárez-Araujo[1(✉)],
and for the Alzheimer's Disease Neuroimaging Initiative

[1] Instituto Universitario de Ciencias y Tecnologías Cibernéticas, Universidad de Las Palmas de Gran Canaria, Las Palmas de Gran Canaria, Spain
carmenpaz.suarez@ulpgc.es
[2] Departamento de Ingeniería Informática y de Sistemas, Universidad de La Laguna, La Laguna, Spain
[3] Instituto Universitario para el Desarrollo Tecnológico y la Innovación en Comunicaciones,, Universidad de Las Palmas de Gran Canaria, Las Palmas de Gran Canaria, Spain

Abstract. Nowadays, there is a population ageing which leads to an increasing of geriatric and non-communicable diseases. One of the major socio-sanitary challenges our society is facing is dementia, with Alzheimer's disease (AD) as the most prevalent one. AD is a progressive neurodegenerative disorder over years, with several stages. One of them is the prodromal one, also called Mild Cognitive Impairment (MCI). Despite the recent advances in diagnostic criteria for AD, its definitive diagnosis is just possible post-mortem because there is nonspecific AD biomarker. Therefore, an early and differential diagnosis of AD is still an issue of high concern. Extensive research looking for appropriate methods of diagnosis has been done.

In this paper, we will present an innovative smart computing solution based on a hybrid and ontogenetic neural architecture, to deal with these challenges. It is an intelligent clinical decision-making system which has a non-neural pre-processing module and a neural processing one. This latter is a Modular Hybrid Growing Neural Gas (MyGNG), developed in this work. MyGNG consists of an input layer a Growing Neural Gas and a labelling layer based on the Perceptron algorithm. These modules are hierarchically organized and have different neurodynamic, connection topologies and learning laws.

Using just neuropsychological tests of 495 patients (150 AD, 345 MCI) from ADNI repository, our proposal has provided very promising results in the early detection of AD versus MCI, reaching values of AUC of 0.95; Sensitivity of 0.89 and Accuracy of 0.81. It is an appropriate diagnosis system for any clinical setting.

Data used in preparation of this article were obtained from the Alzheimer's Disease Neuroimaging Initiative (ADNI) database (adni.loni.usc.edu). As such, the investigators within the ADNI contributed to the design and implementation of ADNI and/or provided data but did not participate in analysis or writing of this report. A complete listing of ADNI investigators can be found at: http://adni.loni.usc.edu/wp-content/uploads/how_to_apply/ADNI_Acknowledgement_List.pdf.

© Springer Nature Switzerland AG 2021
I. Rojas et al. (Eds.): IWANN 2021, LNCS 12862, pp. 223–235, 2021.
https://doi.org/10.1007/978-3-030-85099-9_18

Keywords: Dementia · Alzheimer's disease · Mild cognitive impairment · Artificial neural network · Growing Neural Gas · Diagnosis

1   Introduction

The growth of the ageing population presents a huge social and economic challenge due to the high prevalence of chronic diseases associated with ageing [1]. AD is a progressive and irreversible neurodegenerative syndrome that generates dementia, which proves to be a public healthcare issue in the world with currently about 47 million people having dementia. Out of these 47 million cases, approximately 70% are caused by AD [2, 3]. While ageing is recognized as the main risk factor of AD, its exact etiology, development and evolution are not known yet.

Subjects with AD show memory deficiencies which may also be accompanied by alterations in other cognitive functions. As a result, the progressive deterioration affects situations of the subject's daily life as well as impacting the behavior and emotional state of the subject [3, 4].

Nowadays, no effective treatment against AD is known. However, intervening in the early and even prodromal stages of the disease will notably improve the quality of life, not only of the person with Alzheimer's, but also of the caregiver who will always accompany the patient from the moment of diagnosis [2, 5].

Moreover, in some older people a condition called MCI can be found, characterizing patients with light cognitive deficit but who have not yet produced dementia. People with MCI can still take care of themselves and realize their normal activities. MCI can sometimes be an early sign of AD, yet not everyone with MCI will develop AD, since about 5 − 10% MCI patients convert to dementia annually [6, 7].

The high prevalence of AD and the serious personal, family, socio-sanitary and economic repercussions it implies, indicate that investigating even more into a differential and early diagnosis of AD and MCI is necessary [5]. However, the absence of a biomarker for this pathology causes a substantial level of underdiagnosis, especially in primary care. This, coupled with the non-existence of standardized diagnostic criteria, makes the diagnosis of AD and MCI, respectively, a highly complex problem [3, 8].

Our proposal applies methodologies of the neural computation approach with the aim of facilitating an improved way of early diagnosing AD and MCI. Artificial neural networks (ANNs) are the main information structure in neural computing. They are a parallel and distributed information processing structure that consists of processing elements (neurons) connected to each other [9].

Several studies within this field have provided computational solutions for the diagnosis of dementia. In general, most of these studies focus on the classification of healthy subjects versus dementia [10, 11] or binary classification MCI versus AD [12, 13]. To a lesser extent, multi-class systems have been proposed to classify healthy subjects versus MCI versus AD [14–16] or longitudinal systems to study the progression of healthy subjects to MCI or from MCI subjects to AD [17, 18]. In recent years, there is a predominant use of deep learning techniques [15, 19, 20], but also a great variety of ANNs [21, 22] or even other mathematical methods [23] has been proposed. However, in most of these studies, the application in primary care is not possible since they mainly require expensive and/or invasive tests such as neuroimaging or cerebrospinal fluid [19].

The main aim of this paper is to provide an intelligent and effective computational solution to aid detecting AD versus MCI. We develop an innovative intelligent system, on our proposed new neural architecture, MyGNG. We demonstrate how the proposed system can be considered as a very useful and effective intelligent tool to aid in early and differential diagnosis of AD, essentially loaded with neuropsychological tests. Therefore, our proposed system supports the clinical decision-making process in any clinical setting, especially in primary care.

2 Data Set and Method

2.1 Data Set

Data used in this work was obtained from ADNI database (adni.loni.usc.edu). ADNI was launched in 2003 as a public-private partnership. It offers an extensive database that unifies a multitude of medical tests of different patients over time. The aim of the ADNI study is to detect AD at the earliest possible stage and support advance in intervention, prevention and treatment through new diagnostic methods. It is also a comprehensive study of imaging and omics in AD [24].

In this study, 495 subjects were included, out of which 150 subjects have AD and 345 subjects have MCI. The dataset was obtained from ADNI2 at the baseline and all the subjects respect an exhaustive diagnosis criterion included from ADNI. 202 characteristics for each subject are extracted including demographic characteristics, neuropsychological tests, brain measurements obtained by Magnetic resonance imaging (MRI) and positron emission tomography (PET) and other biomarkers.

Our final data set consists of total score and values of different items corresponding to three neuropsychological tests. (1) The Minimental Status Examination (MMSE) [25], consisting of 30 items which assess various cognitive functions such as orientation, memory, language, comprehension, reading, writing and constructional skills. (2) The Functional Assessment Questionnaire (FAQ) [26] which evaluates the ability to develop complex social activities, the so-called instrumental activities of daily life, through ten questions. (3) The Alzheimer Disease Assessment Scale-cognitive (ADAS-Cog) [27] consisting of 11 subtests that assess cognitive functions like, for example, memory, language and praxis.

Table 1 depicts some information about the demographic features, (age, as the most important risk factor) and test results, as we indicated in previous paragraph. These tests results are, the MMSE test total score (MMSCORE) and three of their items (MMDATE, MMYEAR and MMBALLDL), one question of FAQ that measures the dependence of the subject to make a purchase (FAQSHOP) and one item of ADAS-Cog that examine the long-short cognitive memory (ADAS_Q7). Statistical significance was tested for each feature using the non-parametric test Mann-Whitney U for two independent groups [28]. The dataset was split up in two sets, a training set with 396 subjects and a test set of 99 subjects preserving the percentage of each class.

Table 1. Characteristics of the subjects: demographic features, and test results of the subjects. Acronyms: SD (standard deviation).

	AD	MCI	All
Subjects	150	345	495
Age_{mean} (SD)	74.67 (8.18)	71.56 (7.38)	72.5 (7.77)
Age_{range}	55.6–90.3	55.0–91.4	55.0–91.4
$MMSCORE_{mean}$ (SD)	23.07 (2.08)	27.98 (1.74)	26.49 (2.91)
$MMSCORE_{range}$	19–26	24–30	19–30
$MMDATE_{mean}$ (SD)	1.6 (0.49)	1.08 (0.26)	1.23 (0.42)
$MMDATE_{range}$	1–2	1–2	1 – 2
$MMYEAR_{mean}$ (SD)	1.27 (0.44)	1.0 (0.05)	1.08 (0.28)
$MMYEAR_{range}$	1–2	1–2	1–2
$MMBALLDL_{mean}$ (SD)	1.67 (0.47)	1.14 (0.35)	1.3 (0.46)
$MMBALLDL_{range}$	1–2	1–2	1–2
$FAQSHOP_{mean}$ (SD)	2.78 (1.82)	0.5 (1.14)	1.2 (1.73)
$FAQSHOP_{range}$	0–5	0–5	0–5
$ADAS\_Q7_{mean}$ (SD)	2.4 (1.75)	0.43 (0.85)	1.03 (1.5)
$ADAS\_Q7_{range}$	0–7	0–8	0–8

2.2   Method

We present an intelligent hybrid system shown in Fig. 1. This system is formed by two modules: a non-neuronal pre-processing module followed by a neural processing one. The pre-processing module has two stages: feature ranking and dimension reduction. The former was carried out via a Fast Correlation-Based Filter (FCBF) [29], while, in a second step, Principal Component Analysis (PCA) [30] was applied to the feature vector to reduce its dimension.

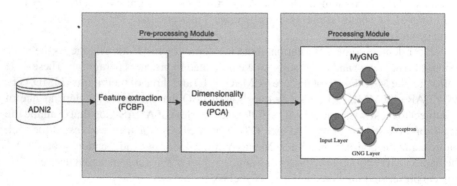

Fig. 1. Intelligent hybrid system diagram.

Pre-processing Module. Datasets can contain unusual data combinations, missing values and redundant information that include noise which may lead to ambiguous results when it comes to AD and MCI detection. Thus, it is imperative to improve the quality of the data before performing the analysis. The aim of this module is to represent the dataset by a subset of features to achieve higher performance and reduce the training time cost [31].

The first stage of the pre-processing module is based on the feature selection FCBF. This algorithm is a hybrid filter and wrap feature selection developed by Yu and Liu in 2003 [29]. It uses symmetric uncertainty (SU) to determine the correlation between features and categories as well as highlighting redundancy between the features. As a result, calculation efficiency, and therefore speed, is improved which improves the recognition rate. Furthermore, this method demonstrates promising results, achieving the highest level of dimensionality reduction and, hence, great ability to identify redundant characteristics to address complex and multi-category situations [29].

A vector of the most relevant features of AD and MCI is obtained from 202 features of all subjects extracted. This vector is formed by six features belonging to the neuropsychological tests shown in Table 1.

The second stage of the pre-processing apply a PCA. This method is an unsupervised dimensionality reduction method, which permits to reduce the size of a data set by projecting the data to low-dimensional space containing most of the original variance. This method produces a series of principal components from a multivariate random data by computing the eigenvectors of its covariance matrix corresponding to the largest eigenvalues, and the projection of the data over the eigenvectors. PCA has been widely employed for data processing [32, 33].

A new set of two-dimensional feature vectors was produced as a result of applying PCA with the six features selected on the previous stage [30]. In Fig. 2 are shown the two components obtained and the percentage of variance explained by each one. As seen in Fig. 2 the first component is for the most part associated inversely proportional to the MMSE test variance and to a lesser extent, directly proportional to the others. Which takes us, according to the meaning of these tests, to the conclusion that this component represents the cognitive symptomatology. The second component is related mainly by the FAQSHOP question variance. This may indicate that this second component is related mostly to the functional symptomatology. Working with two components feature vectors reduces the learning process time and facilitates the analysis and the evaluation of our Intelligent system performance.

Processing Module. The differential detection of AD presented in this work is essentially based on neural computing methods, more precisely a dynamic artificial neural network, the Growing Neural Gas (GNG).

We have proposed MyGNG. This architecture has two main modules: The first one based on an unsupervised and self-organizing module and built with a GNG, and a second one built with a simple perceptron, Fig. 3.

The GNG network was developed by Fritzke in 1995 [34]. GNG is a self-organization map based on a dynamic graph of connected neurons. This graph is initialized with a low number of neurons connected to each other which has the ability to grow and adapt

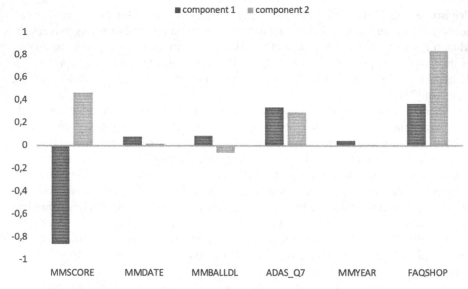

Fig. 2. Values of the two principal components.

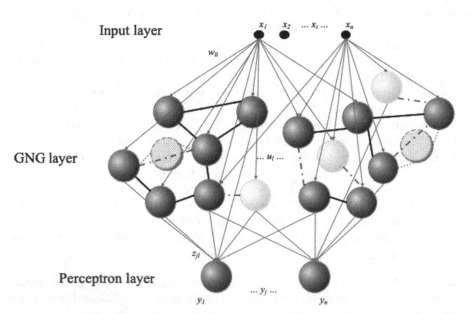

Fig. 3. Structure of a modular hybrid Growing Neural Gas.

to produce a topological learning to clustering the input space. The graph is generated and continuously updated by a competitive learning algorithm [35], where the winner neuron s_1 is established according to the minimal Euclidean distance between the input vector and the neuron's weights (w). The adaptation process is defined by the adjustment of the winner neuron and its direct topological neighbours as exposed in the Eq. 1 and Eq. 2 where e_b and e_n are the learning rates for the winner and neighbours learning, respectively [34].

$$\Delta w_{s_1} = e_b * (w_{s_1} - x) \tag{1}$$

$$\Delta w_{As_1} = e_n * (w_{As_1} - x) \tag{2}$$

$$\Delta error(s_1) = \|w_{s_1} - x\|^2 \tag{3}$$

The neurogenesis process depends on a local error variable calculated for each winner neuron following the Eq. 3. This error permits to identify regions where neurons are not enough adapted to input signals. After a fixed number λ of adaptation steps, a new neuron is inserted between the unit q with the highest error and its neighbour f in the graph that has the maximum error as seen on Eq. 4. Error variables of units q and f are decreased according to a parameter β.

$$w_{new} = 0.5 * (w_q + w_f) \tag{4}$$

Also, the topology is modified by altering connections. A new connection is generated on each adaptation step joining the winner to the second neuron. On the other hand, a connection whose age attribute exceeds the value of the a_max parameter is removed. If a neuron becomes disconnected because of the indicated connection removal step, it will be erased too.

The output layer of MyGNG is represented by a simple perceptron, whose neurodynamic and supervised learning process are given by Eq. 5 and Eq. 6,

$$y_j = \begin{cases} 1 \ iff \ (\sum_l u_l * z_{jl}) \geq \theta \\ 0 \ iff \ (\sum_l u_l * z_{jl}) < \theta \end{cases} \tag{5}$$

$$z_{jl} = z_{jl} + \alpha * \partial * u_l \tag{6}$$

where θ is the threshold, α is the learning rate, ∂ is the output error of the perceptron, u_l is the output of each GNG neuron and z the weights of the perceptron. The parameters u_l will be defined according to the order in which it is close to the winner neuron.

3 Results and Discussion

The results obtained on this work show that the proposed system is a suitable computing tool for the differential diagnosis of AD versus MCI, which as described earlier is a very complex diagnosis problem. The system was tested using three activation neighbour-hoods (AN1, AN2, and AN3) of winner neuron in the GNG module, with zero, two and four neighbour neurons, respectively. The distance between winner and each neighbour in each neighbourhood will be different. The outputs for these three cases are given by Eq. 7, Eq. 8 and Eq. 9.

$$u_l = \begin{cases} 1 \; ifl = \arg\min\left(distance\left(x, w_l\right)\right) \\ 0 \; otherwise \end{cases} \tag{7}$$

$$u_l = \begin{cases} 1 \; ifl = \arg\min\left(distance\left(x, w_l\right)\right) \\ 0.66 \; ifl = second \; \arg\min\left(distance\left(x, w_l\right)\right) \\ 0.33 \; ifl = third \; \arg\min\left(distance\left(x, w_l\right)\right) \\ 0 \; otherwise \end{cases} \tag{8}$$

$$u_l = \begin{cases} 1 \; ifl = \arg\min\left(distance\left(x, w_l\right)\right) \\ 0.8 \; ifl = second \; \arg\min\left(distance\left(x, w_l\right)\right) \\ 0.6 \; ifl = third \; \arg\min\left(distance\left(x, w_l\right)\right) \\ 0.4 \; ifl = forth \; \arg\min\left(distance\left(x, w_l\right)\right) \\ 0.2 \; ifl = fifth \; \arg\min\left(distance\left(x, w_l\right)\right) \\ 0 \; otherwise \end{cases} \tag{9}$$

The learning process of the system was made sequentially. The final MyGNG has the following optimal configuration:

- GNG Module: winnerStep $= 0.2$; neighbourStep $= 0.05$; maxAge $= 6$; maxNodes $= 27$; $\lambda = 1250$; $\beta = 0.5$; d $= 0.99$ and 215 epochs.
- Perceptron Module formed by a single neuron: learningRate $= 0.2$; and just 20 epochs.

In the next step, the optimal configuration of the perceptron was obtained. The performance measurements of our MyGNG have been, for the first stage, the unsupervised metric Calinski [30], for evaluating the GNG module. Calinski measure assesses both cohesion and separation of clusters. After that diverse performance evaluation metrics have been used with the aim of MyGNG assessment: Area Under the Curve (AUC), specificity, sensitivity (or recall), precision and accuracy [36]. The goodness of this system is also shown by means of ROC curves, Fig. 4. We consider the area under the ROC curve as the main metric to consider due to not being affected by unbalanced data sets [36]. AUC values above 0.94 have been obtained for the three cases, achieving more than 0.95 with AN3, the biggest activation neighbourhood as seen in the Table 2. Table 3 shows a little performance comparison of similar AD-MCI detection works. This table provides a brief sample of how the MyGNG achieves a good performance using cheap, non-invasive and non-ionizing diagnostic criteria such as neuropsychological tests.

We can observe that just a few subjects have been misclassified. This misclassification is represented in Fig. 5 where only AD subjects with a lower cognitive distortion (principal component 1) are classified as MCI subjects. Furthermore, this Fig. 5 represents, in a small proportion, the complexity of the problem, the difficulty between separating MCI from AD, and how the perceptron improves the classification with the high-dimensional input vector from the previous GNG layer ($\mathbb{R}^{maxNodes}$).

Table 2. Performance results of MyGNG architecture for the three different activation neighbourhoods. Acronyms: AUC (area under the ROC curve).

Metrics	AN1 $\theta=0.28$	AN2 $\theta=0.16$	AN3 $\theta=0.28$
Accuracy	0.87	0.85	0.88
Precision	0.87	0.87	0.88
sensitivity	0.73	0.91	0.76
Specificity	0.94	0.82	0.94
AUC	0.94	0.94	0.95

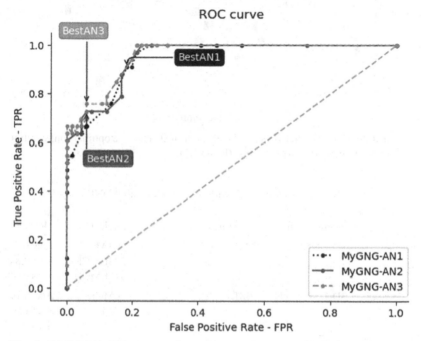

Fig. 4. ROC Curve of the test set for the three different activation neighbourhoods.

4 Conclusions

We have developed a new hybrid neural architecture, the MyGNG, which has allowed us to develop an intelligent system for aiding in the differential diagnosis of AD versus MCI, a very complex problem.

The proposed system has a great discrimination capacity allowing the early detection of AD in any medical setting, which is necessary in order to improve the quality of treatment, the evolution of subjects with AD or MCI and, most importantly, the quality of life for both patients and caregivers.

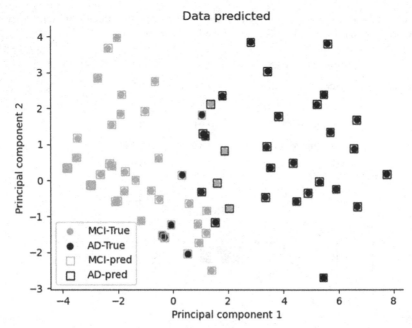

Fig. 5. Comparative label predicted vs real label for the test set of the optimal configuration with an activation neighbourhood of five neurons (BestAN3).

Table 3. Comparative with other works with ADNI.

Works	Neural method	Features	Subjects	Metrics
Basaiaa et al., 2019. [12]	3D-CNN	MRI	294AD 253EMCI 510LMCI	Acc: 0.86, Spe: 0.84, Sens: 0.88
Hosseini et al., 2018. [13]	3D-DSA-CNN	MRI	70MCI 70AD	Acc: 1.0, Spe: 1.0, Sens: 1.0
Our	MyGNG	Neuropsychological tests	345MCI 150AD	Acc: 0.88, Spe: 0.94, Sens: 0.76

Our system can be applied from the earliest stages, such as in primary care, to more advanced stages using non-invasive diagnosis criteria as neuropsychological tests. It is not necessary to apply the complete tests and, in some cases, only one item is required.

Using the FCBF and PCA dimension reduction methods allowed to achieve better results which demonstrates the importance of preprocessing in the system. Also, the activation neighbourhood of the GNG layer resulted in a slight improvement of most performance metrics. The goodness of the results demonstrates the capacity of the system, obtaining similar results to other studies even though they used more expensive and invasive medical tests.

Because of this, we propose to improve our advances to adapt the proposed MyGNG architecture to more complex dementia diagnosis problems such as very early AD detection and differential diagnosis of dementia. Furthermore, others validation systems will be used to test the system, such as a k-fold cross validation.

On the other hand, the Supervised Reconfigurable Growing Neural Gas (SupeRGNG), a novel and improved version of the GNG, is currently being tested. Thanks to its reconfigurable characteristic within the GNG algorithm, this system should be not only faster than the MyGNG but also able to deal with more challenging dementia diagnosis problems.

Acknowledgments. Data collection and sharing for this project was funded by the Alzheimer's Disease Neuroimaging Initiative (ADNI) (National Institutes of Health Grant U01 AG024904) and DOD ADNI (Department of Defense award number W81XWH-12-2-0012). ADNI is funded by the National Institute on Ageing, the National Institute of Biomedical Imageing and Bioengineering, and through generous contributions from the following: AbbVie, Alzheimer's Association; Alzheimer's Drug Discovery Foundation; Araclon Biotech; BioClinica, Inc.; Biogen; Bristol-Myers Squibb Company; CereSpir, Inc.; Cogstate; Eisai Inc.; Elan Pharmaceuticals, Inc.; Eli Lilly and Company; EuroImmun; F. Hoffmann-La Roche Ltd and its affiliated company Genentech, Inc.; Fujirebio; GE Healthcare; IXICO Ltd.; Janssen Alzheimer Immunotherapy Research & Development, LLC.; Johnson & Johnson Pharmaceutical Research & Development LLC.; Lumosity; Lundbeck; Merck & Co., Inc.; Meso Scale Diagnostics, LLC.; NeuroRx Research; Neurotrack Technologies; Novartis Pharmaceuticals Corporation; Pfizer Inc.; Piramal Imaging; Servier; Takeda Pharmaceutical Company; and Transition Therapeutics. The Canadian Institutes of Health Research is providing funds to support ADNI clinical sites in Canada. Private sector contributions are facilitated by the Foundation for the National Institutes of Health (www.fnih.org). The grantee organization is the Northern California Institute for Research and Education, and the study is coordinated by the Alzheimer's Therapeutic Research Institute at the University of Southern California. ADNI data are disseminated by the Laboratory for Neuro Imaging at the University of Southern California.

We would like to thank the anonymous reviewers for their valuable comments, which allowed improving the quality of the paper.

References

1. Alzheimer's Disease International: World Alzheimer Report 2010. Alzheimer's disease International, London (2010)
2. Romo-Galindo, D.A., Padilla-Moya, E.: Utilidad de los test cognoscitivos breves para detectar la demencia en población mexicana. Archivos de Neurociencias **23**(4), 26–34 (2018)
3. World Health Organization: Risk reduction of cognitive decline and dementia: WHO guidelines. World Health Organization (2019)
4. Medina, M., de Arriba-Enríquez, J., Frontera, A., Flores, A., Valero, S.: Informe Anual CIBERNED 2016. Ministerio de Economía, Industria y Competitividad, Instituto de Salud Carlos III, CIBERNED (2017)

5. Grupo Estatal de Demencias: Plan Integral de Alzheimer y otras Demencias (2019–2023). Ministerio de Sanidad, Consumo y Bienestar Social (2019)
6. Grupo de Neurología Cognitiva de la sociedad Valenciana de Neurología COGVAL. Guía de manejo práctico de la enfermedad de Alzheimer, Sociedad valenciana de Neurología (2017)
7. Mitchell, A., Shiri-Feshki, M.: Rate of progression of mild cognitive impairment to dementia–meta-analysis of 41 robust inception cohort studies. Acta Psychiatr. Scand. **119**(4), 252–265 (2009)
8. Erkinjuntti, T., Ostbye, T., Steenhuis, R., Hachinski, V.: The effect of different diagnostic criteria on the prevalence of dementia. N. Engl. J. Med. **337**(23), 1667–1674 (1997)
9. Hecht-Nielsen, R.: Neurocomputing. Addison-Wesley, Boston (1990)
10. Ebrahimi-Ghahnavieh, A., Luo, S., Chiong, R.: Transfer learning for Alzheimer's disease detection on MRI images. In: 2019 IEEE International Conference on Industry 4.0, Artificial Intelligence, and Communications Technology (IAICT), pp. 133–138. IEEE (2019). https://doi.org/10.1109/ICIAICT.2019.8784845
11. Khvostikov, A., Aderghal, K., Benois-Pineau, J., Krylov, A.S., Catheline, G.: 3D CNN-based classification using sMRI and MD-DTI images for Alzheimer disease studies (2018)
12. Basaiaa, S., et al.: Automated classification of Alzheimer's disease and mild cognitive impairment using a single MRI and deep neural networks. NeuroImage Clin. **21**, 101645 (2019). https://doi.org/10.1016/j.nicl.2018.101645
13. Asl, E.H., Gimel'farb, G., El-Baz, A.: Alzheimer's disease diagnostics by a deeply supervised adaptable 3D convolutional network. Front. Bioscience-Landmark **23**(3), 584–596 (2016). https://doi.org/10.2741/4606
14. Ramzan, F., et al.: A Deep learning approach for automated diagnosis and multi-class classification of Alzheimer's disease stages using resting-state fMRI and residual neural networks. J. Med. Syst. **44**(2), 1–16 (2019). https://doi.org/10.1007/s10916-019-1475-2
15. Kruthika, K.R., Maheshappa, H.D.: Multistage classifier-based approach for Alzheimer's disease prediction and retrieval. Inform. Med. Unlocked **14**, 34–42 (2019). https://doi.org/10.1016/j.imu.2018.12.003
16. Cabrera-León, Y., Garcia, P., Ruiz-Alzola, J., Suárez-Araujo, C.P.: Classification of mild cognitive impairment stages using machine learning methods. In: 2018 IEEE 22nd International Conference on Intelligent Engineering Systems (INES), pp. 000067–000072. IEEE (2018). doi: https://doi.org/10.1109/INES.2018.8523858
17. Cui, R., Liu, M., Li, G.: Longitudinal analysis for Alzheimer's disease diagnosis using RNN. In: 2018 IEEE 15th International Symposium on Biomedical Imaging (ISBI 2018), pp. 1398–1401. IEEE (2018). doi: https://doi.org/10.1109/ISBI.2018.8363833
18. Tabarestani, S., et al.: A distributed multitask multimodal approach for the prediction of Alzheimer's disease in a longitudinal study. Neuroimage **206**, 116317 (2019). https://doi.org/10.1016/j.neuroimage.2019.116317
19. Manzak, D., Çetinel, G., Manzak, A.: Automated Classification of Alzheimer's disease using deep neural network (DNN) by random forest feature elimination. In: 2019 14th International Conference on Computer Science and Education (ICCSE), pp. 1050–1053. IEEE (2019). https://doi.org/10.1109/ICCSE.2019.8845325
20. Jiang, J., Kang, L., Huang, J., Zhang, T.: Deep learning based mild cognitive impairment diagnosis using structure MR images. Neurosci. Lett. **730**, 134971 (2020). https://doi.org/10.1016/j.neulet.2020.134971
21. Suárez-Araujo, C.P., García, P., Cabrera-León, Y., Prochazka, A., Rodríguez, N., Fernandez, C.: A real-time clinical decision support system, for mild cognitive impairment detection, based on a hybrid neural architecture. Computational and Mathematical Methods in Medicine (2021)

22. Zhu, H., Adeli, E., Shi, F., Shen, D.: FCN based label correction for multi-atlas guided organ segmentation. Neuroinformatics **18**(2), 319–331 (2020). https://doi.org/10.1007/s12021-019-09448-5

23. Pellegrini, E., et al.: Machine learning of neuroimaging for assisted diagnosis of cognitive impairment and dementia: a systematic review. Alzheimer's Dement. Diagn. Assess. Dis. Monit. **10**, 519–535 (2018). https://doi.org/10.1016/j.dadm.2018.07.004

24. Yao, X., Yan, J.A.G.: Mapping longitudinal scientific progress, collaboration and impact of the Alzheimer's disease neuroimaging initiative. PLoS ONE **12**(11), 1–19 (2017). https://doi.org/10.1371/journal.pone.0186095

25. Rojas-Gualdrón, D.F., Segura, A., Cardona, D., Segura, A., Garzón, M.O.: Análisis Rasch del Mini Mental State Examination (MMSE) en adultos mayores de Antioquia Colombia. Rev. CES Psico **10**(2), 17–27 (2017). https://doi.org/10.21615/cesp.10.2.2

26. Ito, K., Hutmacher, M.M., Corrigan, B.W.: Modeling of functional assessment questionnaire (FAQ) as continuous bounded data from the ADNI database. Pharmacokinet Pharmacodyn. **39**, 601–618 (2012). https://doi.org/10.1007/s10928-012-9271-3

27. Rosen, W.G., Mohs, R.C., Davis, k.L.: A new rating scale for Alzheimer's disease. Am. J. Psychiatry **144**, 1356–1363 (1984). https://doi.org/10.1176/ajp.141.11.1356

28. Mann, H.B., Whitney, D.R.: On a test of whether one of two random variables is stochastically larger than the other. Ann. Math. Stat. **18**(1), 50–60 (1947). https://doi.org/10.1214/aoms/1177730491

29. Yu, L., Liu, H.: Feature selection for high-dimensional data: a fast correlation-based filter solution. In: Proceedings of the 20th international conference on machine learning (ICML 2003) pp. 856–863 (2003)

30. Peña, D.: Componentes Principales. Análisis de datos multivariante. McGraw Hill, Madrid (2003)

31. Reddy, C.K., Aggarwal C.C.: Data Clustering. Chapman and Hall, Boca Raton (2013)

32. García Báez, P., Suárez Araujo, C.P., Fernández Viadero, C., Regidor García, J.: Automatic prognostic determination and evolution of cognitive decline using artificial neural networks. In: Yin, H., Tino, P., Corchado, E., Byrne, W., Yao, X. (eds.) IDEAL 2007. LNCS, vol. 4881, pp. 898–907. Springer, Heidelberg (2007). https://doi.org/10.1007/978-3-540-77226-2_90

33. Sell, S., Widen, G., Prough, D., Hellmich, H.: Principal component analysis of blood microRNA datasets facilitates diagnosis of diverse diseases. PLoS ONE **15**(6), 1–26 (2020)

34. Fritzke, B.: A Growing Neural Gas Network Learns Topologies (1994)

35. Ryotaro, K.: Information enhancement for interpreting competitive learning. Int. J. Gen. Syst. **39**(7), 705–728 (2010). https://doi.org/10.1080/03081071003601421

36. Fawcett, T.: An introduction to ROC analysis. Pattern Recogn. Lett. **27**(8), 861–874 (2006). https://doi.org/10.1016/j.patrec.2005.10.010

Fine-Tuning of Patterns Assignment to Subnetworks Increases the Capacity of an Attractor Network Ensemble

Mario González[1]([✉]), Ángel Sánchez[2], David Dominguez[3], and Francisco B. Rodríguez[3]

[1] SI2Lab, Universidad de las Américas, Quito, Ecuador
mario.gonzalez.rodriguez@udla.edu.ec
[2] E.T.S. Ingeniería Informática, Universidad Rey Juan Carlos, 28933 Madrid, Spain
angel.sanchez@urjc.es
[3] Grupo de Neurocomputacin Biolgica, Dpto. de Ingeniera Informtica, Escuela Politcnica Superior, Universidad Autónoma de Madrid, 28049 Madrid, Spain
{david.dominguez,f.rodriguez}@uam.es

Abstract. It is known that dividing an attractor network into a set of subnetworks whose connectivity is equivalent to the attractor network from which they come, and therefore with the same computational cost, increases the system's recovery capacity. This opens the possibility of optimizing the assignment of pattern subsets to the ensemble modules. The patterns subsets assignment to the network modules can be considered as a combinatorial optimization problem, where varied strategies (i.e. random vs. heuristic assignments) can be tested. In this work, we present a possible heuristic strategy driven by an overlap minimization in the subsets for assigning the patterns input to the modules of the ensemble attractor neural network. In terms of system pattern storage capacity, the assignment driven by the overlap minimization in each subset/module proved to be better than no specific assignment, i.e. distribution of patterns to modules randomly.

Keywords: Ensemble of diluted modules · Structured patterns · Retinal images retrieval · Module input optimization · Overlap driven assignment

1 Introduction

Attractor networks possess many desirable properties, they are dynamical systems able to store patterns (as fixed points) and retrieve information, starting from a stimulus similar to a pattern learned (inside the basin of attraction) [2,15]. Such properties are very useful in scenarios such as pattern denoising and pattern reconstruction. However, the storage capacity of the attractor model is limited, and even more, when patterns are correlated [14]. We have proposed an

© Springer Nature Switzerland AG 2021
I. Rojas et al. (Eds.): IWANN 2021, LNCS 12862, pp. 236–247, 2021.
https://doi.org/10.1007/978-3-030-85099-9_19

Ensemble Attractor Neural Network (EANN) [12] and proved that the retrieval capacity increases (almost triple) when compared with a single attractor network, while keeping the connectivity and computation cost the same [4,10–13]. We have tested the EANN for random unbiased patterns [11,12], as well for structured and biased patterns [4,10,13]. The ensemble attractor learner follows a divide-and-conquer approach, where the attractor network is divided into modules of diluted connectivity. The set of patterns, to feed the EANN, is divided into uniform subsets according to the number of modules in the ensemble, and each pattern subset is assigned to each module. The patterns supplied to each module are randomly chosen from the complete set of patterns to be stored in the EANN. In [13], we explored the ensemble model for fingerprint ridges patterns, finding an optimization of the retrieval capacity in terms of the ensemble components (modules) and connection topology. The retrieval capacity was non-monotonic in terms of the number of modules, and the optimum number of modules (ensuring maximum storage capacity) was found. Given that fingerprint ridges have a two-dimensional (2D) structure, a 2D cross grid topology performed better than a 1D ring topology. The small-world connectivity was also optimized for both 1D and 2D topologies for the attractor ensemble [13].

In this work, we present preliminary results of exploring the EANN in terms of optimizing the input strategy of pattern subsets to modules, following different strategies. The Digital Retinal Images for Vessel Extraction (DRIVE) Dataset [17] is used as input of the EANN system. The DRIVE contains spatially structured patterns, which implies a correlation between patterns. The EANN results helpful for dealing with such patterns. First, an optimization assignment problem arises, i.e. how the pattern subsets are assigned to the ensemble modules, where different assignment strategies can be tested. Second, a pre-processing, semi-supervised-like scenario, where the patterns subsets can be constructed so that each ensemble module, specializes and improves the retrieval for each assigned subset. The EANN has proved to increase the capacity of the single attractor. Given the divide-and-conquer approach of the ensemble learner when partitioning the set of patterns to be assigned to the ensemble modules, we prove that these subsets assignment can be used to improve the retrieval capacity by taking into account the non-homogeneous correlation among patterns within the subsets. This can be handled as an optimization combinatorial problem (i.e., an assignment problem), where a random assignment is compared to an heuristic strategy driven by overlap balancing. Intuitively, the goal of this strategy is to control the correlation equilibrium by minimizing the mean overlap among the patterns within subsets which are assigned to the different modules of the ensemble. In this way, all the modules in the EANN will have a load of patterns as balanced as possible in relation to the correlation (overlap) among the patterns to be stored. In this work, we show how this preprocessing strategy allows the subsets to be assigned by minimizing the correlation/similarity between patterns within each subset, and thus increasing the pattern storage capacity of the EANN.

2   Neural Model

This section presents the neural coding and network dynamics for each individual ensemble module, followed by a schematic representation of the ensemble model.

2.1   Neural Coding and Network Dynamics

The ensemble base learner (module) can be formalized as an attractor network, where the neural state is defined, at any discrete time t, by a set of N binary variables $\boldsymbol{\tau}^t = \{\tau_i^t \in 0, 1; i = 1, \ldots, N\}$, where 1 and 0 represent, respectively, active and inactive states. The network will recover a set of patterns $\{\boldsymbol{\eta}^\mu, \mu = 1, \ldots, P\}$ that have been stored by a learning process. Each patter corresponds a stable fixed point attractor and the network retrieval state satisfies $\boldsymbol{\tau}^t = \boldsymbol{\eta}^\mu$, for large enough time t. The patterns in the DRIVE dataset are encoded as a set of binary variables $\boldsymbol{\eta}^\mu = \{\eta_i^\mu \in 0, 1; i = 1, \ldots, N\}$, according to the probability $p(\eta_i^\mu = 1) = a$, $p(\eta_i^\mu = 0) = 1-a$. Where $a \in (0, 0.5]$ stands for the corresponding average activity ratio of the patterns [6,8].

The synaptic couplings between the neurons i and j are given by the adjacency matrix $J_{ij} \equiv C_{ij} W_{ij}$, where the topology matrix $\boldsymbol{C} = \{C_{ij}\}$ describes the connectivity structure of the neural network and $\boldsymbol{W} = \{W_{ij}\}$ is the matrix with the learning weights. The topology matrix corresponds to an asymmetric random network [1], with a network degree of K, that is each node is connected to a mean of K other nodes. The network is then characterized by the dilution parameter $\gamma = K/N$.

The retrieval of a gesture pattern is achieved through the noiseless neuron dynamics

$$\tau_i^{t+1} = \Theta(h_i^t - \theta_i^t), \quad i = 1, \ldots, N, \tag{1}$$

where

$$h_i^t \equiv \frac{1}{K} \sum_j J_{ij} \frac{\tau_j^t - q_j^t}{\sqrt{Q_j^t}} \tag{2}$$

denotes the local field at neuron i and time t and θ_i is its threshold of firing. In Eq. (2) is introduced the average activity of the neighborhood of neuron i, $q_i^t = \langle \tau^t \rangle_i$, and its corresponding variance, $Q_i^t = Var(\tau^t)_i = \langle (\tau^t)^2 \rangle_i - \langle \tau^t \rangle_i^2$. The neighborhood average is defined as $\langle f^t \rangle_i \equiv \sum_j C_{ij} f_j^t / K$. In Eq. (1) is used the step function $\Theta(x) = 1$ if $x \geq 0$, and $\Theta(x) = 0$, otherwise.

The uniform binary neural model is recovered when $a = 1/2$ [7].

In the sequel the normalized variables are used, the site and time dependence being implicit:

$$\sigma \equiv \frac{\tau - q}{\sqrt{Q}}, \ q \equiv \langle \tau \rangle, \ Q \equiv Var(\tau) = q(1 - q), \tag{3}$$

$$\xi \equiv \frac{\eta - a}{\sqrt{A}}, \ a \equiv \langle \eta \rangle, \ A \equiv Var(\eta) = a(1 - a), \tag{4}$$

where a and q are the pattern and neural activities, respectively. The averages done run over different groups of neurons, and are indicated in each case.

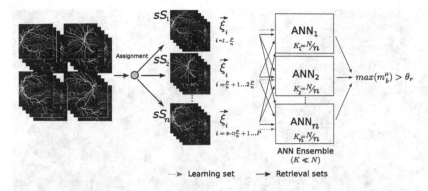

Fig. 1. Schematic representation of the assignment of patterns to the modules of the ensemble of diluted attractor neural networks.

In terms of these normalized variables, the neuron dynamics can be written as

$$\sigma_i^{t+1} = g(h_i^t - \theta_i^t, q_i^t); \quad h_i^t \equiv \frac{1}{K} \sum_j J_{ij}\sigma_j^t, \ i = 1, \ldots, N, \tag{5}$$

where the gain function is given by $g(x, y) \equiv [\Theta(x) - y]/\sqrt{y(1-y)}$.

The weight matrix $\boldsymbol{W}$ is updated according to the Hebb's rule, $W_{ij}^\mu = W_{ij}^{\mu-1} + \xi_i^\mu \xi_j^\mu$. Weights start at $W_{ij}^0 = 0$ and after P learning steps, they reach the value $W_{ij} = \sum_\mu^P \xi_i^\mu \xi_j^\mu$. The network learns $P = \alpha K$ patterns, where α is the load ratio. A threshold is necessary to keep the neural activity close to that of the learned patterns, $\theta^0(a) = \frac{1-2a}{2\sqrt{A}}$ is used, where a corresponds to the mean activity of the learning pattern set, and $A = a(1-a)$ to the activity variance. The threshold changes dynamically in time step t, according to the local neighborhood activity q_i^t, $\theta_i^t(q_i^t) = \theta^0(-\theta^0)$, $q_i^t < 0.5(> 0.5)$.

In order to characterize the retrieval ability of the network modules, the overlap is used, $m \equiv \frac{1}{N} \sum_i^N \xi_i \sigma_i$, which are the statistical correlation between the learned pattern ξ_i and the neural state σ_i.

2.2 Ensemble Attractor Network

Figure 1 depicts schematically the ensemble of attractor neural networks. The single attractor of size $N \times K$, where N is the number of units in the network and K the mean connectivity of each unit. One can see in Fig. 1 that network has been divided in an ensemble of n modules with connectivity K/n, and each module is assigned with a pattern subset. Note that the connectivity in each ANN module is highly diluted with $K \ll N$. It is well-known that diluted networks (K connections per unit instead of N connections, with $K \ll N$), increase the capacity of the attractor network per connection, and additionally the computation is less intensive (each local field only involves a K neighborhood activation) [3,5,12]. This works emphasizes in the assignment process, where the pattern dataset is also divided in n subsets, which will be assigned to each one of the n modules in the ensemble. To evaluate the ensemble performance, the

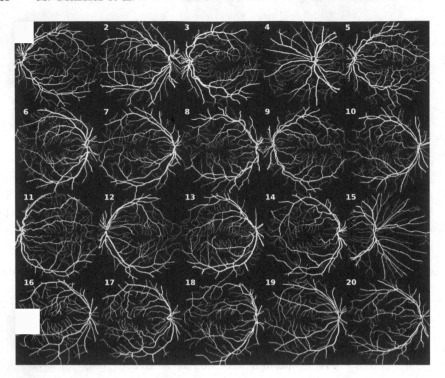

Fig. 2. Binarized and cropped Digital Retinal Images for Vessel Extraction (DRIVE) Dataset. The pattern (image) size is $530 \times 514 = 272420$, which is also the network size N.

retrieval efficiency R is defined as the number of learned patterns that are successfully retrieved $R = \frac{P_r}{P}$, where P_r is the overall number of retrieved patterns that satisfy $m^\mu > \theta_r$, and P is the overall number of patterns presented to the network during the learning phase. One has that $P \geq P_r$. Here, $\theta_r = 0.7$ is used as the retrieval threshold, unless stated otherwise. The mean retrieval overlap M is calculated over all patterns subset $\mu \in 1, 2, \ldots, P$, $M = \langle m \rangle_\mu = 1/P \sum_{\mu=1}^{P} m^\mu$. It is worth noting that in the case of the ensemble, the retrieval pattern load is calculated as $\alpha_R = \frac{P_r}{K_b \times n}$ where n is the number of subnetworks. Thus, we use $K_b \times n = K$ constant for all network ensembles studied, where K is the connectivity of the single "dense" network.

3   Materials and Methods: Approach for the Considered Assignment Problem

3.1   Dataset: Characterization and Analysis of Overlap

Figure 2 depicts the processed dataset used to test the ensemble learning. The patterns come from the Digital Retinal Images for Vessel Extraction (DRIVE) Dataset [17]. This dataset is commonly used for segmentation of blood vessels in retinal images. Retina vascular patterns is a well-known a biometric trait for

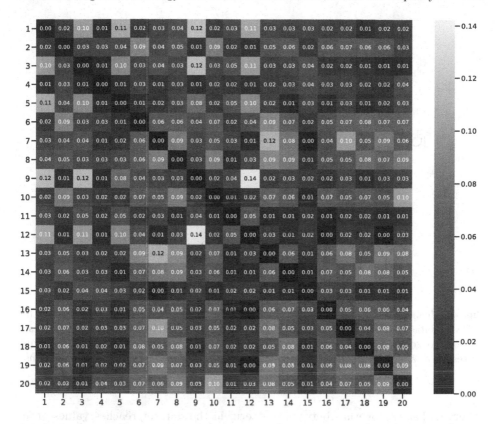

Fig. 3. Overlap matrix $O^{\mu\nu}$ between all patterns in the binarized DRIVE dataset, t, calculated through Eq. 6.

accurate authentication of people but it is also one of the least deployed due to a very low acceptability [18]. The dataset contains 40 images of which 20 have been manually segmented. These 20 images have also been binarized and the image edges with no information have been removed (cropped). The resulting binary patterns are shown in Fig. 2. Each digital retinal image has a size of $530 \times 514 = 272420$ pixels and the size of the pattern is the same as the number of neurons that each ensemble module contains. Thus, the dataset is comprised of $P = 20$ patterns (binary images), of size $N = 272420$.

Figure 3 represents the overlap matrix corresponding to the DRIVE dataset. The overlap matrix entries can be defined as:

$$O^{\mu\nu} = \frac{1}{N} \sum_i^N \xi_i^\mu \cdot \xi_i^\nu. \tag{6}$$

The resulting overlap matrix is of size $P \times P$, with $P = 20$. The overlap of a pattern μ with itself, that is the entries of the overlap matrix, where, $\mathbf{O}^{\mu\nu} = 1$, $\forall \mu = \nu$. For the purpose of calculating the overlap of each pattern with the rest of the dataset, the overlap of a pattern with itself must be removed. One can

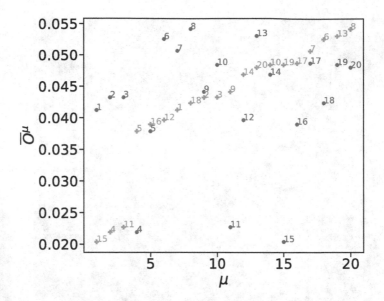

Fig. 4. Mean Overlap of each pattern μ with the rest of $P-1$ patterns, $\overline{O}^{\mu}$, for the DRIVE dataset. The orange crosses represent the patterns ordered from least mean overlap to greatest mean overlap between one pattern and the rest. The blue dots represent a random realization of the mean overlaps for the 20 retinal images patterns.

observe, that the overlap between patterns in the dataset reaches values of at most $O^{\mu=9,\nu=12} = 0.14$, for patterns $\mu = 9$, $\nu = 12$. This is a non-negligible value for the cross-talk noise term, which worsens the performance of the attractor network.

Figure 4 shows the mean overlap of pattern μ with the $P-1$ patterns in the DRIVE dataset, which can be defined as:

$$\overline{O}^{\mu} = \frac{1}{P} \sum_{\nu=1}^{P} O^{\mu\nu}, \ \nu \neq \mu. \tag{7}$$

That is the sum of each row of the overlap matrix in Fig. 3 over the $P-1$ patterns. The mean overlap of each pattern with the rest of the dataset, $\overline{O}^{\mu}$ can be used as a criterion to assign the patterns to the modules in the ensemble. In Fig. 4, the patterns are depicted according their mean overlap with the dataset. In blue dots, the patterns are presented following a random order. In orange crosses, the patterns are presented from minimum to maximum mean overlap with the rest of the patterns in the dataset. One can observe in this figure that patterns 15, 4, and 11 are the ones with lower mean correlation with respect to the rest of the dataset. Thus, a discontinuity in the mean overlap $\overline{O}^{\mu}$ occurs for the rest of the dataset, and this value then increases following an approximate linear behavior.

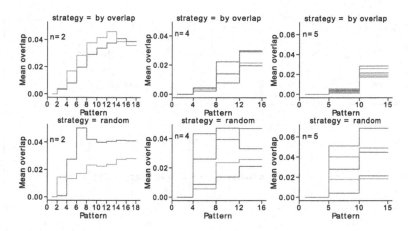

Fig. 5. Example of dynamic pattern assignment to network modules. The first row of panels ($n = 2$, 4, 5 modules), depicts the different selected sets reach a balanced state with similar average overlaps in each selected set. On the contrary, in the second row of panels ($n = 2$, 4, 5 modules), with the random strategy, the state of the final sets is clearly more unbalanced with respect to the average of each set of selected patterns.

3.2   Strategy for Assigning Patterns to Modules

Patterns subset assignment to network modules is a type of combinatorial assignment problem [16]. Our considered problem resembles the subset assignment problem which is applied to data placement in caches [9]. Given the organization of the attractor network into a fixed number of modules, and the partition of the patterns into disjoint subsets, an optimized subset-to-module assignment strategy is needed. This work describes a new pattern assignment strategy for the considered problem. The idea behind our strategy is based on the overlap value within each patterns subset. The patterns are assigned to a subset so that the overlap within each subset is as low and balanced as possible. The assignment algorithm is detailed as follows:

1 Calculate the overlap matrix **O**.
   Start **Pset** with all $P = 20$ binarized DRIVE patterns.
   Start each subset $(S_1, S_2, \ldots S_n)$ with a random seed and remove the seed from the original pattern set **Pset**.
2 Alternately assign a pattern to each subset S_i as follows:
   2.1 Select a pattern candidate μ^c from the remaining patterns in **Pset** and include it in subset S_i.
   2.2 Measure the overlap matrix of the subset (this is equivalent to get a section of the matrix $\mathbf{O}[S_i, S_i]$).
   2.3 Repeat 2.1 and 2.2 for all patterns' candidates μ^c, remaining in the **Pset**.
   2.4 Select as final candidate the pattern μ^c that produces the minimum overlap matrix for the subset, add it to S_i, and remove it from **Pset**.
3 Repeat 2 until no candidates in **Pset** are left.

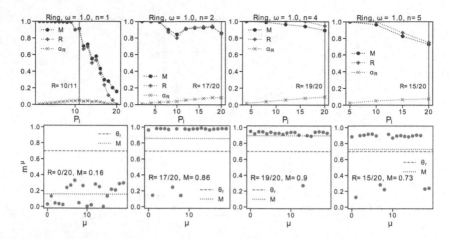

Fig. 6. Macroscopic and microscopic performance of the recovery of the set of 20 retinal images patterns for different number of modules in the EANN ($n = 1$, 2, 4, 5). Top row shows the EANN performance curves M, R, α_R, the maximum value cut-off for the pattern load P, is indicated with the solid red vertical line, and the fraction of retrieved patterns $R = Pr/P$. Bottom row shows the microscopic retrieval of $P = 20$ retinal images patterns, that is the whole dataset is loaded in the network. This corresponds to the load in the last point of the top panels curves. This microscopic retrieval is shown for different number of modules ($n = 1$, 2, 4, 5). (Color figure online)

Note that this algorithm generates disjoint subsets of patterns in the assigning process to the modules of EANN.

The aforementioned process is represented in Fig. 5 for the DRIVE dataset for different number of modules, i.e. $n = \{2, 4, 5\}$. An initial pattern set $Pset$ with 20 binary images must be assigned to the n ensemble modules. Note that n has been chosen to be an exact divisor of **card**($Pset$). The assignment strategy driven by overlap (Fig. 5 top panels) is compared with a random assignment (Fig. 5 bottom panels). The assignment strategy driven by overlap allows a more balanced pattern subsets placing into modules, with the subsets having a similar mean overlap, as well as having a smaller mean overlap when compared with the random assignment. For the case of $n = 2$ modules (Fig. 5 left panels), the overlap is similar for both assignment strategies, however the assignment driven by overlap is more balanced. The effect is more noticeable for a larger number of subsets, as it can be observed in top middle and right panels of Fig. 5, where the value of the mean of the assignment driven by overlap is more distinguishable low than the random assignment for $n = 4$ and $n = 5$ modules.

4   Results

The tested attractor ensemble has $N = 272420$ nodes with total connectivity of $K = 200$, that is a dilution of $\gamma = K/N \approx 0.0007$, and the network topology connectivity is random. Figure 6 shows the retrieval performance

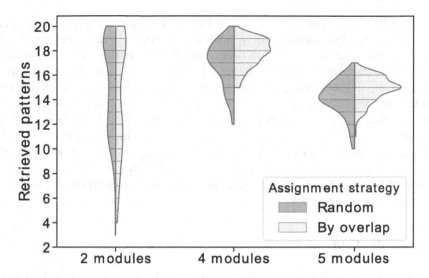

Fig. 7. Retrieval performance for different number of modules $n = 2$, 4, 5, and the two tested assignment strategies (random vs driven by overlap). A hundred realizations of the assignment process were carried out for each configuration and the retrieved number of patterns is compared.

for $n = 1$, 2, 4, 5 ensemble modules, corresponding to modules connectivity $K_b = K/n$ of $K_b = 200$, 100, 50, 40, respectively. Note that all systems are equivalent in terms of network size $N \times K_b \times n = 272420 \times 200$. For a single attractor module ($n = 1$) the optimal retrieval (red vertical line) occurs for a load of $P_l = 11$ patterns, being able to retrieve just $P_r = 10$ of them, as depicted in Fig. 6 top left panel. Loading the whole $P_l = 20$ patterns in a single module, none of them are retrieved (see Fig. 6 bottom-left panel), achieving a mean retrieval overlap of $M = 0.16$. This highlights the difficulties of learning correlated patterns as is the case with the DRIVE dataset.

Increasing the number of modules ($n = 2$, 4, 5) in the ensemble improves the retrieval capacity of the system. In [13], an optimal value appears for the number of modules n in the ensemble, for retrieving fingerprint patterns. In the case of the binarized DRIVE dataset, a maximum retrieval is achieved for $n = 4$ modules. A retrieval of $R = P_r/P_l = 19/20$ (quantity) patterns occurs with a mean retrieval overlap (quality) of $M = 0.9$. This value is higher than the observed for $n = 2$ modules, $R = 17/20$, $M = 0.86$, and for $n = 5$ modules, $R = 15/20$ $M = 0.73$. These preliminary results guarantee a more detailed analysis as the one carried out in [13].

Figure 7 compares both assignment strategies: random vs. driven by overlap. It summarizes the results of 100 simulations for the different cases studied, i.e. assignment strategies and number of modules. A violin plot is constructed comparing for each number of modules ($n = 2$, 4, 5) and the two assignment strategies (random and driven by overlap). The best results correspond to $n = 4$

modules, where the density plots tend to the maximum of the patterns in the dataset $P = 20$. The density curve peak moves towards the total number of patterns in the dataset $P = 20$ and becomes narrow near this value. This clearly shows a better retrieval capacity for $n = 4$ modules. A maximum value can be found ($n = 4$), and increasing further the number of modules worsen the retrieval performance. In practice, the connectivity dilution have a limit, where the modules connectivity worsen their performance [13]. Comparing for each module the two assignment strategies, random vs. driven by overlap, the latter performs better for the DRIVE dataset. Thus, an optimizing strategy for assigning the patterns to the modules, balancing the overlap between patterns in the subsets, improves the network performance. Again, this results need to be checked more extensively in a future work.

5   Conclusions

The attractor network ensemble has proved to increase the retrieval capacity when compared with a single attractor of similar connectivity. This has been observed for random and structured patterns. Structured patterns, such as retinal image vessels, are usually correlated. The correlation among patterns tampers the retrieval performance of the attractor network. The ensemble division into modules, which are assigned with disjoint pattern subsets help solving the correlation issue. In this work, an assignment strategy driven by the minimization of the overlap (correlation) between patterns belonging to each subset was tested. Since the problem of assigning pattern subsets to ensemble modules is a combinatorial problem, we intend to test diverse heuristic strategies and compare the performance of the network for different structured datasets. The strategy driven by overlap minimization was compared with a random assignment strategy, and proved to be better in terms of retrieval performance, achieving a larger number of retrieved patterns. The assignment problem considered in the present scenario for the attractor ensemble, can benefit of preprocessing the subsets, so that the pattern retrieval is maximized. An interesting issue is that there are a number of EANN modules where this strategy works best, which should be investigated in more detail in future work, depending on the specific topology of the subnetworks in the modules. On the other hand, a more extensive investigation of possible new strategies for assigning patterns according to other criteria is also needed for future work.

Acknowledgments. Funded by UDLA-SIS.MGR.21.04, AEI/FEDER TIN2017-84452-R, PID2020-114867RB-I00, RTI2018-098019-B-I00, and CYTED Network 518RT0559.

References

1. Albert, R., Barabási, A.L.: Statistical mechanics of complex networks. Rev. Mod. Phys. **74**(1), 47 (2002)

2. Amit, D.J.: Modeling Brain Function: The World of Attractor Neural Networks. Cambridge University Press, New York (1992)
3. Arenzon, J., Lemke, N.: Simulating highly diluted neural networks. J. Phys. A Math. Gen. **27**(15), 5161 (1994)
4. Dávila, C., González, M., Pérez-Medina, J.-L., Dominguez, D., Sánchez, Á., Rodriguez, F.B.: Ensemble of attractor networks for 2D gesture retrieval. In: Rojas, I., Joya, G., Catala, A. (eds.) IWANN 2019. LNCS, vol. 11507, pp. 488–499. Springer, Cham (2019). https://doi.org/10.1007/978-3-030-20518-8_41
5. Derrida, B., Gardner, E., Zippelius, A.: An exactly solvable asymmetric neural network model. EPL (Europhys. Lett.) **4**(2), 167 (1987)
6. Dominguez, D., González, M., Rodríguez, F.B., Serrano, E., Erichsen Jr., R., Theumann, W.: Structured information in sparse-code metric neural networks. Phys. A Stat. Mech. Appl. **391**(3), 799–808 (2012)
7. Dominguez, D., González, M., Serrano, E., Rodríguez, F.B.: Structured information in small-world neural networks. Phys. Rev. E **79**(2), 021909 (2009)
8. Doria, F., Erichsen Jr., R., González, M., Rodríguez, F.B., Sánchez, Á., Dominguez, D.: Structured patterns retrieval using a metric attractor network: application to fingerprint recognition. Phys. A Stat. Mech. Appl. **457**, 424–436 (2016)
9. Ghandeharizadeh, S., Irani, S., Lam, J.: The subset assignment problem for data placement in caches. Algorithmica **80**(7), 2201–2220 (2018)
10. González, M., Dávila, C., Dominguez, D., Sánchez, Á., Rodriguez, F.B.: Fingerprint retrieval using a specialized ensemble of attractor networks. In: Rojas, I., Joya, G., Catala, A. (eds.) IWANN 2019. LNCS, vol. 11507, pp. 709–719. Springer, Cham (2019). https://doi.org/10.1007/978-3-030-20518-8_59
11. González, M., Dominguez, D., Sánchez, Á., Rodríguez, F.B.: Capacity and retrieval of a modular set of diluted attractor networks with respect to the global number of neurons. In: Rojas, I., Joya, G., Catala, A. (eds.) IWANN 2017. LNCS, vol. 10305, pp. 497–506. Springer, Cham (2017). https://doi.org/10.1007/978-3-319-59153-7_43
12. Gonzalez, M., Dominguez, D., Sanchez, A., Rodriguez, F.B.: Increase attractor capacity using an ensembled neural network. Expert Syst. Appl. **71**, 206–215 (2017). https://doi.org/10.1016/j.eswa.2016.11.035
13. González, M., Sánchez, Á., Dominguez, D., Rodríguez, F.B.: Ensemble of diluted attractor networks with optimized topology for fingerprint retrieval. Neurocomputing **442**, 269–280 (2021)
14. Hertz, J.A., Krogh, J., Palmer, R.: Introduction to the Theory of Neural Computation. Santa Fe Institute Studies in the Sciences of Complexity, vol. 1. Addison-Wesley (1991)
15. Hopfield, J.J.: Neural networks and physical systems with emergent collective computational abilities. Proc. Nat. Acad. Sci. **79**(8), 2554–2558 (1982)
16. Pentico, D.W.: Assignment problems: a golden anniversary survey. Eur. J. Oper. Res. **176**(2), 774–793 (2007)
17. Staal, J., Abramoff, M., Niemeijer, M., Viergever, M., van Ginneken, B.: Ridge based vessel segmentation in color images of the retina. IEEE Trans. Med. Imaging **23**(4), 501–509 (2004)
18. Uhl, A.: State of the art in vascular biometrics. In: Uhl, A., Busch, C., Marcel, S., Veldhuis, R. (eds.) Handbook of Vascular Biometrics. ACVPR, pp. 3–61. Springer, Cham (2020). https://doi.org/10.1007/978-3-030-27731-4_1

A Combined Approach for Enhancing the Stability of the Variable Selection Stage in Binary Classification Tasks

Silvia Cateni$^{(\boxtimes)}$ ⓘ, Valentina Colla ⓘ, and Marco Vannucci ⓘ

Scuola Superiore Sant'Anna, Pisa, Italy
{silvia.cateni,valentina.colla,marco.vannucci}@santannapisa.it

Abstract. Variable selection is an essential tool for gaining knowledge on a problem or phenomenon, by identifying the factors that shows the highest influence on it. It is also fundamental for the implementation of machine learning-based approaches to modelling and classification tasks, by improving performances and reducing computational cost. Furthermore, in many real-world applications, such as the ones in the medical field, a relevant number of variables are jointly observed, but the number of available observations is quite limited. In these cases, variable selection is clearly essential, but standard variable selection approaches become "unstable", as the high correlation among different variables or their similar relevance with respect to the considered target lead to multiple solutions leading to similar performances. In machine-learning based classification, the stability of variable selection, namely its robustness with respect variations in the classifier training dataset, is as important as the performance of the classifier itself. The paper presents an automatic procedure for variable selection in classification tasks, which ensures excellent stability of the selection and does not require any a priori information on the available data.

Keywords: Variable selection · Stability · Binary classification

1 Introduction

The interest of researchers and practitioners for Variables Selection (VS) approaches has increased over the years, due, on one hand, to the increasing diffusion of Machine Learning (ML) techniques and, on the other hand, to the multiplication of data sources and data collection and storage capabilities in any field and discipline. In real world applications, a relatively easier access to large amounts of different data allows development of more complex and reliable models. However, the multiplication of information sources also increases the difficulty of extracting the most important information conveyed by the collected data. In particular, when a classification task is faced in relation to phenomenon or system where poor a-priori knowledge is available, the first problem to address consists in selecting the right input variables of the designed classifier. Selecting an appropriate set of input variables reduces the complexity of the classifier and can also improve the classification accuracy [1]. However, in addition to performance and

© Springer Nature Switzerland AG 2021
I. Rojas et al. (Eds.): IWANN 2021, LNCS 12862, pp. 248–259, 2021.
https://doi.org/10.1007/978-3-030-85099-9_20

computational efficiency, the stability of the adopted VS algorithm must also be taken into careful consideration [2].

A VS approach is stated to be *stable* if it leads to the selection of the same (or very similar) subset of variables even when the so-called training dataset, i.e. the set of data on which VS is performed, changes [3]. In many cases of practical interest, especially dealing with datasets with many variables and a limited number of samples, when the training subset is modified, traditional VS methods lead to different solutions at each iteration. This fact makes the data reduction practically useless for the classifier design, due to lack of replicability in presence of an eventual new dataset. Moreover, no significant contribution is provided to the achievement of a thorough knowledge of the phenomenon or process under investigation.

Therefore, stability becomes a crucial aspect when the VS goal is twofold, i.e. knowledge extraction from raw data and accurate classification performance, which is a very frequent situation in real world application of ML-based binary classifiers. A good VS algorithm should not only improve the performance of the classifier, but also provide stable and reproducible selection results.

In this paper a totally automatic VS approach is proposed, which is capable of selecting the variables that mostly affect the target by combining classic VS methods and, thus, ensuring excellent stability.

The paper is organized as follows: Sect. 2 provides a brief literature review concerning VS; Sect. 3 discusses in detail the stability issue; in Sect. 4 a description of the proposed algorithm is provided. Some numerical results are presented and discussed in Sect. 5, while Sect. 6 provides some concluding remarks and hints for future work.

2 Background on Variable Selection

VS is a significant data pre-processing step that is widely adopted for different applications, such as classification [4, 5], clustering [6, 7] and regression [8, 9]. The importance of selecting the most important variables to be fed as inputs to a ML-based model or classifier is mainly related to the possible presence of variables, which are highly correlated to each other (i.e. *redundant* variables) as well as of variables, which are irrelevant with respect to the considered target [10]. Introducing redundant and irrelevant variables usually decreases the performance of the developed model or classifier. Moreover, an optimal selection of input variables helps the achievement of a deeper understanding of the problem.

In literature, VS techniques can be divided into three main classes: filter, wrapper and embedded approaches [11].

Filters select the best subset of input variables before the application of the classifier [12, 13]. The subset is generated by evaluating the association between input and output and, consequently, the variables are classified on the basis of their relevance to the target through a statistical test [14, 15]. The main advantages of filters are their low computational complexity and their speed. However, being independent on the adopted ML-based model or classifier, they are unable to optimize it. An example of filters is represented by the correlation-based approach, which, firstly, computes the correlation coefficient between each variable and the target. Afterwards, variables are ranked and a subset is selected including the variables showing the highest values of the correlation coefficient [16]. Other commonly applied filter approaches are the chi-square approach [17] and the Information Gain method [18].

The wrapper VS approach was introduced in 1997 by Kohavi and John [19]: it exploits the performance of the learning machine to extract the subset of variables on the basis on their predictive/classification power. Wrappers consider the model as a black box, and this feature makes them universal, as they can be applied using different kind of algorithms [20]. An obvious wrapper method is the exhaustive search, also named *brute force method*, which examines all the combinations of variables. When the number of input variables is significant, this exhaustive approach is not viable. A traditional wrapper method is the Greedy Search strategy [21], which gradually creates the variables subset by adding or eliminating single variables from an initial set. Greedy search can be applied into two directions: Sequential Forward Selection (SFS) and Sequential Backward Selection (SBS) [22]. SFS begins with an empty set of variables, and the variables are iteratively added until a fixed stopping condition is achieved. For instance, in classification tasks, usually the adopted performance index is the classification accuracy of the learning machine. In other words, the search ends when the addition of new variables to the input set does not increase the accuracy of the model. On the other hand, SBS starts with an input set including all the available variables and removes them one by one. The importance of an input variable is determined by removing one of them and calculating the performance of the classifier without having such variables among its inputs. The search end when removing variables from the input decreases the accuracy. SFS is less computationally expensive than SBS, but SBS is impracticable, if the number of potential input variables is too large [23].

Embedded methods perform the variable selection as part of the learning stage and are generally specific of a particular learning machine [24]. Common examples of embedded approaches are Decision Trees (DT) and approaches based on regularization techniques [25]. The main advantage of embedded methods lies in their association to the learning algorithm. Embedded approaches also exploit all the variables to generate a model and then evaluate it to establish the importance of the variables [26].

To sum up, filter VS methods are suitable to deal with very high dimensional datasets, as they are computationally simple, fast and independent on the algorithm employed. Wrapper methods exploit the learning algorithm as a black box assessing its performance for VS, but are subjected to over-fitting and computationally cumbersome. Embedded methods show a lower computational cost with respect to wrappers, but they are specific of a given model or classifier [27].

Recently, several hybrid variable selection approaches have been proposed to exploit their advantages by overcoming their drawbacks [28, 29].

3   The Stability Issue

The stability concept was introduced in 1995 by Turney [30]. Stability is defined as the sensitivity of a VS algorithm with respect to variations in the training dataset. Ignoring the stability issue of the variable selection algorithm can lead to wrong conclusions and unreliable design of a ML-based model or classifier [31–33]. Several papers discuss the fact that using different training sets can lead to select different variable subsets also applying the same VS algorithm [34, 35]. The investigation of stability of VS approaches is related to the need to provide users with a quantitative confirmation that VS is reliable and sufficiently robust with respect to variations in the training data [36]. This requirement is essential especially in real-world applications, where an improved knowledge of the phenomenon under investigation is a further important outcome of the VS. For instance, in monitoring applications [37–39], the identification of the most relevant input variables allows highlighting the factors to monitor so as to early identify and prevent faults and anomalies, but such identification need to be definitive, if it is preliminary to the setup of the hardware for a monitoring system.

The VS output can be represented by different evaluation criteria: a weighted score of each variable, the ranking, or a subset of significant variables, namely a binary vector where the unitary value corresponds to the presence of the feature in the subset [40]. Stability measures can be classified in three categories: stability $by\ subset\ (S_B)$, stability $by\ rank$ and stability $by\ weight$. According to the first definition, the similarity between two weighting vectors is computed through the Pearson's correlation coefficient. Similarly, to quantify the similarity between two variables rankings, the Spearman's rank correlation coefficient [41], also known as"the Pearson correlation coefficient between the ranked variables" is evaluated. These two indices lie in the range [-1, 1] where the unitary value means full direct or inverse correlation, while the null value corresponds to the absence of correlation. Finally, the similarity between two binary vectors b_1 and b_2 can be estimated employing the Tanimoto distance [42], which is defined as:

$$S_B = \frac{|b_1 * b_2|}{|b_1| + |b_2| - |b_1 * b_2|} \tag{1}$$

where $|\bullet|$ represents the vector norm, while $b_1 * b_2$ is the scalar product of the two vectors. The Tanimoto index lies in the range [0; 1], where the unitary value corresponds to two identical vectors, while the null value identifies two completely different vectors.

4 The Proposed Method

The main objective of the proposed approach lies in the creation of a stable and efficient variable selection algorithm for ML-based binary classifiers, which is capable to guarantee the selection of variables that really affect the target. The proposed method is applicable also to the datasets that have relatively few samples and many variables and combines VS selection approaches belonging to two of the three previously described categories, namely filters and wrappers methods.

For the sake of simplicity, in the following we will represent the dataset as a matrix where the rows represent the available samples and the columns the measured variables for each sample.

Firstly, the dataset is shuffled and divided into two parts, 25% of the available data will be used as test set to validate the classifier, while the remaining 75% of the data is used to extract the final variables subset by applying the proposed procedure. The dataset also needs to be preliminarily cleansed by eliminating all the lines where at least one variable is missing, to work with a complete dataset [43, 44].

Subsequently, the necessary redundancy analysis is performed to eliminate redundant variables, which also offers improvement in interpretability of the VS outcome. In this approach redundant variables are detected by applying a method based on the Dominating Set Algorithm (DSA), a method deriving from the graph theory [45, 46]. DSA identifies the highly correlated variables by defining as *correlated* two variables showing a linear correlation coefficient $\rho > 0.95$ and a $p\_value < 0.05$, where the definitions of ρ and p_value derives from classical statistical correlation theory introduced by Pearson at the end of the 19th century [47]. DSA extracts the minimal dominating set of the graph corresponding to the set with the lower number of vertexes: variables of the graph that do not fall inside the minimal dominating set are considered as redundant.

After redundant variables elimination, two VS techniques belonging to filter category are separately applied. The two VS procedures are applied N_F times each and, at each iteration, the intersection of the most significant variable set is recorded. The variables which are included in such intersection with a frequency greater than or equal to 80% are selected.

The reduced dataset is then subjected to N_W different iterations of the two well-known wrapper VS methods: SFS and SBS. The union of the two solutions is stored ate each iteration and the variables which are included in such union with a frequency greater than or equal to 60% are selected. This last subset of variables is the candidate to be the final "winner" variable subset.

The two frequencies values used as threshold (80% and 60%) have been set considering that the filters methods are intrinsically stable, so a higher threshold ensures that only those variables that, for a certain training set, have accidentally "fallen" into the subset are not selected. Furthermore, the filters based reduction is performed prior the wrappers due to two reasons: the first one is that the filters are performed in the pre-processing phase, the second is that they are computationally faster than the wrappers so this preliminary reduction of the variables number also speeds up the next steps.

Finally, both the average accuracy of the classifier and the stability of the approach can be assessed. Similarly, to the training dataset, also the test set undergoes a cleansing stage, but such cleansing is done considering only on the reduced subset of input variables. The overall procedure is schematically represented in Fig. 1.

The proposed VS algorithm is generic and can be executed on any kind of binary or multiclass classifier. In addition, even the classic VS methods that are used here could be replaced with other algorithms belonging to the same category.

The proposed method shows the great advantage of not requiring any *a priori* information on the available database, it is completely automatic and modular and, therefore, adaptable to various problems.

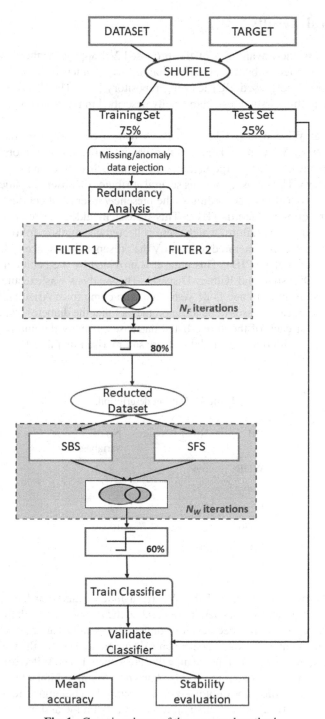

Fig. 1. Generic scheme of the proposed method.

5 Numerical Results

In order to assess the advantages of the proposed VS approach, the described algorithm has been applied to binary classification tasks implemented on different datasets extracted by the largely used UCI learning repository [48]. The datasets, which have been exploited in the pursued tests, are briefly described in the following.

- Breast Cancer Wisconsis (**BCW**): the BCW database comes from the Hospital of the University of Wisconsin. Data refer to patients affected by tumors. The binary classification target refers to the fact that the tumor is benign or malign.
- Cervical (**Cerv**): The dataset contains several attributes on observed patients, who are classified into two classes according to the presence/absence of cervical cancer.
- Heart Failure clinical records (**HF**): This dataset includes the medical records of patients who had heart failure, which were collected during their follow-up period.
- **Heart**: This dataset is generated to identify the presence or absence of heart disease.
- Pima Indians Diabetes (**PID**): This dataset is provided by the National Institutes of Diabetes and Digestive and Kidney Diseases. This analysis was executed on women patients whose minimum age is 21 years and who come from Arizona. Each patient belongs to one of two classes depending on the fact that the diabetes test is positive or not. The sizes of each of the above-listed databases, namely the number of samples and variables considered in each dataset, are summarised in Table 1.

Table 1. Dataset description.

DB	No of samples	No of variables
WDBC	699	9
Cerv.	72	19
HeartF.	299	12
Heart	270	13
PID	768	8

The correlation coefficient and the Wilcoxon index evaluation have been implemented as filter approaches. For each input variable the Pearson's correlation coefficient with the considered target has been evaluated, then the variables are ranked considering this value and the mean value of all coefficients is computed. Finally, the variables which have the coefficient greater than the mean value are selected. The Wilcoxon index, coming from the Wilcoxon rank sum test, is also known as Mann-Whitney test [49], and is a non-parametric test, which does not need to work with data belonging to a specific distribution, differently from other statistical tests that rely on the assumption of a normal data distribution [50]. The Wilcoxon index w_i for the i-th variable is computed through the following steps: firstly the values of the considered variable for all data included in the training dataset ($v_1, v_2 \ldots v_N$) are sorted in ascending order. Then a rank r_W is assigned to each value, which is computed as follows:

$$
r_W = \begin{cases} i & \text{if } v_{i-1} \neq v_i \neq v_{i+1} \\ \frac{\sum_{k=0}^{N} i+k}{N+1} & \text{otherwise} \end{cases} \tag{2}
$$

where N is the number of available input variables.

Finally, the Wilcoxon index is evaluated as the sum of the ranks for the class that includes the smallest number of samples. If the two classes contain an identical number of samples the choice of the class to adopt is arbitrary. In the performed experiments, the iteration parameters are assumed to be all identical, namely $N_F = N_W = 10$. Moreover, 10 independent runs of the proposed procedure have been performed on each dataset in order to calculate the stability of the solutions. The stability is measured through the average Tanimoto distance. This distance is compared to the one calculated by running SFS and SBS as the only VS algorithms (also computed on 10 iterations) to demonstrate that they can encounter instability issues and to emphasize the improvement obtained with the proposed algorithm. Furthermore, the variables selected with the three methods (SFS, SBS, proposed method) are identified in the test set, which is used to validate the classifier. In our tests the classifiers used are a Bayesian classifier [51, 52] and a Support Vector Machine (SVM)-based classifier [53]. The purpose of the developed test is to demonstrate the efficiency of the proposed method in improving the stability of the VS stage independently from the classifier exploited and without negatively affecting the performance of the classifier itself. Therefore, the focus is not on the section of the most suitable classifier. The performance of the classifiers is evaluated through the Overall Accuracy, which is calculated as the ratio between the sum of the correctly classified test values and the total number of test values. The obtained results are shown in Table 2 for the Bayesian classifier and in Table 3 for the SVM-based classifier. In particular, the first column indicates the processed dataset, columns 2–5 report the mean accuracy obtained with the test set using all initial variables, the selected variable by SFS and SBS and the mean accuracy obtained with the proposed procedure, respectively. Finally, the last three columns show the Tanimoto stability measure considering the three different approaches.

Table 2. Results on the tested datasets with Bayesian classifier.

DB	Mean acc All vars	Mean Acc SFS	Mean acc SBS	Mean acc Prop Method	Stab SFS	Stab SBS	Stab Prop Method
WDBC	0.96	0.96	0.97	0.98	0.4	0.6	1
Cerv.	0.94	0.78	0.83	0.94	0.6	0.3	0.8
HeartF.	0.80	0.72	0.77	0.80	0.4	0.6	0.9
Heart	0.85	0.75	0.81	0.85	0.6	0.7	1
PID	0.72	0.72	0.71	0.76	0.5	0.7	0.9

Table 3. Results on the tested datasets with SVM-based classifier.

DB	Mean acc All vars	Mean Acc SFS	Mean acc SBS	Mean acc Prop Method	Stab SFS	Stab SBS	Stab Prop Method
WDBC	0.96	0.96	0.97	0.98	0.4	0.6	1
Cerv.	0.88	0.67	0.76	0.88	0.4	0.5	0.8
HeartF.	0.71	0.71	0.66	0.86	0.6	0.6	0.9
Heart	0.81	0.66	0.78	0.81	0.78	0.64	1
PID	0.80	0.76	0.77	0.80	0.5	0.6	1

The obtained results show that the proposed method ensures excellent stability of the VS and, therefore, also support knowledge extraction form raw data concerning the considered problem/phenomenon without decreasing the performance of the classifier. This superior capability of the proposed approach is shown both in comparison to traditional VS methods and to the case where VS is not applied, i.e. all the available variables are exploited for the classification task. Finally, the times required to execute the VS algorithms have been calculated and are shown in Table 4 where average computation times and their standard deviations (in brackets) over 10 runs are reported. The time is expressed in seconds and it is computed using a Notebook PC with Intel Core i9, CPU speed 2.9 GHz, SDD 512 GB and RAM 16GB.

Table 4. Results of execution time in seconds on the tested datasets with both classifiers.

DB	Prop.Method Bayes-classifier	SFS Bayes-classifier	SBS Bayes-classifier	Prop. Method SVM-classifier	SFS SVM Classifier	SBS SVM classifier
WDBC	4 (1.6)	5.8 (3.8)	4.7 (2.8)	7.1 (2.8)	11.5 (4.0)	7.4 (2.3)
Cerv.	18.3 (8.7)	37.7 (6.0)	12.6 (9.7)	13.8 (5.8)	18.2 (5.6)	7.1 (2.6)
HeartF.	3.8 (4.1)	8.8 (1.8)	5.7 (4.5)	100.3 (21.9)	1165.3 (169.6)	340.2(216.2)
Heart	5.8 (2.1)	8.1 (4.8)	7.7 (3.2)	62.7 (12.9)	654.3 (161.2)	21.3 (24.9)
PID	2.8 (0.5)	3.5 (1.6)	3.7 (2.6)	259.9 (30.8)	1751.2 (218.9)	643.3 (148.6)

Concerning the execution times we can note that, in the cases where traditional methods take longer to provide a solution, the proposed method provides significant savings.

6   Conclusions and Future Work

The paper proposes a novel approach that improves the stability of traditional VS algorithms when applied to binary classification tasks. In fact, the main issue of these algorithms lies in their sensitivity to the variation of the training set, which is a serious problem, especially when the main objective is knowledge extraction concerning the considered system or phenomenon.

The proposed algorithm has been tested on some real data sets and the results demonstrate its efficiency both in terms of accuracy but above all of stability. In fact, the proposed method improves the stability of variable selection compared to classical methods without worsening the accuracy of the classification. A further advantage of this procedure lies in the fact that it is automatic, namely it does not require any a priori information on the considered dataset, and is modular, namely each included VS approach inserted can be replaced with other approaches belonging to the same category.

Future work will focus on the demonstration of the versatility of the proposed approach within other contexts, including multi-class classification problems, as well as on the investigation of the effect of some hyper-parameters of the proposed approach, such as N_F and N_W. Moreover, the proposed approach will be extended to regression problems and will be extensively tested.

References

1. Guyon, I., Elisseeff, A.: An introduction to variable and feature selection. Mach. Learn. **3**, 1157–1182 (2003)
2. Kalousis, A., Prados, J., Hilario, M.: Stability of feature selection algorithms. In: Proceedings of 5th IEEE International Conference on Data Mining (ICDM05). pp. 218–225 (2005)
3. Kalousis, A., Prados, J., Hilario, M.: Stability of feature selection algorithms: a study on high-dimensional spaces. Knowl. Inf. Syst. **12**, 95–116 (2007)
4. Song, Q.B., Wang, G., Wang, C.: Automatic recommendation of classification algorithms based on data set characteristics. Pattern Recogn. **45**(7), 26722689 (2012)
5. Ali, S., Smith, K.: On learning algorithm selection for classification. Appl. Soft Comput. **6**(2), 119138 (2006)
6. Wang, S., Zhu, J.: Variable selection for model-based high dimensional clustering and its application on microarray data. Biometrics **64**, 440–448 (2008)
7. Maugis, C., Celeux, G., Martin-Magniette, M.L.: Variable selection in model-based clustering: A general variable role modeling. Comput. Stat. Data Anal. **53**(11), 3872–3882 (2009)
8. Andersen, C.M., Bro, R.: Variable selection in regression—a tutorial. J. Chemom. **24**(11–12), 728–737 (2010)
9. Mehmood, T., Liland, K.H., Snipen, L., Sæbø, S.: A review of variable selection methods in partial least squares regression. Chemometrics Intel Lab Syst. **118**, 62–69 (2012)
10. Che, J., Yang, Y., Li, L., Bai, X., Zhang, S., Deng, C.: Maximum relevance minimum common redundancy feature selection for nonlinear data. Inf. Sci. **409**, 68–86 (2017)
11. Souza, F., Araujo, R., Soares, S., Mendes, J.: Variable selection based on mutual information for soft sensors application. In: Proceedings of the 9th Portuguese Conference on Automatic Control (Controlo 2010), At Coimbra, Portugal (2010)
12. Cateni, S., Colla, V., Vannucci, M.: A fuzzy system for combining filter features selection methods. Int. J. Fuzzy Syst. **19**(4), 1168–1180 (2017)

13. Sun, Y., Robinson, M., Adams, R., Boekhorst, R., Rust, A.G., Davey, N.: Using feature selection filtering methods for binding site predictions. In: Proceedings of 5th IEEE International Conference on Cognitive Informatics (ICCI 2006) (2006)
14. Degenhardt, F., Seifert, S., Szymczak, S.: Evaluation of variable selection methods for random forests and omics data sets. Brief. Bioinform. **20**(2), 492–503 (2019)
15. Ellies-Oury, M.P., Chavent, M., Conanec, A., Bonnet, M., Picard, B., Saracco, J.: Statistical model choice including variable selection based on variable importance: a relevant way for biomarkers selection to predict meat tenderness. Sci. Rep. **9**(1), 1–12 (2019)
16. Eid, H., Hassanien, A., Kim, T.H., Banerjee., S.: Linear correlation based feature selection for network intrusion detection model. Commun. Comput. Inform. Sci. **381**, 240–248 (2013)
17. Bahassine, S., Madani, A., Al-Sarem, M., Kissi, M.: Feature selection using an improved Chi-square for Arabic text classification. J. King Saud Univ.-Comput. Inf. Sci. **32**(2), 225–231 (2020)
18. Jadhav, S., He, H., Jenkins, K.: Information gain directed genetic algorithm wrapper feature selection for credit rating. Appl. Soft Comput. **69**, 541–553 (2018)
19. Kohavi, R., John, G.: Wrappers for feature selection. Artif Intell. **97**, 273–324 (1997)
20. Dhamodharavadhani, S., Rathipriya, R.: Variable selection method for regression models using computational intelligence techniques. In: Research Anthology on Multi-Industry Uses of Genetic Programming and Algorithms, pp. 742–761. IGI Global (2021)
21. Gokalp, O., Tasci, E., Ugur, A.: A novel wrapper feature selection algorithm based on iterated greedy metaheuristic for sentiment classification. Expert Syst. Appl. **146**, 113176, (2020)
22. S Asdaghi, F., Soleimani, A.: An effective feature selection method for web spam detection. Knowl.-Based Syst. **166**, 198–206 (2019)
23. May, R., Dandy, G., Maier, H.: Review of input variable selection methods for artificial neural networks. In: Suzuki, K. (ed.) Artificial Neural Networks Methodological Advances and Biomedical Applications, pp. 19–44. IntechOpen, London (2011). https://doi.org/10.5772/16004
24. E Genuer, R., Poggi, J.M., Tuleau-Malot, C.: Variable selection using random forests. Pattern Recogn. Lett. **31**(14), 2225–2236 (2010)
25. Breiman, L.: Random forests. Mach. Learn. **45**, 5–32 (2001)
26. Al Janabi, K.B., Kadhim, R.: Data reduction techniques: a comparative study for attribute selection methods. Int. J. Adv. Comput. Sci. Technol. **8**(1), 1–13 (2018)
27. Rodriguez-Galiano, V.F., Luque-Espinar, J.A., Chica-Olmo, M., Mendes, M.P.: Feature selection approaches for predictive modelling of groundwater nitrate pollution: an evaluation of filters, embedded and wrapper methods. Sci. Total Environ. **624**, 661–672 (2018)
28. Cateni, S., Colla, V., Vannucci, M.: A hybrid feature selection method for classification purposes. In: Proceedings - UKSim-AMSS 8th European Modelling Symposium on Computer Modelling and Simulation, EMS 2014, art. no. 7153972, pp. 39–44 (2014)
29. Cateni, S., Colla, V.: A hybrid variable selection approach for NN-based classification in industrial context. Smart Innov. Syst. Technol. **69**, 173–180 (2017)
30. Turney, P.: Techncal note:bias and the quantification of stability. Mach. Learn. **20**, 23–33 (1995)
31. Cateni, S., Colla, V.: Improving the stability of wrapper variable selection applied to binary classification. Int. J. Comput. Inf. Syst. Ind. Manag. Appl. **8**, 214–225 (2016)
32. Yu, L., Ding, C., Loscalzo, S.: Stable feature selection via dense feature groups. In: Proceedings of the ACM SIGKDD International Conference on Knowledge Discovery and Data Mining (2008)
33. Vannucci, M., Colla, V., Sgarbi, M., Toscanelli, O.: Thresholded neural networks for sensitive industrial classification tasks (2009). Lecture Notes in Computer Science (including subseries Lecture Notes in Artificial Intelligence and Lecture Notes in Bioinformatics), 5517 LNCS (PART 1), pp. 1320–1327

34. Loscalzo, S., Yu, L., Ding, C.: Consensus group stable feature selection. In: Proceedings of ACM SIGKDD International Conference on Knowledge Discovery and Data Mining 2009, vol. 1, pp. 567–575 (2009)
35. Cateni, S., Colla, V.: Improving the stability of Sequential Forward variables selection. In: International Conference on Intelligent Systems Design and Applications, ISDA, 2016-June, art. no. 7489258, pp. 374–379 (2016)
36. Fakhraei, S., Zadeh, H.S., Fotouhi, F.: Bias and stability of single variable classifiers for feature ranking and selection. Expert Syst. Appl. **14**(15), 6945–6958 (2014)
37. Zagaria, M., Dimastromatteo, V., Colla, V.: Monitoring erosion and skull profile in blast furnace hearth. Ironmaking Steelmaking **37**(3), 229–234 (2010)
38. Peres, F.A.P., Peres, T.N., Fogliatto, F.S., Anzanello, M.J.: Fault detection in batch processes through variable selection integrated to multiway principal component analysis. J. Process Control **80**, 223–234 (2019)
39. Wang, L., Yang, C., Sun, Y., Zhang, H., Li, M.: Effective variable selection and moving window HMM-based approach for iron-making process monitoring. J. Process Control **68**, 86–95 (2018)
40. Khaire, U.M., Dhanalakshmi, R.: Stability of feature selection algorithm: a review. J. King Saud Univ.-Comput. Inf. Sci., 1–14 (2019, in press). https://doi.org/10.1016/j.jksuci.2019.06.012
41. Spearman, C.: The proof and measurement of association between two things. Am. J. Psychol. **15**, 72101 (1904)
42. Fligner, M.A., Verducci, J.S., Blower, P.E.: A modification of the Jaccard-Tanimoto similarity index for diverse selection of chemical compounds using binary strings. Technometrics **44**(2), 110–119 (2002)
43. Cateni, S., Colla, V., Vannucci, M., Vannocci, M.: A procedure for building reduced reliable training datasets from real-world data. In: Proceedings of the IASTED International Conference on Artificial Intelligence and Applications, AIA 2014, pp. 393–399 (2014)
44. Cateni, S., Colla, V., Vannucci, M.: A fuzzy system for combining different outliers detection methods. In: Proceedings of the IASTED International Conference on Artificial Intelligence and Applications, AIA 2009, pp. 87–93 (2009)
45. Torkestani, J.A., Meybodi, M.R.: Finding minimum weight connected dominating set in stochastic graph based on learning automata. Inf. Sci. **200**, 57–77 (2012)
46. Sampathkumar, E., Walikar, H.B.: The connected domination number of a graph. J. Math. Phys. **13**(6), 607–613 (1979)
47. Pearson, K.: Notes on regression and inheritance in the case of two parents. Proc. R. Soc. Lond. **58**, 240–242 (1895)
48. Asuncion, A., Newman, D. UCI Machine Learning Repository (2007)
49. Siegel, S., Castellan, N.: Nonparametric Statistics for the Behavioral Sciences, Mac GrawHill, New York (1988)
50. Li, J., Liu, H., Tung, A., Wong, L.: In The practical-bioinformatician (2004)
51. Hastie, T., Tibshirani, R., Friedman, J.: The Elements of Statistical Learning. SSS, Springer, New York (2009). https://doi.org/10.1007/978-0-387-84858-7
52. Manning, C.D., Raghavan, P., Schütze, M.: Introduction to Information Retrieval. Cambridge University Press, NY (2008)
53. Christianini, N., Shawe-Taylor, J.C.: An Introduction to Support Vector Machines and Other Kernel-Based Learning Methods. Cambridge University Press, Cambridge, UK (2000)

A Convolutional Neural Network as a Proxy for the XRF Approximation of the Chemical Composition of Archaeological Artefacts in the Presence of Inter-microscope Variability

Catalin Stoean[1,2]([✉]), Leonard Ionescu[1,3] , Ruxandra Stoean[1,2],
Marinela Boicea[3] , Miguel Atencia[4], and Gonzalo Joya[4]

[1] Romanian Institute of Science and Technology, Cluj, Romania
[2] Faculty of Sciences, University of Craiova, Craiova, Romania
{catalin.stoean,ruxandra.stoean}@inf.ucv.ro
[3] Restoration and Conservation Lab, Oltenia Museum, History and Archeology
Section, Craiova, Romania
[4] Universidad de Málaga, Málaga, Spain
{matencia,gjoya}@uma.es

Abstract. The paper puts forward a convolutional neural network model for multi-output regression, which is trained on images from two distinct microscope types to estimate the concentration of a pair of chemical elements from the surface of archaeological metal objects. The target is to simulate the approximation behaviour of the more complex XRF technology, which is used as ground truth in training the model. Experiments investigate the adequacy of learning on either type of data and then using the models to test images coming from each microscope in turn and in combination. Under these terms of performance and flexibility, the technology can be successfully used in the front line of ancient object restoration across laboratories irrespective of the equipment available.

Keywords: Convolutional neural networks · Multi-output regression · Chemical estimation · XRF · Inter-microscope variability · Archaeology

1 Introduction

Historical artefacts undergo complex restoration and conservation procedures in their journey from excavation to museum display. But, in order to decide the best methods, a thorough assessment of the objects must be conducted first [8]. Various partially invasive methods are performed for the elemental analysis regarding alloy composition, proteic nature, acidity, solubility, ink type, color, and measurements of physical, chemical, mechanical and biological degradation. In

© Springer Nature Switzerland AG 2021
I. Rojas et al. (Eds.): IWANN 2021, LNCS 12862, pp. 260–271, 2021.
https://doi.org/10.1007/978-3-030-85099-9_21

opposition to these, several non-invasive, non-destructive qualitative and quantitative approaches can be used to investigate the material structure of objects. The surface of the artefact can be examined through optical analysis (optical and electron microscopes, endoscopes) and photo-fixing (cameras, lighting or irradiation with UV or IR). In this way, the forms of corrosion layers, textures, iridescence, blistering, erosion, deposition, finishing, sanding, polishing, inlaying, watermarks can be determined. On the other hand, direct assessment techniques have been employed in recent years, namely reflectography, radiography, atomic spectrometry - X-ray fluorescence (XRF), and trace analysis.

XRF spectrometry is a method of non-destructive and non-invasive instrumental analysis [10], also suitable for portable devices, that can provide coherent and reliable estimations about the analyzed heritage asset. The primary X-rays are emitted from an X-ray tube and the characteristic X-rays released by the analyzed object, under the impact of the electron beam, come from a maximum depth of 5 µm and are used for elementary chemical analysis at the surface. The measurements can only be made for chemical elements from Be to U. The light elements cannot be analyzed, because the X-rays emitted by them are absorbed by the air. The extensive use of the machine is limited however by its cost, the required training, and a small possibility of radioactivity.

On the other hand, microscopes of distinct types with different magnification and resolution levels are largely available in all museum laboratories. Therefore, provided sufficient microscopic samples of object surfaces, a convolutional neural network (CNN) could learn to approximate the chemical concentrations of the main elements in the composition of the item to resemble the XRF estimation.

The effectiveness of the CNN approach may however assume a repeated, regular way of microscopic data collection in various restoration labs and museums. Nevertheless, this desirable asset is hindered by variation in imaging quality and consistency when taken by different microscopes. Therefore, the aim of the current paper is to train a CNN architecture on images taken by one stereo microscope and one electron device, of distinct performances, using the XRF approximation as ground truth for learning. Several experimental settings are envisaged in order to evaluate the difference between training separately or on the combination of the two microscopic image types for recognizing test examples produced by each machine.

The surface of an object shows the presence of several chemical elements, but the expert restorer solely considers the main one (or two) components, i.e. those with a concentration above 25%. The study therefore considers the analysis of two elements, namely copper (Cu) and iron (Fe), that are present in large concentrations and in a sufficient number of artefacts. A multiple output regression problem is formulated and the CNN model is applied for solving the task.

The paper is structured in the following manner. Section 2 introduces the data set and the two types of microscopic images on the selected pair of chemical elements (Cu, Fe). The appointed CNN methodology for their analysis is presented in Sect. 4, while the state of the art related to recent computational intelligence support for the chemical investigation of the XRF in archaeology is depicted in Sect. 3. The experiments on the various configurations for the training set and the results on every type of microscopic image per studied element are discussed in Sect. 5. Section 6 establishes the final conclusions.

2   Materials

The data are available from the Oltenia Museum - the History and Archaeology Section, Craiova, Romania. The set encompasses artefacts brought for restoration at the museum laboratory during the months January - April 2021.

Every item was examined under the microscope and photographed in the areas adjacent to the XRF point of analysis. Both a stereo microscope and an electron microscope were used. The former is an Olympus SZX-7 optical stereo microscope equipped with a Quick Photo Micro 2.2 digital camera. The latter is a portable LCD digital microscope, model G600. The difference between the two is that, while the electron one is a common, simple device, the stereo optical system of SZX-7 offers a superior quality of the image, especially when used together with the digital camera. The stereoscopic system uses two independent and parallel optical channels, offering color high fidelity, noise reduction, and increased modularity for imaging. A general purpose electron microscope is more accessible in conservation labs everywhere. In this sense, from the practical perspective, it is important to know if the CNN approach is independent of the machine that takes the samples. Hence, we considered 65 objects which were photographed by the stereo microscope and produced 482 images, and 21 artefacts that were given to the electron device and led to 124 images. The chemical investigation of the objects was done by means of a portable Bruker Titan S1 XRF spectrometer, together with the specific software Artax. Each microscopic sample thus has attached the concentration values approximated by the XRF as ground truth.

Figure 1 shows examples of images derived from both types of microscopes. The two elements considered in the analysis, i.e. Fe and Cu, were chosen because most artefacts are built upon the metallurgy principles of strength and performance of either the Bronze or Iron Ages. Also, based on the same production concepts, their role is different in the composition of an ancient object: while Fe is strongly predominant, Cu is generally present as part of an alloy. The XRF estimation of the quantity of the two elements accompanies each image.

3   State of the Art

Deep learning support for microscopy image analysis is performed largely, but with preponderance within the medical domain [3,7,9,18], while architectures for several applications in materials science in general have also been considered [12,13,15]. On the other hand, the XRF output in archaeology has been investigated only by a small number of statistical and artificial intelligence methods. Besides the numerical estimation of the elemental concentrations in the object, the XRF also gives a plot of energy versus photon counts, called a spectrum [4].

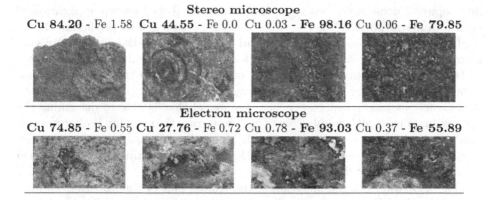

Fig. 1. Samples of images taken from artefacts both from stereo and electron microscopy. The chemical concentrations of Fe and Cu estimated by the XRF are outlined above each image, with the predominant metal highlighted in bold.

In the current literature, the entries on machine learning in tandem with XRF address the sampling or analysis of the XRF spectra. A Monte Carlo algorithm is constructed in [1] to simulate the XRF spectra in application to metal artefacts. The paper [11] also employs the Monte Carlo technique to simulate the XRF spectra; a neural network for multi-output regression subsequently uses the resulting spectra to approximate the chemical concentration of five metals. In the different field of geology, the study [4] puts forward an analysis-by-synthesis auto-encoder that employs XRF spectral data to estimate the composition of several elements from rocks with geochemical assay as the ground truth. The inverse problem of taking the elemental concentrations given by the XRF and using them as predictors for the type of a (ceramic) object is tackled in [2] by means of k-nearest neighbors, decision trees, and learning vector quantization.

In opposition, the current paper attempts to offer a XRF-independent and device-independent tool for approximating the chemical concentrations of the main elements in an archaeological artefact. A CNN is trained on images from two microscopes to output an approximation of the concentrations of Cu and Fe, and the result is compared to the XRF estimate. A primary attempt to appraise the quantity of two metals separately from a data set of stereo microscopy images only has been proposed in [19] and acknowledged the potential of combining microscopy, XRF, and deep learning.

4 Method

The task of concentration estimation is formulated as a multiple output regression problem. Given a set of images $X = \{x_1, x_2, ..., x_m\}$, the assignment is to predict associated targets $y_i^j \in \mathbb{R}$, $i = 1, 2, ..., m$, $j \in \{1, 2\}$. Since the deep network must produce a multi-output result, after the sequence of the convolutional layers, and once the last volume is flattened, the architecture branches into separate dense layers for each desired output. A well known application of such a multi-output CNN is the simultaneous age and gender prediction [14].

In the current task, the targets y_i^1 and y_i^2 correspond to the numerical assessments of the percent of Fe and Cu respectively, which result from the analysis of the i-th microscopic image. In previous work [19], we treated each output as a separate task for the CNN. However, when presented with a new item, it is clearly more efficient to run just one model that is able to determine the approximations of all possibly constituent elements, than testing it on every one model tailored for one particular metal. Moreover, this multi-output approach resembles more the behaviour of the XRF technology in estimating the chemical composition of an artefact.

The CNN takes in the images and the related pair of concentration estimations from the XRF. The practical question that arises at this point is whether the model will be further able to rightly estimate the concentrations, given that test images are potentially produced by a different microscope. This aspect will be debated in the experimental Sect. 5.

Given the limited amount of actual microscopic samples, especially when not combining the images from both microscopes for training, a pre-trained model is used to prevent overfitting, defining mean squared error (MSE) as loss function.

Apart from the regression specific metrics of MSE and mean/median absolute errors (MAE/MedAE), the performance of the model will also be measured through one that allows for a margin of error, called accuracy@t and first introduced in the study [16] for age prediction. An exact value for the elemental concentration is not necessary, as the ground truth itself is an estimation given by the point on which the XRF is applied, where deposits of corrosion might have hindered its approximation [10]. As such, given a margin of error of $\pm t$, the CNN prediction for a sample $x_i \in X$ is deemed correct for output j in comparison to the XRF ground truth $\hat{y}_i^j$ if $|y_i^j - \hat{y}_i^j| < t$. This metric was also applied in the early study [19] and the results were deemed by the experts to be informative for the restoration procedures.

5   Experiments

Different training sets are taken to evaluate the dependence of the results on the microscopic type of input images that are considered. The setup of the experiments is next described and is followed by the results and a discussion about their interpretation.

5.1   Experimental Setup

There are three settings established for training the CNN models. In one of them the Resnet34 and Densenet201 architectures are trained only on samples from stereo microscope, in the second one the training is based only on images from the electron microscope, and in the last one the models are built on the slides coming from both microscopes. In all scenarios, the results from the test set are provided too for all three cases, i.e. only for images from stereo-microscope, only from the electron one, and combined.

Each object has between 1 and 17 microscopical images, depending on its size. The images that appear in the test set belong to objects different than those that have microscopical pictures in the training/validation sets. The distribution of the items between training and test sets is shown in Table 1, both at the image and at the object levels.

Table 1. Number of images and objects for the k-fold cross-validation and for test.

Microscope	Image level		Object level	
	Training/validation	Test	Training/validation	Test
Stereo	413	69	57	8
Electron	97	27	17	4

Figure 2 illustrates the amount of Fe and Cu in microscopical images from each type of device, as they appear both in the training/validation and test sets.

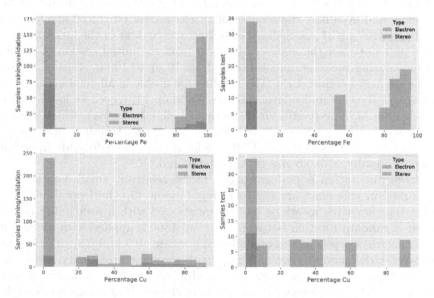

Fig. 2. Sample frequency for images from simple and stereo microscopes for Fe (top row) and Cu (bottom row) and for training/validation items (left plots) and test ones (right plots).

The training/validation set is split using k-fold cross-validation with $k = 5$. For each split, the models learn from the training part and are validated on the remaining 1/5 set. The best model obtained in validation for each of the 5 splits is also applied on the test set. Consequently, the reported output for the validation set, as well as the one for the test set, is computed by averaging the results obtained over the 5 cross-validation rounds. The same data set splits are used for Fe and Cu, as well as for each architecture in turn.

Similar settings are considered for both architectures. All images are resized to 224×224 pixels. An additional final layer is appended to each of the 2 architectures with the aim of maintaining the outputs of the models inside the interval $[0, 100]$. This is done by replacing negative values with 0 and numbers larger than 100 with 100. The 1cycle policy follows the procedure in [17] and uses the implementation in [6]. It is used for the training process in 2 steps. Within the first training session, the model uses a discriminative learning rate for 50 epochs. The learning rate starts from a low value of 1e–05 for the first layers, continues up to 1e–04 for the middle layers, and reaches 1e–01 in the final layers. The model with the lowest validation MSE obtained from each of the cross-validation rounds and each architecture is then reloaded, has all its layers unfrozen and is trained for an additional 10 epochs with a learning rate tuned automatically [6].

For the first training session, we used an additional early stopping criterion of 30 epochs without improvement, but this maneuver appeared in just 13.33% of the cases and even here the number of epochs was only reduced in average by 9 epochs, i.e. taking 37 epochs in the shortest run and 45 in the longest one.

The parameter for the number of epochs from the initial session of training was tuned during pre-experimental setup from 10 up to 100 in steps of 10 using only the Resnet34 architecture. The results were usable in all combinations, but they were relatively stabilized from 50 epochs and up. Still, even for lower number of epochs, the MSE were still viable (although slightly higher), which suggests that the number of epochs could be reduced in the case training times happen to be an issue. Hence, a value of 50 epochs is considered for this important parameter. Finally, a batch size of 32 is considered.

Data augmentation is performed due to the relatively small data set. The options used in this sense are the following: random flip (horizontal and vertical flips together with rotations by 90° are allowed with a probability of 0.5), rotation (a random rotation between −180 and 180° is applied with probability 0.5), symmetric warp (random and allowed between −0.3 and 0.3 with the same probability 0.5), random resize and crop (with the same probability, resizes and crops are applied to images using a zoom of 2; the method, initially proposed in [5], uses points that determine the center of the resulting image and switches from one to another).

The output results are computed as MSE, MAE, and MedAE, for the samples in the test set. The reported results are calculated as average from the outputs of the models obtained from the 5-fold cross-validation as applied on the test samples for each type of image (as concerns the microscope that produced it) in turn. Additionally, we also compute a classification accuracy in which a threshold

t is set to allow a window of error such that if the XRF estimated value for a metal in an image is $\hat{y}_i^j$, the predicted value is considered to be correct if it lies within the range $[\hat{y}_i^j - t, \hat{y}_i^j + t]$.

5.2 Results and Discussion

Table 2 illustrates the MSE, MAE, and MedAE average results from the outcomes on the test set from the 5-fold cross-validation models. Every training set (stereo, electron, and combined) is considered separately and, for each category, the models are applied on the test set that contain images from the stereo microscope, from the electron device, and from the combination of both, showing the results in different rows. The first column, *Test all*, refers to the results on all test samples, both those that originate from the electron and the stereo microscope, and also aggregates the results from Fe and Cu. The next column, *Stereo all*, contains only stereo images, and refers to the results from both metals, whereas the column *Electron all* refers to the corresponding result coming from electron images from the test set. Finally, the columns *Fe all, Cu all* refers to the stereo and electron samples that correspond only to the Fe or Cu measurements, respectively. The remaining columns refer to the indicated subgroups for combinations of a particular metal and a particular device.

As concerns the running times, the entire procedure of training in two steps and tuning for finding the appropriate learning rate, as well as applying the model on the test set, takes 22 min for the combined data for ResNet-34 and 30 min for DenseNet-201. When using only the stereo data, the running times decrease to 15 min for the former architecture and 19 for the latter. For the electron data, the times reduce further to 9.7 min and 11.5, respectively. The application of the models on the test set takes around 4 s for either architecture, which means that for testing one image it takes 0.04 s. All runs and time measurements are made using Google Colab and a Tesla T4 GPU. Testing an image using CPU also in Google Colab takes significantly more, but the running time remains under a second, i.e. 0.31 s.

We next assess the proposed methodology as a classification task, according to the accuracy@t index [16], i.e. when an image is considered to be correctly classified for a metal if the estimation error is less than a threshold t. In our experiments, the threshold that defines the width of the allowed error interval is varied from 1 to 30, and the results are shown in Fig. 3, illustrating the classification accuracy in all discussed scenarios.

By evaluating separately the two types of data stemming from the respective microscopes, it can be seen that the limited number of samples from the electron one is well reflected by the results. When the training and validation is made on the stereo microscope, the test on the data of the same type leads MSE values of 122.8 and 131.9 for ResNet-34 and DenseNet-201, respectively. Conversely, when the training and testing is made on the data from the electron microscope, the corresponding results are of 402.6 and 391.1, respectively. The decrease in quality for the data coming from the electron microscope is additionally caused by the fact that Fe has 11 samples in the test set that have a percentage of 56%,

Table 2. Average MSE, MAE, and MedAE results for both architectures and for each training/validation type in turn.

Trained on	Test all	Stereo all	Electron all	Fe all	Cu all	Fe stereo	Cu stereo	Fe electron	Cu electron
ResNet-34 MSE									
Combined	186.3	117.6	361.7	158.6	213.9	61.6	173.7	406.7	316.8
Stereo	203.6	122.8	410	119.3	287.9	51.5	194.2	292.6	527.4
Electron	1119.2	1399.6	402.6	1647.3	591.1	2120.4	678.9	438.4	366.8
ResNet-34 MAE									
Combined	9	7.2	13.8	8.2	9.9	5.5	8.9	15.1	12.5
Stereo	9.4	6.8	16	7.1	11.6	4.4	9.2	14.2	17.9
Electron	25.6	29.6	15.2	31.3	19.8	37.4	21.8	15.8	14.7
ResNet-34 MedAE									
Combined	4.4	3.9	6.8	4.6	4.2	4.3	3.7	6.8	6.7
Stereo	4.78	3.1	13.1	4.4	6.2	3.1	2.9	11.7	14.5
Electron	21	22.3	11.4	26.8	19	37	21	11.3	11.5
DenseNet-201 MSE									
Combined	158.3	112.5	275.1	131.2	185.3	36.3	188.8	373.7	176.4
Stereo	241.7	131.9	522.2	135.8	347.5	25.3	238.5	418.2	626.2
Electron	1149.3	1446	391.1	1504.3	794.2	1937.1	954.9	398.4	383.8
DenseNet-201 MAE									
Combined	8.2	6.7	12.2	7.5	9	4.7	8.6	14.4	10
Stereo	9.7	6.5	17.9	7.1	12.2	3.5	9.4	16.4	19.5
Electron	26.8	31.1	15.8	30.6	23	36.9	25.4	14.7	16.9
DenseNet-201 MedAE									
Combined	4.2	3.6	7.5	4.2	4.1	3.9	2.7	9	7.1
Stereo	4.1	2.8	16	3.6	5.8	2.9	2.4	15.9	16.2
Electron	20.8	28.7	14.1	23.5	18.2	36.7	21.6	13.2	15.9

while the training data for this metal contains either artefacts that are very low on Fe or pieces with high quantities. Moreover, such lack of samples with an intermediate percentage for Fe occurs also for the stereo one.

The hardest task lies in the recognition of the percentage of Fe in examples coming from the stereo microscope when the training is made only on samples from the electron microscope. There is only a small amount of samples with high percentages of electron Fe in the training, while the number of stereo test images with similarly high percentage is large. At the opposite end, the Cu is better spread for percentages between 25% and 90% on both the electron training and stereo test sets, hence the significantly better results in this scenario.

The results do not show a clear general winner between the two tested architectures, ResNet-34 and DenseNet-201. When learning from the data set with combined images, the results appear to have a slight advantage for DenseNet-201, both in Table 2 and in the Fig. 3. On the other hand, in the case when the training is made only on the data from the electron microscope, the ResNet-34 has better results in general than DenseNet-201. However, the results are not

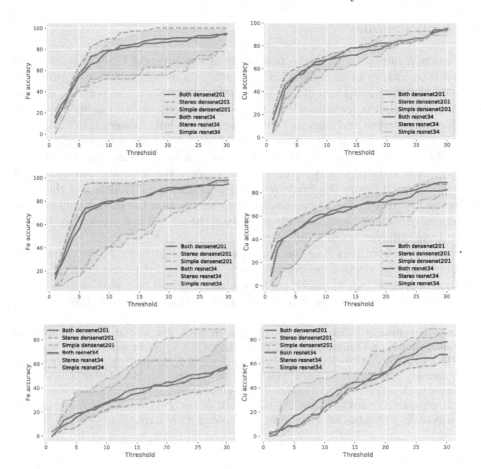

Fig. 3. Classification accuracy as obtained by Densenet201 and Resnet34 for Fe (left column) and Cu (right column), for varied approximation thresholds of the accuracy@t index, when training is performed on combined data (first row), stereo microscope data (middle), and electron microscope samples (bottom).

significantly better for one versus another, hence the running time might prove decisive in preferring ResNet34 for the task.

As a general conclusion on the experimental findings, the ideal case would be if all labs had stereo microscopes available for a high definition output of the object surface. In this situation, with the training performed also only on stereo, the estimation error on new examples would be very low. But, since in the real-world scenario, restoration facilities rather have general purpose devices, having a training made on many samples stemming from various types of microscopes will lead to a good test approximation whatever the device.

6   Conclusions

The current paper explores the possibility of employing a CNN that analyzes microscopy images of archaeological artefacts to simulate the XRF approximation of the chemical elemental concentration present on the surface. A dual output regression is formulated for Fe and Cu and the use of different types of microscopes (stereo and electron) to produce the training images is investigated.

As expected, the results from the models trained on samples originating from the electron microscope are generally poor, demonstrating thus the need to acquire more data of this type, in order to balance the data set. The combined approach (results from the first row in each section from Table 2 and the plots from the first row in Fig. 1) encourage us to believe that the models will be able to generalize well and estimate the quantity of the metals well, even if the images come from different types of microscopes.

Future work will include the consideration of a higher number of samples produced by the electron microscope. It is also intended to use other elements present in archaeological assets, such as silver, tin, lead or silicon, with a corresponding increase in the number of examined artefacts to include them.

Acknowledgement. This work was supported by a grant of the Romanian Ministry of Research and Innovation, CCCDI – UEFISCDI, project number 178PCE/2021, PN-III-P4-ID-PCE-2020-0788, *Object PErception and Reconstruction with deep neural Architectures (OPERA)*, within PNCDI III, by the Spanish Ministry of Science and Innovation, through the Plan Estatal de Investigación Científica y Técnica y de Innovación, Project TIN2017-88728-C2-1-R, as well as the *Plan Propio de Investigación, Transferencia y Divulgación Científica*, Universidad de Málaga.

References

1. Brunetti, A., Fabian, J., Torre, C.W.L., Schiavon, N.: A combined xrf/monte carlo simulation study of multilayered peruvian metal artifacts from the tomb of the priestess of chornancap. Appl. Phys. A **122**, 571 (2016)
2. Charalambous, E., Dikomitou-Eliadou, M., Milis, G.M., Mitsis, G., Eliades, D.G.: An experimental design for the classification of archaeological ceramic data from cyprus, and the tracing of inter-class relationships. J. Archaeol. Sci. Rep. **7**, 465–471 (2016)
3. Deng, S., et al.: Deep learning in digital pathology image analysis: a survey. Front. Med. **14**, 470–487 (2020)
4. Dirks, M., Poole, D.: Incorporating domain knowledge about xrf spectra into neural networks. In: Workshop on Perception as Generative Reasoning, NeurIPS 2019 (2019)
5. Howard, A.G.: Some improvements on deep convolutional neural network based image classification (2013)
6. Howard, J., Gugger, S.: Fastai: a layered api for deep learning. Information **11**(2), 108 (2020)
7. Komura, D., Ishikawa, S.: Machine learning methods for histopathological image analysis. Comput. Struct. Biotechnol. J. **16**, 34–42 (2018)

8. Lins, S.A., Di Francia, E., Grassini, S., Gigante, G., Ridolfi, S.: Ma-xrf measurement for corrosion assessment on bronze artefacts (2019)
9. Mittal, S., Stoean, C., Kajdacsy-Balla, A., Bhargava, R.: Digital assessment of stained breast tissue images for comprehensive tumor and microenvironment analysis. Front. Bioeng. Biotechnol. **7**, 246 (2019)
10. Nørgaard, H.W.: Portable xrf on prehistoric bronze artefacts: limitations and use for the detection of bronze age metal workshops. Open Archaeol. **3**(1), 101–122 (2017)
11. Rakotondrajoa, A., Radtke, M.: Machine learning based quantification of synchrotron radiation-induced x-ray fluorescence measurements - a case study. Mach. Learn. Sci. Technol. **2**, 025004 (2020)
12. Samide, A., Stoean, C., Stoean, R.: Surface study of inhibitor films formed by polyvinyl alcohol and silver nanoparticles on stainless steel in hydrochloric acid solution using convolutional neural networks. Appl. Surf. Sci. **475**, 1–5 (2019)
13. Samide, A., Stoean, R., Stoean, C., Tutunaru, B., Grecu, R.: Investigation of polymer coatings formed by polyvinyl alcohol and silver nanoparticles on copper surface in acid medium by means of deep convolutional neural networks. Coatings **9**, 105 (2019)
14. Savchenko, A.: Efficient facial representations for age, gender and identity recognition in organizing photo albums using multi-output convnet. PeerJ Comput. Sci. **5**, e197 (2019)
15. Schmidt, J., Marques, M.R.G., Botti, S., Marques, M.A.L.: Recent advances and applications of machine learning in solid-state materials science. npj Comput. Mater. **5**(83), 1–36 (2019)
16. Smith, A., Gaur, M.: What's my age?: Predicting twitter user's age using influential friend network and dbpedia (2018)
17. Smith, L.N.: A disciplined approach to neural network hyper-parameters: Part 1 - learning rate, batch size, momentum, and weight decay (2018)
18. Stoean, R.: Analysis on the potential of an ea-surrogate modelling tandem for deep learning parametrization: an example for cancer classification from medical images. Neural Comput. Appl. **32**, 313–322 (2020)
19. Stoean, R., Ionescu, L., Stoean, C., Boicea, M., Atencia, M., Joya, G.: A deep learning-based surrogate for the XRF approximation of elemental composition within archaeological artefacts before restoration (2021)

Implementation of Data Stream Classification Neural Network Models Over Big Data Platforms

Fernando Puentes-Marchal$^{(\boxtimes)}$, María Dolores Pérez-Godoy ,
Pedro González , and María José Del Jesus

University of Jaén, Jaén, Spain
{fpuentes,lperez,pglez,mjjesus}@ujaen.es

Abstract. Streaming is being increasingly demanded because it helps in analyzing data in real-time and in decision making. Over time, the number of existing devices increases continuously, generating a huge amount of data. Processing this data with traditional algorithms is impractical, so it is necessary to apply distributed algorithms in a Big Data context. In this paper, Apache Spark is used to implement some distributed versions of algorithms based on Extreme Learning Machine (ELM). In addition, these algorithms are evaluated with different real and synthetic datasets by performing two experiments. The first one tries to demonstrate that the performance of the distributed algorithms is the same as that of the sequential versions. The second experiment is a study about the behaviour of the algorithms in the presence of concept drift, an important research area within streaming.

Keywords: Datastream · Classification · Extreme learning machine · Big data · Spark streaming

1 Introduction

Nowadays we are in the digital age, where a big number of connected devices are continuously generating a huge amount of information. This number is growing every day, as new devices are appearing and generating more and more data. Machine learning algorithms have traditionally focused on analyzing stored data in a static dataset, in which all data are available from the beginning. However, new devices generating new data appear over time, and other techniques that analyze this information and provide answers in real time are needed to help in decision making. These techniques are known as streaming algorithms.

Over time, new streaming machine learning algorithms or improvements of existing ones have appeared. In [3,5,7] different studies about the state of the art in streaming classification can be seen. There are different types of base models, such as decision trees, rule-based models, nearest neighbor, support vector machines, neural networks and ensembles. However, there are few algorithms

© Springer Nature Switzerland AG 2021
I. Rojas et al. (Eds.): IWANN 2021, LNCS 12862, pp. 272–280, 2021.
https://doi.org/10.1007/978-3-030-85099-9_22

based on neural network models. This fact can be caused by the high computational cost of neural networks, because returning a response takes a long time and, in streaming, the response time must be minimal. Usually, streaming neural network algorithms have a low number of hidden layers in order to reduce the computational cost. Due to the lack of neuronal network streaming algorithms, this work is focused on such algorithms. Specifically, in Extreme Learning Machine algorithms, that is a type of neural network well known by its low computational cost.

In streaming, responses must be returned in real time, so it is important to reduce the computational time to get faster responses. Due to the huge amount of data to be analyzed, applying distributed machine learning techniques in a Big Data context is needed. These techniques reduce the computational cost by distributing the computation over different machines that work in parallel. Nowadays, there are lots of open source platforms that simplify the distributed implementation of streaming algorithms. These solutions are widely used by companies and researchers because some of them provide libraries with algorithms and methods that help in the implementation of machine learning algorithms. The best known streaming platforms are Apache Spark, Apache Kafka, Apache Storm and Apache Flink. There are currently not many implementations of streaming machine learning algorithms in distributed platforms. So, the main contribution of this work is the implementation of distributed versions of some Extreme Learning Algorithms.

This document is organized as follows. Section 2 introduces the extreme learning machine algorithms used as basis. After this, distributed implementations are proposed and explained in Sect. 3. The experimental environment and the results are discussed in Sect. 4. Finally, Sect. 5 outlines the conclusions of the work.

2   Extreme Learning Machine Algorithms

An Extreme Learning Machine (ELM) [4] is a neural network algorithm composed of three layers: input, hidden and output. The hidden layer has L neurons, where L is an input value defined by the user. Each link between layers has an associated weight value and each hidden neuron has a bias value, usually in the interval [−1,1]. In this type of algorithms, input-hidden weight and bias values are randomly generated. The objective is to compute hidden-output weight values based on input data, because the class value of each input instance is known and these weight values are adjusted to get corresponding outputs.

The original ELM algorithm cannot be directly applied on a streaming context because it requires that all the data are available from the beginning. This is not possible in streaming, because the data arrive continuously over time. So, a modification of ELM, capable of processing data by blocks was presented, called Online Sequential Extreme Learning Machine (OS-ELM) [8]. This allows to process the stream like a sequence of blocks. This algorithm has two phases: initialization and sequence. In the initialization phase, the first block is used to initialize the neural network. The rest of blocks are used in the sequence phase, to update the neural network using incremental equations over each block.

After this, new ensemble approaches have been proposed. One of them was the Ensemble of OS-ELM (EOS-ELM) [6], that contains several OS-ELM classifiers. The combining strategy of the ensemble consist on computing the mean of all the outputs. Over time, another approach called Voting based OS-ELM (VOS-ELM) [1] have been proposed, that change the combining strategy to use a majority voting strategy.

More recently, new streaming approaches with a drift detection method based on the ensemble error have appeared. In this work, the implementation of an algorithm based on VOS-ELM with a drift detection method similar to [10], called Concept Drift VOS-ELM (CD-VOS-ELM), is introduced. There are two decision levels that must be defined by the user: warning and drift level. When the error is under the warning level, the model is not updated because it knows the current concept of the stream. When the error is between the warning and drift levels, the model is updated incrementally like in previous algorithms, because it is possible that concept drift is happening. Finally, if the error is over the drift level, there is a concept drift and the current model is discarded. After discarding the model, a new one is created from scratch.

3   Distributed Methods Implemented

This section details the contribution of this work, the implementation of different distributed versions of streaming algorithms. In a previous analysis about streaming platforms [9] we stated that Apache Spark Streaming is recommended to implement distributed streaming algorithms due to his high performance, the machine learning library (MLLIB) and a high amount of documentation, that helps in the implementation. Spark has a data structure called Resilient Distributed Dataset (RDD), that is a dataset distributed between different machines for distributed processing. In this work, the implementation of distributed versions of OS-ELM, EOS-ELM, VOS-ELM and CD-EOS-ELM is introduced, called D-OS-ELM, D-EOS-ELM, D-VOS-ELM and D-CD-VOS-ELM, respectively.

After random initialization, the output of the activation function of all the hidden nodes are computed. There is a computation for each input instance and each hidden node. To increase the process, all of these computations are distributed over Spark nodes. These values are included in a matrix H. In addition, the output of each instance is represented by a matrix Y, in which each row is an instance and each column is a class. The generation of this matrix has also been parallelized.

Once these two matrices have been computed, the algorithms apply some matrix operations defined in the original paper to compute the matrix of the output weights β. These matrix operations include product, inverse, add, subtract and transpose of matrices, with a high computational cost when the amount of data is very large. For this reason, the computation of the matrix operations has been distributed in different machines. Each machine performs a matrix operation over a portion of the matrix. This allows to compute faster and reduces the response time. Previous matrix operations have been implemented as follows:

- Product of two matrices (A·B=C): Rows form matrix A and their row indexes (to reconstruct matrix C) are distributed over Spark nodes. Each Spark node has a copy of entire matrix B, so each node computes a part of C.
- Inverse of a matrix (A^{-1}): This method uses the SVD algorithm implemented in the machine learning library from Spark (MLLIB). SVD decomposes the input matrix A into three matrices (U,V,S). Finally, the equation $A^{-1}=VS^{-1}U^{T}$ is used for distributed computing of the inverse of A.
- Transpose of a matrix (A^{T}): Cells of matrix A and their indexes (row and column to reconstruct resulting matrix) are distributed over Spark nodes. Each Spark node switches row and column indexes of the set of received cells. Finally, resulting matrix is reconstructed by new indexes.
- Addition of two matrices (A+B=C): In this case, cells from matrices A and B are grouped by row and column index, generating a list of A-B-cell pairs. After this, pairs from list and their indexes (row and column to reconstruct matrix C) are distributed over Spark nodes. Each Spark node add the two elements of each received pair. Finally, resulting matrix is reconstructed by new indexes.
- Subtraction of two matrices (A-B=C): The parallelization of this operation follows the same strategy as addition, but for the subtraction.

4 Experimentation and Analysis of Results

Experiments have been performed in a Spark cluster with five machines (a master and four slaves) for data processing. Additionally, a machine with Kafka Broker, Zookeeper and Kafka producer is used to send the collected data to Spark. Each Spark node has an Intel Core i7-2600 3.40 GHz, 8 cores and 4 GB de RAM. The node that contains Kafka, Zookeeper and Kafka producer has an Intel Core i7-8700 3.20 GHz, 12 cores and 16 GB RAM. Also, 1 GB/s Ethernet connections have been used to link all the nodes in a switch device.

For these experiments, some real and synthetic dataset, detailed in Table 1, have been used. In this table, a cell with no number means that the dataset has not been divided into train and test partitions. Real datasets are Satellite Image, Diabetes, Letter and Poker, obtained from the UCI[1] repository. On the other hand, synthetic datasets are SEA and SINE, that have been generated with MOA[2].

Two experiments have been performed in this work. The first experiment uses real datasets to compare the performance of distributed implementation with the original sequential implementations (Table 2), to show that the results are similar in terms of classification error. The experiment has been developed as follows. Spark cluster is started and then a distributed algorithm is run. For each dataset, the algorithm is trained and evaluated 10 times with a different seed each time. Seeds used are 5, 7, 11, 13, 17, 19, 23, 29, 31, 37. The final result is the mean of these 10 values. This process is repeated for each distributed

---

[1] https://archive.ics.uci.edu/.
[2] https://moa.cms.waikato.ac.nz/.

Table 1. Datasets

Dataset	Attributes	Classes	Instances	Train	Test
SEA (Abrupt)	3	2	5.000.000	—	—
SEA (Gradual)	3	2	5.000.000	—	—
SINE	4	2	5.000.000	—	—
SatImage	36	6	6.435	4.435	2.000
Diabetes	8	2	768	576	192
Letter	16	26	20.000	18.000	2.000
Poker	10	10	1.025.010	—	—

algorithm. The experiments have been run only on a cluster with a single node, because the number of instances is not so high and the improvement in time is not visible. The results obtained are shown in Table 3.

As can be seen, the results obtained by the distributed versions are very similar to those of the sequential implementations. The results are not exactly the same because these algorithms have a random initialization and the seeds used by sequential algorithms are not specified in the literature. A symbol—in a cell means that the literature does not indicate the value.

Table 2. Streaming results of original sequential implementations

Dataset	OS-ELM	EOS-ELM	VOS-ELM	CD-VOS-ELM
SatImage	0,111	0,1099	—	—
Diabetes	0,2254	—	0,2176	—
Letter	0,2295	0,236	0,2176	—

Table 3. Streaming results of new distributed implementations

Dataset	L	Block size	D-OS-ELM	D-EOS-ELM	D-VOS-ELM	D-CD-VOS-ELM
SatImage	400	20	0,1295±0,0023	0,1537±0,0062	0,1325±0,0028	0,1325±0,0028
Diabetes	20	20	0,2066±0,0030	0,2153±0,0120	0,2153±0,0120	0,2153±0,0120
Letter	200	500	0,1963±0,0032	0,2628±0,0028	0,1808±0,0043	0,1808±0,0043

The second experiment uses synthetic datasets to evaluate the performance of distributed algorithms in the presence of concept drift with a big amount of data, because real datasets have a low number of instances. In this case, algorithms process the dataset by blocks. Every time a new block is available, it is first used to evaluate (test) the current model, and then used to train a new model. This technique is known as Test-then-Train [2] and generates one result for each block. The experimentation has been developed as follows. The number of cluster nodes changes from 1 to 4. For each number of cluster nodes, each distributed algorithm processes one dataset 3 times. This is because the execution time is so high. Seeds used in experiments are 5, 7 and 11, respectively. The final result for each distributed algorithm is the mean of the 3 executions. This process is repeated with each dataset. The results of these executions are shown in Figs. 1, 2, 3 and 4 and Table 4.

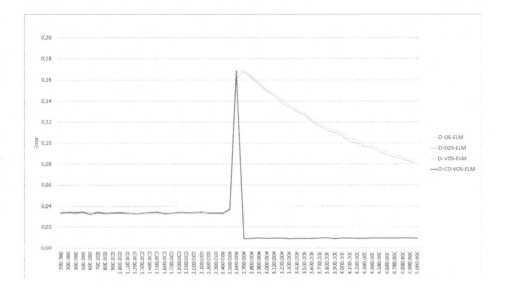

Fig. 1. Test-then-Train results on SEA dataset (Abrupt)

In Fig. 1 the behaviour of each algorithm in an abrupt concept drift can be seen. D-OS-ELM has the highest error, followed by D-EOS-ELM and D-VOS-ELM. This is because they adapt incrementally without having into account the concept drift. The algorithm with best adaptation is D-CD-VOS-ELM due to his drift detection method. When a concept drift is detected, the current model is discarded and a new one is retrained from scratch. Figure 2 shows the error of each algorithm in a gradual concept drift. D-CD-VOS-ELM again has the best behaviour because his drift detection method allows a faster adaptation to the new concept. Another example of abrupt concept drift can be seen in Fig. 3. Finally, the last experiment showed in Fig. 4 shows the performance of these methods with poker dataset. In this case all the algorithms obtain an error around 0.5.

Table 4 shows the total processing time of all the datasets with each algorithm. As can be seen the processing time is reduced with the number of nodes in the Spark cluster. In SEA (Abrupt) the least time is in D-CD-VOS-ELM, because this algorithm is not processing most of blocks due to the error is under the warning level and the algorithm does nothing. For the other datasets, the

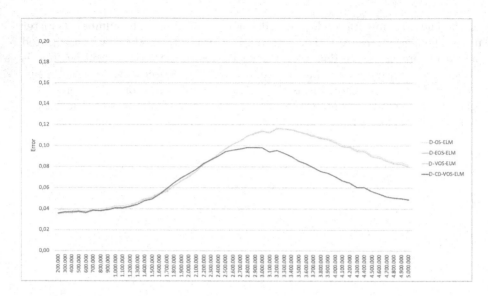

Fig. 2. Test-then-Train results on SEA dataset (Gradual)

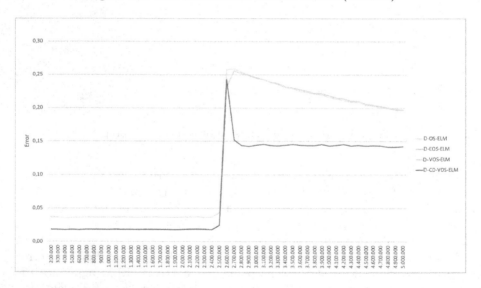

Fig. 3. Test-then-Train results on SINE dataset

algorithm with best behaviour is D-OS-ELM, because the training of a single model is faster than the training of several models. In this case, the training time for D-CD-VOS-ELM is lower due to his drift detection method.

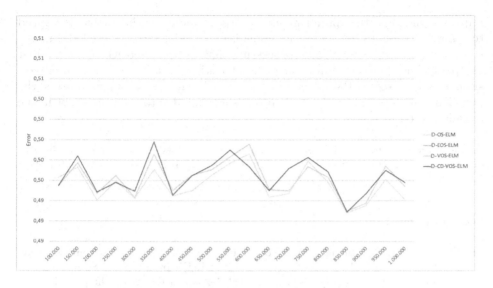

Fig. 4. Test-then-Train results on Poker dataset

Table 4. Streaming training time of distributed implementations (seconds)

Dataset	Block size	Cluster nodes	D-OS-ELM	D-EOS-ELM	D-VOS-ELM	D-CD-VOS-ELM
SEA (Abrupt)	100.000	Local	1.031,58	5.321,76	5.321,76	**442,15**
	100.000	2	732,54	3.630,93	3.630,93	**321,46**
	100.000	4	623,28	3.134,57	3.134,57	**286,77**
SEA (Gradual)	100.000	Local	**1.029,28**	5.206,25	5.206,25	3.593,56
	100.000	2	**731,31**	3.610,35	3.610,35	2.509,50
	100.000	4	**623,46**	3.126,89	3.126,89	2.126,19
SINE	100.000	Local	**1.030,08**	5.321,87	5.321,87	2.886,05
	100.000	2	**739,95**	3.652,33	3.652,33	2.016,07
	100.000	4	**628,72**	3.112,74	3.112,74	1.750,29
Poker	100.000	Local	**259,47**	1.255,76	1.255,76	2.013,18

5   Conclusions

In this work, new distributed implementations of OS-ELM, EOS-ELM, VOS-ELM and CD-VOS-ELM have been introduced. This is because there is a low number of stream neural networks and there are not distributed implementations of these algorithms. To perform these implementations, Apache Spark Streaming has been used. Two comparisons have been performed. The first comparison shows that distributed implementations of the original sequence algorithms generate similar results in terms of classification error, so distributed algorithms are implemented correctly. The second comparison shows that ensemble methods generate more stable results, but the processing time is increased because the algorithms has to train several models each time. This fact shows that it is important to consider the use of a D-OS-ELM or ensemble method depending on the problem. In addition, it can be highlighted that drift detection method improves the algorithm performance because it increases the adaptation speed to a new concept. In this case, the model is only updated if it is needed. Finally, the results obtained show that processing time is decreased when the number of Spark nodes increases, and that it is interesting to use these distributed versions when the size of the dataset is very high. In the case of small datasets, the parallelization does not reduce the processing time due to the time spent in the parallelization process.

Acknowledgements. This work was partially supported by the Spanish Ministry of Science and Innovation under project PID2019-107793GB-I00/AEI/10.13039/501100011033

References

1. Cao, J., Lin, Z., Huang, G.B.: Voting base online sequential extreme learning machine for multi-class classification. In: 2013 IEEE International Symposium on Circuits and Systems (ISCAS2013), pp. 2327–2330. IEEE (2013). https://doi.org/10.1109/ISCAS.2013.6572344
2. Gama, J., Sebastião, R., Rodrigues, P.P.: On evaluating stream learning algorithms. Mach. Learn. **90**(3), 317–346 (2013). https://doi.org/10.1007/s10994-012-5320-9
3. Haneen, A.A., Noraziah, A., Wahab, M.H.A.: A review on data stream classification. J. Phys. Conf. Ser., 012019 (2018). https://doi.org/10.1088/1742-6596/1018/1/012019
4. Huang, G.B., Zhu, Q.Y., Siew, C.K.: Extreme learning machine: a new learning scheme of feedforward neural networks. In: 2004 IEEE International Joint Conference on Neural Networks (IEEE Cat. No. 04CH37541), vol. 2, pp. 985–990. IEEE (2004). https://doi.org/10.1109/IJCNN.2004.1380068
5. Iwashita, A.S., Papa, J.P.: An overview on concept drift learning. IEEE Access **7**, 1532–1547 (2019). https://doi.org/10.1109/ACCESS.2018.2886026
6. Lan, Y., Soh, Y.C., Huang, G.B.: Ensemble of online sequential extreme learning machine. Neurocomputing **72**(13–15), 3391–3395 (2009). https://doi.org/10.1016/j.neucom.2009.02.013
7. Li, L., Sun, R., Cai, S., Zhao, K., Zhang, Q.: A review of improved extreme learning machine methods for data stream classification. Multimedia Tools Appl. **78**(23), 33375–33400 (2019). https://doi.org/10.1007/s11042-019-7543-2
8. Liang, N.Y., Huang, G.B., Saratchandran, P., Sundararajan, N.: A fast and accurate online sequential learning algorithm for feedforward networks. IEEE Trans. Neural Netw. **17**(6), 1411–1423 (2006). https://doi.org/10.1109/TNN.2006.880583
9. Puentes, F., Perez-Godoy, M.D., González, P., del Jesus, M.J.: An analysis of technological frameworks for data streams. In: PRAI (2020). under second review
10. Xu, S., Wang, J.: Dynamic extreme learning machine for data stream classification. Neurocomputing **238**, 433–449 (2017). https://doi.org/10.1016/j.neucom.2016.12.078

Performance Evaluation of Classical Classifiers and Deep Learning Approaches for Polymers Classification Based on Hyperspectral Images

Javier Lorenzo-Navarro[1]([⊠]), Silvia Serranti[2], Giuseppe Bonifazi[2],
and Giuseppe Capobianco[2]

[1] Universidad de Las Palmas de Gran Canaria, Instituto Universitario SIANI,
35017 Las Palmas, Spain
javier.lorenzo@ulpgc.es
[2] Department of Chemical Materials, Environmental Engineering,
Sapienza University of Rome, Rome, Italy
{silvia.serranti,giuseppe.bonifazi,giuseppe.capobianco}@uniroma1.it

Abstract. Plastics are very valuable material for their desirable characteristics being one of them, their durability. But this characteristic turns
plastics into an environmental problem when they end in the environment, and they become one source of contamination that can last for
centuries. Thus, the first step for effective recycling is to identify correctly the types of plastics. In this paper, different classical classifiers
as Random Forest, KNN, or SVM are compared with 1-D CNN and
LSTM to classify plastics from hyperspectral images. Also, Partial Least
Squares Discriminant Analysis has been included as the baseline because
is one of the most widely used classifiers in the field of the Chemometrics community. The images were preprocessed with several techniques
as Standard Normal Variate or Savitzky-Golay Polynomial Derivative to
compare their effectiveness with raw data with the classifiers. The experiments were carried out using hyperspectral images with a 240 bands
spectrum, and six types of polymers were considered (PE, PA, PP, PS,
PVC, EPS). The best results were obtained with SVM+RBF and 1-D
CNN with an accuracy of 99.41% and 99.31% respectively, preprocessing
the images previously with Standard Normal Variate. Also, PCA and
t-SNE methods were tested for dimensionality reduction, but they don't
improve the classifier performance.

Keywords: Polymer classification · Hyperspectral images · Machine
learning · Deep learning

This work was supported in part by the project IMPLAMAC (MAC2/1.1a/265)
financed by the Interreg MAC (European Fund to Regional Development, Macarone-
sian Cooperation).

© Springer Nature Switzerland AG 2021
I. Rojas et al. (Eds.): IWANN 2021, LNCS 12862, pp. 281–292, 2021.
https://doi.org/10.1007/978-3-030-85099-9_23

1   Introduction

The acquisition of images in wavelengths different from the visible by humans allows identifying the surface composition of the objects. This is known as hyperspectral or multispectral imaging depending if the wavelengths bands are respectively continuous or not. The wavelength range in hyperspectral imaging normally corresponds to the Near-infrared (NIR) 0.75–1.4 μm or Short-wavelength infrared (SWIR) 1.4-3 μm. Multispectral images were initially applied for remote sensing with satellite and airborne cameras [18]. With the spread of ground-based hyperspectral cameras, other applications of this technology have emerged as agricultural [34], arts [29], defense [13, 35, 38], medical diagnosis [9, 17, 24, 25] or food quality control [19]. A review of current applications of hyperspectral imaging can be found in [21].

As it was previously mentioned, the environment is one of the current fields where hyperspectral images can play an important role. Two of the most important environmental problems are waste management and marine plastics, which are two sides of the same coin, the extensive use of plastics in our society. Plastics are a common way to refer to a family of organic carbon-chain polymers. They have some properties that make them unique and superior to many others in several applications. Plastics durability is one of its strengths, though at the same time it makes its debris management complicated. So in the recycling of urban waste is necessary to classify the plastic types to process them correctly. Some researchers have proposed several methods to this aim [4, 23, 27, 32, 41]. Another field where plastic classification is needed is in the field of monitoring marine microplastics [33].

One of the most widely used classification methods with hyperspectral images is the PLS-DA [7]. It consists of projecting both the predictive and response variables into low dimensional spaces (latent variables) that model the covariance between them, similar to principal components analysis (PCA). Other methods from the Machine Learning field have also been used in hyperspectral imaging analysis [16, 40].

In this paper, we compare the performance of some Machine Learning methods in a problem of pixel-based polymers classification based on hyperspectral images. Among the considered method are 1-D Convolutional Neural Network (1-D CNN), Long Short Term Memory (LSTM), and PLS-DA. The comparison is carried out with raw and preprocessed data to remove acquisition effects as illumination scatter or reduce the dimensionality. The contributions of this paper are (i) comparison of different machine learning methods for polymer classification, (ii) analysis of the influence of the data preprocessing methods in the classifiers under consideration, and (iii) the novel introduction of a 1-D CNN and LSTM as polymer type classifier.

2   Related Work

In the literature, we can find some works that make use of hyperspectral images for plastics classification. In [23] the authors present a prototype for polymer classification considering 16 types of them. The spectral data were standardized and derivated with Savitzky-Golay filtering and PCA were applied for Linear and Quadratic Discriminant classifiers, that along with Fisher Discriminant classifier and Spectral Angle Mapper were the four compared classifiers. Vidal et al. [37] describe a method for classifying four types of plastic (LDPE, HDPE, PP, and PS). The hyperspectral data are preprocessed applying a Standard Normal Variate (SNV) followed by a Savitzky–Golay first derivative with a second-order polynomial. The classification stage is based on the PLS-DA classifier with six latent variables, and the reported accuracies are 92.59%, 98.71%, 100%, and 100% for each type of plastic, respectively. Amigo et al. [1] focused on the problem of classifying plastics with flame retardants because they modify the reflectance of the polymers. In their work, authors classify five types of plastics with different proportions of retardants. As preprocessing they use SNV and Savitzky-Golay filtering and the classifier is a PLS-DA. In [27], Moroni et al. present a method to differentiate between PET and PVC. Unlike previous works, the preprocessing is carried out with Flat Field (FF) to reduce the dependence on the spectra of the measuring instruments. After that, a Continuum Removal (CR) is used to normalize the spectra. Zheng et al. [41] propose a method to differentiate among six types of plastics. Data from the NIR system is preprocessed applying a Savitzky-Golay filtering and followed by a wavelet transformation. After that, a PCA is computed to identify the most informative wavelengths based on PC loadings. The classification of the six types of plastics is done with five Fisher Discriminant classifiers and the results on 21 samples are 100% of accuracy. In [4], instead of classifying the polymer type in a one-shot, the authors propose a tree hierarchical classifier wherein each node a decision about the plastic types is done based on a PLS-DA classifier.

Multispectral imaging has not been indifferent to the advances in the Deep Learning field. As in many other areas, deep learning has found a field of application in hyperspectral image classification [28]. Chen et al. [10] describe the use of 1-D, 2-D, and 3-D CNN for feature extraction in a hyperspectral remote sensing scenario and compared them with other classical classifiers. For 1-D CNN, the pixel spectra are fed to the network losing the spatial relationship with others pixels. With 2-D CNN, the hyperspectral image is preprocessed with PCA and then, patches around the pixel for each principal component are taken as input to the network. And for 3-D CNN a tridimensional patch is considered that includes spectral and spatial information. Yang et al. [39] propose both 2-D and 3-D CNN along with their recurrent variants (R-2-D-CNN and R-3-D-CNN). As the number of trainable parameters of the networks will be very high due to the number of spectral bands, they propose to make a pixel-based classification using a patch around the pixel. This patch is fed to a 2-D CNN with an input size of $K \times K \times D$, being K the size of the patch and D the number of spectral bands. 3-D CNN is a variation of the previous one, where spectral bands are re-order to keep similar bands closer. The recurrent versions of the previous CNN are two multilevel versions more than recurrent as they are normally understood. Apart from CNN models, other deep learning models, as autoencoders (AE), have been proposed to classify hyperspectral images. Chen et al. [11] make use of AE to obtain a feature vector that is input to a logistic regression model to classify the pixels of an HSI. To reduce the spectral dimension, a PCA is applied to keep only the first several principal components reducing the cube dimension. After that, the input vector of the AE is obtained by applying a flattening operation.

3 Methodology

To assess the performance of the Machine Learning methods, we select six types of commonly used polymers: Polythene (PE), Polyamide (PA), Polypropylene (PP), Polystyrene (PS), Polyvinyl Chloride (PVC), and Expanded Polystyrene (EPS). Samples with pieces of each polymer were prepared (Fig. 1), and a hyperspectral image of each sample was acquired. Table 1 shows the number of polymer samples and the size of the acquired images. The acquisition of the hyperspectral images was done with the line-scan SISUChema XL^{TM} from Specim (Finland) equipped with a 31 mm lens. The spatial resolution of the system is 320 pixels in width. The height depends on the number of plastic particles in the camera tray. A diffuse line unit provides the illumination of the sample, and the calibration of the system is automatically done using internal dark and white references. The spectral range of the system is 1000–2500 nm with a resolution of 6.3 nm, therefore a 240 bands spectrum is obtained for each pixel of the hyperspectral image which has a size of ($height \times 320 \times 240$).

Fig. 1. Samples of polystyrene on the camera tray with a rule as reference.

Each hyperspectral image was manually segmented choosing a threshold value that correctly separates the pixels into background and foreground (plastics). Figure 2 shows the result of thresholding the image shown in Fig. 1. The

Fig. 2. Result of the thresholding of image shown in Fig. 1

Table 1. Image size of the polymer samples and number of background and polymer pixels in each image.

Polymer	Image size	Polymer pixels	Background pixels
PE	480 × 320	26175	127425
PE	482 × 320	29732	124508
PP	48 × 320	30768	123472
PP	482 × 320	23658	130582
PP	482 × 320	17282	136958
PA	480 × 320	22336	131264
PA	482 × 320	24689	129551
PS	482 × 320	23469	130771
PS	482 × 320	29864	124376
PS	482 × 320	27053	127187
PVC	482 × 320	26067	128173
PVC	482 × 320	29104	125136
PVC	480 × 320	23966	129634
EPS	1082 × 320	111688	234552
Total		445851	1903589

number of pixels of background and foreground (plastics) of each image is presented in Table 1. The dataset was created with a random sample of 10% of the pixels of each type of plastic (Table 2)

Table 2. Number of pixels of each polymer type in the dataset.

Polymer	Number of pixels
PE	5590
PP	7169
PA	4701
PS	8037
PVC	7912
EPS	11168
Total	44577

3.1   Data Preprocessing

Due to the effects of illumination and scatter, some preprocessing techniques are applied to the hyperspectral data before obtaining the subsequent classification models. Here below, a brief description of the preprocessing techniques used in this study is given.

Standard Normal Variate (SNV). This method, also known as standardization, transforms the spectrum of each pixel by removing the mean and scaling to unit variance, yielding a signal with zero mean and unitary variance. This process will reduce the effect of the light scattering, and it is among the most widely used methods for scatter correction in near-infrared images [31].

Principal Component Analysis (PCA). Though it is not strictly preprocessing, this technique is widely used in hyperspectral images since they exhibit a high correlation between consecutive bands. So with the PCA preprocessing, a new set of features are obtained that are uncorrelated, and they keep the most of the variability of the spectrum. As the SNV preprocessing, this technique is one of the most used in hyperspectral imagery.

Wavelet Transform. Wavelet transformation has been applied in some applications of hyperspectral images showing an increase in the performance [2,8]. Unlike other transformations as FFT, wavelet transform gives both temporal and frequency information [14], and its results depend on the family of base wavelet used (Haar, Daubechies, ...). In [8] it was found that best results are obtained with Daubechies and biorthogonal, and in [2] the Daubechies bases improve the classification accuracy rates against PCA transformation.

Savitzky-Golay Polynomial Derivative (SG). This preprocessing technique eliminates both additive and multiplicative effects in the data [31]. Savitzky-Golay filter is based on the derivative computation of a polynomial fit in the neighborhood of the point, so a smoothing process is implicit in this method. The higher degree of the polynomial is used, the smaller the smoothing is. With 1st degree polynomial, the additive effect is removed and with 2nd-degree polynomial, the linear tendency of the spectrum is also removed. The degree of the polynomial and the window size around the point to fit it, are design decisions that must be taken according to the data nature.

t-SNE. t-Distributed Stochastic Neighbor Embedding [26] is a non-linear technique for feature reduction based on the minimization of Kullback-Leibler divergence (KL) between the conditional probabilities of the points in the high dimension space and the reduced dimension space. This technique is included in a comparison of different dimensionality reduction techniques in hyperspectral images [22].

4   Experiments and Results

The classification process can be done at the pixel or particle level. In this work, the pixel-based approach has been selected because the number of samples (number of pixels) is higher than particles and the results on both approaches yield similar results when comparing the same classifier [16]. To assess the performance of the classifiers, a hold-out setup was selected with 60% of the samples for training and the rest for testing, and it was repeated five times. In Tables 3 and 4, the reported values of accuracy is the average of the five repetitions.

As it was mentioned previously, PLS-DA is the most widely used classifier to deal with the problem of polymer classification based on hyperspectral images, and to our best knowledge Machine Learning approaches have not been widely tested in this problem. This paper aims to study the performance of some of the most well-known classical classifiers of the Machine Learning field and compare them with two deep learning approaches. Specifically the following classical classifiers are compared: Logistic classifier (Logistic) [3], Decision Trees (Decision Tree) [6,30], Random Forests (Random Forest) [5], Nearest Neighbours (K-NN) [15] Support Vector Machines (SVM) [36] or Neural Networks (MLP) [20]. The hyperparameters of the previous classifiers are: 100 trees for the Random Forest, number of neighbors and C parameter obtained by cross-validation in each holdout repetition for the K-NN and SVM respectively, and two hidden fully connected layers with a number of units equal to the double of the number of inputs for the MLP trained with Adam optimizer ($lr = 0.001$). The PLS-DA classifier performance will be the baseline due to its great acceptance in the Chemometrics community.

As the spectral response of each pixel in the hyperspectral image is a one-dimensional signal, a 1-D Convolutional Neural Network (1-D CNN) is considered as an alternative to classical classifiers. The architecture of the 1-D CNN is: two 1-D convolutional layers with Relu activation followed by a max-pool layer, two 1-D convolutional layers with Relu activation followed by a global average pooling layer, and a final fully connected layer. The assumption of introducing

Table 3. Accuracy for preprocessing methods without dimensionality reduction.

	Raw	SNV	SNV+SG	Wavelet Db7	Average
PLS-DA	81.63	78.33	**97.22**	93.34	87.63
Logistic	96.76	**99.28**	98.91	96.92	97.97
Decision tree	84.48	94.75	**96.70**	88.34	91.07
Random forest	97.64	99.09	**99.41**	97.95	98.52
K-NN	96.73	98.92	**99.17**	96.47	97.82
SVM linear	98.72	99.29	**99.30**	98.78	99.02
SVM RBF	95.27	**99.41**	99.19	94.82	97.17
MLP	97.60	99.31	**99.32**	98.00	98.56
1-D CNN	98.97	**99.31**	**99.31**	98.80	99.10
LSTM	92.73	**98.67**	98.37	67.08	82.73
Average	94.05	96.64	98.69	93.05	95.61

the 1-D CNN is that the initial convolutional layers mimic the pre-processing filters obtaining similar results with raw data. Also, the hyperspectral response of each pixel is an ordered sequence and a recurrent neural network can be considered as a useful approach to classifying the polymer type. In this work, a two-level stacked LTSM is tested with 64 cells in each level and a final fully connected layer. For both models, the optimizer is the Adam with a learning rate of 0.001.

Table 4. Accuracy for preprocessing methods with dimensionality reduction.

	Raw	PCA	t-SNE	SNV+PCA	SNV+t-SNE	Avg
PLS-DA	**81.63**	48.77	52.33	79.90	73.13	67.15
Logistic	**96.76**	58.83	55.54	85.61	89.21	77.19
Decision tree	84.48	61.64	81.79	90.94	**94.72**	82.71
Random forest	97.64	63.24	91.52	97.69	**98.11**	89.64
K-NN	96.73	66.02	91.03	97.30	**98.06**	89.83
SVM linear	**98.72**	61.96	63.94	88.46	93.28	81.27
SVM RBF	95.27	65.46	90.60	**98.40**	97.73	89.49
MLP	**97.60**	46.78	44.38	88.80	65.15	68.54
Avg	93.60	59.09	71.39	90.89	88.67	–

Table 3 and 4 report the average accuracy of each classifier without and with dimensionality reduction, respectively. The number of principal components (PC) with PCA was fixed to keep the 95% of the original dataset variability, resulting in 2 PC when applied to raw data and 7 PC when applied to data preprocessed with SNV. The intrinsic dimension for t-SNE was fixed to 3 in all cases. The best result is obtained with the 1-D CNN with an average accuracy of 99.61% on the 5-holdout tests using as input data the SNV followed by the Savitzky-Golay filtering of quadratic polynomial 1st order derivative. The baseline classifier, PLS-DA, achieves the best performance also for the same pre-processing reaching an accuracy of 97.22%. As the second-best classifier, Random Forest yields an accuracy of 99.41% that confirms the good performance of this type of classifiers compared to deep learning approaches in some problems. PCA preprocessing exhibits on average the worst results because perhaps it is not the best preprocessing method for hyperspectral data as pointed out Cheriyadat and Bruce [12] the nature of this type of data.

The results obtained with the different methods under comparison show that Machine Learning classifiers perform, on average, better than the most used PLS-DA with and without dimensionality reduction (Tables 3 and 4). The introduction of a dimensionality reduction stage in this problem implies a decrease in the performance of the classifiers, and in some cases, the raw data yield the best results (Table 4). It is worthwhile to note that the two best accuracy scores are obtained with Random Forest with SNV and Savitzky-Golay filter, and with SVM with RBF kernel with SNV preprocessing. The latter has the advantage over the former in that there is no need to tune different parameters as a polynomial degree or the neighbor size, unlike the Savitzky-Golay filter. Concerning the deep learning approaches, 1-D CNN yields close results to the two best results but with preprocessed data, so it seems that it is not able to mimic the pre-processing filters. But, 1-D CNN with raw data improves the best performance of PLS-DA with preprocessing (SNV+SG) that implies the elimination of the parameter tuning of the Savitzky-Golay filter.

5   Conclusions

This work has presented a comparison among ten different classifiers, classical ones as Random Forest, SVM, and deep learning approaches as 1-D CNN and LSTM for the problem of polymer classification using as input hyperspectral images. The problem of plastic (polymer) classification has a great interest for correct plastic recycling, thus six of the most widely used polymers are considered. All methods were tested with different types of preprocessed data, from raw data to the most common preprocessing techniques in Chemometrics as SNV or Savitzky-Golay Polynomial Derivative. Some techniques of dimensionality reduction were applied due to the high correlation that may present the spectra bands, but the results don't show a performance improvement of the classifiers. From the results, it can be concluded that both classical (Random Forest and SVM) and deep learning classifiers (1-D CNN) perform quite well in this problem yielding accuracies higher than 99% in a pixel-based classification scenario. For these classifiers, the performance is better than the PLS-DA baseline classifier, which is widely used in polymer classification with hyperspectral images, and whose better value of accuracy is 97.22% against the 99.41% of the Random Forest or the 99.31% of the 1-D CNN.

References

1. Hyperspectral image analysis. A tutorial. Analytica Chimica Acta 896, 34–51, October 2015. https://doi.org/10.1016/J.ACA.2015.09.030
2. Abdolmaleki, M., Fathianpour, N., Tabaei, M.: Evaluating the performance of the wavelet transform in extracting spectral alteration features from hyperspectral images. Int. J. Remote Sens. **39**(19), 6076–6094 (2018). https://doi.org/10.1080/01431161.2018.1434324
3. Bishop, C.M.: Pattern Recognition and Machine Learning. Springer, eidelberg (2006)
4. Bonifazi, G., Capobianco, G., Serranti, S.: A hierarchical classification approach for recognition of low-density (LDPE) and high-density polyethylene (HDPE) in mixed plastic waste based on short-wave infrared (SWIR) hyperspectral imaging. Spectrochim. Acta Part A Mol. Biomol. Spectrosc. **198**, 115–122 (2018). https://doi.org/10.1016/J.SAA.2018.03.006
5. Breiman, L.: Random forests. Mach. Learn. **45**(1), 5–32 (2001). https://doi.org/10.1023/A:1010933404324
6. Breiman, L., Friedman, J.H., Olshen, R.A., Stone, C.J.: Classification and Regression Trees. Wadsworth & Brooks (1993)
7. Brereton, R.G., Lloyd, G.R.: Partial least squares discriminant analysis: taking the magic away. J. Chemom. **28**(4), 213–225 (2014). https://doi.org/10.1002/cem.2609
8. Bruce, L.M., Koger, C.H., Li, J.: Dimensionality reduction of hyperspectral data using discrete wavelet transform feature extraction. IEEE Trans. Geosci. Remote Sens. **40**(10), 2331–2338 (2002)
9. Calin, M.A., Parasca, S.V., Savastru, D., Manea, D.: Hyperspectral imaging in the medical field: present and future AU - Calin, Mihaela Antonina. Appl. Spectrosc. Rev. **49**(6), 435–447 (2014). https://doi.org/10.1080/05704928.2013.838678
10. Chen, Y., Jiang, H., Li, C., Jia, X., Ghamisi, P.: Deep feature extraction and classification of hyperspectral images based on convolutional neural networks. IEEE Trans. Geosci. Remote Sens. **54**(10), 6232–6251 (2016). https://doi.org/10.1109/TGRS.2016.2584107
11. Chen, Y., Lin, Z., Zhao, X., Wang, G., Gu, Y.: Deep learning-based classification of hyperspectral data. IEEE J. Sel. Top. Appl. Earth Observations Remote Sens. **7**(6), 2094–2107 (2014). https://doi.org/10.1109/JSTARS.2014.2329330
12. Cheriyadat, A., Bruce, L.M.: Why principal component analysis is not an appropriate feature extraction method for hyperspectral data. In: IGARSS 2003. 2003 IEEE International Geoscience and Remote Sensing Symposium. Proceedings (IEEE Cat. No.03CH37477). vol. 6, pp. 3420–3422 (2003). https://doi.org/10.1109/IGARSS.2003.1294808
13. Chiang, S., Chang, C., Ginsberg, I.W.: Unsupervised target detection in hyperspectral images using projection pursuit. IEEE Trans. Geosci. Remote Sens. **39**(7), 1380–1391 (2001). https://doi.org/10.1109/36.934071
14. Daubechies, I.: The wavelet transform, time-frequency localization and signal analysis. IEEE Trans. Inf. Theory **36**(5), 961–1005 (1990)
15. Duda, R.O., Hart, P.E., Stork, D.G.: Pattern Classification, 2nd edn. Wiley-Interscience, New York (2000)
16. Duro, D.C., Franklin, S.E., Dubé, M.G.: A comparison of pixel-based and object-based image analysis with selected machine learning algorithms for the classification of agricultural landscapes using SPOT-5 HRG imagery. Remote Sens. Environ. **118**, 259–272 (2012). https://doi.org/10.1016/j.rse.2011.11.020

17. Fabelo, H., et al.: An intraoperative visualization system using hyperspectral imaging to aid in brain tumor delineation. Sensors (Switzerland) **18**(2) (2018). https://doi.org/10.3390/s18020430

18. Goetz, A.F.H.: Three decades of hyperspectral remote sensing of the Earth: a personal view. Remote Sens. Environ. **113**, S5–S16 (2009)

19. Gowen, A.A., O'Donnell, C., Cullen, P.J., Downey, G., Frias, J.M.: Hyperspectral imaging-an emerging process analytical tool for food quality and safety control. Trends Food Sci. Technol. **18**(12), 590–598 (2007)

20. Haykin, S.: Neural Networks; A comprehensive Foundation, 1st edn. Macmillan, New York (1994)

21. Khan, M.J., Khan, H.S., Yousaf, A., Khurshid, K., Abbas, A.: Modern Trends in Hyperspectral Image Analysis: A Review. IEEE Access **6**, 14118–14129 (2018)

22. Khodr, J., Younes, R.: Dimensionality reduction on hyperspectral images: A comparative review based on artificial datas. In: 2011 4th International Congress on Image and Signal Processing. vol. 4, pp. 1875–1883 (2011). DOI: 10.1109/CISP.2011.6100531

23. Kulcke, A., Gurschler, C., Spöck, G., Leitner, R., Kraft, M.: On-Line Classification of Synthetic Polymers Using near Infrared Spectral Imaging. J. Near Infrared Spectrosc. **11**(1), 71–81 (2003). https://doi.org/10.1255/jnirs.355

24. López, S., et al.: A novel use of hyperspectral images for human brain cancer detection using in-vivo samples. In: Proceedings of the 9th International Joint Conference on Biomedical Engineering Systems and Technologies - (Volume 4), pp. 311–320 (2016). https://doi.org/10.5220/0005849803110320

25. Lu, G., Fei, B.: Medical hyperspectral imaging: a review. J. Biomed. Optics **19**(1), 1–25 (2014)

26. van der Maaten, L., Hinton, G.: Visualizing data using t-SNE. J. Mach. Learn. Res. **9**(Nov), 2579–2605 (2008)

27. Moroni, M., Mei, A., Leonardi, A., Lupo, E., Marca, F.L.: PET and PVC separation with hyperspectral imagery. Sensors **15**(1), 2205–2227 (2015). https://doi.org/10.3390/s150102205

28. Paoletti, M., Haut, J., Plaza, J., Plaza, A.: Deep learning classifiers for hyperspectral imaging: a review. ISPRS J. Photogrammetry Remote Sens. **158**, 279–317 (2019). https://doi.org/10.1016/j.isprsjprs.2019.09.006, https://www.sciencedirect.com/science/article/pii/S0924271619302187

29. Polak, A., et al.: Hyperspectral imaging combined with data classification techniques as an aid for artwork authentication. J. Cultural Heritage **26**, 1–11 (2017). https://doi.org/10.1016/J.CULHER.2017.01.013

30. Quinlan, J.R.: C4.5: Programs for Machine Learning. Morgan Kauffman Pub. Inc., Los Altos (1993)

31. Rinnan, Å., van den Berg, F., Engelsen, S.B.: Review of the most common preprocessing techniques for near-infrared spectra. TrAC, Trends Anal. Chem. **28**(10), 1201–1222 (2009). https://doi.org/10.1016/j.trac.2009.07.007

32. Serranti, S., Gargiulo, A., Bonifazi, G.: Characterization of post-consumer polyolefin wastes by hyperspectral imaging for quality control in recycling processes. Waste Manage. **31**(11), 2217–2227 (2011). https://doi.org/10.1016/J.WASMAN.2011.06.007

33. Serranti, S., Palmieri, R., Bonifazi, G., Cózar, A.: Characterization of microplastic litter from oceans by an innovative approach based on hyperspectral imaging. Waste Manage. **76**, 117–125 (2018). https://doi.org/10.1016/j.wasman.2018.03.003

34. Teke, M., Deveci, H.S., Haliloglu, O., Gurbuz, S.Z., Sakarya, U.: A short survey of hyperspectral remote sensing applications in agriculture. In: RAST 2013 - Proceedings of 6th International Conference on Recent Advances in Space Technologies, pp. 171–176 (2013). https://doi.org/10.1109/RAST.2013.6581194

35. Tiwari, K., Arora, M., Singh, D.: An assessment of independent component analysis for detection of military targets from hyperspectral images. Int. J. Appl. Earth Observation Geoinformation **13**(5), 730–740 (2011). https://doi.org/10.1016/J.JAG.2011.03.007

36. Vapnik, V.: The Nature of Statistical Learning Theory. Springer, New York (1999). https://doi.org/10.1007/978-1-4757-3264-1

37. Vidal, M., Gowen, A., Amigo, J.M.: NIR hyperspectral imaging for plastics classification. NIR News **23**(1), 13–15 (2012). https://doi.org/10.1255/nirn.1285

38. Wu, K., Xu, G., Zhang, Y., Du, B.: Hyperspectral image target detection via integrated background suppression with adaptive weight selection. Neurocomputing **315**, 59–67 (2018). https://doi.org/10.1016/J.NEUCOM.2018.06.017

39. Yang, X., Ye, Y., Li, X., Lau, R.Y.K., Zhang, X., Huang, X.: Hyperspectral image classification with deep learning models. IEEE Trans. Geosci. Remote Sens. **56**(9), 5408–5423 (2018). https://doi.org/10.1109/TGRS.2018.2815613

40. Zhang, J., Chen, L., Zhuo, L., Liang, X., Li, J.: An efficient hyperspectral image retrieval method: Deep spectral-spatial feature extraction with DCGAN and dimensionality reduction using t-SNE-based NM hashing. Remote Sens. **10**(2) (2018). https://doi.org/10.3390/rs10020271

41. Zheng, Y., Bai, J., Xu, J., Li, X., Zhang, Y.: A discrimination model in waste plastics sorting using NIR hyperspectral imaging system. Waste Manage. **N.Y.)** **72**, 87–98 (2018). https://doi.org/10.1016/j.wasman.2017.10.015

Hotel Recognition via Latent Image Embeddings

Boris Tseytlin[1] and Ilya Makarov[1,2,3]

[1] HSE University, Moscow, Russia
b.tseytlin@lambda-it.ru, iamakarov@hse.ru
[2] Steklov Institute of Mathematics, St. Petersburg, Russia
[3] Artificial Intelligence Research Institute, Moscow, Russia

Abstract. We approach the problem of hotel recognition with deep metric learning. We overview the existing approaches and propose a modification to Contrastive loss called Contrastive-Triplet loss. We construct a robust pipeline for benchmarking metric learning models and perform experiments on Hotels-50K and CUB200 datasets. Contrastive-Triplet loss is shown to achieve better retrieval on Hotels-50k.

Keywords: Deep metric learning · Image retrieval · Contrastive learning

1 Introduction

In large-scale image-based hotel recognition, the goal is to retrieve hotels from a large database of hotel images. The input is a hotel photo and the retrieved hotel images are expected to be from the same hotel or hotel chain. We approach this task as a deep metric learning problem. In this setting, we train a deep neural network to project images into an informative low-dimension latent space. This space is used for approximate nearest-neighbor retrieval.

The paper is structured in the following way. First we carefully investigate the available approaches. We investigate failure cases of Contrastive and Triplet losses, where they miss out on potentially important information within a triplet. Based on the hypotheses that Triplet loss and Contrastive loss use different information available in a batch we propose the Contrastive-Triplet loss. We construct a benchmarking pipeline for robust model comparisons, ensuring equal conditions for all approaches. The Mean Average Precision at R (MAP@R) metric is used for evaluation. Finally, we experimentally test the proposed approach by comparing the performance of Contrastive-Triplet loss to individual Contrastive and Triplet losses on the CUB200 and Hotels-50k datasets. We finish with a discussion of experimental results. The code for reproducing our experiments is available on Github.[1]

---

[1] https://github.com/btseytlin/metric_benchmarks

© Springer Nature Switzerland AG 2021
I. Rojas et al. (Eds.): IWANN 2021, LNCS 12862, pp. 293–305, 2021.
https://doi.org/10.1007/978-3-030-85099-9_24

Our contributions are two-fold:

1. We find examples where Contrastive and Triplet losses fail to include important information within a batch and formulate the hypothesis that the classic losses use different aspects of similarity.
2. We propose the Contrastive-Triplet loss function which combines Contrastive loss and Triplet loss with no additional computational overhead.
3. For the first time to our knowledge we evaluate a newly proposed Deep Metric Learning approach against the fair benchmarking pipeline by *Musgrave et al.* [17] and open-source the code for reproduction.

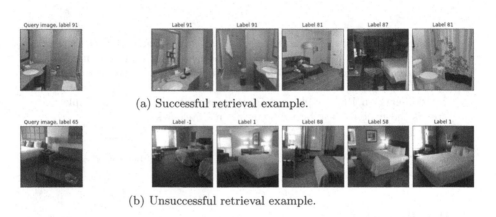

(a) Successful retrieval example.

(b) Unsuccessful retrieval example.

Fig. 1. Retrieval examples for Hotels-50k chain recognition using Contrastive-Triplet loss.

2   Related Work

The tasks of image retrieval, scene recognition and place recognition can be solved using metric learning. Metric learning attempts to map data to an embedding space, where similar data are close together and dissimilar data are far apart. There are two main approaches to deep metric learning: embedding and classification losses.

2.1   Classification

In this setting, a classification model is trained using softmax loss and the embeddings produced by the penultimate layer of the model are used.

The first caveat of this approach is that a model trained for classification does not directly optimize for similarity, which sometimes leads to sub-par results. The second caveat is that image retrieval problems tend to have large numbers of semantic labels, which makes it computationally hard to train a classifier model. Despite that, *Zhai et al.* [27] modify a softmax loss trained classifier for metric learning and show that such approach is very competitive and can be scaled to large numbers of classes.

Deng et al. [3] address the problem that softmax loss does not directly optimize for similarity. They introduce a new loss function ArcFace loss that distributes the data points on a hypersphere. Unlike a generic softmax loss, this loss function directly enforces an angular margin m between embeddings of different classes. Authors achieve great results on face recognition benchmark datasets, which tend to have high inter-class variance and large numbers of clusters.

2.2 Embedding Losses

In this approach a model is trained to explicitly learn an embedding of data into a latent space, where the similarity is maximized for semantically similar data points and minimized otherwise. This is usually achieved by considering pairs, triplets or N-tuplets of images.

Contrastive loss [6] is a classic approach that had wide adoption. The idea behind it is to analyze pairs of embeddings and penalize the embedder model for images of the same label being too far apart and for images of different labels being too close. While training with Contrastive loss, the loss is computed over pairs of images within a batch. A pair with the same label is called a positive pair. A pair with different labels is called a negative pair. The loss is calculated as follows:

$$L_{Contrastive} = [d_p - m_{pos}]_+ + [m_{neg} - d_n]_+ \qquad (1)$$

Where d_p is the distance for the positive pair, d_n is the distance for the negative pair, m_{pos} and m_{neg} are hyperparameters, $[x]_+ = max(0, x)$ is the hinge function.

Another classic approach is Triplet loss [23]. Triplets of images (a, p, n) are selected from each batch, where x_a is an anchor image, p has the same label as the anchor, n has a different label. Triplet loss minimizes the anchor-positive pair distance and maximizes the anchor-negative distance, so that the anchor-positive pair is closer than the anchor-negative pair by some margin $m_{triplet}$:

$$L_{Triplet} = [d(a, p) - d(a, n) + m_{triplet}]_+ \qquad (2)$$

Both Triplet loss and Contrastive loss share the issue of selecting useful triplets or pairs within a batch. The total number of possible triplets in a dataset is $O(n^3)$, but only a tiny fraction of these produce useful gradients. Triplet mining aims to select useful triplets for learning.

Xuan et al. [26] show that sampling the easiest positive and semi-hard negative pairs for triplets leads to better results on datasets with high intra-class variance. An easiest positive image is the closest positive to the anchor in the batch. A semi-hard negative is a negative image that is further from the anchor than the positive image, but within the triplet margin. Such selection pushes each image closer to the most similar image of the same class. This reduces the over-clustering problem, when very different images of the same class are mapped to the same place. Authors indicate that mapping each image close to the closest positive leads to better generalization on unseen data.

Movshovitz et al. [16] argue that it's not enough to select useful triplets from each training batch, but careful sampling of batches is a problem as well. To counter the sensitivity to individual triplets picked into the batch, they propose to learn a small set of proxy points P that approximates the original data distribution. In a supervised setting, where all data points are labelled as belonging to a class, a single proxy is used for each class. Authors extend the NCA loss [4] with proxies, proposing the Proxy-NCA loss. This has the additional advantage over Triplet loss as the margin hyperparameter is no longer needed. This approach was extended [25] to ProxyNCA++ later.

Wang et al. [22] claim that different ranking losses take in account different aspects of similarity. Contrastive loss is based on the similarity between the anchor and the negative example. Triplet loss is based on the difference between the anchor-negative similarity and similarity to positive examples. According to the author each method only uses a specific part of information about a tuple. They propose a multi-similarity loss that attempts to capture all of the information at once and claim that it naturally selects harder pairs.

2.3 Other Approaches

Kim et al. [9] propose an attention-based ensemble model. Multiple attention masks are used after spatial feature extraction, which focuses the model on different regions of the input image. They utilize a divergence loss that promotes each attention mask to learn a different embedding. Similar methods are used for content-based retrieval [21] and automated content editing techniques [5,12].

There were attempts to combine embedding and classification losses for better performance [13]. *Jun et al.* [8] combine the two major approaches by pre-training a DCNN using a classification loss and then fine-tuning the network using Triplet loss.

An loss-agnostic way to improve model performance is to provide the model more useful training samples. *Lin et al.* [11] use a generator network to generate hard negative points from easy negatives, so that the whole distribution of negative samples is covered by the network during training. *Ko et al.* [10] take a different approach for generating hard points: they generate points by linearly interpolating between negative data points during training and picking the hardest point. Other approaches may directly learn metric space transformation via graph embeddings [14,15].

2.4 Reality Check

Musgrave et al. [17] benchmark the models proposed by numerous metric learning papers and find out that much of the claimed progress in the field was caused by flawed experiments. They find that most methods perform roughly like the classic Contrastive loss, Triplet loss or softmax loss approaches. Most of the gains of recent approaches are explained by using newer backbone DNN architectures, optimizing hyper-parameters on test subsets and using flawed accuracy metrics.

3 Proposed Improvements

After analysing previous works on this topic, we formulated the following hypothesis that could be experimentally tested: embedding losses use different aspects of similarity and current embedding losses do not use all of the available information within a batch.

3.1 Contrastive-Triplet Loss

To test the hypotheses that different embedding losses use different information in a batch, we engineer some examples where the classic losses could fail.

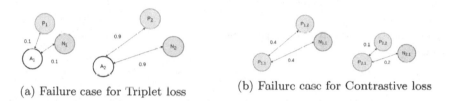

(a) Failure case for Triplet loss   (b) Failure case for Contrastive loss

Fig. 2. Different triplets for which Triplet loss (a) or Contrastive loss (b) produce the same loss value, potentially ignoring important properties of triplets.

Example where Triplet Loss Fails. Consider Triplet loss with $m_{triplet} = 0.1$ and two triplets with the following distances: $d(a_1, p_1) = 0.9$, $d(a_1, n_1) = 0.9$, and $d(a_2, p_2) = 0.1$, $d(a_2, n_2) = 0.1$. For both triplets the loss is equal to 0.1, even though they are different. The information about the positive example being very far from the anchor is ignored in the first triplet. This case is illustrated by Fig. 2a.

Another failure case of Triplet loss is when a triplet produces no gradients. For example consider a triplet with $d(a, p) = 0.3$, $d(a, n) = 0.4$. This is considered an "easy" triplet and produces zero loss, even though the positive example could be pulled closer and the negative could be pushed further away.

Example where Contrastive Loss Fails. Consider Contrastive loss $m_{pos} = 0.2$, $m_{neg} = 0.5$ and pairs with the following distances: $d(p_{1,1}, p_{1,2}) = 0.4$, $d(p_{1,1}, n_{1,1}) = 0.4$, and $d(p_{2,1}, p_{2,2}) = 0.1$, $d(p_{2,1}, n_{2,1}) = 0.2$. For both cases the resulting loss is 0.3, even though in the first case the distances are equal and the example is therefore harder. The information about the relative distance between the positive and the negative examples is ignored. This is illustrated by Fig. 2b.

We attempt to create a loss function for which these failure cases are avoided. We propose a new loss function that combines Contrastive and Triplet loss to

Table 1. Optimal hyperparameters of approaches for the CUB200 dataset (top) and the Hotels-50k dataset chain recognition task (bottom) found via Bayesian optimization. Dashes mark hyperparameters that are not used by an approach.

Approach	m_{pos}	m_{neg}	$m_{triplet}$	$\alpha_{triplet}$	m_{own}	m_{other}	α_{own}	α_{other}	$delay$
Batch-hard Triplet loss (baseline)	–	–	0.289	–	–	–	–	–	–
Contrastive loss	0.330	0.691	–	–	–	–	–	–	–
Contrastive-Triplet	0.030	0.742	0	1	–	–	–	–	–
Approach	m_{pos}	m_{neg}	$m_{triplet}$	$\alpha_{triplet}$	m_{own}	m_{other}	α_{own}	α_{other}	$delay$
Batch-hard Triplet loss (baseline)	–	–	0.396	–	–	–	–	–	–
Contrastive loss	0.111	0.407	–	–	–	–	–	–	–
Contrastive-Triplet	0.080	0.989	0.608	0.884	–	–	–	–	–

use more information about the embedding whilst providing no computational overhead.

Consider a triplet (a, p, n). In addition to Triplet loss, we can also calculate the Contrastive loss for the triplet by taking $d_p = d(a, p)$ and $d_n = d(a, n)$.

By summing these losses, we obtain the Contrastive-Triplet loss:

$$L_{ContrastiveTriplet} = [d(a, p) - m_{pos}]_+ [m_{neg} - d(a, n)]_+$$
$$+ \alpha_{triplet}[d(a, p) - d(a, n) + m_{triplet}]_+ \quad (3)$$

Where $\alpha_{triplet}$ is a hyperparameter weight for the Triplet loss component.

The pairwise distances matrix can be reused when computing both loss components, so there is no computation overhead.

4   Experiments

We follow the fair comparison procedure proposed by *Musgrave et al.* [17] and use the proposed benchmarker software [18] for our experiments. We ensure that all approaches are tested using the same backbone network, BatchNorm parameters, image augmentation and other conditions. The hyperparameters for each approach are optimized via Bayesian optimization first. We also use cross-validation and multiple reproductions to obtain robust estimates of model performance as well as confidence intervals. We use 25 Bayesian optimization iterations for CUB200 and 10 for Hotels-50k instead of 50 due to computation resource limits and time constraints.

4.1 Experiment Setup

Experiments use the PyTorch [1] library with the following procedure:

- The trunk model is an ImageNet [2] pre-trained BN-Inception [7] network.
- The head model is a 1-layer MLP.
- Trunk BatchNorm parameters are frozen during training.
- Embedding dimensionality is 128.
- Batch size is 32. Batches are constructed by sampling 8 classes and randomly sampling 4 images for each class.
- During training, images are first resized so that the shorter side has length 256, then a random crop is made of size between 40 and 256, and aspect ratio between 3/4 and 4/3. Finally, the crop is resized to 227 × 227, and flipped horizontally with 50% probability.
- During evaluation, images are resized to 256 and then center cropped to 227.
- We use separate RMSprop optimizers with a learning rate of $1e - 6$ for trunk and head networks.
- Embeddings are L2 normalized.
- Losses are reduced by averaging all non-zero loss values.
- In case of CUB200, the first half of classes are used as the training set. The second half of classes are used as the test set. In case of Hotels-50k the train-test split is predefined.
- We use 4-fold cross-validation on the training set. Each fold consists of 1/4 training classes and all folds are class-disjoint.
- Training stops when validation accuracy does not improve for 9 consecutive epochs.
  We perform 5 reproduction training runs with the best hyperparameters. Within each reproduction, for each CV split, we load the best model based on validation set error. We use the best models to obtain train and test set embeddings. We concatenate these embeddings into 512-dim embeddings and L2-normalize them. Using these embeddings we test retrieval and report the mean accuracy and confidence intervals.

For Hotels-50k the procedure has the following differences:

- 10 iterations of Bayesian optimization are performed.
- Only 500 batches are processed per epoch.
- For each cross-validation fold, the validation fold only has labels that are present in the training set. This is done to mimic the task of the dataset.

Batch-size can have a significant effect on neural networks, but *Musgrave et al.* [17] demonstrate that increasing batch size from 32 to 256 has little effect to relative rankings of metric learning approaches.

4.2 Accuracy Metrics

We compare solutions using Mean Average Precision at R (MAP@R). For a given query it's defined as follows:

$$MAP@R = \frac{1}{R} \sum_{i=1}^{R} P(i) \qquad (4)$$

Where $P(i)$ = precision at i if the i-th retrieval is correct and 0 otherwise. R is the total number of references that have the same label as the query.

This metric takes in account both the number of correct retrievals and their ranking. We also provide the commonly used $P(1)$ metric, also called Top-1 Accuracy, for comparison. However it should be noted that the metric can be very high even for poorly-clustered samples, as demonstrated in [17].

4.3   Evaluation

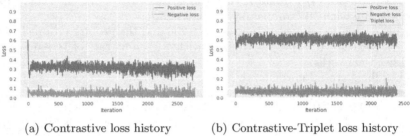

(a) Contrastive loss history   (b) Contrastive-Triplet loss history

Fig. 3. Loss histories for Contrastive loss (a) and Contrastive-Triplet loss (b) when training on CUB200 with the best hyperparameters. The negative loss value is approximately same for both approaches. Positive loss changes considerably in presence of the Triplet loss component. The overall convergence pattern remains the same.

For the best hyperparameters, 5 reproduction iterations are run, following the standard cross-validation scheme. For each reproduction the accuracy score is computed. For each CV partition within a reproduction, the highest-accuracy checkpoint is loaded. The 4 models are used to obtain embeddings. For both train and test sets we concatenate the 128-dim embeddings of the 4 models to get 512-dim embeddings, and then L2 normalize them. We test and report the accuracy of retrieval using these embeddings. In the end, we aggregate the scores of reproductions to obtain mean accuracy metrics and confidence intervals.

4.4   CUB200 Dataset

We benchmark our approaches on CUB200-2011 [24] dataset. The dataset contains photos of birds taken in the wild, with bird species used as labels. It's a commonly used benchmark in metric learning. Just like Hotels-50k, it contains a lot of hard cases of two types:

- images of the same class that are very different visually,
- images of different classes that are very similar visually.

In other words, this dataset is notable for high intra-class variance and high similarity between some classes.

The dataset contains 11,788 images distributed between 200 classes. In accordance with previous literature, we use the first 100 classes for the training dataset, and the last 100 classes for the test dataset.

4.5   Hotels-50k Dataset

Finally, we benchmark on the Hotels-50k [19] dataset. The dataset contains images taken in hotel rooms. Some images are non-professional photos of hotel rooms taken with the TraffickCam app, the rest are professional photos from hotel booking websites. Each photo is labelled with hotel id, hotel chain id and image source (TraffickCam or not). All test images come from TraffickCam, so the task is to identify a hotel or chain given a poor-quality user submitted photo. The dataset provides two tasks: hotel instance recognition and hotel chain recognition. We only approach the hotel chain recognition task.

Due to the large size of the dataset, time and resource constraints, we use a subset of the dataset. For the training set, we remove all hotel chains that have fewer than 100 images and all hotels that have fewer than 10 images. Among the remaining images, we keep only a sample the non-TraffickCam images, such that their number is equal to the number of TraffickCam images. Finally, we remove all hotels from the test set if they are not in the resulting training set.

In the end, the training subset contains 86,936 images from 30,467 hotels of 90 hotel chains. 43,468 images among these come from TraffickCam. The test subset contains 10,900 images from 3,244 hotels of 85 hotel chains. All images in the testing set come from TraffickCam. The final subset we used, as well as the code for recreating it, can is available on Github[2].

To speed up training on this large dataset, we convert the test and train sets into Lightning Memory Mapped Database [20] binary files storing the following key value pairs: $(image\_index, (image, chain\_id, hotel\_id, image\_source))$. LMDB allows multiple concurrent readers to read images from the file. This significantly increases the speed of loading images and training.

4.6   Baseline

For comparison, we reproduce the approach used in the original Hotels 50K paper [19]. A neural network is trained using Triplet loss. Batch-hard mining is used: a miner that samples the hardest positive and hardest negative triplet for each anchor. All losses are averaged, including zero values. All other parameters, including backbone network, batch size, embedding dimension and image augmentations, are the same as for other approaches (described in Sect. 4), to ensure a fair comparison.

---

[2] https://github.com/btseytlin/metric_benchmarks.

5   Results

The benchmark results can be found in Table 2 and Table 3. The optimal hyper-parameters for the CUB200 dataset can be found in Table 1, and for the Hotels-50k dataset in Table 1.

The hypotheses behind Contrastive-Triplet loss was that the different components of the loss might describe different aspects of similarity. If that was true, combining them with optimized hyperparameters would achieved better results.

Table 2. Benchmark results on CUB200.

Approach	MAP@R	MAP@R confidence	P(1)	P(1) confidence
Untrained backbone	0.134	–	0.524	–
Triplet loss (baseline)	0.243	[0.237, 0.249]	0.647	[0.639, 0.655]
Contrastive	**0.260**	[0.257, 0.264]	0.668	[0.664, 0.671]
Contrastive-Triplet	0.258	[0.254, 0.262]	0.670	[0.665, 0.675]

Table 3. Benchmark results on Hotels-50k chain recognition.

Approach	MAP@R	MAP@R confidence	P(1)	P(1) confidence
Untrained backbone	0.023	–	0.175	–
Triplet loss (baseline)	0.029	[0.028, 0.030]	0.255	[0.251, 0.260]
Contrastive	0.031	[0.030, 0.033]	0.268	[0.262, 0.275]
Contrastive-Triplet	**0.039**	[0.037, 0.040]	0.300	[0.290, 0.310]

It does not appear to be the case for CUB200. Loss history plots, shown on Fig. 3, indicate that adding a Triplet loss component does not significantly affect convergence. The negative loss component does not change with addition of the Triplet loss component. Our experiments show that adding a Triplet loss component to Contrastive loss shifts the positive loss margin towards zero, making the positive loss greater in value, while the Triplet loss margin also shifts towards zero. When $m_{triplet}$ is close to zero, Triplet loss only provides penalties when the positive pair is farther away than the negative pair. In that case Triplet loss component pulls positive examples that are too far away closer to the anchor, almost like positive Contrastive loss. For the CUB200 dataset, a combination of Triplet loss and Contrastive loss achieves the same results as Contrastive loss alone. This leads us to believe that either Triplet loss or Contrastive positive loss are redundant in this case. It should be noted that while Contrastive-Triplet loss does not achieve better results on CUB200, the hyperparameter values are much more stable for it than for Contrastive loss, as shown on Fig. 4.

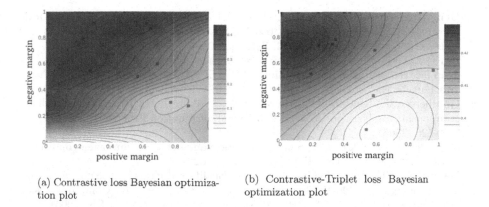

(a) Contrastive loss Bayesian optimization plot

(b) Contrastive-Triplet loss Bayesian optimization plot

Fig. 4. Bayesian optimization plots for Contrastive and Contrastive-Triplet losses on dataset CUB200. Black squares indicate Bayesian trials. Darker colors indicate higher validation set MAP@R. Optimal values for positive and negative margin are much more stable in presence of Triplet loss component.

However, the approach does achieve slightly better results on Hotels-50k dataset. This might be explained by the fact that Contrastive-Triplet loss has more stable hyperparameters. Fewer Bayesian optimization iterations were done for Hotels-50k, which could lead to better results for the method that takes less steps to optimize hyperparameters. Examples of retrieval are provided on Fig. 1. Overall, qualitative analysis indicates that the embedding produced is densely packed, with the distances between random pairs of images being very small, which leads to a lot of false positives. The network is not able to enforce a large margin between hotel chains.

6   Conclusion

In this paper we approached the task of hotel recognition. Having reviewed the existing approaches we investigated the failure cases of Contrastive and Triplet losses and proposed the Contrastive-Triplet loss. We constructed a robust experiment pipeline to ensure consistent and reproducible results. Our experiments indicate that Contrastive-Triplet loss doesn't outperform the baseline on CUB200, but achieves better retrieval results on Hotels-50k than baseline Contrastive and Triplet losses.

References

1. Paszke, A., et al.: Pytorch: an imperative style, high-performance deep learning library. In: et al., H.W. (ed.) Advances in Neural Information Processing Systems 32, pp. 8024–8035. Curran Associates, Inc. (2019)

2. Deng, J., Dong, W., Socher, R., Li, L.J., Li, K., Fei-Fei, L.: Imagenet: a large-scale hierarchical image database. In: 2009 IEEE Conference on Computer Vision and Pattern Recognition, pp. 248–255. IEEE (2009)
3. Deng, J., Guo, J., Xue, N., Zafeiriou, S.: Arcface: additive angular margin loss for deep face recognition. In: Proceedings of the IEEE Conference on Computer Vision and Pattern Recognition, pp. 4690–4699 (2019)
4. Goldberger, J., Hinton, G.E., Roweis, S.T., Salakhutdinov, R.R.: Neighbourhood components analysis. In: Advances in Neural Information Processing Systems, pp. 513–520 (2005)
5. Golyadkin, M., Makarov, I.: Semi-automatic manga colorization using conditional adversarial networks. In: AIST, pp. 230–242 (2020)
6. Hadsell, R., Chopra, S., LeCun, Y.: Dimensionality reduction by learning an invariant mapping. In: 2006 IEEE Computer Society Conference on Computer Vision and Pattern Recognition (CVPR 2006), vol. 2, pp. 1735–1742. IEEE (2006)
7. Ioffe, S., Szegedy, C.: Batch normalization: accelerating deep network training by reducing internal covariate shift. arXiv preprint arXiv:1502.03167 (2015)
8. Jun, H., Ko, B., Kim, Y., Kim, I., Kim, J.: Combination of multiple global descriptors for image retrieval. arXiv preprint arXiv:1903.10663 (2019)
9. Kim, W., Goyal, B., Chawla, K., Lee, J., Kwon, K.: Attention-based ensemble for deep metric learning. In: Ferrari, V., Hebert, M., Sminchisescu, C., Weiss, Y. (eds.) ECCV 2018. LNCS, vol. 11205, pp. 760–777. Springer, Cham (2018). https://doi.org/10.1007/978-3-030-01246-5_45
10. Ko, B., Gu, G.: Embedding expansion: augmentation in embedding space for deep metric learning. In: Proceedings of the IEEE Conference on Computer Vision and Pattern Recognition (2020)
11. Lin, X., Duan, Y., Dong, Q., Lu, J., Zhou, J.: Deep variational metric learning. In: Ferrari, V., Hebert, M., Sminchisescu, C., Weiss, Y. (eds.) ECCV 2018. LNCS, vol. 11219, pp. 714–729. Springer, Cham (2018). https://doi.org/10.1007/978-3-030-01267-0_42
12. Lomotin, K., Makarov, I.: Automated image and video quality assessment for computational video editing. In: AIST, pp. 243–256 (2020)
13. Lomov, I., Lyubimov, M., Makarov, I., Zhukov, L.E.: Fault detection in tennessee eastman process with temporal deep learning models. J. Ind. Inf. Integr. **23**, 100216 (2021)
14. Makarov, I., Kiselev, D., Nikitinsky, N., Subelj, L.: Survey on graph embeddings and their applications to machine learning problems on graphs. PeerJ Comput. Sci. **7**, e357 (2021)
15. Makarov, I., Makarov, M., Kiselev, D.: Fusion of text and graph information for machine learning problems on networks. PeerJ Comput. Sci. **7**, e526 (2021)
16. Movshovitz-Attias, Y., Toshev, A., Leung, T.K., Ioffe, S., Singh, S.: No fuss distance metric learning using proxies. In: Proceedings of the IEEE International Conference on Computer Vision, pp. 360–368 (2017)
17. Musgrave, K., Belongie, S., Lim, S.N.: A metric learning reality check (2020)
18. Musgrave, K., Lim, S.N., Belongie, S.: Powerful benchmarker (2019). https://github.com/KevinMusgrave/powerful-benchmarker
19. Stylianou, A., Xuan, H., Shende, M., Brandt, J., Souvenir, R., Pless, R.: Hotels-50k: a global hotel recognition dataset. In: The AAAI Conference on Artificial Intelligence (AAAI) (2019)
20. Symas: Symas lightning memory mapped database. https://symas.com/lmdb/
21. Tseytlin, B., Makarov, I.: Content based video retrieval system for distorted video queries. In: Proceedings of MacsPro 2020 (2020)

22. Wang, X., Han, X., Huang, W., Dong, D., Scott, M.R.: Multi-similarity loss with general pair weighting for deep metric learning. In: Proceedings of the IEEE Conference on Computer Vision and Pattern Recognition, pp. 5022–5030 (2019)
23. Weinberger, K.Q., Saul, L.K.: Distance metric learning for large margin nearest neighbor classification. J. Mach. Learn. Res. **10**(2), 207–244 (2009)
24. Welinder, P., et al.: Caltech-UCSD Birds 200. Technical report CNS-TR-2010-001, California Institute of Technology (2010)
25. Wern Teh, E., DeVries, T., Taylor, G.W.: Proxynca++: revisiting and revitalizing proxy neighborhood component analysis. arXiv pp. arXiv-2004 (2020)
26. Xuan, H., Stylianou, A., Pless, R.: Improved embeddings with easy positive triplet mining. In: The IEEE Winter Conference on Applications of Computer Vision, pp. 2474–2482 (2020)
27. Zhai, A., Wu, H.Y.: Classification is a strong baseline for deep metric learning. arXiv preprint arXiv:1811.12649 (2018)

Time Series Prediction
with Autoencoding LSTM Networks

Federico Succetti, Andrea Ceschini, Francesco Di Luzio, Antonello Rosato,
and Massimo Panella[✉]

Department of Information Engineering, Electronics and Telecommunications,
University of Rome "La Sapienza", 00184 Rome, Italy
{antonello.rosato,massimo.panella}@uniroma1.it

Abstract. Nowadays, solving prediction problems in green computing is
an open and challenging task, for which solutions based on deep learning
are studied. In this work, we present a forecasting algorithm based on
Long Short-Term Memory networks applied to renewable energy sources
time series prediction. We make use of an encoder-decoder structure to
extract useful representative sequence data, employing a stacked LSTM
architecture for data embedding and successive prediction. By comparing
the performance of the proposed forecasting scheme with a classical two-
layer LSTM structure, we are able to asses the performance of the former
as a robust tool for solving prediction problems in the green computing
framework.

Keywords: Long short-term memory network · Autoencoding · Time
series prediction · Data embedding · Renewable energy sources

1 Introduction

Predicting future values of time series is a frequently studied problem, and over
the past few years a challenging field has been given by the Renewable Energy
Sources (RESs) production. One of the main issues is related to the integration of
high intermittent and stochastic energy production of RESs, such as solar power
and wind energy, into deterministic energy systems, thus demanding an improvement of their own flexibility [13]. Since RESs are more and more widespread,
with photovoltaic (PV) energy being the most common and one of the most
reliable sources, power forecasting plays an important role from this perspective: it allows an efficient distribution of this energy on the grid and enables
to balance the electrical consumption and generation [11]. However, predicting
PV power generation is not an easy task because it mainly depends on weather
conditions, which may be unstable and vary over time. Additionally, as most
of the RESs forecasting problems, seasonality must be taken into account. The
fluctuating behaviour typical of RESs entails several uncertainty issues related
to the difference between predicted and real power.

In this work, an innovative deep neural network (DNN) approach for green
time series forecasting is presented. An LSTM-Autoencoded Network composed

© Springer Nature Switzerland AG 2021
I. Rojas et al. (Eds.): IWANN 2021, LNCS 12862, pp. 306–317, 2021.
https://doi.org/10.1007/978-3-030-85099-9_25

by two stacked LSTM layers is adopted, where the first layer works as an encoder to embed input data and extract meaningful information, while the second LSTM layer acts as a predictor. The original contribution of this paper consists of a two-stages approach in the training modalities of the network. In fact, bearing non-linearity and long-interval datasets typical of RES time series in mind, an initial pre-training phase is conducted in an unsupervised manner to fit the encoder, then the entire network is fine-tuned in a supervised fashion. In the second training stage, the weights of the encoder LSTM layer remain unchanged. In this way, the encoder LSTM could capture the hidden structures among samples adaptively thanks to its long short-term mechanism, leading to better generalization. Our approach is therefore compared to a classical two-layer LSTM, which represents the state-of-the-art in this context. It is shown that our model, which will be denoted in the following as LSTM-Autoembedding, achieves the best performance and improves significantly the error rate and its standard deviation with respect to a vanilla architecture. The LSTM-Autoembedding is easily adaptable to both univariate and multivariate time series, acting as an intelligent feature-extraction tool [8] and offering great flexibility and paving the way for more accurate results in the green computing framework as well as in time series modelling [10].

2 Relevant Literature Summary

Deep Learning (DL) has proven to be the most suitable solution in this field, with several architectures having yielded satisfactory results; relatively recently, Long Short-Term Memory (LSTM) networks have established themselves as a *de facto* standard in time series modelling. They are designed to solve the cited vanishing gradient problem and to retain information for longer periods of time, making them suitable to deal with long-term dependencies and useful for different applications, from forecasting to anomaly detection [9]. The effectiveness of LSTMs, mainly due to their peculiar design based on a memory cell controlling the interactions among different memory units, makes LSTM the most efficient solution to face the vanishing gradient problem typical of Recurrent Neural Networks (RNNs) [12].

With the fluctuations typical of RESs, classical DNNs are easily prone to error when steep variations occur. Moreover, a high number of layers inevitably increases the number of parameters to be optimized, hence the training time too, while large computations among layers still suffer from the vanishing gradient problem. One of the possible ways to tackle these issues consists in introducing an autoencoder (AE) scheme in the network architecture. AEs have gained increasing popularity in time series analysis, because they allow automated feature learning in order to extract a compressed feature representation with minimal human effort. More specifically, an AE takes advantage of embedding to translate high-dimensional vectors into a low-dimensional space, providing a dense feature representation of the input data, learning the hidden structure among them. A plain AE architecture can usually be divided into two steps: (i) an encoding stage, where the input is compressed into a low-dimensional representation; (ii) a decoding stage to reconstruct the original input from the embedded features. Finally, AEs offer great flexibility to sequences of different nature in terms of raw input data, capturing non-linear dependencies automatically and thus enabling true multivariate analysis. For these reasons, AEs are commonly used for unsupervised feature learning in combination with other learning systems.

Energy time series forecasting have received significant attention from many researchers lately and both LSTM and AE networks are commonly used for this task due to their characteristics. We will now briefly revise some of these solutions. Alzahrani et al. [2] propose a two-layer LSTM to predict solar irradiance, overcoming traditional Machine Learning (ML) techniques such as SVM and simple FeedForward Neural Networks. In [5], a stacked AE is used for ultra-short-term and short-term wind speed prediction to better capture non-linearity among data, highlighting the superiority of this approach with respect to other shallow network architectures. The combination of these two models, i.e. Autoencoders and LSTM, can be found in several energy prediction solutions, with enhanced performances against traditional Machine Learning techniques, shallow networks and vanilla LSTMs. For example, in [4] the AE is pre-trained, then the encoder part is detached and employed as a high-level feature extractor in an LSTM network. Afterwards, in a fine tuning phase, only the weights of the LSTM network are trained.

Researchers in [1] propose an Auto-GRU, that is a combination of AE and Gate Recurrent Unit (GRU), a variant of LSTM networks. The Auto-GRU model actually performs better than other models, including vanilla LSTM and the combination of AE and LSTM. Researchers in [3] take a cue from the previous techniques and predict geothermal energy production using an LSTM Sequence-to-Sequence Encoder-Decoder network in a single-stage framework, where both the encoder and decoder are LSTMs and hence they can shrink and expand the input sequence, respectively. Similar architectures are also present in many papers outside the energy domain. An encoder-decoder made up of two LSTM layers is introduced in [14], whose encoder output is then fed into another network with three stacked Fully Connected (FC) layers to predict daily Uber trips in some American cities. However, the encoder-decoder LSTM here is not a typical unsupervised AE, since the decoder network is forced to construct the next few timestamps of the sequence instead of the original input. Again, authors in [12] stacked more than an LSTM-AE layer in a deep fashion, pre-training each encoder-decoder layer in a greedy layer-wise manner.

Nevertheless, none of the previous papers truly investigated the embedding rationale behind an LSTM encoder-decoder structure for PV power production data. In fact, some drawbacks in implementing vanilla LSTM networks are related to their training and inference phases, which are very time consuming, and to the possibility to be stuck in local minima due to random weights initialization, without being able to extract high-level features. On the other hand, a plain combination of classic AE and LSTM may not fully represent the complex dynamics among data in an efficient manner, because of AE's inability to learn long short-term dependencies. Moreover, pure LSTM encoder-decoder architectures significantly vary one another and are not always trained in a two-stages fashion, sometimes changing the network's inner structure when passing from the pre-training phase to the fine-tuning step. For all of the previous reasons, we used as a state-of-the-art benchmark for RESs forecasting a two-layer LSTM architecture with the classic training approach.

3 Proposed Methodology

Time series data are a sequence of consecutive observations recorded in uniform intervals over a period of time. The problem of univariate time series (UTS) forecasting is the most commonly managed approach and consists of predicting future values using previous known samples of the same signal. This UTS problem can be seen as a sequence of scalar numbers used to forecast the future samples. Time series are usually modelled through a stochastic process, which is namely a sequence of real values. In UTS, the goal is to estimate the future samples using only the data available at the current time.

Despite the various advantages cited for the LSTM network, its performance for time series problems is not always satisfactory and, often, the reason is that the supervised learning approach is based on a random initialization of the neurons, making the backpropagation algorithm trapped in different local minima [7]. As already stated, to overcome these challenges and to ensure a more robust prediction scheme in energy related contexts, in this paper an innovative approach is proposed. We describe herein the LSTM-Autoembedding model, which is composed by two stacked LSTM layers. The first LSTM layer (LSTM-1) works as an encoder in order to extract useful and representative embedding for the time series representation in an unfolded state space, while the second LSTM layer (LSTM-2) is the one charged with non-linear modelling to forecast future samples.

Let $S[n]$, with $n > 0$, be the scalar time series to be predicted. Let the current sample at time step n, usually at the end of the day, and all of the previous ones be the known samples to be used for predicting the new ones. The innovative factor of this approach is inherent of the training procedure: to fit the encoder, a pre-training step is conducted where the LSTM-2 works as a decoder to reconstruct the embedded time series data; the encoder-decoder pair is trained to forecast the same current sample that is present at the encoder's input. In this pre-training step, $S[n]$ is the input sequence that is fed into the LSTM-1 layer that acting as encoder; it returns as output a vector $\mathbf{h}(n)$ that has dimension equal to the number of cells H_1 in the encoder layer. The LSTM-decoder with H_2 hidden cells decodes the input sequence $S[n]$ from the embedding vector $\mathbf{h}(n)$. A Fully Connected (FC) layer is used for compiling the data extracted by the previous layers and form the scalar sequence $\tilde{S}[n]$, which is a reconstructed copy of the original. The pre-training network configuration can be seen in Fig. 1.

After pre-training, the network is trained again for the actual time series prediction. In this stage, the input is still $S[n]$ and the LSTM-1 weight, denoted

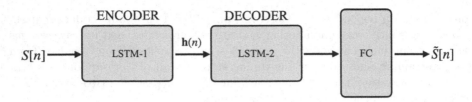

Fig. 1. Pre-training configuration of the proposed DNN.

as W_1, remain unchanged in order to continue to extract the same embedding vector $\mathbf{h}(n)$ from the training sequence. Conversely, in the actual prediction step the weights W_2 of the LSTM-2 layer are trained again together with the FC layer, in order to predict the K samples after the current one and thus resulting in the forecasted sequence $\tilde{S}[n + K]$. The overall pseudo-algorithm is detailed in Algorithm 1.

Algorithm 1. Pseudo-Algorithm of the training procedure

Require: observed time series $S[n]$; a DNN model consisting of two LSTM layers (i.e., LSTM-1 and LSTM-2) and a FC layer.

1: **Data preparation:** time series normalization, data filling, etc.
2: **Pre-training hyperparameters definition:** define H_1, H_2, number of epochs N_{epochs}, etc.
3: **Pre-training setup:** define the input to be encoded by the LSTM-1 layer and also to be reconstructed by the LSTM-2 layer.
4: **Pre-training:** train the network to find the best parameters configuration W_1 for the LSTM-1, with the goal of reconstructing the input sequence with AE.
5: **Forecasting-setup:** initialize the LSTM-1 parameters to W_1, fix the learning rate of LSTM-1 to 0 in order to keep the LSTM-1 parameters equal to W_1 for the whole duration of the training.
6: **Forecasting:** train LSTM-2 (W_2) and FC to return the final predicted output $\tilde{S}[n + K]$

The intuition is that with the encoding, the first layer of the network learns how to extract representative and meaningful features form the input time series and in this way it is employed as an intelligent embedding-extraction tool. After the auto-embedding model is trained, the inference is done with the second training of the network in which the first LSTM layer acts as encoder and the second LSTM layer is the actual forecasting component of the network. The forecasting configuration of the network can be seen in Fig. 2.

4   Experiments

To assess the performance of the proposed approach, we perform a comparison with a standard two-layer LSTM network, which is used herein as a reference

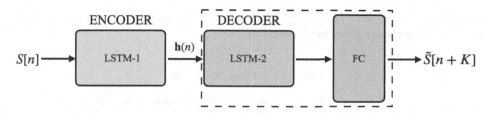

Fig. 2. Forecasting configuration of the proposed DNN. Colours of the LSTM-2 and the FC blocks have changed with respect to Fig. 1 because of the re-trained weights after the pre-training configuration.

benchmark. It is not pre-trained, so the sequence $S[n]$ is fed to the network in which both LSTM layers are going to be trained only once, as in the classic vanilla-LSTM training. Thus, in this case, there is not the fixing of the first LSTM parameters.

Both LSTM models are trained on the same dataset, retrieved from the Measurement and Instrumentation Data Center (MIDC) database, which contains time series data related to real case scenarios. In particular, the photovoltaic (PV) power production plant corresponding to the geographic coordinates $35°92'99.6''$ N, $84°30'95.2''$ W, elevation 245 m is considered, which refers to the 'Oak Ridge National Laboratory', located in Oak Ridge, TN, USA. Irradiance data are measured through a LICOR LI-200 pyranometer sensor at 12.04 m above ground level and the related output power (which represents the time series to be predicted, in kW) is computed by using a system balance of 0.9 and by applying an inverter curve with Maximum Power Point Tracking (MPPT). The considered time series refers to year 2018 and it is sampled on a hourly base (24 samples a day).

A training set of two months is used for the experiments. The test sets, which start after the last available sample of the training set, have a length of 1-day (i.e., 24 samples). To ensure a variation in seasonality, we decided to carry out the aforementioned tests in four different months: May, July, October and December 2018. The first two months are, in general, sunny months, where the sunshine hours are long. On the contrary, in the last two months the weather has, in general, a more variable behaviour, that makes the prediction harder. For each month, the test sets are composed by the 24 samples of the first day of the month. As the samples are predicted all together at the same time, the prediction distance in all models is set to $K = 24$. Before applying the learning procedures, a statistical standardization is carried out on the data, subtracting the mean and scaling by the standard deviation of the training set only.

All networks have been trained using the ADAM algorithm [6] with gradient decay factor 0.9 and mini batch size 1. The additional hyperparameters and training options have been set through the use of a grid search procedure in order to avoid overfitting. This optimization is done for each test set: this means that both networks use the same setup of training options and hyperparameters for a specific test set (May, July, October and December). A summary list of network hyperparameters is reported in Table 1.

Table 1. Network structures

Month	H_1	H_2	N_{epochs}	Initial Learn rate	Learn rate Drop period	Learn rate Drop factor
May	15	30	175	0.01	100	0.4
July	15	45	125	0.007	65	0.8
Oct.	15	30	175	0.01	100	0.4
Dec.	30	40	175	0.005	100	0.6

All the experiments were performed using Matlab® R2020a on a machine provided with an Intel® Core™ i7-3820 64-bit CPU at 3.60 GHz and with 32 GB of RAM, using for training and inference an NVIDIA® GeForce™ GTX 680 GPU at 1.006 GHz and 2048 MB GDDR5 RAM. Considering that the initial hidden state of the network is initialized randomly, 10 runs are performed for each test and the average and standard deviation over the different runs are reported, in order to highlight the robustness of our approach. Two different error measures are reported to evaluate the performance of the models: the Root Mean Square Error (RMSE) and Mean Absolute Error (MAE). RMSE is also used as the loss function to train both networks by the ADAM algorithm. One important remark must be done regarding the error measures. Based on the fact that during the night period the produced PV output power is zero, the RMSE and MAE are computed only considering the hours of sunshine predicted in the test phase. Thus, the predicted PV output power is set to zero during the night period by computing the hours of sunrise and sunset. The numerical results are reported, for each month, in Tables 2, 3, 4 and 5, respectively.

Table 2. Average RMSE and MAE (kW) with standard deviation for May test

Model	RMSE	MAE
LSTM-Autoembedding	7.558 ± 1.057	5.213 ± 0.674
LSTM-Benchmark	7.646 ± 1.225	5.300 ± 0.801

In all cases, the LSTM-Autoembedding achieves the best performance, both in terms of RMSE and MAE. This proves the effectiveness of the autoembedding in extract relevant features in the pre-training stage, that result useful when the prediction is carried out. In the May test set, our approach achieve better

Table 3. Average RMSE and MAE (kW) with standard deviation for July test

Model	RMSE	MAE
LSTM-Autoembedding	7.561 ± 0.793	4.161 ± 0.377
LSTM-Benchmark	8.795 ± 1.550	4.797 ± 0.828

Table 4. Average RMSE and MAE (kW) with standard deviation for October test

Model	RMSE	MAE
LSTM-Autoembedding	3.608 ± 0.527	2.467 ± 0.295
LSTM-Benchmark	4.031 ± 0.938	2.715 ± 0.572

Table 5. Average RMSE and MAE (kW) with standard deviation for December test

Model	RMSE	MAE
LSTM-Autoembedding	6.915 ± 2.776	4.324 ± 1.749
LSTM-Benchmark	10.346 ± 3.724	6.451 ± 2.278

performance than the benchmark with a relative improvement of 1.2% (RMSE) and 1.7% (MAE). Here, the difference between the networks, in terms of performance, is small, since it is a standard sunny day, as reported in Fig. 3. This is not the case of the July test set, as reported in Fig. 4. In fact, the relative improvements are about 16% (RMSE) and 15% (MAE), that are higher with respect to the previous case. The same happens for the October test set (Fig. 5), where the relative improvements are about 12% (RMSE) and 10% (MAE). The biggest difference in performance is achieved in the December test set, in Table 5. It represents an example of hard prediction, as can be seen from Fig. 6. Here, the observed output power is very low and variable (this is probably due to a rainy day). In particular, this case highlights the robustness of our approach with respect to the benchmark one. The relative improvements are of about 50% (RMSE) and 33% (MAE).

Tables 2, 3, 4 and 5 show another important result: the LSTM-Autoembedding is better than the LSTM-Benchmark even in terms of standard deviation, in all cases. This is a further proof of the goodness and robustness of our model. The only case where the standard deviation is high on average is in the December test set. This is due to the variable weather conditions that usually affect the winter months.

In order to give a visual interpretation of the performance of our approach, the predicted output powers are reported in Fig. 3, 4, 5 and 6 together with the observed ones. Figure 3 represents the prediction of the output power related

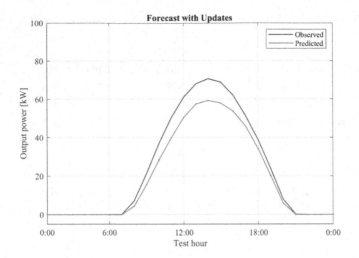

Fig. 3. Predicted (red) by LSTM-Autoembedding and observed (blue) value of output power at the beginning of May 2018. (Color figure online)

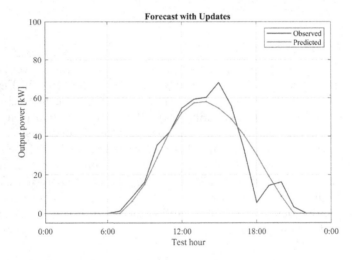

Fig. 4. Predicted (red) by LSTM-Autoembedding and observed (blue) value of output power at the beginning of July 2018. (Color figure online)

to the 1st of May. This is a standard sunny day and the model's prediction is good. In Fig. 4 is reported the prediction for the July test set. Here, the observed output power is not regular, as in the previous case, with a cliff around 18 pm. (this is probably due to a worsening in weather conditions, such as the transition of a cloud). This makes the prediction harder and the model cannot predict the cliff. Figure 5 refers to the October test set. Even in this case, the observed output power is variable. Nevertheless, the prediction is quite good, as reported in Fig. 5. Finally, Fig. 6 represents the predicted output power related to the

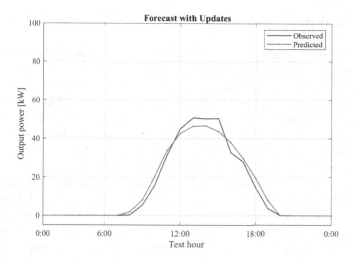

Fig. 5. Predicted (red) by LSTM-Autoembedding and observed (blue) value of output power at the beginning of October 2018. (Color figure online)

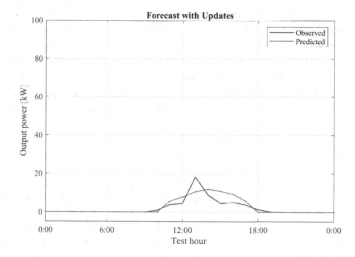

Fig. 6. Predicted (red) by LSTM-Autoembedding and observed (blue) value of output power at the beginning of December 2018. (Color figure online)

December test set. This case represents the hardest one to predict because the observed output power has a low and variable profile. In fact, the prediction is not so good, due to the fact that the predicted curve does not match the spike of the real one and also because it presents a relative high standard deviation, as reported in Table 5.

5   Conclusion

Pushed by the high demand of reliable prediction systems for RESs and energy-related sequences in general, in this work, we presented a novel technique for forecasting in the green computing framework. The innovative contribution of this work lies in using an encoder-decoder structure for a dual stacked-LSTM deep network. In this architecture, the first LSTM layer is used as an encoder to embed and extract information from the input data, while the second LSTM is used as the actual predictor. The whole network is trained with a two-stages approach to ensure its tailoring to the deep network structure.

From a complexity point of view, the LSTM-Autoembedding network differs from the reference model in just one more LSTM layer to train. Of course, the complexity of the network is also affected by the number of LSTM cells employed, hence a deeper assessment on this topic can be conducted in future tests on real data. The pre-training phase can also be performed on a dilated time scale to reduce its computational impact, for example at the beginning of each week or month.

The experimental results demonstrate the goodness of our approach. Accurate predictions of PV output power allow to exploit this energy more efficiently, respecting environmental sustainability, and profitably, ensuring an appropriate return on investment.

In the future, this work can pave the way to the employment of the encoder-decoder structure to more complex architectures. Furthermore, the compression of the information resulting from the encoder-decoder processing can be exploited to enable fast multivariate and even multimodal approaches.

References

1. AlKandari, M., Ahmad, I.: Solar power generation forecasting using ensemble approach based on deep learning and statistical methods. Applied Computing and Informatics (2020)
2. Alzahrani, A., Shamsi, P., Ferdowsi, M., Dagli, C.: Solar irradiance forecasting using deep recurrent neural networks. In: IEEE 6th International Conference on Renewable Energy Research and Applications (ICRERA), pp. 988–994 (2017)
3. Gangwani, P., Soni, J., Upadhyay, H., Joshi, S.: A deep learning approach for modeling of geothermal energy prediction. Int. J. Comput. Sci. Inf. Secur. **18**(1), 62–65 (2020)
4. Gensler, A., Henze, J., Sick, B., Raabe, N.: Deep learning for solar power forecasting – an approach using autoencoder and LSTM neural networks. In: IEEE International Conference on Systems, Man, and Cybernetics (SMC), pp. 002858–002865 (2016)
5. Khodayar, M., Teshnehlab, M.: Robust deep neural network for wind speed prediction. In: 4th Iranian Joint Congress on Fuzzy and Intelligent Systems (CFIS), pp. 1–5 (2015)
6. Kingma, P.D., Ba, J.: Adam: A method for stochastic optimization. In: International Conference on Learning Representations (2014)

7. Längkvist, M., Karlsson, L., Loutfi, A.: A review of unsupervised feature learning and deep learning for time-series modeling. Int. J. Comput. Sci. Inf. Secur. **42**, 11–24 (2014)
8. Maisto, M., Panella, M., Liparulo, L., Proietti, A.: An accurate algorithm for the identification of fingertips using an RGB-D camera. IEEE J. Emerging Sel. Top. Circuits Syst. **3**, 272–283 (2013)
9. Nguyen, H., Tran, K., Thomassey, S., Hamad, M.: Forecasting and anomaly detection approaches using LSTM and LSTM autoencoder techniques with the applications in supply chain management. Int. J. Inf. Manage. **57**, 102282 (2021)
10. Rosato, A., Altilio, R., Araneo, R., Panella, M.: Embedding of time series for the prediction in photovoltaic power plants. In: 2016 IEEE 16th International Conference on Environment and Electrical Engineering (EEEIC), pp. 1–4 (2016)
11. Rosato, A., Panella, M., Araneo, R.: A distributed algorithm for the cooperative prediction of power production in PV plants. IEEE Trans. Energy Convers. **34**(1), 497–508 (2019)
12. Sagheer, A., Kotb, M.: Unsupervised pre-training of a deep LSTM-based stacked autoencoder for multivariate time series forecasting problems. Sci. Rep. **9**, 1–16 (2019)
13. Succetti, F., Rosato, A., Araneo, R., Panella, M.: Deep neural networks for multivariate prediction of photovoltaic power time series. IEEE Access **8**, 211490–211505 (2020)
14. Zhu, L., Laptev, N.: Deep and confident prediction for time series at uber. In: IEEE International Conference on Data Mining Workshops (ICDMW), pp. 103–110 (2017)

Improving Indoor Semantic Segmentation with Boundary-Level Objectives

Roberto Amoroso[✉][iD], Lorenzo Baraldi[iD], and Rita Cucchiara[iD]

University of Modena and Reggio Emilia, Modena, Italy
{roberto.amoroso,lorenzo.baraldi,rita.cucchiara}@unimore.it

Abstract. While most of the recent literature on semantic segmentation has focused on outdoor scenarios, the generation of accurate indoor segmentation maps has been partially under-investigated, although being a relevant task with applications in augmented reality, image retrieval, and personalized robotics. With the goal of increasing the accuracy of semantic segmentation in indoor scenarios, we develop and propose two novel boundary-level training objectives, which foster the generation of accurate boundaries between different semantic classes. In particular, we take inspiration from the Boundary and Active Boundary losses, two recent proposals which deal with the prediction of semantic boundaries, and propose modified geometric distance functions that improve predictions at the boundary level. Through experiments on the NYUDv2 dataset, we assess the appropriateness of our proposal in terms of accuracy and quality of boundary prediction and demonstrate its accuracy gain.

Keywords: Indoor scene understanding · Segmentation · Boundary losses

1 Introduction

Automatically parsing and understanding pictures of indoor scenes is a core problem in Computer Vision, with a variety of applications ranging from augmented reality interfaces to image retrieval and the navigation of mobile robots in indoor spaces. The goal of the task is that of providing detailed information about the objects in a scene, the layout of the space, and how objects interact with each other [28]. One of the core subtasks which need to be solved in this context is that of performing a semantic segmentation over the input image. While most of the indoor understanding literature has focused on the usage of RGBD data [7,9,15], and while most of the semantic segmentation literature has adopted outdoor scenarios [10,18,22,27], some applications require to employ RGB data in indoor contexts. Examples include the understanding of indoor photos taken from mobile phones for augmented reality applications, the processing of pictures taken from social networks and search engines, and every application in which employing a depth camera is not practical.

© Springer Nature Switzerland AG 2021
I. Rojas et al. (Eds.): IWANN 2021, LNCS 12862, pp. 318–329, 2021.
https://doi.org/10.1007/978-3-030-85099-9_26

In such contexts, providing accurate and fine-grained pixel-wise classification without relying on depth data is of great importance. Recently, the research on semantic segmentation models has focused on the introduction of fully convolutional networks [4,16] which leverage convolutional layers and downsampling operations to achieve a large receptive field, while upsampling operations are employed to increase the output resolution. Although this architectural choice is necessary to encode contextual information and deal with objects at large scales, it also leads to feature smoothing across object boundaries, and thus to a degraded quality in the final result. The segmentation results might look blurry and lack fine object boundary details, thus leading to defects in the results of augmented reality applications.

With the aim of improving the quality of semantic segmentation in indoor scenarios, especially in boundary regions, in this paper, we investigate the design of boundary-aware losses for the optimization of semantic segmentation architectures. We start from two recently proposed loss functions, namely the Boundary loss [12] and the Active Boundary loss [21], and design two improved versions that can significantly increase the overall quality of the segmentation at boundary level. In particular, we improve their formulation in the geometric distance between objects and prove that this results in better segmentation accuracy and better predictions in boundary areas. From an experimental point of view, we assess the effectiveness of the proposed losses on the NYUDv2 dataset for indoor semantic segmentation. We quantify and show, through quantitative and qualitative experiments, the role of both losses in the case of indoor scene segmentation and the appropriateness of the proposed variants.

2   Related Work

Localizing semantic boundaries or exploiting boundary information to improve the semantic segmentation has been the focus of several previous studies [1,6,24]. Gated-SCNN [20], for instance, designs a two-stream network to exploit the duality between the segmentation predictions and the boundary predictions, integrating shape information. Other works [3,5,11], instead, learn pairwise pixel-level affinity and monitor information flow across boundaries to preserve feature disparity for semantic boundaries and feature similarity for interior pixels.

While most of these methods [5,11,20] depend on the segmentation model and require re-training, extensive studies [14,26] have proposed post-processing techniques to improve boundary details of segmentation results. DenseCRF [14] considers fully connected CRF models defined at the pixel level to improve segmentation accuracy around boundaries. SegFix [26], instead, proposes a model-agnostic method to refine segmentation maps, by training a separate network to transfer the label of interior pixels to boundary pixels. PointRend [13] presents a rendering approach to refine boundary information by performing point-based predictions at selected locations based on an iterative subdivision algorithm.

Boundary loss (BL) [12] and Active Boundary loss (ABL) [21], finally, propose a model-agnostic end-to-end trainable approach to tackle the problem of semantic segmentation at boundaries. BL promotes the refinement of the semantic boundaries by optimizing the sum of the linear combinations of the regional probability predictions and their distance transforms. ABL monitors the changes in the boundaries of the segmentation predictions and encourages the alignment between predicted boundaries and ground-truth boundaries, leveraging the distance transform of the prediction maps to regularize the network behavior.

Despite the empirical success of boundary-aware approaches in improving segmentation precision, there are still substantial segmentation errors at object boundaries. In this work, we investigate the reciprocal dependency between semantic segmentation and boundary-level objectives to increase the accuracy of semantic segmentation performance.

3   Method

Most of the existing semantic segmentation models can fail to provide correct predictions along semantic boundaries between two different classes, as widely used loss functions (like Cross-Entropy or Lovász-Softmax [2]) do not explicitly deal with the prediction of semantic region boundaries. With the aim of improving the prediction along boundaries in the case of indoor scene segmentation, we investigate the design of loss functions that explicitly model the prediction of semantic boundaries. In particular, we take inspiration from the Boundary loss [12] and the Active Boundary loss [21], two loss functions that already encode the presence of boundary regions in their formulation. Noticeably, all the functions we consider are model-agnostic and can be used during end-to-end training to improve boundary prediction.

Hereafter, we consider a segmentation setting characterized by C classes and input image resolution $H \times W$. $\boldsymbol{P} \in \mathbb{R}^{C \times H \times W}$, instead, will be used to indicate the class probability map predicted by the network. Thorough the rest of the section, given a tensor with spatial support $\boldsymbol{Z}$, the notation $\boldsymbol{Z}_i$ will be employed to denote the value(s) stored at the i-th spatial location of $\boldsymbol{Z}$, thus employing a "flattened" indexing of the two spatial dimensions (Fig. 1).

3.1   Boundary Loss

The Boundary loss was originally proposed by Kervadec *et al.* [12]. It conceptually calculates an integral over the points between regions which capture the proximity of two shapes, and it is inspired by a discrete graph-based optimization technique for computing gradient flows, which introduces a non-symmetric ℓ_2 loss to regularize boundary deviation of the predicted segmentation mask relative to the ground truth. As such, it allows the incorporation of a weighting term between the estimated and expected pixels along a semantic boundary.

The loss can be seen as a weighted average of predicted probabilities over the entire image, as follows:

$$\mathbf{BL} = \frac{1}{N} \sum_{i}^{N} P_i D_i^{\mathsf{T}}, \tag{1}$$

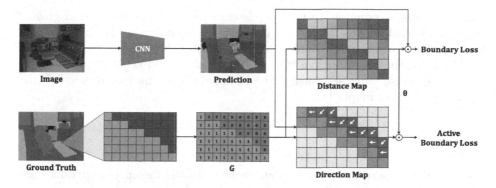

Fig. 1. We consider two loss functions for improving boundary-level predictions in semantic segmentation: (a) a *Boundary loss* which weights pixels predictions according to their distance to semantic boundaries; (b) an *Active Boundary* loss which promotes the alignment between predicted and ground truth boundaries. Best seen in color.

where **BL** indicates the Boundary loss, N is the number of pixels of the input image, and $D \in \mathbb{R}^{C \times H \times W}$ is a distance map that applies a probability weighting. Negative values in $D_i \in \mathbb{R}^C$ will increase the probability of predicting a given class in a pixel, while positive values will discourage the network from predicting a given class in a spatial location.

Given a one-hot ground-truth tensor $G \in \{0,1\}^{C \times H \times W}$, the distance map is usually calculated by means of the distance transform operator, which computes for each positive pixel its distance to the closest zero-valued pixel on the same channel, *i.e.* the closest pixel which does not belong to a given class. In the original formulation of the Boundary loss [12], the distance map was defined as follows:

$$D_i = -\mathrm{Dist}(G_i) \odot G_i + \mathrm{Dist}(1 - G_i) \odot (1 - G_i) \tag{2}$$

where $\odot$ indicates the element-wise multiplication and $\mathrm{Dist}(\cdot)$ is the distance transform. As it can be observed from the above formula, pixels that belong to a class are given a negative weight, thus promoting the prediction of high probability values for that class – while pixels that do not belong to a class are given a positive weight, thus discouraging the network from predicting the same class. When considering the magnitude of the weights, instead, it can be seen that pixels far from the boundaries, for which the $\mathrm{Dist}(\cdot)$ function produces high values, play a larger role in determining the loss in this formulation – while pixels close to the boundary are given less importance. In other words, the network is encouraged to give correct predictions in regions that do not lie close to the boundaries between classes and is allowed to be less precise in boundary regions.

With the aim of increasing the quality of predictions at the boundary level, we propose and investigate variations of the Boundary loss according to two principles: (i) we consider the different role of positive and negative pixels, and devise different weighting strategies for the two classes of pixels, instead of treating them equally as the original loss does; (ii) we replace the distance function with a *proximity* function, so that pixels close to a boundary are given greater importance, and regions that do not lie close to a boundary are given less importance – thus inverting the original spirit of the Boundary loss.

Following the first principle (*i.e.* treating positive and negative pixels differently), we devise two variations of the Boundary loss which correspond to the following distance maps:

$$D_i^+ = -G_i + \text{Dist}(1 - G_i) \odot (1 - G_i), \tag{3}$$

$$D_i^- = -\text{Dist}(G_i) \odot G_i + (1 - G_i). \tag{4}$$

As it can be observed, in the two above variants the distance map values are replaced with constant values which are independent of the distance from the boundary. This is done in the case of pixels that do not belong to the target class (*i.e.*, negative pixels) for D_i^-, and in the case of pixels that belong to the target class (*i.e.*, positive pixels) for D_i^+, respectively. In this manner, greater importance is also given to boundary pixels, compared to the original formulation.

According to the second principle, instead, we replace the concept of distance with that of proximity to the boundaries. To this aim, we devise an inversion function that translates distances to proximities. Our inversion function is defined as $\Phi(x) = \max(x) - x + 1$: as it can be seen, when applied to a distance transform, $\Phi(\cdot)$ returns the maximum value of the original map for pixels connected to a class boundary (for which $x = 1$ holds), and decreases linearly until reaching a minimum value of 1. According to this proximity function, we devise the following two variants of the Boundary loss:

$$\widetilde{D}_i = \text{ReLU}(K - \text{Dist}(1 - G_i)) \odot (1 - G_i) - \text{ReLU}(K - \text{Dist}(G_i)) \odot G_i, \tag{5}$$

$$\widehat{D}_i = \text{Dist}(1 - G_i) \odot (1 - G_i) - \Phi(\text{Dist}(G_i)) \odot G_i. \tag{6}$$

As it can be seen by comparing the two above formulations with the original loss, in the first case the distance function $\text{Dist}(\cdot)$ is replaced with $\text{ReLU}(K - \text{Dist}(\cdot))$, *i.e.* with a proximity function that starts from K and decreases linearly until reaching 0 – while in the second case the full proximity function $\Phi(\cdot)$ is employed. Noticeably, in the second case, the maximum proximity value depends on the size of the object (being a function of the maximum distance in the ground-truth map), while in the first case it is constant.

3.2   Active Boundary Loss

We now turn to the evaluation of a second boundary-aware loss function, namely the Active Boundary loss. This is formulated as a differentiable direction vector prediction problem, which gradually promotes the alignment between predicted boundaries (which in the following will be named, for brevity, PBs) and ground truth boundaries (for brevity again, GTBs). The pipeline for computing the loss can be conceptually divided into two phases.

Phase 1. During this phase, we compute the PBs starting from the probability map predicted by the network and devise a target direction map D^g which will be employed to align PBs with GTBs.

Specifically, boundary pixels of the predicted boundary map are recovered through the computation of the Kullback–Leibler (KL) divergence between the probabilities predicted for adjacent pixels. The i-th pixel of the PB is defined as

$$PB_i = \begin{cases} 1 \text{ if } \exists \mathbb{KL}(P_i || P_j) > \epsilon, j \in \mathcal{N}_2(i); \\ 0 \qquad \text{otherwise,} \end{cases} \tag{7}$$

where $\mathcal{N}_2(\cdot)$ indicates the 2-neighborhood of a pixel, corresponding to the offset $\{\{1,0\},\{0,1\}\}$ (*i.e.*, the pixels to the right and below the current pixel). The threshold value ϵ is calculated dynamically to ensure that the number of boundary pixels in PB is less than $1/100$ of the area of the input image.

The pixels of GTBs are, accordingly, determined by applying Eq. 7 to the one-hot ground-truth tensor and replacing the KL divergence with a simpler equality condition on the class labels between the pixels in $\mathcal{N}_2(\cdot)$.

As a second point, we compute a target direction map containing offset vectors which will encourage pixels on the PBs to move towards pixels of the GTBs. In the original version of the Active Boundary loss, the offset was encoded as a one-hot vector. In our version, we encode the coordinate of the offset vector as a progressive index indicating its position within the 8 neighborhood of a pixel, ranging from 0 (*i.e.* offset $\{-1,-1\}$ or top-left corner) to 8 (*i.e.* offset $\{1,1\}$ or bottom-right corner) following the row-major order, and excluding index 4 which is associated with the central pixel itself.

Formally, the target direction map $D^g \in \mathbb{R}^{H \times W}$ is computed by considering the offset direction which would move a pixel closer to a GTB, *i.e.*:

$$D_i^g = \arg\min_j M_{i+\Delta_j}, \; j \in \{0, 1, ..., 7\}, \tag{8}$$

where $M = \text{Dist}(\text{GTBs})$ is the result of the distance transform applied to GTBs and Δ_j represents the j-th element in the set of directions $\Delta - \{\{-1,-1\}, \{0,-1\}, \{1,-1\}, \{-1,0\}, \{1,0\}, \{-1,1\}, \{0,1\}, \{1,1\}\}$.

Phase 2. By using the KL divergence between the predictions for a pixel i and those for one of its neighbor pixels j as logits in a cross-entropy loss, the predicted boundary at pixel i is pushed towards the pixel j in a probabilistic way. The purpose is to increase the KL divergence between the class probability distribution of i and j while reducing the KL divergence between i and its 8-neighborhood pixels. To this aim, a predicted direction map $D^p \in \mathbb{R}^{8 \times H \times W}$ is computed as follows:

$$D_i^p = \left\{ \frac{e^{\mathbb{KL}(P_i, P_{i+\Delta_k})}}{\sum_{h=0}^7 e^{\mathbb{KL}(P_i, P_{i+\Delta_h})}}, k \in \{0, 1, ..., 7\} \right\}, \tag{9}$$

Employing the predicted and the target direction map, the Active Boundary loss can be defined as a weighted cross-entropy (**CE**) loss, as follows:

$$\mathbf{ABL} = \left(\sum_i \Lambda(M_i) \odot \mathbf{CE}(D_i^p, D_i^g) \odot PB_i \right) \cdot \frac{1}{\sum_i PB_i} \qquad (10)$$

Through the weight function $\Lambda(x) = \frac{\min(x,\theta)}{\theta}$, the distance of the pixel i from the nearest boundary of GTBs is used as weight to penalize its divergence from the GTBs.

Managing Collisions. Noticeably, collisions between offset vectors of neighboring pixels are possible, especially in the case of complex boundary shapes. To address this problem, the original formulation of the Active Boundary loss [21] suggests detaching the gradient flow for all non-boundary pixels. As a result, the gradient is calculated only for the pixels on the predicted boundaries, ignoring all the other pixels.

To overcome any conflicts, we adopted an equivalent strategy. In our implementation, we multiply the result of the weighted cross-entropy loss by the predicted boundary map PB, so that the only pixels that contribute to the loss calculation are the boundary pixels. The final value is the average calculated by dividing the sum of the weighted and masked values of the cross-entropy by the number of predicted boundary pixels.

Finally, the Active Boundary loss is regularized through label smoothing [19], to prevent the network from taking over-confident decisions. During label smoothing, the highest probability of the one-hot target distribution is set at 0.8, while the rest of the distribution is set to 0.2/7. Both values have been empirically determined during our preliminary experiments.

Applying Proximity Function. As in the case of the Boundary loss, we propose to employ a proximity function in place of the distance function when weighting predicted boundary pixels (cfr. Eq. 10). Employing the previously defined proximity function Φ, we propose to modify the Active Boundary loss function as follows:

$$\widehat{\mathbf{ABL}} = \left(\sum_i \Lambda(\widehat{M_i}) \odot \mathbf{CE}(D_i^p, D_i^g) \odot PB_i \right) \cdot \frac{1}{\sum_i PB_i}, \qquad (11)$$

where $\widehat{M}$ is obtained by applying the proximity function to the distance transform applied to GTBs, i.e. $\widehat{M} = \Phi(\text{Dist}(\text{GTB}))$. As it can be observed, also in this case we give more importance to pixels lying close to object boundaries, in order to increase the quality of the prediction at the boundary level. This is in contrast with the original spirit of the Active Boundary loss, which instead promoted pixels far from the boundaries. As the maximum proximity value depends on the size of the ground-truth object mask, the application of the proposed proximity function encourages the network to concentrate on the boundaries of objects with a significant area.

4 Experiments

4.1 Dataset

We conduct our analyses on the image segmentation dataset NYU-Depth V2 [17], which provides densely annotated images of indoor environments. Specifically, the NYU-Depth V2 dataset consists of 1449 RGB-D frames showing interior scenes, acquired through the Microsoft Kinect sensor and with a size of 640×480. Since the distortion of the images has been corrected, they showcase a thin white border which we remove by cropping the original images to a size of 608×448 pixels. We use the segmentation labels provided in [7], in which all labels were mapped to 40 classes. We employ the standard training/test split with 795 and 654 images, respectively, and train our models on RGB images only.

In NYU-Depth V2, ground-truth labels are given as semantic regions, rather than pixel-level segmentation. This occasionally results in thin strips of unlabeled pixels between two adjacent regions and creates an issue when evaluating segmentation results at boundary level. To remedy the issue, we pre-processed the ground truth to remove small unlabeled regions through the median filtering strategy proposed in [23]. Overall, the NYUDv2 is a challenging dataset due to difficult lighting conditions and cluttered scenes.

4.2 Implementation Details and Evaluation Protocol

We train our semantic segmentation models using two loss functions $\mathcal{L}_{bl}$ and $\mathcal{L}_{abl}$, both consisting of the traditional cross-entropy and IoU losses, which are paired with the considered boundary-level losses:

$$\mathcal{L}_{bl} = \mathbf{CE} + \mathbf{IoU} + w_a \, \mathbf{BL},$$
$$\mathcal{L}_{abl} = \mathbf{CE} + \mathbf{IoU} + w_b \, \mathbf{ABL}. \tag{12}$$

Here, $\mathbf{CE}$ is the cross-entropy loss and $\mathbf{IoU}$ refers to the lovász-softmax loss [2], a surrogate IoU loss. While the $\mathbf{CE}$ loss focuses on per-pixel classification, the lovász-softmax loss prevents small objects from being ignored. The weights w_a and w_b regulate the contribution of $\mathbf{BL}$ and $\mathbf{ABL}$ to the final loss, respectively. In particular, our experimental results are obtained by setting w_a to 1 both for the original version of BL and its proposed variants, while w_b is set to 0.8. The loss hyper-parameters K and θ are respectively set to 300 and 50.

In all experiments, we employ a DeepLabV3 [4] with ResNet-50 [8] as our default backbone architecture. Following the training protocol of [25], we use random scaling, crop, left-right flipping, and brightness jittering during data augmentation. We use a plain SGD optimizer, with an initial learning rate of 0.005 and weight decay equal to 0.0005. Training is performed with a mini-batch size of 4 and conducted for 200 training epochs. The learning rate is divided by 10 after 60, 80, 100, and 150 epochs.

Table 1. Quantitative results on the NYUDv2 dataset, when training with the Boundary loss and the proposed variations.

Loss function	Pixel accuracy	Mean accuracy	Mean IoU
CE	64.85	53.37	38.95
CE + IoU	65.16	54.73	39.68
CE + IoU + BL	65.10	**55.05**	39.49
CE + IoU + BL$^-$	64.97	54.15	39.39
CE + IoU + BL$^+$	65.24	54.71	39.55
CE + IoU + $\widetilde{\text{BL}}$	65.30	54.98	39.45
CE + IoU + $\widehat{\text{BL}}$	**65.36**	54.60	**39.84**

4.3   Quantitative Evaluation

Table 1 reports the results obtained on the NYUDv2 dataset when training with the Boundary loss, and with the four proposed variations, in terms of mean intersection-over-union, pixel accuracy, and mean accuracy [16]. As it can be seen, the combination of cross-entropy loss and IoU loss leads to improved results in terms of all metrics, proving that this combination is useful in the domain of indoor segmentation.

When turning to the evaluation of the losses based on BL, we first notice that the combination of cross-entropy, IoU, and Boundary loss leads to an improvement in terms of mean accuracy and to a decrease in pixel accuracy and mean IoU, highlighting that the original loss struggles to improve the results. The usage of the proposed variations that treat positive and negative pixels differently (D^+ and D^- – indicated in Table 1, respectively, as BL$^+$ and BL$^-$), helps to recover this quantitative loss, leading to improved results in terms of accuracy and mean IoU. This also highlights that giving a constant weight to pixels close to the boundary works better than using a distance function which gives more importance to pixels far from a boundary.

Using the proposed variations that employ a proximity function in place of the distance function ($\tilde{D}$ and $\hat{D}$ – indicated in Table 1, respectively, as $\widetilde{\text{BL}}$ and $\widehat{\text{BL}}$) leads to a further improvement in terms of pixel accuracy and mean IoU, with the full proximity function providing the best result on all metrics except the mean accuracy. Figure 2 reports some qualitative samples, comparing the predictions obtained with CE+IoU and those with CE+IoU+BL and CE+IoU+$\widehat{\text{BL}}$.

In Table 2, instead, we turn to the evaluation of the Active Boundary loss, and the proposed variant based on the proximity function. Firstly, we notice that in this case the ABL, in its original formulation, does not show a loss in performance when compared with the CE + IoU baseline. Indeed, a CE+IoU+ABL setting leads to an improvement in terms of pixel accuracy, mean accuracy, and mean

| Image | Ground Truth | CE+IoU | CE+IoU+BL | CE+IoU+$\widehat{\text{BL}}$ |

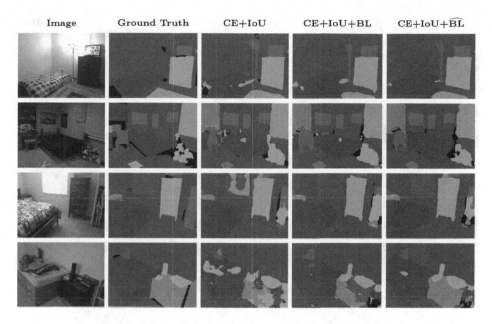

Fig. 2. Qualitative comparison between Boundary loss functions

Table 2. Quantitative results on the NYUDv2 dataset, when training with the Active Boundary loss and the proposed variation.

Loss function	Pixel accuracy	Mean accuracy	Mean IoU
CE	64.85	53.37	38.95
CE + IoU	65.16	54.73	39.68
CE + IoU + ABL	65.18	**54.76**	39.74
CE + IoU + $\widehat{\text{ABL}}$	**65.49**	54.60	**39.99**

IoU. Further, applying the proximity function in place of the distance function significantly increases the performance in terms of pixel accuracy and mean IoU, thus confirming the appropriateness of using a proximity function that gives higher importance to boundary pixels. Finally, in Fig. 3 we show qualitative samples comparing the results obtained when employing the CE+IoU baselines, in comparison with the ABL loss with distance and proximity functions.

| Image | Ground Truth | CE+IoU | CE+IoU+ABL | CE+IoU+$\widehat{ABL}$ |

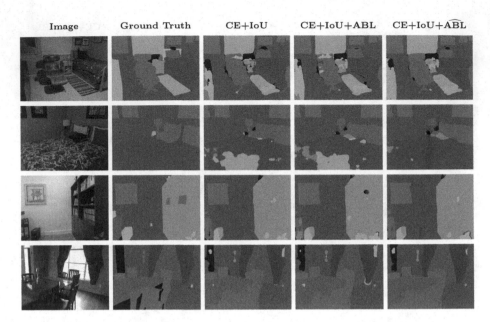

Fig. 3. Qualitative comparison between Active Boundary loss functions

5   Conclusion

We considered the usage of boundary loss functions when training segmentation models in indoor scenarios. To this end, we have considered two recently proposed boundary-level objectives, *i.e.* the Boundary loss, and Active Boundary loss, and proposed the application of a proximity function that gives higher importance to boundary pixels. Through quantitative and qualitative experiments on the NYUDv2 dataset, we have shown that the proposed variation can improve segmentation results at the boundary level.

References

1. Acuna, D., Kar, A., Fidler, S.: Devil is in the edges: learning semantic boundaries from noisy annotations. In: CVPR (2019)
2. Berman, M., Triki, A.R., Blaschko, M.B.: The lovász-softmax loss: a tractable surrogate for the optimization of the intersection-over-union measure in neural networks. In: CVPR (2018)
3. Bertasius, G., Torresani, L., Yu, S.X., Shi, J.: Convolutional random walk networks for semantic image segmentation. In: CVPR (2017)
4. Chen, L.C., Papandreou, G., Schroff, F., Adam, H.: Rethinking atrous convolution for semantic image segmentation. In: CVPR (2017)
5. Ding, H., Jiang, X., Liu, A.Q., Thalmann, N.M., Wang, G.: Boundary-aware feature propagation for scene segmentation. In: ICCV (2019)
6. Ding, H., Jiang, X., Shuai, B., Liu, A.Q., Wang, G.: Semantic correlation promoted shape-variant context for segmentation. In: CVPR (2019)

7. Gupta, S., Arbelaez, P., Malik, J.: Perceptual organization and recognition of indoor scenes from rgb-d images. In: CVPR (2013)
8. He, K., Zhang, X., Ren, S., Sun, J.: Deep residual learning for image recognition. In: CVPR (2016)
9. Hu, W., Zhao, H., Jiang, L., Jia, J., Wong, T.T.: Bidirectional projection network for cross dimension scene understanding. In: CVPR (2021)
10. Huang, Z., Wang, X., Huang, L., Huang, C., Wei, Y., Liu, W.: Ccnet: criss-cross attention for semantic segmentation. In: ICCV (2019)
11. Ke, T.W., Hwang, J.J., Liu, Z., Yu, S.X.: Adaptive affinity fields for semantic segmentation. In: ECCV (2018)
12. Kervadec, H., Bouchtiba, J., Desrosiers, C., Granger, E., Dolz, J., Ayed, I.B.: Boundary loss for highly unbalanced segmentation. In: MIDL (2019)
13. Kirillov, A., Wu, Y., He, K., Girshick, R.: Pointrend: image segmentation as rendering. In: CVPR (2020)
14. Krähenbühl, P., Koltun, V.: Efficient inference in fully connected crfs with gaussian edge potentials. In: NeurIPS (2011)
15. Kundu, A., et al.: Virtual multi-view fusion for 3D semantic segmentation. In: ECCV (2020)
16. Long, J., Shelhamer, E., Darrell, T.: Fully convolutional networks for semantic segmentation. In: CVPR (2015)
17. Silberman, N., Hoiem, P.K.D., Fergus, R.: Indoor segmentation and support inference from rgbd images. In: ECCV (2012)
18. Pang, Y., Li, Y., Shen, J., Shao, L.: Towards bridging semantic gap to improve semantic segmentation. In: CVPR (2019)
19. Szegedy, C., Vanhoucke, V., Ioffe, S., Shlens, J., Wojna, Z.: Rethinking the inception architecture for computer vision. In: CVPR (2016)
20. Takikawa, T., Acuna, D., Jampani, V., Fidler, S.: Gated-scnn: gated shape cnns for semantic segmentation. In: ICCV (2019)
21. Wang, C., et al.: Active boundary loss for semantic segmentation. arXiv preprint arXiv:2102.02696 (2021)
22. Wang, L., Li, D., Zhu, Y., Tian, L., Shan, Y.: Dual super-resolution learning for semantic segmentation. In: CVPR (2020)
23. Xiaofeng, R., Bo, L.: Discriminatively trained sparse code gradients for contour detection. In: NeurIPS (2012)
24. Yu, Z., Feng, C., Liu, M.Y., Ramalingam, S.: Casenet: deep category-aware semantic edge detection. In: CVPR (2017)
25. Yuan, Y., Chen, X., Wang, J.: Object-contextual representations for semantic segmentation. In: ECCV (2020)
26. Yuan, Y., Xie, J., Chen, X., Wang, J.: Segfix: model-agnostic boundary refinement for segmentation. In: ECCV (2020)
27. Zhao, H., Shi, J., Qi, X., Wang, X., Jia, J.: Pyramid scene parsing network. In: CVPR (2017)
28. Zhuo, W., Salzmann, M., He, X., Liu, M.: Indoor scene parsing with instance segmentation, semantic labeling and support relationship inference. In: CVPR (2017)

EvoMLP: A Framework for Evolving Multilayer Perceptrons

Luis Liñán-Villafranca[1], Mario García-Valdez[2], J. J. Merelo[3(✉)],
and Pedro Castillo-Valdivieso[3]

[1] RTI, Granada, Spain
`luis@rti.com`
[2] Instituto Tecnológico de Tijuana, Tijuana, Mexico
`mario@tectijuana.edu.mx`
[3] Universidad de Granada, Granada, Spain
`{jmerelo,pacv}@ugr.es`

Abstract. Designing neural networks for classification or regression can be considered a search problem, and, as such, can be approached using different optimization procedures, all of them with several design challenges: The first and more important is to constrain the search space in such a way that proper solutions can be found in a reasonable amount of time; the second is to take into account that, depending on how the optimization procedure is formulated, the fitness score used for it can have a certain degree of uncertainty. This means that creating a framework for evolving neural networks for classification implies taking a series of decisions that range from the purely technical to the algorithmic at different levels: neural or the optimization framework chosen. This will be the focus of this paper, where we will introduce DeepGProp, a framework for genetic optimization of multilayer perceptrons that efficiently explores space of neural nets with different layers and layer size.

Keywords: Neuroevolution · Backpropagation · MLPs · Software frameworks

1 Introduction

Applying artificial neural networks (ANN) to the solution of classification problems requires establishing their structure in layers and connections between them, the initial parameters (such as initial weights) and a set of learning constants. Using an optimization algorithm to solve at least part of this design problem is an usual approach to this challenge, and evolutionary neural networks [1] have been proved to be an efficient way of searching for the architecture, weights, and other ANN parameters (such as learning constants). This has been demonstrated repeatedly for *shallow* architectures (with a single hidden layer) since late in the previous century [2,3]. However, in most cases, design of the structure and connections between different layers, as indicated by [4], is still

© Springer Nature Switzerland AG 2021
I. Rojas et al. (Eds.): IWANN 2021, LNCS 12862, pp. 330–342, 2021.
https://doi.org/10.1007/978-3-030-85099-9_27

mostly done by hand and left off the evolutionary process. This is mainly due to the above mentioned fact that including this makes search spaces huge, so using rules of thumb (such as the ones detailed in [5], or using certain formulas to set the number of layers) to decide on those parameters, are a way of fixing part of the search space, letting the neural net training algorithm to figure out the weights themselves, whose optimization, in these cases, is able to cover big spans of the search space. Some of these algorithms stop short of setting weights, and leave that to an actual neural net training algorithm. The fitness of the neural net is measured *after* training, thus including training time within the fitness evaluation time. Adding long evaluation time to the size of the search space makes, sometimes, the mixture of evolutionary algorithms with neural networks something that can be approached only with big evaluation budgets.

That high budget required needs to be managed, and this is done in several ways. Usually one of them is to fix a part of the architecture, by choosing a multi-layer perceptron (MLPs) using some well-proven training algorithm. After all, MLPs with a single hidden layer are universal approximators, and have been used extensively for classification and regression problems. Once that part of the search space is covered, the initial weights as well as biases will evolve using an evolutionary algorithm (EA), and some MLP training algorithm such as backpropagation will be used to find the final MLP that's tested and eventually produced as the solution to a problem. This algorithm was proposed in the early years of the century, and called *G-Prop* (as in *Genetic Back-Propagation*), originally presented in [6]. G-Prop evolves a population of data structures representing multi-layer perceptrons initial weights and biases, which are trained and tested to obtain the fitness. This method leverages the capabilities of two classes of algorithms: the ability of EA to find a solution close to the global optimum, and the ability of the back-propagation algorithm (BP) [7] to tune a solution and reach the nearest local minimum by means of local search from the solution found by the EA.

This initial G-Prop algorithm was limited, first, by the fact that most of it had to be programmed from scratch, since there were few (if any) off-the-shelf software that could do this kind of task; additionally, available computational capability limited the size of the search space; this was further limited by the evolution of only single-layer perceptrons. This is why only small problems could be approached, and the evaluation budget used in them was, forcibly, limited.

However, the *memetic* combination of optimization at two levels, the weight level (handled by backpropagation) and the parametrized architecture level (handled by an evolutionary algorithm), is still conceptually new, since not many methods use them. Besides, the implementation, even being open source, is not maintained. This is why in this paper we propose, first, a reimplementation of the G-Prop concept, and second, an extension that solves some problems with this initial method: the inability to work with neural nets with several layers, and also the implicit dealing with the uncertainty in computing the fitness using a stochastic method like neural net training.

Thus, the aim of this paper is to present EvoMLP, a neuroevolution framework that evolves the initial weights, number of hidden layers and hidden layer sizes of a MLP, based on a EA and Stochastic Gradient Descent (SGD) [8]. This algorithm has been used for training deep neural nets and other kind of machine learning algorithms [8]; however, in this case intermediate (or hidden) layers have the same structure, which is the structure of a multi-layer perceptron, justifying our denomination of EvoMLP for this specific method.

In this paper what we will do is to first bring the implementation of the G-Prop concept to current tools and languages, choosing the best suited for the purpose and show the design decisions that were taken in order to do so; since we are using off the shelf software libraries which are in constant evolution, we will also demonstrate, since implementation matters [9], how this change of versions affects (or not) the performance of the algorithm. Apart from that, we will also attempt to characterize the size of problems for which this type of algorithm can be considered useful.

The remainder of this paper is structured as follows: Sect. 2 makes a short overview of the methods to design ANN. In Sect. 3 it is fully described the proposed model. Section 4 describes the results and Sect. 5 draws conclusions.

2   State of the Art

Searching the parameter space of neural networks looking for optimal combinations has been a problem traditionally approached in a limited number of ways, using *incremental algorithms*, which, in general, will depart from a specific architecture, number of layers and elements in every layer, and offer a series of heuristic procedures to add/eliminate hidden-layers and/or neurons from them. This way was, for a certain amount of time, the preferred technique for optimizing the architecture of the neural net along with its weights, according to classical reviews such as the one by Alpaydin [10]. However and simultaneously, a series of evolutionary heuristics were starting to be applied for the same purpose, as revealed by Balakrishnan and Honavar's review [11]. They propose a taxonomy, that classifies evolutionary design of the architecture of neural nets along three different axes (plus one for application domain): genotype representation, network topology, and a third axis that includes basically everything else: "variables of evolution". This classification was much more comprehensive, and included many more degrees of freedom in evolution than simply adding or eliminating neurons. However, it still left some constraints and probably did not emphasize the parameters that are most likely to have the greater influence in the outcome.

This is why, from our point of view, a more precise classification of evolved neural architectures would include:

– Fixed or variable architecture. Regardless of the kind of data structure used to represent it, the relevant matter is if that representation allows a variation of the architectural parameters, that is, adding or eliminating new nodes, layers, or in general, nodes and edges in a graph representation of the architecture.

- Articulation of the neural learning method. There is a whole range of possibilities, from letting the evolutionary process set all weights and other parameters, to using a learning process just to find the success rate, with additional possibilities like evaluating success *before applying learning* (to take advantage of the Baldwin effect [12]), to running a few cycles of learning that will become part of the codified solution.
- How the lack of a "crisp" value for the fitness, is taken into account during evolution. Either from the fact that an stochastic algorithm is used to train the neural net before evaluating fitness, or the fact that the data set (or how it's presented for training) might not be totally fixed but subject to randomness, the fitness of a neural net cannot be pinned down to a single, crisp, number. This randomness in the fitness can be taken into account during the selection phase [13], or not. This is related to having models that can generalize better when classifying unseen data, reducing overfitting.
- Single or multiobjective optimization. In general, the main issue is to get the highest accuracy possible. However, several other factors can be taken into account; in unbalanced data sets, accuracy for every one of the categories must be taken into account separately; besides, it is almost impossible to optimize by generalization, so a proxy for it, size, is instead optimized. All these objectives can be aggregated into a single one (using weights), hierarchized or considered properly as different objectives to be optimized separately.

With these axes in mind, the first one, the variation of architecture, has been the one that has developed the most, lately evolving towards (almost) unconstrained evolution using Neuroevolution of Augmenting Topologies (NEAT), as shown in the recent review by Miikkulainen et al. [4]. Since this blows up the search space (essentially evolving graphs), these methods need computational resources that are really beyond the reach of most labs or individuals. This is the reason why most of the latest publications still use a fixed model for the network architecture, for instance SVM or MLPs, and even, in some cases, fixed number of layers and weights [14]; however, recent papers like the one by Tajmiri et al. [15] already use a representation that is able to accommodate a maximum number of layers, as well as the number of neurons in every layer. This encoding of architecture does not have any place for initial weights, which in the case of G-Prop, were proved to be essential for a good performance, including the emergence of a Baldwin effect [12] during evolution. On the other hand, lately multi-objective algorithms are being explored. Senhaji et al. [16] optimizes performance at the same time that minimizes size using the NSGA-II algorithm. This is a generally good strategy, once again involving, as is usual in multiobjective algorithms, a boost in the size of the search space requiring big evaluation budgets.

More generally, network architecture search algorithms are also model search algorithms [17], a framework for which was recently released by Google. These methods are generally appropriate if you have unlimited evaluation budget or if problems are complex enough that only this kind of algorithms are able to find the correct model.

However, there is a huge amount of moderately-sized problems (with their corresponding datasets), where constrained search can be successful. In this paper we will extend the principles of variation of a MLP architecture through the use of genetic operators as well as codification of initial weights to a modern, standard based implementation, that will also be released as free software. We show how this new EvoMLP method works next. This means it will again use the architecture axis of evolution, although constraining it to a particular type of neural nets so that, by constraining search, we shrink the search space and make finding good architectures easier. Even so, the size of the datasets (and thus problems) that can be approached must be characterized, which we will do in the next sections.

3   Proposed Method

There are two parts in this EvoMLP framework, the "neural" part and the "evolutionary" part. Our objective from the beginning was to use off-the-shelf frameworks as much as possible.

The first line of choice is the programming language. G-Prop was written in C++ mainly because the underlying library used, EO [18], used that language. In this case, we went in the opposite direction. Most popular high-performance machine learning libraries, like TensorFlow, are written in Python. Once we settled for TensorFlow, working with Python was the obvious choice.

There are indeed several evolutionary frameworks written in Python; EvoloPy, for instance [19], includes many hyperheuristics, including EAs. However, DEAP [20] has emerged as a standard for this language, covering all that is needed to evolver multilayer perceptrons, so this is what we chose. This will definitely have some impact in performance [21], however for us researcher time is more important than computer time, and we can always use that time saved to improve the algorithm or the implementation.

TensorFlow is a low-level framework based on representing machine learning models as graphs; we will need a higher-level library to work with multilayer perceptrons. Once again, unlike G-Prop, we will choose the off-the-shelf Keras package [22], a framework for building multi-layer deep learning models In the version used in the initial stages of this research, Keras allowed multiple back-ends, meaning different frameworks for the effective representation of the neural net. That has changed lately, as we will later see. Once again, Keras is characterized for offering a simple API as opposed to a flexible and low-level interface, which is characteristic of TensorFlow or others like PyTorch; this has an impact on performance, but it helps ease the burden of the designers. The fact that it's maintained and updated often also ensures that the software created with it is kept up-to-date. This is important for a software framework like the one we're presenting here.

We need to make a series of decisions on the data structures and functions used in Keras; these are presented below. An individual is coded as a list of *Layers*. Each layer is composed by a matrix of weights and a list of bias (both

Numpy [23] ndarrays) joined together with it's configuration (a Python dictionary) in a Python class. One column of the weight matrix represents all the connections from the previous layer to the nth neuron. All the weights and bias are randomly initialized with a uniform distribution between −1.0 and 1.0. A random proportion of all this genes and biases are muted for all the individuals each generation.

From this configuration, when the moment of evaluation comes, we create a *Sequential* Keras model and append each *Layer* as a *Dense* Keras layer.

There are three stop conditions that will finish the execution of the genetic algorithm: if we reach the maximum number of generations, if after 10 generations there was no improvement in the best solution and if we find the ideal solution (0% error, a single neuron left and 1 on the F2 score). We used these 10 generations as an indication that evolution was stuck and could proceed no further, thus stopping being a better option.

For each generation we clone the best half individuals of the current population and perform all the evolutionary operations to them. Each operation has it own probability to occur chosen when running EvoMLP CLI. For the weights/bias mutation, a percentage of each (selected too with the CLI parameters) are muted randomly. After that, the worst half is replaced by this muted group.

The crossover function will swap the "neurons" together with their connections. Main difference with respect to original G-Prop is that, in this case, there can be several hidden layers, so the connections might be either to output or to another layers. The crossover only occurs when the two models selected for it have the same structure (same number of layers and neurons per layers).

There are several kinds of *mutation* operators: (initial) weights, biases, as well as changing the number of neurons and/or layers. For the neuron mutator, one neuron will be added last in the randomly selected layer, and it will be eliminated in the same way. Since we use fully connected neural networks, it does not really matter where the neuron is added or eliminated. The layer add/eliminate mutator is the main difference with respect to G-Prop, which used only one layer. In this case, only the last hidden layer can be eliminated. When a layer is eliminated, the weights from the previous layer to the eliminated one are kept, adding randomly generated weights and biases if the output layer (newly connected with this previous layer) have more "neurons" than the recently deleted layer. When adding a new hidden layer, the connections between the last hidden layer and the output layer are recycled, and the connections between the newly created layer and the output layer are calculated randomly (running similar fix as when we delete the layer).

We need the selection process, via the fitness function, to exert parsimony pressure, which is why we take into account not only the accuracy score reached after training, but also the overall size of the network using this score:

$$f_s = (\sum_{i=0}^{nhl} nu_i) \times nhl \tag{1}$$

where f_s, is the hidden-layer, or size, score, nhl is the number of hidden layers and nu_i the number of neurons for the layer i). This score is minimized, meaning that the less neurons, the better, but also that less hidden layers are preferred over more hidden layers. This f_s, however, receives a very low weight equivalent to 1% of the accuracy, meaning that it will be only determinant, in practice, if there's a very small difference in accuracy when comparing two individuals of if accuracy is virtually the same.

Finally, the F2 score metric (explained in Sect. 4) is also considered. At the end, the fitness value is a compound of three elements: accuracy, hidden-score and F2 score. As the DEAP framework [20] was used as a base to create the genetic algorithm, we also took advantage of its fitness class to rank the individuals of a population. It performs a lexicographical comparison of the three values, so we chose the order previously mentioned to approach as much as possible to the fitness function used by G-Prop.

We handle uncertainty by *resampling*, that is, re-evaluating all individuals every generation. Every training-testing set will yield a different fitness, which usually have a skewed distribution [13]. However, by repeatedly evaluating them individuals that have a statistically better fitness that the rest will *survive* to the next generation. This method, though simple, is generally adequate and tends to select individuals whose fitness distribution has a lower standard deviation and are less skewed.

The library was packaged and uploaded to the Python package registry, including the scripts that are used to run the experiments here. You can download it directly with `pip install DeepGProp`. It has been released under the GNU GPL v3, and between releases it's also available from its GitHub repository https://github.com/lulivi/dgp-lib.

Since we have implemented EvoMLP using the Python programming language. Tests with pypy, an accelerated, just-in-time version of the regular interpreter were performed, but although it is supposed to accelerate most numerical workloads, it actually was almost twice as slow as the one using the regular interpreter.

4   Results

Initial results comparing EvoMLP with G-Prop under different circumstances were already presented in [24]. In general, allowing the evolution to optimize the number of layers allowed to obtain significantly better results than the original results published by G-Prop. Since then, however, new datasets have been published and we will need to establish a new baseline, as well as characterize the size of problems that are suitable for optimization with this package.

In this paper we will first try to show the performance of the algorithm for this kind of problem, as well as create a baseline for comparison as we evolve the framework and the underlying algorithm. For that purpose, we have chosen spambase as the dataset for all experiments. Taken from the UCI [25] database, it is a highly unbalanced dataset, with a good amount of features, and has been used extensively for benchmarking frameworks and algorithms. In papers such as the one by Duriqi et al. [26], which tests the algorithms implemented in WEKA, the accuracy reported is around 90%, although it's not clear how the data set was split and if it is measured with a part of the dataset unseen before in any way. In order to measure generalization, in our experiments we have followed the PROBEN1 convention [27] which is equivalent to a three-fold cross validation, splitting the dataset in three parts and sequentially using two of them for training and validation, finally testing them with the third part. By testing the models with an unseen part of the dataset, we guarantee that we are measuring its generalization capability, and not overfitting the model to the specific data it has been trained with.

Table 1. Baseline error percentage results for spambase per partition, with validation (V., used by the algorithm) and test (unseen data, used for generalization) results.

Partition	V. best	V. median	V. mean	Test, best	Test, median	Test, average	Test, SD
spambase1	22.70	25.740	26.31867	23.02	26.240	29.47067	5.981871
spambase2	21.30	25.915	30.10948	19.46	27.365	29.20700	6.827490
spambase3	18.78	26.700	28.73122	19.98	28.060	30.19741	5.981871

We will use default parameters, except for the population (64) and the maximum number of generations (32), which have been found by exploration; we try to use a reasonable amount of exploitation with exploration that is more intense for weights, and less intense for the other possibilities of change. This version will use Python 3.8.6, as well as Theano 2.3.1 with a Theano backend; Theano is a good choice, and it was proved to be slightly faster than other backends, like TensorFlow. Results are shown in Table 1. That table represents the average over *all* individuals in the last generation. We should take into account the uncertainty in the evaluation of the fitness via training and testing, so the concept of *best* individual in the last generation includes the same amount of uncertainty; this is why in the table we include the median and the average; in these uncertain environments, median might be a better measure of success reached. This should be essentially considered a baseline value, and we do not want to present it as the state of the art. Looking at published results, these are comparable with those obtained with the Naive Bayes algorithm and shown, for instance, in [26], although the way of measuring them is totally different and we cannot really draw a comparison.

The time needed to reach these results is around 2 h for every run, which is acceptable for us. The spambase problem is mid-size, with many inputs and a sizable dataset, so this might be, in fact, in the limit of the kind of problems that can be approached with this algorithm, unless some improvements in performance (and accuracy) are made. Taking into account that all we have used is 2048 evaluations, it is not such a bad result, leading us to think that increasing the budget would probably obtain better results.

Table 2. Comparison of baseline (Theano-based) and the last version, based on TensorFlow, error percentage results for **spambase** per partition, with validation (used by the algorithm) and test (unseen data, used for generalization) results.

Partition	Val. best	Val. median	Test, best	Test, median	Test, SD
spambase1 Theano	22.70	25.740	23.02	26.240	5.981871
spambase1 TF	20.35	26.960	21.72	27.020	6.004629
spambase2 Theano	21.30	25.915	19.46	27.365	6.827490
spambase2 TF	20.52	41.390	16.42	36.320	5.135031
spambase3 Theano	18.78	26.700	19.98	28.060	5.981871
spambase3 TF	18.52	30.260	19.81	30.715	6.004629

However, another possible way of obtaining better results in one way or another is upgrading the dependencies. As a matter of fact, Keras underwent a change in the last version, being incorporated into the TensorFlow module, instead of being an independent one. That also had as a result eliminating the possibility of using different backends, reducing itself to only one backend: TensorFlow. We need to find out how this will affect the results of the algorithm, so we created a fork of the problem, changing all dependencies from the original version to the one included with TensorFlow, and run again using the same datasets and the same command line. The result is shown in Table 2. The set of last-generation results have been compared using Wilcoxon test, and in all cases difference is significant. However, as you can see, the result with this new version are worse than the original *in median*, although, since the standard deviation is higher, the best values are, in general, better. We should emphasize that the library code is exactly the same, except for a line that imports Keras as part of the TensorFlow library.

Once it is clear that the latest version of TensorFlow offers the best results, we will use it exclusively to check if one of the changes of EvoMLP, being able to evolve the number of layers, really brings any kind of improvement to the overall performance. On one hand, theoretically better results can be obtained; on the other hand, the search space again blows up, so with the same budget you might be, as it were, fishing in a bigger pond with a smaller fishing rod. So let us run an experiment where the number of layers is stuck at one, comparing it with these results. These are shown in Fig. 1.

Although the difference is significant in all three cases, the problem is that it differs on which one is the best; using a single partition would probably hide that. The single-layer version is better in spambase2, the 3-layer version is better in the other two. Overall, however, there is no significant difference between in these three experiments the way we have done it, which probably means that, since we are using the same budget, as we have indicated above, the constrain added of having a single layer makes search in the space of architectures reach further, so we would need more evaluations to really see a difference. We should also take into account that we are using all the individuals in the last generation,

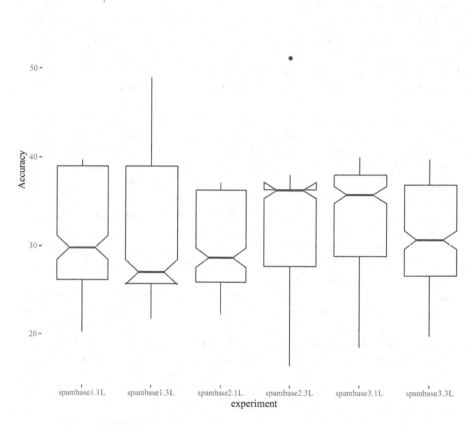

Fig. 1. Comparing test results over the three partitions allowing up to three layers to evolve (results reported above) or fixing the number of hidden layers to 1 (1L).

due to the practical impossibility to select the absolute best, since the evaluation for every individual is affected by the uncertainty in training. The best results seem to indicate that, in some cases, using 3 layers is able to reach a level of accuracy that are just not possible with one layer. However, this is left as an hypothesis to be checked in the future. Besides, since training time is mainly dependent on the number of weights and not the number of layers, the time they take is virtually the same. So, eventually, evolving one or several layers is simply a judgment call that can be done for a number of reasons, including how different representations are done in several hidden layers; performance-wise, however, there is no difference.

5   Conclusions and Future Work

We have introduced EvoMLP, released to the Python ecosystem as DeepGProp, that uses state-of-the-art libraries for evolutionary algorithms and neural nets combining them in a way that can easily design a multilayer perceptron that solves problems up to mid size, such as spambase. We have performed careful tests on the impact of the changes in the upstream libraries; upgrading to Keras 2.4.0 has yielded higher uncertainty in the results obtained by our algorithm, although this has resulted in better exploration and eventually a better *best* results.

In this paper we have proved also that this new library allows us to explore easily the possible space of neural net configurations, with one or several layers, and produces output that can be easily processed to obtain statistical results. This eventually has led to the conclusion that, overall, it is probably enough with evolving MLPs with a single layer as G-Prop did. However, this is again dependent on the fact that we need a better way to evaluate the results than simply using a single evaluation of all individuals in the last generation. To do a proper evaluation, we would need to perform several trainings on the stored initial weights, at least 15, and use all 15 validation results as the fitness, and then compare them statistically as proposed in [28]. This is beyond the simple, proof-of-concept approach in this paper.

Taking into account the double handicap of a low budget and also the uncertainty in fitness, it might be the case that the neural net training algorithm we use is actually responsible for most of the improvement in fitness. Although the generational plot shows that average and best results improve with time, we might need many more generations to get an improvement, and that one might probably be only marginal; since we don't really know what is the optimal value for this dataset, we might have reached that limit, which would explain the small differences obtained with set of varying number of layers.

This is why as a future line of work, we will try to obtain the best results possible by finding the optimal population as well as number of generations. Since this will increase the time needed to train, additional changes will have to be included, possibly sampling the testing set in every generation, which will have the effect of increasing uncertainty, but certainly reducing training time. Sensitivity to changes in the parameters beyond population and number of generations will also have to be investigated. Finally, all possibilities of increasing speed like parallelization or using GPU instructions will also be investigated.

Finding different ways to take uncertainty into account will also be considered, from the simplest one, which is simply re-evaluating the individuals in the last generation and choose only the one that is significantly better than the rest, to introducing it further in the selection process by resampling or, as was shown in [28], take into account all fitness measures taken through all generations to select individuals.

This paper has been developed in an open repository https://github.com/ JJ/2021-cec-deep-g-prop/blob/main/README.md, including this paper, data obtained in the experiments, code, and processed data.

Acknowledgments. Supported in part by project DeepBio (TIN2017-85727-C4-2-P) and PID2020-115570GB-C22.

References

1. Martinez, A.D., et al.: Lights and shadows in evolutionary deep learning: taxonomy, critical methodological analysis, cases of study, learned lessons, recommendations and challenges. Inf. Fusion **67**, 161–194 (2021)
2. Castillo, P., Carpio, J., Merelo-Guervós, J.-J., Rivas, V., Romero, G., Prieto, A.: Evolving multilayer perceptrons. Neural Process. Lett. **12**, 115–127 (2000). https://doi.org/10.1023/A:1009684907680
3. Stanley, K.O., Miikkulainen, R.: Evolving neural networks through augmenting topologies. Evol. Comput. **10**(2), 99–127 (2002)
4. Miikkulainen, R., et al.: Evolving deep neural networks. In: Artificial Intelligence in the Age of Neural Networks and Brain Computing. Elsevier, pp. 293–312 (2019)
5. Qolomany, B., Maabreh, M., Al-Fuqaha, A., Gupta, A., Benhaddou, D.: Parameters optimization of deep learning models using particle swarm optimization. In: 13th International Wireless Communications and Mobile Computing Conference (IWCMC), vol. 2017, pp. 1285–1290. IEEE (2017)
6. Castillo, P.A., Merelo-Guervós, J.-J., Prieto, A., Rivas, V., Romero, G.: G-Prop: Global optimization of multilayer perceptrons using GAs. Neurocomputing **35**, 149–163 (2000). https://doi.org/10.1016/S0925-2312(00)00302-7, http://geneura.ugr.es/pub/papers/castilloNC.ps.gz
7. Williams, D.R.G.H.R.: Learning internal representations by error propagation. Parallel Distrib. Proccess. **1**, 310–362 (1986)
8. Bottou, L.: Stochastic gradient descent tricks. In: Montavon, G., Orr, G.B., Müller, K.-R. (eds.) Neural Networks: Tricks of the Trade. LNCS, vol. 7700, pp. 421–436. Springer, Heidelberg (2012). https://doi.org/10.1007/978-3-642-35289-8_25
9. Merelo, J.J., Romero, G., Arenas, M.G., Castillo, P.A., Mora, A.M., Laredo, J.L.J.: Implementation matters: programming best practices for evolutionary algorithms. In: Cabestany, J., Rojas, I., Joya, G. (eds.) IWANN 2011. LNCS, vol. 6692, pp. 333–340. Springer, Heidelberg (2011). https://doi.org/10.1007/978-3-642-21498-1_42
10. Alpaydin, E.: GAL: networks that grow when they learn and shrink when they forget. Int. J. Pattern Recognit Artif Intell. **8**(01), 391–414 (1994)
11. Balakrishnan, K., Honavar, V.: Evolutionary design of neural architectures - a preliminary taxonomy and guide to literature, AI Research Group, Technical report January 1995, cS-TR 95–01
12. Castillo, P. A.: Lamarckian evolution and the Baldwin effect in evolutionary neural networks (2006). http://www.citebase.org/abstract?id=oai:arXiv.org:cs/0603004
13. Merelo, J.J., et al.: There is noisy lunch: a study of noise in evolutionary optimization problems. In: Rosa, A.C., (eds.) Proceedings of the 7th International Joint Conference on Computational Intelligence (IJCCI 2015), vol. 1, ECTA, Lisbon, Portugal, 12–14 November 2015, pp. 261–268. SciTePress (2015) https://doi.org/10.5220/0005600702610268
14. Ecer, F., Ardabili, S., Band, S.S., Mosavi, A.: Training multilayer perceptron with genetic algorithms and particle swarm optimization for modeling stock price index prediction. Entropy **22**(11), 1239 (2020)

15. Tajmiri, S., Azimi, E., Hosseini, M.R., Azimi, Y.: Evolving multilayer percep- tron, and factorial design for modelling and optimization of dye decomposition by bio-synthetized nano cds-diatomite composite. Environ. Res. **182**, 108997 (2020). http://www.sciencedirect.com/science/article/pii/S0013935119307947

16. Senhaji, K., Ramchoun, H., Ettaouil, M.: Training feedforward neural network via multiobjective optimization model using non-smooth l1/2 regularization. Neuro- computing 410, 1–11 (2020). https://www.sciencedirect.com/science/article/pii/ S0925231220309115

17. Mazzawi, H., Gonzalvo, X.: Introducing model search: An open source platform for finding optimal ml models, Google AI blog. https://ai.googleblog.com/2021/ 02/introducing-model-search-open-source.html. February 2021

18. Merelo-Guervós, J.-J., et al.: Evolving objects. In: Wang, P.P., (ed.) Proceedings of JCIS 2000 (Joint Conference on Information Sciences), vol. I, 2000, pp. 1083–1086. ISBN: 0-9643456-9-2

19. Faris, H., et al.: Evolopy: An open-source nature-inspired optimization framework in python. In: Guervós, J. J. M., et al. (eds.) Proceedings of the 8th International Joint Conference on Computational Intelligence, IJCCI 2016, Vol. 1: ECTA, Porto, Portugal, 9–11 November 2016, SciTePress, pp. 171–177 (2016) https://doi.org/10. 5220/0006048201710177

20. Fortin, F.-A., De Rainville, F.-M., Gardner, M.-A., Parizeau, M., Gagné, C.: DEAP: evolutionary algorithms made easy. J. Mach. Learn. Res. **13**, 2171–2175 (2012)

21. Kim, J., Yoo, S.: Software review: Deap (distributed evolutionary algorithm in python) library. Genetic Program. Evolvable Mach. **20**(1), 139–142 (2019)

22. Chollet, F., et al.: Keras. (2015) https://keras.io

23. van der Walt, S., Colbert, S.C., Varoquaux, G.: The numpy array: a structure for efficient numerical computation. Comput. Sci. Eng. **13**(2), 22–30 (2011)

24. Villafranca, L.L., Guervós, J.J.M.: Deepgprop, Nov. (2020). https://doi.org/10. 5281/zenodo.4287505

25. Dua, D., Graff, C.: UCI machine learning repository. http://archive.ics.uci.edu/ml (2017)

26. Duriqi, R., Raca, V., Cico, B.: Comparative analysis of classification algorithms on three different datasets using weka. In: 2016 5th Mediterranean Conference on Embedded Computing (MECO), pp. 335–338. IEEE (2016)

27. Prechelt, L.: PROBEN1 – A set of benchmarks and benchmarking rules for neural network training algorithms, Fakultät für Informatik, Universität Karlsruhe, D- 76128 Karlsruhe, Germany. Technical report **21/94**, (September 1994)

28. Merelo-Guervós, J.-J.: Using a Wilcoxon-test based partial order for selection in evolutionary algorithms with noisy fitness, GeNeura group, university of Granada, Technical report (2014). https://doi.org/10.6084/m9.figshare.974598

Regularized One-Layer Neural Networks for Distributed and Incremental Environments

Oscar Fontenla-Romero, Bertha Guijarro-Berdiñas,
and Beatriz Pérez-Sánchez(✉)

CITIC and Facultad de Informática, Universidade da Coruña,
Campus de Elviña, A Coruña, Spain
{oscar.fontenla,berta.guijarro,beatriz.perezs}@udc.es

Abstract. Deploying machine learning models at scale is still a major challenge; one reason is that performance degrades when they are put into production. It is therefore very important to ensure the maximum possible generalization capacity of the models and regularization plays a key role in avoiding overfitting. We describe Regularized One-Layer Artificial Neural Network (ROLANN), a novel regularized training method for one-layer neural networks. Despite its simplicity, this network model has several advantages: it is noniterative, has low complexity, and is capable of incremental and privacy-preserving distributed learning, while maintaining or improving accuracy over other state-of-the-art methods as demonstrated by the experimental study in which it has been compared with ridge regression, lasso and elastic net over several data sets.

Keywords: Regularization · Big data · Incremental learning · Distributed learning · Privacy-preserving · Singular value decomposition

1 Introduction

In machine learning, an important issue to consider when training a model is to avoid overfitting which, along with underfitting, is largely responsible for the poor performance of algorithms. Overfitting can happen when, instead of generalizing properly, the model is trying to capture noise that may exist in the training data. Regularization techniques are used to reduce model generalization error by properly fitting a function to a given training set, alleviating

This work has been supported by grant *Machine Learning on the Edge (Ayudas Fundación BBVA a Equipos de Investigación Científica 2019)*, also by the National Plan for Scientific and Technical R&I of the Spanish Government (Grant PID2019-109238GB-C2), and by the Xunta de Galicia (Grant ED431C 2018/34) with the European Union ERDF funds. CITIC is partially funded by "Consellería de Cultura, Educación e Universidades from Xunta de Galicia" (Grant ED431G 2019/01).

© Springer Nature Switzerland AG 2021
I. Rojas et al. (Eds.): IWANN 2021, LNCS 12862, pp. 343–355, 2021.
https://doi.org/10.1007/978-3-030-85099-9_28

overfitting by imposing a preference to learn a smoother function. Most regularization approaches are based on limiting the capacity of models by incorporating a penalty term weighted by a hyperparameter in the loss function. The penalty term should be minimized so as to keep the weights of the model small and so achieve a trade-off between fitting and overfitting the data.

In the current state of the art there are several successful proposals regarding learning methods with regularization. One of the most popular is ridge regression [1], where the mean squared error (MSE) loss function is modified by adding a shrinkage quantity based on the squared magnitude of the parameters as the penalty term. This is usually called L2 regularization. Another important proposal is the lasso [2], which adds the absolute value of magnitude of the parameters as the penalty term. This is usually called L1 regularization. Unlike ridge regression, there is no closed form, and the original implementation involves quadratic programming techniques from convex optimization. A more recent proposal is called elastic net, which emerged as a result of a critique on lasso [3]. The elastic net solution is to linearly combine the penalties of ridge regression and lasso (thereby obtaining the best of both approaches), for which the authors proposed an iterative algorithm called LARS-EN.

In this research, we propose ROLANN as a novel regularized training method for one-layer neural networks (no hidden layers) that uses an L2-norm penalty term. This noniterative supervised method uses a closed-form expression and determines the optimum set of weights by solving a system of linear equations. It presents two interesting properties that differentiate it from other methods:

- Computational complexity depends on the minimum value among the number of inputs and samples of the training set, in contrasts with the majority of methods that are only computationally efficient on one side.
- Incremental and distributed privacy-preserving learning is allowed, which means a perfect fit in federated learning environments.

These characteristics make ROLANN very useful in many different scenarios, for instance, in dealing with data sets with a high number of inputs, as the majority of methods concentrate on reducing only complexity with respect to the number of training samples. Another use could be in internet of things (IoT) scenarios where we can take advantage of edge computing capacities and autonomous learning from data streams in IoT devices. All these scenarios could share the common restriction of a low number of available training samples. For example, in learning from microarray data it is possible to have thousands of inputs and only few hundred samples or, in learning from data streams, it is possible to start from a small training set that will eventually grow over time. In these cases, when the number of inputs is much higher than the number of samples, the number of free parameters in the network just needed to support the inputs may be excessive and will probably involve overfitting on the training data, thus making regularization essential.

2   The Proposed Supervised Training Method

Consider a training data set defined by an input matrix $\mathbf{X} \in \mathbb{R}^{m \times n}$, where m is the number of inputs (including the bias) and n is the number of data instances, while the desired output matrix is $\mathbf{d} \in \mathbb{R}^{n \times p}$. In what follows, we consider only one output (i.e., $\mathbf{d} \in \mathbb{R}^{n \times 1}$) to avoid a cumbersome derivation; however, the extension to multiple outputs is trivial, since each output of the neural network depends solely on a set of independent weights. In this situation, a one-layer feedforward neural network (no hidden layers) is defined by a weight vector (including the bias) $\mathbf{w} \in \mathbb{R}^{m \times 1}$ and the nonlinear activation function at the output neuron $f : \mathbb{R} \to \mathbb{R}$. In this situation, the weights are usually obtained by an iterative process that minimizes the MSE at the output of the network when comparing the real output $\mathbf{y} = f(\mathbf{X}^T \mathbf{w})$ and the desired output $\mathbf{d}$. However, as described in [4], another option is to minimize the MSE measured *before* the activation function, i.e., between $\mathbf{X}^T \mathbf{w}$ and $\bar{\mathbf{d}} = f^{-1}(\mathbf{d})$, as defined by:

$$J(\mathbf{w}) = \frac{1}{2} \left(\mathbf{F} \left(\bar{\mathbf{d}} - \mathbf{X}^T \mathbf{w} \right) \right)^T \left(\mathbf{F} \left(\bar{\mathbf{d}} - \mathbf{X}^T \mathbf{w} \right) \right) \tag{1}$$

where $\mathbf{F} = diag(f'(\bar{d}_1), f'(\bar{d}_2), \ldots, f'(\bar{d}_n))$ is a diagonal matrix formed by the derivative of the f function for the components of $\mathbf{d}$.

Using this error function, the weights $\mathbf{w}$ can be obtained noniteratively by solving the following system of linear equations [4]:

$$\mathbf{Aw} = \mathbf{b} \tag{2}$$

where $\mathbf{A}$ and $\mathbf{b}$ are defined as:

$$\mathbf{A} = \mathbf{XFFX}^T$$
$$\mathbf{b} = \mathbf{XFF}\bar{\mathbf{d}} \tag{3}$$

One popular technique to obtain smoother input-output mappings, and thus avoid overfitting, is regularization, which consists of adding a penalty term to the cost function that conditions the form of the solution. One of the simplest forms of regularization is *weight decay*, also known as *ridge regression* in conventional curve fitting [5]. It consists of adding a new term R to the error function as the sum of squares of the free parameters of the network, i.e.:

$$R = \frac{1}{2}\mathbf{w}^T \mathbf{w} \tag{4}$$

As a consequence, when that term is added to the cost function defined in Eq. 1, we obtain the following new regularized cost function:

$$J(\mathbf{w}) = \frac{1}{2} \left[\left(\mathbf{F} \left(\bar{\mathbf{d}} - \mathbf{X}^T \mathbf{w} \right) \right)^T \left(\mathbf{F} \left(\bar{\mathbf{d}} - \mathbf{X}^T \mathbf{w} \right) \right) + \lambda \mathbf{w}^T \mathbf{w} \right] \tag{5}$$

whose minimum – which can be obtained by deriving this function and equating the result to zero – is at a point $\mathbf{w}$ that satisfies:

$$\mathbf{Aw} + \lambda \mathbf{w} = \mathbf{b} \tag{6}$$

or, equivalently

$$(\mathbf{XFFX}^T + \lambda\mathbf{I})\mathbf{w} = \mathbf{XFF\bar{d}} \tag{7}$$

where λ is a positive scalar that controls the influence of the penalty term in the solution and therefore the smoothness of the fitting function. The hyperparameter λ will be 0 when no regularization is required.

The size of the system of linear equations in Eq. 7 depends on m, as the most expensive operations to solve the equations and obtain $\mathbf{w}$ are calculation of matrix $\mathbf{A}$ and of its inverse, with computational complexity of $O(m^2n)$ and $O(m^3)$, respectively. When m is small, these complexities imply high efficiency, but become computationally demanding when the number of inputs is large, even though the method provides a noniterative way to determine $\mathbf{w}$. Our aim is to obtain $\mathbf{w}$ in the most efficient way possible, irrespective of whether the data contains a greater number of samples than variables or vice versa.

With this goal, we propose using the singular value decomposition (SVD) of matrices [6] to transform the system in Eq. 7. This allows us to obtain a factorization of matrix $\mathbf{XF} = \mathbf{USV}^T$ where $\mathbf{U} \in \mathbb{R}^{m \times m}$ and $\mathbf{V} \in \mathbb{R}^{n \times n}$ are orthogonal matrices, and where $\mathbf{S} \in \mathbb{R}^{m \times n}$ is a diagonal matrix with r nonzero elements, known as the singular values of $\mathbf{S}$, where $r = rank(\mathbf{XF}) \leq min(m, n)$.

Replacing $\mathbf{XF}$ on the left of Eq. 7 gives us:

$$(\mathbf{USV}^T\mathbf{FX}^T + \lambda\mathbf{I})\mathbf{w} = \mathbf{XFF\bar{d}} \tag{8}$$

Since $\mathbf{F}$ is a square diagonal matrix, it holds that $\mathbf{FX}^T = \mathbf{F}^T\mathbf{X}^T = (\mathbf{FX})^T = (\mathbf{USV}^T)^T = \mathbf{VS}^T\mathbf{U}^T$. Substituting $\mathbf{FX}^T$ with $\mathbf{VS}^T\mathbf{U}^T$ in Eq. 8, we get:

$$(\mathbf{USV}^T\mathbf{VS}^T\mathbf{U}^T + \lambda\mathbf{I})\mathbf{w} = \mathbf{XFF\bar{d}} \tag{9}$$

Given the orthogonality of $\mathbf{V}$, it holds that $\mathbf{VV}^T = \mathbf{V}^T\mathbf{V} = \mathbf{I}$, and thus:

$$(\mathbf{USS}^T\mathbf{U}^T + \lambda\mathbf{I})\mathbf{w} = \mathbf{XFF\bar{d}} \tag{10}$$

Equivalently, using $\mathbf{UU}^T = \mathbf{I}$ we further obtain:

$$(\mathbf{USS}^T\mathbf{U}^T + \lambda\mathbf{UU}^T)\mathbf{w} = \mathbf{XFF\bar{d}} \tag{11}$$

which is equivalent to:

$$\mathbf{U}(\mathbf{SS}^T + \lambda\mathbf{I})\mathbf{U}^T\mathbf{w} = \mathbf{XFF\bar{d}} \tag{12}$$

Multiplying on the left by $\mathbf{U}^T$ both sides of the expression become:

$$(\mathbf{SS}^T + \lambda\mathbf{I})\mathbf{U}^T\mathbf{w} = \mathbf{U}^T\mathbf{XFF\bar{d}} \tag{13}$$

To obtain an expression for the weights $\mathbf{w}$ we further multiply on the left by $(\mathbf{SS}^T + \lambda\mathbf{I})^{-1}$, obtaining the following equation:

$$\mathbf{U}^T\mathbf{w} = (\mathbf{SS}^T + \lambda\mathbf{I})^{-1}\mathbf{U}^T\mathbf{XFF\bar{d}} \tag{14}$$

Lastly, multiplying on the left by $\mathbf{U}$ obtains the final solution:

$$\mathbf{w} = \mathbf{U}(\mathbf{SS}^T + \lambda\mathbf{I})^{-1}\mathbf{U}^T\mathbf{XFF}\bar{\mathbf{d}} \tag{15}$$

The computational complexity for calculating this closed-form solution continues to be high, with the previous calculation of SVD($\mathbf{XF}$) and the inverse of ($\mathbf{SS}^T + \lambda\mathbf{I}$) in Eq. 15 as the most expensive operations. However, as already mentioned, the number of nonzero elements in the diagonal matrix $\mathbf{S}$ is r, and thus, the effective dimensions of $\mathbf{U}$ and $\mathbf{S}$ are $m \times r$ and $r \times r$ (note that matrix $\mathbf{V}$ is no longer required in Eq. 15). This allows us to calculate SVD ($\mathbf{XF}$) using an economy-sized decomposition that contains all the relevant information of the regular decomposition, but since it is more compact, it can be calculated more efficiently in time $O(mnr)$ [7]. Moreover, as long as λ is nonzero, ($\mathbf{SS}^T + \lambda\mathbf{I}$) is a diagonal matrix with nonzero elements on the diagonal, and, therefore, the calculation of the inverse lowers complexity to time $O(r)$; this is because all that is needed is to calculate the reciprocals of the main diagonal elements. Under these circumstances, $r \leq min(m, n)$ as the system in Eq. 15 becomes efficient whether $m \gg n$ or $n \gg m$. As a result, the final proposed solution to obtain $\mathbf{w}$ includes regularization, which is noniterative and computationally very efficient, given that its complexity depends on the smallest value between the number of samples in the training set (n) and the dimension of the input space (m).

2.1   Incremental and Distributed Learning

The approach in Eq. 15 can only be used for batch learning when the whole data set $\mathbf{X}$ is available. However, there are three main situations in which batch learning is not possible. The most obvious situation is learning from data streams: we do not want to train the model from scratch each time new data become available, yet we want to add the new knowledge to the previously learnt model. A second situation in which batch learning is not possible is when data are distributed in several locations and cannot be gathered in a single location for privacy reasons. Finally, traditional batch learning algorithms become very inefficient or even inapplicable to very large big-data sets, which is why distributed learning is a solution. Following the distribution scheme presented elsewhere [8], we reformulate the training algorithm proposed in the previous section to allow for distributed/incremental learning using Eq. 15.

In that equation we can distinguish two parts on the right-hand side. On the one hand, we have $\mathbf{XFF}\bar{\mathbf{d}}$, which does not depend on matrices obtained from the SVD of $\mathbf{XF}$. Suppose, at time k, that we have a batch of n examples $\mathbf{X}_k \in \mathbb{R}^{m \times n}$ and that $\mathbf{M}_k = \mathbf{X}_k\mathbf{F}_k\mathbf{F}_k\bar{\mathbf{d}}_k$ is computed to obtain $\mathbf{w}_k$. When new data $\mathbf{X}_p$ become available, the new matrix $\mathbf{M}_{k|p}$ – which combines the information provided jointly by $\mathbf{X}_k$ and $\mathbf{X}_p$ – can be easily obtained by simply adding, to $\mathbf{M}_k$, the term that depends only on the new data block, as was demonstrated elsewhere [9], i.e.:

$$\mathbf{M}_{k|p} = \mathbf{M}_k + \mathbf{X}_p\mathbf{F}_p\mathbf{F}_p\bar{\mathbf{d}}_p \tag{16}$$

On the other hand, a more complex approach is needed for the incremental/distributed calculation of the first part of Eq. 15, i.e., $\mathbf{U}(\mathbf{SS}^T + \lambda \mathbf{I})^{-1}\mathbf{U}^T$, as it depends on matrices $\mathbf{U}$ and $\mathbf{S}$. Let us again suppose that, at time k, we obtain the economy-sized SVD of matrix $\mathbf{X}_k \mathbf{F}_k$, i.e.:

$$SVD(\mathbf{X}_k \mathbf{F}_k) = \mathbf{U}_k \mathbf{S}_k \mathbf{V}_k \qquad (17)$$

And later on we obtain:

$$SVD(\mathbf{X}_p \mathbf{F}_p) = \mathbf{U}_p \mathbf{S}_p \mathbf{V}_p. \qquad (18)$$

Iwen and Ong [10] demonstrated that the matrix $\mathbf{B} = [\mathbf{U}_k \mathbf{S}_k | \mathbf{U}_p \mathbf{S}_p]$ has the same singular values $\mathbf{S}$ and left singular vectors $\mathbf{U}$ as if calculated using the whole data set $\mathbf{X} = [\mathbf{X}_k | \mathbf{X}_p]$, i.e.:

$$SVD(\mathbf{XF}) = SVD([\mathbf{U}_k \mathbf{S}_k | \mathbf{U}_p \mathbf{S}_p]) \qquad (19)$$

This partial SVD merging scheme has been shown to be numerically robust to rounding off errors and corruption of the original data. It is also accurate even when the rank of matrix $\mathbf{XF}$ is underestimated or deliberately reduced.

Finally, Eq. 16 and Eq. 19 allow weights $\mathbf{w}$ to be calculated both incrementally and/or distributively as summarized in Algorithm 1. To perform distributed learning, at each node k and for a given data partition $\mathbf{X}_k$, we only need to compute $\mathbf{M}_k = \mathbf{X}_k \mathbf{F}_k \mathbf{F}_k \bar{\mathbf{d}}_k$ and the matrices $\mathbf{U}_k$, $\mathbf{S}_k$ resulting from the SVD of $\mathbf{X}_k \mathbf{F}_k$. Each node subsequently sends these partial results to a given node to be combined and to obtain the global matrices $\mathbf{M}$, $\mathbf{U}$ and $\mathbf{S}$ according to Eq. 16 and Eq. 19. The weights are then calculated using Eq. 15. Moreover, in the case of very big-data sets we could adopt a hierarchical distribution in which a large network of nodes could compute the basic matrices $\mathbf{M}_i$, $\mathbf{U}_i$ and $\mathbf{S}_i$ from the data available at each node i. Subsequently, some of these nodes can be organised in hierarchical levels such that they obtain partial results from the previous level and be used to calculate new matrices $\mathbf{M}_j$, $\mathbf{U}_j$ and $\mathbf{S}_j$; those matrices are passed through the hierarchy to a final node to obtain the components to compute the global matrices and the weights. The number of levels will depend on the required computational power, thus obtaining a high-level scalable algorithm. Moreover, since no raw data is transmitted among nodes, only among locally computed matrices $\mathbf{M}$, $\mathbf{U}$ and $\mathbf{S}$, the algorithm also guarantees privacy.

To perform incremental learning, we have to combine a partially computed SVD representation of past data with a new partially computed SVD based on recent data. Assuming that matrix $\mathbf{M}_k$ has previously been computed for the past data $\mathbf{X}_k$, the updated matrix $\mathbf{M}_{k|p}$ that adds information from the new block of data $\mathbf{X}_p$ is calculated using Eq. 16. In the same way, if we have already computed $\mathbf{U}_k$ and $\mathbf{S}_k$ using $\mathbf{X}_k$, to obtain the new $\mathbf{U}_{k|p}$ and $\mathbf{S}_{k|p}$ corresponding to the augmented matrix $\mathbf{XF}_{k|p}$, we apply the result in Eq. 19, i.e.:

$$SVD(\mathbf{XF}_{k|p}) = SVD([\mathbf{X}_k \mathbf{F}_k | \mathbf{X}_p \mathbf{F}_p]) = SVD(\mathbf{U}_k \mathbf{S}_k | \mathbf{U}_p \mathbf{S}_p) \qquad (20)$$

As can be seen, to perform incremental learning, only matrices $\mathbf{M}_{k|p}$, $\mathbf{U}_{k|p}$ and $\mathbf{S}_{k|p}$ need to be stored for the next steps. Note that the fact that the size of these matrices is constant over time provides an additional advantage over nonincremental solutions requiring storage of all the raw data and resulting, therefore, in increasingly large volumes of data.

Finally, the incremental and distributed uses of the algorithm can be combined as needed to obtain, for instance, a distributed learning environment that also learns incrementally at each location. In the interest of contributing to reproducible research the Python code is available online[1].

Algorithm 1. ROLANN for incremental/distributed regularized learning

Inputs:

$\mathbf{X}_p \in \mathbb{R}^{m \times s_p}$	▷ New data block with m inputs and s_p samples
$\mathbf{d}_p \in \mathbb{R}^{s_p \times 1}$	▷ The corresponding new block of desired outputs
f	▷ Nonlinear activation function (invertible)
λ	▷ Regularization hyperparameter
$\mathbf{M}_k$	▷ Current $\mathbf{M}$ matrix calculated using other data blocks
$\mathbf{U}_k$	▷ Current $\mathbf{U}$ matrix calculated using other data blocks
$\mathbf{S}_k$	▷ Current $\mathbf{S}$ matrix calculated using other data blocks

Outputs:

$\mathbf{w} \in \mathbb{R}^{m \times 1}$	▷ Optimal weights
$\mathbf{M}_{k|p}$	▷ Updated $\mathbf{M}$ matrix
$\mathbf{U}_{k|p}$	▷ Updated $\mathbf{U}$ matrix
$\mathbf{S}_{k|p}$	▷ Updated $\mathbf{S}$ matrix

```
1: function ROLANN(X_p,d_p,f,λ,M_k,U_k,S_k)
2:     X_p = [ones(1, s_p); X_p];                              ▷ Bias is added
3:     d̄_p = f⁻¹(d_p);                            ▷ Inverse of the neural function
4:     f_p = f'(d̄_p);                             ▷ Derivate of the neural function
5:     F_p = diag(f_p);                                     ▷ Diagonal matrix
6:     if (M_k & U_k & S_k are empty matrices)
7:         [U_{k|p}, S_{k|p}, ~] = SVD(X_p * F_p);                ▷ Economy size
8:         M_{k|p} = X_p * (f_p. * f_p. * d̄_p);
9:     else                                      ▷ Combining previous knowledge
10:         M_{k|p} = M_k + X_p * (f_p. * f_p. * d̄_p);
11:         [U_p, S_p, ~] = SVD(X_p * F_p);
12:         [U_{k|p}, S_{k|p}, ~] = SVD([U_k S_k | U_p S_p]);
13:     endif
14:     w = U_{k|p} * inv(S_{k|p} * S_{k|p} + λI) * (U_{k|p}^T * M_{k|p});
15: end function
```

---

[1] https://github.com/ofontenla/ROLANN.

3   Experimental Results

We present and discuss several results that show the performance and characteristics of ROLANN. The experimental study compares its behaviour with that of some other well-known learning methods available in the literature. Specifically, we focus on similar proposals with minimization of the residual sum of squares plus a penalty term. The aim is to identify the model that achieves the best trade-off between goodness of fit and complexity. ROLANN is therefore compared with the ridge regression [1], lasso [2] and elastic net [3] methods.

For this experimental study, we considered a scenario where regularization could benefit learning. We consider different two-class classification problems involving microarrays, for which the risk of overfitting is high given the low number of training examples and the very high number of input variables. Table 1 summarises their characteristics[2].

Table 1. Description of data sets used in the experimental study.

Data set	Samples	Variables
Lung*	181	12533
Prostate*	136	12600
ALLAML*	72	7130
Breast*	97	24481
Smk	187	19993
Ovarian	253	15154
Gli85	85	2283
Colon	62	2000
CNS	60	7129

* These data sets already contain independent training and test sets.

Experimental study considerations were as follows:

- We employed grid search and 10-fold cross-validation to select the optimal hyperparameter values for each model. We subsequently used an independent test set to evaluate goodness. In some cases the data were already distributed into training and test sets (see data sets denoted * in Table 1) and in those cases the provided test set was used. In all other cases, we employed 70% of

---

[2] All data sets are available for download at:
http://www.broadinstitute.org/cgibin/cancer/datasets.cgi.
http://genomics-pubs.princeton.edu/oncology/.
http://leo.ugr.es/elvira/DBCRepository/.
http://featureselection.asu.edu/datasets.php.

the total samples for cross-validation and the remaining 30% as a test set to evaluate the best configurations selected by cross-validation.
- To check the influence of λ, all learning algorithms were run using different values of this regularization hyperparameter. The optimal value was obtained by an exhaustive grid search using values from the set $\{0.001, 0.002, \ldots, 1, 10, 20, \ldots, 10000, 1 \times 10^5, 5 \times 10^5, 1 \times 10^6, 5 \times 10^6, \ldots, 5 \times 10^{11}, 1 \times 10^{12}\}$.
- For the elastic net, in addition to λ, another hyperparameter had to be tuned, i.e., α. In this case, the optimal hyperparameter configuration was also selected by means of a grid search combining all the already mentioned values of λ with α in the set $\{0.1, 0.2, \ldots, 0.9\}$.
- Both linear and logarithmic sigmoid functions were used as activation functions for the proposed method, in order to determine when the use of a nonlinear activation function meant a performance improvement.
- ROLANN was run in a distributed environment. Four nodes were employed for its execution, for randomly split instances of each data set.

Table 2 shows the validation performance results using the best hyperparameter configurations. The first two columns show the results of ROLANN using logarithmic sigmoid and linear functions. The last row shows the mean accuracy values obtained over all data sets. In order to determine whether the differences in the results are statistically significant the Kruskal Wallis test was applied. For each data set, significantly worse results are underlined. As it can be seen, the proposed method shows a better behavior than the other approaches, since in none of the cases it obtains a result that is significantly worse.

Table 2. Mean Accuracy $\pm$ standard deviation (%) obtained in the validation set for the 10-fold cross-validation using the best hyperparameter configuration for each method.

	$ROLANN_{log}$	$ROLANN_{lin}$	Ridge	Lasso	Elastic net
Lung	100.0 ± 0.0	100.0 ± 0.0	90.8 ± 14.9	90.8 ± 14.9	$\underline{74.2 \pm 20.9}$
Prostate	93.2 ± 0.0	93.3 ± 0.0	$\underline{83.3 \pm 11.3}$	84.3 ± 14.0	89.2 ± 8.6
AMLALL	97.5 ± 0.0	97.5 ± 0.0	$\underline{76.7 \pm 5.9}$	76.7 ± 5.2	96.7 ± 0.0
Breast	64.3 ± 1.83	64.2 ± 3.8	69.5 ± 15.5	68.0 ± 14.5	53.8 ± 4.1
SMK	73.3 ± 15.0	74.8 ± 0.0	$\underline{59.5 \pm 7.4}$	$\underline{58.7 \pm 8.4}$	$\underline{61.8 \pm 1.9}$
Ovarian	100.0 ± 0.0	100.0 ± 0.0	$\underline{91.6 \pm 5.6}$	$\underline{76.7 \pm 8.1}$	35.2 ± 0.0
Gli85	82.7 ± 2.4	82.7 ± 14.6	77.7 ± 16.5	76.0 ± 14.7	27.3 ± 0.0
Colon	86.0 ± 16.9	79.0 ± 21.8	$\underline{72.1 \pm 12.2}$	$\underline{73.0 \pm 16.7}$	74.5 ± 0.0
CNS	68.5 ± 23.1	66.5 ± 0.0	76.5 ± 19.3	74.0 ± 12.9	66.5 ± 0.0
Mean	85.1	84.2	77.5	73.3	64.3

Table 3 shows the results on the independent test sets. Note that, for a given model there may be ties in terms of accuracy for different hyperparameter configurations. All tying configurations were applied over the test set. The last row

Table 3. Mean Accuracy ± standard deviation (%) in the test set for all hyperparameter configurations that were selected as optimal. Best results are boldfaced.

	$ROLANN_{log}$	$ROLANN_{lin}$	Ridge	Lasso	Elastic net
Lung	**98.0 ± 0.0**	**98.0 ± 0.0**	80.5 ± 0.0	96.0 ± 0.0	90.6 ± 0.0
Prostate	**97.1 ± 0.0**	39.7 ± 2.1	76.5 ± 0.0	76.5 ± 0.0	26.5 ± 0.0
AMLALL	**97.1 ± 0.1**	**97.1 ± 0.1**	59.2 ± 1.5	58.8 ± 0.0	94.6 ± 0.0
Breast	71.5 ± 2.6	**75.2 ± 4.0**	36.8 ± 0.0	36.8 ± 0.0	67.1 ± 6.6
SMK	73.2 ± 0.0	**76.8 ± 0.0**	46.4 ± 0.0	46.4 ± 0.0	46.4 ± 0.0
Ovarian	**100.0 ± 0.0**	**100.0 ± 0.0**	84.9 ± 12.1	82.9 ± 0.0	38.2 ± 0.0
Gli85	90.4 ± 2.7	**92.3 ± 0.0**	61.5 ± 0.0	61.5 ± 0.0	38.5 ± 0.0
Colon	**100.0 ± 0.0**	94.7 ± 0.0	71.0 ± 3.0	68.4 ± 0.0	74.7 ± 2.1
CNS	**61.1± 0.0**	**61.1± 0.0**	**61.1± 0.0**	**61.1± 0.0**	**61.1 ± 0.0**
Mean	**87.6**	81.6	64.2	65.4	59.5
Loss	**−2.5**	2.6	13.3	7.9	4.8

(denoted *Loss*) shows, for each learning algorithm, the differences between validation and test accuracy values when all data sets are considered. Best results for each data set are boldfaced.

Analysing Table 3, it can be observed that, ROLANN's results may vary depending on the activation function; however, in no data set the differences are too high except for the Prostate data set. Considering all the methods, it seems that for all data sets except CNS, ROLANN outperforms other algorithms, with differences that are significant for the AMLLAL, Gli85 and Colon data sets. Regarding the CNS data set, all methods achieved test accuracy of 61.1%, amounting to a poor result. Note that the CNS data set presents a high level of overlapping between classes and its classification accuracy is generally poor, as it also occurs with the Breast and SMK data sets. A peculiarity of the Prostate set should also be underlined. The test set was extracted from a different experiment and the test distribution differs significantly from the training distribution. This explains why some classifiers do not generalize properly – as occurred with ROLANN with linear function and elastic net approaches; Tables 2 and 3 show important differences between their validation and test performances, specifically, 93.3% vs 39.7% for ROLANN linear and 89.2% vs 26.5% for elastic net. Analysing the *Loss* results in the last row of Table 3, it can be seen that the smallest differences in accuracy between validation and test sets occurs for ROLANN, indicating a better generalization capacity.

Our results were also compared with others available in the literature [11] and, to our knowledge, the results obtained by ROLANN are, in general, similar or even better. In cases where superior results were reported in the literature, a previous stage of feature selection was always applied. Even so, while this selection stage may be critical for this type of data set [12], the results obtained by ROLANN were occasionally better. This conclusion holds for all the data

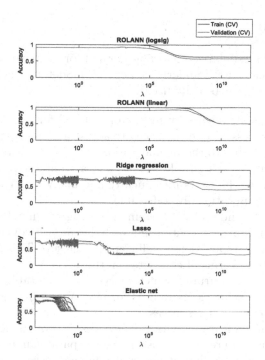

Fig. 1. Prostate data set: accuracy curves as a function of the λ parameter obtained by each model during cross-validation for both the training and test sets.

sets except for Gli85, for which a sparse evolutionary deep net obtained 100% accuracy [13]. For the Colon dataset no result (when using no feature selection) was found to be as good as that obtained by our proposed ROLANN method.

Also a stability analysis of the methods, as function of the regularization parameter λ, was performed. Using the Prostate data set as a representative example of all the results, Fig. 1 shows the influence of several λ values on the accuracy curves obtained during cross-validation for both training and validation sets. Results shows that, in contrast to the other methods, ROLANN has a more stable behaviour when the value of the parameter λ is varied. In addition, for a given value of λ, its behaviour is more homogeneous among the 10 cross-validation executions, especially when compared to the elastic net.

Finally, regarding computational complexity it is worth remembering that ROLANN has some additional advantages over the other methods. First, its complexity depends on the lower value between the number of variables and data which, in certain circumstances, can make it more computational efficient. Second, ROLANN is capable of distributed learning. The data distribution does not affect its performance as it has been shown mathematically, when proving that the distributed and non-distributed solutions are equivalent, and as it has been supported by the experiments carried out for which a distributed learning scheme was used with 4 nodes.

4 Conclusion

We have proposed a regularized learning method for one-layer neural networks. Despite the simplicity of the underlying network model, the method has several advantages that makes it broadly useful:

- It finds the optimal weights by means of a closed form and thus through a *non-iterative* process. It does not need to adjust any *hyperparameter*, beyond the one corresponding to the regularization term. Thus, it requires minimum human intervention, a desirable feature and a competitive advantage when learning from large data sets for which tuning many hyperparameters is difficult or even computationally unfeasible.
- Its complexity depends on the minimum among the number of inputs and samples of the training set, contrasting with the majority of the training methods that are only computationally efficient on one side. This makes ROLANN very competitive in terms of computation time.
- It allows incremental learning, which makes it very suitable for learning continuously on data streams, as well as for big data as batch learning usually demands more computer resources.
- It allows distributed learning with privacy preservation, making it well suited for environments where data must remain separate in multiple locations, whether due to memory limitations or privacy concerns.

Furthermore, as was experimentally corroborated, in terms of accuracy, the method has a performance level comparable or superior to classical state-of-the-art regularization methods, with additional advantages as mentioned above.

Future work is intended to include the incorporation of a forgetting factor to handle a concept drift effect. Another line is the integration of this method as part of the learning procedures for dense layers in a deep network, which could provide a more efficient training in terms of computational time.

References

1. Hoerl, A.E., Kennard, R.W.: Ridge Regression, chapter 8, pp. 129–136 (1988)
2. Tibshirani, R.: Regression shrinkage and selection via the lasso. J. Royal Stat. Soc. Ser. B (Methodological) **58**(1), 267–288 (1996)
3. Zou, H., Hastie, T.: Regularization and variable selection via the elastic net. J. Royal Stat. Soc. Ser. B **67**, 301–320 (2005)
4. Fontenla-Romero, O., Guijarro-Berdiñas, B., Pérez-Sánchez, B., Alonso-Betanzos, A.: A new convex objective function for the supervised learning of single-layer neural networks. Pattern Recogn. **43**(5), 1984–1992 (2010)
5. Bishop, C.M.: Neural Networks for Pattern Recognition. Oxford University Press, New York (1995)
6. Fontenla-Romero, O., Pérez-Sánchez, B., Guijarro-Berdiñas, B.: LANN-SVD: A non-iterative SVD-based learning algorithm for one-layer neural networks. IEEE Trans. Neural Netw. Learn. Syst. **29**(8), 3900–3905 (2018)

7. Golub, G.H., Van Loan, C.F.: Matrix Computations. Johns Hopkins University Press, Baltimore (2012)
8. Fontenla-Romero, O., Pérez-Sánchez, B., Guijarro-Berdiñas, B., Gómez-Casal, M.: LANN-DSVD: A privacy-preserving distributed algorithm for machine learning. Presented at European Symposium on Artificial Neural Networks, Computational Intelligence and Machine Learning (ESANN), pp. 573–578 (2018)
9. Fontenla-Romero, O., Pérez-Sánchez, B., Guijarro-Berdiñas, B.: An incremental non-iterative learning method for one-layer feed forward neural networks. Appl. Soft Comput. **70**, 951–958 (2018)
10. Iwen, M.A., Ong, B.W.: A distributed and incremental SVD algorithm for agglomerative data analysis on large networks. SIAM J. Matrix Anal. Appl. **37**, 1699–1718 (2016)
11. Sánchez-Maroño, N., Fontenla-Romero, O., Pérez-Sánchez, B.: Classification of microarray data. In: Bolón-Canedo, V., Alonso-Betanzos, A. (eds.) Microarray Bioinformatics. MMB, vol. 1986, pp. 185–205. Springer, New York (2019). https://doi.org/10.1007/978-1-4939-9442-7_8
12. Jain, I., Jain, V.K., Jain, R.: Correlation feature selection based improved-binary particle swarm optimization for gene selection and cancer classification. Appl. Soft Comput. **62**, 203–215 (2018)
13. Liu, S., Mocanu, D.C., Matavalam, A.R.R., Pci, Y., Pcchcnizkiy, M.: Sparse evolutionary deep learning with over one million artificial ncurons on commodity hardware. Neural Comput. Appl. **33**(7), 2589–2604 (2020). https://doi.org/10.1007/s00521-020-05136-7

Frailty Level Prediction in Older Age Using Hand Grip Strength Functions Over Time

Elsa Pérez[1], Jose E. Torres Rangel[1], Marta Musté[1], Carlos Pérez[2], Oscar Macho[2], Francisco S. del Corral Guijarro[3], Aris Somoano[4], Cristina Gianella[4], Luis Ramírez[4], and Andreu Català[1(✉)]

[1] CETpD-UPC, Technical University of Catalonia, Vilanova i la Geltrú, Spain
{elsa.perez,andreu.catala}@upc.edu
[2] Consorci Sanitari de l'Alt Penedès i Garraf, Vilafranca del Penedès, Spain
[3] Universidad Politécnica de Madrid, Madrid, Spain
[4] Hospital Central de la Cruz Roja San José y Santa Adela de Madrid, Madrid, Spain

Abstract. Frailty syndrome can be defined as a clinical state in which there is a rise in individual vulnerability, developing an increase in both the dependence of the person and mortality. Frailty is completely related to age. A fundamental factor to apply rehabilitative interventions successfully resides in having a simple and reliable method capable of identifying frailty syndrome.

Frailty indexes (FI) have several sources of uncertainty trough the opinion of the patients, white coat effect and external factors. Moreover, in the clinical practice, the experience of the geriatricians led them to determine an approximation of the frailty level only with a simple handshake. Hand grip strength (HGS) has been widely used in tests by investigators and therapists to be able to diagnose sarcopenia and frailty, as it is a reliable indicator of the overall muscle strength, which decreases with age. Most researches focused mainly on peak HGS, which will not give insight on how the patient's strength was distributed over time. In the present work it is proposed to evaluate HGS behavior over a period of time, and to develop a system based on Machine Learning for the identification of frailty levels using physiological features, FI and the classical signal processing based on statistics of the HGS signals.

The starting hypothesis is that it can be identified the "way" of performing HGS correlated with the level of frailty. To achieve this goal a clinical study was designed and carried out with a cohort of 70 elderly persons, in two Hospitals.

Keywords: Frailty identification · Hand grip strength · Machine Learning

1 Introduction

Frailty syndrome can be defined as a clinical state in which there is a rise in individual vulnerability, developing an increase in both the dependence of the person and mortality when exposed to a stressor. Frailty is completely related to age, being highly prevalent in the elderly, reaching up to 30% in people over 75 years of age.

© Springer Nature Switzerland AG 2021
I. Rojas et al. (Eds.): IWANN 2021, LNCS 12862, pp. 356–366, 2021.
https://doi.org/10.1007/978-3-030-85099-9_29

There are many questionnaires that define various frailty factors, but there is no accepted standardization on this. In addition, these methods require the opinion of the patient, whose criteria may vary depending on the patient, thus generating an imprecise diagnosis. Geriatricians consider that this clinical condition considerably increases health risks [1] and even death [2].

On the other hand, there is evidence through several studies that show that the appearance of frailty can be anticipated, delayed or even avoided [9]. Therefore, a fundamental factor to apply rehabilitative interventions successfully resides in having a simple, effective and reliable method capable of identifying people with frailty syndrome.

At present there is no common criterion to quantify frailty. Most questionnaires are based on asking the patient about various symptoms and noting which ones he or she manifests or perceives [3–5]. One of these methods is that of Fried et al. [17], which involved 5210 people over 65 years of age, who proposed that the frailty phenotype is defined by the presence of three or more of the following symptoms: unintended weight loss, weakness, low resistance, slowness of movement, low activity.

In the 90s it was demonstrated the usefulness of VIG (comprehensive geriatric assessment) [18] to evaluate frailty in the elderly. The VIG is a global diagnostic tool or methodology at all levels of care, it is designed to identify and quantify biomedical and pharmacological data, physical, functional, psychological and social problems that the elderly may present.

Both Fried and other indices or scales exclusively use the maximum value of the grip strength of the hand as one of the symptoms, but in clinical practice the geriatrician uses his experience to make quick diagnoses based on the "form" in which the patient performs a handshake.

1.1 HGS Related Work

Hand grip strength (HGS) has been widely used in tests by investigators and therapists to be able to diagnose sarcopenia and frailty, as it is a reliable indicator of the overall muscle strength, which decreases with age. Results obtained from these tests have been used to verify if HGS can indeed work as a predictor of disability in older men [6]. These tests are tied to recent protocols, such as Southampton protocol or the one proposed by the ASHT (American Society of Hand Therapists), made to try and establish a common ground for different studies.

However, even after updating these protocols recently (as recent as 2015), there is still a lack of consistency when it comes to evaluate HGS over a period of time. There are studies which aim to gather data from other studies that measured HGS to diagnose sarcopenia and frailty and identify the differences in the protocols used [7], which is an important focus for the present research, as the protocol that is to be proposed will use others as means for comparison and innovation.

When a protocol is taken for a specific study, there are a few main elements that can be appreciated and need to be highlighted from the beginning, such as the dynamometer used to measure HGS, which hand was used, the subject's posture, arm position, handle position, how long did the measurement take or how long were the intervals between the measurements. The recommended protocol to follow is the most recent ASHT protocol, as it is the most detailed one, and if a modification should be made, it is to be mentioned [8].

Another parameter which has also shown to have correlation to grip strength is the body mass index (BMI). Again, data was collected with a Jamar dynamometer and using healthy males as subjects aged 20–74 years [9].

Even though a wide range of instruments was used among the majority of studies (Smedley, Martin, Tekdyne, among others), the predominant dynamometer used was de Jamar dynamometer [10].

Regarding sincerity of effort, that is, whether a genuinely maximal effort is being given during clinical strength testing, there are several studies that have examined the force-time curve produced by maximal and submaximal effort [11]. By using a specialized dynamometer with a force transducer (Biopac Instruments), with a test time of 5 s, a 30-s rest interval between trials, the function obtained had the form of a step.

Respecting the time for test, a 6-s test was found to have a higher reliability despite gender or hand dominance, in contrast to a 10-s test, which did not have results as reliable as the first [12].

If HGS was to be measured over time, and plot a strength curve for the same period of the procedure, more valuable information could be obtained regarding how HGS really determines patients' muscle strength, or perhaps, even go as far as being able to diagnose more efficiently frailty or sarcopenia by extracting determined features from it. Some studies studied the slope of the force-time curve related to sincerity of effort with a Jamar dynamometer and following the protocol recommended by the ASHT [13, 14].

Another study that aimed to investigate the force-time characteristics during a sustained maximal grip effort, according to age and clinical condition [15] was consulted, in which a sustained maximal grip was continuously recorded by using a modified Martin vigorimeter. The investigators concluded that the force-time characteristics during a sustained maximal handgrip effort are significantly different according to age and clinical condition. Old patients were characterized by a rather fast decline in muscle work during the first part of sustained grip.

1.2 HGS and the Level of Frailty

In the present work, a system based on Machine Learning for identifying the levels of frailty is developed using the features of the grip force signal in a determined period of time. The objectives of this study are two: to perform the main frailty indexes VIG, Fried, Frail, with a cohort of elderly persons, done by geriatricians, in a transversal pilot together with a designed test of HGS in a period of time, and with the created database to develop different Machine Learning strategies to extract significant information and knowledge useful for the detection of frailty tendencies using the results of only one simple test. The starting hypothesis is that we can identify the "way" of performing HGS correlated with the level of frailty.

2 Material and Methods

The following lines are dedicated to the description of the instrument and the cohort.

2.1 Instrumentation

The instrument used for the present study was a modified Deyard dynamometer, being the modified part the whole electronic circuit, which was replaced by one designed and made by the CETpD, the rest of the model, meaning the mechanical design, remained the same as the original. Thanks to this modification, the dynamometer measures the HGS continuously in time (Fig. 1).

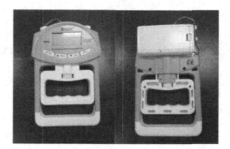

Fig. 1. Modified Deyard dynamometer

The modification includes the ability to store information and Bluetooth connectivity with the IMU (Inertial Measurement Unit) developed by the CETpD [16] 15 for long-term monitoring of human pathological movement.

2.2 Calibration

Calibration was necessary to set the accuracy of the modified version to an acceptable level. For this, weights that ranged from 5 to 40 kg were used (which is more than the max force expected for the tested population), with an increasing rate of 5 kg per trial. The dynamometer was held by two metallic bars, which were placed in the space between the handle and the screen, where no disruption should be presented for the test. A belt was tied to the base for the weights (extra 731.8 g) and to the handle, as centered as possible, note that the belt is made of a non-stretchable material, as to not influence the result of the calibration tests (Figs. 2 and 3).

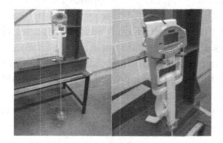

Fig. 2. Calibration process

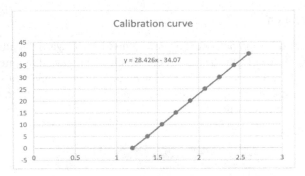

Fig. 3. Calibration curve force (Kg) vs voltage (V)

Its calibration curve resulted as follows:
For which the slope equation for the curve is as shown:

$$y = 28.426 * x - 34.07$$

Considering the weight of the balance used for the calibration trials (731.8 g) it is then:

$$y = 28.426 * x - (34.07 - 0.7318)$$

Where y is the force total (Kg), and x represents the voltage (V) measured.

2.3 Pilot Protocol

The protocol designed includes the cohort, the clinical study, which includes the registration of several frailty indexes, and the performance of 3 HGS test recorded with a modified Deyard dynamometer to store and transmit the produced signals. This protocol was carried out by geriatricians, with a cohort of 70 elderly persons, in two Hospitals, (*Hospital Central de la Cruz Roja San José* and *Santa Adela de Madrid, Consorci Sanitari de l'Alt Penedès i Garraf*). All data were captured in a single visit, where the general inclusion criteria were applied and each participant was assigned their corresponding level of frailty. Geriatricians performed the HGS test and evaluated the following scales in clinical trials: Fried criteria [17], Fragile Vig Index (VIG) [18], Barthel scale [19] and Lawton – Brody scale [20]. The protocol was approved by the "Comité de Ética de la Investigación con Medicamentos de la Comunidad de Madrid" (Ref 47/916546.9/19).

The HGS test consists of 3 trials carried out in a sitting stance take on a chair, forearm placed on top of the leg in neutral position (holding the dynamometer perpendicular to the leg), feet firm on the floor at shoulder-width distance, shoulder adducted, neutrally rotated and using the dominant hand. Encouragement was also one aspect to keep into consideration, as it was used as well. Tests had a duration of 6 s each, and a rest interval of 1 min between tests (Fig. 4).

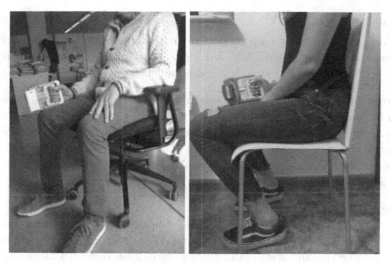

Fig. 4. Protocol position example

2.4 Data Acquisition and Processing

To plot the force-time curves, the data was stored in the memory card inside the IMU and inserted in the PC to run the Matlab script, which acquired the signal, filter it, establish the desired range for treatment, and then segment the resulting signal in three phases: the Force-generation phase (FGP), force maintenance (FM) and the Force-decay phase (FDP) (Fig. 5). These phases will be used to extract different proposed features with a Matlab script, specially designed for this function. These specific characteristics can be identified to truly be able to detect whether a patient is prone to developing frailty in the future or not.

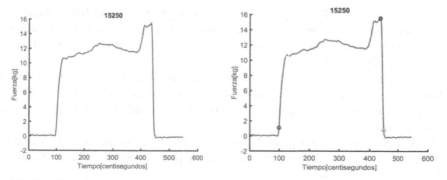

Fig. 5. Filtered signal sample from a patient and the 3 segments of the resulting signal.

2.5 Features

The features to consider for each patient are divided in 2 large groups: Physiological information compiled during the VIG & FRIED Tests performed to each patient and a group of between 1 to 3 HGS signals for each patient.

Physiological Information Compiled During the VIG and FRIED Tests Performed to Each Patient

In total we gather around 92 features from the VIG and Fried Tests from those we only took interest in 5: age, gender, weight, height, ICM. This was because the need was to select as few features as possible that were related with the muscular strength of the patients and that were easy and simple to get.

HGS Signals for Each Patient

First is important to remember that the signal is a non-structured data because it does not have a fixed number of samples and behaves as a time dependent variable. So, the first step was to convert the signal into a structured group of data. To do so we took inspiration in the work of industrial control signal featurization since the HGS could be interpreted as a response to a step input function and the features selected to represent each of the 3 segments (Generation, Maintenance and Decay phases) of the HGS signal were: Initial time, Initial Strength, Final time, Final Strength, Area, Density, Minimum Strength, Time of occurrence of Minimum Strength, Maximum Strength, Time of occurrence of Maximum Strength, Mean Strength, Median Strength, Strength Scope (Last-First), Mean Slope, Median Slope, Maximum Slope, Minimum Slope and OverPeak. Meaning that the HGS Signals were converted into 54 structured features.

Summarizing, each sample of each patient have 59 features. It was decided to work with the samples because we could upgrade our number of observations from 83 patients to 235 samples.

2.6 Targets

The original DDBB possessed 3 possible outputs or diagnosis the ones from VIG, FRIED and Estratos. Each of them had 3 possible output classifications: Frail, prefrail and Sturdy. The ideal distribution of classifications should be 33.33/33.33/33.33 so the more the actual distributions approach to it the better.

The Output of the VIG Diagnosis was selected to use as target, since: FRIED diagnosis had only 1 patient classified as sturdy, Estratos diagnosis depends on both the FRIED and VIG Test and the VIG diagnosis has a good distribution between the frail, prefrail and sturdy patients.

Also, to simplify the number of classifications, a one vs all focus was applied. Meaning that the classifications were changed from prefrail, frail and sturdy (3-class) to frail or not-frail (2-class).

2.7 Structured Data Base Creation

With the features and the targets selected we created a new Data Base that can be use as input for a predictor with the following size: 235 rows (samples) × 60 Columns (59 features and 1 target).

2.8 Predictor Structure

The predictor proposed was a SNN (Shallow Neural Network) available in Matlab as patterned a NN (Neural Network) with 1 hidden layer. The final amount of hidden size or internal neurons of the hidden layer were determined during the training (Fig. 6).

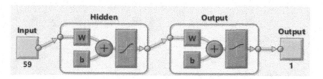

Fig. 6. SNN without training

2.9 Predictor Training

To create the final predictor (Fig. 7), the following steps were followed: a) Separate the Structured DDBB in 3 subsets called train, check and test b) Perform the basic training of an SNN c) Train 10000 SNN for the same hidden size d) train 120 different hidden size. And then the best SNN is picked from 1.200.000 trained SNN. This Final SNN was called FragilNET.

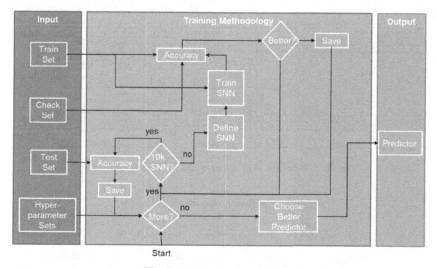

Fig. 7. Training methodology

3 Tests and Results

The confusion matrix of each set of the FragilNET are presented in Fig. 8.

A summary of the data comparations is found in Table 1.

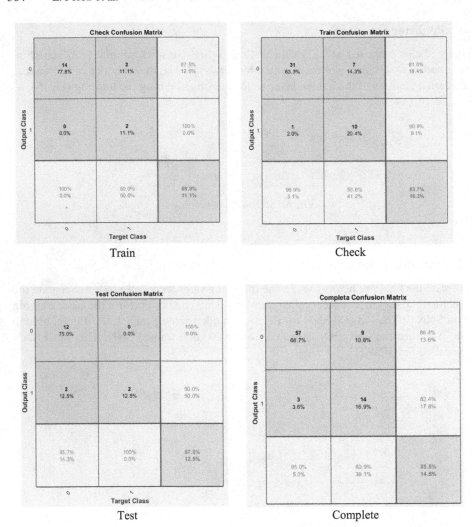

Train

Check

Test

Complete

Fig. 8. Confusion matrix associated with each data set.

Table 1. Confusion metrics comparison.

	Accuracy (%)	Precision (%)	Sensitivity (%)	Specificity (%)
Train	83.7	90.9	58.8	95.9
Check	88.9	100	50	100
Test	87.5	50	100	85.7
Complete	85.5	82.4	60.9	95
Mean ± std	86.4 ± 2.3	80.8 ± 21.8	67.4 ± 22.2	94.2 ± 6.0

4   Conclusions

The protocol design proposed was successfully implemented during the different tests conducted in the population, and the modified Deyard dynamometer was calibrated effectively and yielded satisfactory results for these tests and the resulting force overtime signals were similar to what was expected after consulting past studies that used them as well.

The Data of 83 patients (235 samples) was used to build a SNN called FragilNET that can predict the frailty label with 85,5% of accuracy and a sensibility of 67% using the signal information of the hand strength and the physiological data of the patient.

This research has many layers of development and finally we got the predictor that can relate the signal of hand force to the frailty level.

Even with the good news, we found it convenient to increase SNN training with more iterations, as it is slightly lower than check performance meaning that we hadn't reach the best training performance yet.

All decision to pick the best SNN were automatized. Data preprocessing Methods and how to separate it could work on other signals with similar step-like behaviors.

In order to achieve a support tool to correctly classify with a simple test the fragile condition it is crucial to have a high level of precision in our predictions, that means the correct classification of True Positives (Fragile) among all the subject. A value around 86% corroborates that assertion. On the other hand, and in the same level of importance, it is the fact that we need to minimize the number of False Negatives i.e., being fragile and predict robust. In this case the Sensitivity index that measures this concept has still a low value, around 67%. This is the weakness part of the whole prediction system and further work is needed to improve this sensitivity.

4.1   Recommendations for Future Work

Apply a data augmentation algorithm or get more data to balance the labels. We need more data from frail patients or perform data augmentation strategies like SMOTE to achieve a better balance between frail and robust patients.

Follow the classification strategy of the VIG, FRIED and Estratos index, built a three-class predictor including the "prefrailty level".

Combine all 3 predictors to enhance the final frailty level predictor with a 3-level definition.

We can work also in the redesign of the data base, for example doing all de previous steps to a data set with one observation per patient (only last sample, the average of the samples or the weighted average of the samples).

Acknowledgements. This work was partially supported by the Spanish Ministry of Ciencia, Innovación y Universidades under project RTI2018-096701-B-C22, and by the Catalonia FEDER program, resolution GAH/815/2018 under the project, PECT Garraf: Envelliment actiu i saludable i dependència.

References

1. Campbell, A.J., Buchner, D.M.: Unstable disability and the fluctuations of frailty. Age Ageing **26**, 315–318 (1997)
2. Morley, J.E., et al.: Frailty consensus: a call to action. J. Am. Med. Dir. Assoc. **14**, 392–397 (2013)
3. Collard, R.M., Boter, H., Schoevers, R.A., Oude Voshaar, R.C.: Prevalence of frailty in community-dwelling older persons: a systematic review. J. Am. Geriatr. Soc. **60**, 1487–1492 (2012)
4. Clegg, A., Young, J., Iliffe, S., Olde Rikkert, M.G.M., Rockwood, K.: Frailty in older people. Lancet **381**, 752–762 (2013)
5. Rockwood, K., et al.: A global clinical measure of fitness and frailty in elderly people. Can. Med. Assoc. J. **173**, 489–495 (2005)
6. Giampaoli, S., Ferrucci, L., Cecchi, F., et al.: Hand-grip strength predicts incident disability in non-disabled older men. Age Ageing **28**, 283–288 (1999)
7. Sousa-Santos, A.R., Amaral, T.F.: Differences in handgrip strength protocols to identify sarcopenia and frailty - a systematic review. BMC Geriatr **17**(1), 238 (2017)
8. Richards, L.G., Olson, B., Palmiter-Thomas, P.: How forearm position affects grip strength. Am. J. Occup. Ther. **50**, 133–138 (1996)
9. Alahmari, K.A., Silvian, S.P., Reddy, R.S., et al.: Hand grip strength determination for healthy males in Saudi Arabia: a study of the relationship with age, body mass index, hand length and forearm circumference using a hand-held dynamometer. J. Int. Med. Res. **45**, 540–548 (2017)
10. Desrosiers, J., Bravo, G., Hébert, R., Dutil, E.: Normative data for grip strength of elderly men and women. Am. J. Occup. Ther. Off. Publ. Am. Occup. Ther. Assoc. **49**, 637–644 (1995)
11. Innes, E.: Handgrip strength testing: a review of the literature. Aust. Occup. Ther. J. **46**(3), 120–140 (1999)
12. Kamimura, T., Ikuta, Y.: Evaluation of grip strength with a sustained maximal isometric contraction for 6 and 10 seconds. J. Rehabil. Med. **33**(5), 225–229 (2001)
13. Sindhu, B.S., Shechtman, O.: Using the force-time curve to determine sincerity of effort in people with upper extremity injuries. J. Hand Ther. **24**, 22–30 (2011)
14. Bhuanantanondh, P., Nanta, P., Mekhora, K.: Determining sincerity of effort based on grip strength test in three wrist positions. Saf. Health Work **9**, 59–62 (2018)
15. De Dobbeleer, L., Beyer, I., Njemini, R., et al.: Force-time characteristics during sustained maximal handgrip effort according to age and clinical condition. Exp. Gerontol. **98**, 192–198 (2017)
16. Rodríguez-Martín, D., Pérez-López, C., Samà, A., et al.: A waist-worn inertial measurement unit for long-term monitoring of Parkinson's disease patients. Sensors **17**(4), 827 (2017)
17. Fried, L.P., Tangen, C.M., Walston, J., et al.: Frailty in older adults: evidence for a phenotype. J. Gerontol. A. Biol. Sci. Med. Sci. **56**(3), M146–M156 (2001)
18. Redin, J.M.: Valoración geriátrica integral (I). Evaluación del paciente geriátrico y concepto de fragilidad. ANALES del Sistema Sanitario de Navarra **22**(1), 41–50 (1999)
19. Mahoney, F.I., Barthel, D.W.: Functional evaluation: the barthel index. Md State Med. J. **14**, 61–65 (1965)
20. Carla, G.: The lawton instrumental activities of daily living scale. Am. J. Nurs. **17**(5), 343–344 (2008)

Accuracy and Intrusiveness in Data-Driven Violin Players Skill Levels Prediction: MOCAP Against MYO Against KINECT

Vincenzo D'Amato, Erica Volta, Luca Oneto[✉], Gualtiero Volpe,
Antonio Camurri, and Davide Anguita

DIBRIS Department, University of Genoa, Via Opera Pia 13, 16145 Genoa, Italy
{Vincenzo.DAmato,Erica.Volta,Luca.Oneto,Gualtiero.Volpe,
Antonio.Camurri,Davide.Anguita}@unige.it

Abstract. Learning to play and perform violin is a complex task, that requires a high conscious control and coordination for the player. In this paper, our aim is to understand which technology and which motion features can be used to efficiently and effectively distinguish a professional performance from a student one trading off intrusiveness and accuracy. We collected and made freely available a dataset consisting of Motion Capture (MOCAP), Electromyography, Accelerometer, and Gyroscope (MYO), and Microsoft Kinect (KINECT) recordings of different violinists with different skills performing different exercises covering different pedagogical and technical aspects. We then engineered peculiar features starting from the different sources (MOCAP, MYO, and KINECT) and trained a data-driven classifier to distinguish among two different levels of violinist experience, namely Beginners and Experts. We then studied how much accuracy do we loose when, instead of using MOCAP data (the most intrusive and costly technology), MYO data (which is less intrusive than MOCAP), or the KINECT data (the less intrusive technology) are exploited. In accordance with the hierarchy present in the dataset, we study two different scenarios: extrapolation with respect to different exercises and violinists. Furthermore we study which features are the most predictive ones of the quality of a violinist to corroborate the significance of the results. Results, both in terms of accuracy and insight on the cognitive problem, support the proposal and support the use of the presented technique as an effective tool for students to monitor and enhance their home study and practice.

Keywords: Movement technology · Music education · Music learning technology · Multimodal interactive systems · Motion capture · Electromyography · Kinect · Machine learning · Feature engineering · Feature ranking

© Springer Nature Switzerland AG 2021
I. Rojas et al. (Eds.): IWANN 2021, LNCS 12862, pp. 367–379, 2021.
https://doi.org/10.1007/978-3-030-85099-9_30

1   Introduction

Individual practice is a fundamental – but often problematic – learning process for any student and consequently also in music education. In [22,26] it is studied how the major issues are the students' lack of methodical rehearsals' planning and effective study methodology. Moreover, as shown in [5], the students' learning outcomes improve as they acquired more awareness in their study methodology. In [2] it is studied how students subject to long period of self-studying tend to drop the practice and authors of [15] showed how weekly lessons are not enough to make students more self aware, improve their study methodology, and reduce dropout.

Recent technology can provide and effective support to students individual practice, especially in learning to play and perform music instrument, by automating teachers feedback about the correct execution of movements. The motor learning theory and technology-based systems for analysis can be useful tools in understanding motor skills needed in music performances, monitoring improvements or mistakes, and evaluating learning efficiency [24]. Following these findings, many researchers are focusing on how motion analysis technologies can be used to improve music performances and learning outcomes, also minimizing the risk of injuries [25,36]. Different data sources can be used for this purpose: from Motion Capture data (MOCAP), to Electromyography, Accelerometers, Rotations, and Gyroscopes data (MYO), and to Microsoft Kinect data (KINECT). These data can be exploited by the most recent Machine Learning (ML) techniques in order to extract actionable information and automatize process that are often acquired by years of experience of the teachers. Several contributions in this field have been proposed where these data sources are exploited to study musicians and their musical performance using MOCAP [7,10,12,14], MYO [11,13] and KINECT [29,39] with the purpose of supporting the students individual practice.

The study of body movements in music instrument learning recently (but also in the past [23]) is attracting the interest of many researchers. In fact, improvements in motion analysis technologies have unlocked the shift from qualitative [30] to quantitative [19] approaches. Most of the works study kinematic features of body movements and specific aspects of the motor performance. In Turner-Stokes et al. [34] study, for example, rotation in the upper limb movement in the bowing is investigated. Visentin et al. [35], instead, study biomechanics of left-hand position changes. Baader et al. [3] study bimanual coordination in violinists playing repeatedly a simple tone sequence while Ng et al. [27] study the relationships between the bow, the instrument and the body.

In this study, we want to understand how to help beginner violinists to enhance their motor skills in order to help them during their individual practice. For this purpose, we try to automatically detect if a movement is performed by an experienced violinist or a beginner. This allows both to provide an automatic feedback to the student and to identify what movement features are important to improve beginners' violin skills. Moreover, in this work we want to investigate how less intrusive and cheaper data sources can still produce high recognition performances, enabling the use of these technologies from a large audience. In particular, we will compare for the first time MOCAP (the most intrusive and costly technology) with MYO (a less costly but still intrusive technology) and with KINECT (the less expensive and the most non-intrusive technology). This study is the prosecution of a previous work of the authors [14], where only MOCAP data were exploited. In this paper, we exploited the recording of three renowned violinists, selected by the Royal College of Music of London (RCM), and two beginners. The dataset consists in 5 bow-violin techniques, chosen by teachers of the RCM, from various sources of classical violin pedagogy literature. These exercises focused on several techniques considered important in the training process of a violinist, such as: repertoire pieces, technique on both hands, handling the instrument and articulation studies. Then we propose the combination of carefully crafted features in combination with Random Forest [6] (RF) to lead our classification target. To replicate real application scenarios, we exploited the intrinsic hierarchy present in the dataset individuating two different ones: extrapolation with respect to different exercises and players. Results, both in terms of classification metrics and insight on the problem, will demonstrate the reasonableness of the results obtained as a support tool in the practice of less experienced violists. In particular we will show that the KINECT, while being the less expensive and the most non-intrusive technology, is still able to provide accurate results with respect to use MOCAP and MYO.

The remaining paper is organized as follows. The problem description and related data is reported in Sect. 2. The description of the proposed data-driven methodology is presented in Sect. 3. The results of applying the methods presented in Sect. 3 on the problem described in Sect. 2 is reported in Sect. 4. The feature ranking is reported in Sect. 4.2. Finally, Sect. 5 concludes the paper.

2   Data Description

In this study, we employed the data collected during the H2020 ICT-TELMI Project[1]. The main goals of the project were essentially two: the firs one was to understand how violin playing is learned, and the second was to design technologies able to effectively support the learning phases. Royal College of Music of London (RCM) suggested to collect data regarding a series of typical exercises performed during the learning path of classical violin conservatoire programs. The pedagogical materials was divided into three groups

– posture exercises for beginners, including how to handle the instrument, bow techniques, and fingering;
– techniques studies, including vibrato and different articulation exercises;
– repertoire pieces as examples of expressive performances.

The use of both custom and pre-existing exercises was deliberate and they were selected from different sources

---

[1] http://telmi.upf.edu/.

- some were taken from the standard published catalog of exercises, e.g. Schradieck, Ševčík, and Kreutzer;
- other ones are sourced or adapted from the Associated Board of the Royal Schools of Music (ABRSM) examination syllabus;
- the last ones were customised exercises developed by M. Mitchell, high-level performer and teacher from RCM, to address specific techniques and focus on the capabilities offered by non notated feedback (e.g. bowing exercises).

All the recordings took place at the Casa Paganini InfoMus research centre of the University of Genova[2]. We collected data about 5 violinists (3 experts selected by the RCM and 2 beginners) playing 5 bow-violin techniques such as left hand articulation, bowing techniques and repertoire pieces. Musicians' performance movements-related data were collected using three different sources: MOCAP, MYO sensors, and KINECT. Moreover, as MOCAP allows an extension of markers to track objects, also bow and violin were tracked in order to enrich the details about the movements of the players. The information about the collected data (players, exercises, and data sources) is summarized in Table 1. Table 1 shows that for MOCAP more exercises are available (since at the beginning of the data collection MYO and KINNECT were not available) while the number of players is the same across the different sources. Note also, from Table 1, that more exercises are present for experts with respect to beginners.

Table 1. Information about the collected data: players, exercises, and data sources.

Source		MOCAP	MYO	KINECT
Skill level	n° of violinists	n° of exercises	n° of exercises	n° of exercises
Experts	3	32	29	31
Beginners	2	20	12	12
Total	5	52	41	43

Regarding the MOCAP data, exploiting the experience of the expert players and the teachers of the RCM, we extracted 14 low-level features starting from the MOCAP skeleton data using the EyesWeb XMI platform[3] [9]. These features, according to the literature, potentially fully describe the movements characterizing the skill-level of violinists. These are the 14 low-level features: mean Shoulders' velocity, shoulder low back asymmetry, upper body kinetic energy, left/right shoulder height, bow-violin incidence, distance low/middle/upper bow-violin, hand-violin incidence, left/right head inclination, and left/right wrist roundness. Note that MOCAP require to put markers on both players and violin so intruding into their habits (see Fig. 1a).

---

[2] www.casapaganini.org.
[3] http://www.infomus.org/eyesweb_eng.php.

Physiological data were captured using 2 MYO sensors located on both fore-arms of each musicians, as depicted in Fig. 1b. A MYO device has eight elec-tromyographic (EMG) sensors that measure muscle tension and an inertial mea-surement unit (IMU) with triaxial accelerometer, gyroscope, and magnometer. The accelerometer component measures linear accelerations, the gyroscopes mea-sures angular accelerations, and the magnetometer measures the magnetic fields. Magnetometer exploited in conjunction with accelerometer and gyroscope data to determine the absolute heading.

The KINECT, like the MOCAP, is able to reconstruct a person's skeleton. However, bow and violin positions cannot be tracked using this device and then we miss 4 features with respect to the MOCAP data: the feature regarding bow-violin incidence, and the three features concerning bow-violin distances. Note that KINECT is the most unobtrusive technologies, being also the cheapest, since it can work in the wild with no device to be places on the player.

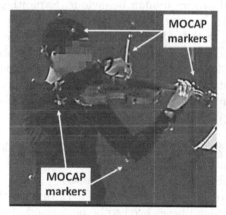 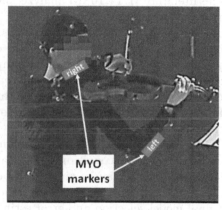

(a) MOCAP sensors on a player.   (b) MYO sensors on a player.

Fig. 1. MOCAP and MYO sensors on a player

As mentioned in the introduction our goal is to understand if it is possible to use MOCAP, KINECT, or MYO data produced by a players to automatically label it as expert or beginner. In particular we would like also to understand the trade off between accuracy and intrusiveness.

3 Methods

The task described in the previous sections can be easily mapped into a binary classification problem [33] where the input are the data of MOCAP, KINECT, or MYO and the output is the experience of the player (expert or beginner). Many algorithms can address binary classification problems [33] but Random Forest (RF) has shown to be one of the most effective ones [6,17,37] expecially in this context [14]. The RF forest is composes by several binary Decision Trees (DTs) built via bagging and boosting [6]. RF is characterized by several hyperparameters: the number of DTs which compose the forest n_t (the larger the better if the computational budget is not an issue), the depth of each DT n_d composing the RF, the cardinality of the random subset of n_v features (over the whole n_f features composing the dataset) to be sampled in the DT node optimization, and the number of sample n_b to be bootstrapped from the total number of samples in the datasets.

In order to leverage on RF for solving our task, we need first to extract and engineer features from the raw data described in Sect. 2. For each data sources (MOCAP, MYO, and KINECT), which is composed by a group of time series (e.g., acceleration over the x-axis collected by the MYO or the upper body kinetic energy collected with MOCAP and KINECT during the performance of the players), we sampled data using fixed-width sliding windows of 10 seconds with overlap of 50% in time. This temporal heuristic has already proven effective in the literature [1,14,16] to analyze and predict human behaviour. Exploiting the literature on the topic [1,4,14,32,38], we extracted a series of measures from these data using sliding windows: statistical measures in time and frequency domains (e.g., mean, signal-pair correlation, and signal magnitude area). Moreover, a new set of features was employed in order to improve the learning performance, including energy of different frequency bands, frequency skewness, and frequency kurtosis. The resulting three datasets has been made freely available for the research community[4] where it possible to find the details of all the extracted features.

Many different metrics can be used in binary classification in order to provide insights about the recognition performances of the model [33]. In this work we will measure performances via overall percentage of accuracy (ACC).

To select the best set of hyperparameters and to estimate the performance of the final model selection and error estimation phases need to be performed [28]. In this work, we exploited resampling techniques where the dataset $\mathcal{D}$ is resampled n_r times splitting it in three independent datasets called learning $\mathcal{L}$, validation $\mathcal{V}$ and test $\mathcal{T}$ averaging the results. $\mathcal{L}$ is used to train the model, $\mathcal{V}$ to estimate the best hyperparameters, and $\mathcal{T}$ to estimate the final performance. In particular, in our work, the complete k-fold cross validation is exploited [28].

Once the best models are trained we still need to get insight over the problem by understanding how these models leverage on the provided data. This step was useful in order to understand if the learning process has also a cognitive meaning, or in other words, if it is able to capture the underline phenomena and not just capture spurious correlation [8,21]. For this purpose we need to analyzed the insights of the models with the knowledge of the domain experts. Feature Ranking is an easy way to address this problem since it allows to detect if an appropriate match between relevant features detected by the algorithm and domain knowledge. This match is a fundamental phase of model checking

---

[4] https://www.dropbox.com/sh/n17nvgahrnq4g5j/AAB4zYEHbKeOCoTkIt40 pdvMa.

and verification, since it should generate results comparable to the knowledge of the domain experts. RF allows to perform this step almost at no extra cost exploiting permutation test and Mean Decrease in Accuracy metric [18,20,31]. Note that, as features we intend the raw feature (e.g. upper body kinetic energy, mean shoulder velocity, etc. for both MOCAP data or KINECT data, or IMU and EMG information for both hands for MYO data) and not a particular engineered one (e.g., mean upper body kinetic energy) since we want to proved high level insights on the problem.

In order to understand the extrapolation capability of the data-driven models, we studied two scenarios

- Leave One Person Out (LOPO): in this scenario the model has been trained with all the subject excepts one that will be exploited to test the resulting model;
- Leave One Exercise Out (LOEO): in this scenario the model has been trained with all the exercises except one that will be exploited to test the resulting model.

Basically the two scenarios just differ in the definitions of the learning, validation and test sets, that are the subset of data exploited for building, tuning and testing the models. For instance, in the LOPO scenario learning, validation and test sets have been created by randomly selecting data from one person to be inserted in the test set, from another person to be inserted in validation set, and from the remaining ones to be inserted into learning set. For the LOEO scenario, we have the same procedure of the LOPO one but where exercise are considered instead of the people.

4   Experimental Results

In this section, we will report the results of applying the methodology presented in Sect. 3 over the data described in Sect. 2. In all the experiments we set: $n_r = 100$, $n_t = 1000$, $n_d = \infty$, $n_b = n$ (where n is the total number of dataset samples), and $n_v \in \{ {}^{1/}\!\sqrt[3]{n_f}, \sqrt{n_f}, {}^{3/}\!\sqrt[4]{n_f} \}$. Experts (violinists 1 to 3) are labeled with $Y = 0$ and beginners (violinists 4 and 5) with $Y = 1$.

4.1   Recognition Performances for LOPO and LOEO

Let us present the results for the LOPO scenario. Table 2 reports the ACC for each violinist using different sources (MOCAP, MYO, or KINECT). From Table 2, we can notice that all the three different sources allows to achieve quite high recognition performances (>78% for both MOCAP and MYO and >74% for KINECT). Therefore, the markers on the bows and violins (which are present just in the case of MOCAP as explained in Sect. 2) are not fundamental to achieve good recognition performances. Using the KINECT, in the other side, allows to drastically reduce the intrusiveness at the expenses of just 4% of ACC. Table 2 also shows which violinists are easier to label correctly as experts or beginners.

For what concerns the experts, subjects 1 and 3 are easily recognised accurately with all the data sources while subject 2 is harder to detect with MYO. KIN-NECT, contrarily to MOCAP and MYO, shows lower performance in average but is more constant over the subjects. For what concerns the beginners, very different recognition performances are obtained using different sources. Indeed, analyzing MOCAP data we can observe how the subject 4 is easy to label while the subject 5 is harder to detect. The opposite behaviour is observed when using the KINECT data while MYO has more constant behavior.

Table 2. ACC for the LOPO scenario using different sources (MOCAP, MYO, and KINECT).

Source		MOCAP		MYO		KINECT	
Expert/Beginner	Violinist	avg	std	avg	std	avg	std
0	1	98.19	0.51	100.00	0.00	89.99	2.26
	2	77.68	2.55	54.57	6.72	96.75	0.92
	3	99.73	0.40	93.33	3.78	80.40	0.39
1	4	88.89	3.05	66.34	9.48	35.21	3.01
	5	34.47	5.90	80.18	5.27	68.08	9.38
Mean		**79.79**	**2.25**	**78.88**	**3.52**	**74.09**	**3.62**

Let us present now the results for the LOEO scenario. Table 3 is the counterpart, for LOEO scenario, of Table 2. Note that we do not have all the data for all the exercises and all the players since not always the three sensors have been positioned and acquires (see '-' in Table 3). From Table 3, it is possible to observe that all the three different sources allows to achieve pretty high recognition performances (>87% for KINECT and >96% for MOCAP and MYO) even if in this case using the KINECT induces a higher loss in performances with respect to the LOPO scenario. Obviously recognition performances in the LOEO scenario are higher than in the LOPO one since we wan to simply extrapolate over the exercises an not over the subjects. As happens before, we can observe how markers placed on violin and bow are not fundamental to achieve good recognition performances since also MYO is able reach good performances. However, using KINECT allows to reduce the intrusiveness at the expenses of just 9% of ACC. Observing Table 3, we can notice how some exercises are more informative and then easier to associate with the correct label (expert or beginner). For instance, right hand exercise performed by experts 1 or 3 are easily recognised accurately with all the data sources. A similar behavior is observable when articulation and left hand technique are performed by the beginner players 5. Unfortunately, violinist 4 is the most penalized exploiting both MYO and KINECT data as 3 out of 5 exercises are missing. Note also that some obtained results may seem counter-intuitive compared to what we might expect. Indeed, we may think that the technique exercise is the most discriminating one in the analysis of the skill-level of each violinist. In a context where only kinetic data are analyzed, this is not true as we not taking into account the quality of sound reproduced by each musician. In fact, technique exercise are performed by everyone in a classic way since they have been learned during the early stages. For this reason technique exercise are less informative since players do not show their movement expressiveness.

Table 3. ACC for the LOEO scenario using different sources (MOCAP, MYO, and KINECT). '-' means that those data (the particular combination of exercise and violinist) have not been collected so the results are not available.

Source			MOCAP		MYO		KINECT	
Expert/Beginner	Violinist	Exercise	avg	std	avg	std	avg	std
0	1	Articulation	100.00	0.00	100.00	0.00	74.50	7.19
		Expressive	100.00	0.00	–	–	87.00	12.55
		Left hand	100.00	0.00	100.00	0.00	97.19	3.37
		Right hand	100.00	0.00	100.00	0.00	100.00	0.00
		Technique	89.83	6.28	–	–	97.76	1.39
	2	Articulation	99.40	0.56	98.00	1.51	99.92	0.83
		Expressive	100.00	0.00	–	–	100.00	0.00
		Left hand	86.23	4.18	98.47	1.50	96.35	3.14
		Right hand	100.00	0.00	85.19	4.91	100.00	0.00
		Technique	88.01	5.02	100.00	0.00	86.00	3.91
	3	Articulation	100.00	0.00	100.00	0.00	99.79	0.47
		Expressive	100.00	0.00	–	–	64.67	7.96
		Left hand	100.00	0.00	99.33	2.01	100.00	0.00
		Right hand	100.00	0.00	100.00	0.00	96.50	7.96
		Technique	99.81	0.40	100.00	0.00	79.03	2.37
1	4	Articulation	100.00	0.00	94.83	1.64	–	–
		Expressive	100.00	0.00	–	–	79.00	9.87
		Left hand	98.56	3.76	95.67	0.82	–	–
		Right hand	87.07	7.97	–	–	–	–
		Technique	100.00	0.00	–	–	59.97	5.07
	5	Articulation	100.00	0.00	99.75	2.50	99.63	0.54
		Expressive	100.00	0.00	–	–	91.50	18.88
		Left hand	100.00	0.00	98.54	0.92	100.00	0.00
		Right hand	100.00	0.00	89.00	1.11	33.08	7.38
		Technique	95.08	0.83	98.40	1.00	87.17	2.82
Mean			**96.98**	**5.31**	**98.15**	**2.08**	**87.85**	**6.30**

4.2 Feature Ranking

In order to understand the relevance of each raw feature, for each source described in Sect. 2, in the classification between expert or beginner players we exploited the methodology presented in Sect. 3. We analized the LOPO scenario which is the most practical one (being able to extrapolate among different players). Table 4 reports the feature ranking of the raw features for each source exploited. Since in the analysis of both MOCAP and KINECT data we leveraged on features extracted from skeletons, they are easily comparable. For MYO they are not so comparable since it measures different aspects of the movements. Table 4 allow us to observe that the most relevant features are often similar between MOCAP and KINECT (e.g., the wrist roundness, the overall upper body kinetic energy, and the hand violin incidence). We also observe that left shoulder height is ranked as unimportant for both MOCAP and KINECT. These results validates the soundness of the proposal: MOCAP and KINECT data can actually extract properties of the movement effectively focusing on physical plausible aspects. For what concerns the MYO results, it is possible to observe that the most relevant features refers to movements performed by left arm (the arm that held the violin) which is the most reasonable result that we expected. The relevant features detected in this work confirm what was previously investigated in [14], where the most predictive MOCAP (and then also KINECT) related features depended mainly on the upper body kinetic energy and on the left hand/arm movements. Finally, domain experts validated our results in terms of feature ranking agreeing with the results achieved by our algorithm. This process highlights how our model learns in an effective way movements concerning to the correct execution of music task.

Table 4. Raw features ranking for the LOPO scenario using different sources (MOCAP, MYO, and KINECT).

Rank	Data		
	MOCAP	MYO	KINECT
	Raw features	Raw features	Raw features
1	Upper body kinetic energy	Left arm rotation	Right wrist roundness
2	Mean shoulder's velocity	Left arm gyroscope	Left wrist roundness
3	Hand violin incidence	Left arm EMG	Hand violin incidence
4	Distance lower bow violin	Right arm gyroscope	Upper body kinetic energy
5	Left wrist roundness	Right arm acceleration	Left head inclination
6	Right shoulder height	Left arm acceleration	Right shoulder height
7	Right head inclination	Right arm EMG	Mean shoulder's velocity
8	Right wrist roundness	Right arm rotation	Right head inclination
9	Shoulder low back asymmetry		Shoulder low back asymmetry
10	Left head inclination		Left shoulder height
11	Bow violin incidence		
12	Distance upper bow violin		
13	Distance middle bow violin		
14	Left shoulder height		

5 Conclusions

The main goal of this work was to understand which technology (MOCAP or MYO or KINECT) and which motion features (that we carefully engineered based on domain experts and literature review) can be used to efficiently and effectively to distinguish a professional violin player from a student trading off intrusiveness and accuracy. For this purpose we first collected and made freely available a dataset consisting of MOCAP, MYO, and KINECT recordings of different violinists with different skills performing different exercises covering different pedagogical and technical aspects. We then engineered peculiar features starting from the different sources (MOCAP, MYO, and KINECT) and trained a data-driven classifier to distinguish among two different levels of violinist experience, namely Beginners and Experts. We then studied how much accuracy do we loose when, instead of using MOCAP data (the most intrusive and costly technology), MYO data (which is less intrusive than MOCAP), or the KINECT data (the less intrusive technology) are exploited in two different extrapolation scenarios (i.e., extrapolating over players and extrapolation over exercises). In the most interesting scenario (i.e., being able to extrapolate over players) we discover that using the most unintrusive technology (i.e., the KINECT) only reduces the recognition performance of 4% (out of 79%), which means that the lost in accuracy is negligible with respect to having a fully unintrusive and afford able supporting tool. We then studied (together with domain experts) that the most predictive raw features ranked by the algorithms to predict the quality of a violinist to corroborate the significance of the results observing how recognition performances depend directly on the confidence with the instrument and mainly on movements of the left hand that holds the instrument. Results, both in terms of accuracy and insight on the cognitive problem, support the proposal and support the use of the proposed technique as a support tool for students to monitor and enhance their home study and practice. In conclusion, we demonstrated how the Microsof KINECT (the less intrusive and the much cheaper device) can be used to provide an affordable and effective application to assist students learning violin.

Acknowledgments. This work is partially supported by the University of Genova through the Bando per l'incentivazione alla progettazione europea 2019 - Mission 1 "Promoting Competitiveness", the EU-H2020-ICT Project TELMI (G.A. 688269), and the EU-H2020-FETPROACT Project ENTIMEMENT (G.A. 824160).

References

1. Anguita, D., Ghio, A., Oneto, L., Parra, X., Reyes-Ortiz, J.L.: Human activity recognition on smartphones using a multiclass hardware-friendly support vector machine. In: International Workshop on Ambient Assisted Living (2012)
2. Aróstegui, J.L.: Educating Music Teachers for the 21st Century. Springer Science & Business Media, Rotterdam (2011). https://doi.org/10.1007/978-94-6091-503-1
3. Baader, A.P., Kazennikov, O., Wiesendanger, M.: Coordination of bowing and fingering in violin playing. Cogn. Brain Res. **23**(2–3), 436–443 (2005)

4. Bao, L., Intille, S.S.: Activity recognition from user-annotated acceleration data. In: International Conference on Pervasive Computing (2004)
5. Barry, N.H.: The effects of practice strategies, individual differences in cognitive style, and gender upon technical accuracy and musicality of student instrumental performance. Psychol. Music **20**(2), 112–123 (1992)
6. Breiman, L.: Random forests. Mach. Learn. **45**(1), 5–32 (2001)
7. Butepage, J., Black, M.J., Kragic, D., Kjellstrom, H.: Deep representation learning for human motion prediction and classification. In: IEEE Conference on Computer Vision and Pattern Recognition (2017)
8. Calude, C.S., Longo, G.: The deluge of spurious correlations in big data. Found. Sci. **22**(3), 595–612 (2017)
9. Camurri, A., Coletta, P., Varni, G., Ghisio, S.: Developing multimodal interactive systems with EyesWeb XMI. In: International Conference on New Interfaces for Musical Expression (2007)
10. Cho, K., Chen, X.: Classifying and visualizing motion capture sequences using deep neural networks. In: International Conference on Computer Vision Theory and Applications (2014)
11. Dalmazzo, D., Ramírez, R.: Bow gesture classification to identify three different expertise levels: a machine learning approach. In: Cellier, P., Driessens, K. (eds.) ECML PKDD 2019. CCIS, vol. 1168, pp. 494–501. Springer, Cham (2020). https://doi.org/10.1007/978-3-030-43887-6_43
12. Dalmazzo, D., Ramírez, R.: Bowing gestures classification in violin performance: a machine learning approach. Front. Psychol. **10**, 344 (2019)
13. Dalmazzo, D., Tassani, S., Ramírez, R.: A machine learning approach to violin bow technique classification: a comparison between IMU and MOCAP systems. In: International Workshop on Sensor-Based Activity Recognition and Interaction (2018)
14. D'Amato, V., Volta, E., Oneto, L., Volpe, G., Camurri, A., Anguita, D.: Understanding violin players' skill level based on motion capture: a data-driven perspective. Cogn. Comput. **12**(6), 1356–1369 (2020)
15. Davidson, J.W.: Visual perception of performance manner in the movements of solo musicians. Psychol. Music **21**(2), 103–113 (1993)
16. DeVaul, R.W., Dunn, S.: Real-time motion classification for wearable computing applications. MIT Technical Report (2001)
17. Fernández-Delgado, M., Cernadas, E., Barro, S., Amorim, D.: Do we need hundreds of classifiers to solve real world classification problems? J. Mach. Learn. Res. **15**(1), 3133–3181 (2014)
18. Genuer, R., Poggi, J.M., Tuleau-Malot, C.: Variable selection using random forests. Pattern Recogn. Lett. **31**(14), 2225–2236 (2010)
19. Goebl, W., Dixon, S., Schubert, E.: Quantitative methods: Motion analysis, audio analysis, and continuous response techniques. In: Expressiveness in Music Performance: Empirical Approaches Across Styles and Cultures, pp. 221–239 (2014)
20. Good, P.: Permutation Tests: A Practical Guide to Resampling Methods for Testing Hypotheses. Springer, New York (2013). https://doi.org/10.1007/978-1-4757-2346-5
21. Guyon, I., Elisseeff, A.: An introduction to variable and feature selection. J. Mach. Learn. Res. **3**(Mar), 1157–1182 (2003)
22. Hallam, S.: The development of metacognition in musicians: implications for education. Br. J. Music Educ. **18**(1), 27–39 (2001)
23. Jacobs, C.: Investigation of kinesthetics in violin playing. J. Res. Music Educ. **17**(1), 112–114 (1969)

24. Magill, R., Anderson, D.: Motor Learning and Control. McGraw-Hill Publishing, New York (2010)

25. Marquez-Borbon, A.: Perceptual learning and the emergence of performer-instrument interactions with digital music systems. In: Proceedings of a Body of Knowledge - Embodied Cognition and the Arts conference (2018)

26. McPherson, G.E., Renwick, J.M.: A longitudinal study of self-regulation in children's musical practice. Music Educ. Res. **3**(2), 169–186 (2001)

27. Ng, K., Larkin, O., Koerselman, T., Ong, B.: i-maestro gesture and posture support: 3D motion data visualisation for music learning and playing. In: London International Conference (2007)

28. Oneto, L.: Model Selection and Error Estimation in a Nutshell. MOST, vol. 15. Springer, Cham (2020). https://doi.org/10.1007/978-3-030-24359-3

29. Rosa-Pujazón, A., Barbancho, I., Tardón, L.J., Barbancho, A.M.: Fast-gesture recognition and classification using kinect: an application for a virtual reality drumkit. Multimedia Tools Appl. **75**(14), 8137–8164 (2016)

30. Ruggieri, V., Katsnelson, A.: An analysis of a performance by the violinist D. Oistrakh: the hypothetical role of postural tonic-static and entourage movements. Percept. Mot. Skills **82**(1), 291–300 (1996)

31. Saeys, Y., Abeel, T., Van de Peer, Y.: Robust feature selection using ensemble feature selection techniques. In: Daelemans, W., Goethals, B., Morik, K. (eds.) ECML PKDD 2008. LNCS (LNAI), vol. 5212, pp. 313–325. Springer, Heidelberg (2008). https://doi.org/10.1007/978-3-540-87481-2_21

32. Sama, A., Pardo-Ayala, D.E., Cabestany, J., Rodríguez-Molinero, A.: Time series analysis of inertial-body signals for the extraction of dynamic properties from human gait. In: International Joint Conference on Neural Networks (2010)

33. Shalev-Shwartz, S., Ben-David, S.: Understanding Machine Learning: From Theory To Algorithms. Cambridge University Press (2014)

34. Turner-Stokes, L., Reid, K.: Three-dimensional motion analysis of upper limb movement in the bowing arm of string-playing musicians. Clin. Biomech. **14**(6), 426–433 (1999)

35. Visentin, P., Li, S., Tardif, G., Shan, G.: Unraveling mysteries of personal performance style; biomechanics of left-hand position changes (shifting) in violin performance. Peer J. **3**, e1299 (2015)

36. Volta, E., Mancini, M., Varni, G., Volpe, G.: Automatically measuring biomechanical skills of violin performance: an exploratory study. In: International Conference on Movement and Computing (2018)

37. Wainberg, M., Alipanahi, B., Frey, B.J.: Are random forests truly the best classifiers? J. Mach. Learn. Res. **17**(1), 3837–3841 (2016)

38. Wang, N., Ambikairajah, E., Lovell, N.H., Celler, B.G.: Accelerometry based classification of walking patterns using time-frequency analysis. In: IEEE Engineering in Medicine and Biology Society (2007)

39. Zlatintsi, A., et al.: In: A web-based real-time kinect application for gestural interaction with virtual musical instruments, pp. 1–6. Sound in Immersion and Emotion (2018)

Features Selection for Fall Detection Systems Based on Machine Learning and Accelerometer Signals

Carlos A. Silva[1,2]([⊠]), Rodolfo García–Bermúdez[1]([⊠]), and Eduardo Casilari[2]([⊠])

[1] Universidad Técnica de Manabí, Manabí, Ecuador
{carlos.silva,rodolfo.garcia}@utm.edu.ec
[2] Departamento de Tecnología Electrónica, Universidad de Málaga, Málaga, España
ecasilari@uma.es

Abstract. Fall among older people is a major medical concern. Fall Detection Systems (FDSs) have been actively investigated to solve this problem. In this sense, FDSs must effectively reduce both the rates of false alarms and unnoticed fall. In this work we carry out a systematic evaluation of the performance of one of the most widely used machine learning supervised algorithm (Support Vector Machine) when using different input features. To evaluate the impact of the feature selection, we use Area Under the Curve (AUC) of Receiver Operating Characteristic (ROC) Curve as the performance metric. The results showed that with four features it is possible to obtain acceptable values for the detection of falls using accelerometer signals obtained from the user's waist. In addition, we also investigate if the impact of selecting the features based on the analysis of a dataset different from the final application framework where the detector will be operative.

Keywords: Fall detection system · Supervised algorithm · Accelerometer · Wearables · Support vector machine · Feature selection

1 Introduction

The World Health Organization (WHO) has estimated a growth in the number of people over 60 years of age worldwide who annually suffer a fall from 688 million in 2006 to two billion by 2050 [1]. Falls are one of the main causes of morbidity and mortality among elderly as they can provoke from damage to wrists to hip fractures or even traumatic brain injuries [2].

Automatic Fall Detection Systems (FDSs) are being actively investigated in order to solve this problem. An FDS can be defined as a binary classification system which must constantly decide if the movements executed by the subject under monitoring correspond to a possible fall or if, instead, they are originated by conventional Activities of Daily Living (ADLs).

The FDSs are traditionally categorized into two groups: context-aware and wearable-based. The first group utilizes image analysis from video-camera recording, Kinect-like devices and/or other environmental sensors, such as pressure sensors or acoustic

© Springer Nature Switzerland AG 2021
I. Rojas et al. (Eds.): IWANN 2021, LNCS 12862, pp. 380–391, 2021.
https://doi.org/10.1007/978-3-030-85099-9_31

sensors. Context-aware methods present not-negligible installation and service costs as well as remarkable operational limitations due to privacy issues, camera blind spots, low device video resolution, little lighting and other visual artifacts [3]. In contrast, wearable FDSs can be transported as an extra garment or seamlessly integrated via software into conventional personal devices (such as smartwatches or even smartphones).

Due to the difficulties of systematically testing a FDS with actual falls experienced by elderly people, current FDS prototypes are typically trained, shaped and evaluated based on the movements (in particular, mimicked falls) normally generated in a controlled laboratory environment. This aspect makes us question the effectiveness of a certain FDS not only when it is applied on real world falls but also when it is extrapolated to detect falls with a dataset different from that used to configure the classifier.

FDS algorithms can be grouped into threshold-based techniques and detectors implemented on supervised learning or Machine Learning (ML) strategies. One of the issues for FDSs based on thresholds is finding an appropriate value for the threshold able to accurately differentiate falls from ADLs [4]. Therefore, supervised learning algorithms are commonly preferred. In this regard, a key element for the definition of any supervised learning is the election of the features with which input data are characterized.

This work carries out a systematic evaluation of the impact of the selection of the input features. The goal is to assess if the selection of features based on the analysis of a certain dataset is a good choice when a different dataset (with different movements and users) is considered. For this purpose, the study focuses on the behavior of a popular machine learning algorithm (Support Vector Machine -SVM-) when it is applied to several public datasets containing accelerometer signals from ADLs and falls.

The remainder of this paper is organized as follows: Sect. 2 reviews related works. Section 3 describes the experimental framework, including the dataset and input features selection. Section 4 presents and discusses the results. Finally, Sect. 5 recapitulates the conclusions of our work.

2 Related Works

An FDS error causes either a false negative or a false positive. The first case implies not detecting a real fall while the second provokes an unnecessary alarm as an ADL is misinterpreted as a fall. An excessive number of false positives or false alarms can cause users to consider the system to be ineffective and useless [5].

SVM is one of the most employed techniques used to implement the fall detection algorithms in wearable systems (refer, for example, to [6] or [7] for two recent reviews on detection strategies for FDSs). Many works have shown that SVM can outperform other typical ML strategies [8, 9].

In 2006, Tong Zhang et al. [10] already proposed a method based on the One-class SVM algorithm. The algorithm was tested with the movement signals of the human body using a tri-axial accelerometer. The tests were carried out with 600 samples (from 6 categories) recorded from 12 volunteers. They obtained between 80 and 100% correct detection rate using the following six features: 1) the interval between the beginning of falling and the beginning of the reverse impact, 2) the average acceleration, 3) the variance of acceleration before the impact, 4) the interval of the reverse impact, 5) the average acceleration, and 6) the variance of acceleration after the impact.

Paulo Salgado et al. [11] tested the SVM algorithm with Gaussian Kernel function using accelerometers signals collected with a smartphone located on the volunteer's torso using four features to determine the falls: 1) angular position, 2) angular rate, 3) angular acceleration and 4) radius curve. The tests showed a detection rate of 96%.

Medrano et al. [12] evaluated several supervised classifiers, including a SVM model with a Radial Basis Function kernel, using the accelerometer signals recorded with a smartphone transported by 10 volunteers, who generated 503 samples of simulated falls and 800 ADLs. Authors concluded that SVM clearly outperformed the other algorithms. Regarding to the information fed into the classifier, they have restricted this work to discriminate the acceleration shape during falls using the raw acceleration values.

Santoyo-Ramón et al. [13] used the UMAFall dataset containing data of accelerometers signals of 19 volunteers. These authors evaluated four algorithms: SVM, k-Nearest Neighbors (KNN), Naive Bayes and Decision Tree using six features: 1) Mean signal magnitude vector, 2) The maximum value of the maximum variation of the acceleration components in the three axes, 3) the standard deviation of the signal magnitude vector, 4) The mean rotation angle, 5) mean absolute difference, 6) the mean module acceleration. They concluded that the SVM algorithm achieved the performance in the detection of falls. In a subsequent work [14] they investigated the most significant features of the accelerometer signals, using the ANOVA tool for the statistical analysis of the performance. They evaluated the algorithms with three datasets, UMAFall [15], SisFall [16], and 'Erciyes' repository by Özdemir et al. [17].

In this work we focused on evaluating the importance of a set of candidates features for seven datasets commonly employed in the related literature. Random Forests (RFs) are a common tool for feature selection in machine-learning classifiers as their easy interpretability allows directly weighting the importance of each candidate feature to represent and characterize the data [18]. Thus, by using a RFs model [19] we determine which are the most relevant statistical features for each dataset. Then, we assess the performance of SVM depending on the dataset employed to select the feature set.

3   Process Description for Testbed

3.1   Data Bases Selection

The tests were carried out with publicly available datasets with accelerometer signals obtained on the volunteers' waist. In the literature, eleven public datasets, presented in Table 1, were found with this criterion. The table indicates the complete number of samples and falls for each dataset.

To characterize each movement sample in the datasets, the features are calculated by focusing on a fixed time interval (an 'observation window') within every sample. As a fall is associated to a sudden peak in the acceleration magnitude caused by the impact against the floor, this window is selected around the instant (±0.5 s) where the maximum value of the acceleration module occurs. For our research we discarded FARSEEING, SMotion, UR Fall and DLR datasets, as no falls (or an insignificant number of falls) were found after applying this windowing techniques to the corresponding traces. In the rest of the datasets, we also ignored those samples in which the acceleration peak was found in the first or last period of 0.5 s of the whole time series (so that a complete observation window of 1 s cannot be properly defined). The datasets and the number of valid samples finally employed in our tests are shown in Table 2.

Table 1. Public datasets with accelerometer signals captured on volunteers' waist.

	Name and reference	Total number of samples	Falls
1	TST Fall [20]	264	132
2	UMAFall [15]	746	208
3	SisFall [16]	4050	1798
4	Erciyes [17]	3297	1821
5	UP Fall [21]	559	255
6	IMUFD [9]	600	210
7	FallAllD [22]	6605	1722
8	DLR [23]	1017	56
9	UR Fall detection [24]	70	30
10	FARSEEING [25]	22	22
11	SMotion [26]	364	2

Table 2. Employed datasets after applying the windowing technique.

	Name	Final number of used samples	Final number of used falls
1	TST Fall	263	132
2	UMAFall	604	186
3	SisFall	4474	1797
4	Erciyes	3147	1819
5	UP Fall	505	234
6	IMUFD	591	210
7	FallAllD	1661	465

3.2 Feature Selection

In this work, we use the six 'candidate' features described in the work [14]. Additionally, we added seven extra features (see [27] for a more complete formal definition). For all the samples (ADLs or falls), the thirteen features were calculated taking into account only the triaxial signals captured by the accelerometer (located on the waist) that are provided by the seven datasets under study. The considered features are:

1. Mean Signal Magnitude Vector of the acceleration vector (***Mean SMV***).

2. The maximum value of the maximum variation of the acceleration components in the three axes (**Max diff**).
3. The standard deviation of the Signal Magnitude Vector (**Std SMV**).
4. The mean rotation angle (**Mean rotation angle**).
5. The mean absolute difference between consecutive samples of the acceleration magnitude (**Mean absolute diff**).
6. The mean acceleration of the magnitude of the vector formed by the acceleration components that are parallel to the floor plane (**Mean body inclination**).
7. Maximum value of the acceleration magnitude (**Max SMV**).
8. Minimum value of the acceleration magnitude (**Min SMV**).
9. Third central moment (skewness or bias) of the acceleration magnitude (**Skewness SMV**).
10. Fourth central moment (kurtosis) of the acceleration magnitude (**Kurtosis SMV**).
11. The mean of the autocorrelation of the acceleration magnitude within the observation window (**Mean autocorrelation**).
12. The standard deviation of the autocorrelation module the acceleration magnitude within the observation window (**Std autocorrelation**).
13. The frequency value at which the maximum of the Discrete Fourier Transform (DFT) of the acceleration magnitude is detected (**Freq DFT max**).

3.3 Classification of the Candidate Features

The capability of the different candidate features to characterize the signals was evaluated and classified through Random Forests classification [19], which fits a number of decision tree classifiers on various sub-samples of the dataset and uses averaging to improve the predictive accuracy while controlling over-fitting. For this study, one hundred trees were used. As a result, a matrix is obtained (see Table 3) with the percentage of importance of each feature for each database. As it can be observed, the relevance of each feature as a discrimination element strongly varies depending on the considered dataset.

From the previous data, aiming at defining a global classification of the features, we compute a global ranking by calculating the mean of the percentage importance value of each feature for each dataset. Figure 1 shows (in descending order) the error bar graphic with represents the mean and the standard deviation of the obtained values.

Table 3. Features importance percentage value for each dataset.

Feature	Erciyes	FallAllD	IMUFD	SisFall	TST Fall	UMAFall	UP Fall
Kurtosis SMV	0.90	3.08	0.55	1.86	0.41	0.37	0.00
Max diff	20.98	17.08	13.32	9.93	5.41	12.84	18.20
Max SMV	25.36	19.07	17.09	14.92	6.26	12.75	15.03
Freq DFT max	0.14	10.36	15.24	1.12	26.96	2.41	0.61
Mean body inclination	1.60	19.84	1.41	1.47	7.41	9.35	0.00
Mean autocorrelation	14.95	7.39	16.02	20.27	4.13	11.96	12.40
Mean rotation angle	1.32	0.83	1.85	7.53	6.59	7.58	6.23
Mean absolute diff	0.49	0.34	0.30	0.15	0.03	3.54	5.43
Mean SMV	0.09	5.36	5.68	0.83	17.23	0.78	1.39
Min SMV	3.43	3.09	0.03	1.17	1.24	4.40	5.85
Std SMV	12.14	5.69	21.36	15.27	13.69	16.36	18.84
Skewness SMV	6.75	5.70	1.31	9.53	1.25	0.89	1.75
Std autocorrelation	11.86	2.15	5.85	15.95	9.39	16.77	14.27

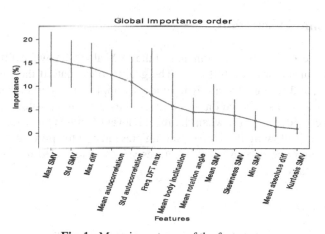

Fig. 1. Mean importance of the features.

Table 4 shows the features ordered by the mean importance percentage. This ranking does not coincide with that provided in [14], which used the ANOVA analysis. In that work authors estimated that the best global variables were: 1) Std SMV, 2) body inclination, 3) max diff, 4) rotation angle, 5) absolute difference and 6) mean SMV.

Table 4. Global feature ranking.

Order	Feature	Mean importance (%)
1	Max SMV	15.78
2	Std SMV	14.76
3	Max diff	13.97
4	Mean autocorrelation	12.45
5	Std autocorrelation	10.89
6	Freq DFT max	8.12
7	Mean body inclination	5.87
8	Mean rotation angle	4.56
9	Mean SMV	4.48
10	Skewness SMV	3.88
11	Min SMV	2.74
12	Mean absolute diff	1.47
13	Kurtosis SMV	1.02

4   Results and Discussion

In this section, we analyze the performance of the SVM algorithm when different criteria to select the input features are followed. The goal is to evaluate if the performance of the ML technique degrades when it is individually applied to a certain dataset, but the selection of the features is based on the analysis of a different repository. In this framework we also consider the case when the most relevant features are selected according to the mean case (following the global ranking presented in the previous tables).

Before training and testing, all the features values were scaled following a typical Z-score normalization [28].

4.1   Model Selection

For the study, we utilized Python and the implementation of the SVM algorithm provided by the *scikit-learn* package [29]. The SVM algorithm was evaluated with the following kernels: linear, polynomial, Radial Basis Function (RBF) and Sigmoid. The RBF kernel offered the best results, so the following tests were based on SVM configured with this kernel.

When training an SVM with the RBF kernel, two parameters must be considered: C and *gamma*. The parameter C, common to all SVM kernels, trades off misclassification of training examples against simplicity of the decision surface. The *gamma* parameter in turn defines the influence of a single training example [29]. The optimal values for the C and *gamma* parameters were set through a "fit" and a "score" method provided by *scikit-learn* package [30].

4.2 Model Training and Evaluation

We evaluated the performance of the SVM algorithm with a variable number of input features (from 1 to 13), taking into the rank obtained for both the global and particular analysis of the datasets. Model training is achieved with 70% of falls and 70% of the ADL while testing is carried out with the remaining 30% of samples. Whenever a new test is triggered, an extra feature is added according to 1) the rank established by the dataset under analysis ('self-order'), 2) the global rank, 3 and 4) the rank defined by the analysis of two particular datasets (SisFall and UMAFall, as they have been frequently utilized by the related literature).

As a performance metric, we use Area Under the Curve (AUC) of Receiver Operating Characteristic (ROC) Curve. The AUC provides an aggregate measure of performance across all possible classification thresholds [31]. Figure 2 shows the ROC AUC values of the evaluations for each dataset for the four feature selection criteria and for the 13 possible combinations of features. Results show that, for almost all datasets and for a low number of features, basing the selection on the global analysis of all datasets leads to a certain increase of the performance of the detection algorithm, when it is compared with the case in which just a single dataset is considered as the unique reference (SisFall and UMAFall) to rank and select the features. This performance increase in the detection algorithm is more remarkable with the FallAllD dataset.

Another important aspect when dealing with ML strategies is the reduction of the number of features, as a lower dimension of the features may ease the implementation of the algorithm in low cost devices with limited computation resources. In this regard, from Fig. 2 we observe that an increase of the number of features beyond 4 or 5 does not imply a significant improvement of the performance metric if the selection of features is based on the global knowledge. The values of AUC are tabulated in Table 5 for the case in which the four most relevant features are selected to characterize the data. The table also shows the sensitivity (Se) and specificity (Sp) values (for the optimal configuration of the SVM), which are also basic metrics to evaluate binary classifiers.

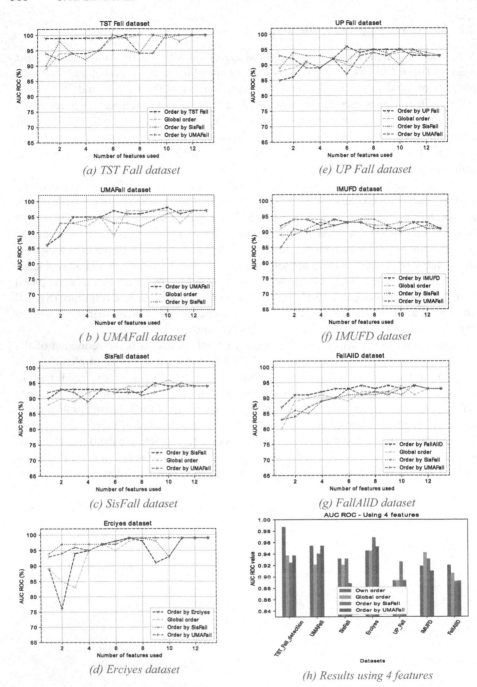

(a) TST Fall dataset

(b) UMAFall dataset

(c) SisFall dataset

(d) Erciyes dataset

(e) UP Fall dataset

(f) IMUFD dataset

(g) FallAllD dataset

(h) Results using 4 features

Fig. 2. AUC ROC for different feature selection criteria and number of features.

Table 5. Sensitivity, specificity and AUC ROC for each dataset applying the 4 most significant features according to the global ranking, the order reccomneded by SisFall and the order derived from the analysis of each dataset.

	Dataset	Global order			Self-order			SisFall order		
		AUC ROC	Se	Sp	AUC ROC	Se	Sp	AUC ROC	Se	Sp
1	TST Fall	93.75	100.0	87.50	98.75	100.0	97.50	92.50	97.50	87.50
2	UMAFall	92.16	87.50	96.83	95.44	96.43	94.44	94.05	92.86	95.24
3	SisFall	92.08	89.26	94.90	93.16	90.19	96.14	93.16	90.19	96.14
4	Erciyes	94.55	97.62	91.48	94.55	97.62	91.48	96.86	97.99	95.74
5	UP Fall	89.30	85.92	92.68	89.30	85.92	92.68	92.63	90.14	95.12
6	IMUFD	94.29	92.06	96.52	91.91	87.30	96.52	93.14	88.89	97.39
7	FallAllD	90.60	89.29	91.92	92.06	88.57	95.54	89.16	85.00	93.31

5 Conclusions

This paper has assessed the capacity of the detection algorithms intended for wearable FDSs to extrapolate conclusions obtained with a certain dataset when they are applied to data obtained with other users and movements. The study is based on the analysis of seven public datasets that contain recorded accelerometer signals captured on the volunteers' waist and the use of AUC ROC as a performance validation metric.

In particular, we analyzed the performance of the SVM algorithm when up to thirteen accelerometer-based features are considered to feed the classifier. Results reveal the difficulties of low dimensional algorithms to detect falls when the selection criteria are merely based on a previous study of a single dataset. This fact highlights the importance of considering a variety of datasets to configure, train and test any fall detection algorithm, as most current datasets have remarkable limitations in terms of the number of experimental subjects and the typology of movements with which they were generated.

On the other hand, the results also show with a small set of well selected features (in this work four features seem to be enough) an acceptable performance can be obtained for fall detection. The results suggest that using a greater number of features to determine if a fall occurs just slightly improves detection effective ratio at the cost of increasing the complexity of the algorithms, which may hamper its implementation on the low cost wearable devices that produce the fall detection decision in real-time.

Funding Information. Research presented in this article has been partially funded by FEDER Funds (under grant UMA18-FEDERJA-022), Universidad de Málaga, Campus de Excelencia Internacional Andalucia Tech and Asociación Universitaria Iberoamericana de Postgrado (AUIP).

Conflicts of Interest. The authors declare no conflicts of interest.

References

1. Yoshida, S.: A global report on falls prevention epidemiology of falls. World Health Organization (2007)
2. Stevens, J.A., Corso, P.S., Finkelstein, E.A.: The costs of fatal and nonfatal falls among older adults. Inj. Prev. **12**, 290–295 (2006)
3. Vallabh, P., Malekian, R.: Fall detection monitoring systems: a comprehensive review. J. Ambient. Intell. Humaniz. Comput. **9**(6), 1809–1833 (2017). https://doi.org/10.1007/s12652-017-0592-3
4. Yacchirema, D., de Puga, J.S., Palau, C., Esteve, M.: Fall detection system for elderly people using IoT and ensemble machine learning algorithm. Pers. Ubiquitous Comput. **23**(5), 801–817 (2019)
5. Igual, R., Medrano, C., Plaza, I.: Challenges, issues and trends in fall detection systems. Biomed. Eng. Online **12**(1), 66 (2013)
6. Ramachandran, A., Karuppiah, A.: A survey on recent advances in wearable fall detection systems. BioMed Research International, vol. 2020. Hindawi Limited (2020)
7. Rastogi, S., Singh, J.: A systematic review on machine learning for fall detection system. Comput. Intell. **4**, 1–24 (2021)
8. Hou, M., Wang, H., Xiao, Z., Zhang, G.: An SVM fall recognition algorithm based on a gravity acceleration sensor. Syst. Sci. Control Eng. **6**(3), 208–214, September 2018
9. Aziz, O., Musngi, M., Park, E.J., Mori, G., Robinovitch, S.N.: A comparison of accuracy of fall detection algorithms (threshold-based vs. machine learning) using waist-mounted tri-axial accelerometer signals from a comprehensive set of falls and non-fall trials. Med. Biol. Eng. Comput. **55**(1), 45–55 (2016). https://doi.org/10.1007/s11517-016-1504-y
10. Zhang, T., Wang, J., Xu, L., Liu, P.: Fall Detection by Wearable Sensor and One-Class SVM Algorithm, pp. 858–863. Springer, Berlin, Heidelberg (2006). https://doi.org/10.1007/978-3-540-37258-5_104
11. Salgado, P., Afonso, P.: Body Fall Detection with Kalman Filter and SVM, pp. 407–416. Springer, Cham (2015). https://doi.org/10.1007/978-3-319-10380-8_39
12. Medrano, C., Igual, R., Plaza, I., Castro, M.: Detecting falls as novelties in acceleration patterns acquired with smartphones. PLoS One **9**(4), e94811 (2014)
13. Santoyo-Ramón, J., Casilari, E., Cano-García, J., Santoyo-Ramón, J.A., Casilari, E., Cano-García, J.M.: Analysis of a smartphone-based architecture with multiple mobility sensors for fall detection with supervised learning. Sensors **18**(4), 1155, April 2018
14. Santoyo-Ramón, J.A., Casilari-Pérez, E., Cano-García, J.M.: Study of the detection of falls using the svm algorithm, different datasets of movements and ANOVA. In: Rojas, I., Valenzuela, O., Rojas, F., Ortuño, F. (eds.) IWBBIO 2019. LNCS, vol. 11465, pp. 415–428. Springer, Cham (2019). https://doi.org/10.1007/978-3-030-17938-0_37
15. Casilari, E., Santoyo-Ramón, J.A., Cano-García, J.M.: Analysis of public datasets for wearable fall detection systems. Sensors (Switzerland), **17**(7), 1513, July 2017
16. Sucerquia, A., López, J.D., Vargas-bonilla, J.F.: SisFall: a fall and movement dataset. Sensors **198**(52), 1–14 (2017)
17. Özdemir, A.T.: An analysis on sensor locations of the human body for wearable fall detection devices: principles and practice. Sensors (Switzerland) **16**(8), 1161 (2016)
18. Dewi, C., Chen, R-C:. Control, and undefined. Random forest and support vector machine on features selection for regression analysis. ijicic.org (2019)
19. sklearn.ensemble.RandomForestClassifier—scikit-learn 0.24.1 documentation. https://scikit-learn.org/stable/modules/generated/sklearn.ensemble.RandomForestClassifier.html. Accessed 16 Apr 2021

20. Gasparrini, S., Cippitelli, E., Spinsante, S., Gambi, E.: A depth-based fall detection system using a Kinect® sensor. Sensors **14**(2), 2756–2775 (2014)
21. Martínez-Villaseñor, L., Ponce, H., Espinosa-Loera, R.A.: Multimodal database for human activity recognition and fall detection. In: Proceedings of the 12th International Conference on Ubiquitous Computing and Ambient Intelligence (UCAmI 2018), vol. 2, no. 19 (2018)
22. Saleh, M., Abbas, M., Le Jeannes, R.B.: FallAllD: an open dataset of human falls and activities of daily living for classical and deep learning applications. IEEE Sens. J. **21**(2), 1849–1858 (2021)
23. Frank, K., Vera Nadales, M.J., Robertson, P., Pfeifer, T.: Bayesian recognition of motion related activities with inertial sensors. In: Proceedings of the 12th ACM International Conference on Ubiquitous Computing, pp. 445–446 (2010)
24. Kwolek, B., Kepski, M.: Human fall detection on embedded platform using depth maps and wireless accelerometer. Comput. Methods Programs Biomed. **117**(3), 489–501 (2014)
25. Klenk, J., et al.: The FARSEEING real-world fall repository: a large-scale collaborative database to collect and share sensor signals from real-world falls. Eur. Rev. Aging Phys. Act. **13**(1), 8, December 2016
26. Ahmed, M., Mehmood, N., Nadeem, A., Mehmood, A., Rizwan, K.: Fall detection system for the elderly based on the classification of shimmer sensor prototype data. Healthc. Inform. Res. **23**(3), 147–158 (2017)
27. Casilari, E., Santoyo-Ramón, J.A., Cano-García, J.M.: On the heterogeneity of existing repositories of movements intended for the evaluation of fall detection systems. J. Healthc. Eng. **2020**, 6622285 (2020)
28. sklearn.preprocessing.scale—scikit-learn 0.24.1 documentation. https://scikit-learn.org/sta ble/modules/generated/sklearn.preprocessing.scale.html. Accessed 19 Apr 2021
29. Version 0.23.2—scikit-learn 0.24.1 documentation. https://scikit-learn.org/stable/whats_ new/v0.23.html#version-0-23-1. Accessed 16 Apr 2021
30. sklearn.model_selection.GridSearchCV—scikit-learn 0.24.1 documentation. https://scikit-learn.org/stable/modules/generated/sklearn.model_selection.GridSearchCV.html. Accessed 16 Apr 2021
31. Clasificación: ROC y AUC | Curso intensivo de aprendizaje automático. https://developers.google.com/machine-learning/crash-course/classification/roc-and-auc?hl=es-419. Accessed 19 Apr 2021

Autonomous Docking of Mobile Robots by Reinforcement Learning Tackling the Sparse Reward Problem

A. M. Burgueño-Romero$^{(\boxtimes)}$, J.R. Ruiz-Sarmiento, and J. Gonzalez-Jimenez

Machine Perception and Intelligent Robotics Group (MAPIR), Department of System Engineering and Automation, Biomedical Research Institute of Malaga (IBIMA), University of Malaga, Málaga, Spain
{ambrbr,jotaraul,javiergonzalez}@uma.es

Abstract. Most mobile robots are powered by batteries, which must be charged before their level become too low to continue providing services. This paper contributes a novel method based on Reinforcement Learning (RL) for the autonomous docking of mobile robots at their charging stations. Our proposal considers a RL network that is fed with images to visually sense the environment and with distance measurements to safely avoid obstacles, and produces motion commands to be executed by the robot. Additionally, since the autonomous docking is in essence a sparse reward task (the only state that returns a positive reward is when the robot docks at the charging station), we propose the usage of reward shaping to successfully learn to dock. For that we have designed extrinsic rewards that are built on the results of a Convolutional Neural Network in charge of detecting the pattern typically used to visually identify charging stations. The experiments carried out support our design decisions and validate the method implementation, reporting a ~100% of success in the docking task with obstacle-free paths, and ~93% when obstacles are considered, along with short execution times (10 s and 14 s on average, respectively).

Keywords: Autonomous docking · Reinforcement learning · Mobile robots · Pattern detection · Reward shaping · CNN · Unity

1 Introduction

We all take care about the level of charge of our phones, hungrily looking for a charging point when they are running out battery so we can keep doing productive things like chatting or sending emails. The same is the case with mobile robots, whose landing in fields like education, housekeeping, health care or entertainment is becoming more and more evident, and which require to keep their batteries charged in order to reliably and autonomously provide their services [1–3]. For this purpose, a fundamental task is that of docking at the charging station. During the robot operation, this occurs when the robot's battery is running out

© Springer Nature Switzerland AG 2021
I. Rojas et al. (Eds.): IWANN 2021, LNCS 12862, pp. 392–403, 2021.
https://doi.org/10.1007/978-3-030-85099-9_32

of charge, or when it is estimated that the battery level is insufficient to perform the remaining tasks. At that moment, the robot must initiate the docking process, which typically consists of the navigation to the area where the charging station is located, the identification of said station, and the approach of the robot towards it until docking takes place.

Over the past few years, different techniques have been proposed to detect the charging station in the environment, typically based on visual information (images coming from cameras), as well as to guide the robot towards it. In this way, it is common to see charging stations incorporating some sort of fiducial marker or pattern to ease their identification (see Fig. 1). Initial works relied on traditional computer vision techniques for edge segmentation, feature extraction, template matching, etc., aiming to detect such pattern [4,5]. However, these approaches suffer from their high parametrization [6], which turns them into inflexible techniques prone to fail in presence of changing lighting conditions, occlusions, etc. Recent visual docking techniques made the move to Convolutional Neural Networks (CNN) [7,8] in order to detect the pattern. Although these methods are more robust against challenging conditions, they require the collection of a vast amount of training data in order to be properly fitted. This, besides being a tedious and highly time-consuming task, can be difficult to carry out in specialized domains, as it is the case of pattern detection.

In spite of the technique used to detect the pattern, in order to dock at the charging station, it is typically implemented a simple algorithm: the robot is instructed to rotate and align the pattern in the center of the image, and then to move forward until docking is complete, making the strong assumption that the path is obstacle-free. An alternative to this approach is the utilization of Reinforcement Learning (RL) algorithms, which have been explored in recent works to automate robots' navigation towards a certain goal using visual information (intensity images) as input data [9,10]. A reward function, needed for the fitting of RL algorithms, evaluates the action performed by the robot in a specific state, and returns a number which sign depends on whether the action it has performed is right or wrong for the task it has been assigned. However, a common issue that recurrently appears in RL problems is solving sparse reward tasks, that is, tasks where the amount of states that return a positive reward is very limited, as is the case of docking at the charging station. Sparse rewards cause the robot not to acquire the information needed to solve the problem, resulting in an unreliable operation.

This work contributes a novel method for the autonomous docking of mobile robots by means of Reinforcement Learning (RL) that deals with the previous issues. Concretely, this method addresses the sparse rewards problem by considering a CNN to detect the charging station pattern in RGB images, and the utilization of those detections to provide extrinsic rewards. This way, the proposed method performs docking by instantiating a RL network that is fed with RGB images and pattern detection results, and that produces actions to move the robot (translations and rotations) towards the charging station. We also consider an additional input to this RL network: distance measurements collected

Fig. 1. Left, charging station for a domestic robot composed of three circles [4]. Middle, station for a drone consisting of a circle with a cross [11]. Right, a charging station identified by two QR codes [5].

by a radial laser scanner, a sensor typically found in robotic platforms and that provides valuable information about the obstacles in the robot surroundings. By doing so we avoid an obstacle-free path assumption and permit the method to successfully operate in more challenging environments.

The training of a RL network requires the deployment of the robot in its working environment to learn by trial-and-error, which demands a long time to achieve robust results, being crashes also possible. To handle this, we have resorted to Unity [12], a video game development framework that permitted us to design realistic virtual environments including robots and charging stations, and to perform a faster RL network training. Regarding the CNN for pattern detection, as previously introduced, its training requires a vast amount of data for fitting a reliable model. In this regard, we propose the utilization of transfer learning [13] and the fine-tuning of a general model for the detection of the particular pattern used in each docking scenario (recall Fig. 1). To carry out such fine-tuning, Unity is also used to generate synthetic training samples in the form of images including the pattern at hand with different sizes, orientations, and lighting conditions.

To validate our proposal, we have carried out extensive tests with a replica of the Giraff Robot [14] (see Fig. 2). The robot was commanded to dock at the charging station, starting from different relative distances and orientations w.r.t. said station. The performance of our proposal has been compared with other methods following other typical RL techniques such as behavior cloning [15], reporting a higher performance. The method implementation is publicly available at https://github.com/AmbroxMr/UnityMLDocking.

2   The Proposed Method for Autonomous Docking

Figure 2 shows the pipeline of our proposal. Once the robot triggers the *docking at the charging station* task, we resort to a RL network, described in detail in Sect. 2.1, to produce the motion commands to reach such goal. In this work we assume that the robot is located in the same room as the charging station, otherwise a prior navigation to said room would be needed. At a certain time instant while executing the docking task, the RL network processes the following

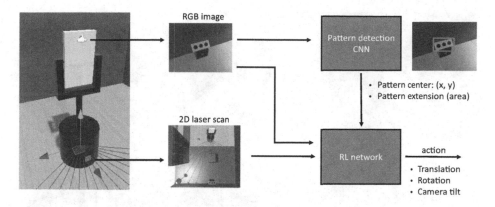

Fig. 2. Pipeline of the proposed method, where the RL network is in charge of processing images, 2D laser scans and pattern detections to produce actions (translations and rotations) until docking is complete.

input data: an image from an RGB camera for visually sensing the environment, distance measurements in the form of a 2D laser scan useful for avoiding obstacles, and the results from a pattern detection CNN (see Sect. 2.3) for facing the sparse rewards problem (see Sect. 2.2). This way, we consider a common robotic platform equipped with an RGB camera and a 2D laser scanner. The Giraff robot, recreated in our experiments, is capable of tilting the camera, but this is not a requirement for our method to work. The 2D laser scanner could be also replaced by other sensor or technique that provides distance measurements such as RGB-D cameras, sonars, stereo-vision systems, etc. With such inputs, the RL network infers an action (motion command), and the process is repeated until docking is completed. Specifically, the possible robot actions are translation (forward/backward), rotation (left/right) and tilt (increase/decrease).

Since we are dealing with RL techniques, it is worth mentioning at this point the learning environment used for the design and validation of the proposed method. Typically, for the sake of generality it is preferred the utilization of environments that randomly change between method executions (different objects and at different locations, different lighting conditions, different charging station and initial robot positions, etc.). For doing so we have resorted to the Robot@VirtualHome tool[1] (see Fig. 3), which provides interesting mechanisms to facilitate working with domestic environments.

2.1 Designing the Reinforcement Learning Network

We have leveraged the Unity ML-Agents Toolkit[2] for the design, training and execution of the RL network. This open-source toolkit allows us to integrate Unity and Python, providing implementations of state-of-the-art Reinforcement

---

[1] https://github.com/DavidFernandezChaves/RobotAtVirtualHome.
[2] https://github.com/Unity-Technologies/ml-agents.

Fig. 3. Randomized virtual scenarios built by the Robot@VirtualHome tool, used for the design and validation of the proposed method.

Learning algorithms. Concretely, ML-Agents offers an implementation of two popular RL algorithms: Proximal Policy Optimization [16] (PPO) and Soft Actor-Critic [17] (SAC).

On the one hand, PPO is an on-policy algorithm which trains a stochastic policy $\pi_\theta(A|S)$, meaning that the policy π is the probability of taking an action $a \in A$, at state $s \in S$, and the network parameters are θ. It explores by sampling actions according to the latest version of this policy, which is updated using intrinsic and extrinsic rewards (adding them). An intrinsic reward determines the current objective function for the learning agent (a successful docking in our case) while extrinsic rewards encourage the agent to achieve that goal. In PPO, new policies use to be close to previous ones, becoming progressively less random during the training phase.

This policy is trained by means of both intrinsic and extrinsic rewards (r_t) that come from the environment at time step t. This way, the value of the policy π_θ, denoted $J(\pi_\theta)$, is the expected discounted sum of rewards obtained by the robot:

$$J(\pi_\theta) = \mathbb{E}_{\pi_\theta}\left[\sum_t \gamma^t r_t\right] \tag{1}$$

where γ is the discount factor, a hyperparameter that quantifies how much importance is given to the rewards.

Thereby, having the rewards r_t from all time steps t within an episode (time steps between a initial state and a terminal one), it is possible to update the policy π_θ computing the gradient of the value J with respect to the policy parameters θ:

$$\nabla_\theta J(\pi_\theta) = \mathbb{E}_{\pi_\theta} \left[\sum_t (\gamma^t r_t) \nabla log \pi_\theta(a_t|s_t) \right] \tag{2}$$

On the other hand, SAC is an off-policy algorithm that add an entropy measure of the policy into the reward to encourage exploration. The idea in this case is to randomly learn a policy that is able to succeed in the assigned task. During the method design phase we have considered both PPO and SAC alternatives in order to choose the most appropriate one for the problem at hand. This analysis is reported in Sect. 3.2.

In spite of the applied RL learning algorithm, the utilization of a reward function is required. In this work it has been defined with positive signals when the robot completes a docking.

2.2 Dealing with the Problem of Sparse Rewards

The task at hand, the autonomous docking of mobile robots, tends to be a sparse reward task. This is due to the fact that the robot only receives a positive reward just when a successful docking is achieved. However, this is an uncommon situation if the robot starts the training phase without any prior information. Sparse reward tasks have been an important subject of research [18,19]. A solution to this problem is *reward shaping*, which consists of adding extra rewards obtained from the environment. Recently, new solutions have explored alternatives to adding new rewards obtained by sensing the environment. One of these is *behavioral cloning* [15], which aims to learn from demonstrations of a real person controlling the robot towards the target. Another is *curriculum learning* [18], which begins the training phase considering a very relaxed version of the problem, getting more complex over time until the robot can solve the initially given task.

As a novelty, our proposal considers a reward shaping solution consisting of the addition of new extrinsic rewards taking advantage of the visual information the robot receives, as well as pattern detection methods. This concept is put into practice by modeling a Convolutional Neural Network that detects the position and extension of the charging station pattern in the image.

Thus, an *extrinsic_reward*($\cdot$) function has been defined, which evaluates the orientation of the detected pattern w.r.t. the camera and its proximity. The former is related to the difference between the center of the pattern $C = (C_x, C_y)$ and the center of the image, while the latter is rated by the area A of the bounding box containing the pattern in the image: a large area means a close pattern and vice versa. The defined function is as follows:

$$extrinsic\_reward(C, I_s, A) = \frac{er_x(C, I) + er_y(C, I) + er_z(A)}{Max_s * 9} \qquad (3)$$

$$er_x(C, I) = \frac{-|C_x - I_w/2|}{I_w/4} + 3, \qquad er_y(C, I) = \frac{-|C_y - I_h/2|}{I_h/4} + 3$$

$$er_z(A) = \frac{A * 3}{Max_a}$$

being $I_s = (I_w, I_h)$ the image size, Max_s the number of maximum steps per episode, and Max_a the maximum possible area of the pattern projected on the image. Notice that these parameters play a normalization role. The functions $er_x(\cdot)$ and $er_y(\cdot)$ are similar, mapping the distance between the center of the pattern and the center of the image, to the range $[1, 3]$ in both the x and y axes. In its turn, $er_z(\cdot)$ maps the distance between the robot and the docking station to the range $[0, 3]$ according to the area of the pattern appearing in the image. This way, this extrinsic reward function provides signals from $2/(Max_s * 9)$ (pattern detected in the corner of the image and far away) to $1/Max_s$ (accomplished docking). Additionally, a negative reward of $-1/Max_s$ is provided when the pattern is not detected, encouraging the agent not to lose sight of the pattern too long. The normalization carried out considering Max_s pursuits the moderation of this extrinsic reward so it does not totally govern the learning process.

2.3   The Pattern Detection Network

In order to detect in images the pattern of the charging station, we propose the utilization of a CNN. These networks exhibit a great performance while detecting objects in images, although they require a heavy training phase that needs, among others, a vast repository of training data. Moreover, they require a fine-tuning to detect specific objects, as is the case of charging station patterns.

To face these issues we propose exploiting transfer learning, along with the generation of synthetic data for fine-tuning the model. For doing so, we relied on the Unity's *Perception*[3] package, which implements a toolkit for generating large-scale datasets. Using this toolkit, synthetic images and their ground truth can be generated, whether for 2D object detection, class segmentation or pose estimation (among others). Additionally, it is possible to model the randomization of different parameters in the environment where the synthetic images generation takes place, as is the case of lighting conditions, colors and textures of objects, etc. (see Fig. 4). Section 3.1 describes the generated dataset in this work.

Regarding transfer learning, this entails the selection of an initial network architecture pre-trained on an extensive dataset to enable the creation of a generalized model [13]. Then, modifications to the pre-existing model are done to fine-tune it for the problem at hand, which includes the utilization of the synthetically generated data for further training the network. Notice that this step

---

[3] https://github.com/Unity-Technologies/com.unity.perception.

needs to be done out of Unity. Although we have employed PyTorch, there are other valid alternatives as Caffe, Tensorflow, etc. Once the network has been trained, Unity permits to import models in the common *.onnx* format by means of Barracuda[4], a lightweight cross-platform Neural Networks inference library.

Fig. 4. Batch of synthetic data for the pattern considered in this work, used for the fine-tuning of the CNN. It is composed of 2 images and its ground truth. Lighting, colours, textures, rotation and scale are randomized parameters.

3   Evaluation

3.1   Implementation Details

The main two decisions to be made in the method implementation are both the RL network and the pattern detection CNN to be used. The network implemented in the Reinforcement Learning algorithm is the CNN architecture proposed by Mnih et al. [20], consisting of three convolutional layers followed by two fully-connected layers with a single output for each valid action.

Regarding the pattern detection CNN, as introduced in Sect. 2.3, in this work we resorted to transfer learning and the Faster R-CNN model with a MobileNetV3-Large FPN backbone as initial network architecture. Said network was pre-trained on Imagenet, a widely used repository of data large enough (1.2M images) to create a generalized model. The fine-tuning of this method was carried out using a synthetic dataset consisting of 2000 images with approximately 5 patterns appearing in them, which are accompanied by their respective ground truth (patterns' bounding boxes), as shown in Fig. 4.

It is also worth mentioning the pattern chosen to identify the charging station, composed of three dark circles in a row over a white rectangle. This pattern has proven to be discriminant enough to be distinguished from other objects in most domestic scenarios, unequivocally identifying the charging station [4]. However, other geometric patterns or even QR codes could be used.

---

[4] https://github.com/Unity-Technologies/barracuda-release.

3.2   Analysis of RL Alternatives

To discern which reinforcement learning algorithm use, SAC or PPO, we analyzed the resources required by each one for training a RL network. SAC demands much more RAM due to the experience buffer it requires, which collects experiences during the training phase. In the context of this work, this becomes unfeasible due to the high size of visual observations. As a consequence, although SAC takes much fewer episodes to teach the robot to dock at its charging base, each iteration is significantly slower than in PPO. These are some of the reasons why it has been decided that PPO is more optimal for this particular problem.

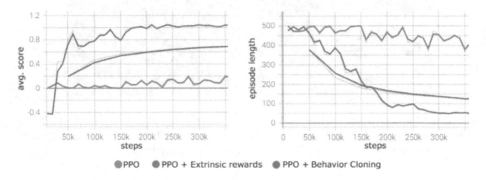

Fig. 5. Average score and episode length (expressed in batches of size 10), computed from the episodes completed in batches of 10k steps, in a 350k steps training phase for PPO, PPO + BC and our proposal.

Moreover, we have analyzed the evolution of two different learning metrics when considering three different RL methods: PP0, PP0 + Behavior cloning, and PPO + Extrinsic rewards (our proposal). For that, these methods have been in a 350k steps training phase each one during approximately 3 h and a half, using a GPU Nvidia GeForce GTX 1660 Super. During the execution of these training phases they were computed the average scores of the episodes completed each 10k steps (the maximum length of an episode is 5k steps), as well as the length of those episodes measured in steps. Figure 5 shows the obtained results. As evidenced by the evolution of the average score obtained by the PPO method, the sparse rewards problem appears. This is due to the robot not consistently getting positive rewards over time, leading in the long term to random movements or even to the robot standing still, not achieving a significant score improvement. When behavior cloning [15] (BC) is considered, a decent score is achieved quickly. However, after some time improvement is no longer happening, as the algorithm is overfitting to the behavior provided in the demo, which normally does not include all possible cases. Finally, our proposal keeps improving longer, converging to a score slightly higher than 1. This reward is split into 1 point when docking is successful (provided as intrinsic reward), and a small reward for looking at the pattern every step (provided as extrinsic reward). As it can be observed, during the very first episodes (until 25k steps), the robot gets negative rewards. We argue that this changes once the algorithm detects that keeping the pattern in sight gives positive rewards. Between 25k and 50k steps, the robot learns that if it gets closer to the pattern, rewards are higher. This happens until the robot actually docks successfully, obtaining a huge reward (1 point) and having little room for improvement. From step 175k, the robot is able to perform autonomous docking, hence converging faster than the competitors.

Regarding the evolution of the length of the episodes for the different methods (right part of Fig. 5), we can see how it remains almost horizontal for PPO, while PPO + BC and our proposal experiment a decrease in said length when the training phase progresses. This is because as both methods are trained, the robot performs the docking in less steps.

3.3   Performance Results

We have evaluated the performance when carrying out docking for two methods: PPO + Behavior cloning and PPO + Extrinsic rewards. The PPO method is omitted, since the resultant RL network was unable to accomplish docking. For this test two different scenarios have been considered: one with obstacle-free paths, and other one with objects placed at random locations between the robot and the charging station. A total of 3000 autonomous docking tasks were carried out in each scenario, giving 100 s to the robot to complete each one. For each task execution they were recorded: the robot initial position and orientation w.r.t. the charging station, the execution time and the docking success.

In the obstacle-free scenarios, our proposal achieved a performance of 99.8% successful docking tasks, resulting in a highly reliable method. Regarding the execution time, it was low: ~10 s on average. In its turn, the PPO + Behavior cloning method reached a 64% of success with an execution time of ~12 s.

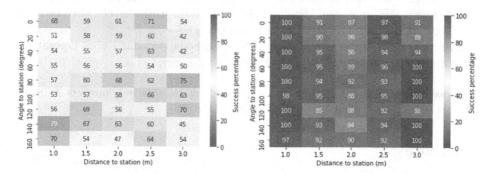

Fig. 6. Average success (expressed as a percentage) when docking at the charging station according to the initial robot distance and orientation w.r.t. said station using: PPO + Behavior cloning (left) and PPO + Extrinsic rewards (right).

As for the scenarios containing obstacles, the results achieved by these methods are shown in Fig. 6. In this figure, the task executions are grouped according to the initial position and orientation of the robot w.r.t. the charging station, aiming to measure how they affect docking. As can be seen, in both cases the robot has a similar success rate regardless of the initial orientation, but the distance has a remarkable effect in our method: the performance is quite high for low distances, it slightly decreases for medium distances, and increases again for larger ones. This can be due to the fact that with a larger distance, it is more probable for the robot to avoid the obstacle. Regardless of this, the average performance of our method is quite superior to the one using BC, a ~93% of successful docking tasks versus a ~59%.

Regarding execution times, they are not affected by the initial orientation, but they tend to increase with growing distances with both methods. The reported averaged times were similar: 17 s for BC and 14 s for our proposal.

4   Conclusions and Future Work

This work has presented a novel method for performing the autonomous docking of mobile robots using a Reinforcement Learning (RL) network. An innovative way to face the sparse reward problem is presented, which considers reward shaping. This consists of providing extrinsic rewards to the RL network, which are built on the output of a Convolutional Neural Network (CNN) in charge of detecting the pattern identifying the charging station. We dealt with the problem of fitting a CNN for detecting a specific pattern by means of transfer learning and synthetic training data generation. This way, the RL network is fed with: images that visually sense the environment, distance measurements for perceiving and avoiding obstacles, and the extrinsic rewards, and produces actions to be carried out by the robot (translations and rotations) in order to accomplish docking. The method has been designed and validated using different tools from Unity. An extensive evaluation has been made, where our proposal achieved a success of ~100% and ~93% in obstacle-free and cluttered paths, respectively, also showing short execution times (10 s and 14 s, respectively).

In future work, we plan to connect Unity with the popular Robot Operating System (ROS) using the *ROS-TCP-Connector* package.

Acknowledgements. This work was supported by the research projects WISER (DPI2017-84827-R) and ARPEGGIO (PID2020-117057).

References

1. Luperto, M., et al.: Towards long-term deployment of a mobile robot for at-home ambient assisted living of the elderly. In: 2019 European Conference on Mobile Robots (ECMR), pp. 1–6. IEEE (2019)
2. Tussyadiah, I.P., Park, S.: Consumer evaluation of hotel service robots. In: Stangl, B., Pesonen, J. (eds.) Information and Communication Technologies in Tourism 2018, pp. 308–320. Springer, Cham (2018). https://doi.org/10.1007/978-3-319-72923-7_24

3. Ruiz-Sarmiento, J.R., Galindo, C., González-Jiménez, J.: Robot@ home, a robotic dataset for semantic mapping of home environments. Int. J. Robot. Res. **36**(2), 131–141 (2017)
4. González-Jiménez, J., Galindo, C., Ruiz-Sarmiento, J.R.: Technical improvements of the Gira telepresence robot based on users' evaluation. In: 2012 IEEE RO-MAN, pp. 827–832 (2012)
5. Wang, Y., et al.: Autonomous target docking of nonholonomic mobile robots using relative pose measurements. IEEE Trans. Industr. Electron. **68**, 1 (2020)
6. Burgue no Romero, A.M., et al.: A collection of Jupyter notebooks covering the fundamentals of computer vision. In: ICERI2020 Proceedings. Online Conference, pp. 5495–5505 (2020)
7. Yahya, M.F., Arshad, M.R.: Detection of markers using deep learning for docking of autonomous underwater vehicle. In: 2017 IEEE I2CACIS, pp. 179–184 (2017)
8. Kriegler, A., Wöber, W.: Vision-based docking of a mobile robot. Tech. rep. Easy-Chair (2021)
9. Ebert, F., et al.: Visual foresight: model-based deep reinforcement learning for vision-based robotic control. arXiv: 1812.00568 [cs.RO] (2018)
10. Tai, L., Paolo, G., Liu, M.: Virtual-to-real deep reinforcement learning: continuous control of mobile robots for mapless navigation. In: 2017 IEEE/RSJ IROS, pp. 31–36 (2017)
11. H3 Dynamics homepage. https://www.h3dynamics.com/. Accessed 20 Apr 2021
12. Juliani, A., et al.: Unity: a general platform for intelligent agents. arXiv:1809.02627 (2018)
13. He, K., Girshick, R., Dollar, P.: Rethinking ImageNet pre-training. In: Proceedings of the IEEE/CVF ICCV, October 2019
14. Gonzalez-Jimenez, J., Galindo, C., Gutierrez-Castaneda, C.: Evaluation of a telepresence robot for the elderly: a Spanish experience. In: Ferrández Vicente, J.M., Álvarez Sánchez, J.R., de la Paz López, F., Toledo Moreo, F.J. (eds.) IWINAC 2013. LNCS, vol. 7930, pp. 141–150. Springer, Heidelberg (2013). https://doi.org/10.1007/978-3-642-38637-4_15
15. Torabi, F., Warnell, G., Stone, P.: Behavioral cloning from observation (2018). arXiv: 1805.01954 [cs.AI]
16. Schulman, J., et al.: Proximal policy optimization algorithms. CoRR arXiv:1707.06347 (2017)
17. Haarnoja, T., et al.: Soft actor-critic algorithms and applications (2019). arXiv: 1812.05905 [cs.LG]
18. Hare, J.: Dealing with sparse rewards in reinforcement learning (2019). arXiv:1910.09281 [cs.LG]
19. Vecerik, M., et al.: Leveraging Demonstrations for Deep Reinforcement Learning on Robotics Problems with Sparse Rewards. Presented at the arXiv:1707.08817 (2018) [cs.AI]
20. Mnih, V., et al.: Human-level control through deep reinforcement learning. Nature **518**(7540), 529–533 (2015)

Decision Support Systems for Air Traffic Control with Self-enforcing Networks Based on Weather Forecast and Reference Types for the Direction of Operation

Dirk Zinkhan[1]([✉]), Sven Eiermann[1], Christina Klüver[2], and Jürgen Klüver[2]

[1] Deutscher Wetterdienst, Offenbach, Germany
{dirk.zinkhan,sven.eiermann}@dwd.de
[2] CoBASC Research Group, 45130 Essen, Germany
cobasc@rebask.de

Abstract. The increasing of air traffic, changing weather conditions, and the requirements of climate protection intensifies the complex problem of finding optimal flight routes to avoid delays. Especially the prediction of weather conditions for the selection of the right direction of operation for runways at airports imply a particular challenge. Because the interpretation of the forecasted weather data requires meteorological expert knowledge, a system is needed, which enables to communicate the results for air traffic controllers in an easily understandable way.

As a decision support system, the Self-Enforcing Network (SEN), a self-organized learning neural network, was developed for the selection of the right direction of operation for runways at the airport of Frankfurt am Main. The SEN processes the forecasted wind situations and generates a recommendation for the selection of a suited direction of operation. These recommendations are communicated through the "Meteorological Airport Briefing web-portal" in a graphical visualization.

Keywords: Self-Enforcing network · Decision support systems · Air traffic controlling · Airport · Direction of operation selection · Ensemble-prediction-system · COSMO-DE-EPS

1 Introduction

The necessity of air traffic control (ATC) has increased, and the optimization of traffic capacity includes principal objectives as reduction of emissions per flight, minimization of late departures and optimal flight routes (e.g. [1]).

The climate changes [2], hazardous weather conditions [3] as well as a pandemic situation like COVID-19 [4] impact the weather prediction and the air traffic control.

Hence, there exist several attempts for the construction of efficient computer-based decision support systems [5–8]. In recent years statistics-based Machine Learning algorithms as decision trees, random forest regressors, Bayesian networks [9–11], and "Deep

© Springer Nature Switzerland AG 2021
I. Rojas et al. (Eds.): IWANN 2021, LNCS 12862, pp. 404–415, 2021.
https://doi.org/10.1007/978-3-030-85099-9_33

Learning-based weather prediction" (DLWP) using Autoencoders (AE), Long-Short Term Memory (LSTM), Convolutional Neural Networks (CNN), or hybrid systems (e.g. [12, 13]) are invested to improve the forecast models and to support the air traffic control.

For the proper operation at international airports the actual weather is a decisive factor involved (e.g., [9, 13–15]), especially because the weather plays an important role for late departures and/or arrivals. In the year 2019 the weather in Europe was e.g., much more responsible for the arrival delays than for the departure delays [16].

Because of the implication of weather conditions, the states of all meteorological data for air traffic must be known and these relevant data are committed by the International Civil Aviation Organization (ICAO) Annex 3 [17].

The data for wind direction and speed, visibility and significant weather phenomena are predicted within a space of 24 or 30 h as Terminal Aerodrome Forecast (TAF) for all international airports.

One of the main problems of air traffic control at an airport is the selection of the right direction of operation on the runways for the starting and landing of the airplanes, according to the respective weather and in particular wind conditions [10]. The basic principle for the selection of a suited operating direction is that the wind should come from the front when airplanes are starting or landing. Tail winds for starting or landing are permissible only if the speed of the wind is just moderate or low, i.e., below a defined threshold.

As the changing of a first chosen direction of operation always takes time and organizational efforts an air traffic control management must have sound decision reasons for keeping the selected direction or changing it.

In cooperation between the department of aviation meteorology of Deutscher Wetterdienst (the National Weather Service of Germany), which provides meteorological services for Frankfurt Airport, one of the major hubs in Europe, and the Research Group CoBASC (Computer Based Analysis of Social Complexity), we have developed an according decision support system [18]. For this purpose, we used a self-organized learning neural network, the Self-Enforcing Network (SEN), as the algorithmic basis for a suited decision support system based on real data of the forecasted wind conditions at Frankfurt Airport.

The basic idea was to insert the wind conditions as inputs into the SEN; the SEN afterwards generates a recommendation for the most suited direction of operation, i.e., if to stay with the direction chosen by the management of air traffic control or to change to another operating direction. Finally, the recommendations of the SEN were compared with the factual decisions of the management.

The decision problem for the management is in particular complicated because the changing of one direction of operation to another takes time due to several organizational procedures. That is why the management not only needs the weather data for a certain point in time but also forecast data for the next time. The forecast data are derived from the COSMO-DE ensemble prediction system (COSMO-DE-EPS), operated by the Deutscher Wetterdienst (DWD). The use of an ensemble forecast system enables to quantify uncertainties or probabilities for the forecasted wind situations. This is an advantage over the use of traditional deterministic forecast models, but on the other hand an additional challenge for the management since the uncertainty has to be incorporated into the decision process.

In this contribution we first present the airport conditions and the developed model. In the next sections the components of SEN and the results are described. Because the air traffic controllers need a rapid analysis and concise visualization, a web-based interface is introduced, which is presented in Sect. 5.

2   The Model Based on Airport Conditions and Weather Data

Frankfurt Airport has three parallel runways that can be used for starting and landing. A fourth runway, the so-called Startbahn-West (west runway), can be used only for starting in one direction and is located nearly orthogonally to the parallel runway system; that is why this runway was not included into our experiments. The three main runways can (and must) be used in that operating direction that the management of air traffic control has chosen. These directions are orientated to 70° (compass degrees), i.e., roughly east-north-east and 250°, i.e., approximately west-south-west. Therefore, the directions are called 07 and 25. These directions (and the according construction of the runways) were chosen because in the region of Frankfurt as in most parts of Middle Europe chiefly winds from Western directions dominate the weather, in particular strong winds with "bad" weather like rain in company.

The weather data necessary for the according decisions are derived, as mentioned, from the COSMO-DE-EPS ensemble prediction System of the Deutscher Wetterdienst (DWD). Since COSMO-DE is a limited area model, this model needs to be nested in a global model to get the lateral boundary condition. To generate the ensemble system, two approaches were combined:

- Using different global models to provide a variation of the initial and boundary conditions
- Variation of certain parameters of the internal model physics.

As a provider of initial and boundary conditions the global model GME of the DWD, the Integrated Forecast System (IFS) of the European Centre for Medium-Range Weather Forecasts (ECMWF), the Global Forecast System (GFS) of the National Centers for Environmental Prediction (NCEP) and the Global Spectral Model (GSM) of the Japan Meteorological Agency (JMA) are used. The variation of the internal model physics incorporates five parameters; for each model configuration one of these parameters is slightly modified. The combination of the four different boundary conditions with the five varied physical parameters amounts to the currently 20 components of the COSMO-DE-EPS system [19].

The weather data necessary for the according decisions are ensemble forecasts for 11 reference positions placed in different distances along the glide path to the airport and on the airport itself. For each position 5 quantiles, i.e., a statistical measure reflecting the spread of the ensemble forecasts, are computed, namely for the "parallel wind component", i.e., the headwind respectively tailwind component of a starting or approaching aircraft. For our model we have used collections of these processed ensemble forecast data from the DWD.

When we speak of "weather data" it is important to note that these are strictly speaking "forecast data", namely predictions about the probable weather conditions at a specific time. Yet for the sake of simplicity, we shall use only the term "weather data".

For the decision support system, the ensemble forecast data are the input vectors for SEN. For the development of the reference types, representing the operation directions at the airport in Frankfurt, the decisions of air traffic controllers based on the weather forecasts were considered. In consequence, the knowledge of several experts (involved meteorologists, air traffic controllers and SEN-developers) was incorporated for the development of the model shown in Fig. 1.

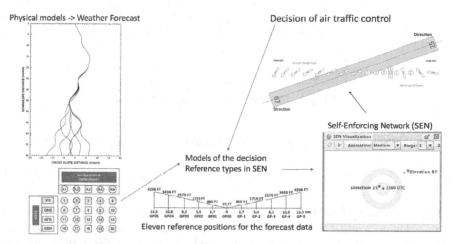

Fig. 1. The model of the decision support system. The geographic reference positions around the airport in Frankfurt/M can be seen in [20].

In the next sections the neural network, the model and results are presented in more details.

3   The Self-enforcing Network SEN and the Methodical Procedure for the Building of Reference-Types

The SEN is a self-organized learning neural network [21]. "Self-organized learning" means that in contrast to supervised learning the network does not get any explicitly given learning goal but must structure the input given to it according to an internal learning logic[1].

The chief function of a SEN is the ordering or classifying respectively of data sets consisting of objects with certain attributes and these data are represented in a "semantical matrix": The rows of the matrix are constituted by the objects and the columns by the

---

[1] The best-known examples of self-organized learning neural networks are the different versions of the "Kohonen Feature Map" (KFM, [22]).

according attributes. The elements of the matrix are numerical values, i.e., the affiliation degree of an attribute to an object.

In Fig. 2 an excerpt of the semantical matrix is shown, containing the attributes (numerical values of the forecasted wind direction at the reference positions along the glide path – GP_) and the forecasted UTC-time as objects.

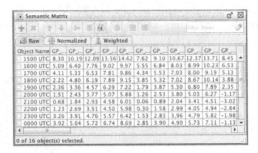

Fig. 2. Excerpt of the semantical matrix.

In the SEN application the weather data had to be accordingly normalized:

$$v_{norm} = \frac{v_{raw} - r_{min}}{r_{max} - r_{min}} * (n_{max} - n_{min}) + n_{min} \tag{1}$$

v_{norm} is the normalized value defined in the interval $[n_{min}; n_{max}]$; r_{min} is the minimum of the value interval of the original not normalized values; accordingly, r_{max} is the maximum; n_{max} and n_{min} are the maximum and minimum for the normalized value interval.

The network SEN is in this case constructed as a two-layered feed forward network, where the objects and the attributes each are a specific layer. Its activation function for this problem is the "Enforcing Activation Function" (EAF):

$$A_j = \sum_{i=1}^{n} \frac{A_i * w_{ij}}{|A_i| + 1} \tag{2}$$

A_j is the activation value of the receiving neuron j, A_i is the output value of the sending neuron i, and w_{ij} is the according weight value.

The operations of a SEN start by analyzing the values of the semantical matrix v_{sm} and transforming the values of the semantical matrix into the weight matrix of the network. If an object **o** does not have the attribute **a** and hence the according semantical value $v_{oa} = 0$, then the weight value $w_{oa} = 0$ and remains so; in all other cases the weight value is

$$w_{oa} = c * v_{oa} \tag{3}$$

c is a "learning rate" used in most neural network learning, i.e., a numerical value that determines the velocity of the learning process.

The learning rule of a SEN that varies the values of the weight matrix according to the problem is:

$$w(t + 1) = w(t) + \Delta w, \text{ and}$$

$$\Delta w = c * w_{oa} \tag{4}$$

where c is again a learning rate as in Eq. (3) and w_{oa} is the according value in the weight matrix. There is no necessity of additional parameter tuning.

A specific methodical procedure when using a SEN is the usage of so-called reference types. These are objects that are in some way representative cases for a class of objects. The task of the SEN is to compare new objects with one or several reference types and in this way to classify the new objects; similar approaches were proposed as "proto-type based machine learning" [23].

In the first step we constructed two reference types for the directions of operation. This means that we defined for each direction a "representative" set of weather data, i.e., a weather situation where the decision for one of the directions is unambiguous. For example, if the dominating wind direction is west wind, then obviously direction 25 must be chosen (condition of head wind for starting and landing); hence such a situation would represent a suited reference type. The normalized values of the reference types define the semantical matrix.

Because there are, as we mentioned, 11 reference positions, and because each reference position is characterized by 5 values for the quantiles, the reference types and the factual situations are represented by vectors consisting of 55 components. The objective values of the reference positions are adjusted by a "cue validity factor" [24].[2] This means that the distances of the reference positions to the airport, the height of the measured wind data, and other factors are considered. The data of a reference position immediately in the neighborhood of the airport have the cue validity factor of 1.0; those of a reference position in the larger distance the value of 0.1.

Figure 3 shows the reference types for the direction 25 and 07 in the semantical matrix.

ε Semantic Matrix												Filter Rows	☑ ☒
⊞ Raw ⊞ Normalized ⊞ Weighted													
Object Name	GP_...	GP_...	GP_...	GP_...	GP_...	GP_...	GP_...	GP_...	GP_...	GP_...	GP_...	GP_...	GP_...
■ Direction 07	-8.28	-8.08	-7.88	-7.50	-7.15	-7.65	-7.49	-7.21	-7.09	-6.86	-7.84	-7.63	-7.32
■ Direction 25	11.35	11.78	12.29	12.65	12.99	11.18	11.30	11.65	11.90	12.17	10.98	11.19	11.45
0 of 2 object(s) selected.													

Fig. 3. Excerpt of the semantical matrix containing the two reference types

The next step is the transformation of the semantical matrix into the SEN that transforms the matrix components according to Eq. (3) and performs its learning process

---

[2] The term "cue validity factor" was introduced by the cognitive psychologist Eleanor Rosch (cf. [25]). The factor values particular important and less important attributes.

according to Eq. (4). After the end of the learning process the vectors of the factual weather situation at a certain time is inserted into the SEN; the SEN computes the ranking and distance to the two reference types and shows in the visualization the results. We used the "input centered type" of the visualization options, which means that the vector representing the factual situation was placed into the center of the visualization plane [18]. For the results shown in the next section the learning rate $c = 0.5$ and the learning process stops after 3 iterations.

4   Results

An additional part of a SEN are different visualization algorithms. For a fast interpretation of the results, the "Map"-, "Ranking" visualizations, and the according computed values are presented.

In both modii the semantical relations are transformed in geometrical ones: the more similar objects are with respect to certain reference types the smaller is the geometrical distance of these objects to the reference types on the grid and vice versa.

In [18] only the ranking values were taken into consideration. Because of the sensitive problem and for the safety, the ranking and the distance must give the same recommendation [26]. If this is not the case, it can be taken as an indication that weather conditions can change, or an unambiguous recommendation is not possible.

In Fig. 4 the "Map Visualization" shows the clustered input data, namely the hourly forecasted data for a day. In this visualization the Euclidean distance is computed between the input vectors and the objects in the semantical matrix.

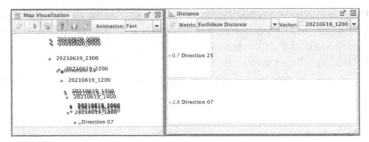

Fig. 4. The Map Visualization of SEN and the computed distance of the input vector with the object name 1500 UTC in relation to the reference types

The crosses in the Map Visualization represent the reference types and the circles the input data. The forecasted weather for 1200 UTC indicates the runway 25 as direction of operation with a distance of 0.7; this means that the forecasted weather condition is similar to the reference type for the direction 25.

The other visualization for the classification of the objects is measured by computing the distance between the final highest activation values of the respective attributes that characterize the objects. In other words, the object in the semantical matrix with the highest activation by an input vector is attracted to the center.[3] The computed result is given as "Ranking". The visualization and the computed ranking are shown in Fig. 5.

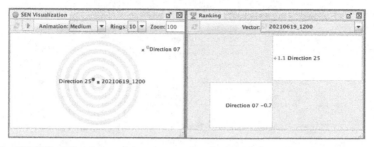

Fig. 5. The SEN Visualization and the computed activation values of the reference types by the given input vector with the object name 1200 UTC

The Ranking confirms in this case the recommendation computed by the Euclidean Distance. One immediately sees that in this (real) case direction of operation 25 should be preferred because its symbol is direct to the center than the symbol of direction 07. The factual decision of air traffic control at Frankfurt Airport at this time was exactly this, namely direction of operation 25 was chosen.

In Fig. 4 the results clustered in the "Map Visualization" show a necessary change of the runways because of the weather circumstances. Between 1200 UTC and 1700 UTC the suited direction of operation is 25. The prediction for 1800 UTC leads to the recommendation shown in Fig. 6.

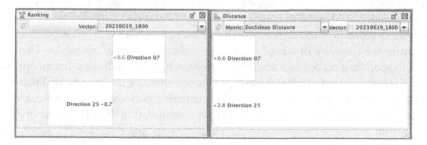

Fig. 6. The recommendation for 1800 UTC based on the weather data

The data stream of weather forecasts is directly inserted into the SEN system that also automatically gives its proposals as output to air traffic control. The real decision processes were compared with the recommendations of SEN over several years.

For example, SEN suggested, based on the weather forecast at 1200 UTC, the direction of operation 07 for 1800 UTC (Fig. 6); the factual decision at 1842 UTC of air traffic control at Frankfurt Airport can be seen in Fig. 7:

---

[3] Readers who are acquainted with the Kohonen Feature Map will see that this method is similar to the well-known "Winner takes all" principle, characteristic for this type of self-organized learning networks. This is only an analogy, because in SEN no winner neuron is computed.

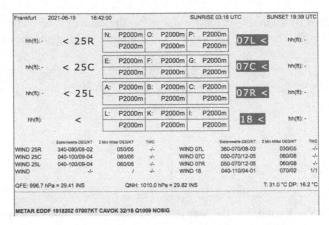

Fig. 7. The factual decision at Frankfurt Airport for 1800 UTC

5 The Web-Based Visualization for Air Traffic Control

Between July 2016 and March 2020, the research project "WxVis4ATC" was conducted under the Federal Aviation Research Program (LuFo) of the Federal Ministry for Economic Affairs and Energy of Germany. Subject of this project was the development of intuitive visualizations of meteorological information or information derived from meteorological data for the use of air traffic controllers.

One intention was to hide the complexity of the system described above and show the output in a condensed and self-explaining graphical display, using color codes showing which operating direction of the runway system is suitable at any point of time over the forecast period.

For the visualization, the activation values must be normalized on a comparable scale, representing the usability of one of the two possible directions of operation. Therefore, a normalization on a percentage scale was chosen, where 0% indicates that an operating direction is not usable at all, 100% indicates the optimum for the respective direction. A value around 50% for either direction may occur during periods of calm or weak winds.

The percentage values for the preferred operating direction ($P_{pref}P_{pref}$), the operating direction with the higher activation value, and the opposite direction ($P_{notpref}P_{notpref}$), are calculated with

$$P_{pref} = 0,5 * \left(1 + e^{-\frac{1}{\Delta}}\right) \tag{5}$$

$$P_{notpref} = 1 - P_{pref} \tag{6}$$

and

$$\Delta = max(A_{07}; A_{25}) - \frac{A_{07} + A_{25}}{2} \tag{7}$$

The preferred direction is determined by higher activation value A_{07} or A_{25}.

Evaluation showed that values between 45% and 55% enable to use any of the two possible directions of operation. Given that, we have a color coding of red for values smaller 45%, orange for values between 45% and 55%, and green for values above 55%. An example for a resulting visualization is shown in Fig. 8.

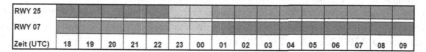

RWY 25																
RWY 07																
Zeit (UTC)	18	19	20	21	22	23	00	01	02	03	04	05	06	07	08	09

Fig. 8. Color-coded visualization based on the calculated percentage values

6 Conclusion

We first presented how powerful the definition - based on expert knowledge - of two reference types is for the decision, which operating direction is best suited for an actual weather condition. Using SEN means that the amount of training data is reduced to two learning vectors, without any loss of quality.

In addition, a color-coded visualization, which allows an easy and effective overview of the results of SEN was implemented and proven to be very helpful in communicating the results of SEN to the end-users.

The data stream of weather forcasts are directly inserted into the SEN system, that automatically gives its proposals in a color-coded visualization as output to Air Control.

Acknowledgment. We thank the Deutscher Wetterdienst, department of Aviation Meteorology and the department of Research and Development, for providing us with the data for our analysis, and to Deutsche Flugsicherung, Air Traffic Control for helpful discussions.

References

1. Avery, J., Balakrishnan, H.: Data-driven modeling and prediction of the process for selecting runway configurations. Trans. Res. Rec.: J. Trans. Res. Board (2600), 1–11 (2016)
2. Lührs, B., Linke, F., Matthes, S., Grewe, V., Yin, F.: Climate impact mitigation potential of European air traffic in a weather situation with strong contrail formation. Aerospace **8**(2), 50 (2021)
3. Taszarek, M., Kendzierski, S., Pilguj, N.: Hazardous weather affecting European airports: climatological estimates of situations with limited visibility, thunderstorm, low-level wind shear and snowfall from ERA5. Weather Clim. Extremes **28**, 100243 (2020)
4. Ingleby, B., et al.: The impact of COVID-19 on weather forecasts: a balanced view. Geophys. Res. Lett. **48**(4), e2020GL090699 (2021)
5. Kulkarni, V.B.: Intelligent air traffic controller simulation using artificial neural networks. In: IEEE Industrial Instrumentation and Control (ICIC), International Conference on 2015, pp. 1027–1031 (2015)

6. Peyronne, C., Conn, A.R., Mongeau, M., Delahaye, D.: Solving air traffic conflict problems via local continuous optimization. Eur. J. Oper. Res. **241**(2), 502–512 (2015)
7. Cruciol, L.L.B.V., Weigang, L., Clarke, J.-P., Li, L.: Air Traffic Flow Management Data Mining and Analysis for In-flight Cost Optimization. In: Lagaros, N.D., Papadrakakis, M. (eds.) Engineering and Applied Sciences Optimization. CMAS, vol. 38, pp. 73–86. Springer, Cham (2015). https://doi.org/10.1007/978-3-319-18320-6_5
8. Silva, W.L., Albuquerque Neto, F.L., França, G.B., Matschinske, M.R.: Conceptual model for runway change procedure in Guarulhos International Airport based on SODAR data. Aeronaut. J. **120**(1227), 725–734 (2016)
9. de Oliveira, M., Eufrásio, A.B.R., Guterres, M.X., Murça, M.C.R., Gomes, R.d.A.: Analysis of airport weather impact on on-time performance of arrival flights for the Brazilian domestic air transportation system. J. Air Trans. Manage. **91**, 101974 (2021)
10. Suzer, A.E., Kaba, A.: A probabilistic-based analysis for wind distribution determination of a runway'. Aircr. Eng. Aerosp. Technol. **93**(2), 284–297 (2021). https://doi.org/10.1108/AEAT-09-2020-0207
11. Stempfel, G., De Visscher, I., Ellejmi, M., Brossard, V., Bonnefoy, A., Treve, V.: Applying machine learning modeling to enhance runway throughput at a big European airport. In: IOP Conference Series: Materials and Science Engineering, Vol. 1024 012106 (2021). https://iop science.iop.org/article/10.1088/1757-899X/1024/1/012106
12. Ren, X., et al.: Deep learning-based weather prediction: a survey, Big Data Res. **23**, 100178 (2021). https://doi.org/10.1016/j.bdr.2020.100178
13. Wang, Y., Zhang, Y.: Prediction of runway configurations and airport acceptance rates for multi-airport system using gridded weather forecast. Trans. Res. Part C: Emerg. Technol. **125**, 103049 (2021)
14. Chen, Z., Wang, Y., Zhou, L.: Predicting weather-induced delays of high-speed rail and aviation in China. Transp. Policy **101**, 1–13 (2021)
15. Rodríguez-Sanz, Á., Cano, J., Rubio Fernández, B.: Impact of weather conditions on airport arrival delay and throughput. Mat. Sci. Eng. **1024**(1), 012107 (2021)
16. Walker, C.: CODA Digest. All-causes delay and cancellations to air transport in Europe. Annual report for 2019. EUROCONTROL (2020)
17. Gonzalo, J., Domínguez, D., López, D., García-Gutiérrez, A.: An analysis and enhanced proposal of atmospheric boundary layer wind modelling techniques for automation of air traffic management. Chin. J. Aeronaut. **34**(5), 129–144 (2021)
18. Klüver, C., Klüver, J., Zinkhan, D.: A Self-enforcing neural network as decision support system for air traffic control based on probabilitstic weather forecasts. In: Proceedings of the IEEE International Joint Conference on Neural Networks (IJCNN). Anchorage, pp. 729–736 (2017). https://doi.org/10.1109/IJCNN.2017.7965924
19. Peralta, C., Ben Bouallégue, Z., Theis, S.E., Gebhardt, C., Buchhold, M.: Accounting for initial condition uncertainties in COSMO-DE-EPS. J. Geophys. Res. **117**, D07,108 (2012)
20. Alberts, I., Zinkhan, D.: iPortWX/WiWi. http://www.deutscher-wetterdienst.de/gsb/mitte/wiwi/index.htm (2012)
21. Klüver, C., Klüver, J.: Self-organized Learning by Self-Enforcing Networks. In: Rojas, I., Joya, G., Gabestany, J. (eds.) IWANN 2013. LNCS, vol. 7902, pp. 518–529. Springer, Heidelberg (2013). https://doi.org/10.1007/978-3-642-38679-4_52
22. Kohonen, T.: Self-Organization and Associative Memory. Springer, Berlin, Heidelberg (2012)
23. Biel, M., Hammer, B., Villmann, T.: Prototype-based models in machine learning. Wiley Interdisc. Rev.: Cogn. Sci. **7**(2), 92–111 (2016)
24. Klüver, C.: Steering clustering of medical data in a Self-Enforcing Network (SEN) with a cue validity factor. In: Proceedings of the IEEE Symposium Series on Computational Intelligence (IEEE SSCI 2016), Athens, pp. 1–8 (2016). https://doi.org/10.1109/SSCI.2016.7849883

25. Rosch, E.: Natural categories. Cogn. Psychol. **4**, 328–350 (1973)
26. Klüver, C.: Self-Enforcing Neworks (SEN) for the development of (medical) diagnosis systems. In: International Joint Conference on Neural Networks (IJCNN). Proceedings of the IEEE World Congress on Computational Intelligence (IEEE WCCI), Vancouver, pp. 503–510 (2016)

Impact of Minority Class Variability on Anomaly Detection by Means of Random Forests and Support Vector Machines

Faisal Saleem Alraddadi$^{(\boxtimes)}$ ⓘ, Luis F. Lago-Fernández ⓘ,
and Francisco B. Rodríguez ⓘ

Grupo de Neurocomputación Biológica, Dpto. de Ingeniería Informática, Escuela
Politécnica Superior, Universidad Autónoma de Madrid, 28049 Madrid, Spain
faisal.alraddadi@estudiante.uam.es
{luis.lago,f.rodriguez}@uam.es

Abstract. The increased connectivity of our world has resulted in a drastic rise of cyberattacks. This has created a dire need for improved security methods that can protect data. Many techniques and technologies have been developed to meet security and privacy demands. Machine learning algorithms are one of such techniques that can be used to detect cyberattacks. In a real network, the attacks represent only a small fraction of the traffic and, therefore, these events can be considered as an anomaly. This article discusses how the anomaly ratio affects results such as the accuracy, the recall, the true positive rate, or the false positive rate when machine learning algorithms are used to detect cyberattacks. Two different algorithms, Random Forests and Support Vector Machines, and two datasets, UNSW-NB15 and CICIDS-2017, are used to carry out this study. We observe that class imbalance affects each algorithm in a very different way. While SVMs fail to recognize the anomalies with acceptable accuracy, RFs seem to be more robust against class imbalance, although in cases of extreme anomaly the detection begins to deteriorate in a similar way. It is, therefore, necessary to investigate new methodologies that solve the problem of detecting attacks when their proportion is very small, and even when this proportion can change dynamically over time.

Keywords: Security and privacy · UNSW-NB15 dataset ·
CICIDS2017 dataset · Severe imbalance · Cyberattacks · Detection
rate · False alarm rate

1 Introduction

Modern-day cyber threats may have slipped past your defense system and found a home in your network. An attack occurs when someone tries to break into a secured system to steal or modify the information or to introduce malicious code. Cybercrime was expected to cost six trillion USD yearly in 2021[1]. Juniper

---

[1] https://cybersecurityventures.com/cybercrime-damages-6-trillion-by-2021.

© Springer Nature Switzerland AG 2021
I. Rojas et al. (Eds.): IWANN 2021, LNCS 12862, pp. 416–428, 2021.
https://doi.org/10.1007/978-3-030-85099-9_34

Research predicts that by 2022, cybercrime will cost over 8 trillion USD, which will represent huge losses for government organizations and private companies alike[2]. Broadly speaking, the categories of network traffic can be divided into normal and malicious flow. In this context, one has to be aware that the percentage of attacks represents only a small fraction of the network traffic in the real world, and therefore attacks can be considered anomalies. Due to the evolution of communication systems, the huge amount of network traffic makes it very hard for a human to notice the presence of small malicious packets. For this reason, it is more and more frequent to use machine learning techniques in order to improve security by automatically notifying security administrators the existence of a potential attack. However, most machine learning algorithms are not designed to cope with extremely unbalanced datasets.

In this article, we study the behavior of Support Vector Machines (SVMs) and Random Forests (RFs) when they are applied to problems of increasing imbalance in the cybersecurity context. To tackle the problem of detecting attacks representing only a small ratio of the total flow, we analyzed several examples of network traffic that contain both attacks and normal traffic. We use two well-known cybersecurity datasets with modern cyberattacks, UNSW-NB15 [1] and CICIDS-2017 [6], altering the ratio of attacks versus normal flow to simulate different anomaly scenarios. Random Forests have been widely used to detect anomalies, and they are accurate, fast to train, and easy to interpret [10]. All these properties lead us to use RFs as the main algorithm in our study. We also consider Support Vector Machines, as they are usually ranked amongst the best performing methods in cyberattack detection while operating quite differently from RFs [10]. Our results show that the RF algorithm works much better than the SVM in the context of anomalies, and that the difference between both algorithms is more apparent as the anomaly ratio decreases. However, the behavior of RFs in cases of extreme anomaly also deteriorates. This is why we postulate that it is necessary to investigate new methodologies that solve the problem of detecting attacks when their proportion is very small, and even more when this proportion can change dynamically over time.

The rest of the article is organized as follows. Section 2 reviews research works related to using RF and SVM for anomaly detection in cybersecurity. In Sect. 3 we analyze the datasets and describe the experimental methodology, including the data preprocessing, the model's description, and the evaluation metrics. Section 4 presents the results in the context of previous works. Finally, in Sect. 5 we draw some conclusions and discuss future work.

2   Related Work

Machine learning algorithms have been widely used to detect cyberattacks, and amongst the most common techniques, we should mention RFs and SVMs. In this section, we review some of the recent literature involving the use of RFs and

---

[2] https://www.juniperresearch.com/press/press-releases/cybercrime-to-cost-global-business-over-8-trn.

SVMs for attack detection in the cybersecurity context, specially those research works carried on with the UNSW-NB15 and the CICIDS-2017 datasets. We decided to focus on these two datasets based on: (i) their public availability, (ii) their relative up to date data, and (iii) the variability in the attack types contained. Most of the recent studies on cyberattack detection have been done using the two aforementioned datasets.

Some of the most representative works using SVMs for cyberattack detection on the UNSW-NB15 and the CICIDS-2017 datasets are the model of D. Jing and H. B. Chen [5] and the DBN-SVM model developed by Zhang et al. [4]. The former showed that a logarithmic scaling applied to the input data improves the results of SVMs trained with the UNSW-NB15 dataset. The latter proposed a model that combines a deep belief network and an SVM. Using a subset of the CICIDS-2017 data containing only four types of attacks along with normal traffic, they showed that their model outperforms traditional machine learning algorithms for real time attack detection.

A representative work that models attack detection using RFs has been recently proposed by I. Ullah and Q. H. Mahmoud [8]. The model contains a two-level intrusion detection system. The first level uses a flow-based anomaly detection model to classify the anomalous network traffic. Then, the anomalous traffic is passed to the second level, where three different techniques are applied to detect the type of anomaly: i) Recursive Feature Elimination to extract the optimal features, ii) Synthetic Minority Oversampling Technique (SMOTE) [15] for oversampling the minority class, and iii) Edited Nearest Neighbors for cleaning the datasets. Finally, an RF classifier is used to recognize the class of the attack. The proposed model achieved very good results in both levels when the CICIDS2017 dataset was used for testing.

Comparative studies including SVMs, RFs and other machine learning models have been carried out by Yang et al. [14], Lopez et al. [7] and Kurniabudi et al. [9]. A model called SAVAER-DNN, based on auto-encoders with regulations was proposed by Yang et al. [14]. They performed a comparative study with other machine learning algorithms, including SVMs and RFs, and concluded that SAVAER-DNN achieved the best results on the UNSW-NB15 dataset. Lopez et al. [7] compared RF, Naive Bayes, K-Nearest Neighbors, and Artificial Neural Networks using part of the CICIDS2017 dataset [6]. They found that RF achieved the best results, outperforming the other models. Kurniabudi et al. [9] analyzed a subset of the CICIDS-2017 dataset containing 20% of the data to determine the optimal number of features to get the best results. They used the Information Gain technique to rank the attributes, and applied five machine learning algorithms to classify the data, grouping similar attacks into a single class. Their findings indicate that the RF classifier can achieve very accurate results with only 22 features.

One has to be aware that cybersecurity threats vary in proportion to normal traffic depending on many aspects and contexts. Furthermore, the proportion of malignant traffic can vary dynamically as a function of time. In some cases the attacks represent a smaller part of the network flow than in others but, in general, malicious traffic can be considered to represent only a very small fraction of the total traffic. However, this is not always the case in the available databases. For example, the UNSW-NB15 dataset contains training and test partitions where the normal and attack classes are roughly balanced. Since most of the recent studies do not consider the effects of the class imbalance, their conclusions might not be valid in a more realistic scenario where the attacks are an anomaly. Thus, to obtain correct results for attack detection in a realistic situation, it is necessary to study how the variability of the attack proportion affects their detection rate. Therefore, in this initial work we analyze the attack detection results for different percentages of anomaly, using RF and SVM applied to the UNSW-NB15 and the CICIDS2017 datasets.

3   Materials and Methods

3.1   Analysis and Review of Datasets

In this section, we analyze the datasets used to carry out our study. For each dataset, we briefly describe the total number of records, the number of attacks versus normal records, and the types of attacks they contain.

UNSW-NB15 Dataset. The UNSW-NB15 dataset was created by the Australian Centre for CyberSecurity [1]. It contains ten types of network flow with normal traffic and nine types of attacks (Fuzzers, Backdoors, Analysis, Generic, DoS, Exploits, Shellcode, Reconnaissance, and Worms). The full dataset contains 2,540,044 records, where the attacks represent only the 12.6% of the whole data (see Fig. 1c). Two additional datasets are provided for training (175,341 records) and test (82,332 records), with the class distributions shown in Figs. 1a and 1b respectively. It is important to note the difference in the attack ratio between the full dataset and the official training/test datasets. While the former is highly unbalanced, in the latter the two classes are roughly balanced and the attacks can not be considered an anomaly. It is also worth noting that the official training/test datasets have been used in most of the existing literature. In order to analyze the effect of the class imbalance, both the official and the full datasets are used in this research.

CICIDS2017 Dataset. The CICIDS-2017 dataset was created by the Canadian Institute for Cybersecurity in 2017 [6]. It contains 15 types of network flow, namely Benign, FTP-Patator, DDoS, SSH-Patator, DoS Slowloris, DoS Slowhttptest, DoS Hulk, DoS Goldeneye, Heartbleed, Web Attack–Brute Force, Web Attack–XSS, Web Attack–SQL Injection, Infiltration, Botnet and Port Scan. Table 1 illustrates all the types of flow in the CICIDS-2017 dataset and the number of records of each type [6]. The dataset contains 2,830,743 records, each described by 80 numerical features. The total representation of attacks is around 20% of the dataset.

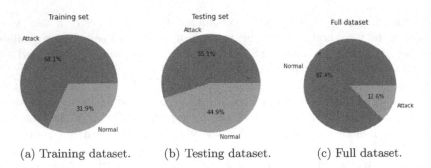

(a) Training dataset.   (b) Testing dataset.   (c) Full dataset.

Fig. 1. Representation of normal and attack flows in the UNSW-NB15 official dataset (training (a), testing (b)), and full dataset (c).

Table 1. CICIDS2017 dataset, number of records of each flow.

Flow type	No. of records	Flow type	No. of records
Benign	2,273,097	DoS Slowloris	5,796
DoS Hulk	231,073	DoS Slowhttptest	5,499
PortScan	158,930	Bot	1,966
DDoS	128,027	Web Attack Brute Force	1,507
DoS GoldenEye	10,293	Web Attack XSS	652
FTP-Patator	7,938	Infiltration	36
SSH-Patator	5,897	Web Attack SQL Injection	21
Heartbleed	11		

3.2   Datasets Preprocessing

We used the UNSW-NB15 dataset and the CICIDS-2017 dataset to mimic real world attacks where the malicious network flow represents a much smaller proportion than the normal network flow. In order to simulate more realistic scenarios, and study the impact that the malignant flow ratio has on its correct detection, we reduce the percentage of attacks in both datasets to reproduce severe anomaly conditions.

UNSW-NB15 Dataset: We use the UNSW-NB15 full dataset. Our analysis revealed that three features had more than 50 percent of their data missing (*attack_cat, ct_flw_http_mthd, is_ftp_login*), and we decided to remove them. We used a label encoder[3] for categorical features. The severe anomaly datasets were generated by drawing a random sample from the UNSW-NB15 full dataset maintaining the same number of records as in the official UNSW-NB15 data (training + test), but reducing the attack ratio to 1%, 2%, 3%, and 12.6% to simulate

---

[3] https://scikit-learn.org/stable/modules/generated/sklearn.preprocessing.Label-Encoder.html

different anomaly scenarios. Then we split each of these sets into a training and a test set with 67% and 33% of the data respectively (as in the official training/test datasets). Table 2 presents the exact number of records for each scenario.

Table 2. UNSW-NB15 dataset, number of records of each network flow in the different anomaly scenarios.

Name of the flow	1% anomaly	2% anomaly	3% anomaly	12.6% anomaly
	No. of records	No. of records	No. of records	No. of records
Normal	255,185	252,608	250,030	225,206
Attack	2,578	5,155	7,733	32,467
Total	257,673	257,673	257,673	257,673

CICIDS2017 Dataset: This dataset has 15 types of traffic flow. However, following [4], we chose only four types of attacks (DoS Hulk, DoS GoldenEye, DoS Slowloris, DoS Slowhttptest) along with normal traffic to carry out our experiments. These attacks represent around 10% of the data. The different sets of severe anomaly are generated by randomly drawing 10% samples from the CICIDS-2017 data, with attack ratios of 1%, 2%, 3%, and 10.1%. We chose 10.1% as the base of our analyses since it is the fraction of attacks, of the four types considered, in the main dataset. Each of the datasets is further divided into training data (80%) and test data (20%). Table 3 presents the number of records of each type of flow in each of the generated datasets.

Table 3. CICIDS-2017 dataset, number of records of each network flow in the different anomaly scenarios.

Flow name	1% anomaly	2% anomaly	3% anomaly	10.1% anomaly
	No. of records	No. of records	No. of records	No. of records
Benign	249,837 (98.99%)	247,583 (98.00%)	244,790(96.99%)	226,895 (89.90%)
DoS Hulk	2,306 (0.91%)	4,611 (1.82%)	6,916 (2.74%)	23,265 (9.21%)
DoS GoldenEye	104 (0.04%)	208 (0.08%)	312 (0.12%)	1,048 (0.41%)
DoS Slowloris	60 (0.02%)	120 (0.04%)	180 (0.07%)	605 (0.23%)
DoS Slowhttptest	54 (0.02%)	109 (0.04%)	163 (0.06%)	548 (0.21%)
Total	252,361 (100%)	252,361 (100%)	252,361 (100%)	252,361(100%)

3.3 Classifier Models

In order to analyze the effect of highly unbalanced datasets on cyberattack detection, we explore the use of two of the most widely used machine learning algorithms in this context: RFs and SVMs.

Support Vector Machines: An SVM is a supervised ML algorithm that uses maximum margin to find the optimal hyperplane that separates two classes [3]. SVMs use the kernel trick to do an implicit projection of the problem data onto a multidimensional space in order to solve non-linear problems. In this article, we train SVMs with the Radial Basis Function (RBF) kernel. Our models depend on two main hyperparameters: the kernel width, γ, and the complexity constant, C, which are tuned using a grid search procedure. We consider $\gamma \in \{10^{-3}, 10^{-4}\}$ and $C \in \{1, 10, 100\}$. We use SVMs only with the UNSW-NB15 dataset. For the experiments ran with the official training/test data, we obtained $\gamma = 0.0001$ and $C = 10$. For all the other tests we obtained $\gamma = 0.0001$ and $C = 1$.

Random Forest: RF is an ensemble based supervised machine learning algorithm. It uses a set of decision trees (estimators or base classifiers) that are grown using some sort of randomization to generate diversity [2]. The opinion of each base classifier is combined using majority voting to get the final ensemble decision. Since RF parameters do not seem to affect the results significantly on the considered data [11] we used typical parameter values in our experiments with the UNSW-NB15 and the CICIDS-2017 datasets. We consider 100 estimators with the Gini splitting criterion. The trees are grown without limiting the maximum depth or the minimum number of samples per node.

3.4   Data Classification and Evaluation Criteria

Evaluating the performance of a machine learning algorithm is an essential step to ensure the algorithm is working perfectly. Thus, a suitable selection of evaluation metrics is important to obtain an optimal classifier for detecting attacks. In this article, we used the detection rate, precision, and false alarm rate. First let us identify the cases of interest, which are the attacks, as positive instances, and the rest of the cases, which are the normal flows, as negative instances. As a result, the four outcomes of an experiment can be described by a two-by-two contingency table, as shown in Table 4. Accordingly, given this contingency table we can define the following quantities and metrics that characterize and evaluate the performance of our classifier:

- True Positives (TP): The number of attack records that are correctly classified as attacks.
- True negatives (TN): The number of normal records that are correctly classified as normal.
- False positives (FP): The number of normal records that are classified as attacks.
- False negatives (FN): The number of attack records that are classified as normal.
- Recall or Detection Rate (DR): The fraction of attack records that are correctly classified as attack:

$$DR = TP/(TP + FN). \tag{1}$$

– Precision: The fraction of predicted attacks that are actually an attack:

$$\text{Precision} = \text{TP}/(\text{TP} + \text{FP}). \tag{2}$$

– F1-Score: The harmonic mean of precision and DR:

$$\text{F1-Score} = 2 \times (\text{Precision} \times \text{DR})/(\text{Precision} + \text{DR}). \tag{3}$$

– False Positive Rate or False Alarm Rate (FAR): The fraction of normal records that are considered as an attack:

$$\text{FAR} = \text{FP}/(\text{TN} + \text{FP}). \tag{4}$$

Table 4. Contingency table for a two-class classification problem.

	True attack	True normal
Predicted attack	True positive	False positive
Predicted normal	False negative	True negative

4   Results

Our initial objective is to address the detection of attacks in conditions similar to certain works in the topic, such as references [13] and [14]. This analysis will serve as a standard or point of reference for our work. Once this initial analysis has been applied, we pose the problem of analyzing how the detection of attacks changes as their proportion decreases. Figure 2 was extracted using RF applied to the official UNSW-NB15 dataset. It shows the relation between precision and recall and compares it with the results of [13] (green circle), and [14] (red circle). The point circled in magenta in the figure represents our results for the selected threshold (numerical values are shown in the column *official* of Table 5). Our result falls between those reached by the works [13] and [14]. We obtain a better result than [14] and a worse result than [13], although all the results are very similar. This coincidence shows that our experimental setup is correctly adjusted for this type of data, and therefore we can start to analyze the problem in the context of severe anomalies. The results of RF applied to the UNSW-NB15 dataset under different anomaly scenarios are also shown in Table 5. Starting with 12.6% of attacks, the detection rate, precision, F1-Score, and FAR are better than for the official data. Moving to an extremely unbalanced class the DR and the F1-Score start to fall until they reach the values 0.8237 and 0.9033 for the 1% anomaly case. The precision and the FAR are almost constant, with values close to 1.0 and 0.0 respectively, for all the anomaly scenarios.

The results of the RF classifier are quite good even for extremely unbalanced data. Note also that the 12.6% problem is easier to solve than the official data

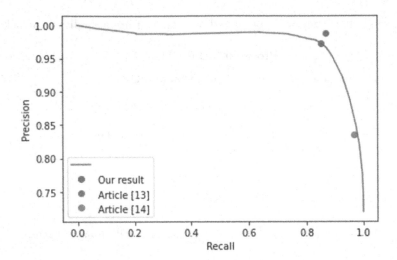

Fig. 2. Precision-Recall curve for the UNSW-NB15 official dataset using RF. (Color figure online)

problem. This fact can also be observed in the results for the SVM classifier, which are shown in the bottom half of Table 5. The same conclusions extracted for the RF, that is, a systematic decrease in measures DR and F1-Score as the ratio of anomalies is reduced, can be drawn for the SVM classifier. Nevertheless, the results for the SVM classifier are worse in all cases (*cf.* 0.7471 vs. 0.9108 DR for the 12.6% case in Table 5).

Table 6 illustrates the results of RF classifiers applied to the CICIDS-2017 dataset. For this problem, we used both binary and multi-class classification. For binary classification, when the attacks represent the 10.1% of the dataset, we obtained excellent results with almost 1.0 DR, precision and F1-Score, and almost 0.0 FAR. When the attack class becomes excessively unbalanced the results start to deteriorate as it happened before with the UNSW-NB15 dataset. Nevertheless, compared to the UNSW-NB15 dataset, the results on CICIDS-2017 are better, which shows that the data complexity of this database is lower (although this must be evaluated in the future in greater depth [12]). In the case of 10.1% of anomalies, we would like to highlight that when we use RF with multiclass-classification (Table 7), the specific attacks DoS Slowlories and DoS Slowhttptest, which only represent around 0.4% of the total traffic, are detected perfectly. However, its detection begins to deteriorate when its representation becomes extremely anomalous. On the contrary, the detection of DoS Hulk attacks, which represent a much larger percentage of the total traffic (around 9%), does not deteriorate as its proportion with respect to the total traffic decreases.

Table 5. UNSW-NB15 dataset, RF and SVM results.

	Metrics	1% anomaly	2% anomaly	3% anomaly	12.6% anomaly	Official
RF	Recall (DR)	0.8237	0.8359	0.8652	0.9108	0.8571
	Precision	1.0000	0.9978	1.0000	0.9986	0.9704
	F1-score	0.9033	0.9097	0.9277	0.9527	0.9102
	FPR (FAR)	0.0000	0.0000	0.0000	0.0001	0.0320
SVM	Recall (DR)	0.3748	0.5149	0.5787	0.7471	0.6072
	Precision	1.0000	1.0000	0.9993	0.9996	0.9418
	F1-score	0.5452	0.6798	0.7330	0.8551	0.7383
	FPR (FAR)	0.0000	0.0000	0.0000	0.0000	0.0459

Table 6. CICIDS-2017 dataset, RF binary classification results.

	Metrics	1% anomaly	2% Anomaly	3% anomaly	10.1% anomaly
RF binary	Recall (DR)	0.8990	0.9425	0.9590	0.9821
	Precision	0.9978	1.0000	0.9986	0.9994
	F1-score	0.9458	0.9704	0.9784	0.9906
	FPR (FAR)	0.0000	0.0000	0.0000	0.0000

Table 7. CICIDS-2017 dataset, RF multi-class classification results.

	Metrics	1% anomaly	2% Anomaly	3% anomaly	10.1% anomaly
Dos hulk	Recall (DR)	0.9826	0.9859	0.9913	0.9954
	Precision	0.9956	0.9989	0.9934	0.9989
	F1-score	0.9890	0.9923	0.9923	0.9972
	FPR (FAR)	0.0000	0.0000	0.0001	0.0001
Dos GoldenEye	Recall (DR)	1.0000	0.8333	1.0000	0.9809
	Precision	0.9545	1.0000	0.9841	1.0000
	F1-Score	0.9767	0.9090	0.992	0.9903
	FPR (FAR)	0.0000	0.0000	0.0000	0.0000
DoS slowloris	Recall (DR)	0.8333	0.875	0.9722	1.0000
	Precision	0.9090	0.9545	1.0000	1.0000
	F1-score	0.8695	0.9130	0.9859	1.0000
	FPR (FAR)	0.0000	0.0000	0.0000	0.0000
Dos Slowhttptest	Recall (DR)	0.9090	0.9545	1.0000	0.9724
	Precision	0.9090	0.9545	0.9428	0.9906
	F1-score	0.9090	0.9545	0.9705	0.9814
	FPR (FAR)	0.0000	0.0000	0.0000	0.0000

5   Conclusions and Discussion

The representation of attacks in network traffic fluctuates. Some types of attacks are minor, while others may be more common, but their representation is much relatively low than that of benign traffic. That is why we refer to these computer-attack-related events as anomalies. In addition, it is necessary to be aware that the proportion of attacks does not remain constant over time, but varies depending on many factors, such as the type of security of the systems, new security holes that are discovered, installation of honeypots and honeynets systems, etc. Thus, in this work, we study what impact this variability of anomalies can have in the context of machine learning systems to detect these attacks. As a first approximation to carry out this study, we analyze the behavior of these machine learning systems with different anomaly ratios. Specifically, we chose imbalance ratios of around 10% and a stronger imbalance of 3%, 2%, and 1% of attacks of the total traffic flow. To analyze and study this effect of low representation of attacks on the results of anomaly detection, we have used RF and SVM algorithms applied on two widely used and modern datasets: UNSW-NB15 and CICIDS2017. The RF and the SVM algorithms are the most widely used in the context of anomaly detection, as we have already commented in the state of the art of this work. We notice that when the anomaly ratio becomes more extreme the performance of both algorithms to detect attacks falls, especially for SVM. Our results show that the UNSW-NB15 dataset complexity is high when the representation of attacks is too low, while the complexity of the CICIDS-2017 dataset is lower. However, this fact must be studied in more detail with different measures that estimate the complexity of the data independently of the precision results obtained using automatic classifiers [12].

This work shows that new methodologies are needed to detect attacks properly and cope with the variability that exists in the proportion of network traffic anomalies. Algorithms need to be improved to adapt to this change in attack ratio appropriately so that their performance is not affected. The performance of algorithms could be enhanced by using different methods such as special algorithms that are designed to solve unbalanced datasets, for example, Synthetic Minority Over-sampling Technique (SMOTE), and Adaptive Synthetic Sampling Approach for Imbalanced Learning (ADASYN) [15–17]. Also, the application of specific normalizations such as those used in [5] for SVM can be another approach to enhance the results with this type of classifiers. Finally, it is important to pay attention to scenarios in which the variation in the number of attacks in relation to the total traffic fluctuates appreciably. In this specific case, new attack detection systems are needed with a dynamic approach that adapts to the change in the representation of attacks over time. One possibility for this scenario could be the one class classification approach due to the fact that it only uses the majority class for training. This scheme represents an advantage over the supervised learning that we have carried out in this work since when training only with benign traffic, possible dynamical fluctuations in the attack rates would not deteriorate its detection so much. However, this should be studied and analyzed in greater detail in future work.

Acknowledgements. This work has been partially funded by Spanish projects MINECO/FEDER TIN2017-84452-R and PID2020-114867RB-I00 (http://www.mineco.gob.es/) and by grant S2017/BMD-3688 from Comunidad de Madrid.

References

1. Moustafa, N., Slay, J.: UNSW-NB15: a comprehensive data set for network intrusion detection systems (UNSW-NB15 network data set). In: 2015 Military Communications and Information Systems Conference (MilCIS), pp. 1–6, November 2015
2. Primartha, R., Tama, B.A.: Anomaly detection using random forest: A performance revisited. In: 2017 International Conference on Data and Software Engineering (ICoDSE), pp. 1–6 (2017)
3. Cervantes, J., Garcia-Lamont, F., Rodríguez-Mazahua, L., Lopez, A.: A comprehensive survey on support vector machine classification: applications, challenges and trends. Neurocomputing **408**, 189–215 (2020)
4. Zhang, H., Li, Y., Lv, Z., Sangaiah, A.K., Huang, T.: A real-time and ubiquitous network attack detection based on deep belief network and support vector machine. IEEE/CAA J. Automatica Sinica **7**(3), 790–799 (2020)
5. Jing, D., Chen, H.B.: SVM based network intrusion detection for the UNSW-NB15 dataset. In: 2019 IEEE 13th International Conference on ASIC (ASICON), pp. 1–4, October 2019
6. Sharafaldin, I., Lashkari, A.H., Ghorbani, A.A.: Toward generating a new intrusion detection dataset and intrusion traffic characterization, pp. 108–116. Science and Technology Publication (2018)
7. Lopez, A.D., Mohan, A.P., Nair, S.: Network traffic behavioral analytics for detection of DDoS attacks. SMU Data Sci. Rev. **2**(1), Article 14 (2019)
8. Ullah, I., Mahmoud, Q.H.: A two-level hybrid model for anomalous activity detection in IoT networks. In: 2019 16th IEEE Annual Consumer Communications & Networking Conference (CCNC), pp. 1–6, January 2019
9. Kurniabudi, Stiawan, D., Darmawijoyo, Idris, M.Y.B., Bamhdi, A.M., Budiarto, R.: CICIDS-2017 dataset feature analysis with information gain for anomaly detection. IEEE Access **8**, 132911–132921 (2020)
10. Sheykhmousa, M., Mahdianpari, M., Ghanbari, H., Mohammadimanesh, F., Ghamisi, P., Homayouni, S.: Support vector machine versus random forest for remote sensing image classification: a meta-analysis and systematic review. IEEE J. Sel. Top. Appl. Earth Observ. Remote Sens. **13**, 6308–6325 (2020)
11. Tyralis, H., Papacharalampous, G., Langousis, A.: A brief review of random forests for water scientists and practitioners and their recent history in water resources. Water **11**(5), 910 (2019)
12. Ho, T.K., Basu, M.: Complexity measures of supervised classification problems. IEEE Trans. Pattern Anal. Mach. Intell. **24**(3), 289–300 (2002)
13. Vinayakumar, R., Alazab, M., Soman, K.P., Poornachandran, P., Al-Nemrat, A., Venkatraman, S.: Deep learning approach for intelligent intrusion detection system. IEEE Access **7**, 41525–41550 (2019)
14. Yang, Y., Zheng, K., Wu, B., Yang, Y., Wang, X.: Network intrusion detection based on supervised adversarial variational auto-encoder with regularization. IEEE Access **8**, 42169–42184 (2020)
15. Chawla, N.V., Bowyer, K.W., Hall, L.O., Kegelmeyer, W.P.: SMOTE: synthetic minority over-sampling technique. J. Artif. Intell. Res. **16**, 321–357 (2002)

16. Santos, M.S., Soares, J.P., Abreu, P.H., Araujo, H., Santos, J.: Cross-validation for imbalanced datasets: avoiding overoptimistic and overfitting approaches [research frontier]. IEEE Comput. Intell. Mag. **13**(4), 59–76 (2018)
17. He, H., Bai, Y., Garcia, E.A., Li, S.: ADASYN: adaptive synthetic sampling approach for imbalanced learning. In: 2008 IEEE International Joint Conference on Neural Networks (IEEE World Congress on Computational Intelligence), pp. 1322–1328, June 2008

Analyzing the Land Cover Change and Degradation in Sundarbans Mangrove Forest Using Machine Learning and Remote Sensing Technique

Ashikur Rahman Khan, Anika Khan, Shehzin Masud, and Rashedur M. Rahman[✉]

Department of Electrical and Computer Engineering,
North South University, Dhaka, Bangladesh
{ashikur.khan01,anika.khan01,shehzin.masud,
rashedur.rahman}@northsouth.edu

Abstract. The purpose of our research work is to understand the efficiency and advantage of applying machine learning technique on remote sensing data collected from one of the largest mangrove forests in the world, named Sundarbans. Our study area was Sundarbans mangrove forest, and we have detected land cover changes in this area. The images we have used were collected from Landsat 8 OLI, ETM+, TM data. After pre-processing the images, we classified them applying the Maximum Likelihood classifier. We got overall accuracy of 80%, 75%, and 77.1% and kappa efficiency 0.80, 0.62, and 0.69 for the years 2001, 2011, 2021 respectively. To determine the overall accuracy and kappa efficiency, we have used confusion matrix. In the last 20 years, Sundarbans mangrove forest has declined by 0.2% due to human settlements, deforestation, natural calamity, increasing water salinity etc.

Keywords: LULC · Classification · Sundarbans · Remote sensing · Landsat image · ArcGIS

1 Introduction

Sundarbans is a collection of naturally made facultative halophytes, widely known as the mangrove forest. These forests are found in hundred and twenty countries all over the world and the maximum amount of South Asian beautiful greenwood is associated in Bangladesh and India. The contiguous forest covers a total area of 10,000 km^2 with 6000 km^2 lying in Bangladesh and the rest 4000 km^2 in India [1, 2] Located in the Ganges-Brahmaputra delta, over 300 flora and 1760 fauna species are found in this World Heritage site. It also attracts a huge number of tourists [3, 4]. An intricate network of river channels covers the forest along with small islands and mudflats formed through the deposition of sediments from the river system. Sundarbans, the largest mangrove forest in the world, serves as a carbon sink, provides shelters from massive damage of intense storms, flood destruction, cyclone barrier, atmospheric imbalance, and a good source of income for about 2.5 million people.

© Springer Nature Switzerland AG 2021
I. Rojas et al. (Eds.): IWANN 2021, LNCS 12862, pp. 429–438, 2021.
https://doi.org/10.1007/978-3-030-85099-9_35

The versatile forest has been decreasing for ages, due to overexploitation and deforestation by humans to create agricultural land, shrimp farming, and natural calamities [5]. While the condition in Bangladesh is already dire, China has also lost 2/3rd of its mangrove forest from Guangdong province [7]. Cyclones have the general capacity of destroying ecosystems, and habitation; and therefore, Sundarbans has been facing greater risk due to being on the front, and experiencing higher wind speeds for its geographical location which leads it being hit by cyclones every 7 to 12 years while smaller disturbances occur at even lesser time intervals [3]. This frequency is problematic since it takes around 10–15 years to reach pre-disturbance levels. Sidr was the most robust cyclone to hit Sundarbans in 2007, and next in 2009, Indian part of Sundarbans was hit by Aila. Depletion in mangroves has become a global concern, thus mapping and monitoring the mangrove has become a vital step for the counties carrying these forests.

Conservation of Sundarbans is crucial since it is already an endangered ecosystem. Climate change inevitably has severe repercussions on it [3]. It has been primarily predicted that the coastal area around the Bay of Bengal will get immersed because of the rise of sea level in the future. So, to better understand what to expect and what not to, it is wise to study the past decades of historical changes in this tropical land. Mangrove mapping, change detection, and biomass estimation, the conservation of the forest demand accurate research results [4].

By remote sensing (RS) an object can be monitored and data regarding it can be noted without having to make any physical contacts or field visits. It comes into play due to the inability to carry out sufficient field investigation in Sundarbans, and the complexity of the area combined with its remoteness, and prevalence of floods make it somewhat inaccessible [6]. RS and satellite imagery has made huge advancements through the decades starting from introduction of sensors, and continues to be the prime source for studies as computational costs became more affordable, and the need for accurate information keeps rising. Therefore, inaccessible parts of the Sundarbans can also be monitored with reliability. Moreover, Landsat datasets can be used to retrieve information for long period of time. Several different aspects such as mangrove extent, canopy closure, LULC, species et cetera have been studied, and the changes in high resolutions can be noticed before, during, and after an event [20].

This study aims to analyze the land use/land cover change (LULC) in total area of Sundarbans in the last 20 years (2001 to 2021), using satellite imagery and remote sensing data. Three cloud-free multi-temporal Landsat Images of 2001, 2011, and 2021 were classified using Maximum Likelihood classification with the help of ArcGIS software which monitored the changes in Mangrove Area, Water Body, Mudflat, Sandy Bench, and Bare Land.

2   Related Works

In paper [4], the authors carried out a study on the Sundarbans to southeast coastal belt of Noakhali Chittagong-Cox's Bazar. 28 Landsat imagery from the years 1976, 1989, 2000 and 2015 were used. Landsat MSS, TM, ETM+, and L8 OLI classified images were found to be 80%, 80%, 87%, and 97% accurate, respectively. Also, perceived changes of Mangrove in Bangladesh were owed to the deforestation, farms built for shrimp & salt production, coastal erosion and sedimentation. A decision-tree learning method for integrating multi-temporal Landsat TM data and ancillary GIS data to identify mangroves in the Pearl River Estuary has been used in this paper [7]. They used C5.0 for UNIX and its Windows counterpart See5 to construct the training set, decision tree training and decision tree rules in the paper. The result shows that from 1988 to 1995 there has been a significant decrease but from 1995 to 2002 there has been an increase in the area, which lead to 45.8 ha reduction. In this paper [11], the authors carried out a study on Khulna and Satkhira region. They collected Landsat images from 1980, 1989, 2002 and 2009. Sensors from Landsat, Multi Spectral Scanner (MSS), Thematic Mapper (TM) and Enhanced Thematic Plus (ETM+) were used. The findings of their research show a decrease from 49% area in 1989 to 29% 2009 in fallow land and 31% to 29% from 1989 to 2009 in mangrove, and increase from 5% in 1989 to 19% in 2009 in homestead and 14% in 1989 to 24% in 2009 in water bodies. As Maximum Likelihood Classification is a prominent classifier in LULC, it was used in paper [10, 13, 14, 17, 19] to secure accuracy between 77.0% to 85.71%. Whereas, unsupervised and supervised classification was used in paper [18] got 78.32% and 81.62% accuracy respectively. The most dominant species reported in [14] is Avicennia sp. In [9], the authors made the Indian part of Sundarbans Biosphere Reserve as their subject of study where they presented a negative correlation between LST and NDVI. The authors in [8] conducted a study on 30 years of Landsat data using CCDC. Results showed that despite the overall stability of the mangrove forest, there was a 25% regressive change owing partially to injurious changes caused by cyclone Sidr and to die- back of Heritiera fomes.

The authors in [12] used cloud-free Landsat 5 TM and Landsat 8 OLI images to study the land cover change for 1998, 2008 and, 2018. ENVI software version 5.3 was used for Image enhancement and classification. The result shows that 80% of the human habitat area has been increased from 1998 to 2018; also 116% of aquaculture has been increased between 1998 to 2008, which are 654 km^2 and 231 km^2, respectively. MLP-Markov Chain-based modeling is used to show the future prediction of land cover change. Land use/land cover change between 1975 and 2006 on south-western part of Indian Sundarbans was presented in this paper [15]. The approximate loss is 0.42% in mangrove coverage. The three (1975, 1990 and 2006) multitemporal cloud-free satellite image (Landsat) was downloaded from United States Geological Service Glovis. The authors of this [16] paper, used freely available Landsat TM of 1989, TM of 2014, and L8 OLI imaginary of 2019 to generate land cover change in the eastern Sundarbans using the maximum likelihood algorithm (MaxLike). Accuracy is reported as 80%, 82.85% and 84.28% respectively. The paper [16] comes out with a predictable output that says 0.44% vegetation cover has been decreased in the past 30 years (1989–2019). As many studies were carried out in this particular region, we have tried to focus on current circumstances only. We have selected last 20 years of data for this study to analyze the changes that has been occurred using the Maximum Likelihood Classifier.

3 Methodology

3.1 Data Acquisition

Our region of interest (ROI) is Sundarbans Mangrove Forest that spread between Bangladesh and India. Its total area consists of 9,200 sq km^2, and a significant part of the forest fall in Bangladesh territory (Fig. 1).

Fig. 1. Location of study area

Our study area lies between 21° 54'–22° 51' latitude and 88° 44'–89° 89' longitude. Heritiera fomes, Excoecaria agallocha, Ceriops roxburghian and Sonneratia apetala are some common trees in this area [4]. The height of mangrove varies from region to region, and on average, it stands 0.9 m and 2.1 m above sea level [3]. Average temperature ranges from 12–25° and average rainfall is 700 mm per year [3]. May to October are rainy seasons, and 80% of rainfall occur at this time. Several factors are reasonable for the growth and development of mangrove forest, such as saline water, sedimentation, ocean tidal etc.

3.2 Image Collection

We have collected twenty-eight level-1 terrain (LIT) Landsat image from United States Geological Survey (USGS) website. This image fell into WGS_1984_UTM_Zone_46N coordinate system. We collected 2021, 2011, 2001 images gradually from Landsat 8 OLI, ETM+7, Landsat 5 TM. Table 1 shows detailed information about the multispectral imaginary. Usually, the dry seasons are the perfect time to collect the satellite image. So, our collected images vary from January to March. The cloud cover of the images we have used in image Pre-processing are less than 5%.

Table 1. Satellite data

Serial Number	Path row	Acquisition Time	Landsat Spacecraft	Cloud Cover	Pixel Size	UTM zone
1	P137 R045	21/01/2001	Landsat 5 TM	0	30	46N
2	P138 R045	5/3/2011	Landsat 7 ETM	0	30	46N
3	P138 R045	4/2/2021	Landsat 8 OLI	0.03	30	46N

3.3 Image Pre-processing

Figure 2 depicts our working policy. At first, we have combined different band image like near-infrared, red, green, blue, and made a composite image. This different band combination helped us to identify different object later on. Then we used ENVI 5.3v Software to perform radiometric calibration pre-processing. It improved the Landsat data by making it sharper and more visible. This process is done by converting the DN (Digital Number) value of the data to the top of atmosphere reflectance. Fast line-of-sight atmospheric analysis of hypercubes also known as FLAASH is an atmospheric correction that corrects visible wavelengths to near infrared regions up to 3 μm. So, we have applied FLAASH in our Landsat images. Then we performed QUAC (Quick Atmospheric Correction). It is also another atmospheric correction that works between VNIR-SWIR range. Finally, we applied the Dark Object Subtraction (DOS) in our pre-processing section to complete it. As the study area is large, so it covers two Landsat scenes. Thus, we had to mosaic the two Landsat images and convert them into one image. After that, we have masked the image according to our area of interest. Finally, after masking, our data is ready for classification. As our data had significantly less cloud cover, so we did not need to perform any cloud masking (Fig. 2).

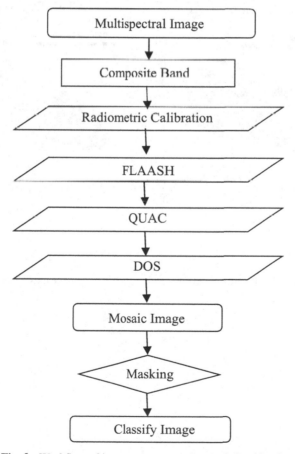

Fig. 2. Workflow of image pre-processing and classification

3.4 Image Classification

We used ArcGIS 10.8 software for image selection and classification. Training samples were collected very carefully from the multispectral image. We have created five different classes to identify different objects. They are Mangrove, Water Body, Mudflat, Sandy Bench, and Bare Land. Training data were collected in the form of polygons. As the study area lies in the coastal region, the water color is different between the open ocean and coastal regions due to sedimentation. So, we had to take data from different locations. On average, we took 50 polygons from each class. However, we have taken more polygons for mangrove and water classes. We used supervised classification for detecting our land cover. Maximum Likelihood Classification (MLC) is a very promising algorithm for classification that we have used by the assist of ArcGIS software. This algorithm is based on two principles. One is, each class sample cells are being distributed in multidimensional space, and another one uses the Bayes theorem for decision making. The classifier classified the images of 2001, 2011, and 2021 years (Figs. 3, 4, 5).

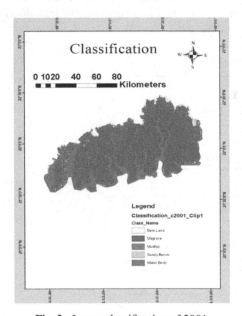

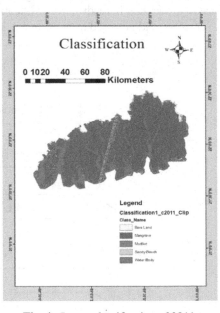

Fig. 3. Image classification of 2001.   **Fig. 4.** Image classification of 2011.

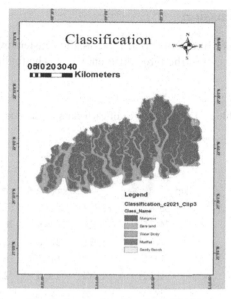

Fig. 5. Image classification of 2021.

3.5 Accuracy Assessment

We have taken 35 points for our validation. It was randomly taken for each different classes. As ground survey was not possible, so we used Google Earth Pro software to choose the validation data. For accuracy assessment, we used confusion matrix. With using it we have found the user accuracy, producer accuracy, overall accuracy and kappa coefficient by the following formulas (Table 2).

$$Overall\ accuracy = \frac{Total\ Number\ of\ Correctly\ Classified\ Pixel\ (Diagonal)}{Total\ number\ of\ Reference\ Pixels} \times 100$$

$$Producer\ accuracy = \frac{Total\ Number\ of\ Correctly\ Classified\ Pixel\ in\ each\ class}{Total\ number\ of\ Reference\ Pixels\ in\ each\ class\ (the\ column\ total)} \times 100\%$$

$$User\ accuracy = \frac{Total\ Number\ of\ Correctly\ Classified\ Pixel\ in\ each\ class}{Total\ number\ of\ Reference\ Pixels\ in\ each\ class\ (The\ row\ total)} \times 100\%$$

$$Kappa\ Efficiency\ (t) = \frac{(TS \times TCS) - \sum(ColumnTotal \times RowTotal)}{TS^2 - \sum(ColumnTotal - RowTotal)}$$

Table 2. Accuracy assessment table consist of user accuracy, producer accuracy, overall accuracy and kappa efficiency.

Landsat	Time	Sample Size	Mangrove PA(%)	Mangrove UA(%)	Water Body PA(%)	Water Body UA(%)	Mudflat PA(%)	Mudflat UA(%)	Bare Land PA(%)	Bare Land UA(%)	Sandy bench PA(%)	Sandy bench UA(%)	Accuracy OA(%)	Accuracy Kappa
TM	2001	35	84.60%	100%	90%	90%	85.70%	60%	50%	66.70%	0%	0%	80%	0.72
ETM	2011	75	67%	97%	81%	100%	83%	50%	100%	60%	100%	10%	75%	0.62
L8 OLI	2021	35	84.60%	91.74	80%	88.80%	57.10%	57.10%	75%	100%	100%	25%	77.10%	0.69

4 Result and Discussion

To calculate our area, we have converted the classified raster image into vector data. Then we calculated the area of the three different years. The findings are shown below (Table 3):

Table 3. Landcover area of each class in our study.

Landcover Class	2001 sq km	2001 %	2011 sq km	2011 %	2021 sq km	2021 %
Mangrove	5684.7	62.28%	5818.5	63.25%	5671.8	61.65%
Water Body	2407.5	26%	2425.8	26.37%	2626.4	28.55%
Bare Land	178.2	1.95%	127.6	1.39%	145.2	1.58%
Mudflat	704.5	7.72%	611.3	6.64%	558.1	6.07%
Sandy Bench	153.2	1.68%	216.5	2.35%	198.3	2.16%
Total area	9128.1	100.00%	9199.7	100.00%	9199.8	100.00%

We can see that the area of mangrove has increased by 134 sq km^2 from 2001 to 2011 but again it deceased by 147 sq km^2 from 2011 to 2021. If we compare it from 2001 to 2021, the result says, total mangrove forest has been deceased by 13 sq km^2 or 0.2% in last 20 years. If we increase the time period the deforestation will surely increase in future (Fig. 6).

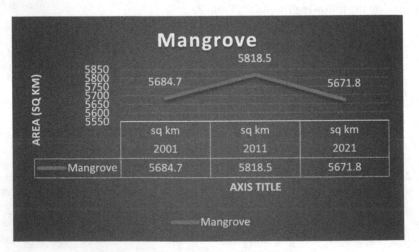

Fig. 6. Mangrove area changes in last 20 years

Global Mangrove Watch [21] is an online platform that provides remote sensing data for mangroves. By using ALOS Palsar and Landsat data it creates a baseline map of mangrove in all over the world. From there, we collected a vector dataset of 2010 to compare with our classification data. Then we clipped the vector dataset to our study area and calculated the total area. The Dataset shows that in our study area 5,608 sq km^2 mangrove forest exists in 2010. In our 2011 year classification, we have found that the mangrove area is around 5818.5 sq km^2. So, our findings are close to the Dataset of Global Mangrove Watch.

We come to know that, in the last 20 years, mangrove forest landcover has decreased by 0.2%. It might not seem a massive loss at first glance but if the time scale increases, then we will gradually observe immense deforestation. Last few years, our government took many reasonable steps to control the loss. There are several reasons for forest declines such as natural calamity, increase of water salinity, human disturbance, forest fire etc. No massive cyclone like Sidr has hit mangrove forest recently, so the decline rate is still low. Government should impose heavy restriction on entering the reserved area of the forest. Besides, mangrove plantation program can also play a significant role to flatten the decline rate of deforestation. We should be more vigilant to protect these halophytes.

5   Limitations and Future Work

The shortcomings of our analysis are that, the Image color band of Open Sea and Coastal area are very different due to sedimentation. As a result, ArcGIS 10.8 software could not segregate them properly and the change detection for Mudflat came out very low. Also, as our study does not include any information related to field visits, the actual situation might affect our predicted accuracy. Our plan for further work is to build a model by using previous year's data that can predict land cover changes in Sundarbans.

6   Conclusion

In our study, we tried to focus on the changes that occurred in the Sundarbans mangrove forest from 2001 to present days. We used high multispectral satellite imagery to conduct the research. Remote sensing is an emerging field of research due to its strong advantage. In our study area, some regions were hazardous to collect data and sample, but we have easily got it by using remote sensing data. From our results, we can see a decline in the mangrove forest. Various factors work for this reduction but we must try our best to stop this deforestation in order to save this beautiful ecosystem. Many researchers have found that mangrove forests are gradually decreasing. So, it is high time we should pay attention to them.

Reference

1. Shimu, S.A., Aktar, M., Afjal, M.I., Nitu, A.M., Uddin, M.P., Mamun, M.A.: NDVI based change detection in Sundarban mangrove forest using remote sensing data. In: 4th International Conference on Electrical Information and Communication Technology (EICT) (2019)

2. Rahman, M.M., Ullah, M.R., Lan, M., Sumantyo, J.S., Kuze, H., Tateishi, R.: Comparison of Landsat image classification methods for detecting mangrove forests in Sundarbans. Int. J. Remote Sens. **34**(4), 1041–1056 (2013)
3. Mandal, M.S.H., Hosaka, T.: Assessing cyclone disturbances (1988–2016) in the Sundarbans mangrove forests using Landsat and Google Earth Engine. Nat. Hazards **102**(1), 133–150 (2020). https://doi.org/10.1007/s11069-020-03914-z
4. Islam, M.M., Borgqvist, H., Kumar, L.: Monitoring mangrove forest landcover changes in the coastline of Bangladesh from 1976 to 2015. Geocarto Int. **34**(13), 1458–1476 (2019)
5. Mondal, S.H., Debnath, P.: Spatial and temporal changes of Sundarbans reserve forest in Bangladesh. Environ. Nat. Res. J. **15**(1), 51–61 (2017)
6. Rahman, M.M., Lagomasino, D., Lee, S., Fatoyinbo, T.: Improved assessment of mangrove forests in Sundarbans east wildlife sanctuary using WorldView 2 and TanDEM-X high resolution imagery. Remote Sens. Ecol. Conserv. **5**(2), 136–149 (2019)
7. Kai Liu, X.L., Shi, X., Wang, S.: Monitoring mangrove forest changes using remote sensing and GIS data with decision-tree learning. Wetlands **28**(2), 336–346 (2008)
8. Awty-Carroll, K., Bunting, P., Hardy, A., Bell, G.: Using continuous change detection and classification of Landsat data to investigate long-term mangrove dynamics in the Sundarbans region. Remote Sens. **11**(23), 2833 (2019)
9. Thakur, S., et al.: Assessment of changes in land use, land cover, and land surface temperature in the mangrove forest of Sundarbans. Environ. Dev. Sustain. **23**(2), 1917–1943 (2020)
10. Rahman, M., Begum, S.: Land cover change analysis around the Sundarbans mangrove forest of Bangladesh using remote sensing and GIS application. JSF **9**(1–2), 95–107 (2013)
11. Sardar, P., Samadder, S.R.: Understanding the dynamics of landscape of greater Sundarban area using multi-layer perceptron Markov chain and landscape statistics approach. Ecol. Ind. **121**, 106914 (2021)
12. Datta, D., Deb, S.: Analysis of coastal land use/land cover changes in the Indian Sunderbans using remotely sensed data. Geo-spatial Inf. Sci. **15**(4), 241–250 (2012)
13. Kumar, M., Mondal, I., Pham, Q.B.: Monitoring forest landcover changes in the Eastern Sundarban of Bangladesh from 1989 to 2019. Acta Geophys. **69**, 561–577 (2021). https://doi.org/10.1007/s11600-021-00551-3
14. Giri, S., et al.: A study on abundance and distribution of mangrove species in Indian Sundarban using remote sensing technique. J. Coast. Conserv. **18**(4), 359–367 (2014). https://doi.org/10.1007/s11852-014-0322-3
15. Kar, N.S., Bandyopadhyay, S.: Tropical storm Aila in Gosaba block of Indian Sundarban: remote sensing based assessment of impact and recovery. Geogr. Rev. India **77**(1), 40–54 (2015)
16. Ghosh, M.K., Kumar, L., Roy, C.: Mapping long-term changes in mangrove species composition and distribution in the Sundarbans. Forests **7**(12), 305 (2016)
17. Debnath, A.: Land use and land cover change detection of Gosaba Island of the Indian Sundarban Region by using multitemporal satellite image. Int. J. Hum. Soc. Sci. **7**(1), 209–217 (2018)
18. Salam, M.A., Ross, L.G., Beveridge, C.M.C.: The use of GIS and remote sensing techniques to classify the Sundarbans mangrove vegetation. J. Agrofor. Environ. **1**(1), 7–15 (2007)
19. Ramteke, I.K., et al.: Land Use/Land Cover Change Dynamics in Coastal Ecosystem of Sundarban Delta, West Bengal-A Case Study of Bali Island (2017)
20. Prusty, B.A.K., Chandra, R., Azeez, P.A. (eds.): Wetland Science. Springer, New Delhi (2017). https://doi.org/10.1007/978-81-322-3715-0
21. Global Watch. https://www.globalmangrovewatch.org/

Correction to: Advances in Computational Intelligence

Ignacio Rojas[iD], Gonzalo Joya, and Andreu Català

Correction to:
I. Rojas et al. (Eds.): *Advances in Computational Intelligence*,
LNCS 12862, https://doi.org/10.1007/978-3-030-85099-9

In the original version of this paper, the affiliation of Gonzalo Joya was presented incorrectly. This was corrected.
It should be read as follows: University of Málaga, Málaga, Spain

In the original version of this paper, the last name of Andreu Català was misspelled and the affiliation was incorrect. These errors were corrected.
The correct spelling is with an accent as follows: Andreu Català
The affiliation is Technical University of Catalonia, Barcelona, Spain

The updated version of the book can be found at
https://doi.org/10.1007/978-3-030-85099-9

© Springer Nature Switzerland AG 2021
I. Rojas et al. (Eds.): IWANN 2021, LNCS 12862, p. C1, 2021.
https://doi.org/10.1007/978-3-030-85099-9_36

Author Index

Printed in the United States
by Baker & Taylor Publisher Services